Professional ADO.N
Programming with SQL S
Oracle®, and MyS

Professional ADO.NET 2
Programming with SQL Server 2005,
Oracle®, and MySQL®

Wallace B. McClure

Gregory A. Beamer

John J. Croft IV

J. Ambrose Little

Bill Ryan

Phil Winstanley

David Yack

Jeremy Zongker

WILEY

Wiley Publishing, Inc.

Professional ADO.NET 2 Programming with SQL Server 2005, Oracle®, and MySQL®

Published by
Wiley Publishing, Inc.
10475 Crosspoint Boulevard
Indianapolis, IN 46256
www.wiley.com

Copyright © 2006 by Wiley Publishing, Inc., Indianapolis, Indiana

Published simultaneously in Canada

ISBN-13: 978-0-7645-8437-4
ISBN-10: 0-7645-8437-5

Manufactured in the United States of America

10 9 8 7 6 5 4 3 2

1B/RW/RR/QV/IN

Library of Congress Cataloging-in-Publication Data is available from the publisher.

About the Authors

Wallace B. McClure

Wallace B. McClure graduated from the Georgia Institute of Technology in 1990 with a bachelor of science degree in electrical engineering. He continued his education there, receiving a master's degree in the same field in 1991. Since that time, he has done consulting and development for such companies as Coca-Cola, Bechtel National, Magnatron, and Lucent Technologies, among others. Products and services have included work with ASP, ADO, XML, and SQL Server, as well as numerous applications in the Microsoft .NET Framework. Wally McClure specializes in building applications that have large numbers of users and large amounts of data. He is a Microsoft MVP and an ASPInsider, and a partner in Scalable Development, Inc. You can read Wally's blog at `http://weblogs.asp.net/wallym/`.

Gregory A. Beamer

Gregory A. Beamer is a solutions architect specializing in Microsoft Internet technologies. Greg got involved in programming in the early 1990s with Visual Basic 3 and has stayed on the leading edge of Microsoft Internet technologies since the Denali beta (ASP 1.0). Greg first worked with .NET with the PDC 2000 beta and has been on both the SQL Server 2005 and .NET 2.0 betas since spring 2003. When Greg is not working, he spends his time with his wife, Tiffany, and their four daughters, Rebecca, Emily, Annabelle, and Miranda.

John J. Croft IV

John J. Croft IV graduated from the Georgia Institute of Technology in 1991, receiving a bachelor's degree in mechanical engineering. He then spent five years consulting for large companies, including Coca-Cola, BellSouth, and MCI. Work at these companies primarily involved C and C++ programming and object-oriented systems analysis. His various clients have included both Fortune 100s and small startup companies. Their problems have ranged drastically, from large databases and executive information systems to lithotripter control and satellite telemetry. Croft has completed projects with Java, XML, and, recently, C# and .NET applications. He is a partner in Scalable Development, Inc.

J. Ambrose Little

Ambrose is the editor-in-chief of the ASPAlliance, an ASPInsider, and a Microsoft ASP.NET MVP who currently works as a Web architect for a large credit union in Tampa, Florida. Previously, he worked as a consultant at Verizon, creating XML Web Services and middle-tier components, and for BOK Financial's Web Services department creating ASP.NET applications for their intranet. His pre-.NET programming experience consists mostly of developing Web applications using ASP and VB COM/DCOM for several years. He has a bachelor's degree in medieval European history, which remains an interest. Apart from developing software, he enjoys movies, reading, writing, foosball, chess, tennis, badminton, and spending time with his wonderful family.

Bill Ryan

Bill currently works as a senior software developer for TiBA Solutions in Greenville, SC. He is also a Windows Embedded MVP, has served on Macromedia's Flash Advisory Board, and helps run two popular .NET Focused Web sites (www.devbuzz.com and www.knowdotnet.com) and his blog www.msmvps.com/WilliamRyan. After earning his master's degree in business administration, Bill began work as a statistical analyst, but quickly realized that his true love was programming. He has worked in multiple industries, including financial services/securities, manufacturing, health care, pharmaceuticals, and, currently, consulting. Bill is a frequent speaker at user's group meetings, has spoken at multiple Microsoft Code Camps, and has hosted multiple MSDN Webcasts. Although technologically related things consume most of his time, Bill's other interests include cult films, economics, Freemasonry, cuckoo clocks, and, most important, his girlfriend, Kim, and her daughter, Sarah.

Phil Winstanley

Phil Winstanley is a Web applications developer working for Portfolio Europe, located in Manchester, England. He has been involved with ASP.NET since its inception, and has developed a deep understanding of the platform. As a Microsoft MVP (Most Valuable Professional), member of the ASPInsiders, co-owner of Microsoft Web Developers UK, and the North West England Regional Director for the .NET Exchange, Phil is deeply embedded in the development community and works closely with the Web Platforms team at Microsoft, regularly visiting the developers in Redmond, Washington.

David Yack

David is the president of Colorado Technology Consultants, Inc. He is a hands-on technology consultant with solid management experience in privately held and Fortune 500 companies and has over 15 years of experience in the IT industry. David is currently responsible for leading Colorado Technology Consultants' focus on Microsoft .NET technologies. David is an active participant in the Microsoft development community, ranging from the Denver .NET user group to Microsoft's Public Communities, such as www.asp.net and http://aspalliance.com. David is the leader of the South Colorado .NET user group. David is recognized by Microsoft as a .NET MVP (Most Valuable Professional).

Jeremy Zongker

Jeremy Zongker is a software development manager who works primarily on data-driven ASP.NET applications with Microsoft SQL Server databases. He is a Microsoft Certified Solutions Developer for .NET and a 2004 MVP for ASP.NET. Jeremy is the founder and senior developer for Trilitech, LLC, a Broken Arrow, Oklahoma, software development company.

Credits

Acquisitions Editor
Bob Elliott

Development Editor
Gabrielle Nabi

Production Editor
William A. Barton

Technical Editor
Anand Narayanaswamy

Copy Editor
Luann Rouff

Editorial Manager
Mary Beth Wakefield

Vice President and Publisher
Joseph B. Wikert

Project Coordinator
Michael Kruzil

Graphics and Production Specialists
Carrie Foster
Denny Hager
Jennifer Heleine
Alicia B. South

Quality Control Technicians
Amanda Briggs
John Greenough

Media Development Specialists
Angela Denny
Kit Malone
Travis Silvers

Proofreading and Indexing
TECHBOOKS Production Services

For my wife, Ronda, my two children, Kirsten and Bradley, and the rest of my family.

—*Wallace B. McClure*

To my loving wife and four daughters, and to God, without whom the aforementioned miracles would not be possible.

—*Greg Beamer*

To my wife, Valerie, for her support, and to my boys, Jack and Conor, for their patience on the weekends while I was writing.

—*John J. Croft IV*

To my mom and stepfather, for putting up with me all of these years and always being there. To my girlfriend, Kim, and her daughter, Sarah, for always being able to make me smile.

—*Bill Ryan*

For my wife, Julie, and my two great kids, Drew and Jacqueline.

—*David Yack*

For my wife, Jeanette, for her support, patience, and understanding during the many hours I worked on this book.

—*Jeremy Zongker*

To my caring father and mother, my loving brother, and to the Almighty, for giving me the power to work every day.

—*Anand Narayanaswamy,*
Technical Editor

Acknowledgments

The initial planning and thinking about this book began during a discussion of SQL Server futures in July 2001. The discussion was with Rob Howard during a trip to Microsoft to discuss the first book I was working on at that time. After that, I stayed involved in what was happening in ADO.NET by going to the SQL Server Yukon Technical Preview in Bellevue, Washington, in February 2002 and by working with the ASP.NET and SQL Server teams at Microsoft since July 2003.

Shortly after the excitement of talking with Bob Elliott at Wiley about this book wore off, it became apparent that I would need to put together an author team that knew about the problems Microsoft was trying to solve with ADO.NET Version 2. It is fortunate that I had recently been named a Microsoft MVP and an ASPInsider. Based on memberships in those groups, I was able to work with and gain the respect of Jeremy Zongker, Ambrose Little, and Phil Winstanley. From that group, I was able to meet David Yack, William (Bill) Ryan, and Gregory Beamer. Adding these six people to John Croft and myself, we created a really good group to work with. I want to thank them for working together very well, for working quickly, and for examining the new features that are provided by ADO.NET 2 that are of particular interest to developers and readers of this book.

Personally, I would like to thank Bob Elliott for keeping me focused on what was going on and working with us to develop this book. Our thanks also go out to the editorial staff at Wiley. Their help keeping us on track as "life happened" was appreciated. The work of our technical editor, Anand Narayanaswamy, was impressive, and his attention to detail was great. Many other people behind the scenes have worked hard on the book. By pulling this group together, Wiley created a team that was dedicated to creating the best possible book on ADO.NET Version 2. For that, we are truly appreciative.

— *Wallace B. McClure and the author team*

Contents

Contents

Contents

Contents

Contents

Contents

Contents

Introduction

Thank you for purchasing *Professional ADO.NET 2*. We know you have a lot of options when selecting a programming book and are glad that you have chosen ours. We're sure you will be pleased with the relevant content and high quality you have come to expect from the Wrox Press line.

What This Book Is About

A few years ago, Microsoft released the 1.0 Framework of ADO.NET and revolutionized the way we access data. It was a drastic change that took some getting used to, but for the most part, developers who made the switch love it. It's now over three years later, and ADO.NET 2.0 is here. It provides all the same features that we've come to love in ADO.NET 1.0 and adds some new ones to provide even more functionality and make repetitive, mundane tasks much simpler. Throughout this book, we dig deeply into many of these new features.

As you start reading, you'll notice that several chapters go beyond ADO.NET, focusing more on Microsoft SQL Server 2005. This is because the two are very tightly related. Many of the new features in ADO.NET 2.0 are designed to be used with Microsoft SQL Server 2005, and many of the new features found in SQL 2005 require ADO.NET 2.0 to get the most benefit from them. It wouldn't be practical to speak strictly about ADO.NET without providing some basic working knowledge about what's new in SQL 2005. Most people will likely move to both technologies around the same time, so this additional information should be very beneficial.

Who Should Buy This Book

As mentioned previously, this book contains information about both ADO.NET 2.0 and Microsoft SQL Server 2005. It is useful for a wide variety of people, including IS managers, project managers, developers, database administrators, system architects, business analysts, and software testers. Of course, because it focuses on developing applications using ADO.NET, software developers will benefit most from it.

Because this book focuses primarily on the new features of ADO.NET 2.0, prior knowledge of ADO.NET 1.0, general .NET development, and Microsoft SQL Server is assumed. In order to completely use the information in this book, you will need a copy of Visual Studio 2005 and Microsoft SQL Server 2005.

How to Use This Book

To provide consistency throughout the book and help you quickly identify important pieces of information, several standards have been used. We recognize that many developers have their own naming conventions. However, we are using the naming conventions recommended by Microsoft, at http://msdn.microsoft.com/library/en-us/cpgenref/html/cpconnamingguidelines.asp, which should also be compatible with the default rules in Fx Cop.

We have employed a standard format for highlighting code. Any time a code example is presented for the first time, it appears with a gray background, like this:

```
Private Sub HelloWorld()
   Response.Write("Hello World")
End Sub
```

Any time a section of code is presented again, it appears without the gray background:

```
Private Sub HelloWorld()
   Response.Write("Hello World")
End Sub
```

We highlight important information by having it appear in a box, like this:

> **This is an important fact.**

Notes or tips appear in italics, like this:

This is a note.

Because this is a book written by programmers for programmers, it includes a lot of code samples. If you want to download these samples, you can do so from our Web site, at www.wrox.com. The code samples in the book are provided in VB.NET, but C# samples are also available for download from the Web site.

We tried our best to ensure that this book was error-free, but every once in a while, errors slip through. To keep you informed of necessary corrections, you can find the complete errata on our Web site. If you discover an error that hasn't been reported yet, please let us know by going to www.wrox.com.

What This Book Covers

The following list provides a breakdown of the topics covered in each chapter:

❑   **Chapter 1**—A brief history of data access technologies so you can see why some of the features are needed. It also touches on the major design goals of ADO.NET 2.0 and highlights what is covered in the rest of the book.

- ❑ **Chapter 2**—Basic database design concepts, primarily in Microsoft SQL Server 2005. It also covers creating databases, tables, and views following third normal form and the importance of primary and foreign keys. It shows you how to optimize performance using indexes and other methods, and in general provides you with a solid foundation for developing database-driven applications.

- ❑ **Chapter 3**—The basics of creating a connection, executing a query, and returning a result. It also digs deeply into many of these areas, showing best practices and techniques for optimizing your code. It covers scenarios for which it may or may not be appropriate to use features such as DataSets and DataViews. It also covers the various options for persisting data back to a database, and introduces new techniques in ADO.NET 2.0. Finally, it introduces the new APIs available for schema discovery and connection pooling.

- ❑ **Chapter 4**—Delves into the new data types available in the 2.0 Framework, and discusses the appropriate situations in which to use them.

- ❑ **Chapter 5**—Covers many of the new features available for XML integration. It offers a brief overview of how XML evolved, the numerous designer enhancements and new features available in XmlReader and XmlWriter, and introduces the XPathDocument as the new standard for storing XML documents. It details new validation features and highlights many of the performance gains available in this framework, and provides a roadmap to where XML technologies are heading.

- ❑ **Chapter 6**—Looks into the new transactional capabilities available in the ADO.NET 2.0 Framework and how to integrate them with Microsoft SQL Server 2005 and other data sources. It covers locking, replication, and other design issues.

- ❑ **Chapter 7**—Covers the details of data binding. It shows how to use the ADO.NET 2.0 design time programmability features in Visual Studio.NET. It also shows off the new TableAdapters and DataConnectors. You will see how you can data bind not only to database queries, but to Web services, business objects, and other sources.

- ❑ **Chapter 8**—In this chapter, you learn how to create a custom ADO.NET managed provider. Step by step, you'll create your own provider, including the various interfaces for creating connections, commands, readers, and adapters.

- ❑ **Chapter 9**—Shows the new TSQL language enhancements available in Microsoft SQL Server 2005. It also covers how these new features tightly integrate with the ADO.NET 2.0 Framework.

- ❑ **Chapter 10**—Covers the details of integrating the new Microsoft SQL Server 2005 features into a client application using ADO.NET 2.0. In this chapter, you learn about the new asynchronous support features, the capability to return multiple result sets from a query, and how to initiate bulk copies. You also learn how to use the new caching features, create your own user-defined data types, and explore various new APIs for working with Microsoft SQL Server 2005.

- ❑ **Chapter 11**—Shows how to use many of the new CLR capabilities of Microsoft SQL Server 2005. You'll learn how to create CLR code in stored procedures, how to use CLR objects for data types, and how to debug your CLR code in Microsoft SQL Server 2005.

- ❑ **Chapter 12**—Provides a detailed description of how to create a Notification Services application in Microsoft SQL Server 2005. It starts from the beginning, assuming no prior experience with notification services, and shows how to create an application from the ground up, including how to interface with that application from custom .NET code.

❑ **Chapter 13**—Shows off the message queuing functionality in the .NET 2.0 Framework by introducing the Service Broker. It covers the feature set and the various options and describes how to use them to develop scalable applications.

❑ **Chapter 14**—Displays how to use the full text search capabilities of Microsoft SQL Server 2005. It provides a background on full text searches, covers the new features available and how to enable them, and describes the best practices for using them.

❑ **Chapter 15**—Many tools are available for retrieving data and presenting it in various ways. This chapter covers some of the most common tools, such as Crystal Reports, Microsoft SQL Reporting Services, OLAP, and other business analysis tools, and shows how to best use them with Microsoft SQL Server 2005.

❑ **Chapter 16**—MySQL is an option for data storage that is rapidly growing in popularity. In this chapter, you examine the new provider available for MySQL and learn how to best utilize it to maximize performance and scalability.

❑ **Chapter 17**—Shows how to best use Oracle in the ADO.NET Framework. It shows off the features specific to the Oracle Managed provider in ADO.NET 2.0. It covers topics such as blobs, clobs, bfiles, packages, and transactions.

Providing Feedback

This book wouldn't have been possible without the hard work of many people. We know our readers work hard for their money and have high expectations regarding the quality of the books they purchase. We have strived to exceed those expectations, but are always looking for ways we can improve. We would love to hear your feedback. If you would like to report an error, let us know what you did and did not like about various sections, or suggest what you'd like to see in future versions, please contact us via our Web site, at www.wrox.com. Once again, thank you for your purchase and we hope you enjoy the book.

History of Data Access

Over the years, many APIs have been released, all of which work toward the goal of providing universal data access. Universal data access is the concept of having a single code base for accessing data from any source, from any language.

Having universal data access is important for four reasons: First, developers can easily work on applications targeting different data stores without needing to become experts on each one. Second, developers can have a common framework for data access when switching between programming languages, making the transition to new languages easier. This is especially important in the .NET Framework, in which developers are expected to be able to easily switch between VB.NET and C#. Third, it enables developers to more easily write a single application that can be deployed against multiple data stores. Finally, it provides a level of abstraction between the application and direct communication to the database to simplify the code the average developer needs to write.

Microsoft has conducted surveys to determine which key factors companies are looking for in a data access layer. They came back with four main points, which they have tried to implement in their databases and data access components:

❑ **High performance** — As any developer knows, performance can make or break almost any application. No matter how much a data access layer may simplify accessing the data, it absolutely must perform nearly as well or better than the alternatives before it becomes a viable solution for the majority of applications.

❑ **High reliability** — If a component consumed by an application is buggy or occasionally stops working, it is perceived by the users as an error in that application. In addition to being a liability and annoyance to the company that implemented the application, it also reflects very poorly on the developer(s) who wrote the application. Any issues, such as memory leaks, that cause unreliable results are unacceptable to the development community. It's also very important to the support personnel that it be fairly maintenance-free. No one wants to have to reboot a server on a regular basis or constantly apply patches just to keep an application running.

❑ **Vendor commitment** — Without the widespread buy-in of vendors to build drivers/providers for their products, any universal data access model wouldn't be universal. Microsoft could provide the drivers for some of the most common vendor products, but it really takes an open, easily extensible model in order to gain widespread acceptance. No matter how much companies try to avoid it, almost all of them become "locked-in" to at least a handful of vendors. Switching to a vendor that supports the latest data access components is not really an option, so without widespread buy-in from vendors, a data access model cannot succeed.

❑ **Broad industry support** — This factor is along the same lines as vendor commitment, but includes a wider arena. It takes more than the data access model to be able to easily create good applications with it; it also requires good tools that can work with the data access model. Furthermore, it requires backing by several big players in the industry to reassure the masses. It also requires highly skilled people available to offer training. Finally, of course, it requires willing adoption by the development community so employers can find employees with experience.

Steady progress has been made, improving databases and universal data access over the last few decades. As with any field, it's important to know where we've come from in database and data access technologies in order to understand where the fields are heading. The following section looks at some early achievements.

The Early Days

In the 1950s and early 1960s, data access and storage was relatively simple for most people. While more advanced projects were under development and in use by a limited number of people, the majority of developers still stored data in flat text files. These were usually fixed-width files, and accessing them required no more than the capability to read and write files. Although this was a very simple technique for storing data, it didn't take too long to realize it wasn't the most efficient method in most cases.

CODASYL

As with the Internet, databases as we know them today began with the U.S. Department of Defense. In 1957, the U.S. Department of Defense founded the *Conference on Data Systems Languages*, commonly known as *CODASYL*, to develop computer programming languages. CODASYL is most famous for the creation of the COBOL programming language, but many people don't know that CODASYL is also responsible for the creation of the first modern database.

On June 10, 1963, two divisions of the U.S. Department of Defense held a conference titled "Development and Management of a Computer-Centered Data Base." At this conference, the term *database* was coined and defined as follows:

> **A set of files (tables), where a *file* is an ordered collection of entries (rows) and an *entry* consists of a key or keys and data.**

Two years later, in 1965, CODASYL formed a group called the List Processing Task Force, which later became the Data Base Task Group. The Data Base Task Group released an important report in 1971 outlining the *Network Data Model*, also known as the *CODASYL Data Model* or *DBTG Data Model*. This data model defined several key concepts of a database, including the following:

- ❑ A syntax for defining a schema
- ❑ A syntax for defining a subschema
- ❑ A data manipulation language

These concepts were later incorporated into the COBOL programming language. They also served as a base design for many subsequent data storage systems.

IMS

During the same period CODASYL was creating the Network Data Model, another effort was under way to create the first hierarchical database. During the space race, North American Rockwell won the contract to launch the first spacecraft to the moon. In 1966, members of IBM, North American Rockwell, and Caterpillar Tractor came together to begin the design and development of the Information Control System (ICS) and Data Language/I (DL/I). This system was designed to assist in tracking materials needed for the construction of the spacecraft.

The ICS portion of this system was the database portion responsible for storing and retrieving the data, while the DL/I portion was the query language needed to interface with it. In 1968, the IBM portion of this system (ICS) was renamed to *Information Management System,* or *IMS*. Over time, the DL/I portion was enhanced to provide features such as message queuing, and eventually became the transaction manager portion of IMS. IMS continued to evolve and was adopted by numerous major organizations, many of which still use it today.

Relational Databases

Both the Network Data Model from CODASYL and IMS from IBM were major steps forward because they marked the paradigm shift of separating data from application code, and they laid the framework for what a database should look like. However, they both had an annoying drawback: They expected programmers to navigate around the dataset to find what they wanted — thus, they are sometimes called *navigational databases*.

In 1970, Edgar Codd, a British computer scientist working for IBM, released an important paper called "A Relational Model of Data for Large Shared Data Banks" in which he introduced the *relational model*. In this model, Codd emphasized the importance of separating the raw, generic data types from the machine-specific data types, and exposing a simple, high-level query language for accessing this data. This shift in thinking would enable developers to perform operations against an entire data set at once instead of working with a single row at a time.

Within a few years, two systems were developed based on Codd's ideas. The first was an IBM project known as *System R*; the other was *Ingres* from the University of California at Berkeley. During the course of development for IBM's System R, a new query language known as *Structured Query Language (SQL)* was born. While System R was a great success for proving the relational database concept and creating SQL, it was never a commercial success for IBM. They did, however, release SQL/DS in 1980, which was a huge commercial success (and largely based on System R).

The Ingres project was backed by several U.S. military research agencies and was very similar to System R in many ways, although it ran on a different platform. One key advantage that Ingres had over System R that led to its longevity was the fact that the Ingres source code was publicly available, although it was later commercialized and released by Computer Associates in the 1980s.

Over the next couple of decades, databases continued to evolve. Modern databases such as Oracle, Microsoft SQL Server, MySQL, and LDAP are all highly influenced by these first few databases. They have improved greatly over time to handle very high transaction volume, to work with large amounts of data, and to offer high scalability and reliability.

The Birth of Universal Data Access

At first, there were no common interfaces for accessing data. Each data provider exposed an API or other means of accessing its data. The developer only had to be familiar with the API of the data provider he or she used. When companies switched to a new database system, any knowledge of how to use the old system became worthless and the developer had to learn a new system from scratch. As time went on, more data providers became available and developers were expected to have intimate knowledge of several forms of data access. Something needed to be done to standardize the way in which data was retrieved from various sources.

ODBC

Open Database Connectivity (ODBC) helped address the problem of needing to know the details of each DBMS used. ODBC provides a single interface for accessing a number of database systems. To accomplish this, ODBC provides a driver model for accessing data. Any database provider can write a driver for ODBC to access data from their database system. This enables developers to access that database through the ODBC drivers instead of talking directly to the database system. For data sources such as files, the ODBC driver plays the role of the engine, providing direct access to the data source. In cases where the ODBC driver needs to connect to a database server, the ODBC driver typically acts as a wrapper around the API exposed by the database server.

With this model, developers move from one DBMS to another and use many of the skills they have already acquired. Perhaps more important, a developer can write an application that doesn't target a specific database system. This is especially beneficial for vendors who write applications to be consumed by multiple customers. It gives customers the capability to choose the back-end database system they want to use, without requiring vendors to create several versions of their applications.

ODBC was a huge leap forward and helped to greatly simplify database-driven application development. It does have some shortfalls, though. First, it is only capable of supporting relational data. If you need to access a hierarchical data source such as LDAP, or semi-structured data, ODBC can't help you. Second, it can only handle SQL statements, and the result must be representable in the form of rows and columns. Overall, ODBC was a huge success, considering what the previous environment was like.

OLE-DB

Object Linking and Embedding Database (OLE-DB) was the next big step forward in data providers, and it is still widely used today. With OLE-DB, Microsoft applied the knowledge learned from developing ODBC to provide a better data access model. OLE-DB marked Microsoft's move to a COM-based API, which made it easily consumable by most programming languages, and the migration to a 32-bit OS with the release of Windows 95.

As with any code, ODBC became bulky through multiple revisions. The OLE-DB API is much cleaner and provides more efficient data access than ODBC. Oddly enough, the only provider offered with its initial release was the ODBC provider. It was just a wrapper of the ODBC provider and offered no performance gain. The point was to get developers used to the new API while making it possible to access any existing database system they were currently accessing through ODBC. Later, more efficient providers were written to access databases such as MS SQL Server directly, without going through ODBC.

OLE-DB Providers

OLE-DB is also much less dependent upon the physical structure of the database. It supports both relational and hierarchical data sources, and does not require the query against these data sources to follow a SQL structure. As with ODBC, vendors can create custom providers to expose access to their database system. Most people wouldn't argue with the belief that it is far easier to write an OLE-DB provider than an ODBC driver. A provider needs to perform only four basic steps:

1. Open the session.
2. Process the command.
3. Access the data.
4. Prepare a rowset.

OLE-DB Consumers

The other half of the OLE-DB framework is the OLE-DB consumer. The consumer is the layer that speaks directly to the OLE-DB providers, and it performs the following steps:

1. Identify the data source.
2. Establish a session.
3. Issue the command.
4. Return a rowset.

Figure 1-1 shows how this relationship works.

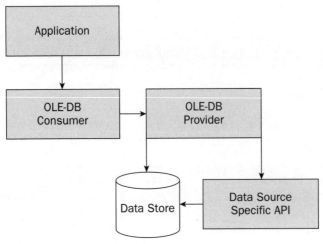

Figure 1-1

Data Access Consumers

Developers who use languages that support pointers — such as C, C++, VJ++, and so on — can speak directly to the ODBC and OLE-DB APIs. However, developers using a language such as Visual Basic need another layer. This is where the data access consumers such as DAO, RDO, ADO, and ADO.NET come into play.

DAO

With the release of Visual Basic 2.0, developers were introduced to a new method for accessing data, known as *Data Access Objects (DAO)*. This was Microsoft's first attempt to create a data consumer API. Although it had very humble beginnings, and when first released only supported forward-only operations against ODBC data sources, it was the beginning of a series of libraries that would lead developers closer to the ideal of Universal Data Access. It also helped developers using higher-level languages such as Visual Basic to take advantage of the power of ODBC that developers using lower-level languages such as C were beginning to take for granted.

DAO was based on the JET engine, which was largely designed to help developers take advantage of the desktop database application Microsoft was about to release, Microsoft Access. It served to provide another layer of abstraction between the application and data access, making the developer's task simpler. Although the initial, unnamed release with Visual Basic 2.0 only supported ODBC connections, the release of Microsoft Access 1.0 marked the official release of DAO 1.0, which supported direct communication with Microsoft Access databases without using ODBC. Figure 1-2 shows this relationship.

DAO 2.0 was expanded to support OLE-DB connections and the advantages that come along with it. It also provided a much more robust set of functionality for accessing ODBC data stores through the JET engine. Later, versions 2.5 and 3.0 were released to provide support for ODBC 2.0 and the 32-bit OS introduced with Windows 95.

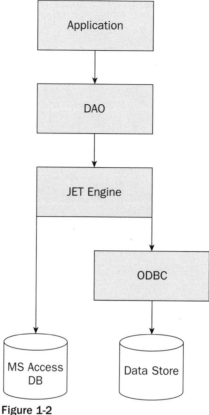

Figure 1-2

The main problem with DAO is that it can only talk to the JET engine. The JET engine then communicates with ODBC to retrieve the data. Going through this extra translation layer adds unnecessary overhead and makes accessing data through DAO slow.

RDO

Remote Data Objects (RDO) was Microsoft's solution to the slow performance created by DAO. For talking to databases other than Microsoft Access, RDO did not use the JET engine like DAO; instead, it communicated directly with the ODBC layer. Figure 1-3 shows this relationship.

Removing the JET engine from the call stack greatly improved performance to ODBC data sources. The JET engine was only used when accessing a Microsoft Access Database. In addition, RDO had the capability to use client-side cursors to navigate the records, as opposed to the server-side cursor requirements of DAO. This greatly reduced the load on the database server, enabling not only the application to perform better, but also the databases on which that application was dependant.

RDO was primarily targeted toward larger, commercial customers, many of whom avoided DAO due to the performance issues. Instead of RDO replacing DAO, they largely co-existed. This resulted for several reasons: First, users who developed smaller applications, where performance wasn't as critical, didn't want to take the time to switch over to the new API. Second, RDO was originally only released with the Enterprise Edition of Visual Basic, so some developers didn't have a choice. Third, with the release of

ODBCDirect, a DAO add-on that routed the ODBC requests through RDO instead of the JET engine, the performance gap between the two became much smaller. Finally, it wasn't long after the release of RDO that Microsoft's next universal access API was released.

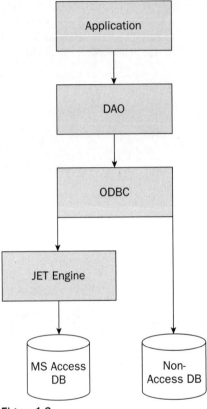

Figure 1-3

ADO

Microsoft introduced ActiveX Data Objects (ADO) primarily to provide a higher-level API for working with OLE-DB. With this release, Microsoft took many of the lessons from the past to build a lighter, more efficient, and more universal data access API. Unlike RDO, ADO was initially promoted as a replacement for both DAO and RDO. At the time of its release, it (along with OLE-DB) was widely believed to be a universal solution for accessing any type of data — from databases to e-mail, flat text files, and spreadsheets.

ADO represented a major shift from previous methods of data access. With DAO and RDO, developers were expected to navigate a tree of objects in order to build and execute queries. For example, to execute a simple insert query in RDO, developers couldn't just create an `rdoQuery` object and execute it. Instead, they first needed to create the `rdoEngine` object, then the `rdoEnvironment` as a child of it, then an `rdoConnection`, and finally the `rdoQuery`. It was a very similar situation with DAO. With ADO, however, this sequence was much simpler. Developers could just create a command object directly, passing in the connection information and executing it. For simplicity and best practice, most developers would still create a separate command object, but for the first time the object could stand alone.

As stated before, ADO was primarily released to complement OLE-DB; however, ADO was not limited to just communicating with OLE-DB data sources. ADO introduced the provider model, which enabled software vendors to create their own providers relatively easily, which could then be used by ADO to communicate with a given vendor's data source and implement many of the optimizations specific to that data source. The ODBC provider that shipped with ADO was one example of this. When a developer connected to an ODBC data source, ADO would communicate through the ODBC provider instead of through OLE-DB. More direct communication to the data source resulted in better performance and an easily extensible framework. Figure 1-4 shows this relationship.

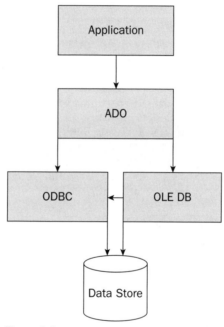

Figure 1-4

In addition to being a cleaner object model, ADO also offered a wider feature set to help lure developers away from DAO and RDO. These included the following:

❑ **Batch Updating** — For the first time, users enjoyed the capability to make changes to an entire recordset in memory and then persist these changes back to the database by using the UpdateBatch command.

❑ **Disconnected Data Access** — Although this wasn't available in the original release, subsequent releases offered the capability to work with data in a disconnected state, which greatly reduced the load placed on database servers.

❑ **Multiple Recordsets** — ADO provided the capability to execute a query that returns multiple recordsets and work with all of them in memory. This feature wasn't even available in ADO.NET until this release, now known as *Multiple Active Result Sets (MARS)*.

In addition to all of the great advancements ADO made, it too had some shortcomings, of course. For example, even though it supported working with disconnected data, this was somewhat cumbersome. For this reason, many developers never chose to use this feature, while many others never even knew it existed. This standard practice of leaving the connection open resulted in heavier loads placed on the database server.

The developers who did choose to close the connection immediately after retrieving the data faced another problem: having to continually create and destroy connections in each method that needed to access data. This is a very expensive operation without the advantages of connection pooling that ADO.NET offers; and as a result, many best practice articles were published advising users to leave a single connection object open and forward it on to all the methods that needed to access data.

ADO.NET

With the release of the .NET Framework, Microsoft introduced a new data access model, called *ADO.NET*. The ActiveX Data Object acronym was no longer relevant, as ADO.NET was not ActiveX, but Microsoft kept the acronym due to the huge success of ADO. In reality, it's an entirely new data access model written in the .NET Framework.

ADO.NET supports communication to data sources through both ODBC and OLE-DB, but it also offers another option of using database-specific data providers. These data providers offer greater performance by being able to take advantage of data-source-specific optimizations. By using custom code for the data source instead of the generic ODBC and OLE-DB code, some of the overhead is also avoided. The original release of ADO.NET included a SQL provider and an OLE-DB provider, with the ODBC and Oracle providers being introduced later. Many vendors have also written providers for their databases since. Figure 1.5 shows the connection options available with ADO.NET.

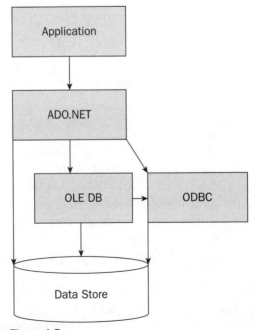

Figure 1-5

With ADO.NET, the days of the recordset and cursor are gone. The model is entirely new, and consists of five basic objects:

- ❏ **Connection** — The `Connection` object is responsible for establishing and maintaining the connection to the data source, along with any connection-specific information.

- ❏ **Command** — The `Command` object stores the query that is to be sent to the data source, and any applicable parameters.

- ❏ **DataReader** — The `DataReader` object provides fast, forward-only reading capability to quickly loop through the records.

- ❏ **DataSet** — The `DataSet` object, along with its child objects, is what really makes ADO.NET unique. It provides a storage mechanism for disconnected data. The `DataSet` never communicates with any data source and is totally unaware of the source of the data used to populate it. The best way to think of it is as an in-memory repository to store data that has been retrieved.

- ❏ **DataAdapter** — The `DataAdapter` object is what bridges the gap between the `DataSet` and the data source. The `DataAdapter` is responsible for retrieving the data from the `Command` object and populating the `DataSet` with the data returned. The `DataAdapter` is also responsible for persisting changes to the `DataSet` back to the data source.

ADO.NET made several huge leaps forward. Arguably, the greatest was the introduction of truly disconnected data access. Maintaining a connection to a database server such as MS SQL Server is an expensive operation. The server allocates resources to each connection, so it's important to limit the number of simultaneous connections. By disconnecting from the server as soon as the data is retrieved, instead of when the code is done working with that data, that connection becomes available for another process, making the application much more scalable.

Another feature of ADO.NET that greatly improved performance was the introduction of connection pooling. Not only is maintaining a connection to the database an expensive operation, but creating and destroying that connection is also very expensive. Connection pooling cuts down on this. When a connection is destroyed in code, the Framework keeps it open in a pool. When the next process comes around that needs a connection with the same credentials, it retrieves it from the pool, instead of creating a new one.

Several other advantages are made possible by the `DataSet` object. The `DataSet` object stores the data as XML, which makes it easy to filter and sort the data in memory. It also makes it easy to convert the data to other formats, as well as easily persist it to another data store and restore it again.

ADO.NET 2.0

Data access technologies have come a long way, but even with ADO.NET, there's still room to grow. The transition to ADO.NET 2.0 is not a drastic one. For the most part, Microsoft and the developers who use ADO.NET like it the way it is. In the 2.0 Framework, the basic design is the same, but several new features have been added to make common tasks easier, which is very good for backward compatibility. ADO.NET 2.0 should be 100% backwardly compatible with any ADO.NET 1.0 code you have written.

With any 2.0 product, the primary design goal is almost always to improve performance. ADO.NET 1.0 does not perform poorly by any means, but a few areas could use improvement, including XML serialization and connection pooling, which have been reworked to provide greater performance.

In the 2.0 Framework, Microsoft has also been able to improve performance by introducing several new features to reduce the number of queries that need to be run and to make it easier to run multiple queries at once. For example, the bulk insert feature provides the capability to add multiple rows to a database with a single query, instead of the current method of inserting one at a time. This can greatly reduce the amount of time it takes to insert a large number of rows.

Another example is the capability to be notified when data changes and to expire the cache only when this happens. This eliminates the need to periodically dump and reload a potentially large amount of data just in case something has changed. The introduction of *Multiple Active Result Sets (MARS)* provides the capability to execute multiple queries at once and receive a series of results. Removing the back and forth communication that is required by executing one query at a time and waiting for the results greatly improves the performance of an application that needs this functionality. If you prefer to do other work while waiting for your data to return, you also have the option of firing an asynchronous command. This has been greatly simplified in the 2.0 Framework.

Another major design goal is to reduce the amount of code necessary to perform common tasks. The buzz phrase we all heard with the release of .NET Framework 1.0 was "70 percent less code" than previous methods. The goal with the .NET 2.0 Framework is the same: to reduce the amount of code needed for common tasks by 70% over .NET 1.0. We'll leave the decision as to whether this goal was met or not to you, but after reading this book and using ADO.NET for awhile, you should notice a significant decrease in the amount of code needed to write your application.

The rest of the enhancements are primarily new features. For example, there is now a database discovery API for browsing the schema of a database. Also offered is the option of writing provider-independent database access code. This is very beneficial if you sell applications to customers who want to run it against numerous data sources. Keep in mind that the queries you write still must match that provider's syntax.

Summary

Now that you know some of the history behind how technologies such as ADO.NET and Microsoft SQL Server have evolved, you should have a clearer vision of where these technologies are heading. Throughout this book, we will cover the new features of these technologies in great depth and lay out the roadmap describing where many of them are heading. This release is just another major stepping-stone on the path to efficient universal data access.

For More Information

To complement the information in this chapter, take a look at the following resources:

❑　*Funding a Revolution: Government Support for Computing Research,* by the Computer Science and Telecommunications Board (CSTB), National Research Council. Washington, D.C.: National Academy Press, 1999. www.nap.edu/execsumm/0309062780.html.

❑　**Network (CODASYL) Data Model (Course Library)** — http://coronet.iicm.edu/ wbtmaster/allcoursescontent/netlib/library.htm

❑　**"Technical Note — IMS Celebrates 30 Years as an IBM Product,"** by Kenneth R. Blackman. www.research.ibm.com/journal/sj/374/blackman.html.

2

Standardized Database Objects and Design

Database design is probably one of the most misunderstood areas of database work. It's also one of the most vital. In this chapter, we'll share our experiences and the lessons we've learned working with both large and small projects. We'll cover the basics of maintainable, normalized design, and offer general guidelines, including useful tips and tricks. You won't find much code in this chapter—just a lot of very useful advice.

Creating Databases

Before you delve into your favorite database editor and start banging out tables left, right, and center, it's important to understand the job at hand. If you've reached the stage in application development where you're ready to start building the databases, then you already have a good idea of what the job entails. This section explains how you should go about initially laying out your tables once you understand the structure of your applications and their requirements.

In an ideal world, every database would be fully normalized, optimized for speed, and designed to make security integral to the structure. Of course, we don't live in an ideal world. Many of the databases out there are slow, unmanageable lumps of goo. Never fear. Together, we can make the world a better place by designing resilient databases that easily cope with the evils of feature creep, the inane promises of our marketing teams, and the abysmal quality of the data that many users seem to think is production-ready.

The key to keeping your life simple is to do the work up front. Because the database is usually the most vital part of any application, it's important to set it up correctly now—to avoid heartache later. Trying to make changes to a long-standing database is incredibly difficult and usually results in breaking other systems. Once a database is in production use, it becomes very difficult to change. In other words, any mistakes made during design will be there weeks, months, and even years down the line, which doesn't do much for the original developer's reputation.

Before you start work on a database, make sure you possess all of the facts regarding the applications that will be using it. The more information you can gather about the uses for the database, the better you can design it to suit those needs. Here are some of the questions you should ask before proceeding:

❑   Do you understand all of the logical units (objects) of the applications using the database?

❑   What are the ways in which people will want to query/manage the data now?

❑   Does the data structure support all of the functionality needed in your applications?

❑   Where are the applications going in their next versions, and do you need to make provisions for that now?

Once you have the answers to these questions, you'll be nearly ready to jump in and run some CREATE commands against your database server. First, though, you should lay out all the logical units (objects) of your solution on paper to show how they will be represented as objects in your applications and tables in your database. You'll learn more about this in greater detail later, in the section called "Normalizing."

Figure 2-1 shows a portion of the table structure for the Northwind database, which ships with SQL Server 2000, viewed as a Database Diagram.

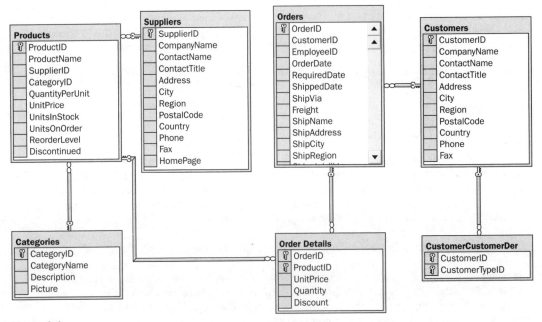

Figure 2-1

By first creating the design on paper, you'll be able to identify and solve numerous problems and challenges. Then, after you have the design, run through the preceding questions again to ensure that you have covered all the bases.

Naming Conventions

Just as important as a solid database design is the naming of your tables, views, and stored procedures. Misnaming or poorly naming your database objects can result in a lot of heartache for both yourself and anyone who has to maintain your applications later.

While choosing a naming convention is a personal decision, we'll show you the conventions we use and explain why we use them. That way, you can make an informed decision about which convention to adopt. Keep in mind, however, that the most important rule in naming conventions is *consistency*. In the following sections, we'll go into detail about naming tables and stored procedures; for now, however, here are a few general rules regarding all database objects:

- ❑   *Do* use Pascal Case.
- ❑   *Don't* let the name get too long. Remember: You'll have to read it and type it.
- ❑   *Don't* use Hungarian notation — in other words, don't prefix objects such as tables with "tbl".
- ❑   *Don't* abbreviate or use acronyms.

Tables

Naming your tables can be very difficult, and if it's not done correctly, it can result in much confusion down the line. Always use Pascal Case when naming your tables. This means that the first letter of each word is capitalized (for example, `CustomerOrders` and `IntranetUsers`). This is the best way to differentiate between SQL keywords such as `SELECT`, `UPDATE`, and `DELETE` in your SQL statements and your table names, which will always be in Pascal Case, and it makes all your queries very easy to understand at a glance.

Hungarian notation should not be used when naming your tables. It's easy to discover what type an object represents in your database server — for example, a table can only be a table, so why bother to name it as such? Tables should be named with plurals, such as `Orders` instead of `Order`. Treat each row of a table as an individual *thing,* such as an order. The table is the bucket for all these individual rows, so it's named plurally. When a table has multiple words, only the last word should be plural. For example, `OrderItems` is preferable to `OrdersItems`, as the table contains a list of *Order Items*, not a list of *Orders Items*.

All tables should be named in relation to their scope. This is especially important if the tables are located in a shared database. Name your tables so they relate to the application in which they will be used or to the functionality that they control. For example, a table of users for an intranet should be named `IntranetUsers`.

Table names should never contain numbers. If you find yourself considering the creation of a table with numbers in the name, it's likely your design is not normalized; consider moving the "number" into a new column within the table itself. A good example of this would be a table listing sales items, which could be grouped together by year. The wrong way to do this would be to name the tables `Sales2003`, `Sales2004`, and so on. Instead, a column should be added to a generic `Sales` table called `Year`, and the values `2003` and `2004` should be placed against the relevant records.

Ensure that no underscores or spaces find their way into your table names. Using Pascal Case for your tables negates the need for underscores in table names, and spaces are only supported by some database servers, so they should be avoided at all costs. Observing these rules will enable you to easily move your entire database schema among many different relational database management servers (just in case you ever get bored).

The following few sections will walk you through naming conventions for every part of a table's structure and its associated objects. Just to clarify what we're talking about, here's the CREATE script for a table in SQL Server:

```
CREATE TABLE [Customers] (
  [CustomerId] [int] IDENTITY (1, 1) NOT FOR REPLICATION  NOT NULL ,
  [CustomerName] [nvarchar] (50) COLLATE SQL_Latin1_General_CP1_CI_AS NULL ,
  [CustomerAddress] [nvarchar] (50) COLLATE SQL_Latin1_General_CP1_CI_AS NULL
  CONSTRAINT [PK_CustomersFirstForm] PRIMARY KEY  CLUSTERED
  (
   [CustomerId]
  )  ON [PRIMARY]
) ON [PRIMARY]
GO
```

Columns

When naming the columns in your tables, keep in mind that the columns already belong to a table, so it is not necessary to include the table name within the column names.

That said, the primary keys in any table should be the only exception to the preceding rule of not including the table name in a column. If your table is IntranetUsers, then the primary key column should be named IntranetUsersId. This helps avoid any ambiguity in any queries written subsequently. The location of *Id* in your column name can appear at either the beginning or the end of the name, so IdIntranetUsers would also be acceptable. Use whichever you prefer—just remember to be consistent throughout your entire database schema.

Foreign keys should match the column they're referencing exactly, so if you had a column in your IntranetUserSettings table that referred to the primary key IntranetUsersId in the IntranetUsers table, then you would name it IntranetUsersId. Carefully consider the naming of other columns that just store data and not keys.

Any Boolean fields should pose a question, such as IsPhotographed or HasOwnTeeth, to which True or False provides a clear answer. (We'll ignore NULL because that's just awkward.)

DateTime fields should contain the word DateTime, so a field for storing the *Created DateTime* for a row should be called CreatedDateTime. If a column is only storing a Time, then it should be named appropriately (CreatedTime, for example).

It is not necessary to use the word "number" in columns of type integer and other numeric columns, as their data type should show this. This rule can be ignored if names seem ambiguous within the scope of your table. In addition, string columns should not have "string" or "text" in their name.

Columns storing ambiguous data such as time periods or speeds should also contain within the name the measurements used for the units, such as PriceUSDollars, SpeedMilesPerHour, or LeaveRemainingInDays.

It's important to take into account not only the names of the columns, but also the data type assigned to them. Only use what's nessesary. If you're storing smaller numbers in SQL Server, use the tinyint or smallint data types instead of the int data type.

Triggers

Triggers should always have a prefix to distinguish them from stored procedures and tables. Choose a self-explanatory prefix you're comfortable with, such as Trig.

All trigger names should include both the table name they're referencing and the events on which they're fired. For example, a trigger on the IntranetUsers table that needs to be fired on both an INSERT and a DELETE would be called TrigIntranetUsersInsertDelete:

```
CREATE TRIGGER TrigIntranetUsersInsertDelete
ON IntranetUsers
FOR INSERT, UPDATE, DELETE
AS
    EXEC master..xp_sendmail 'Security Monkey',
        'Make sure the new users have been added to the right roles!'
GO
```

Here is a reference table you can use to check your triggers for conformance to the naming conventions.

Table	Insert	Update	UpdateInsert
Customers	TrigCustomers Insert	TrigCustomer Update	TrigCustomers UpdateInsert
IntranetUsers	TrigIntranet UsersInsert	TrigIntranet UsersUpdate	TrigIntranetUsers UpdateInsert

Stored Procedures

Everyone likes to do things their own way, and the practice of naming stored procedures is no different. Still, there are some things to keep in mind when naming stored procedures. Use the following questions to create the best possible stored procedure names:

❑ **Will the name be easy to find within the database, both now and when there are a lot more procedures?**

If the procedure is specific to the application that's using it, then it's in the right place and doesn't need to be named specifically. However, if the procedure is in a general or shared database, then it should be named with respect to the application it's related to by prefixing the procedure with the name of the application, such as ReportingSuite, EcommerceWebsite or Intranet.

❏ **Does the name relate to the object on which the actions are being performed?**

The scope of the procedure is the most vital part of its name. If the procedure is adding customers to a table, then it should contain the word `Customer` in its name. If the procedure is referring to invoices, then it would include the name `Invoice`.

❏ **Has the procedure been named in a way in which its action can be identified?**

Whether the stored procedure is performing a simple `SELECT`, `INSERT`, `UPDATE`, or `DELETE`, or whether it's performing a more complicated task, you need to pick a name for the action it's performing.

For example, if you're inserting rows into the `Customer` table, you would use, say, `Add` or `Insert`. However, if the procedure is performing a more complicated task, such as validating a username and password, then it would include the word `Validate` in its name.

A procedure that would insert a new record into the `Customers` table via the `Intranet` application should be called `IntranetCustomerAdd` or `CustomerAdd` depending on whether it's inside the `Intranet` database or in a shared/generic database. The procedure to validate the username and password of an intranet user should be called `IntranetUserValidate`.

A procedure that's selecting a specific customer from the intranet should be called `IntranetCustomerSelect` or `IntranetCustomerGet`, depending on your preferences.

If you were to write a procedure for the `Accounting` application that needed to return a report of all the invoices for a certain customer, it should be called `IntranetCustomerInvoiceGet`, as shown in the following example:

```
CREATE PROC [IntranetCustomerInvoiceGet]
(
        @CustomerId Int
)
AS
SELECT *
FROM CustomerInvoices
WHERE CustomerId = @CustomerId
GO
```

If you're working in a multicompany environment, it can also be a good idea to prefix all of your stored procedures with the name of your company, such as `BadgerCorp_IntranetCustomerAdd` (this is one of the few circumstances in which underscores could be used).

> If you're using SQL Server, do not prefix your stored procedures with "sp_" or "xp_" as this is what SQL Server uses for its internal stored procedures. Not only will this make it difficult to differentiate your custom stored procedures from the database-generated ones, but it will also slow down your applications, as SQL Server checks inside the "Master" database for anything prefixed with "sp_" or "xp_" before looking inside the specified database. If you're using another database server, make sure your procedure names will not clash with any system-specific names.

The following list provides some examples of well-named procedures. These are some of the stored procedures from the ASP.NET 2.0 SQL Server Provider. Although they violate some of the rules mentioned earlier (there's a rather liberal use of underscores, for example), they do show how clarity can easily be achieved when simple rules are followed in even the most complicated of schemas:

```
aspnet_Membership_ChangePasswordQuestionAndAnswer
aspnet_Membership_CreateUser
aspnet_Membership_FindUsersByEmail
aspnet_Membership_FindUsersByName
aspnet_Membership_GetAllUsers
aspnet_Membership_GetNumberOfUsersOnline
aspnet_Membership_GetPassword
aspnet_Membership_GetUserByEmail
aspnet_Membership_GetUserByName
aspnet_Membership_ResetPassword
aspnet_Membership_SetPassword
aspnet_Membership_UpdateLastLoginAndActivityDates
aspnet_Membership_UpdateUser
aspnet_Roles_CreateRole
aspnet_Roles_DeleteRole
aspnet_Roles_GetAllRoles
aspnet_Users_CreateUser
aspnet_Users_DeleteUser
```

The following table provides a quick reference for the naming conventions of stored procedures.

Table	Select	Insert	Delete	Update	Custom
Customers	Customer Get	CustomerAdd date	Customer Delete	CustomerUp	Customer Custom
IntranetUsers	Intranet UserGet	Intranet UserAdd	IntranetUser Delete	IntranetUser Update	Intranet UserCustom

Primary Keys

Every table has a primary key (or at least *should* have one). A primary key enables each row to be uniquely identified by a column or combination of columns.

As already stated, a primary key identifies a row of data in a table, but it does more than that. It also enforces constraints upon the table, enabling checks to be made by the database server to ensure that the data in a row is unique among the other rows in the table by having a different primary key.

The primary key can be defined on just one column or across several and can be set on different data types. Primary keys are usually assigned a numeric data type, although some people also use unique identifiers such as GUIDs. To create a primary key, take a look at the following code sample:

```
CREATE TABLE jobs
(
    job_id  smallint
        IDENTITY(1,1)
```

```
        PRIMARY KEY CLUSTERED,
    job_desc          varchar(50)      NOT NULL
        DEFAULT 'New Position - title not formalized yet',
    min_lvl tinyint NOT NULL
        CHECK (min_lvl >= 10),
    max_lvl tinyint NOT NULL
        CHECK (max_lvl <= 250)
 )
```

Here's a sample for creating a GUID primary key on a table:

```
CREATE TABLE Globally_Unique_Data
(guid uniqueidentifier
    CONSTRAINT Guid_Default
    DEFAULT NEWID(),
Employee_Name varchar(60),
CONSTRAINT Guid_PK PRIMARY KEY (Guid)
 )
```

When the primary key is only on one column, then things are quite straightforward. It's not possible to have two rows with the same value within the primary key column.

If the primary key is made up of multiple columns, it's the combination of values in each column defined as a primary key on the row that make up the unique key. It's possible for values to be repeated within the same primary key column; however, the combination of values across all the primary key columns has to be unique.

> **Try to avoid using GUIDs within your primary keys; they are slower to search for than numeric fields such as Int. GUIDs are primarily used in replication scenarios in which an identity must remain unique so that data may be merged successfully. Moreover, it's easier to remember to type 1 than it is to remember to type 77B3E758-36D1-4890-A4A7-130A71FA07D5.**

Foreign Keys

When you have multiple tables in a database, it's more than likely that they're related in some way, and databases control relationships between tables with *foreign keys*. A foreign key normally matches a primary key in a table. The table of the primary key can be a different table or the same table.

Here's an example of a primary key/foreign key relationship. Suppose you have two tables, Customers and CustomerPets, and inside the Customers table is a column named CustomerId, which is a numeric data type and is set as the primary key of the Customers table. Inside the CustomerPets table is a CustomerPetId column, which is the primary key of that table, but there is also a CustomerId column. The CustomerId column in the CustomerPets table is joined to the Customers table via a relationship, with the primary key being in Customers and the foreign key being in CustomerPets, as shown in Figure 2-2.

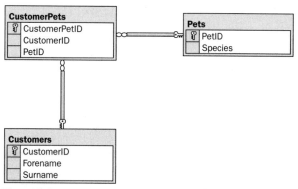

Figure 2-2

Unlike single-column primary keys, it's possible for foreign key columns to have duplicate entries; this enables the formation of one-to-many relationships, and enables us, as in the previous example, to associate a customer with more than one pet.

As stated previously, it's possible for a foreign key to reference the primary key in the same table. This is especially useful when your table lists parent/child relationships. For example, it would be quite simple to build a family tree from a single table of People that has a primary key of PersonId and two foreign keys of MotherId and FatherId, as shown in Figure 2-3.

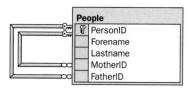

Figure 2-3

If you normalize your databases, you will already have many foreign keys; they are, if you'll excuse the pun, the key to normalization.

Creating a foreign key is very simple. This code shows how to create a key between Customers and CustomerPets:

```
ALTER TABLE Customers
ADD CONSTRAINT fk_customer
FOREIGN KEY (CustomerId)
REFERENCES CustomerPets (CustomerId)
GO
```

Indexes

While indexes are not essential to database design, they are something worth considering. Indexes enable the database server to quickly scan your tables for information, making search operations much faster than the same tables without indexes.

When designing your tables, you need to think about how they will be used, especially which tables will be heavily searched or joined into extensively. Once you've worked this out, it's relatively easy to go into the tables and assign indexes to the columns that are heavily used.

Indexes enable the database to search only a small part of the data, rather than the entire table. Thus, they make searching tables much faster, and the benefits can be huge in terms of performance. Keep in mind that tables with indexes will be slower when calling the INSERT, UPDATE, and DELETE statements, so indexes should only be added to tables that really need fast access.

The columns that should have indexes are those referenced in JOIN or WHERE statements. Primary keys in SQL Server automatically have indexes assigned to them, but not on foreign keys, so you'll need to assign these manually. When you're ready to optimize your current or new systems, always try to apply some indexes to your tables. You could well see dramatic increases in performance.

Views

More often than not, you'll be working with a normalized database schema; and when working with a normalized schema, one of the major drawbacks is the complexity of queries. Views are a great way to hide that complexity by presenting your code with clean, tidy result sets.

Views enable you to look at a table, or a number of tables, in whatever way you want. They act like tables in terms of running CRUD operations against them, but the underlying data might not actually exist in the format in which it's represented. Views enable you to easily abstract your data from the real database layout or to present compiled views of data.

Views also enable you to encapsulate complex queries across many tables and return just the data you need, which can be very useful when you have a fully normalized database and wish to retrieve data that's ready for the presentation layer (after all, you don't need all those primary and foreign keys if you're just showing some search results).

Help with Normalization

You can use Views to normalize data that's all mashed together in the same tables, such as using a SELECT DISTINCT on a textual column of a table that's not normalized to give you a lookup table of the values within:

```
Create View AllCustomerTypes

As

Select Distinct CustomerType
From Customers

Go
```

Performing a select on all of the columns in the `AllCustomerTypes` query returns a normalized list of all possible Customer Types:

```
CustomerType
-------------------------------------------------------
Adored
Beloved
Tolerated
```

Enforcing Security

By only allowing access to your database with views, you can completely control the data that your users are allowed to see, while hiding the real data and database schema from them. An example of this might be allowing your sales assistants to see what type of pets someone has, but not the customer's address:

```
Create View ViewCustomersListPets

As

Select CustomerId, P.PetName
From CustomerPets CP
    Join Pets P
        On P.PetId = CP.PetId

Go
```

In this example, anyone searching for information on the customer can only gain access to the view and thus only the information exposed by the view. The salespeople can only run queries like this:

```
Select CustomerId, PetName
From ViewCustomersListPets
Where CustomerId = 1
```

The query would return data like the following:

```
CustomerId  PetName
----------- ---------------------------------------------
1           Dog
1           Rat
```

As you can see, views can be used to lock down the kind of access you provide to your applications, making your database a much safer environment to let users loose on.

Creating Compiled Views of Data (Reports)

Views are great for creating compiled sets of data from your database. For example, if you wish to know the percentage of your customers that have a cat, then it's quite easy to throw a query together to do this, but there's no need to repeat this SQL in every statement that needs the percentages:

```
Create View CustomerPetPercentages

As

Select PetName, (Convert(Numeric(5,2),Count(PetName))/(Select
Convert(Numeric(5,2),Count(PetName)) From Pets)) * 100 AS 'Percentage'
From dbo.CustomerPets CP
    Join dbo.Pets P
        On P.PetId = CP.PetId
Group By PetName

Go
```

Running a SELECT on the view returns a compiled "View" of the data in both the CustomerPets table and the Pets table. It also performs some calculations, and it's all wrapped up in the view:

PetName	Percentage
Badger	20.00000000
Dog	20.00000000
Giraffe	20.00000000
Rat	40.00000000

In conclusion, views can be very useful for encapsulating business logic and compiling data to make it more user-friendly in a reusable fashion. They can be used liberally with no impact on your database schema in terms of a small performance hit.

Normalizing

This is a topic that is often overcomplicated, but is actually quite simple when you understand it. The best way to describe normalizing a database is think of it as breaking your data down to its logical units, i.e., the smallest possible objects that make up your data. Then, for each one of them, you need to make sure that it lives in it's own table, that the data is not replicated, and that the table in some way relates to other tables where appropriate.

Why Normalize Data?

Normalization isn't just a fad — it's probably the most important part of database design. Without it, you can get into a real mess — if not right now, when you need to make changes to your schema by adding more functionality or by fixing design flaws.

Data should be normalized to remove repeated or redundant data. Doing this instantly reduces the amount of space your databases need to occupy, as well as speeds up scans of your tables — with the free bonuses of gaining increased maintainability and scalability.

By reducing the amount of repeated data, the chance of finding errors in your data is dramatically decreased simply because there is less data to contain errors.

Types of Normalization

There are many different degrees of normalization in both academic and real-world settings. In most cases, the different levels of normalization are linear — for example, there are the nth Normal Forms, whereby First Normal Form is the simplest, and the Third Normal Form is more complicated.

There are four main forms of normalization. Each one represents a different level of normalization — from not normalized at all to the nirvana of normalization.

First Normal Form

With the first form, the goal is to remove any repeated groups of data from any tables. That's an easy concept to grasp: If you've got the same few text labels appearing in a table, then they need to be normalized into their own table, and a foreign key should be added to the table that is storing your data. In addition, if you have multiple columns in a table storing the same type of information, this should also be hived off to a separate table. Remove repeated groups of data.

Second Normal Form

Using the second form, all rows containing the same information should have that information hived out to separate tables with foreign keys linking the data.

Third Normal Form

When trying to achieve the third normal form, all columns in the table that are not directly dependant on the primary key should be removed and placed in their own tables, with foreign keys creating relationships between the tables.

Domain\key Normal Form

This form is the nirvana of normalization. As mentioned previously, databases cannot be more normalized than they are when they're in the Domain\key normal form. Each row of every table has its own identifying column.

Real-world Normalization

Outside of the academic world, there is one form of normalization: The one that works for you for the current project in the allowed time frame.

If you're a masochist and have been given enough time to use the Domain\key model, give it a whirl. However, if your boss is breathing down your neck with a mandate to finish the application yesterday, sometimes it's better to just go with what works with the least amount of effort, and deal with the consequences later.

In 99 percent of the cases, the Second Normal Form is the level you should try to achieve in your projects. It offers the best level of maintenance without too much of a compromise on performance.

Designing a Normalized Database

To create a normalized database, you first need to understand the applications that will be using your database and how they need to work, their feature sets, and any further modifications or features that are to be implemented with future releases. Once you understand the applications, you can begin to map out the database structure.

First, write down a list of all the "things" in your applications, be they customers, pets, products or countries — each of these items will need their own table. Second, work out the different ways in which you need to pull all the data together to provide the kind of information you will need. For example, if you want to know which of your customers in England have a pet badger and bought your kitten warmers, you must have a Purchases table. If you don't, you'll need to add one. Third, map out all of your tables on paper or using a database design tool, such as the diagram tool in SQL Server 2000 Enterprise Manager. Fourth, sit down with each of the application-specification documents again, going through each of the features you require and making sure your database can provide it. If you identify any feature that the database can't fulfill, rethink your design so that it can. Once you've gone through the fourth step a few times, you should be ready to start creating your tables, so dive in, remember the rules, and follow your design.

Ensuring Quality Data

While the primary focus of this chapter has been on the physical structure of database schemas, it's equally important to ensure that the data you're storing is of as high a quality as possible, and that the data you're storing is what you actually need (or will need in the future) — the schema is just a way of holding it.

If you're at the beginning of a project and you're about to start putting the database together, look carefully at your application design document (if there is one that bears any relation to the actual application, and not just the sales teams' interpretation), and make sure you understand the functionality required inside out.

Run through each feature and try to visualize the database; you'll soon see where you need one-to-many relationships, where you'll need fast tables to search, and where you'll need to version your records. All of this needs to be factored into your schema before you dive in and put the database together.

Validating the quality of your data is probably the most important aspect of database design after the layout of your tables. If your data is corrupted or has invalid values, then all of the applications running off the database are susceptible to unknown outcomes, and potentially could crash.

We once wrote a Web application that was built on top of a company's existing product database. The application worked perfectly for months until all of a sudden errors started to occur whenever a search was run against the database server. It became apparent that one of the products on the system had been entered with a ridiculous price of several billion dollars, and the search query (which was doing a bit of price manipulation) didn't like it one bit.

The erroneous data took the application down. If that data had been validated before it went into the database, the crash would never have occurred; and a site would not have been offline for several hours. You know that validation is important, but how can you go about mapping out the validation routines? Basically, you need to ask questions about every column in the database that isn't a primary or foreign key.

Consider some hypothetical examples: Could you let someone put any type of date into a Purchases table? (Were you selling computers in 1930?) Could you have sold them in the future? (Do your customers own a time machine?)

Similarly, what are the realistic prices for your product range if you have one. Would you really sell one of your supercomputers for $29.99? (You may have seen the "bargains" on Amazon occasionally when the odd electrical item is accidentally priced at less than a dollar, causing panic buying and much merriment among the technology community.)

You should perform similar checks against data in the e-mail address column. (For example, you shouldn't have an address without the "@" character in them.) All of these checks and more should be built into your applications, but they should also be in your database server. *Check constraints* can enforce any business rule you like on whatever columns you like in your tables.

For example, in the following table of products, we don't want any products on the database that are priced less than $10,000 or greater than $1,000,000. You can see the check constraint called CK_ProductPrice that shows this business rule:

```
CREATE TABLE [Products] (
    [ProductId] [int] IDENTITY (1, 1) NOT NULL ,
    [ProductName] [nvarchar] (50) COLLATE SQL_Latin1_General_CP1_CI_AS NULL ,
    [ProductPrice] [money] NULL ,
    CONSTRAINT CK_ProductPrice CHECK (ProductPrice >= 10000 And ProductPrice <=
100000),
    CONSTRAINT [PK_Products] PRIMARY KEY  CLUSTERED
    (
        [ProductId]
    )  ON [PRIMARY]
) ON [PRIMARY]
GO
```

Now suppose someone tried to insert a row into the database that doesn't pass our check constraint, such as the following:

```
Insert Into Products
(ProductName,ProductPrice)
Values
('My Socks',5)
```

The database will very helpfully throw out a check constraint conflict error message, preventing those socks from ever appearing in the products list:

```
INSERT statement conflicted with COLUMN CHECK constraint 'CK_ProductPrice'. The
conflict occurred in database 'ADO.NET', table 'Products', column 'ProductPrice'.

The statement has been terminated.
```

To summarize, the database should be designed around the data and required functionality of your applications. That way, you'll get the database that you need, and your boss will shower you with lavish praise.

Making a Flat Database Normalized

More often than not, you'll find databases or portions of a database that are not normalized and which look a lot more like a spreadsheet than something on which you'd base your company's future.

If it's possible to change the way in which the database is structured without seriously affecting the applications that depend on it, and it's cost-effective, then you can reap the benefits of converting a flat design to a relational design.

> Be aware that migrating database schemas is a very expensive operation to undertake, especially if nothing is currently broken.
>
> Before any migration is even considered, consider the popular adage "If it's not broken, don't fix it."
>
> Not only do you have to design the new schema, you also need to migrate any old data, in addition to redesigning, deploying, and testing dependant applications.
>
> Migration is no small or easy job.

So where do you begin with the conversion? It all depends on the circumstances. Some designs can be easily changed over if they're not used by other applications, whereas others will be tightly integrated with applications, which will need all their data access operations abstracted away from the database itself before you can make any changes.

When there are no dependent applications sucking the data out of your database, then changing the way your tables are structured is quite easy. You can create a new schema and have it run in parallel to your existing design, or you can migrate the existing design over to a new schema.

When running in parallel, you'll need to duplicate the changes in the one database to ensure that they are reflected in the other.

Abstracting away from your databases is the best way in which a parallel system can be managed. One way in which this can be achieved is by creating stored procedures for all of your data access methods and having those stored procedures feed in to both of your databases at the same time, thereby abstracting from the actual tables. In other words, you can have the legacy applications continue to work fine with the old database until you have the time to migrate them to the new database, while any new applications can take advantage of the new database schema and all the loveliness it provides.

Figure 2-4 shows this system design.

Migrating from one schema to another is much more difficult to achieve successfully because not only do you have to ensure that the schema is spot-on, you also have to ensure that all of the applications dependant on your database are happy living on the new schema and that they work as expected.

While migrating the schema can be very challenging, it's nothing compared to reshaping your data, which is very difficult.

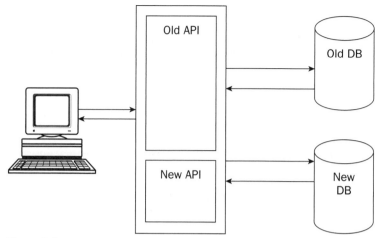

Figure 2-4

Performing data migration requires an explicit knowledge of the data within your database. Once you understand all the ways in which the data is used, you can begin to work out the best way to migrate it to any new schema. Keep in mind that dependencies might exist on data that you don't think relevant at the time, so proceed carefully and begin the migration with the most important (top-level) tables first, and then work your way down.

The easiest way to perform the migration is to write a SELECT statement for each of the "objects" in your new schema that extracts the existing data from the current database, enabling you to easily drop it into your new schema:

```
Insert Into NewDatabase.Customers
( Id, FirstName, LastName )
Select CustomerId, Firstname, Lastname -Other 50 columns not needed in new schema!
From OldDatabase.Customers
```

Some other ways in which this can be done include using Data Transformation Services (DTS) or the Bulk Copy Program (BCP). Once you've decided how you want to perform the migration, it's a good idea to script it all up so that the process can not only be automated, but also tested heavily.

The basic rules are as follows:

1. Define all of the objects in your application(s) design.

2. Create a normalized schema from your object list to represent the new database.

3. Migrate data from the old database to the new database.

4. Create a clean set of stored procedures to access your new schema, with the option of simultaneously maintaining the data in your old schema if it's needed.

5. Test until your fingers are bleeding and your applications squeak with glee.

To summarize our brief tour of migration, keep in mind that it is difficult, and often costs more than sticking with what you've got.

A Black Cloud on the Horizon

While you're normalizing your tables, it's a good idea to keep performance in the back of your mind. For every table you normalize, you'll be adding overhead to your queries and slowing down any applications that will use your database.

You should Draw the line at a few things. For example, there's little point to normalizing data that is incidental to the rows in which it's stored. An example of this is the AddressLine2 column in the Customers table. It could be moved out into its own table, and just referenced with a foreign key in the Customers table. This would make the table more normalized, but at a cost: Every time you need to get the full address of a customer, you have to reference two tables instead of just one, so the gain is too small to justify normalizing it.

After you've normalized your database, there is a performance hit, but that can be worked around with some clever trickery. One thing you can do is have denormalized versions of your data in separate tables, using triggers on the normalized tables to maintain (insert, update, and delete) records in the denormalized table.

Add all the indexes that are appropriate and search directly against the denormalized table to get the Ids for the records you need. It's also useful to only keep "live" data in the denormalized table. This way, your working set (what's in the table) is smaller, which will make searching against the table much faster.

This may not be the most "normalized" way of designing databases, but in the real world, performance is typically much more important than academic design principals. This way, you get the best of both worlds.

In short, normalize where it makes sense, denormalize if you need performance, and don't be afraid to play around with indexes on your tables — they will give you massive increases in performance for many of your tables.

Working with Someone Else's Database

More often than not, you won't be able to choose the database structure you're using, so you need to be able to make the best of a bad situation. We recently worked on a project for which we were hired to develop a fully interactive Web site on top of an existing database. Upon receiving some samples of the database tables, we were horrified to realize that there was no schema — not a bad one, but none at all.

One of the tables had over 260 columns. It even had multiples of some columns inside the same table. This is an extreme example, but tables are often allowed to grow larger over time with no thought given to maintenance or the amount of data, and thus, hard disk space, they are using up. In this case, it was almost as though someone had taken an Excel sheet and placed it into a database server, hoping for the best.

The following sections explain some of the ways you can get around bad database design and ensure that your applications don't creak in the same way that the database might.

Don't Make It Worse

It's easy to fall in to the trap of "going along" with what's already in place — in fact, sometimes you might not have a choice, but if do have any control over the shape of the data your working with and the objects within a database, try not to compound the problem.

As tempting as it might be to just add one more column, think long and hard before doing so. Before you know it, you'll have a table like the monstrosity described in the preceding section, with hundreds of columns, all just added on as "one more column."

One very simple way you can avoid making this mistake is by making sure the structure you're adding is going into its own normalized tables where appropriate, using the primary key in the "bad" tables (if it's got one) to join into your normalized tables.

Abstraction is the way to get around making things any worse. Leave the database alone if you can and move outside of the database server and into your code. Views, DataSets, and custom business objects all help achieve this, as described in the following sections.

Using Views for Database Abstraction

Views are provided to enable subsets or compiled pages of data. They can be used to return whatever "schema" you wish from the existing schema.

By placing views that impersonate a highly normalized schema between your applications and a badly designed database, you gain all of the benefits of normalization with an almost insignificant performance cost.

An example of this would be combining the "CustomerPet1" and "CustomerPet2" columns from the "Customers" table to retrieve a distinct list of all of the Pets on the database:

```
Create View CustomerPets

As

Select DISTINCT CustomerPet1 As PetName
From dbo.Customers
Where Not CustomerPet1 Is Null
Union
Select DISTINCT CustomerPet2 As PetName
From dbo.Customers
Where Not CustomerPet2 Is Null

Go
```

Running a SELECT on the CustomerPets view would return a ResultSet something like this:

```
PetName
----------
Badger
Dog
Giraffe
Kitten
Llama
```

As you can see, you've gained a normalized view of the data without a normalized database — it's cheating, but sometimes it's the only way to get what you want.

Using ADO.NET to Create a Normalized View of the Data

The ADO.NET DataSet is a very powerful object that can be used to create a full in-memory representation of your database schema, or any database schema you wish. This enables you to abstract a poor database design into a tidy normalized in-memory DataSet.

Creating a DataSet with multiple tables and relationships is achieved by using `DataRelation` objects with constraints enforced by `UniqueConstraint` and `ForeignKeyConstraint` objects, enabling you to build a fully relational database, all in-memory. Figure 2-5 shows the structure of a DataSet.

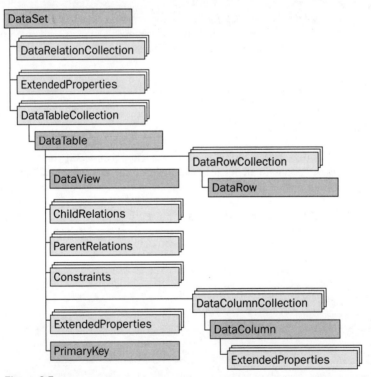

Figure 2-5

By using ADO.NET DataSets, not only do you get a normalized version of your data, you also get loads of other cool features, which are covered in depth throughout Chapter 3.

In ADO.NET 1.0 and 1.1, the DataSet is very large and slow. For ADO.NET 2.0, many optimizations have been added under the hood to make the DataSet a real contender in the framework for both speed and features, including a new indexing engine and the option to use binary serialization. You can find more detailed explanations of using the new ADO.NET 2.0 DataSet features in Chapter 3.

Building Strongly Typed Business Objects

It will often be the case that you'll have no control over the database, meaning the only area of the applications that you can edit is the code itself. Other times, changes may be planned for the database but are not yet in place, so all you can do is prepare from them.

By using strongly typed business objects, you can build a consistent, highly normalized schema for your data, no matter what data source it's originating from. In addition, you can enforce a structured API to work against, as well as house all the business rules inside your objects.

As the business objects exist separately from the databases from which their data is being retrieved, they can take any form of schema you wish — they can match the database exactly or be completely different.

For example, you may have a flat table in the database with two columns containing a pet. However, your object model can represent the data in a different way; for example, there would be nothing to stop your Customers from having a Collection of Pet objects.

Figure 2-6 shows a denormalized table.

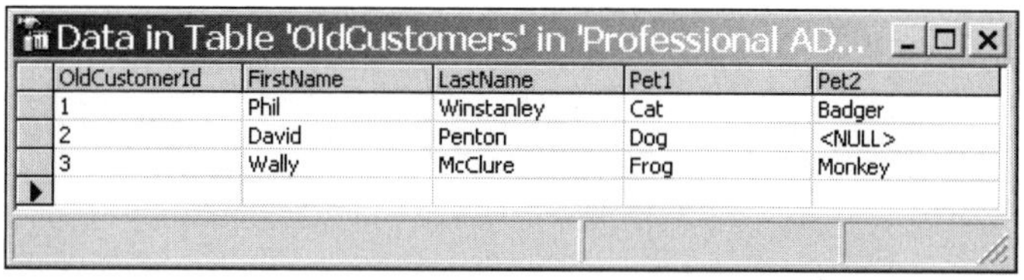
Data in Table 'OldCustomers' in 'Professional AD...

OldCustomerId	FirstName	LastName	Pet1	Pet2
1	Phil	Winstanley	Cat	Badger
2	David	Penton	Dog	<NULL>
3	Wally	McClure	Frog	Monkey

Figure 2-6

It's quite simple to expand this denormalized design into a fully normalized in-code representation of the objects as so:

```
'This is the Representation of our Customers
Public Class Customer

    'Our Customers can have as many pets as they like in
    'this pet collection
    Private _Pets As PetCollection
    Public Property Pets() As PetCollection
        Get
            Return _Pets
        End Get
        Set(ByVal value As PetCollection)
            _Pets = value
        End Set
    End Property

End Class

'Here is the Pet object, even though there isn't one in
'the database
```

```
Public Class Pet

    Private _Name As String
    Public Property Pets() As String
        Get
            Return _Name
        End Get
        Set(ByVal value As String)
            _Name = value
        End Set
    End Property

End Class

'This is a collection for the Pets
Public Class PetCollection
    Inherits System.Collections.CollectionBase

    Public Overridable Function Add(ByVal value As Pet) As Integer
        MyBase.List.Add(value)
    End Function

    Default Public Overridable Property Item(ByVal index As Integer) As Pet
        Get
            Return DirectCast(MyBase.List.Ttem(index), Pet)
        End Get
        Set(ByVal value As Pet)
            MyBase.List.Item(index) = value
        End Set
    End Property

End Class
```

Bringing Them Together

Once you have your custom Views feeding data into the ADO.NET DataSet(s), from which your business objects are then reading their data via a well-structured API, you can forget that underneath all your code there's a mess lurking in the darkness (the Database from Heck), or rather, you can forget about it for now.

Going back to the database from Hades introduced at the beginning of this section, we used the methods outlined in this chapter to normalize the single table into 14 separate tables. This was achieved by taking the data in its raw format, parsing it out, placing the values into a custom business object (with all of the business rules in place to validate the data), and then injecting them into the clean database schema.

By abstracting away from the database itself, you achieve a level of separation that lends itself to N-Tier design. After all, what's the good of a perfectly normalized database without applications that can talk to it?

Your ultimate goal when working around bad database design is to make it as easy as possible to migrate the old design to a new design with as little impact as possible on your applications. Ideally, you should not have to change your applications, other than switching their connection strings or data sources to a normalized version of your database when the time arises.

As hard as a job might look, you can normalize anything, given enough time and enough effort. It's usually worth it for the sake of your sanity if nothing else.

To Delete or Not to Delete . . .

When a record is deleted, it's clear that the data it represents is irretrievably lost without the use of restoring database backups. In many circumstances, it's not a problem that the data has been removed, but as soon as you're asked to report on data that is no longer there, you'll be in a pickle.

> *Some laws require that certain types of data be stored indefinitely, and other laws require aspects of data to be deleted when it's no longer relevant. Be sure to check with your appropriate departments if there is any risk of running afoul of the law.*

There are several ways in which you can ensure that you never delete your records, thereby ensuring that they're always available to be reported on and queried.

Archiving the data into a different database is a simple way to ensure your current working sets of data are kept clean by only storing the most recent data. By maintaining another database with the same schema as your current set, you can easily transfer data across and maintain it for full reporting and queries.

Compiling your data into statistics where appropriate and just storing the compiled statistics instead of the raw data is another very easy way to ensure that all of your data is kept intact as you remove old information from the live tables.

Other ways in which you can preserve data is by versioning records, via version numbers, Boolean (bit) fields indicating the current row, or by using *date spans* that indicate a range of dates in which the data is valid. This method can be somewhat cumbersome because your tables never actually shrink in size; nothing is ever deleted, not to mention the fact that you have extra columns storing versioning information.

Getting at the Data from Your Code

There is one additional area that needs to be covered before we close this chapter: how your applications should access the databases and schemas you've slaved over.

Don't lock your applications into specific databases if you don't have to — you never know when you might be forced to switch to Oracle, DB2, or even ... Progress(!).

Luckily, ADO.NET 2.0 offers some fantastic new features that enable you to write database-independent code, meaning that you can get on with writing your applications while the Oracle guy can work out its oddities and the DB2 girl can decipher the ways of that Database server; your code needn't care.

Using the Abstract Factory model to write your code instantly decouples your applications from the database they're talking to with next to no cost. This completes the "good design" model that you're implementing within your databases and extends it into your business logic tiers.

The interfaces in ADO.NET 2.0 are shown in the following table with their `SqlClient` implementations.

35

SqlClient Class	Base Class	Generic Interface
SqlConnection	DbConnection	IDbConnection
SqlCommand	DbCommand	IDbCommand
SqlDataReader	DbDataReader	IDataReader/IDataRecord
SqlTransaction	DbTransaction	IDbTransaction
SqlParameter	DbParameter	IDbDataParameter
SqlParameterCollection	DbParameterCollection	IDataParameter Collection
SqlDataAdapter	DbDataAdapter	IDbDataAdapter
SqlCommandBuilder	DbCommandBuilder	
SqlConnectionStringBuilder	DbConnectionStringBuilder	
SqlPermission	DBDataPermission	

Using interfaces in your code means that you're decoupling from the data source. However, a slight cost is incurred, and that cost is one of changing the way you write any ADO.NET code — for example, this SqlClient code:

```
Dim Conn As SqlConnection = New SqlConnection("connstring")
Dim Comm As SqlCommand = New SqlCommand(Conn, "commandtorun")
Comm.Connection = Conn
Comm.CommandText = "commandtorun"
Comm.CommandType = CommandType.StoredProcedure
Dim DS As DataSet = New DataSet()
Dim SqlDataAdapter DA = New SqlDataAdapter(Comm)
Conn.Open()
DA.Fill(DS)
Conn.Close()
Conn.Dispose
```

After being rewritten to take advantage of the Abstract Factory approach, it would look like the following:

```
Dim Conn As IDbConnection = GetConnection()
Dim Comm As IDbCommand = New IDbCommand()
Comm.Connection = Conn
Comm.CommandText = "commandtorun"
Comm.CommandType = CommandType.StoredProcedure
Dim DS As DataSet = New DataSet()
Dim IDbDataAdapter DA = New IDbDataAdapter(Comm)
Conn.Open()
DA.Fill(DS)
Conn.Close()
Conn.Dispose
```

The second example doesn't use any classes from the `System.Data.SqlClient` namespace, meaning it's completely generic and can be pointed at any database server just by changing what connection is loaded up from the `GetConnection()` method. We cover this in much more detail in Chapter 3.

Summary

This chapter has covered a very large area, so it has necessarily sacrificed depth for breadth. The information contained here should provide the building blocks you need to meet your own design challenges. As you do more research to determine which methodologies and techniques best suit your own situation, keep the following points in mind:

❑ Only use the advice in this chapter if it's relevant to you and your business needs. The rules outlined here are only general guidelines. You need to work out what is best suited for your business.

❑ Be consistent in whatever you do, be it naming conventions or schema design.

❑ Once you pick a direction, you'll be stuck with it, so think long and hard before you do anything.

❑ If it's not broken, don't fix it. Rather, if it's not going to break, don't fix it!

❑ Remember that you're not (usually) paid to write good code but to write code within the deadline.

Now that the design is out of the way, it's time to get your hands dirty and write some code. Chapter 3 is a whistle-stop tour of all the basic ADO.NET features out there and how to best use them.

For More Information

To complement the information in this chapter, take a look at the following resources:

❑ **MSDN library, "Normalization"** — `http://msdn.microsoft.com/library/default.asp?url=/library/en-us/createdb/cm_8_des_02_2oby.asp`

❑ **Wikipedia, "Normalization"** — `http://en.wikipedia.org/wiki/Database_normalization`

❑ **Database Knowledge Base, "Database Design"** — `http://database.ittoolbox.com/nav/t.asp?t=349&p=349&h1=349`

3

ADO.NET Essentials

In this chapter, we delve into the essential ADO.NET features and explore the best practices surrounding them. We do all of this in a provider-independent way; the code and principles covered here should work for SQL Server, Access, Oracle, MySQL and a whole host of other database servers.

As you move through the chapter, you'll be taken through the code to build a basic Data Access Layer, or *Helper*, before you actually move on to implementing many ADO.NET features.

Each point in this chapter is presented to you in the form of a self contained method. Each method not only shows you how to do something, it also proves to you that it works, and it even lets you change the settings to point to your own databases and providers to test the sample code against them. This chapter should be worked through in a linear manner, as the initial base classes need to be built to provide a platform on which all of the other methods reside.

As you read this chapter, you may notice that we stray somewhat from the subject of ADO.NET. This is because development as a whole needs to be taken into consideration when creating ADO.NET code.

> Your code can still be specific to the provider you are using. The code in this chapter has been written in a provider-independent way so it can be applied to any of the providers. You don't have to switch all your code around!

Not Another ADO Release!

Autumn (or fall, depending on which side of the Atlantic you live on) 2005 marks the arrival of the .NET Framework 2.0. In the past, new releases of ADO meant immense amounts of hair-tearing, tears, and murderous thoughts at the prospect of uprooting your existing code and rewriting it in the new format.

Never fear, this release of ADO.NET won't force you to rewrite anything. Your old code should work under the new Framework (unless you're still using any of the bugs they've fixed—but you wouldn't do that . . . would you?).

No Revolutions

The new ADO.NET API is the same as before; it hasn't been turned upside down. In fact, the existing API has been carefully extended so that the code and applications you've written in 1.0 or 1.1 should continue to work without *any* change.

All of the features introduced in ADO.NET 2.0 can be used incrementally. In other words, if you want to use one of the new features, all you need to do is add on to your existing code; you don't have to switch to a whole new API model. In general, you can preserve your existing code base, only adding the things you need for one particular feature in one part of your application.

We're telling the truth—the API still works!

Obsolete APIs

With every release of .NET, Microsoft has a bit of a spring clean, and this release is no different. They've killed off a few of the methods, types, and properties. What we said earlier still applies, however: Any old code you have with methods or types that have been deprecated or made obsolete will continue to run under ADO.NET 2.0, even if it has references to APIs that have been removed in .NET Framework 2.0. There is one catch: You can't recompile those applications with obsolete APIs under .NET 2.0 with the references remaining.

For example, take something simple, such as this Console application, which was originally built in .NET 1.0 under Visual Studio 2002. It instantiates the `System.Data.OleDb.OleDbPermission` class with a blank constructor, which was made obsolete in .NET 1.1 and remains obsolete in .NET 2.0:

```
namespace DotNetHosting
{
Sub UseObcoleteClass

    Dim ODP As New System.Data.OleDb.OleDbPermission

End Sub
}
```

The preceding code compiled (and still compiles) in .NET 1.0 without any problems. If, however, you attempt to compile the same code under .NET 1.1 or 2.0, the compiler will not be particularly nice to you, presenting you with a rather colorful compilation error:

```
'Public Sub New()' is obsolete: 'OleDbPermission() has been deprecated.  Use the
OleDbPermission(PermissionState.None) constructor.
```

When you run into that kind of exception and you want to compile your application under that version of the Framework, you must change your code to bypass the compiler errors. In the case of the preceding example, you can see that the compiler error that was thrown also describes the fix you should perform.

This issue only exists, however, if you wish to recompile your applications. You don't need to recompile them, of course, just to have them run under a new version of the Framework. In fact, if you've already installed .NET 2.0, it's likely that many of your .NET applications are already running under it. (You can confirm this by checking the value of `System.Environment.Version.ToString()`. It will tell you the version of the Framework under which your applications are running.)

As long as you don't recompile your applications, they will continue to work fine under any version of the Framework. You can force an application to run under a specific version of the Framework very easily with the addition of an entry to the application's configuration file (`app.config/web.config`) that defines the version of the Framework the application is to run under:

```
<startup>
    <supportedRuntime version="v1.1.4322" />
</startup>
```

In short, you don't need to recompile your existing applications to take advantage of the 2.0 release of the .NET Framework. In fact, you're probably already running existing applications that were developed in .NET 1.0 and 1.1 under .NET 2.0. Moreover, if you need to recompile your existing applications in .NET 2.0, you'll have to clean up anything that has been removed from the Framework.

Try your applications under .NET 2.0. You might find they work flawlessly and that you can take complete advantage of the performance increases in both ADO.NET 2.0 and the Framework in general at no cost.

> **We can't guarantee your code will work. Microsoft says it should, but of course, we all know their track record on that point — it means they may be writing some future notes of their own.**

APIs in Their Twilight Months

As well as dealing with types and methods that have been removed in .NET 2.0 or previous incarnations of the Framework, .NET 2.0 introduces changes of its own, marking many types and methods as obsolete — in other words, they won't work in future versions of the Framework.

In the past, Microsoft has dealt harshly with the deprecation of members and types. In the transition between .NET 1.0 and .NET 1.1, types and members marked as obsolete would not compile under 1.1. With .NET 2.0, types and methods that have the mark of death placed on them by the Microsoft Grim Reaper are not being blocked outright. Rather, the compiler will provide warnings, informing developers of the API's impending death.

What this means for you, the developer, is that you can continue to use the APIs that have been placed on death row. However, you already know that the code won't compile in .NET 2.0, so be forewarned.

A full list of all the changes between all versions of the .NET Framework can be found at `www.gotdotnet` `.com/team/changeinfo/default.aspx`.

As an example of this deprecation and warning system, take a look at the following code, which uses the `SqlParameterCollection.Add(string,string)` method signature that has been marked as obsolete in .NET 2.0:

```
Sub SqlSqlCommandAddParameter()

    Dim SqlComm As New System.Data.SqlClient.SqlCommand

    SqlComm.Parameters.Add("@Socks", "Smelly");

End Sub
```

By default, the code will compile and run without any issues under .NET 2.0, but the compiler will output a warning that indicates the method signature has been marked as obsolete. The warning looks like this:

```
'Public Function Add(parameterName As String, value As Object) As
System.Data.SqlClient.SqlParameter' is obsolete: 'Add(String parameterName, Object
value) has been deprecated.  Use AddWithValue(String parameterName, Object value).
```

Think of the warning as a death knoll ringing on the APIs that have been marked as obsolete.

To be completely accurate, the preceding code may or may not compile, depending on the settings of your build environment and whether warnings are treated as errors. If it doesn't compile cleanly, you'll need to change the code to use new or alternative methods suggested by the compiler in the error message.

If you find yourself receiving compiler warnings, change your code. It's not worth the hassle down the line after you've forgotten all about the code and then find yourself needing to change its functionality or fix a bug (not that our code ever has any. . .), or discovering that it won't even compile on future versions of .NET.

The Generic Factory Model

If you don't know what the Generic Factory Model is and you develop against different database servers, then you're in for a real treat. Microsoft has outdone themselves with ADO.NET 2.0 and come to the rescue of all multiplatform database developers.

One day you might be developing against a SQL server; the next you might be developing against an Oracle server. It's possible down the line you'll be asked to develop against a fridge freezer. Whatever your data source, ADO.NET 2.0 gives you a provider-agnostic platform on which to build your applications, meaning you can write your code once and have it work on any data source you wish.

The Generic Factory Model is an architecture that enables access to any database, from one set of code. ADO.NET 2.0 has that architecture plumbed right into the Framework, so you can use it too.

Inside the `System.Data.Common` namespace are some lovely new classes that enable us to make platform-independent code very easily, but before we get our hands dirty, we'll quickly run through the Generic Factory Model.

Providers

During the Dark Ages (when our only Framework was .NET 1.0), there were three providers in the form of the following namespaces:

- ❏   `System.Data.SqlClient`

- ❏   `System.Data.Odbc`

- ❏   `System.Data.OleDb`

In those days, we were encouraged by samples all across the Internet, in books, and by our peers to directly use the most appropriate set of classes from the correct namespace. Doing this was problematic, however, because after a specific provider such as SqlClient was hard-coded into the application, the code could no longer be used to look at an Oracle database server using the OracleClient provider. In other words, we were locked into a single provider, and when our bed was made — as the saying goes — we had to lie in it.

If you wanted to write platform-agnostic code in the olden days (nearly three long years ago), you'd have to use a bit of black magic, interfaces, and a switch statement:

```
Public ReadOnly Property Connection() As System.Data.IDbConnection
    Get
        Select Case OldGenericFactoryHelper.Provider
            Case "SqlClient"
                Return New System.Data.SqlClient.SqlConnection
            Case "Odbc"
                Return New System.Data.Odbc.OdbcConnection
            Case "SqlClient"
                Return New System.Data.OleDb.OleDbConnection
            Case Else
                Return Nothing
        End Select
    End Get
End Property
```

As you can see, the method returns an interface of type `IDbConnection`, which is a generic implementation of the `Connection` class that all provider-specific classes implement (`SqlConnection`, `OdbcConnection`, and so on). This approach enabled you to code against the interfaces, rather than the specific providers, but it always felt a little dirty.

Any application employing this approach had a design that was completely platform-independent. The data access architecture is shown in Figure 3-1.

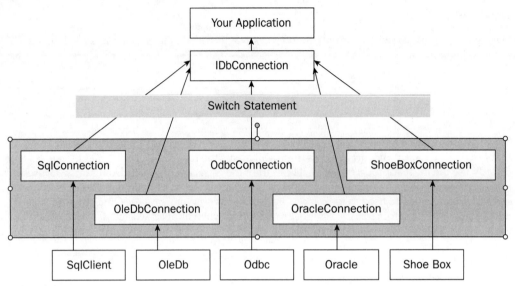

Figure 3-1

One of the main problems with this model was that each time a provider was added to the system, the switch statement had to be altered. The fun didn't stop there, though. You also needed switch statements for all of the other provider-specific classes, such as those that implement IDbCommand, so that your applications could retrieve the right Command class (SqlCommand, OleDbCommand, OdbcCommand, and so on).

Although this wasn't a massive problem, and the approach generally worked well, the ADO.NET 2.0 team at Microsoft came up with a much better solution, called the Generic Factory Model, described in the next section.

ADO.NET to the Rescue

ADO.NET 2.0 solves the aforementioned problem by introducing Factories into the Framework. Just like a real factory, a Factory takes in raw materials and produces fully working products. In this case, the raw materials are the providers we want to use, and the products are the provider-independent classes we need.

The provider-independent classes include DbConnection, DbCommand, and DbParameter, as well as a whole host of other classes. The way they are used is very similar to the way they were used in the old model, but they come from a Factory built into the Framework — you don't have to write the code yourself.

The new architecture is shown in Figure 3-2.

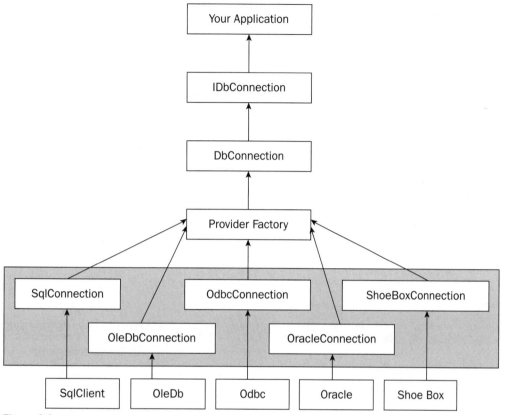

Figure 3-2

In other words, you no longer have to code any switch statements. Better yet, the .NET Framework will do all the hard work for you. For example, if you want a SqlClient connection object, all you need is the following:

```
Public Shared Function GetConnection(ByVal providerName As String)
    Return
System.Data.Common.DbProviderFactories.GetFactory(providerName).CreateConnection()
End Function
```

If you want a command object, then it's as simple as calling `CreateCommand()` on the Factory returned by `GetFactory()`. This code is much cleaner and self-maintaining. You never have to modify it, even to use new providers — they just appear to your code automatically.

See how all of this makes life easier? We're speaking one language only, that of the provider-agnostic class implementations. Now let's go into a little more detail regarding the real-world implementation of ADO.NET 2.0 Provider Factories.

DbProviderFactories

The Factory is the key to the Generic Factory Model; without it, there would be no model. It's the creator of all of your classes, and it's the place where all of the real work happens.

The .NET Framework is shipped with a bundle of Factory implementations in the box. They're defined in the machine.config file inside the Framework folders. You can access the machine.config file and take a look for yourself:

```
C:\WINDOWS\Microsoft.NET\Framework\v2.0.50727\CONFIG\machine.config
```

There are five providers out of the box, but as with everything else in the .NET Framework, this is customizable — you can easily add your own providers to extend the list on any machine with the Framework installed. The five built-in providers are listed in the following table.

Name	Invariant	Type
Odbc Data Provider	`System.Data.Odbc`	`System.Data.Odbc.OdbcFactory`
OleDb Data Provider	`System.Data.OleDb`	`System.Data.OleDb.OleDbFactory`
OracleClient Data Provider	`System.Data.OracleClient`	`System.Data.OracleClient.OracleClientFactory`
SqlClient Data Provider	`System.Data.SqlClient`	`System.Data.SqlClient.SqlClientFactory`
SQL Server CE Data Provider	`Microsoft.SqlServerCe.Client`	`Microsoft.SqlServerCe.Client.SqlCeClientFactory`

As mentioned previously, it's very easy to add your own providers. There are various places where you can define a provider so it can be used, including the machine.config, app.config, and web.config files. Just add a small section to one of the configuration files (and have the provider installed on the machines in question!):

```
<DbProviderFactories>
      <add name="Odbc Data Provider" invariant="System.Data.Odbc" description=".Net
Framework Data Provider for Odbc" type="System.Data.Odbc.OdbcFactory, System.Data,
Version=2.0.0.0, Culture=neutral, PublicKeyToken=b77a5c561934e089" />
</DbProviderFactories>
```

Extensibility is the operative word here. The Generic Factory Model is easy to use, easy to implement, and very easy to justify.

Generic Factory versus Specific Providers

Decisions, decisions. The new features thrown at the feet of .NET developers in ADO.NET 2.0 are extensive and formidable, so in order to help you decide if the shift is worth it, we'll briefly run through the pros and cons of the Generic Factory Model (in comparison to directly accessing a provider such as SqlClient).

Pros

Here are some reasons to use the Generic Factory Model:

❑   Even if you just use one provider today, your code can be moved to another provider without any effort later, saving you and your company both time and money.

❑   The potential market for your applications is massively increased. Some shops will only use Oracle or DB2, for example. By giving your client the option of any provider, you widen your scope to customers that are currently outside your reach.

❑   You and your development team only need to know one API; the specifics of each provider can be abstracted away, enabling you and your colleagues to concentrate on the applications. Plus, using the Generic Factory Model will leave loads of room in your head to watch Internet Flash animations relating to woodland creatures and fungi.

Cons

Of course, there are always some disadvantages too:

❑   There's a good chance you already know your data provider inside out. If you work with SQL Server, you'll know the SqlClient namespace. If you decide to move to the provider model, you'll have to learn an entirely new data access API.

❑   If your current applications contain data access code that is not provider-agnostic (generic) and you decide to go the generic provider route, you'll have to either rewrite all your existing data access code or maintain both the old provider-specific code and any new provider-generic code.

❑   While the majority of your data Access code in ADO.NET 2.0 can be provider-agnostic, huge swathes of your applications are still not generic. For example, any exception thrown from a database server will still be specific to the provider from which it's been thrown, meaning you have to deal with all the "special cases" for every provider manually.

Applications can be weighed against one another in terms of maintainability, security, and performance. For some people, maintainable code is more important than secure code, whereas for others, security is the primary concern. For the majority of developers, however, performance is the only thing they need to worry about — in other words, the only thing the boss will notice.

Writing a Helper Class

While it's perfectly possible to add data access code everywhere you need to access the database server in your applications, it's much better practice to encapsulate all of your data access code inside some form of Data Access Layer, which we will explore by building a Helper class for all of our data access code.

Beginning with this section, proceed in a linear fashion through the chapter. The Helper Class created in this section is used throughout the rest of the chapter to illustrate many aspects of ADO.NET 2.0.

If you don't like the idea of reading the code in this section, download the source code from the Web site and load the Chapter 3 solution into Visual Studio. Then play to your heart's content.

The first thing we need to do is create a class to store our Generic Factory Helper. Ours is called `GenericFactoryHelper` and it started out in life looking just as shown here:

```
Imports System
Imports System.Data
Imports System.Data.Common

Namespace CodeSamples

    Public Class GenericFactoryHelper

    End Class

End Namespace
```

Our Generic Factory is designed to run through static properties and methods, meaning that applications need not instantiate our Factory to gain access to its functionality. In addition, you may notice that the class has included the `System.Data.Common` namespace. This is where all the generic functionality is encapsulated in the .NET Framework.

The following property returns a list of all the possible Factories as defined in the Machine and Application configuration files:

```
Public Shared ReadOnly Property AllFactories() As DataTable
    Get
        Return DbProviderFactories.GetFactoryClasses()
    End Get
End Property
```

As you can see, the type of data that this returns is a data table. Inside that data table are several columns.

While it's nice to be able to retrieve a list of the available providers, it's much more useful to retrieve an instantiation of a Generic Factory from a specific provider. The following property gets the current Factory. At the moment, this is specified (hard-coded) in the property as a string. However, it could be fed from a configuration entry somewhere, or even from the user interface, enabling users to specify the type of database system to which they wish to connect.

```
Public Shared ReadOnly Property CurrentFactory() As String
    Get
        Return "System.Data.SqlClient"
```

```
        End Get
    End Property
```

The next method combines the `CurrentFactory` property we've already created with a call to `DbProviderFactories.GetFactory()`. This method actually returns the Factory for use in our applications — in this case, an instance of the SqlClientFactory:

```
Public Shared ReadOnly Property Factory() As DbProviderFactory
    Get
        Return DbProviderFactories.GetFactory(CurrentFactory)
    End Get
End Property
```

In addition to the preceding method, we offer a way to create a specific Factory from a provider name, like this:

```
Public Shared ReadOnly Property GetFactory(ByVal providerName As String) As
DbProviderFactory
    Get
        Return DbProviderFactories.GetFactory(providerName)
    End Get
End Property
```

Having an instance of a Factory is all well and good, but we need more from our Factory Helper. We need it to produce connections, commands, parameters, and many more objects. Luckily for us, it's just a simple matter of calling the correct method on the Factory to retrieve an instantiated, fully functional provider generic class.

To retrieve an instance of `DbConnection`, which is actually just a wrapper for our provider-specific connection class (`SqlConnection`), we can create a method that enables us to specify a provider name and returns the appropriate `DbConnection` class:

```
Public Shared ReadOnly Property GetConnection(ByVal proverName As String)
As DbConnection
    Get
        Return
GenericFactoryHelper.GetFactory(proverName).CreateConnection()
    End Get
End Property
```

The next method call is simply used to return a provider-specific `DbConnectionStringBuilder` class. It returns this from the factory specified in `CurrentFactory`:

```
Public Shared ReadOnly Property ConnectionStringBuilder() As
DbConnectionStringBuilder
    Get
        Return Factory.CreateConnectionStringBuilder()
    End Get
End Property
```

As you'll see, the next method we implement does something a little bit more interesting than just returning an instantiated class. It actually returns the correct connection string for the provider we're using.

Because each database server likes its connection strings its own way, the following method uses the type of the Factory class currently being used to determine which connection string to return via a switch statement. It then uses a provider-specific DbConnectionStringBuilder from the preceding method to create a connection string.

> *For more information on connection string builders, see the section entitled "Intelligent Connection Strings."*

For each of the providers you wish to support, add your connection details where appropriate. The following section of code shows a Property that dynamically returns the correct connection string, based on the Provider being used.

> **For more information on connection strings, see the section entitled "Connection Strings."**

```vb
Public Shared ReadOnly Property ConnectionString() As String
    Get
        Dim Csb As New DbConnectionStringBuilder
        Select Case Factory.ToString()
            Case "System.Data.SqlClient.SqlClientFactory"
                Csb.Add("Server", "localhost")
                Csb.Add("Integrated Security", "SSPI")
            Case "System.Data.Odbc.OleDbFactory"
                Csb.Add("Provider", "sqloledb")
                Csb.Add("Data Source", "localhost")
                Csb.Add("User Id", "myUsername")
                Csb.Add("Password", "myPassword")
            Case Else
                Throw New System.NotImplementedException("The Provider was
not catered for, try adding your provider into the switch.")
        End Select
        Return Csb.ToString()
    End Get
End Property
```

Once we have our Factory, we can start using it to get all the operation-specific classes. The following method uses the Factory to return a new instantiated DbConnection class:

```vb
Public Shared ReadOnly Property Connection() As DbConnection
    Get
        Return Factory.CreateConnection()
    End Get
End Property
```

What good is a connection if we can't send commands to it? The following method uses the Factory to return a provider-generic DbCommand object:

```
    Public Shared ReadOnly Property Command() As DbCommand
        Get
            Return Factory.CreateCommand()
        End Get
    End Property
```

Occasionally, we'll need to populate a `DataSet` using a `DataAdapter`, or save data to a database via a `DataAdapter`. This method returns a generic `DbDataAdapter` from the Factory to be used in your applications:

```
    Public Shared ReadOnly Property DataAdapter() As DbDataAdapter
        Get
            Return Factory.CreateDataAdapter()
        End Get
    End Property
```

It's also quite useful to have a `CommandBuilder` for dynamically building commands:

```
    Public Shared ReadOnly Property CommandBuilder() As DbCommandBuilder
        Get
            Return Factory.CreateCommandBuilder()
        End Get
    End Property
```

Of course, any command worth its salt needs parameters. This method returns a generic `DbParameter` object back to the application:

```
    Public Shared ReadOnly Property Parameter() As DbParameter
        Get
            Return Factory.CreateParameter()
        End Get
    End Property
```

Data Sources

It's all well and good knowing we can connect to whatever platform we desire with only the flick of a switch, but we really need to know what we can connect to — what's on the network around us.

Using some of the new features baked into ADO.NET 2.0 — specifically, the `GetDataSources` method — we can get a full listing of all the data sources available to us.

> **At the moment, the only provider that actually implements** `GetDataSources()` **is the** `SqlClientFactory`. **Implementations for** `OdbcFactory`, `OleDbFactory`, **and** `OracleFactory` **are currently not available.**

On a machine with the SQL Server client tools, you can manually list all the SQL Server instances on the network, like this:

```
C:\>osql -L

Servers:
    (local)
    Badger\BadgerBadger
    Mushroom

C:\>
```

While that's useful, keep in mind that you can't guarantee that a user will have the SQL Client tools installed on his or her machine. Thus, the ADO.NET team has come up with a way for you to get this information directly from the Framework, using the DbDataSourceEnumerator.

It's quite simple to get a list of all the available data sources for each provider by using the DbDataSourceEnumerator. In the following example, we run through each of the Factories and then, for each one, we print out all the available data sources:

```
Sub EnumerateSources()

    Dim Dt As DataTable = CodeSamples.GenericFactoryHelper.AllFactories
    Dim Dr As DataRow

    For Each Dr In Dt.Rows

        Try

            Dim Dbp As DbProviderFactory =
DbProviderFactories.GetFactory(Dr("InvariantName").ToString())

            Debug.WriteLine(Dr("InvariantName").ToString())

            If Dbp.CanCreateDataSourceEnumerator Then

                Dim Dse As DbDataSourceEnumerator =
Dbp.CreateDataSourceEnumerator()
                Dim DataSources As DataTable = Dse.GetDataSources()
                Dim DataSource As DataRow
                Dim source As String = String.Empty

                For Each DataSource In DataSources.Rows

                    source = DataSource("ServerName").ToString()
                    If Not DataSource("InstanceName") Is Nothing Then
                        source = source & "\" &
DataSource("InstanceName").ToString()
                    End If
                    If Not DataSource("Version") Is Nothing And Not
DataSource("Version").ToString() = String.Empty Then
                        source = source & " - Version " &
DataSource("Version").ToString()
                    End If
```

```
                    Debug.WriteLine(source)

                Next
            End If
        Catch ex As Exception
        End Try
    Next

End Sub
```

What this shows on our network is a list of all the different SQL Servers. Of course, what you see will depend on the makeup of your network. You may see nothing, or you may see hundreds of database server instances:

```
System.Data.Odbc
System.Data.OleDb
System.Data.OracleClient
System.Data.SqlClient
Badger\BadgerBadger - Version 8.00.194
Mushroom\ - Version 8.00.194
Snake\
```

Why is it useful to know the different database servers?

You can use the preceding code to create a "poor man's cluster," whereby you can check each of the entries in a specific provider, looking for a database server that is online or contains the information you're looking for, enabling your applications to be resilient to servers being taken offline.

You could also build a server selection into your applications. For example, you may have development and live servers. By giving your test team the capability to quickly change the database servers they're connected to, they can look after themselves without the necessity of developer involvement.

> *Enumeration for SQL Server 2005 is turned off by default. For more information, check out the section covering Server Enumeration in Chapter 10.*

Connection Strings

Everybody needs connection strings at one time or another, and while they're incredibly simple to construct and use, they're also often misunderstood.

ADO.NET offers three ways to create your connection strings. First, you can specify a simple string, like this:

```
Dim ConnectionString As String = "server=localhost;uid=Phil;pwd=ItsASecret;Initial
Catalog=MyDb"
```

The second way is by using the new `ConnectionStringBuilder` classes built into each of the providers (the rest of this section focuses on this topic). The third way is to use the `ConnectionStringCollection` and the `ConnectionStrings` section of `ConfigurationSettings`.

Before moving on, it's important to understand the different options open to you regarding the connection strings for your provider. Familiarize yourself with the documentation for your chosen provider.

A very comprehensive list of connection strings is available from the following Web site: www .carlprothman.net/Default.aspx?tabid=81.

Connection String Collection

With .NET 2.0, there's a new way to store and use your connection strings in the Framework. Microsoft has brought together the configuration files (app.config and web.config), as well as the managed System.Configuration API to give us a really neat way of loading our connection strings.

Under the Configuration section in the config files is a new element called `connectionStrings`. This is where all the connection strings for your applications can live:

```
<connectionStrings>
  <add name="UserDatabase"
    providerName="SqlClient"
    connectionString="server=localhost;uid=myuser;pwd=mypassword"
  />
</connectionStrings>
```

Once your connection strings are stored inside the configuration files, it's simple to actually get at them. The following line of code shows the retrieval of a connection string:

```
ConfigurationManager.ConnectionStrings("UserDatabase").ToString()
```

The `ConfigurationManager` class lives inside the `System.Configuration` namespace.

Remember: Before you create another entry in the `appSettings` section of your configuration files, if you're adding a connection string, create it in the `connectionStrings` section.

Always try to encrypt your connection strings. That way, if someone does manage to take a peek inside your configuration files, they still have to decrypt the strings before they can be used.

Intelligent Connection Strings

The first thing to remember with the `ConnectionStringBuilder` classes is that they do their own thing. What you tell them you want is not necessarily what you get.

This disobedience can be demonstrated quite easily with a small amount of code. In the following listing, three parameters are passed into the `ConnectionStringBuilder` for the `SqlClient` class: `"Server"`, `"uid"`, and `"pwd"`. What actually comes out of the `ConnectionStringBuilder`, however, are `"Data Source"`, `"User ID"`, and `"Password"`, respectively:

```
Sub ShowStringBuilderManipulation()

    If CodeSamples.GenericFactoryHelper.CurrentFactory.ToString() <>
"System.Data.SqlClient" Then

        Throw New Exception("This test requires the Factory to be running from the
System.Data.SqlClient provider, it's currently running as " +
CodeSamples.GenericFactoryHelper.CurrentFactory)

    End If

    Dim Csb As DbConnectionStringBuilder =
CodeSamples.GenericFactoryHelper.ConnectionStringBuilder

    Csb.Add("Server", "localhost")
    Csb.Add("uid", "myUsername")
    Csb.Add("pwd", "myPassword")

    Dim actual As String = Csb.ConnectionString
    Dim expected As String = "Data Source=localhost;User
ID=myUsername;Password=myPassword"

    If expected <> actual Then
        Throw New Exception("The expected does not match the actual!")
    End If


End Sub
```

This happens because the `ConnectionStringBuilder` for the `SqlClientFactory` knows which parameters are optimal for its performance, and it changes the values we used, converting them to the right version.

Provider-Specific Connection Strings

Each database server allows connections in different ways, and while they all share common features such as "username" and "password," the way those features are implemented varies among providers. Some common examples of differences for the four main providers are listed in the following table.

	Odbc	OleDb	SqlClient	OracleClient
Database Server	Server	Data Source	Server or "Data Source"	Server or "Data Source"
Username	UID	User ID	UID or User ID	User ID
Password	PWD	Password	PWD or Password	Password
Should Integrated Security Be Used?	Trusted_ Connection	Integrated Security	Trusted_Connection or "Integrated Security"	Integrated Security

Table continued on following page

	Odbc	OleDb	SqlClient	OracleClient
Database/Catalog to Connect to	Database	Initial Catalog	Database or Initial Catalog	
Use Connection Pooling		OLE DB Services	Pooling	Pooling

Table courtesy of http://msdn.microsoft.com/library/en-us/dnvs05/html/vsgenerics.asp?frame=true#vsgene_topic6.

If you need to support multiple providers from the same code base, it's a pretty simple procedure to have code dynamically build the appropriate connection string for your providers, as shown here:

```
Public Shared Function LoadTheRightConnectionString() As String

    Dim Actual As String = String.Empty
    Dim Expected As String = String.Empty
    Dim Csb As DbConnectionStringBuilder =
CodeSamples.GenericFactoryHelper.ConnectionStringBuilder

    Select Case CodeSamples.GenericFactoryHelper.Factory.ToString()

        Case "System.Data.SqlClient.SqlClientFactory"

            Csb.Add("Server", "localhost")
            Csb.Add("uid", "myUsername")
            Csb.Add("pwd", "myPassword")
            Expected = "Data Source=localhost;User
ID=myUsername;Password=myPassword"


        Case "System.Data.OleDb.OleDbFactory"
            Csb.Add("Provider", "sqloledb")
            Csb.Add("Data Source", "localhost")
            Csb.Add("User Id", "myUsername")
            Csb.Add("Password", "myPassword")
            Expected = "Provider=sqloledb;Data
Source=localhost;Password=myPassword;User ID=myUsername"

        Case Else

            Throw New Exception("The provider is not supported!")


    End Select

    If Expected <> Actual Then

        Throw New Exception("The Value does not match that which was expected.")
```

```
        End If


        Return Nothing

    End Function
```

Conditionally Adding Connection String Parameters

It's quite common to want to dynamically construct the connection string, and it's simple to do using the ConnectionStringBuilder, as shown in the following example:

```
Public Sub ConditionallyAddParameters()
    Dim Csb As System.Data.Common.DbConnectionStringBuilder =
CodeSamples.GenericFactoryHelper.ConnectionStringBuilder

    If Csb("Initial Catalog").ToString = String.Empty Then
        Csb.Add("Initial Catalog", "Northwind")
    End If

    Dim actual As Boolean = (Csb.ContainsKey("Initial Catalog") AndAlso
(Csb("Initial Catalog").ToString = "Northwind"))

    Dim expected As Boolean = True

    If expected <> actual Then
        Throw New Exception("Did not return the expected value.")
    End If
End Sub}
```

As you can see by using a conditional statement and the Add method, it's a trivial matter to add any parameters that you require, combining the flexibility of a dynamically constructed connection string with the power and intelligence of the ConnectionStringBuilder classes.

Provider-Specific Connection String Parameters

In the previous section, you saw how parameters can be conditionally added to your stored procedures. It's worth noting, however, that the individual providers have sets of parameters that are added by default and cannot be removed at runtime. This can be seen in the following code sample, which builds on top of our Factory Helper class.

The following method clears all of the parameters from the ConnectionStringBuilder and manually removes both the pwd and password parameters. The ContainsKey method is then called against pwd, which has not been added, but explicitly removed. However, the value still returns true.

```
Public Sub ShowDefaultParametersAlwaysExist()

    If Not (CodeSamples.GenericFactoryHelper.CurrentFactory =
"System.Data.SqlClient") Then
```

```
        Throw New Exception("This test requires the Factory to be running from the
System.Data.SqlClient provider, it's currently running as " +
CodeSamples.GenericFactoryHelper.CurrentFactory)
    End If

    Dim Csb As System.Data.Common.DbConnectionStringBuilder =
CodeSamples.GenericFactoryHelper.ConnectionStringBuilder

    Csb.Clear()
    Csb.Remove("pwd")
    Csb.Remove("Password")
    Dim actual As Boolean = Csb.ContainsKey("pwd")
    Dim expected As Boolean = True

    If expected <> actual Then
        Throw New Exception("Did not return the expected value.")
    End If
End Sub
```

The reason why the preceding code always returns true is because the SqlClient Connection-
StringBuilder has some default parameters that are always available. You can easily produce a full list
of these default parameters using our Factory Helper and the following code:

```
Public Sub PrintAllDefaultParameters()
    Dim Dt As System.Data.DataTable = CodeSamples.GenericFactoryHelper.AllFactories

    For Each Dr As System.Data.DataRow In Dt.Rows
        Dim Dbp As System.Data.Common.DbProviderFactory =
System.Data.Common.DbProviderFactories.GetFactory(Dr("InvariantName").ToString)

        Dim Csb As System.Data.Common.DbConnectionStringBuilder =
Dbp.CreateConnectionStringBuilder
        Console.WriteLine(Dbp.ToString)

        For Each Key As String In Csb.Keys
            Console.WriteLine(Key + " = " + Csb(Key))
        Next
    Next
End Sub
```

For your convenience, the following table lists all of the default parameters and values for each of the
Factories shipped with ADO.NET 2.0.

SqlClientFactory		OracleClientFactory	
Data Source		Data Source	
Failover Partner		Persist Security Info	False
AttachDbFilename		Integrated Security	False
Initial Catalog		User ID	
Integrated Security	False	Password	

SqlClientFactory		OracleClientFactory	
Persist Security Info	False	Enlist	True
User ID		Pooling	True
Password		Min Pool Size	0
Enlist	True	Max Pool Size	100
Pooling	True	Unicode	False
Min Pool Size	0	Load Balance Timeout	0
Max Pool Size	100	Workaround Oracle Bug 914652	False
Asynchronous Processing	False		
Connection Reset	True	**OleDbFactory**	
MultipleActiveResultSets	True	File Name	
Replication	False	Provider	
Connect Timeout	15	Data Source	
Encrypt	False	Persist Security Info	False
Load Balance Timeout	0	OLE DB Services	-13
Network Library			
Packet Size	8000	**OdbcFactory**	
Application Name	.Net SqlClient Data Provider	Dsn	
Current Language		Driver	
Workstation ID			
User Instance	False		
Context Connection	False		

Because of the provider-specific implementations of the ConnectionStringBuilder, you can't just add any old rubbish to the connection string. If you do, it will complain bitterly:

```
Public Sub AddIllegalParameters()
    Dim Csb As System.Data.Common.DbConnectionStringBuilder =
CodeSamples.GenericFactoryHelper.ConnectionStringBuilder
    Dim ExpectedError As String = String.Empty
    Dim ActualError As String = String.Empty

    Try
        Csb.Add("My", "Socks")
    Catch Ex As System.ArgumentException
        ActualError = Ex.Message
        ExpectedError = ("Keyword not supported: 'My'.")
```

```
        End Try

        If ExpectedError <> ActualError Then
            Throw New Exception("The error thrown was not one we expected.")
        End If
    End Sub
```

Alas, our socks are rejected from the database connection string and cast into cyber-oblivion.

Connections

The first code sample in this section should probably be called "Hello Database" because that's essentially what you're doing when you open a connection to a database — you're introducing yourself, shaking hands, and preparing for a lengthy discussion.

ADO.NET enables you to make introductions to the databases around you in a very easy manner, regardless of what they are.

Opening a Connection (and Making Sure It's Open)

Before you do any database work, it's likely you'll need to open a connection to the database in question. Here's how to do it:

```
Public Sub OpenConnection()
    Dim Conn As System.Data.Common.DbConnection =
CodeSamples.GenericFactoryHelper.Connection
    Dim actual As System.Data.ConnectionState
    Using Conn


        Try
            Conn.ConnectionString =
CodeSamples.GenericFactoryHelper.ConnectionString
            Conn.Open()
            actual = Conn.State
            Conn.Close()
        Finally
        End Try

    End Using

    Dim expected As System.Data.ConnectionState = System.Data.ConnectionState.Open

    If expected <> actual Then
        Throw New Exception("Did not return the expected value.")
    End If

End Sub
```

When you're doing any database work, it's important to only have the connection open as long as it's absolutely necessary so that it can be used by others when needed. Get in, do your stuff, and get right out again.

Closing a Connection (and Making Sure It's Closed)

Many developers don't give a thought to closing their connections, but closing a connection is just as important — if not more so — than opening one. If your code for closing connections is buggy or faulty, you might run out of available connections and your applications can grind to a halt under heavy use.

> **A bug in .NET 1.0 affected the calling of** `.Dispose()` **on the** `Connection` **object: It did not always internally call the** `.Close()` **method. This meant that applications that were not explicitly calling** `.Close()` **were leaving open connections left, right, and center. Fortunately, the bug was eradicated in .NET 1.1 and has not resurfaced in .NET 2.0.**

The following code example does its utmost to ensure that a connection is closed, returned to the connection pool (where it's in use), and has its managed and unmanaged resources released so that the garbage collector can do its thing:

```
Public Sub CloseConnection()
    Dim Conn As System.Data.Common.DbConnection =
CodeSamples.GenericFactoryHelper.Connection
    Dim actual As System.Data.ConnectionState = System.Data.ConnectionState.Closed
    Conn.ConnectionString = CodeSamples.GenericFactoryHelper.ConnectionString
    Using Conn


        Try
            Try
                Conn.Open()

                If Conn.State <> System.Data.ConnectionState.Open Then
                    Throw New Exception("Connection nott opened")
                End If

            Catch Ex As System.Data.Common.DbException
                Throw New Exception(Ex.Message)
            Finally
                If Not (Conn.State = System.Data.ConnectionState.Closed) Then
                    Conn.Close()
                    actual = Conn.State
                End If
            End Try


        Finally
        End Try

    End Using

    Dim expected As System.Data.ConnectionState =
System.Data.ConnectionState.Closed
```

```
        If expected <> actual Then

            Throw New Exception("Did not return the expected value.")

        End If
    End Sub
```

The preceding code creates a `Connection` object and assumes everything went well with that creation, and then moves into a `using()` statement, which ensures that the object specified will be disposed of when we are finished with it. Once inside the `using()` statement, the code is wrapped with a `Try...Catch...Finally...` statement, which enables us to catch any errors that might have occurred and enforce the closing of the connection.

Even if you don't do anything else, always make sure that you close and dispose of your connection objects when you're finished with them; this will return the connections to a pool (if one's being used) and release any unmanaged resources the instance is using. As we've just shown, the easiest way to do this is by employing a `Using` statement that will call `Dispose()` when we're finished with the objects in question.

> *If you employ the `Using` object statement, the .NET Framework will ensure that the object is disposed of even if an exception is thrown inside the `Using` object statement, meaning your instance will always be cleaned up.*

Managing Exceptions

Yes, they happen, even in your code.

When using ADO.NET, it's possible to get errors from all over the place, especially from your databases, so it's very important to have robust and extensive error reporting built into your applications.

Each provider in the Framework offers its own set of information. For example, the `SqlException` offers the `Procedure` property, which gives you the Sql that has been run that caused the exceptions.

In the following example, you can see how it's possible to collect detailed error information from the `SqlException` class (take particular note of the bold section):

```
Public Sub HandleAProviderException()
    Dim Conn As System.Data.Common.DbConnection =
CodeSamples.GenericFactoryHelper.Connection
    Conn.ConnectionString = CodeSamples.GenericFactoryHelper.ConnectionString
    Dim Comm As System.Data.Common.DbCommand = Conn.CreateCommand
    Comm.CommandText = ("NORTHWIND.dbo.RaiseAnError")
    Comm.CommandType = System.Data.CommandType.StoredProcedure
    Conn.Open()
    Dim Dt As System.Data.DataTable = New System.Data.DataTable
    Try
        Dt.Load(Comm.ExecuteReader)
    Catch Ex As System.Data.SqlClient.SqlException
        Dim ExceptionDetails As String = String.Empty
        Console.WriteLine("Class: " + Ex.Class)
        Console.WriteLine("Data: ")
        For Each Key As String In Ex.Data.Keys
```

```
                    Console.WriteLine(Key + " = " + Ex.Data(Key).ToString)
            Next
            Console.WriteLine("ErrorCode: " + Ex.ErrorCode)
            Console.WriteLine("Procedure: " + Ex.Procedure)
            Console.WriteLine("Server: " + Ex.Server)
            Console.WriteLine("State: " + Ex.State)
            Console.WriteLine("Message: " + Ex.Message)
            Console.WriteLine("HelpLink: " + Ex.HelpLink)
        End Try
        Conn.Close()
    End Sub
```

The preceding code calls a stored procedure that is primed to throw an exception, as shown here:

```
CREATE PROCEDURE [dbo].[RaiseAnError] AS

RAISERROR( 'This is an Exception', 16, 1)

GO
```

On encountering a `SqlException`, the code inspects the `SqlException` and pulls out all the details it can from inside the exception:

```
Class: 16
Data:
HelpLink.ProdName = Microsoft SQL Server
HelpLink.ProdVer = 08.00.0194
HelpLink.EvtSrc = MSSQLServer
HelpLink.EvtID = 50000
HelpLink.BaseHelpUrl = http://go.microsoft.com/fwlink
HelpLink.LinkId = 20476
ErrorCode: -2146232060
Procedure: RaiseAnError
Server: localhost
State: 1
Message: This is an Exception
HelpLink:
```

The `Class` property shows how valuable this information can be; it exposes information that enables the application to give users more detailed error messages.

The following table shows the varying levels of severity at which errors can occur in SQL Server.

Severity Level	Connection Is Closed	Generates SqlException	Meaning
10 and below	No	No	Informational messages that do not necessarily represent error conditions.

Table continued on following page

Severity Level	Connection Is Closed	Generates SqlException	Meaning
11–16	No	Yes	Errors that can be corrected by the user — for example, by retrying the operation with amended input data.
17–19	No	Yes	Resource or system errors
20–25	Yes	Yes	Fatal system errors (including system errors)

Table courtesy of http://msdn.microsoft.com/library/default.asp?url=/library/en-us/dnbda/html/daag.asp.

When you're using the Generic Factory approach, you have two options when catching exceptions: Either you can make do with a generic exception class, which enables you to step into the provider-specific exception layers via the InnerException property of the Exception class, or you can interact directly with the provider-specific exceptions, as shown here:

```
Public Sub CatchAGenericException()
    Dim Conn As System.Data.Common.DbConnection =
CodeSamples.GenericFactoryHelper.Connection
    Conn.ConnectionString = CodeSamples.GenericFactoryHelper.ConnectionString
    Dim Comm As System.Data.Common.DbCommand = Conn.CreateCommand
    Comm.CommandText = ("SELECT * FROM NORTHWIND.dbo.TableDoesntExist")
    Comm.CommandType = System.Data.CommandType.Text
    Conn.Open()
    Dim Dt As System.Data.DataTable = New System.Data.DataTable
    Try
        Dt.Load(Comm.ExecuteReader)
    Catch Ex As System.Data.Common.DbException
        Throw New Exception("A DbExeption was thrown with the message '" +
Ex.Message + "'")
    Catch Ex As System.Exception
        Throw New Exception("An Exception was thrown with the message '" +
Ex.Message + "'")
    End Try
    Conn.Close()
End Sub
```

While the exception might be of type DbException, it still contains all the information you would expect from the provider-specific exception. An example that shows this is detailed here:

```
Public Sub CatchAGenericExceptionInDetail()
    Dim Conn As System.Data.Common.DbConnection =
CodeSamples.GenericFactoryHelper.Connection
    Conn.ConnectionString = CodeSamples.GenericFactoryHelper.ConnectionString
    Dim Comm As System.Data.Common.DbCommand = Conn.CreateCommand
    Comm.CommandText = ("SELECT * FROM NORTHWIND.dbo.TableDoesntExist")
    Comm.CommandType = System.Data.CommandType.Text
    Conn.Open()
    Dim Dt As System.Data.DataTable = New System.Data.DataTable
```

```
    Try
        Dt.Load(Comm.ExecuteReader)
    Catch Ex As System.Data.Common.DbException
        Console.WriteLine(Ex.GetType.ToString)
        Console.WriteLine(Ex.Message)
        Console.WriteLine(Ex.StackTrace)
        Console.WriteLine(String.Empty)
    Catch Ex As System.Exception
        Throw New Exception("An Exception was thrown with the message '" +
Ex.Message + "'")
    End Try
    Conn.Close()
End Sub
```

What this generates is very detailed error information directly from the provider, but wrapped up in a neat little package, DbException:

```
System.Data.SqlClient.SqlException
Invalid object name 'NORTHWIND.dbo.TableDoesntExist'.
   at System.Data.SqlClient.SqlConnection.OnError(SqlException exception, Boolean
breakConnection)
   at System.Data.SqlClient.SqlInternalConnection.OnError(SqlException exception,
Boolean breakConnection)
   at System.Data.SqlClient.TdsParser.ThrowExceptionAndWarning(TdsParserStateObject
stateObj)
   at System.Data.SqlClient.TdsParser.Run(RunBehavior runBehavior, SqlCommand
cmdHandler, SqlDataReader dataStream, BulkCopySimpleResultSet bulkCopyHandler,
TdsParserStateObject stateObj)
   at System.Data.SqlClient.SqlDataReader.ConsumeMetaData()
   at System.Data.SqlClient.SqlDataReader.get_MetaData()
   at System.Data.SqlClient.SqlCommand.FinishExecuteReader(SqlDataReader ds,
RunBehavior runBehavior, String resetOptionsString)
   at System.Data.SqlClient.SqlCommand.RunExecuteReaderTds(CommandBehavior
cmdBehavior, RunBehavior runBehavior, Boolean returnStream, Boolean async)
   at System.Data.SqlClient.SqlCommand.RunExecuteReader(CommandBehavior
cmdBehavior, RunBehavior runBehavior, Boolean returnStream, String method,
DbAsyncResult result)
   at System.Data.SqlClient.SqlCommand.RunExecuteReader(CommandBehavior
cmdBehavior, RunBehavior runBehavior, Boolean returnStream, String method)
   at System.Data.SqlClient.SqlCommand.ExecuteReader(CommandBehavior behavior,
String method)
   at System.Data.SqlClient.SqlCommand.ExecuteDbDataReader(CommandBehavior
behavior)
   at System.Data.Common.DbCommand.ExecuteReader()
   at CodeSampleTests.Exceptions.CatchAGenericExceptionInDetail()
```

As the preceding code is quite generic, it might not give you what you need when trapping exceptions, so it's important to note you can still catch provider-specific exceptions before falling back on generic methods. The following code briefly details the way in which you can build a comprehensive exception trap for exceptions that originate from each of the providers you want to support.

The importance of this can't be underestimated; oftentimes, you get very similar sorts of errors occurring on different database systems, and it's very handy to group them together so your front-end users see a neat, consistent error regardless of the provider they're using. Here's the code:

```
Public Sub CatchAProviderSpecificException()
    Dim Conn As System.Data.Common.DbConnection =
CodeSamples.GenericFactoryHelper.Connection
    Dim Comm As System.Data.Common.DbCommand = Conn.CreateCommand
    Conn.ConnectionString = CodeSamples.GenericFactoryHelper.ConnectionString
    Comm.CommandText = ("SELECT * FROM NORTHWIND.dbo.TableDoesntExist")
    Comm.CommandType = System.Data.CommandType.Text
    Conn.Open()
    Dim Dt As System.Data.DataTable = New System.Data.DataTable
    Try
        Dt.Load(Comm.ExecuteReader)
    Catch Ex As System.Data.SqlClient.SqlException
        Throw New Exception("A SqlException was thrown with the message '" +
Ex.Message + "'")
    Catch Ex As System.Exception
        Throw New Exception("An Exception was thrown with the message '" +
Ex.Message + "'")
    End Try
    Conn.Close()
End Sub
```

Trapping exceptions can be quite easy, and developers find them vital for debugging applications throughout the development cycle. Remember, however, that most users won't know what the exceptions mean, so it's generally best to hide them from end users unless you know they're qualified to deal with them.

Provider-Specific Features

We know we have a connection and we've introduced ourselves. Now we want a little bit more information. We're using the Provider Model, though, so we don't actually know what we're dealing with. We can, however, by using a little forethought, build a degree of intelligence into our code so that any provider-specific functionality is still available to us:

```
Public Sub GetSqlConnectionStatistics()
    If Not (CodeSamples.GenericFactoryHelper.CurrentFactory =
"System.Data.SqlClient") Then
        Throw New Exception("This test requires the Factory to be running from the
System.Data.SqlClient provider, it's currently running as " +
CodeSamples.GenericFactoryHelper.CurrentFactory)
    End If
    Dim SqlConn As System.Data.SqlClient.SqlConnection =
CType(CodeSamples.GenericFactoryHelper.Connection,
System.Data.SqlClient.SqlConnection)
    Dim Stats As System.Collections.Hashtable
    Using SqlConn


        SqlConn.ConnectionString =
CodeSamples.GenericFactoryHelper.ConnectionString
        SqlConn.Open()
        Stats = CType(SqlConn.RetrieveStatistics, System.Collections.Hashtable)
        SqlConn.Close()

        For Each Key As String In Stats.Keys
```

```
                    Console.WriteLine(Key + " = " + Stats(Key).ToString)
            Next

        End Using

        Dim actual As Integer = Stats.Count
        Dim expected As Integer = 18

        If actual <> expected Then

            Throw New Exception("Did not return the expected value.")

        End If

    End Sub
```

The output of this method looks something like this:

```
NetworkServerTime = 0
BytesReceived = 0
UnpreparedExecs = 0
SumResultSets = 0
SelectCount = 0
PreparedExecs = 0
ConnectionTime = 0
ExecutionTime = 0
Prepares = 0
BuffersSent = 0
SelectRows = 0
ServerRoundtrips = 0
CursorOpens = 0
Transactions = 0
BytesSent = 0
BuffersReceived = 0
IduRows = 0
IduCount = 0
```

What's really cool about this is that while you can generally use a provider-generic solution, there's nothing to stop you from using provider-specific code within your generic application so long as you understand that it might not work with all providers. Obviously, the preceding code is just a sample. The possibilities are endless — from exception trapping all the way to using database-specific object types.

For more provider-specific code, check out Chapters 9, 10, 11, 16, and 17.

Schema Metadata

While it's possible to directly access many database servers and check the schema (layout) of their databases, each database server — be it Oracle or SQL Server — gets information in different ways. The *ADO.NET schema metadata system* provides the application developer with easy access to the schemas with a consistent provider-agnostic API.

This section covers schema information in great detail, describing the different types of information you can retrieve and showing some ways in which it can best be used.

Available Information

There is a good deal of variation between the different providers, both in how they implement T-SQL and how they fit together. With the schema metadata system, you can query for schema information and interrogate the different database servers regarding their layout.

The metadata information available depends entirely on the way each provider has been implemented. In SQL Server, for example, it's possible to get quite a bit of information, ranging from the structure of tables (columns and data types) to the reserved words for the Server. In other providers, you can get similar information, but it might not be in the same format. The thing to remember with schema metadata is that it can very well be different for each provider.

To produce a list of what is available for all the providers installed on your system, you can run the following code in conjunction with the `GenericFactoryHelper` defined previously. What this code does is run through each provider, querying the schema metadata, retrieving the list of metadata collections that are available, and then displaying them to the console:

```
Public Sub SchemasAvaliable()
    Dim Dt As System.Data.DataTable = CodeSamples.GenericFactoryHelper.AllFactories
    For Each Dr As System.Data.DataRow In Dt.Rows
        Dim Dbp As System.Data.Common.DbProviderFactory =
System.Data.Common.DbProviderFactories.GetFactory(Dr("InvariantName").ToString)
        Try
            Dim Conn As System.Data.Common.DbConnection = Dbp.CreateConnection
            Dim Schema As System.Data.DataTable
            Using Conn

                Conn.ConnectionString =
CodeSamples.GenericFactoryHelper.ConnectionString
                Conn.Open()
                Schema =
Conn.GetSchema(System.Data.Common.DbMetaDataCollectionNames.MetaDataCollections)
                Conn.Close()

            End Using

            Console.WriteLine(Dbp.ToString)
            For Each SchemaRow As System.Data.DataRow In Schema.Rows
                Console.WriteLine(SchemaRow(0).ToString)
            Next

        Catch Ex As Exception
            Console.WriteLine("Failed for " + Dbp.ToString + " - " + Ex.Message)
        End Try
    Next
End Sub
```

Here you can see the list that the `SqlClientFactory` returns. The items listed can be queried individually to reveal more information about the data to which they pertain.

SqlClientFactory
MetaDataCollections
DataSourceInformation
DataTypes
Restrictions
ReservedWords
Users
Databases
Tables
Columns
Views
ViewColumns
ProcedureParameters
Procedures
ForeignKeys
IndexColumns
Indexes

This table shows all the top-level information that is available for the `SqlClientFactory` provider. As you can see, there is a wealth of information. The following sections describe some areas you might find useful.

DataTypes

The mapping for each data type is stored in the metadata, too, with all of the properties that the Framework and database servers need to translate between .NET-specific types and provider-specific types.

DataSourceInformation

Inside this section of the schema, you'll find information used by the provider-specific `DbCommandBuilder` to construct T-SQL (Transact-SQL) commands and add parameters to queries. Other information can also be contained within this section, but for now we'll just cover the default information returned by the main providers and briefly discuss what each one means.

CompositeIdentifierSeparatorPattern

This represents the separator when referencing the different objects on the server — for example, a table called `Publishers` owned by `Phil` in a database called `Northwind` on a server called `Badger` on SQL Server is expressed like this:

```
Badger.Northwind.Phil.Publishers
```

The separator pattern identifies the "." used to break up the individual elements. The entry for this value inside the SQL Server schema is as follows:

```
<CompositeIdentifierSeparatorPattern>\.</CompositeIdentifierSeparatorPattern>
```

DataSourceProductName

This is more of a label than anything that's actually used; it contains what you expect it to — the name of the type of server to which you're connected. The SQL Server entry is as follows:

```
<DataSourceProductName>Microsoft SQL Server</DataSourceProductName>
```

GroupByBehavior

This is a direct reflection of the `System.Data.Common.GroupByBehavior` enumerator. The possible values are shown in the following table.

ExactMatch	4
MustContainAll	3
NotSupported	1
Unknown	0
Unrelated	2

The SqlClient Provider defaults to Unrelated, as shown here:

```
<GroupByBehavior>2</GroupByBehavior>
```

IdentifierCase

The case sensitivity of identifiers is controlled by this property and it maps straight into the enumerator `System.Data.Common.IdentifierCase`, whose values are shown in the following table.

Insensitive	1
Unknown	0
Sensitive	2

The default value for Sql Client is as follows:

```
<IdentifierCase>1</IdentifierCase>
```

IdentifierPattern

This is a regular expression that specifies the pattern to which the provider requires its identifiers to conform.

The SQL Server provider has a regular expression that looks like this:

```
<IdentifierPattern>(^\[\p{Lo}\p{Lu}\p{Ll}_@#][\p{Lo}\p{Lu}\p{Ll}\p{Nd}@$#_]*$)|(^\[
[^\]\0]|\]\]+\]$)|(^\"[^\"\0]|\"\"+\"$)</IdentifierPattern>
```

OrderByColumnsInSelect

This is a normal Boolean value that signifies whether SELECT statements should also perform an ORDER BY, which mirrors each of the values in the SELECT statement. For example, a SELECT with OrderByColumnsInSelect set to true might look like this:

```
SELECT Badger, Mushroom, Snake
FROM Internet
ORDER BY Badger, Mushroom, Snake
```

The default behavior in the SQL Server provider is false:

```
<OrderByColumnsInSelect>false</OrderByColumnsInSelect>
```

ParameterMarkerFormat

This is a string that identifies a mask for parameters:

```
<ParameterMarkerFormat>@{0}</ParameterMarkerFormat>
```

ParameterMarkerPattern

Each database server prefixes its parameters in a specific way; this regular expression checks the parameter name with its prefix attached (an "@" character in the case of the SQL Server provider):

```
<ParameterMarkerPattern>@[\p{Lo}\p{Lu}\p{Ll}\p{Lm}_@#][\p{Lo}\p{Lu}\p{Ll}\p{Lm}\p{N
d}\uff3f_@#\$]*(?=\s+|$)</ParameterMarkerPattern>
```

ParameterNameMaxLength

This does exactly what you'd expect it to do from its name. The default SQL Server value for this one is as follows:

```
<ParameterNameMaxLength>128</ParameterNameMaxLength>
```

ParameterNamePattern

This is another regular expression that tells the DbCommandBuilder the format in which parameter names must appear. For SQL Server, the default is as follows:

```
<ParameterNamePattern>^[\p{Lo}\p{Lu}\p{Ll}\p{Lm}_@#][\p{Lo}\p{Lu}\p{Ll}\p{Lm}\p{Nd}
\uff3f_@#\$]*(?=\s+|$)</ParameterNamePattern>
```

QuotedIdentifierPattern

Yep — another regular expression. This one confirms that the identifiers inside the `DbCommandBuilder` conform to the format the provider needs. In the case of SQL Server, this is `[Identifier]` and is expressed like this:

```
<QuotedIdentifierPattern>(([^\[]|\]\])*)</QuotedIdentifierPattern>
```

QuotedIdentifierCase

The case sensitivity of parameters is controlled by this property and maps straight into the enumerator `System.Data.Common.IdentifierCase`, where all the values are as follows:

Insensitive	1
Unknown	0
Sensitive	2

The default value for Sql Client is shown here:

```
<QuotedIdentifierCase>1</QuotedIdentifierCase>
```

StatementSeparatorPattern

Almost all database servers enable the user to execute multiple statements in the same execution. This option lets the command builder split those individual statements in a larger execution. SQL Server uses the semicolon (;) character, as shown here:

```
<StatementSeparatorPattern>;</StatementSeparatorPattern>
```

StringLiteralPattern

Literal strings are required all over the place. For example, they make this query work and distinguish between operators and strings:

```
Select Badger From Internet Where Annoyance = 'Massive'
```

On SQL Server, this is expressed with apostrophes and enforced with the following regular expression:

```
<StringLiteralPattern>'(([^']|'')*)'</StringLiteralPattern>
```

SupportedJoinOperators

This translates into one of the values for the `System.Data.Common.SupportedJoinOperators` enumerated type, which has several options:

FullOuter	8
Inner	1
LeftOuter	2

None	0
RightOuter	4

The value for SQL Server is 15, which means it's a combination of the enumerated types above (8 + 1 + 2 + 0 + 4), as shown here:

```
<SupportedJoinOperators>15</SupportedJoinOperators>
```

Restrictions

While having the metadata is useful, it's pointless if you can't search it. With *restrictions,* you can query the schema information, searching for specific entries just as you would search for data in your database tables.

Each object type in the database has different items you can search against. To get a full list of each type and its associated number, run the following code:

```
Public Sub ListAllRestrictionsAvaliable()
    Dim Dt As System.Data.DataTable = CodeSamples.GenericFactoryHelper.AllFactories
    For Each Dr As System.Data.DataRow In Dt.Rows
        Dim Dbp As System.Data.Common.DbProviderFactory = Nothing
        Try
            Dbp =
System.Data.Common.DbProviderFactories.GetFactory(Dr("InvariantName").ToString)
            Dim Conn As System.Data.Common.DbConnection = Dbp.CreateConnection
            Dim Schema As System.Data.DataTable
            Using Conn

                Conn.ConnectionString =
CodeSamples.GenericFactoryHelper.ConnectionString
                Conn.Open()
                Schema =
Conn.GetSchema(System.Data.Common.DbMetaDataCollectionNames.Restrictions)
                Conn.Close()

            End Using

            Console.WriteLine(Dbp.ToString)
            For Each Column As System.Data.DataColumn In Schema.Columns
                Console.Write(Column.ColumnName)
                Console.Write("" & Microsoft.VisualBasic.Chr(9) & "")
            Next
            Console.WriteLine(String.Empty)
            For Each SchemaRow As System.Data.DataRow In Schema.Rows
                For Each Column As System.Data.DataColumn In Schema.Columns
                    Console.Write(SchemaRow(Column.ColumnName).ToString)
                    Console.Write("" & Microsoft.VisualBasic.Chr(9) & "")
                Next
                Console.WriteLine(String.Empty)
            Next
        Catch Ex As Exception
            If Not (Dbp Is Nothing) Then
```

```
                      Console.WriteLine("Failed for " + Dbp.ToString + " - " +
        Ex.Message)
                    End If
             End Try
        Next
    End Sub
```

This code returns a lot of information, but we'll focus on just one piece of it for the moment. Following are the results for tables in the Sql Server Provider, detailing the columns available to us for querying.

RestrictionName	RestrictionDefault	RestrictionNumber
Catalog	TABLE_CATALOG	1
Owner	TABLE_SCHEMA	2
Table	TABLE_NAME	3
TableType	TABLE_TYPE	4

As you can see from the results produced in the preceding table, we can query the database in which tables are stored (TABLE_CATALOG), the owner of the table (TABLE_SCHEMA) and the table name (TABLE_NAME), as well as the table type (TABLE_TYPE), be it user or system created.

We don't actually write a SELECT statement to do this. Rather, we change the way in which we call the GetSchema() method to tell it what we're looking for and which objects to search by, passing in a string array of appropriate restrictions. For example, if we want to determine whether the pubs database contains a table called publishers, we'd set up a string array, like this:

```
Dim Restrictions(4) As String
Restrictions(0) = "pubs" 'TABLE_CATALOG
Restrictions(1) = Nothing 'TABLE_SCHEMA
Restrictions(2) = "publishers" 'TABLE_NAME
Restrictions(3) = Nothing 'TABLE_TYPE
```

The indexes of the string array directly relate to the RestrictionNumber shown in the preceding table (+1, as we're in 0-based arrays).

Once we have the string array, we can actually run the query, but our GetSchema() method call has changed slightly to include the keyword "Tables", which could easily be replaced by any of the items returned from SchemasAvailable() above:

```
Schema = Conn.GetSchema("Tables",Restrictions)
```

What this then returns is a list of every table that matches our restrictions. In this case, there's only one:

TABLE_CATALOG	TABLE_SCHEMA	TABLE_NAME	TABLE_TYPE
pubs	dbo	publishers	BASE TABLE

What happened behind the scenes was that the Framework actually queried the SQL Server with the following:

```
select TABLE_CATALOG, TABLE_SCHEMA, TABLE_NAME, TABLE_TYPE from
INFORMATION_SCHEMA.TABLES where TABLE_CATALOG = 'pubs' and TABLE_SCHEMA =
TABLE_SCHEMA and TABLE_NAME = 'publishers' and TABLE_TYPE = TABLE_TYPE
```

Notice how for each of the restrictions we specified, the SQL was added; and for the ones we ignored, the default value was used instead, due to some intelligence baked into the Framework. The .NET Framework takes the query specified in the Schema Metadata file, as shown below, and converts it into the desired query, as shown above. If you inspect the following query, you'll see that the parameters are specified as {n}, which is why it's important to pass in your restrictions in the right order:

```
select TABLE_CATALOG, TABLE_SCHEMA, TABLE_NAME, TABLE_TYPE from
INFORMATION_SCHEMA.TABLES where TABLE_CATALOG = {0} and TABLE_SCHEMA = {1} and
TABLE_NAME = {2} and TABLE_TYPE = {3}
```

If you don't care about a particular item in the query, you can just set its parameter to null. If it follows the highest number you do care about, just omit it completely. For example, if you wanted only the tables in the pubs database, your restrictions could look like this:

```
Dim Restrictions(1) As String
Restrictions(0) = "pubs" 'TABLE_CATALOG
```

To summarize, if you ever need to query the schema information, it's a good idea to use restrictions to limit your results to only what you need.

Reserved Words

All database languages have words that are operational or expressional. A very small sample of the reserved words in SQL Server includes the following:

```
EXCEPT
PERCENT
ALL
EXEC
PLAN
ALTER
EXECUTE
PRECISION
EXISTS
```

Yawn! There are a lot of these. Using the schema metadata, you can query the reserved words to identify which ones should not be used when constructing queries or picking names for your database provider. To query the data, it's a simple matter of taking the preceding code and changing the query request to the following:

```
Schema = Conn.GetSchema("ReservedWords")
```

This query has already been written for you and can be found in the sample code called "AllReservedWords".

Source of the Schema Information

The schema information is pulled directly from the database server to which the provider you're using is pointing. The queries are tucked away inside the provider itself, enabling information to be looked up from the database server.

The .NET providers for SqlClient, OleDb, and ODBC have these queries and other information embedded as resources inside the System.Data.dll stored in C:\WINDOWS\Microsoft.NET\Framework\v2.0.50215. OracleClient information is inside the System.Data.OracleClient.dll in the same location.

Each provider has its own XML file inside its associated assembly, which details how all the schema information is retrieved from the database server:

❑ System.Data.SqlClient.SqlMetaData.xml

❑ System.Data.OleDb.OleDbMetaData.xml

❑ System.Data.Odbc.OdbcMetaData.xml

❑ System.Data.OracleClient.OracleMetaData.xml

The following table shows the queries sent to the different servers to get both a list of tables and a list of views for each provider.

	SqlMetaData.xml	OracleMetaData.xml
Tables	select TABLE_CATALOG, TABLE_SCHEMA, TABLE_NAME, TABLE_TYPE from INFORMATION_SCHEMA.TABLES where TABLE_CATALOG = {0} and TABLE_SCHEMA = {1} and TABLE_NAME = {2} and TABLE_TYPE = {3}	SELECT OWNER, TABLE_NAME, DECODE(OWNER, 'SYS', 'System', 'SYSTEM', 'System', 'SYSMAN', 'System','CTXSYS', 'System','MDSYS', 'System','OLAPSYS', 'System', 'ORDSYS', 'System','OUTLN', 'System', 'WKSYS', 'System','WMSYS', 'System','XDB', 'System','ORDPLUGINS', 'System','User') AS Type FROM ALL_TABLES WHERE OWNER={0} AND TABLE_NAME={1} ORDER BY OWNER, TABLE_NAME
Views	select TABLE_CATALOG, TABLE_SCHEMA, TABLE_NAME, CHECK_OPTION, IS_UPDATABLE from INFORMATION_SCHEMA.VIEWS where TABLE_CATALOG = {0} and TABLE_SCHEMA = {1} and TABLE_NAME = {2} order by TABLE_CATALOG, TABLE_SCHEMA, TABLE_NAME	SELECT * FROM ALL_VIEWS WHERE OWNER={0} AND VIEW_NAME = {1}

As you can see, different providers are configured to return similar data, but in a very different structure. When using the schema information, it's important to understand that the different providers offer different levels and quality of information.

> It's always a good idea when using GetSchema() to cache your results where possible. That way, you can greatly increase the performance of your applications.

Uses for Schema Metadata

Schema information offers many possible uses, from custom reporting solutions to object relationship mappers.

It's now possible in a platform-independent way to query the layout of databases and then use the information to build visual representations of that data either as reports or by constructing user interface elements.

You can also use the schema information to discover the constraints applied to columns of data, such as the allowed length and data format, to automatically validate data in your user interface before even attempting to pass it through to the database.

Commands

Once you have an open connection to the database server of your choice, the next step is to simply run some SQL against the server. To do this, as you're probably aware, you need to use Command objects.

Commands are the vehicle by which the majority of your database work happens, so it's worth getting very familiar with them. The following sections go through the basics of getting a Command object and then using it, and detail some of the modifications made to the Command object in ADO.NET 2.0.

DbCommand from a Factory

When using the Factory Model, it's important to get the right Command object, and the simplest way to do that is to call the CreateCommand() object, which will return a DbCommand:

```
Public Sub CheckCommandFromProvider()
    Dim actual As String = CodeSamples.GenericFactoryHelper.Command.ToString
    Dim expected As String =
CodeSamples.GenericFactoryHelper.GetFactory(CodeSamples.GenericFactoryHelper.Curren
tFactory).CreateCommand.ToString
    If expected <> actual Then
        Throw New Exception("The values do not match")
    End If
End Sub
```

DbCommand from a DbConnection

It's also possible to create a Command object directly from a DbConnection object, meaning you can get a provider-specific implementation of a Command object while keeping the provider-agnostic approach and references:

```
Public Sub CheckCommandFromConnection()
    Dim actual As String =
CodeSamples.GenericFactoryHelper.Connection.CreateCommand.ToString
    Dim expected As String =
CodeSamples.GenericFactoryHelper.GetFactory(CodeSamples.GenericFactoryHelper.Curren
tFactory).CreateCommand.ToString
    If expected <> actual Then
        Throw New Exception("Did not return the expected value.")
    End If
End Sub
```

Make sure you use this approach to create a command when you have a connection available.

Provider-Specific Commands

If you're not using the Factory Model, it's perfectly possible to grab a Command object from the provider of your choice—for example, the SqlCommand if you're using the SqlClient provider:

```
Public Sub GetCommandFromProvider()
    Dim Comm As System.Data.SqlClient.SqlCommand = New
System.Data.SqlClient.SqlCommand
    If Comm Is Nothing Then
        Throw New Exception("The Command object was null.")
    End If
End Sub
```

While it's easy to do this, please try to avoid it if possible and use the provider-independent (Generic Factory Model) approach.

QuoteIdentifier and UnquotedIdentifier

Quoted identifiers help database servers know when you're talking about objects, such as tables and columns, and when you're talking about literal strings.

In SQL Server, there are two types of quoted identifier: [Square Brackets] and "Quotation Marks." The quotation marks are used differently depending on whether QUOTED_IDENTIFIER is set to On or Off. When set to On, anything inside quotation marks is treated as an object, such as a table or column; when set to Off, characters inside quotation marks are treated as literal strings, such as "Phil".

Why does this matter to you as a developer? Well, depending on the settings of your queries, you may need to quote any objects so that they're not mixed up with their literal string representations. ADO.NET 2.0 provides a couple of methods that hang off the Command object to enable you to do this.

Hidden away in the Schema Metadata files for your provider, buried within the `DataSourceInformation` section, there is an entry for `QuotedIdentifierPattern`. In the case of the SqlServer provider, this is `(([^\[]|\]\])*)`, a regular expression specifying that the string passed in to it should be surrounded by [square brackets]. What the `QuoteIdentifier` method does is take in our string `"Phil"` and use the regular expression to output a properly formatted string:

```
Public Sub UseQuoteIdentifier()
    Dim CommB As System.Data.Common.DbCommandBuilder =
CodeSamples.GenericFactoryHelper.CommandBuilder
    Dim actual As String = CommB.QuoteIdentifier("Phil")
    Dim expected As String = ("[Phil]")
    If expected <> actual Then
        Throw New Exception("Values do not match")
    End If
End Sub
```

As well as being able to quote identifiers, it's also possible to remove any quote mark characters from the identifiers, meaning that you can translate both ways (Database → UI and UI → Database) for any parameters or keywords you wish to use:

```
Public Sub UseUnquoteIdentifier()
    Dim CommB As System.Data.Common.DbCommandBuilder =
CodeSamples.GenericFactoryHelper.CommandBuilder
    Dim actual As String = CommB.UnquoteIdentifier("[Phil]")
    Dim expected As String = ("Phil")
    If expected <> actual Then
        Throw New Exception("Values do not match")
    End If
End Sub
```

Using `QuoteIdentifier` and `UnquoteIdentifer` enables you to dynamically build compliant SQL statements with very little effort. What use they have outside the world of dynamic SQL, however, is not yet known.

Adding DbParameters to a DbCommand

Creating and adding parameters using the Factory Model is relatively simple. It's just a matter of calling the `CreateParameter()` method on the `Command` object and then assigning the parameters any relevant values before appending it to the `Parameters` collection on the `Command` object:

```
Public Sub CreateAndAddParameter()
    Dim Comm As System.Data.Common.DbCommand =
CodeSamples.GenericFactoryHelper.Connection.CreateCommand
    Dim Prm As System.Data.Common.DbParameter = Comm.CreateParameter
    Prm.ParameterName = CodeSamples.GenericFactoryHelper.FormatParameter("Socks")
    Prm.Value = ("Smelly")
    Comm.Parameters.Add(Prm)
    Dim expectedCount As Integer = 1
    If expectedCount <> Comm.Parameters.Count Then
        Throw New Exception("Did not return the expected count.")
    End If
    Dim expectedValue As String = ("Smelly")
```

```
            If expectedValue <> Comm.Parameters(0).Value Then
                Throw New Exception("Did not return the expected value.")
            End If
    End Sub
```

You might think it's odd that this section has been included in the book, but it's important to understand how ADO.NET and specifically *adding parameters* has changed with .NET 2.0.

When adding a parameter now, you should never add it through the `Add(string,object)` signature. That method has been deprecated. Instead, add parameters to a `ParameterCollection` object via the `Add(DbParameter)` overload.

Parameters Are Not Generic

Different providers take their parameters in different ways, and coding for each eventuality can be quite difficult.

The providers use each database's native syntax and positioning information for laying out their parameters. Some are *positional* (that is, the index to which they are added in the `Parameters` collection directly correlates to where in the SQL statement they will be used), and others are *named* (a named parameter goes to a specific place).

The following table lists each of the default providers, with positioning and marker information.

Provider	Named/Positional	Parameter Marker
SqlClient	Named	`@parmname`
OracleClient	Named	`:parmname (or parmname)`
OleDb	Positional	`?`
Odbc	Positional	`?`

Table courtesy of http://msdn.microsoft.com/library/en-us/dnvs05/html/vsgenerics.asp?frame=true#vsgene_topic4.

When you are writing a system that should be database-independent, it's important to remember the preceding table. You have to code for these differences in parameters.

Fortunately, it's very easy with the schema information for a provider to format the parameter automatically. The parameter marker is stored inside the `ParameterMarkerFormat` field of the `DataSourceInformation` section.

Here is a method that demonstrates automatically formatting a parameter with the correct marker:

```
    Public Shared Function FormatParameter(ByVal ParameterName As String) As String
        Dim Conn As DbConnection = Connection
        Conn.ConnectionString = ConnectionString
        Dim ParameterMarkerFormat As String
```

```
        Using Conn
            Conn.Open()
            ParameterMarkerFormat =
    Conn.GetSchema("DataSourceInformation").Rows(0)("ParameterMarkerFormat").ToString
            Conn.Close()
        End Using
        Return String.Format(ParameterMarkerFormat, ParameterName)
    End Function
```

An example showing the exact use of the preceding code follows. Here, you can see a parameter name being passed into `FormatParamater`, and a string delimited with @ being returned from it:

```
Public Sub ProviderSpecificParameter()
    Dim Comm As System.Data.Common.DbCommand =
CodeSamples.GenericFactoryHelper.Connection.CreateCommand
    Dim Prm As System.Data.Common.DbParameter = Comm.CreateParameter
    Prm.ParameterName = CodeSamples.GenericFactoryHelper.FormatParameter("Socks")
    Prm.Value = ("Smelly")
    Comm.Parameters.Add(Prm)
    Dim expectedCount As Integer = 1
    If expectedCount <> Comm.Parameters.Count Then
        Throw New Exception("Did not return the expected count.")
    End If
    Dim expectedValue As String = ("Smelly")
    If expectedValue <> Comm.Parameters(0).Value Then
        Throw New Exception("Did not return the expected value.")
    End If
End Sub
```

As you can see, by using the built-in Schema Metadata, we can infer the marker and actually place it into our parameters dynamically at runtime, depending on the provider we're using.

Now that markers have been dealt with, we turn to the positional side of things. There's just one simple rule to follow here: Make sure the order of the parameters never changes and that all of the positional SQL you write takes parameters in the same order.

ExecuteNonQuery

While much of your ADO.NET code will be retrieving data from data sources, it's also quite useful to be able to push data into the database in the form of inserts and updates. This is exactly what `ExecuteNonQuery` is for.

`ExecuteNonQuery` can be used in conjunction with output parameters and return codes, as detailed in the section "Output Parameters, Return Codes, Scalars, and DataReaders," and it offers the added functionality of returning the number of rows affected by any commands executed with it.

ExecuteReader

You'll often just need a load of data to display onscreen, such as search results or the items for a drop-down list; and the `ExecuteReader` method is meant for such scenarios. It offers the best and fastest approach for reading large amounts of data. Here is a sample showing the use of `ExecuteReader`:

```
Private Shared Sub DoReader()
    Using Conn As System.Data.SqlClient.SqlConnection = New
System.Data.SqlClient.SqlConnection
        Using Comm As System.Data.SqlClient.SqlCommand = New
System.Data.SqlClient.SqlCommand
            Using Reader As System.Data.SqlClient.SqlDataReader =
Comm.ExecuteReader
                While Reader.Read
                    'Do Stuff
                End While
            End Using
        End Using
    End Using
End Sub
```

Make sure that you're using a `Reader` and not a `DataSet` when you just need forward-only read access to data.

Filling a DataSet or DataTable without a DataAdapter

There is now fantastic support in the Framework for filling DataTables and DataSets directly from Readers. No longer do you need a DataAdapter just to get information from your SQL Server tables to an in-memory DataSet.

Here is a brief example showing the population of a DataTable with a Reader:

```
Private Shared Sub FillDataTable()
    Using Conn As System.Data.SqlClient.SqlConnection = New
System.Data.SqlClient.SqlConnection
        Using Comm As System.Data.SqlClient.SqlCommand = New
System.Data.SqlClient.SqlCommand
            Using Reader As System.Data.SqlClient.SqlDataReader =
Comm.ExecuteReader
                Dim Dt As New DataTable
                Dt.Load(Reader)
            End Using
        End Using
    End Using
End Sub
```

System.Data.CommandBehavior

When calling an `ExecuteReader`, there's an overload that takes in one of the `CommandBehavior` enumerated types and acts accordingly. The different options are described in the following sections.

CloseConnection

When you employ the `CloseConnection` option on creation of a Reader, you'll ensure the connection is cleaned up after the Reader has been disposed of, but remember that you need to close your Reader in order for it to close the connection!

Default

Surprisingly enough, `Default` is what you get if you haven't specified a value. It's also one of the options you can choose.

KeyInfo

When `KeyInfo` is specified, ADO.NET will return all the primary key information, along with the tables in the Reader.

SchemaOnly

The `SchemaOnly` enumerated type does exactly what it says on the can — it just returns information about the columns in the tables that are used in the queries.

SequentialAccess

This option should only be selected when reading binary data from databases, as it allows for the streaming of files from columns in the database.

SingleRow

If you're just bringing one row back from the database, choose this option. Some of the .NET providers actually optimize the query to take advantage of the low volume of data being moved around.

SingleResult

When this option is specified, just one result set is returned.

ExecuteScalar

Quite commonly, all you'll want is a single value from the database, as when you select a field for a record based on its identifier. When all you need is one value, use `ExecuteScalar`.

An object of type `System.Object` is returned from `ExecuteScalar`, and you must cast the value out to the appropriate type (that is, the one you're expecting, such as `int` or `string`):

```
Private Shared Sub ExecuteScalar()
    Using Conn As System.Data.SqlClient.SqlConnection = New
System.Data.SqlClient.SqlConnection
        Using Comm As System.Data.SqlClient.SqlCommand = New
System.Data.SqlClient.SqlCommand
            Dim o As Object
            o = Comm.ExecuteScalar()
        End Using
    End Using
End Sub
```

Make sure that all single-field, single-row selects use `ExecuteScalar` when writing your ADO.NET code.

Output Parameters, Return Codes, Scalars, and DataReaders

More often than not, you want to get something from the database server, be it the ID of a newly added record or an error code from a statement. Four options are open to you as an ADO.NET developer, and we'll run through them in the following sections, detailing where they are best used and where they are best avoided.

Three of the options—Output, InputOutput, and ReturnCode—are detailed in the `System.Data.ParameterDirection` enumerated type. The fourth is the DataReader.

Output Parameters

Output parameters act just like normal parameters on the `Command` object. However, the database can specify the value to return with them. It's possible to have multiple output parameters on commands, and using them precludes the need to return a ResultSet of information (a row of data) from the database and place it into a DataReader or DataTable to get at the values. Output parameters are best used to return IDs from newly added rows or to return several values at once where only one row of data is being referenced. Here's an example:

```
Public Sub OuputParameter()
    Dim Comm As System.Data.Common.DbCommand =
CodeSamples.GenericFactoryHelper.Connection.CreateCommand
    Comm.CommandType = System.Data.CommandType.StoredProcedure
    Comm.CommandText = "Northwind.dbo.AddEmployee"
    Dim FirstName As System.Data.Common.DbParameter = Comm.CreateParameter
    FirstName.ParameterName =
CodeSamples.GenericFactoryHelper.FormatParameter("FirstName")
    FirstName.Value = ("Phil")
    FirstName.Direction = System.Data.ParameterDirection.Input
    Comm.Parameters.Add(FirstName)
    Dim LastName As System.Data.Common.DbParameter = Comm.CreateParameter
    LastName.ParameterName =
CodeSamples.GenericFactoryHelper.FormatParameter("LastName")
    LastName.Value = ("Winstanley")
    LastName.Direction = System.Data.ParameterDirection.Input
    Comm.Parameters.Add(LastName)
    Dim EmployeeID As System.Data.Common.DbParameter = Comm.CreateParameter
    EmployeeID.ParameterName =
CodeSamples.GenericFactoryHelper.FormatParameter("EmployeeID")
    EmployeeID.Direction = System.Data.ParameterDirection.Output
    Comm.Parameters.Add(EmployeeID)
    Using Conn As System.Data.Common.DbConnection =
CodeSamples.GenericFactoryHelper.Connection
        Conn.ConnectionString = CodeSamples.GenericFactoryHelper.ConnectionString
        Comm.Connection = Conn
        Comm.Connection.Open()
        Comm.ExecuteNonQuery()
        Comm.Connection.Close()
    End Using

    Dim ActualObject As Object = Comm.Parameters("EmployeeID").Value
    Dim ActualValue As Integer = 0
```

```
            If (Not (ActualObject Is Nothing)) Then
                ActualValue = CType(ActualObject, Integer)
            End If
            Dim ValueWeDontWant As Integer = 0
            If ValueWeDontWant = ActualValue Then
                Throw New Exception("The values match!")
            End If
    End Sub
```

The corresponding SQL looks like this:

```
Alter Proc AddEmployee
(
 @EmployeeID int = Null Output,
 @FirstName nVarChar(20),
 @LastName nVarChar(20)
)
As
Insert Into Northwind.dbo.Employees
(
 FirstName,
 LastName
)
Values
(
 @FirstName,
 @LastName
)
Set @EmployeeID = Scope_Identity()
Go
```

Return Codes

Return codes are very similar to output parameters in that they're accessible via a parameter. However, there can be only one return code per command, meaning they're best used to report on the status of an execution. For example, when updating a record, it would be prudent to have three return codes:

> 1 = Success
>
> 2 = Record Not Found
>
> 3 = Unexpected Error

Using the value retrieved by the return code, you can then act accordingly within your applications by either throwing specific exceptions or alerting the user to what has happened:

```
Public Sub ReturnCode()
    Dim Comm As System.Data.Common.DbCommand =
CodeSamples.GenericFactoryHelper.Connection.CreateCommand
    Comm.CommandType = System.Data.CommandType.StoredProcedure
    Comm.CommandText = "Northwind.dbo.UpdateEmployee"
    Dim FirstName As System.Data.Common.DbParameter = Comm.CreateParameter
    FirstName.ParameterName =
CodeSamples.GenericFactoryHelper.FormatParameter("FirstName")
```

```
        FirstName.Value = ("Phil")
        FirstName.Direction = System.Data.ParameterDirection.Input
        Comm.Parameters.Add(FirstName)
        Dim LastName As System.Data.Common.DbParameter = Comm.CreateParameter
        LastName.ParameterName =
    CodeSamples.GenericFactoryHelper.FormatParameter("LastName")
        LastName.Value = ("Winstanley")
        LastName.Direction = System.Data.ParameterDirection.Input
        Comm.Parameters.Add(LastName)
        Dim EmployeeId As System.Data.Common.DbParameter = Comm.CreateParameter
        EmployeeId.ParameterName =
    CodeSamples.GenericFactoryHelper.FormatParameter("EmployeeId")
        EmployeeId.Value = (1)
        EmployeeId.Direction = System.Data.ParameterDirection.Input
        Comm.Parameters.Add(EmployeeId)
        Dim ReturnValue As System.Data.Common.DbParameter = Comm.CreateParameter
        EmployeeID.ParameterName =
    CodeSamples.GenericFactoryHelper.FormatParameter("ReturnValue")
        EmployeeID.Direction = System.Data.ParameterDirection.ReturnValue
        Comm.Parameters.Add(EmployeeID)
        Using Conn As System.Data.Common.DbConnection =
    CodeSamples.GenericFactoryHelper.Connection

            Conn.ConnectionString = CodeSamples.GenericFactoryHelper.ConnectionString
            Comm.Connection = Conn
            Comm.Connection.Open()
            Comm.ExecuteNonQuery()
            Comm.Connection.Close()
        End Using

        Dim ActualObject As Object = Comm.Parameters("ReturnValue").Value
        Dim ActualValue As Integer = 0
        If (Not (ActualObject Is Nothing)) Then
            ActualValue = CType(ActualObject, Integer)
        End If
        Dim ValueWeDontWant As Integer = 0
        If ValueWeDontWant <> ActualValue Then
            Throw New Exception("The values don't match")
        End If
    End Sub
```

The preceding code executes the following SQL:

```
        Create Proc UpdateEmployee
        (
            @EmployeeID int,
            @FirstName nVarChar(20),
            @LastName nVarChar(20)
        )
        As
        --Check for the Records Existence
        If Not Exists (Select Null From Employees Where EmployeeID = @EmployeeID)
```

```
                    Return 2; -- Record Doesn't Exist!

        --Update the record
        Update Employees
        Set FirstName = @FirstName,
        LastName = @LastName
        Where EmployeeId = @EmployeeId

        --Make sure it was updated
        If @@RowCount = 1
                Return 1; -- Success!
        --If the Procedure got to here, something went very wrong....
        Return 3
Go
```

Scalars

Scalars are a bit trickier to classify because, unlike output parameters and return codes, they're not tied into parameters. Rather, they are actually a single value returned in a result set from the database server returned from a SELECT statement. The code looks like this:

```
Public Sub ExecuteScalarSingleValue()
    Dim Comm As System.Data.Common.DbCommand =
CodeSamples.GenericFactoryHelper.Connection.CreateCommand
    Comm.CommandType = System.Data.CommandType.StoredProcedure
    Comm.CommandText = "Northwind.dbo.ExecuteScalarSingleValue"
    Dim ActualObject As Object = Nothing
    Using Conn As System.Data.Common.DbConnection =
CodeSamples.GenericFactoryHelper.Connection

        Conn.ConnectionString = CodeSamples.GenericFactoryHelper.ConnectionString
        Comm.Connection = Conn
        Comm.Connection.Open()
        ActualObject = Comm.ExecuteScalar
        Comm.Connection.Close()
    End Using
    Dim ActualValue As Integer = 0
    If (Not (ActualObject Is Nothing)) Then
        ActualValue = CType(ActualObject, Integer)
    End If
    Dim ValueWeDontWant As Integer = 0
    If ValueWeDontWant <> ActualValue Then
        Throw New Exception("The Values don't match")
    End If
End Sub
```

The preceding code runs the following SQL:

```
CREATE PROC ExecuteScalarSingleValue
As
Select 1
Go
```

87

DataReaders

The fourth option available to you is to use a DataReader to return the values. The advantage of DataReaders is that many developers are familiar with them, although they seem a bit like overkill for just one or two values:

```
Public Sub ExecuteReaderSingleValue()
    Dim Comm As System.Data.Common.DbCommand =
CodeSamples.GenericFactoryHelper.Connection.CreateCommand
    Comm.CommandType = System.Data.CommandType.StoredProcedure
    Comm.CommandText = "Northwind.dbo.ExecuteScalarSingleValue"
    Dim reader As System.Data.Common.DbDataReader = Nothing
    Dim ActualValue As Integer = 0
    Using Conn As System.Data.Common.DbConnection =
CodeSamples.GenericFactoryHelper.Connection

        Conn.ConnectionString = CodeSamples.GenericFactoryHelper.ConnectionString
        Comm.Connection = Conn
        Comm.Connection.Open()
        reader = Comm.ExecuteReader(System.Data.CommandBehavior.SingleRow)
        Using reader

            While reader.Read
                ActualValue = reader.GetInt32(0)
            End While
        End Using
        Comm.Connection.Close()
    End Using
    Dim ValueWeDontWant As Integer = 0
    If ValueWeDontWant <> ActualValue Then
        Throw New Exception("The Values don't match")
    End If
End Sub
```

In terms of performance, all of the preceding options operate at a very similar speed, so the choice is not one of performance but personal preference and appropriateness to the code you're writing.

For more information on performance comparisons, view this guide at MSDN: `http://msdn` `.microsoft.com/library/en-us/dnbda/html/bdadotnetarch031.asp?frame=` `true#bdadotnetarch031_topic5`

DataSet

The ADO.NET Framework has the DataSet. If you're a hardened .NET developer already, you probably *hate* the DataSet, but we implore you to read on. The DataSet is faster, meaner, and an all-around much nicer chap than it used to be.

When writing code against databases, you'll commonly want to have relationships between tables and chunks of data. The ADO.NET DataSet enables you to represent data in memory in a rich relational model, supporting relationships, key constraints, and a whole host of other features.

In our experience, we've seen the DataSet misused more often than not. Keep in mind that it is *not* meant for all data usage in the Framework, that it does have some overhead, and that if you just need to pull data from a database and display it to a user without any form of data manipulation, you do not need to use the DataSet.

Having a DataSet is all well and good, but you've got to put some data inside it to make it useful. In this section, we briefly discuss the three ways you can populate a DataSet: manually, with DataAdapters, and with DataReaders.

Manually Populating a DataSet

It's perfectly possible, although generally ill advised, to populate a DataSet manually by adding columns and rows to the DataSet tables in code.

An example of when you might want to populate a DataSet manually is a scenario in which no Reader or DataAdapter is available for the data source. For example, if you're reading values from a custom hardware device, you may grab values via the serial interface and then need to store them in a bucket somewhere. The DataSet is a great general bucket for data, so by using the `Rows.Add(DataRow)` method, you can use the DataSet to hold your information without any Reader or Adapter:

```
Public Shared Sub AddRowToDataSet()
    Dim Ds As DataSet = New DataSet
    Ds.Tables.Add(New DataTable)
    Ds.Tables(0).Columns.Add(New DataColumn("Id"))
    Ds.Tables(0).Columns.Add(New DataColumn("Name"))
    Dim Dr As DataRow = Ds.Tables(0).NewRow
    Dr("Id") = 0
    Dr("Name") = "Phil"
    Ds.Tables(0).Rows.Add(Dr)
End Sub
```

If a DataAdapter or DataReader is available for your data source, don't add rows manually or we'll send the programming police around to arrest you for crimes against common sense.

> When you find yourself in a situation that requires you to add rows manually to a DataSet and you think it would be worthwhile, consider writing your own Data Adapter, which you can reuse.

Using DataAdapters

More often than not, your data sources will operate in a very complex manner, meaning that a level of translation needs to occur to convert the provider-specific chunks of data into .NET-compatible DataRows and DataTables. The `DataAdapter` for a given provider will do all the hard work for you.

Each provider that ships with the .NET Framework has its own DataAdapter, which converts provider-specific data into a .NET version.

An example of using a DataAdapter to populate a DataSet is shown here:

```
Public Shared Sub DoAdapter()
    Dim Ds As New DataSet
    Using Conn As New System.Data.SqlClient.SqlConnection
```

```
        Using Comm As New System.Data.SqlClient.SqlCommand
            Dim Da As New System.Data.SqlClient.SqlDataAdapter(Comm)
            Da.Fill(Ds)
        End Using
    End Using
End Sub
```

It's worth noting that a DataAdapter does much more than simply convert data source mush into a DataSet; it also hosts a whole range of features for shoving the DataSet back into the provider-specific mush.

Using DataReaders

A new addition to ADO.NET is the capability to populate DataSets directly from DataReaders. With this new functionality, the clearly defined lines between using DataReaders and using DataSets have become somewhat blurred. The best practices to follow when using these objects remains to be seen.

Here is a quick code snippet showing how to populate a DataSet using only a DataReader:

```
Public Sub LoadFromReader()
    Dim table As New DataTable("Orders")
    Using Conn As DbConnection = CodeSamples.GenericFactoryHelper.Connection
        Dim Comm As DbCommand = CodeSamples.GenericFactoryHelper.Command
        Comm.CommandText = ("Select * From Orders")
        Using Reader As DbDataReader =
Comm.ExecuteReader(CommandBehavior.CloseConnection)
            table.Load(Reader)
        End Using
    End Using
End Sub
```

DataTable

In previous versions of ADO.NET, the DataTable was the "poor relative" of the DataSet, a smaller and less powerful version with quite a few problems. In ADO.NET 2.0, however, the DataTable is now a first-class citizen within the Framework. It can operate completely independently of the DataSet.

Most of the time when people are creating DataSets, they're only populating one table within that DataSet. It's quite common to only want a flat representation of data, so it didn't make sense to use a DataSet every time you needed to grab a flat set of data. Now, under ADO.NET 2.0, you can use the DataTable all by itself.

Under 1.0 and 1.1, the developer had to jump through rings of fire just to get a DataTable into its simplest form, XML. The new Framework has made this much easier.

Bear in mind that while you can now expose the DataTable as a parameter, or return a value for a Web Service, only .NET 2.0 clients will be able to use DataSets with XML serialization.

RowState

While it goes completely against all best practices and defies most of the rules laid down by the ADO.NET team, people often want a way to manually set the RowState for specific rows in their DataTables. In ADO.NET 2.0, new methods have been added to enable this.

You now have explicit control for RowState using the `SetAdded()` and `SetModified()` methods, meaning you can override the DataRow's default behavior.

The following example shows this new explicit control and how you can use it:

```
Public Sub SetModified()
    Dim OrigonalTable As System.Data.DataTable = New System.Data.DataTable
    OrigonalTable.TableName = "InternetSightings"
    OrigonalTable.Columns.Add("AnimalOrFungiName")
    OrigonalTable.Columns.Add("TimesSpotted")
    Dim BadgerRow As System.Data.DataRow = OrigonalTable.NewRow
    BadgerRow("AnimalOrFungiName") = "Badger"
    BadgerRow("TimesSpotted") = "More than you can possibly imagine."
    OrigonalTable.Rows.Add(BadgerRow)
    OrigonalTable.AcceptChanges()
    If System.Data.DataRowState.Unchanged <> OrigonalTable.Rows(0).RowState Then
        Throw New Exception("Not Equal")
    End If
    OrigonalTable.Rows(0).SetModified()
    If System.Data.DataRowState.Modified <> OrigonalTable.Rows(0).RowState Then
        Throw New Exception("Not Equal")
    End If
End Sub
```

DataView

It's now possible to take the data from a DataView and convert it directly to a standalone DataTable object, which reflects exactly the schema and content of the DataView. To achieve this, you use the `ToTable()` method of the DataView:

```
Public Sub ToTable()
    Dim OrigonalTable As System.Data.DataTable = New System.Data.DataTable
    OrigonalTable.TableName = "InternetSightings"
    OrigonalTable.Columns.Add("AnimalOrFungiName")
    OrigonalTable.Columns.Add("TimesSpotted")
    Dim BadgerRow As System.Data.DataRow = OrigonalTable.NewRow
    BadgerRow("AnimalOrFungiName") = "Badger"
    BadgerRow("TimesSpotted") = "More than you can possibly imagine."
    OrigonalTable.Rows.Add(BadgerRow)
    Dim MushroomRow As System.Data.DataRow = OrigonalTable.NewRow
    MushroomRow("AnimalOrFungiName") = "Mushroom"
    MushroomRow("TimesSpotted") = "Just the twice, normally after spotting
Badgers."
    OrigonalTable.Rows.Add(MushroomRow)
    Dim SnakeRow As System.Data.DataRow = OrigonalTable.NewRow
    MushroomRow("AnimalOrFungiName") = "Snake"
    MushroomRow("TimesSpotted") = "Just the once, and crikey, what a scare I had!"
```

```
        OrigonalTable.Rows.Add(SnakeRow)
        Dim Dv As System.Data.DataView = New System.Data.DataView
        Dv.Table = OrigonalTable
        Dv.RowFilter = "AnimalOrFungiName = 'Badger'"
        Dim ToTableTable As System.Data.DataTable = Dv.ToTable
        Dim expected As Integer = 1
        Dim actual As Integer = ToTableTable.Rows.Count
        If expected <> actual Then
            Throw New Exception("The number of rows returned was not the number
expected.")
        End If

        If "Badger" <> ToTableTable.Rows(0)("AnimalOrFungiName").ToString Then
            Throw New Exception("The AnimalOrFungiName was not the value we expected.")
        End If
End Sub
```

The preceding example shows you how to create a table from a DataView. This, in and of itself, isn't very useful, but the table can then be used anywhere else, such as on a Web service or saved to disk.

Serialization

The ADO.NET team has finally paid attention to the crying and whimpering of ADO.NET developers around the world. In ADO.NET 1.0 and 1.1, DataSets would always serialize into an XML text format, even when you explicitly told them to binary serialize. In ADO.NET 2.0, the Framework now listens to your demands as a developer and actually binary serializes the DataSets when you tell it to.

The benefits of this serialization format are massive, especially in the areas of remoting and Web services, where it is quite common to pass DataSets between endpoints across the wire. There is less processing time at both ends, but the greatest gain is on the receiving end of any transfer, as it does not need to be parsed and is deserialized directly into memory.

In addition to experiencing reduced processing time, less memory is used both at runtime and when saving DataSets to disk. This is because the footprint of the DataSet is much smaller when expressed in a binary format.

Because the DataSet is smaller in its binary serialized format, it will clearly use less bandwidth when it's moved over the wire than it would XML Serialization. This is true in almost all real-world scenarios; however, be aware that this is not always the case.

Binary serialization will actually make the DataSet larger when serialized than with XML Serialization when you have a single-row, single-table DataSet. The majority of the information that is serialized in this case is metadata describing the structure of the DataSet and its tables.

In general, using binary serialization makes it possible to get about 80 times the current performance from the same applications, depending on the amount of data they move across the wire.

Keep in mind that you don't have to use binary serialization. In fact, the default will still be XML so that all of your existing .NET 1.0 and 1.1 applications continue to work even when hosted under the .NET 2.0 Framework.

> **Warning: If you try to send a binary serialized DataSet to an application hosted under .NET 1.0 or .NET 1.1, the process will fail. Those Frameworks cannot deserialize binary format DataSets!**

Here's an example that shows how to binary serialize a DataSet and then read back the serialized file:

```
Dim ds As DataSet = New DataSet
Dim FileName As String = ("C:\testbinary.bin")
Dim cs As String = "Data Source=localhost;Integrated Security=SSPI;Initial
Catalog=Northwind"
Dim sql As String = "SELECT * FROM Employees"
Dim cn As System.Data.SqlClient.SqlConnection = New
System.Data.SqlClient.SqlConnection(cs)
Dim cmd As System.Data.SqlClient.SqlCommand = New
System.Data.SqlClient.SqlCommand(sql, cn)
Dim da As System.Data.SqlClient.SqlDataAdapter = New
System.Data.SqlClient.SqlDataAdapter(cmd)
da.Fill(ds, "TestTable")
ds.RemotingFormat = SerializationFormat.Binary
Dim myFormatter As System.Runtime.Serialization.IFormatter = New
System.Runtime.Serialization.Formatters.Binary.BinaryFormatter
Dim myStream As System.IO.Stream = New System.IO.FileStream(FileName,
System.IO.FileMode.Create)
myFormatter.Serialize(myStream, ds)
Dim ds1 As DataSet = New DataSet
ds1.RemotingFormat = SerializationFormat.Binary
Dim myFormatter1 As System.Runtime.Serialization.IFormatter = New
System.Runtime.Serialization.Formatters.Binary.BinaryFormatter
Dim myStream1 As System.IO.Stream = New System.IO.FileStream(FileName,
System.IO.FileMode.Open)
ds1 = CType((myFormatter1.Deserialize(myStream1)), DataSet)
```

Whenever you need to move large DataSets across the wire, it's certainly worthwhile to tweak the code a little so that it moves binary serialized DataSets across and not XML serialized DataSets.

DataTableReader

Microsoft has come up with a little class called the `DataTableReader`, which is essentially a very thin object sitting on top of the DataTable; it's a representation of the table's data as a `DbDataReader`, meaning you can stream data straight out of a DataTable.

Streaming

With the new streaming functionality built into the DataTable, not only can you stream into a DataTable using the `Load(IDataReader)` method:

```
myDataTable.Load(Reader)
```

but you can also get a DataReader out of a DataTable, enabling you to stream in and out of tables:

```
Dim Reader As DbDataReader = myDataTable.CreateDataReader()
```

There's no longer a need to use a StreamReader in your code when dealing with DataTables.

Namespace Qualified Tables

In ADO.NET 1.0 and 1.1, it was not possible to add multiple tables with the same name into different namespaces, even though it should have been. In ADO.NET 2.0, this bug has been fixed, so you can now perform the operation, like this:

```
Public Sub NamespaceQualifiedTables()
    Dim Ds As System.Data.DataSet = New System.Data.DataSet
    Dim TheTable As System.Data.DataTable = New
System.Data.DataTable("TheSameTableName")
    TheTable.Namespace = ("OneNamespace")
    Ds.Tables.Add(TheTable)
    TheTable = New System.Data.DataTable("TheSameTableName")
    TheTable.Namespace = ("AnotherNamespace")
    Ds.Tables.Add(TheTable)
    Dim expected As Integer = 2
    Dim actual As Integer = Ds.Tables.Count
    If expected <> actual Then
        Throw New Exception("The number of tables found was not the number
expected.")
    End If
End Sub
```

If you tried to run the preceding code under .NET 1.1, the Framework would run the following error at runtime:

```
A DataTable named 'TheSameTableName' already belongs to this DataSet.
```

What this means is that you can have many tables with the same name inside the same DataSet as long as they are all contained in different namespaces. This is useful when dealing with XML, where it's quite common to find many instances of the same schema repeated throughout an XML document.

Indexing Engine

When using ADO.NET 2.0, you get a warm, fuzzy feeling like something good is about to happen but you're not quite sure what. You notice this feeling the most when it comes to the speed of your applications.

One place where performance has been increased is with the indexing engine, which has been completely rewritten for ADO.NET 2.0. The changes aren't visible in terms of the API, but you will notice them in your applications' speed.

You'll see the greatest increase in performance when performing inserts into DataTables. In ADO.NET 1.0 and 1.1, the indexing worked perfectly well for small DataSets, but as larger DataSets were thrown at the engine, it started to creak a little because the method of indexing didn't scale very well.

All this has changed in ADO.NET 2.0. The method is now much faster and causes a reduced number of allocations, meaning you'll see much less garbage collection and less tree allocations through the Garbage Collector. In addition, memory usage is lower and the amount of information added to the large object heap has been greatly reduced as the segments are reused to store row and index information.

Other areas in the Framework that have greatly benefited from changes made to the indexing engine include any tables with constraints and relationships, any tables with primary keys, and DataViews when sorting.

In all, you should see a significant increase in performance by just hosting your existing 1.0 and 1.1 applications under the .NET 2.0 Framework.

DataSet, DataTable, DataReader, or an Object?

Use the right tool for the right job — that's been the mantra in engineering shops for many years, and the same applies to the world of ADO.NET.

The DataSet is almost always larger than a collection of objects that match the DataSet's structure in memory.

To help you choose the right tool for the right job, we've drawn up a simple task-oriented guide.

Showing Data to Users without any Manipulation

Use a Reader if all you need to do is bind data up to a grid or show the details of a product. Why bother with a bulky DataSet? You don't need relationships, you don't need state management (changes to rows), and you certainly don't need multiple tables. A simple forward-only Reader will do the job in the most efficient way.

Editing Data That Lives in One Table

This one isn't quite as clear-cut. If you don't really need the change management that the DataSet offers, and usually you won't, then just use a Reader to get the data back from your data source and use `ExecuteNonQuery()` to update any data that the user changes.

Editing Data Spread across More Than One Table

Use a DataSet. It's exactly what it was designed for — managing the complex relationships between many tables and their respective rows of data.

Editing Continuously Updated Data for Which the Chance of Collisions Is High

Again, use the DataSet. It has very cool change management and tracking systems built into it. Combine a DataSet with the DataAdapter and you'll be laughing all the way to the bank.

Getting One Value from a Database

Use an object, employ the use of `ExecuteScalar()`, or use an output parameter to get your value. There's no need for a DataReader or a DataSet. The extra code they both require isn't worth considering for a single value, not to mention the fact that DataSets are usually slower.

Basically, don't use a battering ram when there's a doorbell!

Summary

You should take away a few key points from this chapter. First, learn the ADO.NET 2.0 API. Make sure you understand all of the different classes and what they are meant for. If you understand the basics, then you will be in the right position to use the new features to their fullest.

Second, remember to keep the schema in mind when you are asked to create reports. The simple way in which you can interrogate the schema means that it's very easy to build flexible reporting applications.

Last, get to know the Web. While this book delves deeply into many ADO.NET topics, there are always more out there.

For More Information

To complement the information in this chapter, take a look at the following resources:

- ❑ **Microsoft Data Access and Storage Developer Center**—http://msdn.microsoft.com/data/

- ❑ **Microsoft DataWorks Blog**—http://blogs.msdn.com/dataaccess/

- ❑ **Angel Saenz-Badillos' Blog (member of the ADO.NET team at Microsoft)**—http://blogs.msdn.com/angelsb/

- ❑ **Microsoft SQL Server FAQ, an online SQL Server community**—www.sqlserverfaq.com/

- ❑ **SQL Server Community, another great online community**—www.sqlservercentral.com/

Standard Data Types

In the course of development, data-oriented programmers, even when they have no formal training in data types, quickly become familiar with them — or at least an integral subset that they use on a day-to-day basis. Among these, the most common is by far the *string*. This is because virtually every other data type can be expressed in this format, as is easily evidenced in XML. Not far after that come the *integer* and the *Boolean*.

These three data types make up the vast majority of data types used in data-oriented programming. This is mostly because data-oriented applications are driven by information that is most often expressed using a human language. Human language, written human language, uses strings of characters as a medium for communicating information, so it is only natural that a data-driven computer application would mimic that by storing information as strings of characters.

Integers are a natural runner-up because the most basic applications of mathematics involve integers — counting, adding, subtracting, and so on. And the Boolean type springs from a basic fundamental of human existence: truth or non-truth. Similarly, computers again mimic the human understanding of the world in making use of these core means of expression.

Of course, we are also fascinated by the concept of time; humans started measuring and recording it early in our history, so we also often need and find ways to represent measurements of time and date in our applications. In addition to time, we have to deal with a few other kinds of data, some of which relate to human life and some of which are peculiar to computing.

This chapter describes how these and other data types are handled by Microsoft's SQL Server, which is the de facto relational database system for Microsoft programmers. We'll then consider the System.Data.SqlTypes namespace's use of data types and compare how standard .NET data types interact with these and ADO.NET in general to facilitate communication with a data storage system.

Data Types in SQL Server

First we'll consider the ways in which SQL Server stores character data. There are two basic variations in this type, fixed-length and variable-length storage, but there is a bit more to it than that. In this and the following sections, specifications relate to SQL 2005; however, most of the statements hold true for the existing, equivalent SQL 2000 types. Where available, the equivalent SQL-92 specification synonym is provided in parentheses next to the SQL Server type.

CHAR (CHARACTER)

The character (CHAR) type indicates fixed-length storage, meaning that the length you specify for it will be used for all of the values stored in a column or variable of that type. For example, if you specified CHAR(20), every row in a table containing that column would use 20 characters, regardless of whether you only specified two characters—the remaining 18 would be stored as blank spaces.

In terms of storage size, each character equates to 1 byte, so if you had 100 rows using the 20-character column just described, you would be using 4,000 bytes. Usage of this type is specified by CHAR followed by an optional length indicator in parentheses. If no length is specified, except in CAST statements, one-character length is assumed. In CAST statements, 30-character length is assumed. The maximum length for this type is 8,000.

This column is rarely used except when all of the values for a column are expected to have the same length. For example, if you had a two-letter code for each row, then you might choose CHAR(2), as is often done when storing U.S. state abbreviations. In most cases, however, character data is variable, so you would use the next type.

VARCHAR (CHAR VARYING or CHARACTER VARYING)

VARCHAR is probably the most useful type in SQL Server. This is because it stores character data, which can represent most data, and because it doesn't waste unnecessary space for data that varies considerably in length from row to row. As the name suggests, VARCHAR is used when you wish to declare that a column or variable will contain a variable length of characters.

To use the type, you specify the name followed by the maximum length allowed in parentheses. For example, VARCHAR(1024) indicates a maximum length of 1,024 characters. It also has the same presumed length as CHAR does if you omit the length specification. The beauty of VARCHAR, though, is that it will only use the space actually required by values, instead of padding values with trailing spaces as CHAR does. This means that, while more difficult to estimate actual storage size, you can optimize the space used and you won't have to bother with trimming blank spaces from stored strings when using the values in code.

"If you store this" in a VARCHAR(50), only 19 bytes would actually be stored. If you're studious, you might notice that there are only 17 characters in that string. The reason why 19 bytes are used to store it is because SQL Server uses 2 extra bytes to store the actual length of the row's data for that column. This doesn't mean you can only put 48 characters in the column—it just means that if you fill it up, 52 bytes will be used, not 50.

VARCHAR, like CHAR, has a maximum length of 8,000, which is good for all but the most verbose of us. But if you need storage larger than 8,000 characters, you'll have to supersize your type to the one covered next.

TEXT and VARCHAR(MAX)

Traditionally, in SQL Server, the TEXT type is what has been used to handle those potentially very large bunches of characters that you need to store, such as, for instance, this book (or even this chapter). In cases where you expect your requisite storage for a single row to exceed 8,000 characters, choose this type.

Of course, to mix things up, the SQL Server team decided to do a switcheroo on us with 2005. For some reason, perhaps because it makes sense, they've created the VARCHAR(MAX) type, which is, for all intents and purposes, the same thing as the TEXT type. Both are used to store highly variable, potentially large character data up to 2 GB — well, actually 1 byte less than that (2^{31}-1, that is, 2,147,483,647 bytes).

In fact, the VARCHAR(MAX) type is intended to replace the TEXT type. This means that, likely in the next version (after 2005), if applications are still using TEXT, they will not be directly portable without modification. Keep this in mind while developing new applications on SQL Server 2005.

National Character Storage

If you are a developer who is already familiar with SQL Server, then you are probably wondering why we have not mentioned national (international, really) character storage. It is usually covered with the corresponding non-Unicode types. We felt that, since the Unicode (national) types are the same as their related non-Unicode types, with the one caveat that (owing to the fact that Unicode uses 2 bytes per character) you are limited to half as many characters as their non-Unicode brethren, there is really no need to go over them in depth — you can simply look at the non-Unicode types and know that the Unicode are the same with the caveat just mentioned.

Said another way, NCHAR and NVARCHAR are limited to 4,000 characters, and NTEXT — now NVARCHAR(MAX) — is limited to about one billion (2^{30}-1, aka 1,073,741,823) characters. Why, oh, why would you want to cut your storage size in half? The answer is in the SQL-92 synonyms for these types — the keyword "national." These types store characters in Unicode format, which allows sufficient combinations of bits to represent all written languages' characters.

As you can see, you will want to use these types when you will be globalizing your application. Some people recommend always using national types, but sometimes we know that an application is never going to be globalized, so there really is no reason to over-engineer your application to provide for a situation that will never happen.

INT (INTEGER)

INT is for numbers what VARCHAR is for characters — that is, it is far and away the most commonly used numerical type. This is because it serves as an integer (great for counting and other whole-number operations) and can represent a range of possible numbers that is large enough for most needs and still small enough to not be a storage problem.

INT is a 32-bit (4-byte) number type. As such, it can represent numbers from negative two billion (-2^{31}) to positive two billion (2^{31}-1).

BIGINT

This type is the big brother to all of the other integer types. Being a 64-bit number (8 bytes), it can represent from about negative nine quintillion to positive nine quintillion (-2^{63} to 2^{63}-1). Clearly, you need to use this type when you expect your integer data to represent integer numbers larger than two billion. If you need something larger than nine quintillion, well, then you're out of luck. It is hoped that the national deficit won't grow that big for a while yet.

SMALLINT

If BIGINT is the big brother, SMALLINT is the middle sibling. Being a 16-bit (2-byte) number has its advantages, but these days, it just seems to get overlooked. Everybody's always talking about 32-bit this and 64-bit that, but what about good ol' 16 bit? Unfortunately, the range of numbers for this type is too restrictive for most applications; at one time, negative to positive 32,000 (-2^{15} to 2^{15}-1) was considered plenty, but not anymore.

TINYINT

The baby brother, this 1-byte integer is so small that it is only useful for numbers up to 255. It's great for those situations in which you have a well-known, limited number of values, such as, for instance, when you are storing the numerical representation of constant enumeration values.

DATETIME (TIMESTAMP)

The DATETIME type is another one of those indispensable types you find yourself using in almost every table, almost certainly every database, if for nothing else but logging purposes. It is obvious how this type is used. The key thing to note is the difference between this type and its smaller sister, covered next.

DATETIME is stored as two 4-byte integers (that pesky INT shows up again). The first integer accounts for the number of days before or after the system base date, which is the first of January, 1900. The last 32-bit number keeps track of the number of milliseconds after zero hundred hours.

Valid dates for this type range from January 1, 1753, all the way to the last day of the year in 9999, and its tracking of milliseconds gives it an accuracy to 3.33 milliseconds, rounding to increments of .000, .003, and .007 seconds. When you need to keep accurate time logs or keep dates far into the future or past, this is the type you need.

SMALLDATETIME

SMALLDATETIME differs from its big sister in two key ways—precision and range. Because it is stored as two 2-byte integers (so there is a use for 16-bit integers after all!), it only keeps a precision down to the minute and can only store dates between January 1, 1900 and June 6, 2079. It uses the first 2 bytes to store the days after 1900 and the latter 2 to watch the minutes after midnight.

You will want to use this type anytime you know its range will not be overshot and when you need precision to the minute only. As a rule of thumb, opt for the type requiring smaller storage when it makes sense to do so.

REAL (FLOAT(24)) and FLOAT (FLOAT and DOUBLE PRECISION)

REAL and FLOAT are both floating-point data types. As such, any values within their ranges cannot be represented exactly; hence, they are called approximate numbers. The n in the FLOAT(n) syntax stands for the number of bits used to store the mantissa of the float number in scientific notation.

In both SQL Server 2000 and 2005, SQL Server uses n to determine storage size. If n is less than or equal to 24, then SQL Server stores and treats it as a four-byte number, precise up to seven digits. If n is greater than 24, then it is treated as an 8-byte number with precision up to 15 digits. Because the range of these numbers is most precisely and easily expressed in scientific notation, they are listed in the following table.

Type	Range
FLOAT	- 1.79E + 38 to -2.23E - 38, 0 and 2.23E -38 to 1.79E + 38
REAL	-1.18E - 38, 0 and 1.18E - 38 to 3.40E + 38

NUMERIC and DECIMAL (DEC and DEC(p,s))

Apart from the name, NUMERIC and DECIMAL are pretty much the same thing, so it is really just a matter of personal choice, although to more closely resemble the SQL-92 standard, you may want to stick with DECIMAL. In addition, DECIMAL is what the corresponding types are called in both the SqlTypes namespace and the .NET primitive.

The syntax for both enables you to specify the precision, which is the total number of digits to the left and right of the decimal point. The second number you can optionally specify when declaring one of these is the *scale*, which is a way to limit the number of digits to the right of the decimal point. The maximum precision is 38; the maximum value of the scale is limited to the specified precision. Thus, DECIMAL(14, 7) would give a precision of up to 14 digits, only 7 of which can be on the right side of the decimal.

In terms of storage, these types vary based on the precision. Starting with 5 bytes for a precision up to 9, the storage space increases 4 bytes for every additional nine to ten digits. The range of these numbers is proportional to the precision as well, being about 10 to the power of the precision, so if we consider the default value, 18, for the precision and the default scale of zero, that would give you a range of about plus or minus one quintillion, using 9 bytes to store it. Following is a table showing the relation of precision to range and storage size:

Precision	Maximum Range	Storage Size (in Bytes)
1-9	$-10^9 + 1$ to $10^9 - 1$	5
10-19	$-10^{19} + 1$ to $10^{19} - 1$	9
20-28	$-10^{28} + 1$ to $10^{28} - 1$	13
29-38	$-10^{38} + 1$ to $10^{38} - 1$	17

As you can see, DECIMAL gives you the broadest range of numbers with the greatest degree of accuracy, but this comes at the price of hefty storage requirements (for a number, anyway). To use this number type appropriately, you have to consider what you need in terms of precision and scale.

If you are a business developer, you will rarely need this type because for smaller, less precise non-integer numbers, you can use a small float and save space. For the most part, the only time you really need precise and accurate decimal storage is when you are dealing with money, in which case you have the money types that SQL Server provides, which provide a friendly abstraction to the DECIMAL type.

MONEY and SMALLMONEY

Despite the names, the MONEY and SMALLMONEY are just handy exact numeric types. MONEY is roughly equivalent to DECIMAL(16,4) in range, precision, and scale, but it does save you a byte in storage and gives you a friendly way to deal with numbers in that category. Of course, you shouldn't abuse this type—only use it when you are storing monetary values to prevent potential confusion.

Having a range that spans negative to positive 9.22 trillion should pretty much cover any monetary numbers you will come across, unless you are dealing with the U.S. government. Conversely, you would think that Microsoft would have to up the range with the next release after 2005 or maybe come up with a BIGMONEY type that roughly corresponds to the BIGINT range.

SMALLMONEY, ironically named, will give you, roughly, a range of plus or minus 215,000, just enough to buy a license or two of SQL Server. This type would be an adequate salary column for many of us—of course, you couldn't keep track of CEOs or senators with it. For both MONEY and SMALLMONEY, SQL Server keeps track to four decimal places, or to one ten-thousandth of the applicable unit of currency.

BINARY, VARBINARY, IMAGE, and VARBINARY(MAX) (BINARY VARYING)

Many developers (especially those without a computer science degree) are afraid of binary storage. This is probably because it is an unknown, at least in terms of standards and readability. If you don't have a program that understands the bits, it is just a bunch of numerical gibberish. Put another way, you can't open it in NotePad. (Well, you can, but it usually won't mean much to you unless you're into Kabbalah.) It is a black box, and you can't look at it very meaningfully in Query Analyzer or easily pull reports from it.

On the other hand, your computer likes it. The computer doesn't require any special extra information to store or process it. It is the lingua franca of computers today, the only thing they speak natively. It's simple and efficient, and we kind of like it for that reason as well. There are no complicated decisions to make, no worrying about code pages, globalization, floating points, precision, ranges, or scale. The only decision to be made is how many bytes to permit.

You see, binary storage isn't so bad, and it certainly has its place in your computing environment. Probably the most common use of these types is to store images, Word, and PDF documents. For any scenario in which you have an application that stores data in a proprietary data format, you can use one of these types to store it in the database. In fact, if you are feeling particularly obtuse, you could store a string in this type, but only do that if you don't care to read it back out easily. The point is that it is the most versatile type because, ultimately, anything that can be stored in a computer can be stored in this type.

As you might expect, BINARY and VARBINARY differ only in that the former is a fixed-length type and the latter is a variable-length type. In that sense, it is exactly like CHAR and VARCHAR. In fact, the analogy extends further to the IMAGE and VARBINARY(MAX) types. Just like TEXT and VARCHAR(MAX), IMAGE and VARBINARY(MAX) differ only in name.

For BINARY and VARBINARY, the maximum size is 8,000 bytes. For BINARY, the storage size is exactly the same as the specified size. For VARBINARY and IMAGE (now VARBINARY(MAX)), the actual storage size will be the actual number of bytes provided plus 2 bytes to record that length (just like the variable character data). And, again, use IMAGE/VARBINARY(MAX) in cases where storage will vary to be greater than 8,000 bytes.

Using BINARY to Store Flags

Another handy use for the BINARY type is persisting bit flags, such as a .NET flags enumeration. In case you're not aware of it, .NET enables you to apply the Flags attribute to an enumeration so that developers can combine different values of the enumeration; without the Flags attribute, enumeration members are mutually exclusive constants.

Internally, a flags enumeration is stored as a set of bits, where each place in the binary number can be used as one flag. Because the default underlying type for enumerations is Int32, you can have up to 32 flags for a typical flags enumeration (one flag per bit). Of course, you can use an Int64 if you need more flags. In any case, you can store these kinds of enumerations directly into a BINARY(4) column in SQL Server, as that will directly store the value of those 32 bits for you.

A typical enumeration (non-flags) might look something like this:

```
Public Enum NoFlags
    Option1 = 1
    Option2 = 2
    Option3 = 3
End Enum
```

A flags enumeration would look something like this:

```
<Flags()> _
Public Enum FlagsEnum
    None = 0
    Place1 = 1
    Place2 = 2
    Place3 = 4
    Place4 = 8
    Place5 = 16
    Place6 = 32
    Place7 = 64
    Place8 = 128
    NamedCombo = Place1 Or Place2 Or Place3
End Enum
```

If you were going to store these enumerations in SQL Server, you could use a BINARY(4) column for the flags enumeration and a VARCHAR(20) for the non-flags enumeration. Here's some sample code to illustrate how you might write such values to SQL Server given these options:

```
Public Sub UpdateEnums()
  Dim recsAffected As Integer = 0
  Using conn As New SqlConnection(NorthwindConnString)
    Using cmd As New SqlCommand()
      cmd.Connection = conn
      cmd.CommandText = "UPDATE Orders " & _
        "SET Flags = @Flags, SomeOption = @SomeOption " & _
        "WHERE OrderID = @OrderId"
      Dim flags As New SqlParameter("@Flags", SqlDbType.Int)
      flags.Value = DirectCast(FlagsEnum.Place7 Or _
      FlagsEnum.NamedCombo, Int32)
      Dim someOption As New SqlParameter("@SomeOption", SqlDbType.VarChar)
      someOption.Size = 20
      someOption.Value = NoFlags.Option2.ToString()
      cmd.Parameters.Add(flags)
      cmd.Parameters.Add(someOption)
      cmd.Parameters.AddWithValue("@OrderId", 10262)
      cmd.Connection.Open()
      recsAffected = cmd.ExecuteNonQuery()
    End Using
  End Using
  Console.WriteLine("{0} Records Affected by Enums Update", recsAffected)
End Sub
```

Note a few things about the preceding code. We're using the `Int` `SqlDbType`, even though the column is defined as `BINARY(4)`. This is because we're going to let SQL Server handle the conversion from the `INT` value to `BINARY`.

If you try, for instance, using the `BitConverter` class to convert the `Int32` to bytes, it will work as far as .NET is concerned, but the value will not be usable in SQL Server itself because the `BitConverter`. `GetBytes` will get a 4-byte array with the bytes in reverse order from how they appear in the enumeration/integer — that is, byte one will be the rightmost 8 bits, byte two the next rightmost 8 bits, and so on.

In the previous case, this comes out to be 0x47000000 in SQL Server instead of the correct 0x00000047. That's a huge difference because the flags are reversed, so we just pass the value to SQL Server as the underlying integer value and SQL Server will correctly cast it to `BINARY(4)` for us. Besides that, it's less code this way.

When saving the non-flags enum, we chose to store the string named value instead of the underlying integer value. This is just to make it easier to understand with database reporting and query tools. `System.Enum` overloads the `ToString` method to return the named value.

Note a few of the new features of .NET 2.0. Visual Basic now has a `Using` statement that ensures (like the `using` statement in C#) that `Dispose` is called on the objects being "used." The `SqlCommand` `.Parameters.Add` method has deprecated the overload that takes just the name of the SQL parameter and a value in favor of a new method called `AddWithValue`, so you should use this when you want to let ADO.NET infer the other details of a parameter.

Figure 4-1 shows what those columns might look like in Query Analyzer after running the preceding code.

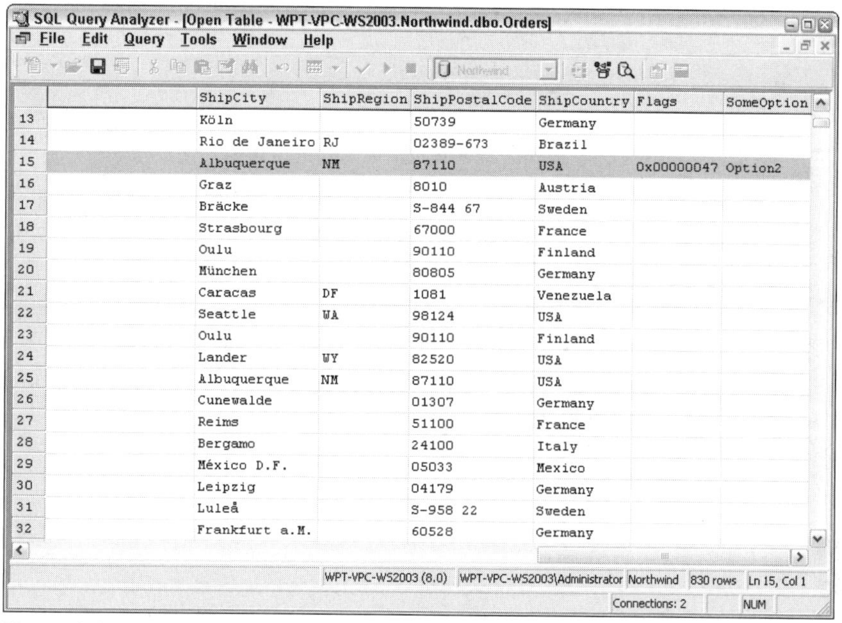

Figure 4-1

Note how Query Analyzer represents the binary column as a hexadecimal number. In this case, it is 0x00000047, which is 00000000 00000000 00000000 01000111 if we convert this number to its binary representation (broken down to bytes for readability). This is correct — the flags we set are Place1, Place2, and Place3 (as the NamedCombo value), and the Place7 value. Remember that the places are read from right to left.

Unfortunately, there's no easy way to display the BINARY column values as the actual binary representation, but you can easily convert hexadecimal (base16) into binary (base2) using the Windows Calculator's scientific functions. Just select the Hex option, enter 47 (in our case), and then select the Bin option to see the corresponding binary value.

Of course, the key here is that you can work with the Flags column using bitwise operators in SQL Server as well, not just in .NET. The only difference (apart from syntax, of course) is that in .NET, you'll have the friendly named values of your flags enumeration to work with. In SQL Server, you'll have to check the flags by comparing the literal values (in hexadecimal form).

To read these values back out of SQL Server, the following code will suffice:

```
Public Sub ReadEnums()
  Dim ourFlags As FlagsEnum
  Dim ourOption As NoFlags
  Using conn As New SqlConnection(NorthwindConnString)
    Using cmd As New SqlCommand()
      cmd.Connection = conn
      cmd.CommandText = "SELECT CAST(Flags AS INT), SomeOption " & _
        "FROM Orders " & _
        "WHERE OrderID = @OrderId"
```

```
            cmd.Parameters.AddWithValue("@OrderId", 10262)
            cmd.Connection.Open()
            Dim dr As SqlDataReader = cmd.ExecuteReader()
            If dr.Read() Then
                ourOption = DirectCast(System.Enum.Parse(GetType(NoFlags), _
                dr.GetString(1)), NoFlags)
                ourFlags = DirectCast(dr.GetInt32(0), FlagsEnum)
            End If
            dr.Close()
        End Using
    End Using
    Console.WriteLine("Retrieved Option is {0}.", ourOption.ToString())
    Console.WriteLine("NamedCombo is Set: {0}.", _
      ((ourFlags And FlagsEnum.NamedCombo) <> 0))
    Console.WriteLine("Place7 is Set: {0}.", _
      ((ourFlags And FlagsEnum.Place7) <> 0))
    Console.WriteLine("Place8 is Set: {0}.", _
      ((ourFlags And FlagsEnum.Place8) <> 0))
End Sub
```

Note two things in this code. First, in our SELECT statement, we cast the Flags value as an INT. Again, we're letting SQL Server do the work of converting the binary value back into the underlying integer that our enumeration uses. This way, we can simply directly cast that integer value to our flags enumeration.

Second, we use System.Enum.Parse in order to create our non-flags enumeration value from its string named value. Note that there is an overload of that method that will let you specify case insensitivity. You might want to use this overload if you are populating that column in SQL Server through other means that might not get your enumeration values' cases right.

As you can see, BINARY is a handy way to store flags values. In the examples here, we've contrasted it with how you might choose to store a constants enumeration. In any case, it is fairly easy to persist such values, and doing so makes them easy to work with both in SQL Server and in .NET.

We should note here that you could simply store the Flags in an INT column. In fact, SQL Server won't allow two operands of a bitwise operator to be binary (as strange as that sounds), so you have to cast the Flags column to an INT anytime you want to use it as part of a bitwise operation. Consider the following:

```
UPDATE Orders SET Flags = Flags | 0x00000008
```

This won't work if Flags is of type BINARY, so you'd have to cast it like so:

```
UPDATE Orders SET Flags = CAST(Flags AS INT) | 0x00000008
```

If that's enough to make you want to make the Flags column an INT, then we'd suggest at least creating a user-defined type called FLAGS based on the INT type. That way, you can make the purpose of the column clear by its type while still getting the advantages of not having to cast it to an INT for bitwise operations. Both options are included in the companion code samples.

Because we usually do more modification and comparison of our flags types in .NET code, we prefer to store the flags as BINARY in order to make it immediately clear to anyone looking at the data that it is not just another integer. Furthermore, it could be argued that visually converting hexadecimal into binary is easier than converting from decimal into binary.

BIT

Every attempt at categorization needs an "other" category. After all, it just doesn't do to have a category that contains only one specific. Accordingly, the next few sections represent our homage to that illustrious compromise.

A *bit* is an exact numeric type, but from a programmer's perspective, it is more of an "other" type because it is most often used to represent a Boolean value. It could also be categorized under binary storage, as it is the most basic binary unit. But we put it here to focus on common usage.

Apart from saying it is a very useful type, there's not a whole lot more to say. Use it whenever you need a single Boolean, yes/no, or on/off value (consider using flags, as shown previously, if you have multiple bit values to store). Actually, if you make it nullable, it can serve as a trinary value, but that can cause some complications when you are using it as a Boolean in your code, so if that is how you are using it, don't make it nullable and give it a meaningful default (stick with 0/false, if you are not sure). If you need more options than a binary digit value provides, use a TINYINT instead.

Not only can these be represented as Booleans in your code outside of SQL Server, SQL Server also lets you use True and False as symbols to represent 1 and 0, respectively. In addition, as its name implies, the storage size for BIT is 1 bit, although SQL Server will allocate 1 byte for every eight BIT type columns in a table (kind of its own internal flags storage).

TIMESTAMP

You may have noticed that the SQL-92 synonym listed for DATETIME in the preceding section is TIMESTAMP. This is because TIMESTAMP in SQL Server does not comply with the SQL-92 standard; this may change in the future, but for now just think of TIMESTAMP as simply a row version type. Its purpose is just to provide a way to further distinguish two potentially identical sets of data, which can be useful in code if you want to easily provide optimistic concurrency handling.

It is *not* useful to use as a key. While a primary key is used to identify a set of data as unique, it is also often used as a foreign key in relationships. Although TIMESTAMP does help with the first purpose, it greatly obstructs the second because every update to a row requires a corresponding update of all related records. Therefore, do not use TIMESTAMP as part of a primary key, at least for referential purposes.

Books Online recommends using the synonym ROWVERSION for data type definition statements because it's possible that the meaning of TIMESTAMP will change in the future. Moreover, ROWVERSION serves the purpose of the type better. This type uses 8 bytes of storage.

SQL_VARIANT

Simply put, do not use this type. There are very few situations in which it would be useful, far too many caveats to list, and, ultimately, this type doesn't offer much more than VARBINARY. If you need something that functions as a variant that will work in most cases, use VARCHAR or NVARCHAR. After all, what is XML if not character data? To report on data of this type, you will likely have to cast to VARCHAR anyway (it shows up as <Binary> in Enterprise Manager if you don't, for example).

Apart from the various complications of using SQL_VARIANT (fully expounded in Books Online), there is an ideological objection to using this type. You have numerous great alternatives that are optimized for specific types of data, so unless you truly need a catch-all column, opt for the more specific type. It will always be a better choice in the long run.

UNIQUEIDENTIFIER

You have to wonder why they didn't just call this type GUID. Needless to say, that is exactly what it is, and GUID is what most computer folks call a type of this definition. In any case, it is a 16-byte type with 32 characters, and we use that term (character) loosely because as you can guess, it obviously isn't 32 characters in the 8-bit meaning of the word. This is because it is actually 32 hexadecimal digits (0–9, a–f), each of which is represented by 4 bits.

You can create new values for it within SQL Server by using the NEWID function or by specifying a string literal consisting of those 32 digits separated into five groups. The first group contains 8 digits, the second through fourth contain 4 digits each, and the final group contains 12, like so: 3a5d99ef-ab3c-d4e5-f68a-9203da93921b.

This type works great as an easy-to-use, guaranteed-unique identifier, so it is a good artificial primary key when you may need to use the same schema in disparate databases and replicate data between them. If you use an "identity" (or auto-number) integer value as your artificial primary key, you can easily run into replication issues whereby multiple rows have the same integer value. GUIDs will always be unique, so you won't have this problem.

Of course, they're not quite as friendly to work with in code and do have other drawbacks. First, they are four times larger than an INT IDENTITY column. Second, they are not efficiently sorted and cannot be used in a GROUP BY or COUNT DISTINCT. Third, indices on these columns are significantly slower than those on integers. To summarize, unless you need to ease replication in a distributed situation, you probably ought to stick with using your typical integer identity column.

XML

A new feature of SQL Server 2005, the XML data type, enables SQL Server to work with XML in a much more meaningful manner than in previous versions. This new type enables querying and modification of XML in place in SQL Server. If an XML column has schemas specified, it can efficiently be used in queries and joined upon. The maximum storage size for items in a column of this type is 2 GB.

TABLE and CURSOR

These last two types are only applicable in the database. Covering them in depth in an ADO.NET book doesn't really make sense. Suffice it to say that TABLE is a great type to use in a stored procedure to temporarily store a result set when you need to, for example, page data on the server side. CURSORs are useful when you need to loop through a row set on the server, but with 2005, you'll be able to do this more efficiently using managed code. CURSORs should generally be avoided and used only as a last alternative.

Data Types in ADO.NET and .NET

Now that we've looked at the types in SQL Server, let's consider the types available to us in .NET and, specifically, ADO.NET.

SqlTypes

The types in the `SqlTypes` namespace are what the SQL ADO.NET provider uses to work with data within the managed environment. For instance, a `SqlDataReader` will read the bytes from SQL Server into a `SqlType` when you request a column value from it. These types implement related explicit cast operators to enable you to convert from, for example, a `SqlString` to a `System.String` with a statement like this:

```
myStringVar = DirectCast(dr("SomeColumn"), String)
```

Because of this capability, some advocate the use of `SqlTypes` in code that works with SQL Server using ADO.NET. If your code uses `SqlTypes`, no casting will be needed between ADO.NET and your code, so it would theoretically increase performance. Whether or not such an increase would be noticeable in most applications is debatable.

Another feature of these types is that they have a built-in "not set" option, even for those `SqlTypes` that correspond to .NET value types. This is made possible by their implementation of the `System.Data.SqlTypes.INullable` interface. This interface simply specifies that implementers provide a read-only `IsNull` property. Ultimately, this means that, for instance, an integer can have a null (not set) value and that you can check the `IsNull` property on `SqlInt32` in order to determine whether the field has been set. Taking this approach can reduce confusion when a particular field is nullable in the database but its corresponding .NET type does not allow for nulls because it is a value type.

The only real objection we have with this approach, apart from the "Sql" name, is that it ties you to types that are not primitive types in the .NET Framework. Any code for which you use your types would need to account for that fact, and you'd have to give those types special handling all over the place, instead of only when you are talking to ADO.NET. For instance, if you try to access the `Value` property on a `SqlType` and the value is null, it will throw a `SqlNullValueException`, so anywhere you access the values of your types, you'll need to check the `IsNull` property first to ensure they're not null.

Furthermore, the great performance shown by many applications indicates that the performance impact from converting to and from `SqlTypes` in your data layer must be negligible. If it really were a problem, we'd all be using them. Therefore, unless you really need to squeeze that last drop out, we would not use these types for performance reasons alone.

On the other hand, if your application's domain types are only used as data transfer objects, and you want an easy way for value type values to be nullable, using `SqlTypes` might be a viable option for you. It really depends on how you plan to use your types and whether you're willing to work with casting your type members or using the `IsNull` and `Value` properties when you need to use them as part of code that expects .NET primitive types.

To illustrate the differences between using `SqlTypes` for your domain objects' type members and using primitive .NET types, consider the following examples. The first example shows an `Order` class using standard, primitive .NET types:

```
Public Class Order
  Private _orderID As Int32
  Public Property OrderID() As Int32
    Get
      Return _orderID
    End Get
    Set(ByVal value As Int32)
      _orderID = value
    End Set
  End Property

  Private _customerID As String
  Public Property CustomerID() As String
    Get
      Return _customerID
    End Get
    Set(ByVal value As String)
      _customerID = value
    End Set
  End Property

  Private _orderDate As DateTime
  Public Property OrderDate() As DateTime
    Get
      Return _orderDate
    End Get
    Set(ByVal value As DateTime)
      _orderDate = value
    End Set
  End Property

  Private _freight As Decimal
  Public Property Freight() As Decimal
    Get
      Return _freight
    End Get
    Set(ByVal value As Decimal)
      _freight = value
    End Set
  End Property

  Private _shipName As String
  Public Property ShipName() As String
    Get
      Return _shipName
    End Get
    Set(ByVal value As String)
      _shipName = value
    End Set
  End Property
End Class
```

Now consider the same class using `SqlTypes`:

```
Public Class SqlOrder
  Private _orderID As SqlInt32
  Public Property OrderID() As SqlInt32
    Get
      Return _orderID
    End Get
    Set(ByVal value As SqlInt32)
      _orderID = value
    End Set
  End Property

  Private _customerID As SqlString
  Public Property CustomerID() As SqlString
    Get
      Return _customerID
    End Get
    Set(ByVal value As SqlString)
      _customerID = value
    End Set
  End Property

  Private _orderDate As SqlDateTime
  Public Property OrderDate() As SqlDateTime
    Get
      Return _orderDate
    End Get
    Set(ByVal value As SqlDateTime)
      _orderDate = value
    End Set
  End Property

  Private _freight As SqlMoney
  Public Property Freight() As SqlMoney
    Get
      Return _freight
    End Get
    Set(ByVal value As SqlMoney)
      _freight = value
    End Set
  End Property

  Private _shipName As SqlString
  Public Property ShipName() As SqlString
    Get
      Return _shipName
    End Get
    Set(ByVal value As SqlString)
      _shipName = value
    End Set
  End Property
End Class
```

Not much is different between them. In fact, for the most part, you simply insert `Sql` somewhere into the type name to work the magic—assuming, of course, that you have imported/used the `System.Data` namespace in your file. The one exception, in this case, is `SqlMoney`. There is no money type in .NET, but you can represent money using the `System.Decimal` type.

The real differences, however, become apparent when you begin using these types. The following code illustrates this to some degree:

```
Sub WriteOrder(ByVal myDataReader As SqlDataReader)
  Dim order As New Order
  order.OrderID = myDataReader.GetInt32(0)
  If Not myDataReader.IsDBNull(1) Then _
   order.CustomerID = myDataReader.GetString(1)
  If Not myDataReader.IsDBNull(2) Then _
   order.OrderDate = myDataReader.GetDateTime(2)
  If Not myDataReader.IsDBNull(3) Then _
   order.Freight = myDataReader.GetDecimal(3)
  If Not myDataReader.IsDBNull(4) Then _
   order.ShipName = myDataReader.GetString(4)

  Console.Write(order.OrderID & vbTab)
  Console.Write(order.CustomerID & vbTab)
  Console.Write(order.OrderDate.ToShortDateString() & vbTab)
  Console.Write(order.Freight.ToString("f2") & vbTab)
  Console.Write(order.ShipName)
  Console.WriteLine()
End Sub
```

In this case, you can see that you have to check for `DBNull` before assigning types that might be null. If any of these values are `DBNull`, you simply leave the default value that can be set when the class is instantiated. For our purposes, these will be the default values for the types used, but you could specify different ones in your class definitions.

Now look at the same functionality using our `SqlOrder` class:

```
Sub WriteSqlOrder(ByVal myDataReader As SqlDataReader)
  Dim order As New SqlOrder
  order.OrderID = myDataReader.GetSqlInt32(0)
  order.CustomerID = myDataReader.GetSqlString(1)
  order.OrderDate = myDataReader.GetSqlDateTime(2)
  order.Freight = myDataReader.GetSqlMoney(3)
  order.ShipName = myDataReader.GetSqlString(4)

  Console.Write(order.OrderID.Value.ToString() & vbTab)
  If Not order.CustomerID.IsNull Then _
   Console.Write(order.CustomerID.Value.ToString() & vbTab)
  If Not order.OrderDate.IsNull Then _
   Console.Write(order.OrderDate.Value.ToString() & vbTab)
  If Not order.Freight.IsNull Then _
   Console.Write(order.Freight.Value.ToString() & vbTab)
  If Not order.ShipName.IsNull Then _
   Console.Write(order.ShipName.Value.ToString())
  Console.WriteLine()
End Sub
```

Note that we didn't have to check for DBNull when we got the values from the SqlDataReader because the data reader takes care of that for us. However, now we have to check the IsNull property prior to using any properties that are nullable in the database. Anywhere that you use these values, you'll need to check that property beforehand if you want to avoid a possible SqlNullValueException. Granted, in many cases where a property can validly have a not set value, you'll probably want to do some special handling in the user interface to display something other than a default value, regardless of whether or not you are using SqlTypes.

Other Alternatives

Essentially, the advantage that these types offer, apart from easier and faster interaction with the data layer, is a way to indicate that a value type is not set. You can achieve this same effect using primitive types and boundary values. Primitive value types have a MinValue static property that returns the lower boundary value for that type. In fact, DateTime instances are initialized to this value by default. You can set your instances of other primitive value types to their respective MinValue values if you want them to be not set by default. Then, in your data tier, you simply substitute DBNull.Value for these when talking to the database.

Some might criticize this approach as the "magic number" approach, but it is reliable if you plan appropriately. Rarely do you actually need to store the lower boundary value of a type — if you are at the boundary under normal conditions, you need to upgrade the type. Therefore, the chances of ever needing this value as a valid value for an instance are virtually non-existent, and even if you do have unusual cases in which you anticipate that might happen, you can simply add extra handling, such as a separate Boolean value to indicate whether a variable is set.

In fact, it is this last approach that the C# team is taking with their new support (in v2.0) for what they call *nullable types*. They are introducing the capability to make any value type nullable using a new type modifier (?). You can add this type modifier to any type name to indicate that you want it to be nullable. Doing so gives it two new properties: HasValue and Value. Like SqlTypes, if you try to access Value directly when it has not been set, it will throw an exception, but unlike SqlTypes, it is not limited to a subset of value types and is not designed with SQL Server (or any particular database) in mind.

The C# team has gone to great lengths to create meaningful operator overloads so that using nullable types is almost as natural as using standard .NET types. One such feature that we particularly see great use for is the new *null coalescing operator,* represented by a double question mark (??). This operator works with reference types, too, so you could, using our previous example, account for null values very easily, like so:

```
Console.WriteLine(order.CustomerID ?? "Unspecified");
```

This is the same as saying if CustomerID is not set, print "Unspecified"; otherwise, print the value of CustomerID. A similar effect can be achieved by using C#'s ?: operators or VB's IIf function, but this is much more compact. Furthermore, don't forget that it works with those nullable value types using the same syntax. Very cool!

If you're not into C#, you can still use nullable types; they're just not quite as snazzy and are far less easy to use. Both VB and C# support generics, and the new Nullable<T> generic type in the Framework is what underpins the new C# language features. The problem is that you'll still have to do a lot of the same handstands that you have to do with SqlTypes or using the magic number technique, i.e., the constant checking for `HasValue`/`IsNull`/`Magic Number` before you access the value. C# does nearly all of this grunt work for you, which is possibly the best *practical* benefit that C# has going for it. To illustrate further, the following code shows how you would use nullable types in VB:

```
Dim x As New Nullable(Of Integer)(125)
Dim y As New Nullable(Of Integer)(33)
Dim z As Nullable(Of Integer) = _
  IIf(x.HasValue And y.HasValue, _
  New Nullable(Of Integer)(x.Value + y.Value), _
  New Nullable(Of Integer)())
```

The same thing in C# would be:

```
int? x = 125;
int? y = 33;
int? z = x + y;
```

As usual, VB keeps its reputation for being verbose, while C# keeps its reputation for being compact, even obscure. Whether or not V3 of VB will come up with a new, more "readable" way to handle nullable types is an open question. One thing's for sure: Users who like C# already are going to like it even more because of these features.

One final alternative for nullable types is an open-source code library called, believe it or not, *nullable types* (`http://nullabletypes.sourceforge.net/`). This library enables nullable type support from V1.0 on; and, as far as we can determine, it is Common Type Specification–compliant, so you could happily expose those types in a public API without worrying about the less frequently used languages not being able to handle them. If that is important to you, this library will definitely remain useful for you even after the release of .NET 2.0.

Ultimately, your decision as to what types you want to use in your .NET code (for interacting with your database) depends largely on how you plan to use those types and, to a lesser extent, on whether or not your database schema even allows for nulls. If you have a database helper layer or an object persistence layer, the benefits of using `SqlTypes` over other alternatives are almost non-existent. However, if you're doing it by hand, it might save you some work to use `SqlTypes` to avoid dealing with the `DBNull` issue. If all you are looking for is nullable value types, though, you should consider the other alternatives given here.

Mapping SQL Server Data Types to .NET

Lastly, we thought it would be useful to provide a table that maps the SQL Server data types to their .NET counterparts to help you choose what to use when writing your ADO.NET code.

SQL Server Type	SqlDbType	DbType	SqlType	.NET Primitive
BIGINT	BigInt		SqlInt64	Int64
BINARY	Binary		SqlBinary SqlBytes	Byte[]

SQL Server Type	SqlDbType	DbType	SqlType	.NET Primitive
BIT	Bit	Boolean	SqlBoolean	Boolean
CHAR	Char	AnsiString FixedLength	SqlString SqlChars SqlStreamChars	String Char[]
DATETIME	DateTime	Date DateTime Time	SqlDateTime	DateTime
DECIMAL	Decimal	Decimal UInt32 UInt64 VarNumeric	SqlDecimal	Decimal
FLOAT	Float	Double	SqlDouble	Double
IMAGE	Image		SqlBinary SqlBytes	Byte[]
INT	Int	Int32 UInt16	SqlInt32	Int32
MONEY	Money	Currency	SqlMoney	Decimal
NCHAR	Nchar	StringFixed Length	SqlString SqlChars SqlStreamChars	String Char[]
NTEXT/ VARBINARY (MAX)	Ntext		SqlString SqlChars SqlStreamChars	String Char[]
NUMERIC	Decimal		SqlDecimal	Decimal
NVARCHAR	NvarChar	String	SqlString SqlChars SqlStreamChars	String Char[]
REAL	Real	Single	SqlSingle	Single
SMALL-DATETIME	SmallDateTime		SqlDateTime	DateTime
SMALLINT	SmallInt	Int16 SByte	SqlInt16	Int16
SMALLMONEY	SmallMoney		SqlMoney	Decimal
SQL_VARIANT	Variant	Object	Object	Object
SYSNAME	NVarchar		SqlString	String
TEXT/ VARCHAR(MAX)	Text		SqlString SqlChars	String Char[]

Table continued on following page

SQL Server Type	SqlDbType	DbType	SqlType	.NET Primitive
TIMESTAMP	Timestamp		SqlBinary	Byte[]
TINYINT	TinyInt	Byte	SqlByte	Byte
UNIQUE-IDENTIFIER	UniqueIdentifier	Guid	SqlGuid	Guid
VARBINARY	VarBinary	Binary	SqlBinary SqlBytes	Byte[]
VARCHAR	VarChar	AnsiString	SqlString SqlChars	String Char[]
XML	Xml		SqlXml	XmlDocument XmlNode XmlElement String

Summary

This chapter described in detail the different types that are available to you in SQL Server, as well as the various types that you can use within ADO.NET, including the caveats and benefits of different approaches to dealing with data types in .NET. We looked at the most commonly used types, particularly variable character, integer, and date time types, but we also looked at less frequently used types. You learned about using SqlTypes and nullable types and how they can make database development easier. In other chapters, you'll see in more detail how you can use these data types in your code to work efficiently, both during design and at runtime.

For More Information

To complement the information in this chapter, take a look at the following resources:

❑ **SQL Server 2005 Books Online** — http://go.microsoft.com/fwlink/?LinkId=44375

❑ **MSDN article, "System.Data.SqlTypes namespace"** — http://msdn2.microsoft.com/library/System.Data.SqlTypes

❑ **MSDN article, "Nullable Types (C# Programmer's Reference)"** — http://msdn2.microsoft.com/library/1t3y8s4s(en-us,vs.80).aspx

5

ADO.NET Integration with XML

Extensible Markup Language, usually referred to as XML, is a very simple and flexible format for defining data and data structures. It has been an important tool for developers for years and is rapidly becoming the standard for exchanging data between applications and platforms due to its extreme flexibility and the ease with which it can be consumed by any operating system.

What makes XML so flexible is the fact that it's a metalanguage. Unlike ridged languages such as HTML that follow a defined format, metalanguages describe the format of another language. By providing a language to describe the format of the data, XML enables you to create an infinite number of types of XML documents to store almost any type of data you may have.

In addition to the extremely flexible format, XML has another huge advantage over other data storage formats: it is not application- or operating-system–specific. XML is typically stored as seven-character ASCII text that can be interpreted by any platform or application. Compared to other formats, it is easily readable by humans, and readers usually find that what the data elements represent is intuitive.

All of these advantages have led to XML being widely integrated into the .NET Framework. As a .NET developer, you see it everywhere. Sometimes you are explicitly working with it, such as when working with configuration files or performing XSL transformations. Other times, it is being used by the .NET Framework almost invisibly to you, such as when working with a dataset, or when writing and calling XML Web Services. Either way, knowing how to work with XML and how XML integrates with the .NET Framework are important skills and essential building blocks for understanding how ADO.NET works.

What This Chapter Covers

This chapter provides a brief overview of what XML features were available in the 1.x Framework. You will learn about enhancements to the `XmlReader` and `XmlWriter` objects that help simplify and consolidate much of the functionality in the 1.0 Framework. You will also examine some of the designer enhancements that help provide a better user experience, and then learn about the `XPathDocument`, which has envolved into a more feature-rich object for working with and editing XML documents. Finally, you will learn about the performance gains with the 2.0 Framework and what new features you can expect to see in future releases of the .NET Framework.

You should have previous experience with XML before reading this chapter. In addition, in order to run the examples provided, you will need a copy of Microsoft Visual Studio 2005. Most of the examples build from the XML file and XSD schema that follow, which are also available for download from this book's Web site at www.wrox.com. The XML file is an XML representation of a few records from the pubs sample database included with Microsoft SQL Server:

```xml
<?xml version="1.0" encoding="UTF-8"?>
<pubs>
  <titles name="The Busy Executive&apos;s Database Guide" pub_id="1389"
price="19.99">
    <authors au_lname="Green" au_fname="Marjorie"/>
    <authors au_lname="Bennet" au_fname="Abraham"/>
  </titles>
  <titles name="Cooking with Computers: Surreptitious Balance Sheets" pub_id="1389"
price="11.95">
    <authors au_lname="O'Leary" au_fname="Michael"/>
    <authors au_lname="MacFeather" au_fname="Stearns"/>
  </titles>
  <titles name="You Can Combat Computer Stress!" pub_id="0736" price="2.99">
    <authors au_lname="Green" au_fname="Marjorie"/>
  </titles>
  <publishers pub_id="0736" pub_name="New Moon Books"/>
  <publishers pub_id="0877" pub_name="Binnet &amp; Hardley"/>
  <publishers pub_id="1389" pub_name="Algodata Infosystems"/>
</pubs>


<?xml version="1.0"?>
<xsd:schema xmlns:xsd="http://www.w3.org/2001/XMLSchema">
<xsd:element name="pubs">
  <xsd:complexType>
    <xsd:sequence>
      <xsd:element ref="titles" maxOccurs="unbounded"/>
      <xsd:element ref="publishers" maxOccurs="unbounded"/>
    </xsd:sequence>
  </xsd:complexType>
</xsd:element>
<xsd:element name="titles">
  <xsd:complexType>
    <xsd:sequence>
      <xsd:element ref="authors" maxOccurs="unbounded"/>
    </xsd:sequence>
    <xsd:attribute name="name" type="xsd:string"/>
```

```
      <xsd:attribute name="pub_id" type="xsd:integer"/>
      <xsd:attribute name="price" type="xsd:float"/>
   </xsd:complexType>
</xsd:element>
<xsd:element name="publishers">
  <xsd:complexType>
     <xsd:attribute name="pub_id" type="xsd:integer"/>
     <xsd:attribute name="pub_name" type="xsd:string"/>
  </xsd:complexType>
</xsd:element>
<xsd:element name="authors">
  <xsd:complexType>
     <xsd:attribute name="au_lname" type="xsd:string"/>
     <xsd:attribute name="au_fname" type="xsd:string"/>
  </xsd:complexType>
</xsd:element>
</xsd:schema>
```

Where XML Is Today

When XML was first introduced to the majority of developers not too many years ago, it was promoted as the solution to every data storage and application interoperability problem. So far, it has fallen short of this universal solution, but it has still proven itself very useful.

Data Exchange

Since XML was introduced, it has been applied to a wide variety of purposes. Probably the most significant of these is a format for exchanging data between applications. Before XML, the standard means of exchanging disconnected data was either a flat text file or some form of delimited text file such as CSV. Often it was much worse, such as a propriety binary data format. Over the last few years, the standard has been shifted to using XML. This greatly simplifies the process of exchanging data between apps by providing a single standard that is easy to parse and easily human readable. It also provides a means to easily convert the data from the format of one application to that of another by using stylesheets.

XML Web Services

Providing a standard format for exchanging data was a huge step forward, but that is only half of the equation. The other half is providing a standard method for easily transmitting this data between applications. XML Web Services have expanded on these features to provide an easy way for applications to connect to one another and transfer data. This was very difficult to do before when the calling and receiving applications were not written in the same programming language or running on the same operating system. Because XML Web Services are typically run on top of a Web server using HTTP or HTTPS, it is very easy for businesses to migrate to XML Web Services. They are now the standard means for transmitting data across the Internet in real time.

The .NET Framework has abstracted away the details of calling XML Web Services to the point that you don't really even need to know XML to use them. It has done this by automatically generating the proxy classes that handle all the work. To call a Web service, you simply add a Web reference and refer to it in code as if you were calling a local DLL. To write a Web service, you just add a few attributes to your class and methods. This ease of use has made XML Web Services particularly appealing to .NET developers.

Configuration Files

Another area in which XML has been widely implemented is configuration files. In Windows 3.x, most configuration settings were stored in flat configuration files. With the release of Windows 95, Microsoft moved to storing all Windows and application settings in the system registry, enabling it to function as a single repository that could be accessed via common APIs. Unfortunately, as the registry's size grows, the performance degrades; and if the registry became corrupt, it was very difficult to recover. With the introduction of the .NET Framework, Microsoft moved to using XML files as the primary store for configuration settings. This combined the benefits of having an easily deployable, human readable text file along with the capability to use common APIs to work with the data. It also cleaned up some security holes by no longer requiring the application that needs to read the configuration files to have access to the registry.

.NET developers have followed this model, storing their configuration settings as XML. This has been accomplished in one of two ways. The first method stores them in default configuration files that are automatically inherited by the application, such as app.config, machine.config, or web.config. The second method stores them in separate configuration files that are then read by the application. With either approach, customizing the application settings is much easier than previous methods.

Text Markup

XML is also commonly used to mark up text designed for display to make it easier to change the display format. One example common to .NET developers is the use of XML comments, which enable developers to document their code in a structured format using XML. This XML is extracted during compilation to produce an XML output file. This output file can be parsed via code or transformed using XSLT to output the documentation in any format desired. A common tool for doing this is NDOC, an open-source utility for producing MSDN and other styles of documentation from the XML file.

XML has also become very popular with the recent increase of Web logs, or *blogs* for short. Bloggers write log entries that are stored as XML and can be easily presented on a Web site as HTML or consumed and consolidated with other Web logs and presented in pretty much any format desired.

The preceding examples are just a few of the more popular uses of XML today. There are far too many uses to list them all, and more are being invented every day. You can see how quickly it has gained popularity over the last few years and how important it is to understand how to work with it and where it can be used.

Design Goals for System.Xml 2.0

A wide variety of changes have been made to System.Xml in the 2.0 release of the .NET Framework. Most of these enhancements revolve around just a few design goals, which you'll look at more closely throughout the chapter:

- ❑   Improved performance

- ❑   Improved schema support

- ❑   Enhanced security

- ❑   Better usability

XmlReader and XmlWriter

The XmlReader and XmlWriter classes introduced in the 1.0 version of the .NET Framework are extremely valuable tools to most XML developers. They allow very quick, forward-only reading and writing of XML files. In the 2.0 Framework, Microsoft has introduced some new features for these classes that make working with them even easier.

Factory Methods

Some new static creation methods are available for both the XmlReader and XmlWriter classes. These methods are designed for a number of purposes. One of these is to simplify development by not requiring the developer to know which XmlReader and XmlWriter to use.

Currently, if you want to simply read an XML file with no special options, you don't create an XmlReader; you create an XmlTextReader. Similarly, you may create an XmlNodeReader or XmlValidatingReader. Each of these XmlReaders are optimized to perform their specific tasks. If the same course is followed as new optimizations are added, so are more classes, which overcomplicates working with XmlReaders. The same is true for the XmlWriters. The static create methods have greatly simplified this. To read an XML file from one source and write it to another, your code will now be as simple as this:

```
Dim reader As XmlReader
Dim writer As XmlWriter

reader = XmlReader.Create("pubs.xml")
writer = XmlWriter.Create("output.xml")

While reader.Read()
    writer.WriteNode(reader, True)
End While

reader.Close()
writer.Close()
```

The preceding example is great for replacing the XmlTextReader, but it's not really optimized for other tasks such as validation. The create methods are overloaded in order to handle these optimizations. There is an XmlReaderSettings class for setting the options for the XmlReader, and an XmlWriterSettings class for doing the same with the XmlWriter. Both of these have several properties you can set, ranging from validating the document or filtering out nodes, to simply formatting the document the way you want it to appear. Following is an example of some of the tasks you can perform by using these settings classes:

```
Dim reader As XmlReader
Dim writer As XmlWriter
Dim readerSettings As New XmlReaderSettings()
Dim writerSettings As New XmlWriterSettings()

readerSettings.IgnoreComments = True
readerSettings.Schemas.Add(Nothing, "pubs.xsd")
readerSettings.ValidationType = ValidationType.Schema

writerSettings.OmitXmlDeclaration = True
writerSettings.Indent = True
writerSettings.NewLineOnAttributes = True

reader = XmlReader.Create("pubs.xml", readerSettings)
writer = XmlWriter.Create("output.xml", writerSettings)

While reader.Read()
    writer.WriteNode(reader, True)
End While

reader.Close()
writer.Close()
```

This example tells the reader not to process any comments and performs schema validation against the pubs.xsd file by setting the corresponding properties. Similarly, it tells the writer not to write the XML declaration line, to indent all of the XML elements, and to add line breaks for each attribute. Doing this makes the XML output easier to read by humans, but increases the output size. This is just an example of what can be done. You can use these and the other settings in any combination you desire to get the precise output you want.

One of these new settings that is particularly worthwhile is ConformanceLevel. In version 1.0 of the .NET Framework, the XmlReader and XmlWriter were not conformant to the XML 1.0 standard by default. With the 2.0 Framework, you can choose the conformance level by setting the ConformanceLevel property. You can set this option to document or fragment conformance, or choose auto to have it auto-detect depending on the nodes encountered.

Conversion Between XML Types and Framework Types

Converting between XML schema types and .NET Framework types is a fairly routine task that wasn't as simple as it could be in the 1.0 Framework. Before, it was necessary to use the XmlValidatingReader and XmlConvert in order to perform the conversion. The 2.0 Framework simplifies this task with the introduction of several new ReadContentAs... methods. For example, to return the price of a book, you could use ReadContentAsDouble to return the value without having to later convert it to a double. The following example shows how you could calculate the total price of all of the books from the XML example provided at the beginning of the chapter:

```
Dim reader As XmlReader
Dim totalPrice As Double = 0
reader = XmlReader.Create("pubs.xml")
While reader.Read()
    If reader.IsStartElement() = True And reader.Name = "titles" Then
        reader.MoveToAttribute("price")
        totalPrice += reader.ReadContentAsDouble()
    End If
End While
```

Of course, the same is true when using the XmlWriter. The Framework now has the capability to convert between CLR data types and XML schema types. The following example shows how you can programmatically write out an XML document containing attributes of types string and double using the new WriteValue() method:

```
Dim writer As XmlWriter
writer = XmlWriter.Create("output.xml")
writer.WriteStartDocument()
writer.WriteStartElement("pubs")
writer.WriteStartElement("titles")
writer.WriteStartAttribute("name")
writer.WriteValue("The Busy Executive&apos;s Database Guide")
writer.WriteEndAttribute()
writer.WriteStartAttribute("price")
writer.WriteValue(19.99)
writer.WriteEndAttribute()
writer.WriteEndElement()
writer.WriteEndElement()
writer.Close()
```

Other XmlReader Enhancements

In addition to the items already mentioned, there are several other enhancements to the XmlReader. Most of these aren't revolutionary, but they will save you some time and are worth mentioning:

❑ **ReadSubTree** — This method will return a new XmlReader instance containing the current node and all of its child nodes. You can then call the Read method in it to loop through each child node. Once the new XmlReader has been closed, the original XmlReader will advance to the next node past the results of the subtree.

❑ **ReadToDescendant** — This method advances the current XmlReader to the descendent node with the specified name if a match is found. It will also return a Boolean indicating whether the match was found. This provides a much easier way of quickly getting to a specific node.

❑ **ReadToNextSibling** — This method provides an easy means for skipping over all of the child nodes to access the next sibling node with the specified name.

Designer Enhancements

Several enhancements to the XML designer make it easier to use. These range from simple coloring of the elements, attributes, and values to fully integrated XSL debugging. In this section, you will learn how to use these features to work more efficiently.

XML Designer

Figure 5-1 shows many of the features that make working with the XML designer easy. Please note that the color features mentioned do not appear in this black-and-white figure.

❏ XML nodes are now collapsible and expandable, much like .NET code or how Internet Explorer renders XML.

❏ The open and close tags of the node being edited are bolded, as shown in the last `titles` node in the figure.

❏ Any lines changed since the last time the XML document was saved are easily identifiable by the yellow highlighting to the left of the line. This is indicated on the last `titles` node shown in the figure.

❏ Any lines saved since the XML document was opened in the editor are now highlighted in green. See the first `publishers` node shown in Figure 5-1.

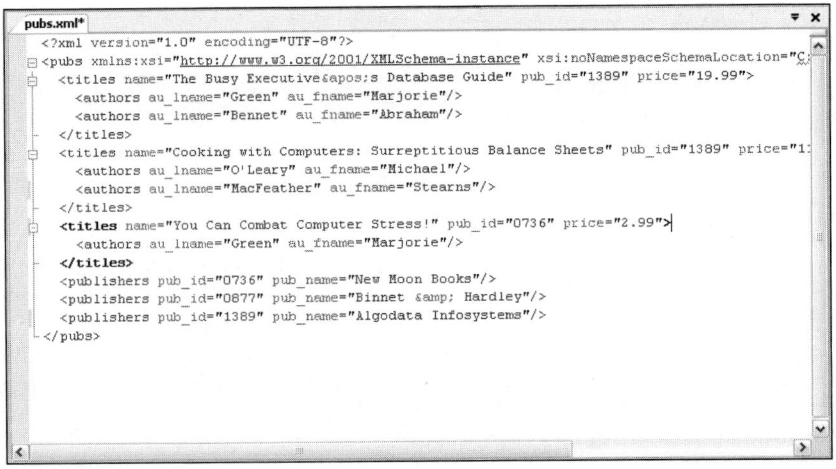

Figure 5-1

❑ You can easily override the schema and stylesheets you wish to use for debugging without modifying the actual XML document by setting the values in the document properties window.

❑ When you have specified a schema document to validate against, you will receive intellisense indicating which elements and attributes are available.

❑ Real-time well-formedness checks are available, which indicate any errors with red squiggles and an error in the error list.

❑ Real-time XSD validation is offered, indicating errors with blue squiggles and a warning in the error list.

❑ You now have the capability to quickly jump between start and end XML tags by using CTRL+].

❑ There is a go to Definition option when right-clicking on a node for quickly hopping to the XSD Schema.

❑ You can easily preview the XSL transformations by using the Show XSL Output option from the XML menu.

XSL Debugging

Because an XSL document is also an XML document, you have all of the features mentioned previously when working with XSL documents. You also have an extra feature that is very helpful: the capability to debug XSL transformations.

To begin debugging an XSL document, open it in the designer. Then open the properties window and specify the values for the input document and output document. After doing so, set a breakpoint in the XSL document the same way you would in code. Notice in Figure 5-2 that only the `xsl:value` element is highlighted. This is because the breakpoints are set at the node level, not the line level.

Once the breakpoint is set, click the Debug XSL option from the XML menu or click the run button from the XSL toolbar to begin debugging. The debugger will begin running the transformation, showing the output in a new window opened to the right of the XSL document. You then have the capability to step into your transformation just as you would with code and see your XSL document as it is forming.

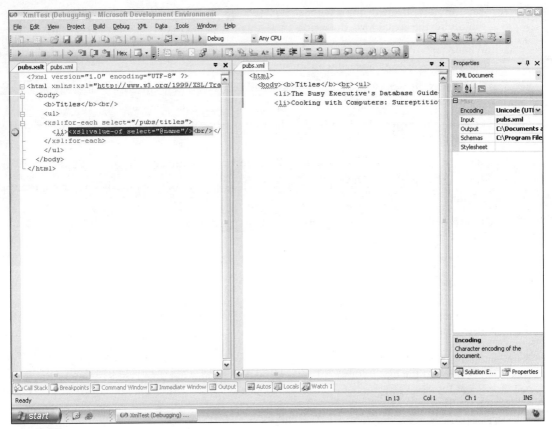

Figure 5-2

XSD Enhancements

Just as with XSL, an XSD document is also an XML document, so the designer for XSD documents supports all of the same features as the XML designer. Other than this, there aren't any enhancements to the XSD designer, but several features make working with XSD documents easier. Most of these revolve around validating the XML document against a schema and were mentioned previously in the section on XML designer features.

There is one feature we haven't covered yet, however. You no longer need to manually write the XSD document. If you already have an XML document but not an XSD, Visual Studio will generate one for you. To do this, load the XML document in the designer and from the XML menu, choose Create Schema. This will generate the XSD schema based upon the patterns detected in the XML document and automatically associate the XML document with the newly generated XSD. It may still be necessary to open the XSD schema and change or add some of the restrictions, but it is definitely a major time saver. Already have a DTD or XDR schema associated with the document? No problem; it will convert it to XSD for you.

Security

Security was not a major focus of the 1.0 release of System.Xml. As a result, a few vulnerabilities exist in the 1.0 Framework. These have been corrected in the 2.0 release.

Denial of Service Attacks

In the 1.0 Framework, it is possible to launch a denial of service attack with DTDs using a method known as *internal entity expansion*. This basically refers to performing a recursive definition of an entity, as in the following example:

```
<!DOCTYPE myEntity [
    <!ENTITY hw0 "Hello World">
    <!ENTITY hw1 "&hw0;&hw0;">
    <!ENTITY hw2 "&hw1;&hw1;">
    <!ENTITY hw3 "&hw2;&hw2;">

    ...
    <!ENTITY hw99 "&hw98;&hw98;">
    <!ENTITY hw100 "&hw99;&hw99;">
]>
<myEntity>&hw100;</myEntity>
```

This will cause the words "Hello World" to be repeated 2^{100} (1,267,650,600,228,229,401,496,703,205,376) times, either causing extreme memory usage or completely taking down the server. Nonetheless, this is a completely legitimate DTD instruction, and any attempt to close this vulnerability would also likely eliminate needed DTD capabilities. To compensate for this, the XmlReaderSettings class now contains a ProhibitDTD property for disabling DTD parsing when it is not needed. This fix was released as a patch for the 1.1 Framework in July 2004, but is now integrated with the 2.0 Framework.

Code Access Security

One of the components that makes the .NET Framework secure is *Code Access Security (CAS)*. It enables the machine administrator to set policies that define how much access a block of code has to the system, based upon the source of that code.

CAS works by gathering evidence about the assembly and assigning it to a code group based upon that evidence. Some examples of this evidence would be where the source document was loaded from — the local machine, a network share, a URL, and so on. If it was loaded from a URL, another factor would be that URL. By default, the code group to which an assembly is assigned is based on its security zone: Local Machine, Local Intranet, Internet, Restricted, or Trusted. You can also define your own code groups.

Each code group is defined by a single membership condition. The zones listed previously are an example of a membership condition, but additional ones include the following:

❏ All Code

❏ Application

❏ Application Directory

❏ Domain Application

❏ GAC (Global Assembly Cache)

Chapter 5

❑ Hash

❑ Publisher

❑ Site

❑ String Name

❑ URL

You can also define custom membership conditions. The final step is to define the permission set that the code group has. This can range widely, from writing to the hard drive, printing, accessing the registry, accessing the Web, and so on. You can configure these settings through the Framework Configuration MMC by loading %Systemroot%\Microsoft.NET\Framework\v2.0.XXXXX\Mscorcfg.msc.

All of these same features available for code security are now available for XML security. For example, when you load an XML document using the XmlReader, an Evidence property is populated with all of the relevant information about where the document came from. The document is then prevented from performing any actions that are not defined by the code group to which it is assigned, such as loading malicious URLs. This evidence is passed up the chain of any classes using the XmlReader, ensuring code access security throughout the XML classes.

XPathDocument

The XPathDocument is not new in version 2.0 of the Framework. It was the preferred data store for XML data that was to be used to perform XPath queries or XSL transformations. There are several new features to the XPathDocument in the 2.0 Framework, however, and this section covers some of the more dramatic changes.

Editing

The reason why the XPathDocument was the preferred data store for XPath queries and XSL transformations in the 1.0 Framework is because it offered a significant performance gain over the XmlDocument class. However, it was often necessary to edit the XML document in some way before performing the transformation. When this situation arose, the best approach was typically to create an XmlDocument, make the changes, and use it as the store for the query. By doing this, you would lose the performance benefits associated with using the XPathDocument. This is no longer a problem.

What makes the XPathDocument so much faster is that it does not have the XML 1.0 serialization constraints, so it can treat the document as just data. Now the XPathNavigator API, has been enhanced to extend cursor-style editing capabilities to the XPathDocument. It does this by reflecting the data within the XPathDocument to manipulate the XML. With this enhancement, the XPathDocument can continue to not be bound by these constraints, and deliver high performance while still being fully editable.

This is a different approach from before and it takes some getting used to, but once you see a few examples it should start to make sense. Let's start by looking at a very simple example. Let's rename the publisher "New Moon Books" to "Full Moon Books". Start as usual by creating a new XmlDocument and loading the pubs.xml file we've been using for all of the examples. Call the CreateNavigator method to get an XPathNavigator for the document and then use the SelectSingleNode method of this navigator to select the publisher with pub_id of 0736. This query will return another XPathNavigator object. You can now use the `SetValue` method of this navigator to change the value to "Full Moon Books". Finally, call the Save function on the original `XPathDocument` to save the results to the output file. Your code should look something like this:

```
Dim doc As System.Xml.XmlDocument
Dim navigator As System.Xml.XPath.XPathNavigator

doc = New System.Xml.XmlDocument()
doc.Load("pubs.xml")

navigator = doc.CreateNavigator.SelectSingleNode _
    ("/pubs/publishers[@pub_id='0736']/@pub_name")

navigator.SetValue("Full Moon Books")
doc.Save("output.xml")
```

Run the code and you'll notice that the publisher's name has been replaced. It was possible to do the same thing with the `XmlDocument` class in the 1.0 version of the Framework, but you didn't get the same performance benefits. Moreover, the result in this case would have been an `XmlNode` or `XmlNodeList` if you used the `SelectNodes` method, which does not offer all of the functions that the `XPathNavigator` does, such as the capability to run another query on the results.

Usually, the changes that need to be made to the XML document are not as simple as swapping out a value for a single property. For example, you may need to add a new publisher altogether. The `XPathNavigator` class makes this easy to do by exposing the `AppendChild` method. This method returns an instance of an `XmlWriter` object for writing new nodes. This is very convenient because most developers should already be familiar with the `XmlWriter`, eliminating the need to learn a second method of writing nodes.

Let's give it a try. Start out as you did in the previous example by creating a new `XmlDocument` and loading the pubs.xml file. Again create an `XPathNavigator` by calling the `SelectSingleNode` method, but this time just select the "/pubs" node. Now call the `AppendChild` method of the navigator object to create an `XmlWriter` instance. With the writer, call the `WriteStartElement` method to create a new publishers element. Then call the `WriteAttributeString` method to specify the pub_id and pub_name attributes, and the `WriteEndElement` method to close the publishers element. Don't forget to call the `Close` method of the writer to push the changes back to the navigator object. Finally, once again call the `Save` method of the document to save the changes to the output file:

```
Dim doc As System.Xml.XmlDocument
Dim navigator As System.Xml.XPath.XPathNavigator
Dim writer As System.Xml.XmlWriter

doc = New System.Xml.XmlDocument()
doc.Load("pubs.xml")
navigator = doc.CreateNavigator.SelectSingleNode("/pubs")
writer = navigator.AppendChild()
writer.WriteStartElement("publishers")
writer.WriteAttributeString("pub_id", "1234")
writer.WriteAttributeString("pub_name", "Wrox Press")
writer.WriteEndElement()
writer.Close()
doc.Save("output.xml")
```

If you view the output, you should see the new publisher as the last child of the pubs element. If you don't want the new node to be added as the last child, alternatives are available to AppendChild, including InsertBefore, InsertAfter, and PrependChild.

Now that you've learned how to replace a single value or insert a single node, let's take a look at how to do a bulk change to a document. The Select method of the XPathDocument returns an XPathNodeIterator that contains a collection of XPathNavigator objects that you can use to run sub-queries. This sounds more complicated than it is. Basically, it's as simple as the for each statement in the following example, which returns an XPathNavigator for each result of the original query. With this collection of XPathNavigators, you can easily loop through the results and make changes throughout the entire document.

That is exactly what the following example demonstrates. It shows how to find all of the titles written by Marjorie Green, remove any co-authors, and add a new co-author of Stearns MacFeather to each title. Begin as you did for the other two examples by creating an XmlDocument and loading the pubs.xml file. Then call the Select method to execute a query that returns all of the titles written by Marjorie Green. Wrap a for each statement around that call to return an XPathNavigator for each result. With this editor, call the SelectSingleNode method to find a co-author that isn't Green (if one exists), which will return a new XPathNavigator. Ensure that you received a result back by checking whether the new editor is null. If so, call the DeleteSelf method of that navigator to remove the co-author. Now all that is left to do is to add the co-author of Stearns MacFeather to each title. The original editor is still pointing at the title node, so call the AppendChild as you did in the previous example to create a new authors node. Set the attributes, close the writer, and save the document. Your code should like similar to this:

```
Dim doc As System.Xml.XmlDocument
Dim navigator, navigator2 As System.Xml.XPath.XPathNavigator
Dim writer As System.Xml.XmlWriter

doc = New System.Xml.XmlDocument
doc.Load("pubs.xml")

For Each navigator In _
    doc.CreateNavigator.Select("/pubs/titles[authors/@au_lname='Green']")

    navigator2 = navigator.SelectSingleNode("authors[@au_lname!='Green']")
    If Not IsNothing(navigator2) Then
        navigator2.DeleteSelf()
    End If

    writer = editor.AppendChild()
    writer.WriteStartElement("authors")
    writer.WriteAttributeString("au_lname", "MacFeather")
    writer.WriteAttributeString("au_fname", "Stearns")
    writer.Close()
Next

doc.Save("output.xml")
```

Open the output file and notice that for every title for which Marjorie Green was an author, any co-authors have been removed and Stearns MacFeather has been added. The other title records were left untouched.

Validation

Earlier, you learned how easily you can validate an XML document while reading it in by using the `ValidationType` property of the `XmlReaderSettings` class. Here, we'll look at how you can validate an XML document that is being created while it is still in memory. This is accomplished by using the `Validate` method exposed by the `XmlDocument` class.

XmlSchemaSet

Before we can look at validating XML output, we must first look at another new class in the 2.0 Framework: the `XmlSchemaSet` class. In the 1.0 Framework, schemas were loaded into an `XmlSchemaCollection`, which was used for storing schemas used by the `XmlValidatingReader`. In the 2.0 Framework, both the `XmlSchemaCollection` and `XmlValidatingReader` have been retired. This accomplishes a number of things, including the following:

❑ **Retiring support for the Microsoft XDR format** — The `XmlSchemaSet` only supports W3C XML Schemas now. The `XmlSchemaCollection` also supported the proprietary XDR format.

❑ **Improving performance by reducing the number of compiles** — The `XmlSchemaCollection` would perform a compile after each schema was added. With the `XmlSchemaSet`, a single compile occurs by manually calling the Compile method after all of the schemas have been added.

❑ **Elimination of schema islands** — The `XmlSchemaCollection` improperly handled multiple schemas by treating them as separate "islands," making all imports and includes only scoped to that particular schema. The `XmlSchemaSet` adds any imported schema to the schema set and treats the whole set as one logical schema.

❑ **Support of multiple schemas for a single namespace** — With the `XmlSchemaCollection`, each namespace could have only one schema. The `XmlSchemaSet` supports multiple schemas for the same namespace as long as there are not any type conflicts.

Validating Input and Output

Let's start by loading the code from the previous example. In the declarations section, declare a new `XmlSchemaSet` and `ValidationEventHandler` object. We'll look at the `XmlSchemaSet` more closely in a minute. Add pubs.xsd to the schema set and call the `Compile` method. After loading the `XmlDocument`, add the schema set to the document. Then set the handler object to a new `ValidationEventHandler` instance pointing to a new method called `ValidationCallback` that you will create in a moment. This method will log the validation errors to a TextBox on the form. Finally call the `Validate` method of the `XmlDocument` object, passing in the handler to validate the input document and log the errors.

The code to update the XML document is the same as in the previous example. When the changes are complete, call the `Validate` method of the `XmlDocument` object again, passing in the handler. This will allow you to validate the output document before saving it to disk. Optionally you could create a second handler to use a different method to log the validation errors to the changed document rather than the original document. Finally you need to create the `ValidationCallback` method and add code to append the contents of the Message property of the `ValidationEventArgs` to the `TextBox`. Your code should look like the following:

```
Private Sub Button1_Click(ByVal sender As Object, ByVal e As EventArgs)
    Dim doc As System.Xml.XmlDocument
    Dim navigator, navigator2 As System.Xml.XPath.XPathNavigator
    Dim writer As System.Xml.XmlWriter
    Dim schemaSet As System.Xml.Schema.XmlSchemaSet
    Dim handler As System.Xml.Schema.ValidationEventHandler

    schemaSet = New System.Xml.Schema.XmlSchemaSet()
    schemaSet.Add(Nothing, "pubs.xsd")
    schemaSet.Compile()

    doc = New System.Xml.XmlDocument()
    doc.Load("pubs.xml")
    doc.Schemas = schemaSet
    handler = New System.Xml.Schema.ValidationEventHandler(AddressOf _
        ValidationCallback)

    TextBox1.Text += "Validating Input:" + System.Environment.NewLine
    doc.Validate(handler)

    For Each navigator In doc.CreateNavigator().Select( _
        "/pubs/titles[authors/@au_lname='Green']")

        navigator2 = navigator.SelectSingleNode("authors[@au_lname!='Green']")
        If Not IsNothing(navigator2) Then
            navigator2.DeleteSelf()
        End If

        writer = navigator.AppendChild()
        writer.WriteStartElement("authors")
        writer.WriteAttributeString("au_lname", "MacFeather")
        writer.WriteAttributeString("au_fname", "Stearns")
        writer.Close()
    Next

    TextBox1.Text += "Validating Output:" + System.Environment.NewLine
    doc.Validate(handler)
    doc.Save("output.xml")
End Sub

Public Sub ValidationCallback(ByVal sender As Object, ByVal e As _
    System.Xml.Schema.ValidationEventArgs)

    TextBox1.Text += e.Message + System.Environment.NewLine
End Sub
```

If you run this, you'll notice that you receive the exact same results as the previous example. This is because the document is valid, so the validation callback never gets called. To see the validation in action, simply change one of the line's output by the writer to output an invalid value, such as the author's last name:

```
writer.WriteAttributeString("au_lname2", "MacFeather")
```

Run the code again and you'll see two error messages stating the following: `The 'au_lname2'` `attribute is not declared`. You can also change the original pubs.xml document to cause the input validation to fail, which will be caught by the first `Validate` method.

Schema Inference

Validating the XML output of your code is very important in most situations. Unfortunately, you don't always have an XSD document to validate against. When this is the case, you can do the next best thing and allow the Framework to infer an XSD schema from an existing XML document. This is relatively simple to do now using the `XmlSchemaInference` class — as simple as replacing the following two lines of code:

```
schemaSet = New System.Xml.Schema.XmlSchemaSet()
schemaSet.Add(Nothing, "pubs.xsd")
```

You need to first declare a new inference object and an `XmlReader`. At the location where you remove the two preceding lines, add a line to load the `XmlReader` from the same `pubs.xml` file the `XmlDocument` is reading. Set the inference object to a new instance of the `XmlSchemaInference` class and populate the schema set by calling the `InferSchema` method of the `XmlSchemaInference` object. Close your reader. You now have a schema you can use to validate your new XML against. You should receive the same results as the previous example after substituting the two lines above with the following lines:

```
Dim reader As System.Xml.XmlReader
Dim inf As System.Xml.Schema.XmlSchemaInference
reader = System.Xml.XmlReader.Create("pubs.xml")
inf = New System.Xml.Schema.XmlSchemaInference()
schemaSet = inf.InferSchema(reader)
reader.Close()
```

Change Notification

Whenever changes are made to the `XmlDocument`, events are raised to which you can add handlers to perform custom actions. Examples might be altering the values of an item being inserted, sending notifications when an item is deleted, and so on. Six events are provided for handling these scenarios. The first three are `ItemDeleting`, `ItemInserting`, and `ItemUpdating`. All three of these fire before the change has taken place. They are useful for actions such as performing validation of the data before allowing the change to take place. The other three are `ItemDeleted`, `ItemInserted`, and `ItemUpdated`. When these events fire, it is too late to modify the data, but they are very useful for actions such as logging. The following code builds upon the preceding example. You need to make the document declaration global and add two new methods: one for `ItemDeleted` and another for `ItemInserted`. In each of these, add a line to display the `OldValue` of each node that was deleted or the `NewValue` of the item that was inserted:

```
Dim WithEvents doc As System.Xml.XmlDocument

Private Sub Button1_Click(ByVal sender As System.Object, ByVal e As _
    System.EventArgs) Handles Button1.Click

    Dim editor, editor2 As System.Xml.XPath.XPathEditableNavigator
    Dim writer As System.Xml.XmlWriter
```

```
    doc = New System.Xml.XmlDocument()
    doc.Load("pubs.xml")

    For Each navigator In doc.CreateNavigator().Select( _
        "/pubs/titles[authors/@au_lname='Green']")

        navigator2 = navigator.SelectSingleNode("authors[@au_lname!='Green']")
        If Not IsNothing(navigator2) Then
            navigator2.DeleteSelf()
        End If

        writer = navigator.AppendChild()
        writer.WriteStartElement("authors")
        writer.WriteAttributeString("au_lname", "MacFeather")
        writer.WriteAttributeString("au_fname", "Stearns")
        writer.Close()
    Next

    doc.Save("output.xml")
End Sub

Public Sub doc_ItemDeleted(ByVal sender As Object, ByVal e _
    As System.Xml.XmlNodeChangedEventArgs) Handles doc.NodeRemoved

    TextBox1.Text += "Deleted Item: " + e.OldValue + System.Environment.NewLine()
End Sub

Public Sub doc_ItemInserted(ByVal sender As Object, ByVal e _
    As System.Xml.XmlNodeChangedEventArgs) Handles doc.NodeInserted

    TextBox1.Text += "Inserted Item: " + e.NewValue + System.Environment.NewLine
End Sub
```

XSLT Improvements

As stated at the beginning of this chapter, one of the major design goals for this release of System.Xml is improved performance. The XslCompiledTransform class has been completely rewritten with this goal in mind. The 1.0 release of this class was written primarily based on MSXML 3.0. It performed pretty well, but there was still a lot of room for improvement. Since then, MSXML 4.0 has been released, which introduced several new optimizations to improve performance that the 2.0 framework benefits from.

The primary way it does this is by compiling the XSLT into IL code and using the Just In Time compiler to compile and run the IL against the XML document. Doing this means it takes a little bit longer to compile the XSLT stylesheet, but it runs much faster. In addition, by explicitly compiling the XSLT stylesheet and then running it against the source document, you can compile it a single time and run it repeatedly. This greatly improves performance when you need to transform numerous documents. The following code shows how to create an XslCompiledTransform, compile the stylesheet, and execute the conversion against an XML document:

```
Dim xslt As System.Xml.Query.XsltCommand

xslt = New System.Xml.Query.XsltCommand()
xslt.Compile("pubs.xslt")
xslt.Execute("pubs.xml", "output.html")
```

Performance

All of the features we've looked at so far have made working with XML much easier, but probably few would disagree that the greatest improvement for XML in the 2.0 Framework is raw performance. We already described the efforts made to improve performance in the previous sections, such as minor tweaks made to optimize the most common code paths in all of the XML classes. You also saw how the XSLT processor has been completely rewritten to provide far better performance. You can see the result of all these efforts in Figure 5-3.

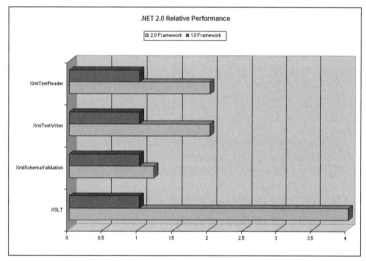

Figure 5-3

Where XML Is Heading

It's hard to know for sure where XML or any rapidly advancing technology is going to be in as little as five years from now. The examples in this section describe some of the features and standards still in development and a sample of what we're likely to see in the next few years. These features are not included in the .NET 2.0 release but will likely be included in the next version.

XPath 2.0

One of the standards that is right around the corner but wasn't finalized in time to be added to the .NET 2.0 Framework is XPath 2.0. For those who aren't already familiar with XPath, it is a query language for XML that is designed for selecting a subset of the XML document. It uses a syntax very similar to a file path, but with the capability to perform filters, calculate aggregates, and carry out other functions within it.

XPath 2.0 expands on these capabilities and introduces some new ones. The biggest change you'll notice is that the syntax has moved away from a simple path definition to what is known as a FLWOR (pronounced "flower") statement. FLWOR stands for For, Let, Where, Order, Return. It's very similar to the Select, Where, and Order By clauses of a SQL statement. By moving to this syntax, it is much easier to get the output you desire because it enables you to create and nest loops, store values in variables and manipulate them, sort the results, and define the exact output format.

XSLT 2.0 and XQuery

XSLT 2.0 and XQuery are two new emerging formats that are supersets of XPath 2.0. They are somewhat competing technologies, and currently it is looking like XQuery is going to become the new standard for querying and manipulating XML data.

One advantage XSLT 2.0 has is that it is built upon the XSLT 1.0 standard that many developers are currently using and have grown attached to. XSLT 2.0 does not have a lot of radical changes planned other than support for XPath 2.0 statements. It is also XML-based, which can be a plus for dynamically generating queries.

XQuery, on the other hand, is not XML-based, although there is an XML form of it called XQueryX. The XQuery syntax is much easier for most people to read, and with the current definition, it can perform all of the same tasks as XSLT. XQuery offers one huge advantage, though: It can be used to query virtualized data sources (that is, data sources such as SQL Server or objects in memory that are not stored as XML by default but can be converted to XML on demand). Due to these advantages, Microsoft's plans at the time this book was written are to focus on providing XQuery support and to continue to maintain XSLT 1.0 support but not build XSLT 2.0 support in the .NET Framework.

XML Views

One problem when working with XML is that, typically, the data source from which you retrieve the original data, or to which you want to save the data, is something other than XML, such as a SQL server. Currently, you have to write code to query the database, parse the results, and build the XML. If you plan to alter the XML document, you need to track the changes and then write code to perform the necessary update, inserts, and deletes to the original data store. If this is an operation that is going to be used frequently, you may choose to write this code as an XML Provider. Regardless of your approach, you still have to write the code.

Wouldn't it be nice if there were a generic component that could do this for you? That is exactly what XML Views are designed to do. They use declarative maps to transform the data instead of requiring custom code for each application. You create three maps: The first map is the XSD schema of the resulting XML you would like to work with. The second map defines your data source with information such as the tables and fields you will use and their primary and foreign keys. The third map links the other two maps together and provides the field-to-field mapping between them.

Now that all of these maps are defined, the XML View has everything it needs to enable you to query the original data store using XQuery and return the results as XML. It will also track any changes made to the XML document and can persist them back to the data store—all of this without requiring you to write the custom conversion code. As an added bonus, because the maps are in a declarative format, they can be changed without recompiling the application.

ObjectSpaces

ObjectSpaces is what every developer can't wait to get their hands on. It will allow you to declare your business objects in code and create maps very similar to XML Views that allow you to relate your business objects to database objects. You can probably guess what this means. No more writing data access code! Of course it won't be applicable in all situations, but it should significantly reduce the amount of code that is necessary to write for standard business applications. Unfortunately ObjectSpaces is still a ways away. It is currently planned for the next version of Visual Studio, currently codenamed Longhorn.

Summary

It is hoped that you can see how the many new features for working with XML in .NET 2.0 can save you time and improve the performance, scalability, and security of your applications. XML is still rapidly developing and new uses are found for it every day. The expanding use of XML as a standard means of sharing data between application shows no sign of slowing down. XML Web Services are continuing to evolve. Emerging technologies described in the previous section are going to expand the implementation of XML within the .NET Framework, and the current enterprise architecture techniques continue a trend toward Service Oriented Architecture (SOA). All of these factors will help ensure the future expansion of XML—and along with it, the need to be able to efficiently work with XML. The new features in this release of the Framework and in future versions will continue to make it easier to perform everyday tasks related to XML.

For More Information

- ❑ **Microsoft XML Developer Center**—http://msdn.microsoft.com/XML/default.aspx
- ❑ **MSDN .NET Framework Class Library (System.XML Namespace)**—http://msdn .microsoft.com/library/en-us/cpref/html/frlrfsystemxml.asp
- ❑ **Arpan Desai's Weblog**—http://blogs.msdn.com/arpande/

6

Transactions

Many aspects of computing adhere to the old adage "the more things change, the more they stay the same." Conceptually, this is a pretty good description of transaction processing in both ADO.NET 2.0 and Yukon. Don't get us wrong, there are some tremendous enhancements and improvements in both areas, but fundamentally, transaction processing is very similar to what it used to be like in the past. This time, though, the devil is in the details.

With respect to the enhancements in the 2.0 Framework, we'll be blunt: Transactions pre–ADO.NET 2.0 left a little to be desired. Or, as Wintellect Member and .NET Guru Dino Esposito put it, most of the new features under the 2.0 Framework are evolutionary, not revolutionary.

Establishing client-side transactions was not that difficult, and the average developer could pick it up in a few hours. Furthermore, a ton of resources were available and even Microsoft's Data Access Application Block included support for them. However, they were limited in many regards. You had basic features such as savepoints, rollbacks, and other traditional features, but transactions often occur on the database side, rather than the client side. That doesn't change in the 2.0 Framework per se. The *really* impressive changes are related to distributed transactions. Previously, if you wanted to use distributed transactions (transactions that span more than one database), you had some work to do. You had to dive deep into COM+, an area in which many .NET developers feared to tread. In the 2.0 Framework, the ADO.NET team has given us the System.Transactions namespace. At the time of this writing, there are approximately 20 classes in this namespace, and several enumerations, delegates, and interfaces. It has a companion namespace, System.Transactions.Configuration, which is small (it contains only three classes in total), but it helps with configuration issues (something that was ostensibly the most difficult part of dealing with distributed transactions under COM+).

Basic Concepts

Before we continue, you should familiarize yourself with a whole slew of concepts. The first is the basic notion of a transaction. Instead of giving you a textbook definition, let's run through an example. Suppose you're updating a record composed of both parent and child information.

Maybe you decide to add a new account at your bank and at the same time change your address. The address information would be stored in the parent record and the new account information would be stored as a new child record. Essentially, four scenarios are possible here:

- ❑ The parent record commits but the child doesn't.

- ❑ The child record commits but the parent doesn't.

- ❑ They both commit.

- ❑ Neither of them commits.

If you built your tables with the proper constraints, the second scenario is off the table. However, there *will* be situations in which tables have not been constructed the way you want them. Ideally, we need the third or fourth scenario to occur, but how do you accomplish this? If you're the "roll your own" type, you start writing code and you keep on writing. And writing and writing. At the end of the day, your solution will work a lot less well than if you did it the "right" way — using transactions. As such, let's define a *transaction* as a group of actions that we want to either succeed or fail together.

A.C.I.D

You won't get very far into any transaction discussion before the acronym *A.C.I.D.* comes up. Here's what the different parts of the acronym stand for:

- ❑ **Atomicity** — Everything is considered to be part of the same unit. In the preceding example, the new account and the address update belong to the same unit, not two separate units (although they are physically different).

- ❑ **Consistency** — This means simply that the state of the database is not unchanged if the transaction does not complete. In other words, there are no half-committed transactions, orphaned records, or the like.

- ❑ **Isolation** — This is not the same as isolation levels, although the two are related. This essentially means that what goes on in this transaction doesn't affect other transactions or processing.

- ❑ **Durability** — This is the notion that once the transaction has completed, it will be saved to the database correctly.

When you hear about transactions, the most common example is how ATMs work. You insert your card and make a request. Money is debited from one account and either credited to another or dispensed. If anything fails, you don't get your money. If transaction processing didn't occur in this scenario, you could have some serious problems (or benefits, depending on the error). Suppose your account was debited but the other account wasn't credited. You'd lose the withdrawal amount. If the reverse happened, the other party(ies) (the banks) would lose the withdrawal amount. Either way, if this kind of mistake happened a lot, confidence in ATMs would plummet and no one would use them.

You can find a great Weblog entry that shows the flaw in this example (visit Scott Allen's blog, at `http://odetocode.com/Blogs/scott/archive/2005/02/27/1061.aspx`). What happened to Scott was that the entire transaction processed, but the money never came out. However, the transaction was committed and the money was deducted from his account. It's not clear exactly what caused the failure, but from Scott's description, it sounds like a durability problem. Suffice it to say that all four characteristics of a successful transaction are equally important. Each needs to occur in order for transactions to work.

Let's talk now about how to *enlist* a transaction. You can do this in two ways: through volatile enlistment and through durable enlistment. These are fancy-sounding concepts, but they're actually pretty straightforward. *Volatile enlistment* is a mechanism whereby nondurable resources will not be reclaimed. *Durable enlistment*, conversely, is what occurs with resources that will need to be reclaimed.

Conceptually, the difference is about the same as between NotePad® and Word XP®. If you are typing a NotePad document and the power goes out, you will lose everything you've typed since the last time you did a save. With newer versions of Word, when the system comes back up, it will inform you that there was a problem and recover what you were doing to the state it was in when the power went out.

Remember A.C.I.D.? Durability is the "D" in that acronym. If you can risk the durability, then volatile enlistment is a good choice. If you're wondering why you would want any risk, consider the fact that true durability can be expensive in terms of hardware and resources, and in many situations you don't need ultradurable transactions.

On the other hand, if you need absolute assurance as far as durability, then your only option is durable enlistment. One good example is a transactional file system, but you can probably think of others. In most instances, volatile enlistment will suffice, but the distinction is worth mentioning. To have *truly* durable transactions, well, as the old expression goes: "There's no such thing as a free lunch." Still, you can get pretty close on the cheap.

Transaction Types

The next thing to understand in terms of background information is local or simple transactions versus distributed transactions (transactions that span more that one data store). You can have transactional processing in areas other than traditional RDBMS systems, but that's where you see them the most. Currently, Microsoft has added transaction support for Microsoft Message Queues (MSMQ) and may well expand it to include file system support. Depending on where you work, you probably work with more local transactions than distributed transactions. The distinction is pretty simple—if your transaction spans only one database or data store (Message Queues, for example, a cornerstone of Service Oriented Architecture, are now often involved in transactions), then it's a simple transaction. If it spans more than one database, be it on one or many servers, then it's a distributed transaction.

In terms of complexity, local transactions are infinitely easier to work with than distributed transactions. The reason should be readily evident. With one database, you are dealing with a very minimal set of variables, whereas distributed transactions span many more. In its simplest form, a simple transaction could be run against a database that resides on the same computer as the application. Accordingly, there would be only one file and only one table. Because everything is on the same computer, the application and database may or may not even be on a network. Conversely, in a distributed scenario, your application could be running on x numbers of computers spanning y number of databases residing on z number of networks.

In a distributed transaction, you may hit x number of databases, where security, network connectivity, and everything else can cause problems. If you use distributed transactions, you'll likely be amazed that they actually work at all, let alone work as superbly as they do. (Think about it: Compare the number of times the ATM has worked correctly from a transactional point of view—even if it didn't give you any money—compared with the number of times it hasn't. Sure, glitches occur, but it's very rare to have problems with accounts being debited or credited.)

Isolation Levels

Stated simply, an *isolation level* is the level at which any given transaction is isolated from any other transaction. There is an inverse relationship between isolation levels and data correctness. A lower isolation level minimizes the problems associated with concurrency (namely, locking), but this is achieved at the expense of correct data (phantom, nonrepeatable reads). The higher the isolation level, the more accurate your data can be assumed to be, but the more risk you subject yourself to in regard to concurrency.

One of the really interesting features about `IsolationLevel` is that once you set it, you can change it at any time. If you specify a `ConnectionString` for instance, and have an open connection, you can't specify a change to it midstream and have the effects take. This is not the case with `IsolationLevel`. Moreover, once the changes have been made, they don't apply to anything that's already been executed, but they will apply to everything that happens afterward. To be perfectly honest, we've worked quite a bit with transactions and have never had a need for this functionality. Still, it's cool that it's there.

At the time of this writing, six isolation levels are defined in the `Transaction` object, as specified in the MSDN documentation:

Member Name	Description	Value
Chaos Supported by the .NET Compact Framework.	The pending changes from more highly isolated transactions cannot be overwritten.	16
ReadCommitted Supported by the .NET Compact Framework.	Shared locks are held while the data is being read to avoid dirty reads, but the data can be changed before the end of the transaction, resulting in nonrepeatable reads or phantom data.	4096
ReadUncommitted Supported by the .NET Compact Framework.	A dirty read is possible, meaning that no shared locks are issued and no exclusive locks are honored.	256
RepeatableRead Supported by the .NET Compact Framework.	Locks are placed on all data that is used in a query, preventing other users from updating the data. Prevents nonrepeatable reads but phantom rows are still possible.	65536
Serializable Supported by the .NET Compact Framework.	A range lock is placed on the dataset, preventing other users from updating or inserting rows into the dataset until the transaction is complete.	1048576
Unspecified Supported by the .NET Compact Framework.	An isolation level other than the one specified is being used, but the level cannot be determined.	–1

Remember that a given provider—OleDb, for example—doesn't know what data source you're connecting to. Therefore, you can use OleDb for instance, to connect to a SQL Server or Oracle database and because the back ends respectively support transactions, you can specify transactions and everything will be fine. Comma-Separated Value files can also be connected via OleDb, and while NotePad is a very useful tool in many instances, transactional support has never been one of its strong points. In other words, client-side transaction processing is only going to be as accessible and useful as the underlying data source provides. We don't think we've ever used a relational database that didn't support transactions, but they may be out there, so be forewarned to look into this before getting too deep into transactions.

Creating a Local Transaction

In its simplest form, creating and using transactions is very simple. The following example shows how this is facilitated:

```
Imports System.Data
Imports System.Data.SqlClient

Dim tn as SqlTransaction
Dim sql as String = "INSERT INTO Employees1(EmpID) VALUES (@UserID)";
Dim cn as new SqlConnection(CONNECTION_STRING)
Try
  If  cn.State <> ConnectionState.Open Then
      Cn.Open
   End If
Catch ex As SqlException
    Debug.Assert(False, ex.ToString())
    tn = cn.BeginTransaction
Dim cmd as New SqlCommand(sql, cn, tn)
cmd.Paramaters.Add("@UserID", SqlDbType.Int)
cmd.Paramaters(0).Value = 314
Try
  Dim I as Integer = cmd.ExecuteNonQuery
   For x As Integer = 0 To 10
      cmd.Parameters("@UserID").Value = 315 + x)
      cmd.ExecuteNonQuery()
Next
    tn.Commit
Catch ex as SqlException
tn.Rollback
    End Try
End Try
```

Another question that comes up a lot has to do with save points. *Save points* are mechanisms by which you can specify points in a transaction so that you can roll back to them. This is particularly helpful for very long transactions in cases where you have a specific failure and you don't want to rollback everything, just a portion of it. To use a save point, it couldn't be easier than this:

```
tx.Save("SomeName")
```

Now let's look at a slightly more complex scenario. Suppose you had a dataset to update that you were very sure would update without any problems. Afterward, you had another dataset that you weren't so sure about. In case of an exception, though, you want to only move past the first save point (admittedly, we can't come up with a scenario like this, but it works well for illustrative purposes):

```
Imports System.Data
Imports System.Data.SqlClient

 Try
```

```
        tx.Save("FirstSave")
        tx = cn.BeginTransaction()
            da.AcceptChangesDuringUpdate = false
        da.Update(ds)
                tx.Save("SecondSave")
        da.Update(SomeOtherDataSet)
                    tx.Commit()
 Catch ex as SqlException
        tx.Rollback("SecondSave")
  System.Diagnostics.Debug.Assert(false, ex.ToString())
 End Try
```

The preceding example is not the only way to accomplish local transactions though. SQL Server, for instance, provides its own flavor of SQL with control statements included. This is known as T-SQL. Most major RDBMS implementations have a similar language available. As such, you can set the `SqlCommand` object's `CommandType` property to *Text* and set the command text to the following to accomplish the same result:

```
BEGIN TRANSACTION
    --Perform everything here
 COMMIT
IF @@ERROR <> 0  BEGIN
   ROLLBACK
END
```

Functionally, you get to the exact same place. However, in the preceding example, all transaction logic is handled on the server. Personally, we have a strong preference for the latter. It's more force of habit than anything else (along with some superstitious fear) because to date, we have yet to run into any real problems using the client-side transaction object. However, as a matter of comfort, it just seems like there's a lot (i.e., the Network) in between the client application and the database, and handling it on the database is the safest way to go. Should you avoid client-side transaction processing? Hardly. David Sceppa, author of the *Microsoft ADO.NET (Core Reference)*, which is unquestionably the best book on the subject, quotes Stevie Wonder in Chapter 10: "When you believe in things that you don't understand, then you suffer. Superstition ain't the way." Take Stevie's advice.

> *The first version of Microsoft ADO.NET (Core Reference) covered the 1.0/1.1 Framework, and is absolutely indispensable for those learning ADO.NET. The author dedicates a good portion of Chapter 11 to distributed transactions. Another title that covers enterprise applications in .NET is* Enterprise Services with the .NET Framework: Developing Distributed Business Solutions with .NET Enterprise Services, *by Christian Nagel, which covers a lot on the subject of distributed transactions. We mention this because it used to be a real pain to work with distributed transactions but now it isn't.*

Before we delve much further into the subject, we'll give you one last warning: Things are winding down with the 2.0 Framework and at the time of this writing, we don't think any functional changes are on the table. However, if changes do occur, they will likely be rather pronounced, due to the complexity of the subject matter. Bill Ryan, for example, wrote an article for "15 Seconds" in September 2004 (www.15seconds.com/issue/040914.htm) and as of this writing, it is completely outdated.

In order to show you how much easier things have gotten recently, we need a comparison point. Therein lies a little bit of the problem. In order to do anything with distributed transactions in the previous version of the Framework, we'd need to spend a good bit of time explaining what is happening and why. Because much of what is available in the 2.0 Framework was put there *precisely* to address (alleviate is probably a more fitting word) the issues related to distributed transactions in the 1.0/1.1 Frameworks, we don't cover it here. Believe us, you aren't missing much. If you're a glutton for punishment, they're still available, but use them for a few hours and you'll be a convert to the newer way of handling things.

Distributed Transactions

According to MSDN, distributed transaction processing systems are "designed to facilitate transactions that span heterogeneous, transaction-aware resources in a distributed environment." In practice, what that typically means is that distributed transactions are transactions that span more than one data source. Until recently, they were for the most part exclusive to database systems, but functionality has been expanded to included other resources such as Microsoft Message Queues (MSMQ). Back in the days when networks weren't common and every computer in an office was effectively an isolated island, distributed transactions were unknown to most developers (and we're not talking about all that long ago — at least one of the authors of this book worked in a large office 10 years ago that had a majority of its computers unlinked to a network). We're not suggesting that no developers dealt with transactions (simple or distributed) back then, but it definitely was more the exception than the norm. However, that changed quickly as desktop databases or spreadsheets became major bottlenecks to productivity. Network-available databases became a lot more affordable and an increasing number of developers/ companies started creating applications with networked databases.

Previously, for example, you might have had a few different software packages that were used by different departments. Sales and Human Resources, for instance, might have used use two totally different primary software packages, both of which used different back-end databases, but data from one might have been dependent on data in the other. Similarly, if a salesperson leaves a company and notifications aren't sent to the sales department, then it's possible that someone in that department might assign a task to them or give them credit for something. Although this is a fictitious example, it's not hard to conceive of a scenario you encountered in your own career where one database was dependent on another one.

As such, in a very short period of time, distributed transactions went from being something only a few, very sophisticated developers had to deal with, to something that was pretty commonplace at most mid- to large-size companies.

In the 1.x Framework, using a client-side transaction looks something like the following:

```
Imports System.Data
Imports System.Data.SqlClient

Private Function OldSchool() as Boolean
   DIM  IsConsistent as BOOLEAN = false;
   DIM oldSchoolTrans AS ICommittableTransaction = Transaction.Create()
   Using (cn as  new SqlConnection(CONNECTION_STRING))

        Dim sql as String = "DELTE CATEGORIES"
             Dim cmd as new SqlCommand(sql, cn)
             cn.Open()
        cn.EnlistTransaction((ITransaction)oldSchoolTrans);
      Try
             cmd.ExecuteNonQuery()
             IsConsistent = true
                Return true
```

```
CATCH (ex as SqlException)

            //You can specify additional error handling here
            //This is where you'd rollback your transaction
            Return (ex.ToString.Length < 1)
        cn.Close()
        End Try

    End Using
End Function
```

This is an example of a "simple" transaction but it's pretty much the standard approach you use with simple transactions under the 1.x Framework. Why didn't we show a distributed transaction example? There's a lot more involved in getting one working and there's nothing simple about them, and because this book is about ADO.NET 2.0, well, keep reading.

Distributed Transactions in ADO.NET 2.0

In most of the examples so far, we've referenced the System.Data.SqlClient library, which is the native library for SQL Server. However, that library isn't of much use in distributed transaction scenarios because you probably aren't working with SQL Server across the board. Do you think that if you called an Oracle database it would have any clue what @@Error is? As such, the starting point here is the System.Transactions namespace. Out of the box, this isn't a referenced assembly, so you'll need to add a reference to it in order to use it. You can do this by selecting the Project menu item, then Add Reference, and then System.Transactions under the .NET tab, as shown in Figure 6-1.

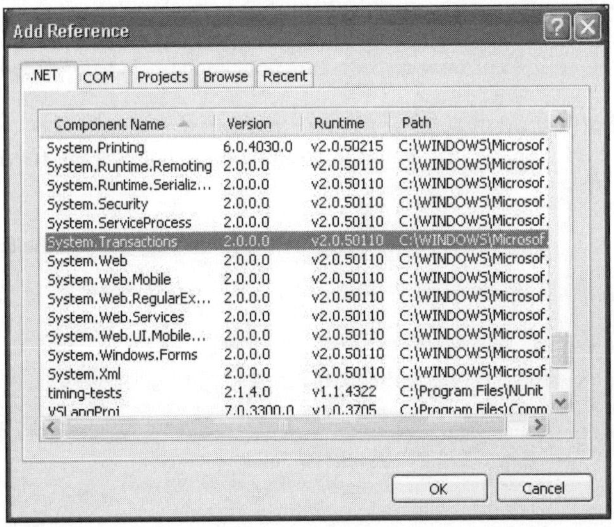

Figure 6-1

Note that at the time of this writing, Oracle, SQL Server, and MSMQ were the only data sources provided under the TransactionScope object. If you need to use another DB, then it's COM+ for you—although in all likelihood, it's virtually assured that other vendors will provide support for it.

In order for distributed transactions to work correctly, remember to adhere to the following order:

1. Create Transaction.

2. Create Connection.

3. Dispose Connection.

4. Call TransactionScope's Complete() method.

5. Dispose Transaction.

Here's how you would create a simple transaction:

```
Dim ConnectString as String = @"Data Source=.\SQLExpress;Integrated
Security=True;AttachDBFilename=C:\xxxxxxxxxxxxxxxx.mdf";private void
btnTryTransaction_Click(object sender, EventArgs e)
{
  TimeSpan ts = new TimeSpan(0, 0, 5);//Didin't do this yet - should have taken it
out.
  TransactionScope scopeObject = new TransactionScope();
  string sql = "INSERT INTO tb_Customers(Customer_ID, Customer_FirstName,
Customer_LastName) VALUES (@CustID, @FirstName , @LastName)";
       using (scopeObject)
       {
              using (SqlConnection cn = new SqlConnection(ConnectString))
              {
                     SqlCommand cmd = new SqlCommand(sql, cn);
                     cmd.Parameters.Add("@CustID", SqlDbType.Int, 4).Value = 8;
                     cmd.Parameters.Add("@FirstName", SqlDbType.VarChar,
50).Value = "William";
                     cmd.Parameters.Add("@LastName", SqlDbType.VarChar,
50).Value = "Gates";
                     cn.Open();
                     cmd.ExecuteNonQuery();
                     cmd.Parameters.Clear();
                     cmd.CommandText = "SELECT COUNT(*) FROM tb_Customers";
                     System.Int32 Result = (int)cmd.ExecuteScalar();//7 Records
after Successful Insert
                     cn.Close();
//Open a connection to a Different Sql Server database,  MSMQ, Oracle etc and do
something there.
              }
              scopeObject.Complete(); //At this point, the transaction is
committed
       }
              MessageBox.Show(GetTotalCount().ToString());
       }

Private Function GetTotalCount() As Integer
   Dim cn As New SqlConnection(CONNECTION_STRING)
   Dim cmd As New SqlCommand("SELECT COUNT(*) FROM tb_Customers", cn)
   cn.Open()
   Dim i As Integer = CType(cmd.ExecuteScalar, Int32)
   cn.Close()
```

```
       Return i
    End Function
```

Regarding the defaults — the default isolation that will be used is serializable, and the default timeout on the transaction is 60 seconds, or 1 minute. However, you will probably come across scenarios in which you want completely different settings. For this, the `TransactionOptions` class comes to save the day:

```
Dim transactionOption as new TransactionOptions()
transactionOption.IsolationLevel = System.Transactions.IsolationLevel.Snapshot
     'Set the transaction timeout to 30 seconds
     'In reality, you'd probably want to get this from a .Config setting
     'For resource file
     transactionOption.Timeout =   new TimeSpan(0, 0, 30);
     Dim  ts =  new TransactionScope(TransactionScopeOption.Required,
transactionOption);
```

Other than `Timeout` and `IsolationLevel`, there isn't much you can do with this, but it is a straightforward way to manipulate these settings.

Back when we first loaded the Alpha bits of Whidbey, things were a little more complex (hats off to Angel Saenz-Badillos and the whole ADO.NET team for making it ever easier). Previously, there was a property named `Consistent` (actually, the property is still there, but you don't have to constantly set it). At each pass through your code, you'd set it to false if something failed. At the end, when the code exited the block and the scope was disposed, if the `Consistent property` was set to true, everything would commit. If it was false, it would roll back. Compared to what you had to previously do, it was a walk in the park, but it was still a little short on elegance. Now, when you are done and you are sure you want to commit everything, you simply call the `Complete` method and voilà, everything is committed.

Presently, you can and should call the `Complete` method of the TransactionScope object to finish off the transaction. You can still set the `Consistent` property, but the latest Whidbey build indicates that it has already been deprecated.

One of the downsides to being an early adopter of new software is that features you spend time learning change dramatically or are deprecated. Depending on the specific item, this can be pretty dramatic. Author Bill Ryan, for instance, spent a lot of time writing articles and giving presentations on the TransactionScope object, much of whose functionality was changed or deprecated even before the first beta was released.

In the following example, only one data store is being used. As such, this transaction is operating as a local transaction. However, suppose we make a slight modification to this code, such that another data store were used:

```
Public Sub Test()
        Dim cn As New SqlConnection(CONNECTION_STRING)
        Dim sql = "SELECT COUNT(*) FROM SomeTable"
        Dim cmd As New SqlCommand(sql, cn)
        cmd.Parameters.Add("@CustID", SqlDbType.Int, 4).Value = 8
        cmd.Parameters.Add("@FirstName", SqlDbType.VarChar, 50).Value = "William"
        cmd.Parameters.Add("@LastName", SqlDbType.VarChar, 50).Value = "Gates"
```

```
        cn.Open()
        cmd.ExecuteNonQuery()

        Dim i As Integer = CType(cmd.ExecuteScalar, Integer)
        cn.Close()
    End Sub
```

What would happen is very interesting. At first, a local transaction would be created. When the second connection was created and opened, it would be automatically enlisted into a distributed transaction.

If you don't want to use the `TransactionScope` and you want to do things manually, a great new feature simplifies things:

```
IDBConnection.EnlistTransaction
```

Therefore, each derivation of this—`SqlConnection`, `OracleConnection`, and so on—has the capability of manually enlisting the transaction, although as far as we know, `System.Data.SqlClient` is the only provider in beta that has actually implemented it.

Monitoring Transactions and Their Performance

As mentioned previously, there's an inverse relationship between performance and accuracy in respect to isolation level. Another thing to remember is that distributed transactions require a lot more monitoring, so there is obviously more overhead associated with them. At any rate, you will no doubt want to monitor them at some point.

The easiest way to accomplish this is visually. Select Start ⇨ Control Panel ⇨ Administrative Tools ⇨ Component Services ⇨ Component Services (Under Console Root) ⇨ Computers ⇨ My Computer ⇨ Distributed Transaction Coordinator. You should see something like what is shown in Figure 6-2.

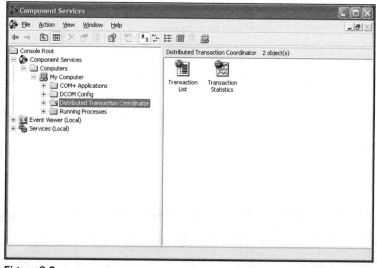

Figure 6-2

From there, you can select either the Transaction List (which will show you all currently running distributed transactions), or Transaction Statistics (which will show you the performance statistics of any given transaction). In most instances, the latter will be much more useful, as shown in Figure 6-3.

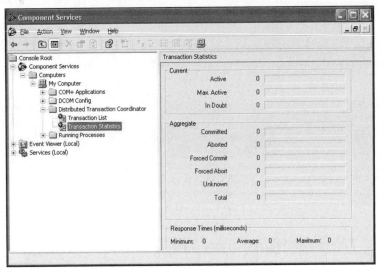

Figure 6-3

Keep in mind, however, that what you are viewing here are distributed transactions, not local ones. If a local transaction has been promoted/enlisted, then it will become visible. Remember that this is the "Distributed Transaction Coordinator" — hence, its use is for monitoring distributed (not local) transactions.

How Does This Affect Local Data?

As a regular in most of the .NET-related newsgroups, author Bill Ryan sees questions about using System .Data.DataSet objects and transactions just about every day. Many developers new to ADO.NET create a transaction, call Update on a IDBDataAdapter object, and somewhere before completion it fails. The transaction in the database is rolled back, but the changes that were successfully updated in the DataSet are lost.

To understand why this is a problem, you need to understand how IDBDataAdapter objects work and what the AcceptChanges method does to a given DataRow. More problems in ADO.NET have been created by not understanding this than anything else we've seen, so we're going to cover it in detail here.

When you call Fill on a IDBDataAdapter object, the RowState of every row is Unchanged unless you set AcceptChangesDuringFill to false. The default is true, which makes sense. If you aren't familiar with RowState or AcceptChanges, this may not be clear yet, but bear with us.

When the Update method of an adapter is called, it walks through each row and looks at the row's RowState. Currently, the RowState enumeration is defined as follows in the MSDN Documentation:

Member Name	Description	Value
Added— Supported by the .NET Compact Framework.	The row has been added to a `DataRowCollection` and `AcceptChanges` has not been called.	4
Deleted— Supported by the .NET Compact Framework.	The row was deleted using the `Delete` method of the `DataRow`.	8
Detached— Supported by the .NET Compact Framework.	The row has been created but is not part of any `DataRowCollection`. A `DataRow` is in this state immediately after it has been created and before it is added to a collection, or if it has been removed from a collection.	1
Modified— Supported by the .NET Compact Framework.	The row has been modified and `AcceptChanges` has not been called.	16
Unchanged— Supported by the .NET Compact Framework.	The row has not changed since `AcceptChanges` was last called.	2

As such, the default `RowState` of a row after calling `Fill` is `Unchanged`. If you delete it, it will change to `Deleted`.

> *Many newcomers to ADO.NET often get confused with the* `Remove` *and* `Delete` *methods.* `Remove` *physically takes the row out of the collection. For example, if you have 10 rows, call* `Remove` *on 10 of them. You now have 0 rows. If you have 10 rows, call* `Delete` *on 10 of them — you still have 10 rows until* `AcceptChanges` *is called. We've seen at least 50 people run into major problems removing rows when they meant to delete them but didn't and then wondered why their updates didn't work.*

If you create a new row and add it to a `DataTable` object, its `RowState` will be `Added`. If you change an existing row, its `RowState` will be set to `Modified`. If you create a new row but forget to add it to a table's `Rows` collection, then its `RowState` is `Detached` — and as such, isn't part of the `DataTable`'s `Rows` collection.

Moving on, when you call `Update`, the adapter iterates through the given table you specify. If you pass in a `DataSet` to the adapter and don't specify a `DataTable`, it will default to the one with the 0th index. If you pass in just a `DataRow`, only it will be used. If you pass in an array of `DataRows`, then it will behave just like a `DataTable`'s `Rows` collection.

At each iteration, the `RowState` is examined. For each `RowState` of `Added`, the `UpdateCommand`, if one is specified, is used. Note that you don't *have* to specify a valid `Update`, `Delete`, or `Insert` command. However, if you don't have a valid command but a `Rowstate` is in the Collection that is `Updated`, `Modified`, or `Deleted`, then an exception will be thrown. No exceptions will be thrown if you don't add one of those commands as long as you never call `Update` — or when you do, they aren't needed. Otherwise, they will throw an exception. That said, each row is examined, the corresponding command is examined, and the adapter fires the respective command using the row provided. Upon successful completion, the `AcceptChanges` method of the `DataRow` is called, which effectively resets its `RowState` to `Unchanged`.

If the `Rowstate` was `Deleted`, then it is removed from the `Collection`. If it's modified, the original values are now what the proposed values were just prior to the update. By default, if an exception is thrown, then everything stops and no more attempts are made at updates.

Remember the old rule of "Where there's smoke, there's fire." If you use any of the visual tools to configure a `IDBDataAdapter` object and you get warnings at the end of the wizard (they typically will tell you that one or more of the commands could not be generated), it's unwise to ignore it (although many people do). The most likely cause of this is that either the table used in the query lacks a primary key or you are using a Join. (Many RDBMS purists will tell you that every table should always have a primary key. While this is an extreme position, it's hard to argue that ensuring each table has a key isn't a good habit. Sure, in some rare cases it may be unnecessary, but the downside to having a key when you don't need it is small, whereas the downside to not having a key when you should is huge.) If you need to join data, it's probably a much better idea to fill both tables and join them client side using a `DataRelation` object (author Bill Ryan has an article on how to do this, available at www.knowdotnet.com/ articles/datarelation.html. Either way, if you get an error when trying to configure your `IDBDataAdapter` object, you can't count on calling the Adapter's `Update` method and having it work. It may, but chances are good some aspect of it won't work. If this happens, take it as a canary in a coal mine — somewhere out there, your database probably needs some attention.

However, there is a `ContinueUpdateOnError` property for each adapter implementation, which, if an error is caused, will just proceed with the next row. For example, if you had 100 rows with a "changed" `RowState`, and the row 98 caused an error, you'd have 97 successful changes in the database and only three rows in your `DataSet` with changes (assuming you were *not* inside a transaction). If you specified `ContinueUpdateOnError`, you'd have 99 successful updated records, but only *1* row with changes in it.

However, if this occurred inside a transaction, you'd have a serious problem. From the client side, nothing would be different, but in the first examples, you'd have 97 rows with `AcceptChanges` called on them, which would reset their `Rowstate` to `Unchanged`, but when the transaction rolled back, no changes would be present in the database, which would cause those changes to be effectively lost.

So how do you get around this? First, you need to use the `GetChanges()` method of a `DataSet` and then pass in the result to your `IDBDataAdapter`. If successful, commit your transaction and call `AcceptChanges` on the entire `DataSet`. This has some potential problems because it's possible that the power could go out between the commit statement and the `AcceptChanges`, but fortunately this all happens so fast that such a situation is highly unlikely. Here is an example of how to do this:

```
Private Sub Test()
      Dim da As New SqlDataAdapter("SELECT * FROM SOMETABLE")
      Dim ds As New DataSet
    Dim dt As New DataTable
     ds.Tables.Add(dt)
    Dim cn As New SqlConnection(CONNECTION_STRING)
     Dim tx As SqlTransaction
     Try
          tx = cn.BeginTransaction
          da.Update(ds.GetChanges)
          tx.Commit()
          ds.AcceptChanges()

    Catch ex As SqlException
          tx.Rollback()
```

```
                    System.Diagnostics.Debug.Assert(False, ex.ToString)

            Finally
                cn.Close()
        End Try

    End Sub
```

Now you can do away with the intermediate step of getting the changes, and just specify the `AcceptChangesDuringUpdate` property of the adapter as false. This will prevent the adapter from calling `AcceptChanges` on each row as it updates them. Here's an example of how this works:

```
Private Sub Test()
        Dim da As New SqlDataAdapter("SELECT * FROM SOMETABLE")
        Dim ds As New DataSet
      Dim dt As New DataTable
        ds.Tables.Add(dt)
        Dim cn As New SqlConnection(CONNECTION_STRING)
        Dim tx As SqlTransaction
        Try
            tx = cn.BeginTransaction
            da.AcceptChangesDuringUpdate()
            da.Update(ds.GetChanges)
            tx.Commit()
            ds.AcceptChanges()

        Catch ex As SqlException
            tx.Rollback()
            System.Diagnostics.Debug.Assert(False, ex.ToString)

        Finally
            cn.Close()
        End Try

    End Sub
```

Nested Transactions

You can nest `TransactionScope` objects if you need to. There are two ways to do this. For lack of better terminology, we'll call these the "obvious" and the "less obvious" ways. The obvious way entails simply creating another `TransactionScope` object inside the first one:

```
Dim transactionScope As New System.Transactions.TransactionScope
Using transactionScope
    Try
       da.Update(ds.Tables(0))
       da2.OrdersTableAdapter.Update(ds)
         transactionScope.Complete()
   Using transactionScope2
     Try
        da3.Update(ds.Tables(0))
        da4.OrdersTableAdapter.Update(ds)
          transactionScope2.Complete()
```

```
        Finally
            ds.Tables(0).SuspendValidation = False
        End Try

    End Using
    Finally
        ds.Tables(0).SuspendValidation = False
    End Try
End Using
```

As you can see, you can do a single nesting but you can take it as deep as you want:

```
Dim transactionScope As New System.Transactions.TransactionScope
Using transactionScope
Try
da.Update(ds.Tables(0))
da2.OrdersTableAdapter.Update(ds)
transactionScope.Complete()
Using transactionScope2
Try
da3.Update(ds.Tables(0))
da4.OrdersTableAdapter.Update(ds)
transactionScope2.Complete()
Using transactionScope3
Try
da5.Update(ds.Tables(0))
da6.OrdersTableAdapter.Update(ds)
transactionScope3.Complete()

Finally
ds.Tables(0).SuspendValidation = False
End Try
End Using
Finally
ds.Tables(0).SuspendValidation = False
End Try

End Using
Finally
ds.Tables(0).SuspendValidation = False
End Try
End Using
```

The less obvious way entails using one scope, calling a function that in turn contains another scope:

```
Dim transactionScope As New System.Transactions.TransactionScope
Using transactionScope
Try
da.Update(ds.Tables(0))
da2.OrdersTableAdapter.Update(ds)
transactionScope.Complete()
ScopeExample()
Finally
ds.Tables(0).SuspendValidation = False
```

```
      End Try
      End Using

      Public Sub ScopeExample()

      Dim transactionScope As New System.Transactions.TransactionScope
      Using transactionScope
          Try
      da.Update(ds.Tables(0))
      da2.OrdersTableAdapter.Update(ds)
      transactionScope.Complete()

      Finally
      ds.Tables(0).SuspendValidation = False
      End Try
      End Using
      End Sub
```

Transactions in Web Services

Without a doubt, one cool feature of transaction processing is the wrapping of Web Services as serviced components. It makes sense if you think about it. We use Web Services to update data and retrieve it, so why wouldn't the requirements of transactions apply here if we were to use Web Services as a fully functioning communications layer? We begin with an example of a Web Service and explain what it does:

```
<%@ WebService Language="VB" Class="TransactionSamples" %>
<%@ assembly name="System.EnterpriseServices" %>

Imports System
Imports System.Data
Imports System.Data.SqlClient
Imports System.Web.Services
Imports System.Web.Util
Imports System.EnterpriseServices

Public Class TransactionSamples Inherits WebService

 <WebMethod(TransactionOption := TransactionOption.RequiresNew)> _
Public Function InsertRecord(keyValue As Integer) As Integer

     Dim sql As [ String = "INSERT INTO TESTTABLE(KeyField) VALUES (KEYVALUE)"
     Dim cn As New SqlConnection("Integrated
Security=SSPI;database=xxxxxxx;server=xxxxxxxxxx")
     Dim cmd As New SqlCommand(sql, cn)

     cmd.Connection.Open()
     Return myCommand.ExecuteNonQuery()
  End Function

 <WebMethod(TransactionOption := TransactionOption.RequiresNew)> _
Public Function DELETERecord(keyValue As Integer) As Integer

     Dim sql As String = "DELETE FROM TestTable WHERE KeyField = keyvalue"
```

```
        Dim cn As New SqlConnection("Integrated
Security=SSPI;database=xxxxxxx;server=xxxxxxxxxxx")
        Dim cmd As New SqlCommand(sql, cn)

        cmd.Connection.Open()
        Return myCommand.ExecuteNonQuery()
    End Function


<WebMethod(TransactionOption := TransactionOption.RequiresNew)> _
Public Function DELETERecord(keyValue As Integer) As Integer

        Dim sql As String = "UPDATE TestTable SET LastUpdated = GetDate() WHERE
KeyField = keyvalue"
        Dim cn As New SqlConnection("Integrated
Security=SSPI;database=xxxxxxx;server=xxxxxxxxxxx")
        Dim cmd As New SqlCommand(sql, cn)

        cmd.Connection.Open()
        Return myCommand.ExecuteNonQuery()
    End Function
End Class
```

It's hoped that you're thinking this looks really simple. It is. Basically, you just need to add a reference to `EnterpriseServices` and then use some minor attributes. All you need in order to make a method participate in a transaction is to add the `<WebMethod(TransactionOption := TransactionOption .RequiresNew)>` attribute. Actually, you can use any of the `TransactionOptions`, but in this case, `RequiresNew` makes the most sense.

Flow-Through Transactions

One of the newest features that we've come across is what's known as *flow-through transactions*. While a thorough discussion of these could alone span multiple chapters, it's worth a brief discussion. With the advent of Yukon, database logic can now be hosted inside the database server and run through the Common Language Runtime (CLR). Essentially, that means that anything you can write in VB.NET or C# can be stored and used inside Yukon, so you could conceivably have a client-side transaction that updates a database table and calls a CLR stored procedure, which in turn updates a totally different database. CLR stored procedures run in different processes, so previously, even if you were to roll back your client transaction, it would remain inaccessible as far as the CLR procedure was concerned and vice versa. Although it's a fairly complex mechanism, ADO.NET 2.0 will provide a way for transactions to flow through so that a rollback or a commit will span the entire contents of the transaction, both the client-side code and anything executed by the CLR routine.

Getting System.Transactions to Work Correctly

Along the way, we've had some problems getting the new distributed transactions to work, most of which had little to do with the code itself and a lot to do with operating systems and service packs. The following table provides a quick rundown of what is necessary as of the time of this writing:

OS	Requirements
Windows 2000 (Professional)	Service Pack 4
Windows XP	Distributed transactions are disabled by default. They will need to be enabled in order to use System.Transactions fully.
Windows XP SP2	Install Hotfix Q828758.
Windows 2003 (Server)	Both COM+ and DTC support.

Summary

The ADO.NET Team has made life a lot easier for a lot of people. In the past, distributed transactions were often reserved for the realm of 3:33t K0d3rz and the like. (This syntax is often used by Hackers to avoid getting filtered by filtering software. 3:33t K0d3rz is 'H4x0r' for the Elite Coder.) Many developers weren't even aware that they were possible. Many developers tried "rolling their own" solutions, which often created more problems than it solved. Many developers stuck their heads in the ground and pretended that the problems didn't even exist. Prior to COM+, distributed transactions were not much fun to work with. COM+ made things a lot easier. Then .NET simplified the process somewhat but it also complicated it in the sense that now you had to learn the behavior of ADO.NET objects like the DataSet and IDbDataAdapter object.

Therefore, while much of the ADO.NET 2.0 features are evolutionary, the System.Transactions namespace packs a lot of bang for the buck. Not only does it make a lot of previously excruciatingly difficult functionality accessible to the common developer, System.Transactions also makes it pretty fun. By having a consistent and intuitive interface for dealing with transactions and distributed transactions, there will no doubt be a lot more people using them. Furthermore, Microsoft has expanded support for providers such as Oracle and MSMQ, and the Windows file system is rumored to be in the pipeline. There are similar rumors of other major players, such as IBM, extending this functionality to its popular DB2 database. As such, dealing with transactions and distributed transactions is about to get a whole lot more interesting.

Please check the Wrox Web site (at www.wrox.com) for updates to this chapter or for additional information.

For More Information

To complement the information in this chapter, take a look at the following resources:

- ❑ **DataWorks Weblog (straight from the ADO.NET Team)** — http://blogs.msdn.com/dataaccess/

- ❑ **John Papa's Blog** — http://codebetter.com/blogs/john.papa/default.aspx

- ❑ **Sahil Malik's Blog** — http://codebetter.com/blogs/sahil.malik/default.aspx

- ❑ **Frans Bouma's Blog** — http://weblogs.asp.net/fbouma/

- ❑ **Andres Aguilar's Blog** — http://weblogs.asp.net/aaguiar

7

Data Binding

This chapter explores how data binding can be used to improve the quality of applications you build and to increase the speed with which you develop them. Data binding has evolved significantly over the past few releases of .NET as well as in the world of programming as a whole. The .NET Framework, along with ASP.NET and Windows Forms, provide some of the most progressive ideas regarding how to bind your user interface control to data, regardless of the data's source.

> **Data binding defined:** *The programming task of retrieving data from a data source, gluing it to a user interface control, allowing manipulation, including sorting and paging, and optionally changing the data and the synchronization of such changes with the original data source. All of this is accomplished with minimal code creation on the part of the developer.*

In the past, data binding was limited to quick and dirty prototypes, literally binding data to the database query result set that was returned from your database query. You still have that option, but it is now possible to bind to your business objects (commonly called *middle-tier*), which enables one or more layers of abstraction between the application and the database. This can be important depending on the type of application you are building and your own architecture philosophies.

This chapter describes how to use a variety of the mechanisms .NET provides for binding your user interface to your data, and associated techniques to speed up your application development using ADO.NET and Visual Studio.

Windows Forms versus Web Applications

At some point, every developer has the same dream: You begin coding and regardless of your choice of a Windows Forms application or an ASP.NET Web application, all of the things you have learned work equally well in either environment. Usually the dream ends with either a sensation of falling forever or the alarm clock going off. Those of us who have been around a while recognize this as the holy grail of programming, although we realize that it is not likely to happen because of the significant differences in the two development environments.

ASP.NET is almost completely stateless and more request/response-centric. Windows Forms applications, on the other hand, retain state in memory on the client and user interaction that is not request/response-based. These differences lead to a divergence of techniques used in each of the environments. This is definitely true for data binding, as you bring together the user interface with one or more data sources.

As we make our way through data binding, not only will we discuss the capabilities of these two environments, but we'll also explore the differences between the two as well. We will try hard to not confuse you with terms such as "data source" and "DataSource." While they are similar, they are also very different. We will try to explain what we mean by that as we push forward through the two worlds of data binding.

In a perfect world, there would not be such a drastic difference between the programming styles of Windows Forms applications and ASP.NET applications. Some of this can be attributed to environmental differences, some of it to differences in object models and concepts. Furthermore, we can't overlook the fact that some of this difference boils down to a lack of coordination between the different development teams.

The Concept of Data Binding

Whether you use ASP.NET applications or Windows Forms, the high-level concept is the same. You get data from somewhere — your database, a file that you load, XML, an application class that is a business object, or from a far-off Web Service that exposes access to data hidden in a remote system. Regardless of the source, you can generically refer to it as a *data source*.

Data is not very interesting unless you are doing something with it: displaying it, manipulating it, or simply interworking it into a composite with other data. With respect to data binding, we are interested in the visual display and manipulation by the end user of an application.

The ultimate goal of data binding is to provide an efficient way to "glue" a data source to user interface controls that enable users to interact with the data without any knowledge of where the data resides, and to automate, optimize, and reduce the amount of effort and code the developer must create to accomplish the binding of data.

Options for Getting the Data

One of the difficult decisions you must make in developing your applications is which technique you will use to define the interaction with your actual data source. Many would argue that you should pick one and only use that one technique. Personally, we're of the opinion that the world is not that black and white, and it's considerably valuable to think through your data access strategy. We think each of the techniques has its place, which is why so many exist in the product.

The following table highlights the salient pros and cons of each technique you can use to bind to your data source. Use this table with the rest of the book and with your personal application architecture beliefs when deciding what type of application you are building.

Bind To?	Pros	Cons
Database via Dynamic SQL	• Easy to build using drag and drop capabilities in Visual Studio. • Reduced deployment on the database side compared with using stored procedures.	• SQL statements are embedded inside pages of the application and must be duplicated if the same access is required in multiple parts of the application. • Security benefits of stored procedures are not obtained. • It's not possible to tune or modify SQL without deployment of the application. • Syntax errors are not detected until runtime because they're not precompiled by the SQL engine.
Database via SQL Stored Procedures	• SQL statements are not embedded in each page, only the reference to the stored procedure is embedded in each page. • Depending on the SQL engine, some performance improvement may be obtained by the database engine's ability to precompile when a stored procedure is cataloged. If nothing else, DBA or another performance tuning expert can manipulate the query independent of code modifications during performance tuning. • Minor database changes can be hidden from the application by simple modification of the stored procedure, i.e., it doesn't require an application change.	• If business logic is required now or in the future, it will have to be stored either on each page or in the stored procedure, or the code will have to be redesigned to accommodate the business logic. It provides no capability to include "business logic" that is not repeated on each page. Typically, the impact of this isn't seen during initial development but as the application evolves and more rules are developed. • Deployment can be more complex because stored procedures must be deployed at the same time as the code

Table continued on following page

Bind To?	Pros	Cons
Business Objects	• Provides a layer of abstraction on top of a data source, enabling business rules to evolve as the application matures. • Clean separation of the UI from the source of the data and tasks involved in data management. • Rules are consistently implemented and logic is not embedded in each page. • Much of the business object code could be generated to reduce required development and to promote consistency. • Allows use of language capabilities such as inheritance and partial classes to reduce the amount of code and ensure consistency.	• Typically takes longer to develop and can't be created using simple drag and drop techniques.
Web Services	• Like business objects, can provide a higher level of abstraction from the ultimate data source. • Can be wrapped with business objects and the page or form would never know it was a remote service. • Typically, not an all-or-nothing approach and adds nicely to an overall architecture, especially in a broader SOA (Service Oriented Architecture) approach to system integration and service aggregation	• Not drag and drop development. • Can consume more time than typical n-tier business object usage due to complexities involved in Web Service invocation and passing of data.
XML Data	• Can provide a rich capability to express hierarchical data and associated relationships. • Great for readability and interoperability with other applications and systems. Often used for storing things such as site maps. • With increased support in the database to treat XML as a first-class citizen, more and more hybrid relational/XML-centric applications will be built.	• XML does not reflect the same strict relational properties or achieve the same level of performance of traditional relational data from a database.

One-Way Binding versus Two-Way Binding

One-way data binding is easy—we've been doing that for years. Some would argue it has never been robust enough for the high standards needed for enterprise applications. One-way data binding is simply retrieving data from a data source and gluing it to the user interface. Two-way data binding is where it really starts to get interesting because you are taking data to the user interface and all the way back to the data source after users have had a chance to manipulate the data.

Two-way data binding introduces new challenges that arise when a user starts editing (changing) data and then tries to replace it in the data source, which other users are also trying to access for their purposes. *Data concurrency* can become a major issue when you start trying to implement two-way data binding. Retrieval of data is typically easier to accomplish than updating of data because the latter involves things like default values for data and constraints that can occur on data (for example, you may want a column to contain a value that's within the valid range or a set of data defined by a constraint). All of this has to be taken into consideration when you're trying to synchronize backup data that was presented on the user interface from the one-way data binding.

In some ways, Windows Forms applications have the upper hand because they're typically allowed to keep a lot more state information than an ASP.NET application. In a Windows Forms application, without having to retrieve additional data, you can keep original data available for concurrency or a determination of what changed without the same concern that ASP.NET applications have about limiting the amount of data they send to and from the client browser. ASP.NET applications are stateless, which becomes a much bigger issue because now you have to decide where you do the determination of what changed and concurrency checks in the application.

Writing a SELECT statement or something that retrieves data is easy. Dealing with inserts/updates with the possibility of missing values not provided by the user, and values that need to be defaulted, is much more complex. To ensure that we maintain the integrity of our data, we also have to include validation to ensure that somewhere in the pipeline we are validating the data and communicating to the user what needs to be corrected prior to allowing any modification to take place.

As if all that is not enough, we also need a strategy for handling concurrent updates of the data and making sure our strategy is imposed by the controls facilitating the update of the data. Should we just allow overwrites of existing data regardless of whether it was changed by another user? Or do we implement some form of concurrency testing to warn or prevent the new user from overwriting a change? You will find that ADO.NET 2.0, along with the .NET Framework, goes a long way toward providing a set of capabilities that achieves the goal of two-way data binding without major coding on the developer's part.

Now that we've covered some of the high-level aspects of data binding, it's appropriate to start examining the specific details of ASP.NET applications and Windows Forms applications.

Data Binding in ASP.NET

ASP.NET has supported one-way data binding since version 1.x on many of its controls, such as DataGrid and DataList. In version 1.x, you are left on your own when it comes to retrieving the data and binding that to the control. If you have three controls on the page that need the same data, you are responsible for getting each one to its own data.

Often, data doesn't need to be retrieved for each request. For example, product catalog information that is the same for each request can be cached to reduce the number of times you have to go to the database. Again, in version 1.x, all of that was left in your hands to code and to determine how best to ensure that you wrote an efficient application.

ASP.NET 2.0 brings along a new set of controls, concepts, and strategies that can be used in data binding in your Web application. The biggest change is a new control called a *Data Source*. The data source manifests itself in several derived classes/controls that we will be discussing here that provide access to your data and provide the mechanism for dropping them on a page and binding your other controls to the data source. These new data source controls become your facilitators for providing one- and two-way data binding with the controls on your page. New controls such as `DetailView`, `GridView`, and others combined with the Data Source controls now enable you to do everything declaratively using drag and drop, properties, and markup. In addition, they don't require writing any code in order to use them. However, they all still support a rich programmable interface when required. These controls are ASP.NET built-in controls, and they completely implement two-way data binding.

Benefits of the Data Source Concept

One of the benefits of the data source control concept is that it reduces the tendency that developers have of retrieving the same data multiple times on the page. One of the challenges that people face when they start componentizing their controls on a page, whether they are using server controls or user controls, is how to manage data when multiple controls on the page need access to the same data. Whether it's customer information or product information, you need to retrieve that from the database.

All too frequently, each control will independently go to the data source and retrieve that data. The data source concept helps streamline that process by providing a consistent mechanism that enables the application to drop the data source onto the page and tell it what data to get; then controls that need access to that data simply assign that data source control as the `DataSourceID` for that visual control (for example, `DropDownList`).

Custom control developers need to learn how to enable their custom controls to be able to leverage the new data source controls, so they don't fall back on simply retrieving the data again. The advantage is realized by using a consistent model, as well as sharing data sources across controls on a page as much as possible.

The data source concept also provides opportunities to be extended as appropriate. For example, you might be able to make custom DataSource controls that are application specific to make it easier for your development team to use them on the pages. The data source concept enables you to do this without requiring new developers to learn a proprietary new concept.

Data Source Controls Provided with ASP.NET 2.0

The following Data Source controls are provided out of the box with ASP.NET:

Data Source Control Name	Description
SqlDataSource	Provides support for accessing and manipulating SQL relational databases. This is not just Microsoft SQL Server–specific and will work with other databases, including Oracle, IBM DB2, and MySQL.
AccessDataSource	Inherits from SqlDataSource and provides a specialized implementation for working with Microsoft Access databases. Provides only retrieval access and no support for insert, update, or delete operations.
XmlDataSource	Provides support for accessing XML data that is either tabular or hierarchical. Support for Transformation and Xpath filtering is provided. Paging is not available, but caching is, and modification support is provided by directly calling the Save method. Derives from HierarchicalDatasourceControl instead of DataSourceControl.
ObjectDataSource	Provides for interaction with your business objects that expose properties and query/update style methods. Provides a business layer abstraction on top of the true data source, which is typically a SQL engine from one of the vendors. Enables you to use data-binding concepts while still maintaining an n-tier approach to your architecture.
SiteMapDataSource	Provides access to data managed by the Site Map Provider. Allows starting at a specific location in the Site Hierarchy, but does not support modification, sorting, paging, or caching. Derives from HierarchicalDatasourceControl instead of DataSourceControl.

Passing Parameters to Data Source Controls

A lot of thought went into the passing of parameters to DataSource controls to supply the runtime parameters for actions such as selecting, filtering, inserting, and deleting on a DataSource. For example, if you have a grid that you want to fill with customers from a user-selected state only, you could have a drop-down and use a ControlParameter to filter the grid. The recognition that not all data retrieval is for every row in a data source, or that parameters from a client cookie, a query string, or other supported parameter types would be useful, demonstrates the improved level of support and the reduced amount of custom code required.

In prior versions of ASP.NET most of this could not be done declaratively and required lots of custom code to achieve the same results now possible. This capability will streamline parameter management and it goes a long way toward the goal of reduction of hand-coded filters and other command strings simply to pass along to a data source to ensure retrieval of the correct information.

Each of the DataSource controls uses parameters for some aspect of its operations. The most common uses are for Select, Update, Delete, and Filter parameters. All Parameter types are inherited from the type System.Web.UI.WebControls.Parameter and each is contained within a ParameterCollection. The following table contains a list of the parameters that are provided with the framework.

Parameter Type	Description
ControlParameter	This allows a simple method to get a parameter from a control on a page by specification of the control id and the property of the control to fetch.
CookieParameter	This allows pulling value from a cookie that is sent from the client on the request.
SessionParameter	This provides retrieval from the user's session of a parameter value.
ProfileParameter	This allows retrieval from a user's profile.
QueryStringParameter	This allows retrieval from the HTTP query string that was passed with the request.
FormParameter	This allows retrieval from posted form data or other properties on the Request Object. For example this could pull the value from a hidden field.

Validation of Parameter Data

One of the shortfalls of parameters is that they don't validate the data passed to them. For example, if you need a value to be within a certain range, you must validate that on your own. In addition, this must be done in the context of the type of DataSource control you are using. For example, if you are using the SQLDataSource, you will validate by looking at the Parameters collection of the Command instance that is passed in the event arguments:

```
protected void SqlDataSource1_Selecting(object sender,
SqlDataSourceSelectingEventArgs e)
{

if (e.Command.Parameters["@CountryCode"].Value== null)
{
Response.Write("You must pass a country");
e.Cancel = true;
return;
}
if ((string) e.Command.Parameters["@CountryCode"].Value != "US")
{
Response.Write("You must select US as the country");
e.Cancel = true;
}
}
```

In the preceding example, we have implemented the Selecting event from the SQLDataSource control. Because the Selecting event gets control prior to the execution of the SelectCommand, you are able to perform any type of pre-validation and, if necessary, prevent the query from running.

The point of the example is not to prescribe a validation approach but to provide an example of how you would use the Selecting event and how you can use the Cancel property on the SQLDatasourceSelectingEventArgs to indicate to the control that you wish to prevent the query from being performed.

Data Source Caching

Data Source caching enables the Data Source control to save a copy in the ASP.NET cache of the data retrieved by the select command for future use. For example, if you had a Data Source control that was used to load product category information into a drop-down, that information does not change frequently so there is no need to have the database access performed each time the control is used.

Using the caching option on the Data Source control means the data would be retained in the ASP.NET cache for a period of time specified on the Data Source control and utilized by the controls on the page without incurring a database access request.

A complete discussion of ASP.NET caching capabilities is beyond the scope of this book. It basically provides an application-wide, in-memory repository to store items for up to the life of the ASP.NET application. Unlike a user session that is specific to single users, items stored in the ASP.NET Cache are available to all users of the application. The lifetime of items in the ASP.NET Cache is based on a number of factors, including expiration policies established when the item was added. If you are on a Web farm (multiple servers supporting a single application), each server on the Web farm has its own local ASP.NET Cache and is not synchronized with the other servers on the farm.

Another important thing to understand is that these cached items are stored in the *private* cache area, not in the public cache area that is accessible to your application. When it is stored in the cache by the Data Source control, the cache key is generated to ensure that it is unique for the type of control being used. For example, if you are using a SQL DataSource, the key will contain the SelectCommand that is used, and if you are using an ObjectDataSource, it will contain the type name and the method.

If you use a control on multiple pages with exactly the same settings, it will share the copy of the cached data, as you might expect. Minor changes such as extra spaces in the SQL query can cause the Data Source to keep a separate copy of the data in the cache.

Another scenario in which you end up with multiple DataSets in cache is when you use parameters — for example, if you passed a country code to a Data Source control that was used to populate a drop-down list of states. Regardless of whether you use it as a parameter to a SQLDataSource or an ObjectDataSource, each different parameter value will result in a different dataset being put in the cache.

By default, caching is not enabled on the DataSource control. You must enable it by setting the EnableCaching property to true. This is not appropriate for all types of data. For example, data that changes frequently is not a good candidate to be cached by the DataSource control.

You can control how long the data is stored in the Cache by using duration, expiration policies, and events to tie it all the way to data in your SQL Server database. The following table describes some of the key properties that control caching on the DataSource controls.

Property	Description/Comments
CacheDuration	Time in seconds that the Data Source control will keep the data in ASP.NET Cache after the SelectMethod is invoked.
CacheExpirationPolicy	Establishes whether the expiration is a sliding window or an absolute time.

Table continued on following page

Property	Description/Comments
CacheKeyDependency	Used to define a key that is used by another cached object (Object #2), so that if that object (Object #1) is removed from cache this object/(Object #2) should be removed also. For example, if you had a CatalogData key that all other catalog data was dependent on and you wanted to force a refresh of all data, you would merely delete the CatalogData object from cache, and all dependent items would be removed.
SQLCacheDependency	Specifies a semicolon-delimited list of connection string/table name pairs that define dependencies on a SQL database.

Making Your Cache Dependent on SQL Data

SQLCacheDependency enables you to set up a cache dependency based on your SQL Server data. The advantage of this is that it avoids having to refresh cache data at a specific time, regardless of whether the source of the data has changed.

SQLCacheDependency will work with SQL 7, SQL 2000, and SQL 2005. In SQL 2005, it is optimized and uses the full Notification Services capabilities of the database engine to perform the notification.

In order to use SQLCacheDependency, you must enable it on both the database and the specific table. There are currently two standard ways to accomplish this: You can use the aspnet_regsqlcache command-line utility that ships with the Framework, or you can do it programmatically via the SQLCacheDepenedencyAdmin class that is part of the System.Web.Caching namespace.

Choosing a Caching Technique

A discussion on using the ASP.NET cache would not be complete without a discussion of when you should use the different types of caching available in ASP.NET. In addition to the caching capabilities in the DataSource control, ASP.NET also enables you to do different types of caching: page-level caching, user-control caching, and programmatically by using the Cache object directly.

Page-level caching allows the same cached copy of a page to be delivered to requestors based on duration as well as query string to determine how long page contents are cached and how many different instances of the page are kept. User-control caching allows the same style of control, but only for the region that is rendered for that user control: all other content on the page is regenerated on each request. Data Source caching provides the capability to store the raw data from a query and does not cache any of the rendered output that the controls using the data create.

Type of Caching	When to Use/Comments
Page-level caching	This is great to use when all of the content on the page does not vary on a request-by-request basis. For example, if you present a product information page, and no pricing or any other information varies by user, then you could probably use page-level caching and vary your caching by the product ID to enable each product to be cached.

Type of Caching	When to Use/Comments
User-control caching	This approach is appropriate when only a region of a page contains content that is the same for each request.
Data Source caching	This option is great for caching data that feeds a specific control on the page. The capability to turn on SQL Cache Dependency on a Data Source provides a convenient way of refreshing the cached data if the underlying data source changes.
Direct storage in ASP.NET Cache	This is great for data that is not necessarily used with a single control, or has other reasons for existence. It requires additional code to load and to maintain data in cache compared to other caching approaches.

One of the other features that page and user-control offer is *vary by caching*. This type of caching enables you to keep multiple copies based on query string, session, or other custom methods.

The ASP.NET UI Controls

Regardless of the DataSource control that you choose, the end target is one of the many controls that come standard with Visual Studio or one of those custom controls that choose to work with the DataSource capabilities.

The following table describes some of the new controls in Visual Studio 2005 that are designed to leverage the capabilities of the Data Source concept for data binding:

Control	Description/Comments
GridView	GridView is the DataGrid all grown up. It picks up where DataGrid fell short and provides robust capabilities to show a table of data. If the Data Source control supports it, it will provide sorting, paging, and even in-place editing of the rows of data. This control should be considered for places where you used DataGrid in prior versions.
DetailsView	Making its debut appearance in ASP.NET 2.0, the DetailsView provides a much needed capability to quickly provide a table view of a single row from a data source. When enabled, it allows the adding and editing of data. Pair this control up with the GridView to provide a master detail view of data.
FormView	At first, we thought FormView existed simply to confuse us as to when to use this instead of DetailsView. In reality, it provides more ability to control the layout of the data. Like DetailsView, it can also be used to facilitate master–detail scenarios.

In addition to the controls highlighted above, most of the standard controls such as DropDownList, DataList, Repeater, and others have been upgraded to be able to take advantage of the data source concept. You can also extend the concept into your own controls or extend the existing controls to add capabilities that are required for your specific project. For example, you could easily define your own class that inherits from DropDownList and adds special features that are relevant to your own project.

If you're building a custom control from scratch, you could tie into the Data Source concept so users would have a consistent way of binding data. A more complete discussion of this is beyond the scope of this book.

SQLDataSource Control

The SQLDataSource provides the capability to interact with the database directly to either execute SQL text commands or invoke stored procedures on the target database. Although the name suggests that this control is applicable only for Microsoft SQL Server, that's not the case at all. The SQLDataSource is capable of interacting with any ADO.NET data provider.

Configuring the SQLDataSource Using the Wizard

After dragging a SQLDataSource onto your Web Form, the SQLDataSource Configuration Wizard will start up and begin to prompt you for the options required to let the control know how to access the data.

All of the options you can set via the wizard you can also set programmatically, or from the properties page, or simply on the element in the markup:

1. **Configuring the ConnectionString:** The first step in the wizard is establishing the connection to your database. This is where you will be prompted to select an existing connection string or to create a new one, as shown in Figure 7-1.

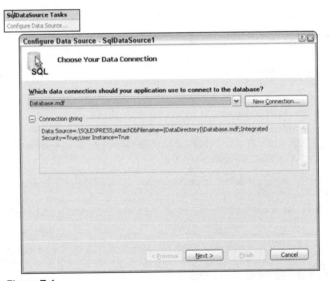

Figure 7-1

2. **Configuring where to save the ConnectionString:** The most important decision you will make now is where to store the connection string (see Figure 7-2). You can either store the connection string on the markup for the control, or have it update your application configuration (Web .config) and insert an entry in the new <connectionStrings> section. The best practice here is to utilize the configuration file to prevent duplication of the settings on each data source.

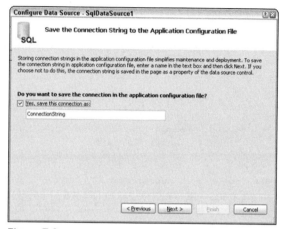

Figure 7-2

If you were to peek into web.config after the wizard runs, you would see the connection string that was added to the new `<connectionString>` section that is new for .NET 2.0, as shown in Figure 7-3.

```
<configuration xmlns="http://schemas.microsoft.com/.NetConfiguration/v2.0">
    <appSettings/>
    <connectionStrings>
        <add name="ConnectionString"
            connectionString="Data Source=.\SQLEXPRESS;AttachDbFilename=|DataDirectory
            providerName="System.Data.SqlClient" />
    </connectionStrings>
```

Figure 7-3

3. In this step, you will configure the columns of the SELECT statement that will be used or indicate that you desire to use a custom query or stored procedure (see Figure 7-4).

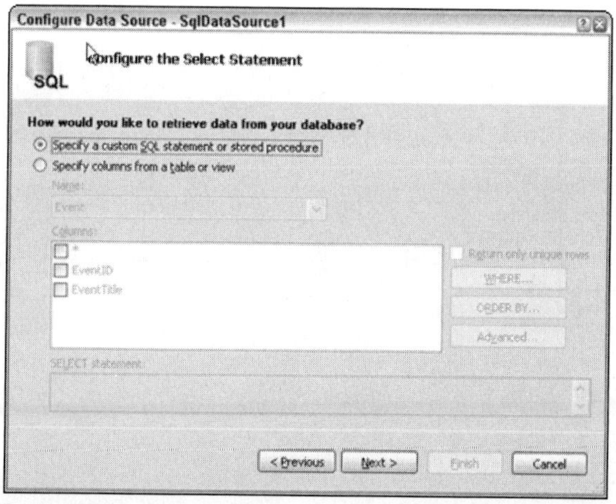

Figure 7-4

Keep in mind that if you select the columns here, the query will be embedded on the aspx page markup and will be duplicated if you have other pages that use the same query.

Now is a good time to reiterate that using SQL embedded will ultimately result in increased maintenance costs. It is recommended that larger applications, at a minimum, use stored procedures or the `ObjectDataSource` with either your own business objects or typed datasets and table adapters.

Another important thing to consider here is that if you select "*", you will get back every column for the table. If you only needed two of the columns, this would be wasting resources, especially if you are enabling caching of the results.

Additionally, if you are using a control like `GridView` and have the Auto Generate Columns option turned on, the columns that appear on your page could change in the future simply by someone adding a column to the table. While some might view that as a benefit to using the "*" approach, you might expose some data that you did not intend to show the end user. Another problem that might occur is that your page formatting might suffer when new fields are added.

4. **Configuring the Custom Select, Insert, Update, or Delete:** Either by typing in a SQL statement or by using Query Builder, this page (see Figure 7-5) enables you to define the commands separately for `SELECT`, `UPDATE`, `INSERT`, and `DELETE`.

If you need to use parameters in your SQL statement, you must specify them as placeholders in your query, as shown below:

```
Select eventid, eventtitle from event where eventid = @eventid
```

By specifying a placeholder for a parameter, the wizard will take you to a new page that enables you to configure a source for the parameters you defined.

Alternatively, you can select the stored procedure radio button, which enables you to select from existing stored procedures. If you have not defined any stored procedures in your database, this list will not be enabled. You would have to add your stored procedures and then rerun the configuration on the `SQLDataSource` control in order to see them.

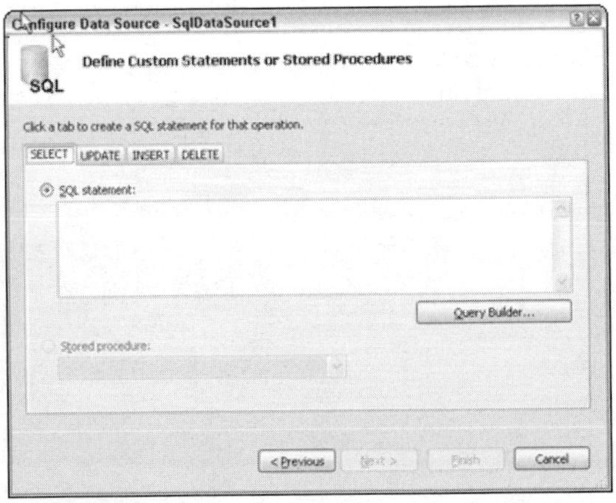

Figure 7-5

Configuring by Using the Property Page

Selecting one of the Query properties on the Property Page will bring up the dialog shown in Figure 7-6, enabling you to modify the query. You can also use this dialog to establish and modify the parameters that populate data for the query.

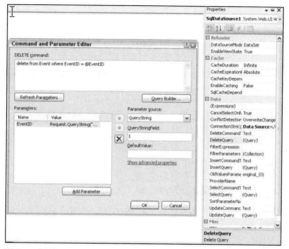

Figure 7-6

You should pay particular attention to your parameters regardless of the type of DataSource control you are using. Make sure you handle cases in which the value is not available, or have provided a default value property setting for each parameter. If you fail to set the default value and the value is not available (null) you will receive an error in most cases if you do not handle it as part of your processing.

Dragging and Dropping a Table

Some do it on purpose, others do it by accident, but we all try dragging a table from Server Explorer onto the Web form. When you drag a table from a database connection listed in Server Explorer (see Figure 7-7) onto a Web form, Visual Studio automation will kick in.

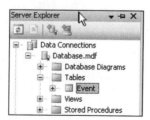

Figure 7-7

After you drag and drop the Event table onto the Web form, Visual Studio will generate markup to add a `GridView` and a `SQLDataSource` to the form (see Figure 7-8). While convenient for demos or quick-and-dirty prototypes, the significant drawback of this technique is that you end up with SQL sprinkled throughout all of your pages.

```
<asp:GridView ID="GridView1" runat="server" AutoGenerateColumns="False"
    DataSourceID="SqlDataSource1"
    EmptyDataText="There are no data records to display.">
    <Columns>
        <asp:BoundField DataField="EventID" HeaderText="EventID"
            ReadOnly="True" SortExpression="EventID" />
        <asp:BoundField DataField="EventTitle"
            HeaderText="EventTitle" SortExpression="EventTitle" />
    </Columns>
</asp:GridView>
<asp:SqlDataSource ID="SqlDataSource1" runat="server"
    ConnectionString="<%$ ConnectionStrings:ConnectionString %>"
    ProviderName="<%$ ConnectionStrings:ConnectionString.ProviderName %>"
    SelectCommand="SELECT [EventID], [EventTitle] FROM [Event]">
</asp:SqlDataSource>
```

Figure 7-8

This technique is best reserved for prototypes or what will later be converted to either stored procedure or business objects.

Key Properties of the SQLDataSource

The following table describes a subset of the key properties of the SQLDataSource control and some associated comments regarding their use. Consult the MSDN documentation for a complete list of every property on the control.

Property	Description/Comments
DataSourceMode	Controls how the data is retrieved either in a DataSet or using a DataReader. If controls that use the DataSource require control over paging and sorting, DataSet is required or it will generate an error. If you only require a simple population of a control, using a DataSet would not provide any advantage over using the DataReader and the DataReader will typically perform better in this case.
CancelSelectOnNullParameter	This gives you control if the Select should happen when any value within the select parameter collection is null. This can be powerful to control the query from happening but it can also be tough to debug if you aren't careful with your selection of parameters. For example, if you have a state and country drop-down, you don't want to do the query if the user hasn't picked a country yet; therefore, if country is null, you don't want the Select query to fire.
ConflictDetection	Only applies during Update or Delete operations and specifies whether the control should try to detect changes in the underlying data source. The default value is Overwrite and will not do checks of the current values on the underlying data.

Property	Description/Comments
ProviderName	ProviderName enables you to specify a different ADO.NET provider using the invariant name. This defaults to System.Data.SqlClient, but it can be set to any registered provider. For example, Oracle would be System.Data.OracleClient.

Beware of Provider-Specific Syntax

The SelectCommand, UpdateCommand, InsertCommand, and DeleteCommand properties all provide the SQL strings that are passed to the active provider set using the ProviderName property. These strings are sensitive to the specific SQL syntax supported by the provider. For example, parameters are specified to the SQLClient provider using "@MyParm". However, if you were using ODBC or OleDb, the parameter would be specified with a placeholder of "?" instead of "@".

The provider-specific nature of the commands highlights an important disadvantage associated with using the SQLDataSource in your applications, as it ties them directly to the provider you choose. Many believe that this lack of abstraction on top of your data is reason enough to not use this type of control. Conversely, on the positive side, because the syntax is specific to a provider, you can leverage provider capabilities without having to dumb down your syntax to a common specification that typically would preclude use of vendor-specific features.

One way to partially mitigate some of your exposure to this problem is to define a library of DataSource controls that inherit from SQLDataSource and are used by your developers. These controls can specify all of the necessary provider-specific information. This would be more business-centric controls — for example, ProductDataSource. While under the covers it is just a SQLDataSource, the developer could drag it from the Toolbox and use it without setting any of the properties unless required to deviate from the typical settings. This is also a way to promote consistency across your pages and prevents specific SQL or SP calls from littering the pages. An even more advanced version of this concept could be leveraged using tools such as CodeSmith or other code-generation helpers to build these based on templates for all of the data objects in your ultimate data source.

The following is a class that inherits from SQLDataSource and presets the values of several of the properties. If this is placed in a separate class library and referenced by an ASP.NET project, it will auto-register in the toolbox and allow drag and drop onto the page preconfigured. This simple example only begins to show some of the creative ways you can reduce redundancy. In the derived class, you could easily check the provider and include variations of the SQL as necessary for the syntax of the database:

```
using System;
using System.Data;
using System.Web.UI;
using System.Web.UI.WebControls;
using System.Web.Configuration;
using System.Configuration;
using System.ComponentModel;
using System.Collections;
namespace testCacheLib
{
```

```
//[ ToolboxData("<{0}:EventListDataSource    runat=server></{0}:EventListDataSource
>")]
 [ToolboxData("<{0}:EventListDataSource  runat=server></{0}:EventListDataSource>")]
public class EventListDataSource : System.Web.UI.WebControls.SqlDataSource
{
    public EventListDataSource()
    {
        this.SelectCommand = "SELECT [EventID], [Title], [EventDate] FROM [Events]";

    }

    protected override void OnInit(EventArgs e)
    {
        try
        {
            ConnectionStringSettings conString =
            WebConfigurationManager.ConnectionStrings["ASPNETDBConnectionString1"];
                this.ConnectionString = conString.ConnectionString;
                this.ProviderName = conString.ProviderName;
        }
        catch
        { }

    }

  }
}
```

The following example shows what the markup would look like using a typical SQLDataSource. Note that the query is inline. If this were used on more than one page, each one would have the redundant query inline:

```
<asp:SqlDataSource ID="SqlDataSource1" runat="server"
        ConnectionString="<%$ ConnectionStrings:ASPNETDBConnectionString1 %>"
        ProviderName="<%$ ConnectionStrings:ASPNETDBConnectionString1.ProviderName
%>"
        SelectCommand="SELECT [EventID], [Title], [EventDate] FROM [Events]">
    </asp:SqlDataSource>
```

The following code shows what the markup would look like using the custom control class derived from a SQLDatasource, and has the queries specified in the class:

```
        <cc1:EventListDataSource ID="eventDS1" runat="server">
        </cc1:EventListDataSource>
```

As you can see from the preceding example, this can reduce the redundancy and centralize the settings. It would also allow for many more creative things to be done inside the derived class. The fact that it allows drag and drop from the toolbox preconfigured is also a plus.

ObjectDataSource Control

The ObjectDataSource is one of the most powerful feature additions to data binding in ASP.NET 2.0. It provides a declarative method of using objects in your data binding. Previously, if you wanted to bind to objects, you did it either programmatically or via cryptic "eval" statements in your page HTML markup. The `ObjectDataSource` control provides the glue, like all other Data Source controls, between your object (the data source) and your UI elements, such as a `GridView`.

The `ObjectDataSource` provides the means to further abstract your application from the specifics of your data storage strategy. With the `SQLDataSource`, if you want to insert business logic, you would have to either write it in SQL or use a managed CLR object in the database. The `ObjectDataSource`, however, enables you to create middle-tier objects to interact with, which can implement more sophisticated business logic shared across all aspects of your user interface. This type of strategy is even more important if you are building an application that might expose multiple UI faces — for example, an application that has a Smart Client, a Web, and a Mobile client.

Like other `DataSource` controls, `ObjectDataSource` supports the full range of parameters to pass information to selects, updates, and deletes. The `ObjectDataSource` also extends the capability to utilize the Cache for information returned from the `Select` method. You can also still get access to the powerful event model, which can be used to validate query parameters and handle errors that occurred in the process of executing the queries.

Keep in mind that this control can be used for binding to almost any data object; it's not limited to binding to only data retrieved from a database. You can bind to data that is calculated, generated, or pulled from a remote Web Service. You can also use this control to call your own utility methods or pass through to built-in methods. For example, using the new `GetSchema` support in ADO.NET, you can create a drop-down of every table in your database. This would be appropriate for utility-type applications, and demonstrates the value of being able to invoke a broad number of object methods and to facilitate binding to the data returned by them.

If your only excuse for not using the `ObjectDataSource` is that you feel overwhelmed by the thought of using it or you think it might be overly complex, you are not alone. We had similar feelings when we first used it. After experimentation with all of the various options, however, we're no longer intimidated. Unless we were doing a simple throwaway application, it would be hard to justify not using the `ObjectDataSource` over some of the other controls such as `SQLDataSource`. After all, remember that some of the investment you make up front you gain back as you maintain your application over the course of its life.

Several chapters could be written on the `ObjectDataSource` and the related philosophy on application architecture, but here we will try to give you an idea of how it fits with the overall data-binding strategy in Visual Studio, leaving those academic discussions for another time:

```
<asp:ObjectDataSource ID="ObjectDataSource1" runat="server" CacheDuration="600"
    EnableCaching="True" SelectMethod="GetData" TypeName="MyBusinessObject">
        <SelectParameters>
            <asp:QueryStringParameter DefaultValue="US" Name="state"
                QueryStringField="State" Type="String" />
        </SelectParameters>
</asp:ObjectDataSource>
<asp:GridView ID="GridView1" runat="server" DataSourceID="ObjectDataSource1"/>
```

Key Properties of the ObjectDataSource Control

The following table describes a subset of the properties of the `ObjectDataSource` control and some associated comments regarding their use. Consult the MSDN documentation for a complete list of all of the properties on the control.

Property	Description/Comments
ConflictDetection	Use to CompareAllValues or OverwriteChanges.
DataObjectTypeName	Partially or fully qualified type string that specifies the data type that can be used as a parameter for the various commands.
SelectMethod	Identifies the method to be called when select action is invoked on the data source control. This method can return an IEnumerable or a DataSet. If the method returns a DataSet, it can be cached using the automatic caching capability using EnableCaching=true.
UpdateMethod	Identifies the method to be called when an update is required by the data source. Parameters to this method are identified by the UpdateParameters collection.
InsertMethod	Method called to insert data; parameters are identified by the InsertParameters property.
DeleteMethod	Method called to delete data; parameters are identified by the DeleteParameters property.
MaxiumRowsParameterName	Identifies the parameter on the SelectMethod that will identify the maximum number of rows to retrieve when data paging is enabled.
SelectCountMethod	Method that ObjectDataSource will call to get a count of rows.

Key Events on the ObjectDataSource

In order to allow you greater control over what happens on an ObjectDataSource, several events are exposed that enable you to tap into the life cycle of the control. Events provide the necessary hooks to enable you to capture, evaluate, and perform both preprocessing and post-processing actions during the life cycle of the ObjectDataSource. The following table represents a subset of the public events on the control:

Event	Description/Comments
Deleted	Occurs after the delete operation has already been completed.
Deleting	Occurs before a delete operation happens.
Inserted	Occurs after the new data has been inserted.
Inserting	Occurs prior to the insert operation happening.
ObjectCreated	Occurs after the object identified by TypeName is created.
ObjectCreating	Occurs before the object identified by TypeName is created.
ObjectDisposing	Allows notification that the TypeName object is being disposed.

Event	Description/Comments
Selecting	Occurs before the select operation is performed. This would be a good place to validate that parameters for select are valid. You can use the Cancel flag in the EventArgs if you need to cancel the query, as demonstrated earlier in the SQLDataSource control.
Selected	Occurs after the select operation has completed. This is a good place to handle errors that were raised as a result of the query.
Updating	Occurs before the update is invoked.
Updated	Occurs after the update has occurred.

Note that events are only called if you are not using Static (shared in VB) methods. If you are using static methods, then the events are not invoked as part of the processing life cycle.

One way that you can use the events is to trap errors that occur during invocation of the methods. For example, if the SelectMethod threw an exception, the user would receive the error on the page. Instead, you can hook into the Selected event, which happens after the SelectMethod is attempted, and evaluate the Exception parameter of the ObjectDataSourceStatusEventArgs that is passed to the event handler. The following example simply forces it to ignore the error. However, you can add whatever logic is appropriate for your application.

```
protected void ObjectDataSource1_Selected(object sender,
        ObjectDataSourceStatusEventArgs e)
{
    if (e.Exception != null)
        e.ExceptionHandled = true;
}
```

Supporting Paging

In order to support paging on an ObjectDataSource control, you must set the following properties on the control:

Property	Description/Comments
EnablePaging	This must be set to true to indicate that you want to support paging. Other conditions, below, must also be set up in order for this to not produce an error.
StartRecordParameterName	This is the name of the parameter for the SelectMethod that the object will use to know what record to start at during execution of the select method.
MaxRecordsParameterName	Specifies the parameter on the SelectMethod that contains the number of records that will be retrieved.
SelectCountMethod	Used to retrieve a total row count when paging is enabled.

Building a Class to Work with ObjectDataSource

The first order of business is understanding what can be the target of an `ObjectDataSource` control. The target class can expose either *static methods* (shared in VB) or *instance methods*. If the class implements static methods, an instance of the class is not required each time the data source is participating in the page life cycle.

> *Objects invoked by the* `ObjectDataSource` *are not kept around for the life of the Web request. If you require expensive startup or state information, you must find alternative methods to maintain or load the information so it does not happen each time your object is instantiated by the* `ObjectDataSource` *control.*

In the following example, we are going to build a simple business object that will be implemented using two classes. The first class will be a data class that contains public properties and operations that act on those data elements. The second class will be our business object class, which implements the methods we will use to select, update, insert, and delete data by our data source. We could also easily accomplish this with one class, combining the two together. There are pros and cons for both approaches, which are beyond the scope of this book. Keep in mind also that in a real application, these classes would contain additional business rules that are excluded here because they are not required to illustrate how the `ObjectDataSource` works.

C# Data Class Sample Code

The following class implements the data class and contains all the properties for the data object:

```
using System;
using System.Data;
using System.Configuration;
using System.Web;
using System.Web.Security;
using System.Web.UI;
using System.Web.UI.WebControls;
using System.Web.UI.WebControls.WebParts;
using System.Web.UI.HtmlControls;

/// <summary>
/// Represents the data object for Events
/// </summary>
public class EventData
{

    private int       m_EventID = 0;
    private string    m_EventTitle = "";

  public EventData()
  {

  }

  public int EventID
  {
     get
     {
        return m_EventID;
```

```
        }
        set
        {
            m_EventID = value;
        }

    }

    public string EventTitle
    {
        get
        {
            return m_EventTitle;
        }
        set
        {
            m_EventTitle = value;
        }

    }
}
```

C# Business Object Class Sample Code

The following class is an example of a database class that implements methods that will interact with ADO.NET and return instances of the preceding data class or a `DataTable` as appropriate:

```
using System;
using System.Data;
using System.Configuration;
using System.Web;
using System.Web.Security;
using System.Web.UI;
using System.Web.UI.WebControls;
using System.Web.UI.WebControls.WebParts;
using System.Web.UI.HtmlControls;

/// <summary>
/// Summary description for EventLogic
/// </summary>
public class EventLogic
{
 public EventLogic()
 {

 }

 public static DataTable SelectData()
 {
     return new DataTable();
 }

 public static EventData SelectData(int EventID)
 {
```

```
    //*Go get data from somewhere here....

    return new EventData();
}

public static void InsertData(EventData data)
{
    //do insert of data to actual data source here
}

public static void UpdateData(EventData data)
{
    //do update logic here
}

public static void DeleteData(int EventID)
{
    //do delete logic here
}

}
```

Using Your Objects on the Page

Using your objects with an `ObjectDataSource` is just a drag-and-drop from the toolbox away. All you have to do is drag an `ObjectDataSource` onto the Web form and it will automatically start the Configuration Wizard (see Figure 7-9).

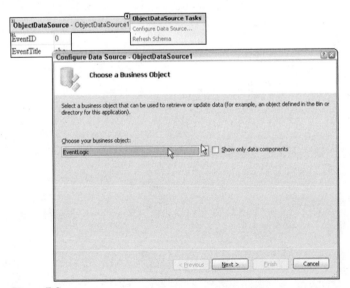

Figure 7-9

The Configuration Wizard will first prompt you to pick which class you want to use by presenting you with a drop-down menu of all of the classes referenced by your project. For a large project, this list can be rather tedious to wade through. It is hoped that a future release will provide more flexibility in how you pick your class to avoid searching through hundreds of referenced classes. If this becomes too tedious, you aren't limited to using the wizard, as all of the options can be set via the properties page for the ObjectDataSource, declaratively through markup, or programmatically in your code behind.

One thing to note is that unlike with the SQLDataSource, you do not have to specify any connection string information. All of this is assumed to be managed by the object you are connecting to and is not configured by the ObjectDataSource.

Defining the Methods to Use

Now that we have picked the object, the next step (see Figure 7-10) is to define which method we will use for selecting data. The wizard makes this easy by providing a drop-down list of all the available methods. If you're like us, you will probably forget to mark a method as public and wonder why it doesn't show up in the list. Yes, each method shown must be public — keep in mind that ObjectDataSource uses reflection to invoke these methods.

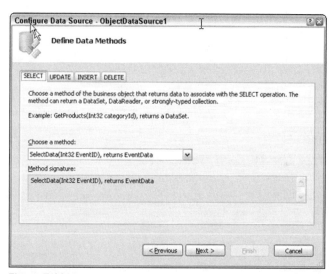

Figure 7-10

You are not required to call your select method "select" and your delete method "delete" — you are free to call your methods whatever is appropriate for your application. You can also have multiple methods on an object and determine which one to use based on the setup of the ObjectDataSource. For example, you could have a SelectByProductCategory and a SelectByProductManager — each having a different audience and probably used on different pages.

Defining the Parameters

If your object requires one or more parameters, the next page in the wizard (see Figure 7-11) will help you configure where the parameters will be passed. Remember from our prior discussion of Data Source parameters that these can come from a variety of sources, including a query string, another control, or a cookie. Using the wizard, you can configure each parameter that is required by the object method. These will be stored in the `SelectParameters` collection on the markup if you were to look at it on the source view. One common thing you might do here is pull the value from another control on the page — for example, a drop-down list that is used to filter a detail `GridView`.

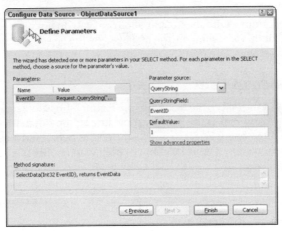

Figure 7-11

If your Insert or Update takes a data type object, it will most likely be able to identify that and set the property for you as you go through the wizard. Otherwise, you must specify the `DataObjectTypeName` manually via the property.

Modifications after the Wizard Completes

Don't worry if you forget to specify something or the wizard closes before you are done — you can access all of the settings later by either rerunning the configure data source or using the properties from the Property panel, as shown in Figure 7-12.

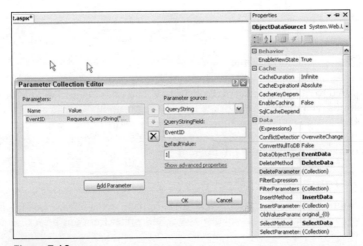

Figure 7-12

If you look under the hood at the markup generated by the wizard, as shown in Figure 7-13, you will see it has added an `ObjectDataSource`, and each of the properties are set as you instructed via the wizard.

```
<asp:ObjectDataSource ID="ObjectDataSource1" runat="server" SelectMethod="SelectData"
    TypeName="EventLogic" DataObjectTypeName="EventData" DeleteMethod="DeleteData"
    InsertMethod="InsertData" UpdateMethod="UpdateData">
    <SelectParameters>
        <asp:QueryStringParameter DefaultValue="1" Name="EventID" QueryStringField="EventID"
            Type="Int32" />
    </SelectParameters>
    <DeleteParameters>
        <asp:QueryStringParameter DefaultValue="1" Name="EventID" QueryStringField="EventID"
            Type="Int32" />
    </DeleteParameters>
</asp:ObjectDataSource>
```

Figure 7-13

Binding to a Control

Regardless of the type of `DataSource` control you are using, the `DataSource` does not render any user interface elements. In order for the data to show up, you must identify this data source on the `DataSource` property of a UI element such as the `GridView`. Most likely, you have already done this because when you add a `GridView` it will prompt you to find the `DataSource` or create a new one.

Table Adapter and Typed DataSets

The typed `DataSet` designer has been reinvented for Visual Studio 2005 and is now separate from the XML Schema editor. While having a schema for the typed dataset is still a cornerstone of its implementation, it was important to enable the `DataSet` designer to evolve on a separate course.

Figure 7-14 shows the design view of two tables in a typed dataset. Notice at the bottom of the table the table adapter methods that have been defined for that table.

One of the architectural decisions you will make in building an application is whether you use typed datasets in your application. In addition to the capability to define the `DataSet` and related tables, you can now define a type-safe data access layer using `TableAdapters`. A simple way of looking at a table adapter is to think of it as a type-safe `DataAdapter`. For example, if the `SelectCommand` were defined to select by `ProductID`, a `FillByProductID` method would be defined and a typed parameter of `ProductID` would be on the method. Like typed `DataSets`, the `TableAdapters` are designer-generated by Visual Studio.

By default, the `TableAdapter` will inherit from Component and will encapsulate a `Data Adapter`. This means that while it looks and smells like a `Data Adapter`, you will get an `InvalidCastException` if you try to cast a `TableAdapter` to a `DataAdapter` object. Note that you can change the base class of the generated `TableAdapter` to be a custom project-specific class that inherits from Component. You do this by setting the base class property in Dataset Designer. Doing this in a project would allow common capabilities to be shared across all of your `TableAdapters`. This is a great way to make sure your favorite helper methods are always available.

When you add a `DataSet` to your project and select the Configure option on a table, the `TableAdapter` Configuration Wizard will help you add methods to the Typed `DataSet`. If you already have a Dataset defined you can still leverage the `TableAdapter` Configuration Wizard on existing datasets.

Figure 7-14

Once configured and defined, a Typed Dataset can be utilized on a page by dragging an `ObjectDataSource` onto the page and pointing it at the Typed Dataset.

From an architectural perspective, this technique provides one more layer of separation than is provided by directly using the `SQLDataSource`. By having that layer of abstraction, you could also share your typed datasets easily across projects and gain more continuity in data access. Without getting stuck on the debate of whether an object or a typed dataset approach is better architecture, there is a general consensus that using either is more robust than doing direct SQL queries from the page, as `SQLDataSource` encourages.

DBDirect Methods

In addition to the `InsertCommand`, `UpdateCommand`, and `DeleteCommand`, a `TableAdapter` defines type-safe methods that can be called to directly manipulate the database via Insert, Update, and Delete calls. The Insert and Update methods will take as arguments all of the fields of a particular table. You can turn off the creation of these methods by setting the `GenerateDBDirectMethods` property to `false`. Figure 7-15 shows an example of an Insert DBDirect method.

```
[System.ComponentModel.DataObjectMethodAttribute(System.ComponentModel.DataObjectMethodType.Insert, true)]
public virtual int Insert(string StateCode, string StateName, string CountryCode) {
    if ((StateCode == null)) {
        throw new System.ArgumentNullException("StateCode");
    }
    else {
        this.Adapter.InsertCommand.Parameters[0].Value = ((string)(StateCode));
    }
    if ((StateName == null)) {
```

Figure 7-15

A word of caution with these methods: If you use these directly in your code, any change to add columns to your table will require all calling applications to be updated to the new method signature, because they require the full set of parameters.

To avoid this, either define an overloaded method that takes the old number of arguments and defaults the new values, or simply create a new public method that takes a row object instead of the individual column values. Figure 7-16 shows an example.

```
namespace WindowsApplication7.DatabaseDataSetTableAdapters
{
    public partial class StateTableAdapter
    {
        public virtual int Insert(DataSet1.StateRow stateRow)
        {
            return Insert(stateRow.StateCode, stateRow.StateName, stateRow.CountryCode);
        }
    }
}
```

Figure 7-16

In the preceding example, we create a partial class that will join together with our generated `TableAdapter`. We add our own `Insert` method, which takes a `StateRow` instead of the individual fields. This new method is simply a pass-through to the generated `Insert` method that Visual Studio built and requires all the columns as individual parameters to the method. Because the new method we defined takes a single parameter, the `StateRow` object will not be required to change any calling code if we add a new column, as long as it has a default value defined.

Configuring the Connection

As you did when configuring a `SQLDataSource`, the first thing you will do is determine what connection string will be used to interact with the database for the `TableAdapter` method calls, as shown in Figure 7-17.

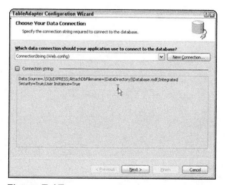

Figure 7-17

Configuring How to Get the Data

Next you will choose between using inline SQL statements or stored procedures, as shown in Figure 7-18. If you select stored procedures, you can either use either existing stored procedures or have the wizard create them for you.

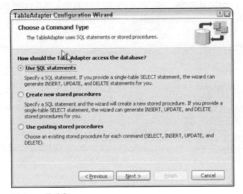

Figure 7-18

Configuring Advanced Options

If you check the Generate Insert, Update, and Delete Statements option, as shown in Figure 7-19, the wizard will attempt to generate `Insert`, `Update`, and `Delete` statements based on your select query.

Refresh the Data Table will cause the data to be reloaded after `insert` and `update` statements. This may not always be appropriate for every application, and in fact can lead to unnecessary overhead in applications for which the data is no longer needed after the insert or update is completed.

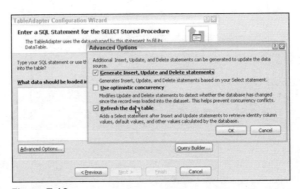

Figure 7-19

Configuring Stored Procedure Names

If you have decided to use existing stored procedures or create stored procedures, this panel (see Figure 7-20) will enable you to specify the names for each type of command. Additionally, you will be able to view the script that will be used to define the stored procedures to the database.

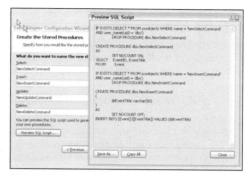

Figure 7-20

Configuring Methods to Generate

One task the wizard will do for you is define basic methods for your table, as shown in Figure 7-21. In addition to these methods, you have the option of adding additional methods later.

Figure 7-21

Generating DataSource Controls

You might have noticed that the data source concept does a good job of reducing the amount of code you have to write to get your data to show on the screen. It also provides the flexibility to choose an approach that is appropriate for your application architecture. What you might not realize yet is that there is very little out of the box that helps you avoid creating these data sources repeatedly. If you had 10 pages that needed a drop-down list containing states or countries, you would be defining 10 Data Source controls, one on each page.

At first, this might not sound all that bad, and in fact it might not even be required all at once — it might creep up on you during the maintenance of your application. Granted, some of this could be dealt with by using User Controls to create page fragments that you reuse on each of the 10 pages, but that approach is not always appropriate.

One of the more powerful solutions you have for this problem is custom data sources in a library that can be reused across the project. You can further enhance that idea by combining your custom data sources with a powerful code generator such as Code Smith, or use other custom techniques — for example, XML/XSLT or a custom application built to generate the controls. These could be configured using metadata from either your object model or data model.

Once you create this library, you could register it on the ToolBox and then your developers would have a simple drag-and-drop approach to adding preconfigured DataSource controls to their pages. This would reduce the redundant work, and it would promote consistency across the pages that use the same type of control. The benefits would likely pay off the first time you had to do maintenance and only had to change one control instead of 10 pages.

So what do we mean by code generation? Well, typically programmers are more and more developing code that will go out and do the data access for you. You see a lot of this directly in Visual Studio 2005, where the wizards are generating code that saves you time and yet still preserves the type-safe nature that promotes quality code.

If you are already using some form of code generation for your data access layer, you could expand the capabilities of your code-generation process to also generate a `DataSource` class. For example, if you are using `SQLDataSource`, you could generate a `ProductDataSource` that inherits from `SQLDataSource` but also automatically sets its properties to be specific to a Product Data Source. This can then be added to the ToolBox and less experienced developers could drag and drop them onto a page for use. This would avoid having the developer reinvent the definition on each page where a similar Data Source is used.

You don't have to do code generation to use this concept. The key is building a common library that contains customized versions of the data source controls, whether you are using a SQL data source, the XML data source, or the object data source. These are then referenced and used in your ASP.NET applications.

Using this custom library, you can derive your own custom class from a SQL data source, a XML data source, or any of the data source controls. Leverage the power of what was already created in terms of the functionality of those controls, but name them in a way that would be meaningful to your development team. Why would you want to do this? By promoting consistency and ease of use, you will see the reward in a more maintainable system that gets to market faster.

By deriving your own classes, you can set the properties the way you want, you can assign meaningful names, and you can enjoy a nice library of controls in the Toolbox, which enables you to simply drag them onto the page. For example, suppose you had a product table and you wanted to have a product data source. By default, a user would drag a SQL data source and repeatedly set the different properties on that control.

By then deriving your own class, you can set those properties in the code (in the derived class); and because it is available in the toolbox, all a user has to do to use the product data source is drag that onto the page. No further manual setting of the properties is required. If you need to change some of the properties on that control later, you have a simple place to do that — you aren't hunting through the code. We believe this is a best practice because simply putting a SQL data source on the page doesn't provide you with a data access layer.

Windows Forms Applications

Windows Forms applications continue to evolve their data-binding strategy with .NET 2.0, including a reduction in complexity, which enables a developer to more easily get the data to show on the form. ASP.NET data binding focuses on binding only the data-oriented properties—Windows Forms enable you to bind almost any property of a control to a data source property. This rich capability can be used to control not only the data that is displayed, but the size, color, and many other aspects of the control.

Keep in mind the differences between the execution environments for ASP.NET and a Windows Forms application. These differences are most noticeable in the way that a Windows Forms application is built on a nonrequest/response basis. This leverages the fact that it is allowed to maintain state easily between user interactions with controls.

Added to Visual Studio 2005 is a new Data Source window that will act as the focal point for all data sources defined to your Windows Forms project. Using the Data Source Configuration Wizard, it is easy to add new sources and configure them for your project. Sources for binding are very flexible, requiring the minimal implementation of the IList interface or one of the ADO.NET data containers such as the DataTable, DataView, etc. The Data Source Window is not just limited to Database-related binding, as you will see when we describe further details about how it works.

It will be clear from your first impression that typed Datasets have improved considerably in the area of usability, and that they are here to stay. In fact, there is no equivalent to the ASP.NET SQLDataSource control that encourages direct database access from your form. You are, however, encouraged to use the Data Source window and to bind to data that is retrieved either via your own custom object or through a Data Component (a typed Dataset and a type-safe DataAdapter).

BindingSource is a new component control that is designed to simplify binding to data, including typed Datasets, Web Services, and custom business objects. Paired with the BindingSource is a new control called the BindingNavigator that provides VCR-like navigation on your BindingSource.

One major change in Windows Form applications is that designer-generated code is no longer intermixed with your code, but instead placed in a formname.designer.cs file. This eliminates the problem in prior versions whereby the generated code could possibly step on your custom code. This capability is supported thanks to the new support for partial classes that was added in .NET 2.0. If you are interested in what happens under the hood, take a peek and browse through the file as you make changes to your application. That can be a great way to understand how some of the parts work together.

Another area highlighting the differences between the capabilities of ASP.NET and Windows Forms involves the loading and saving of data. In an ASP.NET application, the DataSource controls manage the load and save of the data. The BindingSource, while it will pull data from the source, it expects that you have loaded the data into it. Likewise, it expects you to manage the persistence of the data, because you might not necessarily be binding to a persistable object. Ultimately, you are responsible for the code to populate and load the object that is associated with the BindingSource that you are using.

As you start to explore how binding in Windows Forms works, remember that all of this happens in real time and no request/response happens like it does in an ASP.NET application. With that in mind, let's start exploring the changes in more detail.

Where Did My Data Components Go?

Prior to Visual Studio 2005, the toolbox used to have a Data section that contained `SqlConnection`, `SqlCommand`, and so on. These low-level components are no longer available on the toolbox because they promote use of untyped components and the Windows Forms team is pushing hard to convert people to the new model. You will notice that after you add a typed Dataset and Table Adapter to your project, they will automatically show up in the toolbox after your next project build.

The underlying components such as `SqlConnection` and others are still around, and if you are an old dog that can't learn new tricks, you can add them back to your toolbox manually. Doing so, however, would be like doing math with an abacus instead of a calculator. Using the typed capabilities or object references, which are also typed, will promote more robust applications.

Dragging and Dropping a Table

You already saw in ASP.NET that if you drag a table from Server Explorer, it generates a bunch of code for you, but it isn't very robust or useful in production applications. The Windows Forms team took a different approach. They decided not to provide this capability and instead want you to add a new Data Source in the Data Source window.

You can also drag and drop a table from the Server Explorer window onto the `DataSet` designer surface and it will create the table in the `DataSet` and create an associated `TableAdapter` that contains the basic `Fill` method. This will also cause it to show up in your Data Source window.

Once you have defined an item to the Data Source window, you then have the ability to drag and drop that on a form, after which automation will kick in to add a `DataGridView` and associated binding objects that are appropriate.

If you take a second and think about it, this is actually a much more logical process because not only does it allow database-related Data Sources, it also allows for other sources to be corralled into a single window that manages their binding options and allows for drag and drop onto a form.

Data Sources

The Data Source window is new in 2.0 and provides a central focal point for your Data Sources. Unlike Server Explorer, which is not project-specific, the Data Source window only contains data sources that are specific to your active project.

If you are confused about how the Data Source window differs from the Server Explorer window, think of Server Explorer as a list of all your raw database sources. This could be generated from multiple servers. A table in a database on Server Explorer might contain 10 columns, of which only 5 are used on the data source when it is defined on the Data Source window. It is further possible that Table A and Table B are joined together to create a single data source on the Data Source window, whereas they physically exist as two tables on the Server Explorer database list. Items that appear in the Data Source Window are not just database-related data sources. They can also be objects or collections of objects that were configured by the Data Source Configuration Wizard.

Unlike ASP.NET, there is no set of "Data Source" controls that you drag onto your form. Data Sources are interacted with using the new Data Source window, which enables you to drag and drop all or part of a given Data Source onto your form surface. The following table describes the data source types supported:

Data Source	Description/Comments
Database	Allows binding via typed datasets to an SQL provider.
Web Service	Allows for binding to a Web Service via adding a reference.
Object	Allows for referencing an object and easy binding.

In addition to simply keeping a list of the data sources, the Data Source Window also enables you to configure how the source will be rendered when you drag it onto a form. We will discuss this in more detail when we use the Data Source Configuration Wizard in the following section.

Selecting the Type of Data Source

Figure 7-22 shows the empty Data Sources window and the first step of the Data Source Configuration Wizard, which walks you through the selection of a new source. The goal of this wizard is to define a new Data Source that will be listed in your Data Source window and will be available for use in this project to place on forms.

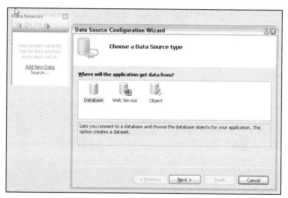

Figure 7-22

Adding and Using a Database Data Source

As shown in Figure 7-23, you choose from an existing connection or add a new connection. After input of the connection options, it will save the connection in the list and you can choose to move ahead. This is where you will choose the provider (e.g., SQL Server, Oracle, etc.).

Next, you will be prompted to save the connection string in your application configuration file. This is important because it will externalize the connection string from your code and allow it to be changed as needed at runtime.

Figure 7-23

Depending on which Data Source (Provider) you choose, the configuration screen options will vary. For example, SQL Server Database File will look different from a typical SQL Server connection, which would have prompted you for the name of the server instead of the name of the file.

Referencing a Local Database File

If the file you choose is a Local SQLExpress database file that is located outside the project, you will be prompted to add the file to the project and modify the connection, as shown in Figure 7-24.

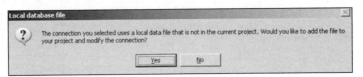

Figure 7-24

Make sure this is really what you want to do because it will take a copy of the database and place it in your project directory. This means that if you have three applications that use the same file, you would end up with three separate copies, and changes made in one project would not be reflected in the other projects.

Choosing Your Database Objects

The next step in the configuration process is to choose what items you want to use from your database. The dialog shown in Figure 7-25 enables you to select one or more tables, including the columns you want included.

If you just created a new database that does not have any objects defined, you may get confused because the panel will appear but you won't have anything to select. You need to define your objects and then re-enter the wizard in order to be able to select items.

After you complete this wizard, a new typed dataset will have been added to your project.

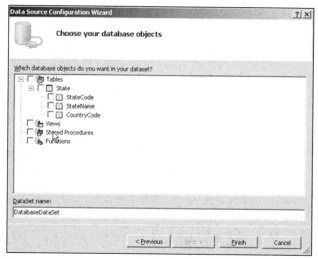

Figure 7-25

Adding and Using an Object Data Source

Selecting Object as the Data Source type enables you to bind to the public properties of any class, or any class that supports the IList interface (for example, `DataView`, `Array`, `ArrayList`, and `Collection`). Figure 7-26 shows you the wizard dialog that will allow you to pick the object you wish to bind to.

Windows Forms are not able to bind to a `DataReader` or `IEnumerable` because they are forward only.

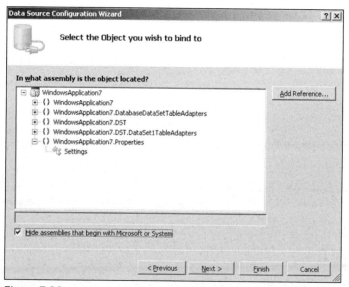

Figure 7-26

Choosing the Type of Control for a Data Source

Now that you have a data source available in your Data Source window, you can customize it prior to dragging it onto a form. Customization enables you to select how you want the item to render when it is placed on a form — for example, a `DataGridView` or a `Details`. Figure 7-27 shows how, by using the drop-down list on the Data Source window, you can make your selection.

Figure 7-27

Additionally, for each property, you can select how you want it to be displayed (or not displayed), as shown in Figure 7-28.

Figure 7-28

You must have a form active in design mode; otherwise, you will not be prompted for these formatting/ display options.

The options shown for each column are based on the item type. Visual Studio enables you to customize that list by selecting the Customize option at the end of the list, and it will walk you through the available options. You can build and add custom controls to the list as long as they follow the specific interface requirements. A full discussion of this is beyond the scope of this book, but it is covered in detail in the MSDN documentation. This capability enables you to plug custom controls into your own applications and use them in an integrated manner with the data-binding capabilities of Visual Studio.

The Windows Form UI Controls

The following table describes two of the new controls in Visual Studio 2005 that are designed to leverage the capabilities of the Data Source concept for data binding:

Control	Description/Comments
DataGridView	Replaces the DataGrid control from previous versions and adds additional capabilities.
BindingNavigator	The BindingNavigator control provides VCR-like controls for navigating through either a grid or detail view of the data.

BindingSource

The BindingSource control is a component control that is the workhorse of the data-binding engine in a Windows Forms application. The BindingSource is the glue between a data source and the UI element that it is binding to, and it acts as an intermediary to ensure a smooth two-way flow of data. The BindingSource is a nonvisual control and does not render any user interface itself.

By design, the BindingSource provides simplification by shielding you from having to deal directly with concurrency management, change notification, and other services, which are encapsulated in the BindingSource control.

If you were to try to find the ASP.NET equivalent, the closest you would get is the DataSource controls (SqlDataSource, ObjectDataSource, etc.). These provide similar glue between the user interface element and the item acting as the data source.

It's possible you have used this control and didn't even know it. Each time you drag a new item from the Data Source window onto the form surface, Visual Studio 2005 will create a BindingSource object instance for you and place it in the component area at the bottom of the form.

Notice in Figure 7-29 that a BindingNavigator instance was also created. As we briefly discussed previously, the BindingNavigator control was designed to interact with a BindingSource to provide VCR-style navigation across the data.

Figure 7-29

If you were to look at the code that is generated or if you decide to programmatically add a BindingSource instance to your code, you would see the following to establish the data source:

```
masterBS.DataSource = dsEvents;
masterBS.DataMember = "Event";
childBS.DataSource = masterBS;
childBS.DataMember = "EventSessionRelation";
```

The following table describes some of the key properties of the BindingSource component:

Property	Description/Comments
AllowNew	True when the user is allowed to add new rows to the BindingSource. If the data source implements IBindingList, the data source will determine the value for this property. This is auto-set to false if the data source is read-only, fixed-size, or does not have a default constructor.
Current	Gets the current item from the data source.
Filter	If the data source implements the IBindingListView, a filter string can be set to filter the list. A NotSupported exception will be thrown if the data source does not support filtering.
DataSource	Establishes the actual data that will be managed by the BindingSource. If the object referenced contains multiple lists (e.g., DataSet), you must also set the DataMember property to indicate the specific list within the source you wish to manage.
DataMember	Specifies the list within a data source that the BindingSource will manipulate.

BindingList

BindingList is a generic implementation of the IBindingList interface and focuses on making binding to business objects easier. Generics are a new feature in .NET 2.0 that enable building strongly typed collections with less code. The following example code builds a BindingList specifically for the object Event, and ensures that all instances returned or added to the collection are of that type:

VB

```
dim bindingList as BindingList(of Event)
```

C#

```
BindingList<Event> bindingList = new BindingList<Event>();
```

BindingNavigator

The BindingNavigator is a visual control that provides a consistent method to navigate data associated with a BindingSource. The typical user interface for a BindingNavigator resembles VCR buttons.

When a BindingNavigator is added to a form and associated with a BindingSource, several of the common functions are tied to the BindingSource for you. For example, operations such as MoveFirst, MoveNext, and so on will be connected, and happen without added coding required.

While a BindingNavigator is convenient, you are not required to use it just because you want to navigate through the data associated with the BindingSource. You can use other navigational controls (see Figure 7-30) or simply call the methods on the binding source programmatically.

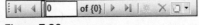

Figure 7-30

Summary

Regardless of the controls you use, your choice of ASP.NET or Windows Forms, the capabilities to help you bind data in .NET 2.0 far exceed the prior version, and, we believe, many of the competing products on the market.

Use what you have learned here as the foundation for building more advanced data binding in your applications. Take the opportunity of using controls such as the `ObjectDataSource` that abstract your application from doing direct access to the database to build more robust and scalable applications, while still maintaining the rapid development capabilities that data binding directly to the database provided in past versions.

Use your creativity to extend the capabilities to make it work with your team and your specific business application. Visual Studio 2005 and .NET 2.0 provide a rich foundation that can easily be extended.

For More Information

To complement the information in this chapter, take a look at the following resources:

❑ **MSDN Data Access and Storage Developer Center, article titled "Bind Your Data in ASP.NET Whidbey," by Steven A. Smith** — http://msdn.microsoft.com/data/dataaccess/ aspnet/default.aspx?pull=/library/en-us/dnaspp/html/aspnet-bindyourdata.asp

❑ **MSDN Data Access and Storage Developer Center, article titled "ASP.NET 2.0 and Data-Bound Controls: A New Perspective and Some New Practices," by Dino Esposito** — http://msdn .microsoft.com/data/dataaccess/aspnet/default.aspx?pull=/library/en-us/ dnaspp/html/databound.asp

8

Building a Custom
ADO.NET Data Provider

Although most developers will find the out-of-the-box ADO.NET providers sufficient for most projects (because the major database vendors supply such providers and/or support the OLE DB or ODBC technology for which there are 2.0 providers), it's helpful to understand what goes into creating such a provider to better understand how best to use them. In addition, you will sometimes want to get or store data in a data store for which there are currently no ADO.NET providers. This chapter elucidates the seemingly dark details of how you might go about creating a provider for such a data source.

For the purposes of demonstration, and because we think it could be darned useful, we chose to implement a sample ADO.NET provider for Active Directory. Our own experience has been that the API for ADSI, LDAP, and Active Directory in general is unfriendly, often obscure, and carries a significant learning curve for developers who are not already familiar with it. It also seems that the technology is somewhat of a stepchild for Microsoft. Yes, they provide it — even recommend it for some applications — but the developer experience when using it versus other Microsoft technologies (such as ADO.NET and SQL Server) is unpleasant. The directory services API provided in the .NET Framework only perpetuates this unfamiliar and difficult API.

We were hoping that Microsoft would create an ADO.NET provider for Active Directory with version 2 of the Framework, but either they don't think it should or needs to be done or they don't see a viable way of doing it. In any case, we chose to create one ourselves, not only to demonstrate the process of creating a custom ADO.NET provider but also to inspire some motivated developers out there to take the idea and run with it, improving it far beyond the simplistic implementation provided in this chapter. Nonetheless, even the simple implementation provided here could prove to be useful for developers who only need to use Active Directory as a data store for user information.

A Brief Overview

As you saw in Chapter 3, ADO.NET 2 has a few new, nice features that help programming against a generic data source. Naturally, this means that builders of ADO.NET providers will have to support these new features. In addition, the .NET Framework as a whole has moved away from interface-based polymorphism to base class–based, and ADO.NET is no exception. The new `System.Data.Common` namespace has all the base classes you need on which to base your custom provider. The following table lists the key items that are part of our implementation. Also included are the related interfaces from version 1, where applicable.

> *For those of you not familiar with Active Directory, it is a directory-based, extensible data store that Microsoft provides. The most common use of Active Directory is for user authentication, authorization, and profile information in a Microsoft domain. Along with this, it typically stores information about the computers and printers in the domain and how they can interact with each other. However, other applications can extend it, defining custom schemas to store other information.*

Provider Classes

ADO.NET Interface	ADO.NET Base Class	AdsProvider Class
IDbConnection	DbConnection	AdsConnection
IDbCommand	DbCommand	AdsCommand
IDataReader	DbDataReader	AdsDataReader
IDataAdapter IDbDataAdapter	DbDataAdapter DataAdapter*	AdsDataAdapter
	DbProviderFactory	AdsFactory
	DbConnectionStringBuilder	AdsConnectionStringBuilder
IDataParameterCollection	DbParameterCollection	AdsParameterCollection

*Note that version 1 did have a base class for the DataAdapter, from which the new DbDataAdapter inherits.

In addition to the evolution from interfaces to base classes, ADO.NET 2 also provides a generic way to discover metadata about your data source, as covered in the "Schema Metadata" section in Chapter 3. As you may recall, it is the `DbConnection` class that provides the API to retrieve this metadata, so the `AdsConnection` class provides implementations of those methods to retrieve metadata about the `AdsProvider`.

That more or less covers the high-level items you need to think about when implementing a custom provider. For the rest of this chapter, we'll explore how each of these items were implemented in the `AdsProvider` to further illustrate how this familiar, common API can be put into action for data sources that don't otherwise support it.

AdsConnection

We're starting with `AdsConnection` because all of the other classes depend upon it; therefore, any ADO.NET provider should — no, must — implement it. Any data sources that don't have an ADO.NET provider will have some way of "connecting" to them and accessing the data that they contain. If one were to create a file system–based provider, one might use the classes in the `System.IO` namespace as the underlying technology to access the data source. If one were to use a data source that provided COM servers for data access, one would likely use COM Interop to do the actual data access. If one had a Win32 library as the only way to access the data source, one would likely create external API calls using the extern or `DllImportAttribute` functionality of the .NET Framework. The point we're illustrating here is that unless you have an entirely new data source written in and for the .NET Framework, most likely what you'll be doing with your custom ADO.NET data provider is packaging up a previously extant API in the friendly, familiar, and common API that ADO.NET provides.

What we've done with the `AdsProvider` is no different. Given that Microsoft has already provided a .NET wrapper around ADSI with the `System.DirectoryServices` namespace, it seemed only natural to package that API with our provider. Therefore, what we've done for the `AdsConnection` class is wrap binding to a `DirectoryEntry` object as the root object for any commands that are run against the provider.

Back to the beginning. The first thing that you will need to do is create a class and derive from `System .Data.Common.DbConnection`, like this:

```
Public NotInheritable Class AdsConnection
    Inherits DbConnection
```

We've declared it as `NotInheritable` (sealed in C#) because we don't want to allow anyone to subclass it. When creating an API, you want to put some thought into these kinds of issues. While sealing it might limit its extensibility, it also limits your support surface. In other words, you prevent a whole slew of support issues that might crop up unexpectedly from a customer extending your API. In addition to that, sealing your types or even just type members can improve performance in .NET.

Next, you will likely need a few fields on your connection to store any state you need during the lifetime of the object:

```
Private _connectionString As String
Private _rootPath As String
Private _username As String
Private _password As String
Private _persistSecurityInfo As Boolean = False
Private _integratedSecurity As Boolean = False
Private _root As DirectoryEntry
Private _state As ConnectionState = ConnectionState.Closed
Shared nameCategories As Specialized.ListDictionary = _
  New Specialized.ListDictionary
Shared tableColumns As Specialized.ListDictionary = New Specialized.ListDictionary
Shared mdCols As Specialized.ListDictionary = New Specialized.ListDictionary
Private _disposed As Boolean
```

What we've done here is create fields for the various parts of the connection string (as well as the connection string itself). In addition, you can see the root field that stores the root directory entry mentioned previously. The state field stores the current state of the connection, which you'll need to implement the State property and the ChangeState event.

The Shared (static in C#) fields are used as caches for the metadata information to improve performance retrieving that data. For most providers, this won't be necessary, but because we use this data for each command, we thought it more efficient to do it this way as opposed to retrieving it from our metadata data source each time. Finally, the disposed field is there to simply support best practices when using the disposable pattern.

While it is not required, you will likely want to support the familiar constructors for a connection object as shown here:

```vb
Public Sub New()
    Me.New(String.Empty)
End Sub

Public Sub New(ByVal connectionString As String)
    MyBase.New()
    Me.ConnectionString = connectionString
End Sub
```

Because the second constructor in the preceding code shows setting the ConnectionString property, let's take a quick look at that and some other properties:

```vb
Friend ReadOnly Property RootEntry() As DirectoryEntry
    Get
        Me.EnsureNotDisposed()
        Return Me._root
    End Get
End Property

Public Overrides Property ConnectionString() As String
    Get
        Me.EnsureNotDisposed()
        Return Me._connectionString
    End Get
    Set(ByVal value As String)
        Me.EnsureNotDisposed()
        If (value Is Nothing) Then
            Throw New ArgumentNullException("ConnectionString", _
                "Connection string cannot be null.")
        End If
        Me._connectionString = value
    End Set
End Property

Public Overrides ReadOnly Property Database() As String
    Get
        Return Me._rootPath
    End Get
End Property

Public Overrides ReadOnly Property State() As ConnectionState
```

```
            Get
                Me.EnsureNotDisposed()
                Return Me._state
            End Get
        End Property

        Public Overrides ReadOnly Property DataSource() As String
            Get
                Me.EnsureNotDisposed()
                Return Me._rootPath
            End Get
        End Property

        Public Overrides ReadOnly Property ServerVersion() As String
            Get
                Return String.Empty
            End Get
        End Property

        Public Overrides ReadOnly Property ConnectionTimeout() As Integer
            Get
                Return 0
            End Get
        End Property
```

As you can see, most of these properties override a property on the base class. Some of them may not be supported by your data source. You will have to decide the best way to handle those. What we have decided to do is liken the data source and database to the root directory entry, so for the DataSource and Database properties, we simply return the root path. In SQL Server, the DataSource is the server instance and the Database is a database on the server instance.

The ServerVersion property only makes partial sense for our provider (we could get, for example, the OS version number, as Active Directory versions are tied to the OS), but we chose to just skip the property for simplicity's sake. We took a similar approach with the ConnectionTimeout property, just returning zero. You could, of course, throw NotImplementedExceptions for such cases, but as a best practice, we don't throw an exception unless code could not meaningfully continue.

The State property is obvious, one to which we have already alluded. It simply returns the current state for the connection. This provider only supports the Open and Closed option on that enumeration, but that is managed elsewhere.

Of all the properties, the most significant is the ConnectionString because it has the most meaning in differentiating one connection from another. It supplies all of the details needed for the connection to connect to the data source. In the case of the AdsProvider, it is only necessary to specify the data source (root path) and what credentials to use to connect to Active Directory. We tried to maintain a semblance to SQL Server connection strings, so Data Source equates to the root path; User ID and Password are used, as are Integrated Security and Persist Security Info. For example, to connect to the root user's container in a test Active Directory instance, you could use Data Source=CN=Users,DC=AdsTest,DC= local;Integrated Security=SSPI and it would connect to that root path using the process identity.

Related Considerations

To further extend the standard database metaphor, you could probably let Data Source be the domain controller to connect to and then use the `Database` property to specify a root object on that DC. To the extent possible, we have tried to map directory concepts to relational database concepts for this provider. The reasoning behind this goes back to the introduction for this chapter — we think most .NET developers are familiar with relational databases and ADO.NET, and are not familiar with Active Directory, LDAP, ADSI, and other directorylike technologies.

The point of the `AdsProvider` is to provide a familiar interface into an unfamiliar technology, thereby reducing the learning curve to start using that technology. Naturally, there will be an impedance mismatch, much like there is between relational databases and object-oriented technologies, that will limit our ability to do this. Some functionality of both technologies will be sacrificed to achieve the common interface.

For the purposes of this book, we have attempted to provide an ADO.NET API to manage users and computers in Active Directory. While we understand that Active Directory is the epitome of extensibility, its most common use tends to be managing these kinds of objects, and because most applications that use Active Directory do so to provide integrated security within the enterprise and a centralized user data store, we have only bothered with supporting basic user management in this sample provider.

That's not to say that this approach could not be extended. In fact, we'd love to see it extended and optimized, but our chief purpose here is to demonstrate a custom ADO.NET provider, so the implementation provided is sufficient.

Once you have a connection created and have set the connection string, the next thing you typically do is open the connection; so we'll look next at the implementation of the `Open` method in the `AdsConnection`:

```
Public Overrides Sub Open()
    Me.EnsureNotDisposed()
    Me.ParseConnectionString(Me._connectionString)
    If (Me._rootPath Is Nothing) Then
        Throw New NullReferenceException("Root path not set.")
    End If
    Me._root = New DirectoryEntry(("LDAP://" + Me._rootPath))
    If Not Me._integratedSecurity Then
        Me._root.Username = Me._username
        Me._root.Password = Me._password
        Me._root.AuthenticationType = (AuthenticationTypes.Secure _
            And AuthenticationTypes.Sealing)
    End If
    If Not Me._persistSecurityInfo Then
        Me._username = Nothing
        Me._password = Nothing
    End If
    Me.ChangeState(ConnectionState.Open)
End Sub
```

The first thing we did here was ensure that the connection has not been disposed of. Because it is essential to provide a mechanism to dispose of unmanaged resources that are used in managed components, the DbConnection implements the IDisposable interface, which we'll look at later. For now, we can assume it has not been disposed, so the next operation is parsing the connection string.

Assuming the connection string could be parsed correctly, the root object is then created from the root path given in the connection string, and the security binding options are set for our connection to the directory. Finally, the state of the instance is changed to Open; and at that point, the connection is ready for use with a command.

Let's look briefly at how the connection string was parsed:

```
Private Sub ParseConnectionString(ByVal value As String)
    Dim connString As AdsConnectionStringBuilder = New AdsConnectionStringBuilder
    connString.ConnectionString = value
    Me._rootPath = connString.DataSource
    Me._username = connString.UserId
    Me._password = connString.Password
    Me._integratedSecurity = ((Not (connString.IntegratedSecurity) Is Nothing) _
            AndAlso (connString.IntegratedSecurity.ToUpper = "SSPI"))
    Me._persistSecurityInfo = connString.PersistSecurityInfo
End Sub
```

When we first wrote the code for this method, we manually parsed out the connection string, which worked fine. However, after we implemented a connection string builder for our provider, it was much easier to simply use it to get the needed values out of the connection string, letting it handle the gory details of parsing the string.

The other significant operation in the Open method is the first call to change the state of the connection:

```
Friend Sub ChangeState(ByVal newState As ConnectionState)
    Dim preState As ConnectionState = Me._state
    Me._state = newState
    RaiseEvent StateChange(Me, New StateChangeEventArgs(preState, newState))
End Sub
```

As you can see, this is a simple matter of setting the current state of the connection and raising the StateChange event to let any subscribers know whether the state was changed. Note here that the visibility is Friend (internal in C#). You do not want to let users of the connection change the state directly—it should be something that happens organically as operations that are performed on the connection change its state. However, you may want to let other types in your assembly change the state, as they work closely with it (and you have complete control over that).

The next operation typically performed on a connection is closing and, often, disposing of it after the client code is done using it:

```
Public Overrides Sub Close()
    Me.EnsureNotDisposed()
    If (Not (Me._root) Is Nothing) Then
        Me._root.Close()
    End If
    Me.ChangeState(ConnectionState.Closed)
```

207

```
    End Sub

    Protected Overrides Sub Dispose(ByVal disposing As Boolean)
        If Not _disposed Then
            If Not disposing Then
                Me._connectionString = Nothing
                Me._rootPath = Nothing
                Me._username = Nothing
            End If
            If (Not (Me._root) Is Nothing) Then
                Me._root.Dispose()
            End If
            Me._root = Nothing
            Me._state = ConnectionState.Closed
            Me._disposed = True
        End If
        MyBase.Dispose(disposing)
    End Sub
```

The Close method closes the connection on the root Active Directory entry and then changes the state of the connection to Closed. The Dispose method does more or less the same thing, but it also nulls the reference types and sets the connection state directly.

Note that the dispose pattern is implemented on the base class, so it is only necessary to override the Dispose method that takes a Boolean parameter. This is part of the dispose pattern — the Boolean value indicates whether the method is being called from the implementation of IDisposable.Dispose (in which case the argument is true) or whether it is being called from the destructor, in which case the argument will be false and it will be unnecessary to null managed resources (because they'll be immediately cleaned up anyway).

Those are the key, most frequently used methods on connection objects, but there are a few others you need to think about when you're implementing a provider:

```
    Protected Overrides Function CreateDbCommand() As DbCommand
        Me.EnsureNotDisposed()
        Return New AdsCommand(String.Empty, Me)
    End Function

    Public Overrides Sub ChangeDatabase(ByVal databaseName As String)
        Me.EnsureNotDisposed()
        Me._rootPath = databaseName
        If (Not (Me._root) Is Nothing) Then
            Me._root.Path = databaseName
        End If
    End Sub

    Protected Overrides Function BeginDbTransaction(ByVal isolationLevel As
    IsolationLevel) As DbTransaction
        Throw New NotSupportedException("Transactions are not supported.")
    End Function
```

The CreateDbCommand is a new one. As you might imagine, it simply creates an instance of the provider's DbCommand implementation. Note that it is Protected, so it will only ever be called by the DbCommand type and its derived classes. What it does is force you to implement the `IDbConnection.CreateCommand` method. By creating an abstract (`MustOverride` in VB) method, the `DbConnection` can implement the `IDbConnection` interface for you and still force you to implement it.

The `ChangeDatabase` method should do whatever it takes to connect to a different database on your source. In our case, we allow this to change the path on the root directory entry. The `BeginDbTransaction` (much like the `CreateDbCommand`) forces you to do something with the `BeginTransaction` method. In the case of the `AdsProvider`, we're not supporting transactions, and because that is something that could definitely interfere with expected semantics, we throw a `NotSupportedException` to let the consumer know that this data source is not transactional.

That's about it for the `DbConnection`, unless you want to support the new metadata discovery API that ADO.NET 2 provides. If you do, you will need to implement three more methods:

```
Public Overloads Overrides Function GetSchema() As DataTable
    Return Me.GetSchema("MetaDataCollections", Nothing)
End Function

Public Overloads Overrides Function GetSchema(ByVal collectionName As String) As
DataTable
    Return Me.GetSchema(collectionName, Nothing)
End Function

Public Overloads Overrides Function GetSchema(ByVal collectionName As String, _
  ByVal restrictionValues() As String) As DataTable
    Return Nothing
End Function
```

We're not sure why the designers chose to force inheritors to implement all three, as the expected meaning of the first two will always be the same — that is, the one with no parameters returns the `MetaDataCollections` schema with no restrictions, the one with the single string parameter returns the requested schema with no restrictions, and the third returns the requested schema with the given restrictions. In other words, the implementation for the first two should always be the same for all inheritors — to call the third implementation, which actually has the guts of the `GetSchema` operation. But, alas, if you don't override all three, the first two will throw `NotImplementedExceptions`.

In any case, we've omitted the code for the `GetSchema` method for brevity and because it is rather simplistic in that all it does is use the `DataSet`'s `ReadXmlSchema` and `ReadXml` methods to load up some static XML resources in the assembly that describe the requested metadata. It also sticks that metadata into the `mdCols` Shared (static in C#) field to speed future retrieval.

Once you have implemented the properties and methods just covered, you should have a connection implementation that will work with the ADO.NET 2.0 model. The next type we'll cover is the connection string builder, simply because it is often used directly in conjunction with setting up the connection itself.

AdsConnectionStringBuilder

Our implementation of the `DbConnectionStringBuilder` is fairly straightforward because the base class does most of the hard work for you. All you need to do is add any strongly typed properties that you would like users of the builder to have handy; however, there is one quirk.

By default, if you attempt to get a value out of the builder that has not been set, it will throw an exception. We're not sure we buy this approach because it is out of sync with the other dictionary collections in the Framework, which will simply return null. This may catch you off-guard if you're not prepared for it. The good news, we suppose, is that they provide you with a try method that you can use to attempt to get a value out of it without causing an exception. This is the approach we used with the accessors for the strongly typed properties we exposed.

Interestingly, we used Reflector to look at the `SqlConnectionStringBuilder`, and it has private fields for each of the properties. You can see how this would improve performance (you don't have to do a lookup on the dictionary for each access), but as far as we could tell, if you set the connection string directly, the fields were not being set, in which case you may have set a value in a connection string, but it won't show up by accessing those properties.

For simplicity's sake, we just stuck with using the `TryGetValue` method in our accessors. Note that to remove a value, you just need to set it to null. The following code presents the complete class to give you an idea of what you might want to do with this type:

```
Public Class AdsConnectionStringBuilder
    Inherits Common.DbConnectionStringBuilder

    Public Sub New()
        Me.New(Nothing)
    End Sub

    Public Sub New(ByVal connectionString As String)
        MyBase.New(False)
        If (Not (connectionString) Is Nothing) Then
            Me.ConnectionString = connectionString
        End If
    End Sub

    Public Property DataSource() As String
        Get
            Dim o As Object = Nothing
            MyBase.TryGetValue("Data Source", o)
            Return CType(o, String)
        End Get
        Set(ByVal value As String)
            MyBase.Item("Data Source") = value
        End Set
    End Property

    Public Property UserId() As String
        Get
            Dim o As Object = Nothing
            MyBase.TryGetValue("User Id", o)
            Return CType(o, String)
        End Get
        Set(ByVal value As String)
            MyBase.Item("User Id") = value
        End Set
    End Property

    Public Property Password() As String
```

```
        Get
            Dim o As Object = Nothing
            MyBase.TryGetValue("Password", o)
            Return CType(o, String)
        End Get
        Set(ByVal value As String)
            MyBase.Item("Password") = value
        End Set
    End Property

    Public Property PersistSecurityInfo() As Boolean
        Get
            Dim o As Object = Nothing
            If MyBase.TryGetValue("Persist Security Info", o) Then
                Return Convert.ToBoolean(o)
            Else
                Return False
            End If
        End Get
        Set(ByVal value As Boolean)
            MyBase.Item("Persist Security Info") = value
        End Set
    End Property

    Public Property IntegratedSecurity() As String
        Get
            Dim o As Object = Nothing
            MyBase.TryGetValue("Integrated Security", o)
            Return CType(o, String)
        End Get
        Set(ByVal value As String)
            MyBase.Item("Integrated Security") = value
        End Set
    End Property
End Class
```

AdsCommand

Next to the connection, the command type is the most integral to ADO.NET. You are up a creek without a paddle if you don't have the command type, so that's what we'll look at in this section.

As with the connection, you will need to inherit from the corresponding base class in `System.Data` `.Common`, and you will probably want to provide constructors with the familiar signatures, as shown here:

```
Public NotInheritable Class AdsCommand
    Inherits DbCommand

    Public Sub New()
        MyBase.New()
    End Sub

    Public Sub New(ByVal commandText As String)
```

```
        Me.New(commandText, Nothing)
    End Sub

    Public Sub New(ByVal commandText As String, ByVal connection As AdsConnection)
        MyBase.New()
        Me._commandText = commandText
        Me._connection = connection
    End Sub
```

Before proceeding, note some of the design decisions we made with the command class, as it is so integral to the entire show. First, we chose not to support parameters. We do not recommend this for a commercial provider because ADO.NET is geared toward using them and best practices are to use them as opposed to inline values. Our choice on this point was purely one of expediency. We did have to create the `AdsParameterCollection` class all the same because the `DataAdapter` expects it to be there, but it is nothing more than a placeholder that is always empty. It exists only to keep the `DataAdapter` happy.

Second, although we wanted to reduce the impedance mismatch as much as possible, we did not preserve standard SQL syntax for criteria statements, instead opting for what you must use with the `DirectorySearcher` class, which is somewhat different, although not difficult to grasp. In addition, we have no quoted identifiers, so you can't use a comma in a value.

Again, both of these were matters of expediency; in a commercial implementation (or even in one developed for an internal production system), we would expect to see these difficulties overcome. The good news is that if your data source supports these features by default (that is, you don't have such an impedance), then it is easier to implement the command.

If you want to support standard T-SQL syntax (at least as much as possible for your data source) and your data source does not support it itself, you will need to write algorithms to parse the commands and turn them into something meaningful for your data source. In the case of the `AdsProvider`, this means parsing out the "columns" as properties on the `DirectoryEntry`.

For the "table" in the command text, we interpret that to mean an arbitrary structure that we have defined as part of our schema. In order to simplify interaction with Active Directory, we have defined a couple of simple schemas based on two object categories in Active Directory: the user and the computer. Thus, there is an abstract Users "table" that will operate against objects in Active Directory in the "user" object category; similarly, there is a Computers "table" that will act on objects in the "computer" category.

Thus, if you select from the Users table, we add `objectCategory=user` to the filter on the directory searcher, and if you update something in the Computers table, we add `objectCategory=computer` to the searcher we use to pull back the entries being updated. In this way, we hide the unfamiliar concepts of object categories, entries, searchers, and so on from the users of the provider. Users can use familiar command syntax working against what appear to be tables and columns that seem to make sense for something they might have defined in a relational database themselves.

With these things in mind, let's look at some of the code behind the `AdsCommand` and what you might want to know when implementing a command type yourself:

```
    Public Overrides Property CommandText() As String
        Get
            Me.EnsureNotDisposed()
            Return Me._commandText
        End Get
        Set(ByVal value As String)
            Me.EnsureNotDisposed()
            Me._commandText = value
        End Set
    End Property

    Public Shadows Property Connection() As AdsConnection
        Get
            Me.EnsureNotDisposed()
            Return Me._connection
        End Get
        Set(ByVal value As AdsConnection)
            Me.EnsureNotDisposed()
            Me._connection = CType(value, AdsConnection)
        End Set
    End Property

    Protected Overrides Property DbConnection() As DbConnection
        Get
            Me.EnsureNotDisposed()
            Return Me._connection
        End Get
        Set(ByVal value As DbConnection)
            Me.EnsureNotDisposed()
            Me._connection = CType(value, AdsConnection)
        End Set
    End Property
```

The preceding code shows some properties that are pretty essential to any meaningful use of the command type. You will need to use CommandText to know exactly what the user wants to do with the data. You will need the Connection and DbConnection properties because they deal with connecting to the data source.

The interesting thing to note here is that Microsoft chose to keep the existing interface-based API while adding the base class–based approach. By default, the base class exposes the IDbCommand.Connection for you, and it provides you with the protected DbConnection property so that you can tell it what to return for the IDbCommand.Connection property. This is the same approach used with the CreateCommand method on the connection.

Note, however, that if you want to return a strongly typed command as an instance of your provider's connection type, you will need to hide (shadow) the base Connection property and expose one of your own type, as we have done above (this is, by the way, the same approach that the SqlCommand takes).

The beauty of this approach is that if you have a reference of type AdsCommand and you access the Connection property, it will return a strongly typed AdsConnection, but if you have a reference of type DbCommand or IDbCommand and access the Connection property, it will still return the AdsConnection; it just won't be typed as an AdsConnection. Pretty nifty, eh?

Other properties you will want to consider when implementing `DbCommand` are listed below:

```vbnet
Protected Overrides Property DbTransaction() As DbTransaction
    Get
        Throw New NotSupportedException("The operation is not supported.")
    End Get
    Set(ByVal value As DbTransaction)
        Throw New NotSupportedException("The operation is not supported.")
    End Set
End Property

Public Overrides Property CommandTimeout() As Integer
    Get
        Me.EnsureNotDisposed()
        Return Me._commandTimeout
    End Get
    Set(ByVal value As Integer)
        Me.EnsureNotDisposed()
        Me._commandTimeout = value
    End Set
End Property

Public Overrides Property CommandType() As CommandType
    Get
        Me.EnsureNotDisposed()
        Return CommandType.Text
    End Get
    Set(ByVal value As CommandType)
        Me.EnsureNotDisposed()
        If (value <> CommandType.Text) Then
            Throw New NotSupportedException("Only text commands are supported.")
        End If
    End Set
End Property

Public Overrides Property UpdatedRowSource() As UpdateRowSource
    Get
        Return UpdateRowSource.None
    End Get
    Set(ByVal value As UpdateRowSource)
        If (value <> UpdateRowSource.None) Then
            Throw New Exception("Only UpdateRowSource.None is supported.")
        End If
    End Set
End Property

Protected Overrides ReadOnly Property DbParameterCollection() As
DbParameterCollection
    Get
        Return New AdsParameterCollection
    End Get
End Property

Public Overrides Property DesignTimeVisible() As Boolean
```

```
        Get
            Return False
        End Get
        Set(ByVal value As Boolean)

        End Set
End Property
```

Again, we disallow the DbTransaction property because we don't support transactions. In our case, CommandType will always be Text, as we don't support TableDirect or StoredProcedure. UpdatedRowSource is mostly applicable to commands that support parameters, so we only support None. We don't want to support a design-time experience, so we set DesignTimeVisible to false.

DbParameterCollection is the infamous property we mentioned previously—an always empty collection. Unfortunately, even though we don't support parameters, we *had* to create our own parameter collection for this because there is no way to create one otherwise (well, you could probably use Reflection, but it's generally not a good idea to make your code dependent upon hidden members in types you don't control).

Some of the ancillary methods that you will want to think about are as follows:

```
    Public Overrides Sub Prepare()
        Me.PrepareCommand()
    End Sub

    Public Overrides Sub Cancel()
    End Sub

    Protected Overrides Function CreateDbParameter() As DbParameter
        Throw New NotSupportedException()
    End Function
```

We've abused the meaning behind Prepare a bit because it is supposed to attempt to create a compiled version of the command on the data source, which makes sense in the context of something like SQL Server, where you might want to have the command prepared before executing it. In our case, we call PrepareCommand, a private method we defined that does the actual parsing of the command text and the creation of the DirectorySearcher that will be used (if necessary). In a sense, it is akin to what Prepare might do on a relational data engine such as SQL Server.

For Cancel, we simply do nothing because the docs on the interface say, more or less, that Cancel should not throw an exception if it fails. Because, in effect, it will always fail for the AdsCommand, we take that to mean that we should not throw an exception; rather, we should just do nothing, as there is no corresponding concept for our data source.

For CreateDbParameter, we do, in fact, throw an exception. We do this because it is more meaningful than a NullReferenceException, which is what will be thrown if someone calls CreateParameter, expecting it to return a parameter, and tries to act upon that reference. Instead, we want to let the user know immediately that it is not supported.

Naturally, if you are supporting parameters, you will simply return a new instance of your parameter from this method, and you would want to hide the CreateParameter method in order to return a strongly typed parameter of your provider's parameter type (as previously demonstrated with the `Connection` property).

What follows are the key methods, without which a command type would be mostly useless. First, we'll look at the reader (select) methods:

```
Public Shadows Function ExecuteReader() As AdsDataReader
    Return Me.ExecuteReader(CommandBehavior.Default)
End Function

Public Shadows Function ExecuteReader(ByVal behavior As CommandBehavior) As
AdsDataReader
    Me.EnsureNotDisposed()
    Me.EnsureConnectionOpen()
    Me.PrepareCommand()
    Return New AdsDataReader(Me)
End Function

Protected Overrides Function ExecuteDbDataReader(ByVal behavior As CommandBehavior)
As DbDataReader
    Return Me.ExecuteReader(behavior)
End Function
```

Let's point out immediately that we are, again, following the hiding pattern previously described. For common methods for which you want to return your own type of data reader type, you need to hide (shadow) the base class's implementation and provide your own, strongly typed implementation. Yet, again, we also override the base's `ExecuteDbDataReader` in order for calls to the hidden methods to work as well.

The implementation itself is rather simple, which may not be what you'd expect from this method. We ensure that the command is not disposed, that the connection is open, and that the command is prepared, and then we simply return a new data reader. It really is that simple because the data reader's Read method is what really does the funky stuff to read each row from the data source, as you'll see in the following section.

```
Public Overrides Function ExecuteScalar() As Object
    Me.EnsureNotDisposed()
    Me.EnsureConnectionOpen()
    Me.PrepareCommand()
    Dim result As SearchResult = Me._searcher.FindOne
    Dim scalarValue As Object = Nothing
    If (Not (result) Is Nothing) Then
        Dim de As DirectoryEntry = CType(result.GetDirectoryEntry, DirectoryEntry)
        scalarValue = de.Properties(Me._propertyLookup(0)).Value
    End If
    Return scalarValue
End Function
```

`ExecuteScalar` is nothing more than a request to get the first row's left-most column value in the result of the command. For `AdsProvider`, this means using the `FindOne` command on the `DirectorySearcher` object that was set up in the `PrepareCommand` method and then getting the value of the first property loaded.

Now for the gooier commands: INSERT, UPDATE, and DELETE. For these, developers typically call the ExecuteNonQuery method on the command, which is what we'll look at next:

```vb
Public Overrides Function ExecuteNonQuery() As Integer
    Dim rowsAffected As Integer = 0
    Dim dr As AdsDataReader
    Me.EnsureNotDisposed()
    Me.EnsureConnectionOpen()
    Me.PrepareCommand()
    Select Case (Me.Type)
        Case CommandTypeOption.Insert
            Dim passwordIdx As Integer = Me.FindPasswordInProps, _
              idIdx As Integer = Me.FindIdInProps
            If (idIdx = -1) Then
                Me.Missing("the identifier for the object")
            End If
            Dim isUserClass As Boolean = (Me._objectCategory = _
              Me._connection.GetObjectCategory("Users"))
            If ((passwordIdx = -1) _
                        AndAlso isUserClass) Then
                Me.Missing("the password for the user")
            End If
            Dim newItem As DirectoryEntry = _
              Me._connection.RootEntry.Children.Add((Me._propertyLookup(idIdx) + _
              ("=" + Me._values(idIdx))), Me._objectCategory)
            Dim i As Integer
            For i = 0 To Me._propertyLookup.Length - 1
                If (Me.CanSetValue(Me._properties(i)) _
                            AndAlso ((Not (Me._values(i)) Is Nothing) _
                            AndAlso (Me._values(i) <> String.Empty))) Then
                    newItem.Properties(Me._propertyLookup(i)).Value = Me._values(i)
                End If
            Next
            newItem.CommitChanges()
            If isUserClass Then
                ' set password
                newItem.Invoke("SetPassword", _
                  New Object() {Me._values(passwordIdx)})
                ' set account as normal/enabled
                newItem.Properties("userAccountControl").Value = 512
                newItem.CommitChanges()
            End If
            rowsAffected = 1
        Case CommandTypeOption.Delete
            dr = New AdsDataReader(Me)
            While dr.Read
                dr.CurrentEntry.DeleteTree()
                rowsAffected += 1
            End While
        Case CommandTypeOption.Update
            dr = New AdsDataReader(Me)
            While dr.Read
                Dim entry As DirectoryEntry = dr.CurrentEntry
                Dim i As Integer
                For i = 0 To Me._properties.Length - 1
```

```
                          If Me.CanSetValue(Me._properties(i)) Then
                              entry.Properties(Me._propertyLookup(i)).Value = _
                                  Me._values(i)
                          ElseIf ((Me._properties(i).ToUpper = "PASSWORD") _
                                      AndAlso (Not (Me._values(i)) Is Nothing)) Then
                              entry.Invoke("SetPassword", New Object() {Me._values(i)})
                          End If
                      Next
                      entry.CommitChanges()
                      rowsAffected += 1
                  End While
              Case Else
                  Throw New InvalidOperationException(_
                      "Invalid command type for specified operation.")
          End Select
          Return rowsAffected
      End Function
```

Again, before starting any real operation with this method, we make sure that the command and connection are in a state that is valid for command execution. The next step, in the case of this provider, is to determine the kind of command being executed, because these require distinct operations on the data source. For a source such as SQL Server, which has built-in functionality to handle the commands itself, this might be a simple call to ExecuteNonQuery on the data source. But for this provider, we are working against a data source that doesn't understand these commands, so we have to parse them.

For the insert command, a couple of constraints are being checked. First, we require what our friendly schema is calling "Id" — which actually maps to the common name (CN) in Active Directory, which is the closest thing akin to an Id that objects have within their containers. Technically, the closest thing would be the fully distinguished name of the object; however, we are abstracting that away from users so that the object will be added to the root path specified in the connection string.

For example, you might set the data source to CN=Users, DC=AdsTest, DC=local, in which case new items would be added to the Users container; and within that container, it is only necessary to have a CN that is unique within the container; hence, it is somewhat akin to a single-value artificial primary key in a database table, which is often given the name "Id."

In addition to the constraint to have an Id, if the item being inserted is inserted into the abstract Users table we have defined (which maps to an object category of "user"), we require the calling code to specify a password as well. After looping through the other properties specified in the command and setting them on the new directory entry, we invoke the SetPassword method to set the password for the user, and we set the user control flags to normal. At that point, the user should be good to go.

Deletes were the easiest to write. The code uses the AdsDataReader to get the results from the specified criteria, loops through, and deletes each one calling the DeleteTree, which might be dangerous if any objects that match the search are containers. However, because we set the object category to non-container categories, this should not be a problem.

Updates, as usual, are a mishmash of deletes and inserts, though not in the same way that they are with, say, SQL Server. In our case, the similarity with deletes is that we use the AdsDataReader to get the records to update, and the similarity with inserts is that it loops through the properties derived from the command text and sets them.

Finally, just to clarify, the `CommandTypeOption` enumeration and `Type` property that we're using to determine the type of command to execute is something specific to this provider. The code for that enumeration, the `PrepareCommand` method, and other provider-specific implementation details can be found in the downloadable code samples. We won't be going over them here because they're not terribly pertinent to the chapter's focus and are somewhat involved and lengthy, which would detract from the purpose of this chapter. The curious can dig into the code.

AdsDataReader

In the preceding section, you saw that the `ExecuteReader` method basically just creates an instance of the `AdsDataReader`. This is because the work of executing the reader itself falls within the scope of the `AdsDataReader` type. The first thing we'll look at here is the constructor for this type. Note that the type, like the others, inherits from the appropriate base class:

```
Public Class AdsDataReader
    Inherits Common.DbDataReader

    Friend Sub New(ByVal command As AdsCommand)
        MyBase.New()
        If (command Is Nothing) Then
            Throw New ArgumentNullException("command")
        End If
        Me._command = command
        Me._results = Me._command.Searcher.FindAll
        Me._reader = Me._results.GetEnumerator
    End Sub
End Class
```

The constructor itself is declared as `Friend` (`internal` in C#), which means that only code in the `AdsProvider` assembly can execute it. This is, in fact, what we want because users do not expect to be able to directly instantiate a reader — that operation only makes sense in the context of a command executing it.

Note two things within the constructor. First, you see that the `FindAll` method is executed on the command's directory searcher instance. Technically, a data reader should endeavor to only pull back one row at a time from the data source, but for simplicity's sake, we chose to simply get all of the results at once. As far as users are concerned, they still have to use the reader in the same way they would otherwise — we don't give them access to the full results at once; they must use the `Read` method or get an enumerator to loop through them.

Second, the code gets an enumerator from the `SearchResultCollection` returned by the `FindAll` method. This makes it easy to provide the reader semantics, as it is basically a fancy enumerator for the result set.

Now, if you were to type into Visual Studio 2005 that you wanted to inherit from `DbDataReader`, it would prompt you to implement all of the abstract members of the base type. And if you did this, you might easily be overwhelmed with the number of methods for which you have to provide implementations. Thankfully, most of these have very simple and similar implementations that involve getting the value of a column at a specified index and casting it to an appropriate type. These are the many `Get<Type>(ByVal ordinal As Integer)`, where `<Type>` is the name of some primitive .NET type. The following code shows a subset of these to give you an example:

```
Public Overrides Function GetBoolean(ByVal ordinal As Integer) As Boolean
    Return Convert.ToBoolean(Me(ordinal))
End Function

Public Overrides Function GetByte(ByVal ordinal As Integer) As Byte
    Return Convert.ToByte(Me(ordinal))
End Function

Public Overrides Function GetDateTime(ByVal ordinal As Integer) As DateTime
    Return Convert.ToDateTime(Me(ordinal))
End Function

Public Overrides Function GetInt32(ByVal ordinal As Integer) As Integer
    Return Convert.ToInt32(Me(ordinal))
End Function

Public Overrides Function GetString(ByVal ordinal As Integer) As String
    Return Convert.ToString(Me(ordinal))
End Function
```

For each of these, the indexer is called. In this implementation, the indexer looks up the property name at the specified index in the command text select list and gets the value of the property from the current search result. The indexers (default properties in VB) are shown here:

```
Default Public Overloads Overrides ReadOnly Property _
    Item(ByVal ordinal As Integer) As Object
    Get
        Dim name As String = Me._command.UserProperties(ordinal)
        Return Me(name)
    End Get
End Property

Default Public Overloads Overrides ReadOnly Property Item(ByVal name As String) _
    As Object
    Get
        If (Me._reader.Current = Nothing) Then
            Throw New InvalidOperationException(_
                "There is no row at the current position.")
        End If
        If Not Me._current.Contains(name) Then
            Return Nothing
        End If
        Return Me._current(name)
    End Get
End Property
```

The integer indexer gets the name of the user property from the command object (UserProperties is an internal/Friend accessor to the string array that was parsed from the select list in the command's PrepareCommand method). It then calls the string indexer, which attempts to look up the property in the _current field, which is actually a hash table that we put together for the current row (entry) in the result set in the Read method. We'll look at that next:

```vb
Public Overrides Function Read() As Boolean
    If Me._reader.MoveNext Then
        Me.LoadRow(CType(Me._reader.Current, DirectoryServices.SearchResult))
        Return True
    Else
        Return False
    End If
End Function

Private Sub LoadRow(ByVal result As DirectoryServices.SearchResult)
    Me._currentEntry = result.GetDirectoryEntry
    If (Me._current Is Nothing) Then
        Me._current = New Hashtable(Me._command.UserProperties.Length)
    End If
    Dim i As Integer
    For i = 0 To Me._command.UserProperties.Length - 1
        If (Not (Me._command.AdPropertyLookup(i)) Is Nothing) Then
            Me._current(Me._command.UserProperties(i)) = _
                Me._currentEntry.Properties(Me._command.AdPropertyLookup(i)).Value
        End If
    Next
End Sub
```

Because we're relying on the built-in enumerator of the SearchResultCollection, all we have to do is enumerate to its next entry using the MoveNext method. If it returns true, there is another result; otherwise, we're done. If there is another result, we load the row into the aforementioned hash table, using the user-specified properties for keys. In either case, we return a Boolean value indicating, as the user of a data reader would expect, whether the reader was able to read another row from the data source.

User Properties versus Active Directory Properties

It is important to use the user-specified property names because, in addition to defining an abstract table for object categories, we have also created new, more user-friendly names for the properties. This is a further attempt to familiarize an unfamiliar technology, so, for instance, instead of forcing users of the provider to know that "l" stands for city/locality in Active Directory, we let them specify "City" and map that to "l" for them.

The complete schema that the provider supports can be discovered from the Tables and Columns metadata collections that this provider supports. We've listed both of the XML files for these below to give you a good idea of how this mapping of abstract table and column (property) names to the actual Active Directory schema occurs.

Tables

```xml
<?xml version="1.0" encoding="utf-8" ?>
<Tables>
    <Tables>
        <Name>Users</Name>
        <ObjectCategory>user</ObjectCategory>
        <Comment>User accounts.</Comment>
    </Tables>
    <Tables>
```

```
            <Name>Computers</Name>
            <ObjectCategory>computer</ObjectCategory>
            <Comment>Computers.</Comment>
        </Tables>
</Tables>
```

Columns

```xml
<?xml version="1.0" encoding="utf-8"?>
<Columns>
    <Columns>
        <Table>Users</Table>
        <FriendlyName>City</FriendlyName>
        <AdName>l</AdName>
        <AdsDbType>7</AdsDbType>
        <Comment>City/locality.</Comment>
    </Columns>
    <Columns>
        <Table>Users</Table>
        <FriendlyName>Password</FriendlyName>
        <AdName>userPassword</AdName>
        <AdsDbType>7</AdsDbType>
        <Comment>Password--write only.</Comment>
    </Columns>
    <Columns>
        <Table>Users</Table>
        <FriendlyName>Country</FriendlyName>
        <AdName>c</AdName>
        <AdsDbType>7</AdsDbType>
        <Comment>Country.</Comment>
    </Columns>
    <Columns>
        <Table>Users</Table>
        <FriendlyName>Department</FriendlyName>
        <AdName>department</AdName>
        <AdsDbType>7</AdsDbType>
        <Comment>Department/work group.</Comment>
    </Columns>
    <Columns>
        <Table>Users</Table>
        <FriendlyName>Description</FriendlyName>
        <AdName>description</AdName>
        <AdsDbType>7</AdsDbType>
        <Comment>Description.</Comment>
    </Columns>
    <Columns>
        <Table>Users</Table>
        <FriendlyName>DisplayName</FriendlyName>
        <AdName>displayName</AdName>
        <AdsDbType>7</AdsDbType>
        <Comment>Display Name</Comment>
    </Columns>
    <Columns>
        <Table>Users</Table>
        <FriendlyName>DistinguishedName</FriendlyName>
```

```
        <AdName>distinguishedName</AdName>
        <AdsDbType>7</AdsDbType>
        <Comment>Fully-Qualified Hierarchical Name in ADS.</Comment>
</Columns>
<Columns>
        <Table>Users</Table>
        <FriendlyName>EmailAddress</FriendlyName>
        <AdName>mail</AdName>
        <AdsDbType>7</AdsDbType>
        <Comment>Primary Email Address.</Comment>
</Columns>
<Columns>
        <Table>Users</Table>
        <FriendlyName>FirstName</FriendlyName>
        <AdName>givenName</AdName>
        <AdsDbType>7</AdsDbType>
        <Comment>First Name.</Comment>
</Columns>
<Columns>
        <Table>Users</Table>
        <FriendlyName>Groups</FriendlyName>
        <AdName>memberOf</AdName>
        <AdsDbType>7</AdsDbType>
        <Comment>Comma-delimited group list.</Comment>
</Columns>
<Columns>
        <Table>Users</Table>
        <FriendlyName>Id</FriendlyName>
        <AdName>cn</AdName>
        <AdsDbType>7</AdsDbType>
        <Comment>Common name unique identifier within object space.</Comment>
</Columns>
<Columns>
        <Table>Users</Table>
        <FriendlyName>Initials</FriendlyName>
        <AdName>initials</AdName>
        <AdsDbType>7</AdsDbType>
        <Comment>Initials</Comment>
</Columns>
<Columns>
        <Table>Users</Table>
        <FriendlyName>LastName</FriendlyName>
        <AdName>sn</AdName>
        <AdsDbType>7</AdsDbType>
        <Comment>Last Name.</Comment>
</Columns>
<Columns>
        <Table>Users</Table>
        <FriendlyName>LogonName</FriendlyName>
        <AdName>userPrincipalName</AdName>
        <AdsDbType>7</AdsDbType>
        <Comment>Windows 2000+ Logon Name</Comment>
</Columns>
<Columns>
```

```
      <Table>Users</Table>
      <FriendlyName>MainPhone</FriendlyName>
      <AdName>telephoneNumber</AdName>
      <AdsDbType>7</AdsDbType>
      <Comment>Main telephone number.</Comment>
</Columns>
<Columns>
      <Table>Users</Table>
      <FriendlyName>NTLogonName</FriendlyName>
      <AdName>sAMAccountName</AdName>
      <AdsDbType>7</AdsDbType>
      <Comment>Pre-Windows 2000 Logon Name</Comment>
</Columns>
<Columns>
      <Table>Users</Table>
      <FriendlyName>OfficeName</FriendlyName>
      <AdName>physicalDeliveryOfficeName</AdName>
      <AdsDbType>7</AdsDbType>
      <Comment>Name of physical location/office.</Comment>
</Columns>
<Columns>
      <Table>Users</Table>
      <FriendlyName>State</FriendlyName>
      <AdName>st</AdName>
      <AdsDbType>7</AdsDbType>
      <Comment>State/province.</Comment>
</Columns>
<Columns>
      <Table>Users</Table>
      <FriendlyName>StreetAddress</FriendlyName>
      <AdName>streetAddress</AdName>
      <AdsDbType>7</AdsDbType>
      <Comment>Mailing Street Address</Comment>
</Columns>
<Columns>
      <Table>Users</Table>
      <FriendlyName>Title</FriendlyName>
      <AdName>title</AdName>
      <AdsDbType>7</AdsDbType>
      <Comment>Job Title</Comment>
</Columns>
<Columns>
      <Table>Users</Table>
      <FriendlyName>Company</FriendlyName>
      <AdName>company</AdName>
      <AdsDbType>7</AdsDbType>
      <Comment>Company Name</Comment>
</Columns>
<Columns>
      <Table>Computers</Table>
      <FriendlyName>ComputerName</FriendlyName>
      <AdName>cn</AdName>
      <AdsDbType>7</AdsDbType>
      <Comment>Computer's name.</Comment>
```

```
        </Columns>
        <Columns>
            <Table>Computers</Table>
            <FriendlyName>Description</FriendlyName>
            <AdName>description</AdName>
            <AdsDbType>7</AdsDbType>
            <Comment>Computer's description.</Comment>
        </Columns>
        <Columns>
            <Table>Computers</Table>
            <FriendlyName>DnsName</FriendlyName>
            <AdName>dNSHostName</AdName>
            <AdsDbType>7</AdsDbType>
            <Comment>Computer's name in DNS.</Comment>
        </Columns>
        <Columns>
            <Table>Computers</Table>
            <FriendlyName>OSHotfixLevel</FriendlyName>
            <AdName>operatingSystemHotfix</AdName>
            <AdsDbType>7</AdsDbType>
            <Comment>Hotfix level for OS.</Comment>
        </Columns>
        <Columns>
            <Table>Computers</Table>
            <FriendlyName>OSName</FriendlyName>
            <AdName>operatingSystem</AdName>
            <AdsDbType>7</AdsDbType>
            <Comment>Operating system name.</Comment>
        </Columns>
        <Columns>
            <Table>Computers</Table>
            <FriendlyName>OSServicePack</FriendlyName>
            <AdName>operatingSystemServicePack</AdName>
            <AdsDbType>7</AdsDbType>
            <Comment>Service pack applied to OS.</Comment>
        </Columns>
        <Columns>
            <Table>Computers</Table>
            <FriendlyName>OSVersion</FriendlyName>
            <AdName>operatingSystemVersion</AdName>
            <AdsDbType>7</AdsDbType>
            <Comment>Operating system version.</Comment>
        </Columns>
        <Columns>
            <Table>Computers</Table>
            <FriendlyName>Role</FriendlyName>
            <AdName>machineRole</AdName>
            <AdsDbType>7</AdsDbType>
            <Comment>Server, Workstation, or DC.</Comment>
        </Columns>
    </Columns>
```

As we see it, the column names that we use are more intuitive and "friendly" for a developer to use, eliminating the need to look up the sometimes obscure property names in the Active Directory schema.

You can see how a developer familiar with an RDBMS such as SQL Server could look at this schema and know how to write an appropriate command in T-SQL syntax to perform some operation against the Active Directory using the `AdsProvider`.

Other AdsDataReader Members

There are a few other `DbDataReader` members that implementers will need to think about. A few of these are properties that should have fairly simple implementations:

```
Public Overrides ReadOnly Property Depth() As Integer
    Get
        Return 0
    End Get
End Property

Public Overrides ReadOnly Property FieldCount() As Integer
    Get
        Return Me._command.UserProperties.Length
    End Get
End Property

Public Overrides ReadOnly Property HasRows() As Boolean
    Get
        Return (Me._results.Count > 0)
    End Get
End Property

Public Overrides ReadOnly Property IsClosed() As Boolean
    Get
        Return Me.disposed
    End Get
End Property

Public Overrides ReadOnly Property RecordsAffected() As Integer
    Get
        Return Me._results.Count
    End Get
End Property
```

`Depth` is supposed to return the depth of nesting for the current row. Because the `AdsProvider` is limited to single-table queries, the depth will always be zero. `Field count` is simply the number of fields in the result set, and for that, the length of the user properties string array is returned. The `HasRows` and `RecordsAffected` properties simply get related values off of the search result collection, and the `IsClosed` property should indicate whether or not the reader is in a readable state. For this implementation, the value is indicated by whether or not the reader has been disposed, which brings us to the other methods for consideration:

```
Public Overrides Sub Close()
    Me.Dispose(True)
End Sub

Public Overrides Function GetDataTypeName(ByVal ordinal As Integer) As String
```

```vb
        Return Me.GetFieldType(ordinal).FullName
    End Function

    Public Overrides Function GetFieldType(ByVal ordinal As Integer) As Type
        Me.LoadTypes()
        Return Me._types(ordinal)
    End Function

    Public Overrides Function GetName(ByVal ordinal As Integer) As String
        Return Me._command.UserProperties(ordinal)
    End Function

    Public Overrides Function GetOrdinal(ByVal name As String) As Integer
        Dim i As Integer
        For i = 0 To Me._command.UserProperties.Length - 1
            If (name = Me._command.UserProperties(i)) Then
                Return i
            End If
        Next
        Return -1
    End Function

    Public Overrides Function GetSchemaTable() As DataTable
        Throw New Exception("The method or operation is not implemented.")
    End Function

    Public Overrides Function GetValues(ByVal values() As Object) As Integer
        If (values Is Nothing) Then
            Throw New ArgumentNullException("values")
        End If
        Dim numValues As Integer
        If (values.Length < Me._command.UserProperties.Length) Then
            numValues = values.Length
        Else
            numValues = Me._command.UserProperties.Length
        End If
        Dim i As Integer = 0
        For i = 0 to numValues - 1
            values(i) = Me(i)
        Next
        Return numValues
    End Function

    Public Overrides Function IsDBNull(ByVal ordinal As Integer) As Boolean
        Return (Me.GetFieldType(ordinal) Is GetType(DBNull))
    End Function

    Public Overrides Function NextResult() As Boolean
        Return Me.Read
    End Function

    Public Overrides Function GetEnumerator() As IEnumerator
        Return New DirectoryEntryEnumerator(Me)
    End Function
```

The first method in the preceding code is the `Close` method. Obviously, this method should do whatever is meaningful for the provider to close itself. In the case of this provider, this means cleaning up the result set, which is what `Dispose` will do. For this case, `Close` and `Dispose` do the same thing, as they likely will in most readers, as there is no corresponding command to reopen it.

The next two methods listed are related to getting field type information about particular columns. To get this information, which the data adapter uses, the `AdsProvider` queries the schema that we've defined (shown previously) for the properties specified in the select list. Once it has that, it returns the data type information for the requested field.

`GetName` and `GetOrdinal` are also two peas in a pod that perform the inverse of each other. `GetName` will get the name of the column/property at the given ordinal. `GetOrdinal` gets the ordinal of the column/property with the given name.

`GetSchemaTable` returns a rather heavy table of schema information about the columns in the result set. We chose not to implement it because many of the fields that are expected in this schema are not terribly meaningful in the context of this provider — they'd be more meaningful for a relational data source. In addition, it will more or less get a subset of what is provided through the connection's `GetSchema` methods, so we did not see any real value in providing it.

`GetValues` will fill the given object array with values from the current row whose ordinals correspond to the indices in the given array. Note that it will only ever get up to the number of fields in the result set, regardless of the size of the given array. It will also return the actual number of values copied.

`IsDbNull`, as its name implies, will get whether or not the value of the column at the given ordinal is a `DbNull`. It never will be for this provider, but we provided a simple implementation all the same.

`NextResult` simply does what `Read` does — advances the reader to the next result. However, if your provider supports batches of SQL statements, this should advance to the results of the next statement in the batch.

Last, `GetEnumerator` is just an implementation of `IEnumerable`. In the case of this provider, we built a simple enumerator that in essence does exactly the same thing as the reader itself, call `Read` on the current reader when the `MoveNext` method on the enumerator is called. Because a reader is basically an enumerator, this is something of a redundant operation, but it is good because it exposes the reader as the more generic `IEnumerable` interface for things like data binding.

That wraps it up for what you need to do for the data reader. Unfortunately, most of it is just busywork, implementing a ton of very simplistic methods for the sake of ease of use for the users. The most meaningful methods are `Read` and `Close`, though certain others (such as `GetFieldType`) are important in order for the data adapter to function.

AdsDataAdapter

At this point, you technically could quit and have a fairly useful provider, enabling the key common data access APIs that ADO.NET provides; however, some would argue that the real value added for ADO.NET is the built-in goo for dealing with data in the `DataSet` and `DataAdapter` objects. In fact, `DataAdapter` was the only base class implementation that the 1.x versions of .NET provided. Therefore, if you want to make all the record set–oriented programmers happy (who probably make up the majority of programmers today), you need to seriously consider implementing the data adapter.

Thankfully, the good folks at Microsoft have made implementing a data adapter very easy. In fact, you could probably get away with implementing just one method, but to provide some other common features, you'll also want to do a few more things. First, you'll want to create strongly typed properties for the four commands the adapter deals with:

```
Public Shadows Property SelectCommand() As AdsCommand
    Get
        Return DirectCast(MyBase.SelectCommand, AdsCommand)
    End Get
    Set(ByVal value As AdsCommand)
        MyBase.SelectCommand = value
    End Set
End Property

Public Shadows Property InsertCommand() As AdsCommand
    Get
        Return DirectCast(MyBase.InsertCommand, AdsCommand)
    End Get
    Set(ByVal value As AdsCommand)
        MyBase.InsertCommand = value
    End Set
End Property

Public Shadows Property DeleteCommand() As AdsCommand
    Get
        Return DirectCast(MyBase.DeleteCommand, AdsCommand)
    End Get
    Set(ByVal value As AdsCommand)
        MyBase.DeleteCommand = value
    End Set
End Property

Public Shadows Property UpdateCommand() As AdsCommand
    Get
        Return DirectCast(MyBase.UpdateCommand, AdsCommand)
    End Get
    Set(ByVal value As AdsCommand)
        MyBase.UpdateCommand = value
    End Set
End Property
```

To do this, you just need to hide (shadow) the base class's implementation of these properties and expose your own, as shown in the preceding code. It is very straightforward — just declare them as your provider's command type and then set and get the same properties on the base class.

Next, you'll want to offer the familiar constructors that developers have come to know and love:

```
Public Sub New()
    MyBase.New()
End Sub

Public Sub New(ByVal selectCommand As AdsCommand)
```

```
        MyBase.New()
        Me.SelectCommand = selectCommand
    End Sub

    Public Sub New(ByVal selectCommandText As String, ByVal connection As
    AdsConnection)
        Me.New(New AdsCommand(selectCommandText, connection))
    End Sub
```

And let's not forget to inherit from the new `DbDataAdapter`:

```
Public Class AdsDataAdapter
    Inherits Common.DbDataAdapter
```

Finally, and most importantly, you will likely want to handle the `OnRowUpdating` event:

```
Protected Overrides Sub OnRowUpdating(ByVal value As Common.RowUpdatingEventArgs)
    Dim row As DataRow = value.Row
    Dim cmd As AdsCommand = DirectCast(value.Command, AdsCommand)
    If Not row.Table.Columns.Contains("Id") Then
        Throw New NotSupportedException(_
          "Updates require an Id to be specified in the select list.")
    End If
    Select Case (value.StatementType)
        Case StatementType.Insert
            Dim i As Integer
            For i = 0 To cmd.Properties.Length - 1
                If Not DBNull.Value.Equals(row(i)) Then cmd.SetValue(i, row(i))
            Next
        Case StatementType.Update
            cmd.SetKeyFilter(DirectCast(row("Id"), String))
            Dim i As Integer
            For i = 0 To cmd.Properties.Length - 1
                If cmd.CanSetValue(cmd.Properties(i)) And Not _
                  DBNull.Value.Equals(row(i)) Then
                    cmd.SetValue(i, row(i))
                End If
            Next
        Case StatementType.Delete
            cmd.SetKeyFilter(DirectCast(row("Id", _
              DataRowVersion.Original), String))
        Case Else
            Throw New NotSupportedException(String.Format(_
              "Row updating statement type '''{0}''' not supported.", _
                value.StatementType.ToString))
    End Select
End Sub
```

In handling this event, you will want to do anything necessary to prepare the various commands to execute against the given data row. Notice that we say "prepare." You do not want to actually execute the commands in this method, as that will cause them to be executed twice. This event is raised prior to executing the needed command for the data row.

Without going into too much detail about this provider's implementation, suffice it to say that for all of them, we have the artificial constraint that the commands use the single-value key constraint ("Id," mentioned earlier). This just makes it easy to find the entry that we want to update. A more sophisticated implementation will possibly want to select based on the entire original row values in order to implement the concurrency handling that is provided in the data adapter and data sets.

In addition, if you are supporting parameters with the data adapter, you will want to implement the `DbCommandBuilder`, which can be used to build a command based on the parameters of the `SelectCommand`. Because we're not supporting parameters, we didn't implement that class, but we did provide similar functionality by adding a `BuildUpdateCommands` method to the `AdsDataAdapter`:

```
Public Sub BuildUpdateCommands()
    If (Me.SelectCommand Is Nothing) Then
        Throw New NotSupportedException("No select command has been specified.")
    End If
    Me.InsertCommand = _
        Me.SelectCommand.BuildAdapterCommand(AdsCommand.CommandTypeOption.Insert)
    Me.UpdateCommand = _
        Me.SelectCommand.BuildAdapterCommand(AdsCommand.CommandTypeOption.Update)
    Me.DeleteCommand = _
        Me.SelectCommand.BuildAdapterCommand(AdsCommand.CommandTypeOption.Delete)
End Sub
```

As you can see, the code calls the `BuildAdapterCommand` internal (Friend) method on the select command, which copies the properties specified in the select list for updating, and sets other values to prepare each command for the type of statement it deals with.

Once you have done these few things, your provider should be ready to support the CRUD functionality that the data adapter helps out with. Now you have a full-featured ADO.NET provider. If you want to enable your provider to be used in generic coding, however, you still have a couple of steps to go.

AdsFactory

The first step is to implement the `DbProviderFactory` class. Luckily, this is the easiest of all the provider classes to implement. You'll probably be tired after implementing the others and be disappointed that you still have more to do, but never fear, this one is a cake walk. First, as you've come to expect, you will need to derive from the correct base:

```
Public NotInheritable Class AdsFactory
    Inherits Common.DbProviderFactory
```

Next, you implement a handful of methods to get instances of your provider's implementation:

```
Public Overrides Function CreateCommand() As Common.DbCommand
    Return New AdsCommand
End Function

Public Overrides Function CreateConnection() As Common.DbConnection
    Return New AdsConnection
```

```
    End Function

    Public Overrides Function CreateConnectionStringBuilder() As
    Common.DbConnectionStringBuilder
        Return New AdsConnectionStringBuilder
    End Function

    Public Overrides Function CreateDataAdapter() As Common.DbDataAdapter
        Return New AdsDataAdapter
    End Function

    Public Overrides Function CreateCommandBuilder() As Common.DbCommandBuilder
        Throw New Exception("The method or operation is not implemented.")
    End Function

    Public Overrides Function CreateDataSourceEnumerator() As _
      Common.DbDataSourceEnumerator
        Throw New NotSupportedException("DataSource enumerator is not supported.")
    End Function

    Public Overrides Function CreateParameter() As Common.DbParameter
        Throw New NotSupportedException("Parameters are not supported.")
    End Function

    Public Overrides Function CreatePermission(ByVal state As _
      Security.Permissions.PermissionState) As Security.CodeAccessPermission
        Return New System.DirectoryServices.DirectoryServicesPermission(state)
    End Function
```

Most of these are one-line operations. For the few things our provider doesn't support, we throw exceptions. One thing we haven't covered is the DataSourceEnumerator. If your provider supports enumerating data sources, you will want to implement this class. It only has one method, GetDataSources, which should return a DataTable describing the various data sources for your provider in your environment. For instance, SQL Server will get instances running in the network domain, which can be used in, for example, a drop-down list to select a particular data source.

The only other method that might not be obvious is CreatePermission—this method should create the code access permission needed for your data source, if one is defined. In the case of the AdsProvider, because we're using Active Directory, we return a DirectoryServicesPermission. If nothing else, you could return a SecurityPermission instance just to let a consuming application continue normally.

The last thing you need to do is declare a static (Shared) field in your factory class of the type of your factory class, named "Instance." It has to be static, public, and named "Instance"; otherwise, ADO.NET won't be able to use your factory. An example from AdsFactory follows:

```
    Public Shared ReadOnly Instance As New AdsFactory
```

Getting Ready for Use

Now that you have your factory all ready to go, you need to register it with ADO.NET so that it knows how to load it. This means adding it to the `DbProviderFactories` element in machine.config, like so:

```
<add name="Active Directory Data Provider" invariant="System.Data.AdsProvider"
    description=".Net Framework Data Provider for Active Directory"
    type="System.Data.AdsProvider.AdsFactory, System.Data.AdsProvider,
    Version=1.0.0.0, Culture=neutral, PublicKeyToken=null" />
```

(Note that the code lines here were wrapped due to page-width constraints.) The `name` is just a friendly name for your provider, and the `description` is just informational as well. The `invariant` attribute is what will need to be passed into the `DbProviderFactories.GetFactory` method to get the `Instance` (mentioned above) of your provider's factory.

The `type` attribute needs to be the full type name, including assembly name, into which your provider is built. This is used to bind to it and load it up dynamically, so your assembly itself will need to be where the runtime can locate it. For most shrink-wrapped providers, this will be in the Global Assembly Cache. However, because the `AdsProvider` is not strongly signed, it can be in another binding location, such as in the consuming application's private executable directory (for example, the /bin directory for ASP.NET apps or the same directory as the EXE for Windows Forms or console applications).

Note that if you will be distributing your provider, you should give it a strong name and even build an installer that will install it into the GAC and modify the machine.config file to add it as a registered provider. Commercial providers may want to take it a step further and work on the design-time experience for their components, and Microsoft has a good VSIP program (`http://msdn.microsoft.com/vstudio/extend/`) to help such vendors integrate well into Visual Studio.

At this point, you should be able to use your provider as you would any other ADO.NET providers, even using the new factory and discoverability features that ADO.NET 2.0 provides. Please refer back to Chapter 3 for more information on how to take advantage of these key features.

Summary

In this chapter, you examined the code we used to create a custom ADO.NET provider for ADO.NET 2.0. The key takeaways are the implementation of `DbConnection`, `DbCommand`, and `DbDataReader`, though providing support for the other base classes in the `System.Data.Common` namespace will make your provider more fully featured.

The key features that this version of ADO.NET brings to the table for data providers are the new base classes, the new metadata exploration API, and the connection string builder. All of these work together to provide a much more compelling story for writing data-store agnostic code, which can easily take advantage of standard data-access functionality from any number of providers, including those that may not otherwise have a familiar .NET interface, such as Active Directory.

For More Information

To complement the information in this chapter, take a look at the following resources:

❑ **"Improving Managed Code Performance," from** *Improving .NET Application Performance and Scalability*—`http://msdn.microsoft.com/library/default.asp?url=/library/en-us/dnpag/html/scalenetchapt05.asp`

❑ **Angel Saenz-Badillos' Blog (member of the ADO.NET team at Microsoft)**—`http://blogs.msdn.com/angelsb/`

❑ **SQL Server Community, another great online community**—`www.sqlservercentral.com/`

9

T-SQL Language and Enhancements

Any discussion of Transact-SQL (T-SQL) would be incomplete without at least some background on how it came to be. Over 30 years ago, a brilliant computer scientist named E. F. Codd embarked upon a methodology that would enable people to uniformly and conveniently extract data from data stores that fit his *relational data model*. Entire books have been dedicated to relational database theory and Codd's work, but suffice it to say that Structured Query Language (pronounced either "See-quel" or "S-Q-L," depending on who you ask) is the well from which T-SQL grew.

> *For more information on the Structured Query Language Specification, please visit* www.faqs.org/docs/ppbook/c1164.htm.

SQL was vastly different from what we traditionally think of in terms of "programming languages," although there are certainly some differences. Specifically, in traditional programming languages, you specified what you wanted to have happened one item at a time. Nothing (other than exceptions) happened that you didn't instruct the program to do. A good illustration of this concept is the story of the professor who conducts an exercise for each first-semester student. He takes a pitcher of water and a bucket and sits them on top of his desk. He then instructs each student to write down the process of pouring the water into the bucket. For each student, he then proceeds to do exactly what that student has written down, nothing more and nothing less. Each year, a huge mess is made. He does this because it precisely mimics the "procedural" language process. The SQL equivalent would be to say "fill the bucket" and then let the students figure out how, and then actually fill the bucket. Not exactly inverses but very close.

Perhaps the best illustration of this distinction was made by Dr. C. J. Date in his book *What Not How: The Business Rules Approach to Application Development* (2000). Traditionally, programmers write code that item by item issues instructions, which in turn issue other instructions, repeating this process until a program is created. Ten different developers can easily achieve the exact same result using 10 different methods because there are always different ways to get to a given result. For instance, let's say that the object at hand were to have the computer output the value 5. This could be accomplished in any of the following ways:

❑ You could declare some variables and add them together, like this:

```
Int32 a = 0;
Int32 b = 1;
Int32 c = 2;
Int32 d = 3;
Return a + b + c + d
```

(We simply added 0 for illustration purposes; in real life this would make little sense.)

❑ You could simply declare an `Int32` variable and initialize with the value 5, and then you would return that value:

```
Int32 d = 5;
Return d;
```

❑ Another approach might be to take a number greater than 5 and subtract whatever value is necessary to get to 5, and then return that number:

```
Int32 a = 10;
Int32 b = 5;
Return a - b;
```

❑ Similarly, you could create a simple `for` loop:

```
Int32 i = 0;
for(i = 0; i < 5; i++){
)
return i;
```

❑ You could also use other loops, such as the `while` loop:

VB.NET

```
Dim i As Int32 = 0
While i < 5
    i += 1
End While
Return i
```

C#

```
Int32 i = 0;
while(i < 5)
    i++;
return i;
```

❑ In addition, just to reinforce the potential variety, you could use a recursive loop:

VB.NET

```
Dim i As System.Int32 = 0
i = Make5(i)
Private Shared Function Make5(ByVal i As System.Int32) As Int32
```

```
        If (i = 5) Then
            Return i
        Else
            i += 1
            Return Make5(i)
        End If
    End Function
```

C#

```
System.Int32 i = 0;
i = Make5(i);

private static System.Int32 Make5( System.Int32 i)
{
    if(i == 5) return i;
    else {
      i++;
      return Make5(i);
    }
}
```

We could go on and on, but the point we're trying to make is that with traditional language approaches, there's virtually an infinite number of ways to get to a given result. As such, these are, in Date's terms, "how" type approaches because they define very specifically how a given result is to be achieved. Each one will yield the same result, but as you can see, how you get there varies greatly.

SQL, conversely, while every bit a "real" programming language, takes essentially the opposite approach. For instance, given a table called Items with one column, ItemValues, that contains 20 unique values, one of which is equal to the number 5, there are only a few ways to get the value because you tell the database what you want, and it determines how to get it for you. Essentially, you retrieve that value using the following query:

```
SELECT Values FROM Items WHERE ItemValues = '5'
```

Because the Items table contains only one column, you could achieve the same result using the "*" character (which tells the database to SELECT every column value). In a production environment, you should develop an aversion to using SELECT * queries unless you are absolutely positive you need the values from all of the columns. While it's certainly easier to use SELECT * instead of spelling out each column name individually, it's wasteful and inefficient if you don't need the data.

Your two alternatives to retrieving the value 5 would be either

```
SELECT * FROM Items WHERE ItemValues = '5'
```

or

```
SELECT Values FROM Items WHERE ItemValues > '4' AND Values < '6'
```

The key concept here is that SQL statements define what data you want returned — *not* how you go about retrieving the data. SQL has matured greatly since its inception into a very powerful language. However, some potential shortcomings with SQL need to be overcome in any viable relational database management system. The first problem is that not all vendors implement the specification precisely. For instance, Microsoft Access(r) has an IsNull function that returns a Boolean value indicating whether or not a given value is Null, while the IsNull implementation of other major vendors such as Microsoft SQL Server and Oracle behaves completely differently. Moreover, because SQL only concerns itself with the "what" aspect of the data, many control structures aren't available to you. As such, absent a specialized subset of SQL such as Microsoft's T-SQL or Oracle's PL/SQL, many common processing tasks would be impossible. For instance, ANSI SQL lacks support for such common programming tasks as loops and/or control flow statements or variable declarations. It also lacks any straightforward mechanism for implementing more advanced programming techniques such as recursion.

An In-Depth Look at T-SQL

As mentioned earlier, while ANSI SQL is very powerful, it's not well suited to many programming tasks. T-SQL is Microsoft's superset of SQL, providing the best of both worlds. You can use pure SQL statements when that's all you require, but for situations in which you need more power and flexibility, T-SQL is there for you.

Most of us had a course or five on relational database theory when we were in college, and if our professors did their jobs right (and we did our homework), we learned to normalize our data. We also learned about the concept of separating our applications into tiers. A typical midsize enterprise application has a UI or Presentation layer, a business or API layer, a Data Access layer, and, depending on your design, a back-end layer where stored procedures are stored.

> **Where and how these layers are drawn is the subject of endless debate. Stored procedure advocates recommend doing as much data access processing on the back-end tier because changes can be made to the application without requiring that the application be recompiled. Other reasons cited are security and performance, to name a few. For a really interesting contrarious opinion, Frans Bouma has laid forth a very thought-provoking "anti-stored" procedure argument that can be found at** http://weblogs.asp.net/fbouma/archive/2003/11/18/38178.aspx.

By and large, when people think of T-SQL, they invariably think of stored procedures. While it's true that T-SQL is very common in most developers' stored procedure code, you do not need to use stored procedures to use T-SQL. You can create a procedure with T-SQL using only the base SQL used in the preceding example:

```
CREATE PROCEDURE usp_Return5FromItems
AS
    SELECT * FROM Items WHERE Values = '5'
```

However, this would be a pretty lame stored procedure for more reasons than one. The worst thing about it is that the value 5 is hard-coded, so if you need a procedure to return other numbers — say, 1 to 100 — you'd need 100 different procedures to accommodate this requirement. This would create a maintenance nightmare, take eons of extra time to code, and provide no real value other than isolation. This is the first area in which T-SQL provides benefit — variable declaration.

To declare a variable in T-SQL, you create a name for it (beginning with the @ character), specify the type, and, if you want to keep it real, add a size where applicable and the parameter direction. For instance, if our `Values` column were `Varchar 5` and we didn't specify a length on the parameter, then someone could pass in a 50-character string, which you can guess is going to cause problems. The following code cleans up the preceding procedure and makes it a little more flexible:

```
CREATE PROCEDURE usp_GetMatchingValues
        @MatchValue VARCHAR(5)   INPUT
AS
SELECT ItemValues
FROM Items
WHERE ItemValues = @Matchvalue
```

We just dramatically improved our query so that it accommodates virtually any `varchar` value that could match our values in the database. If the user tries to pass in a value greater than five characters, then there will be a match problem. The important point is that we just avoided having to write 100 different procedures, each of which would be virtually identical other than the hard-coded number. Let's improve it a little more. Suppose you want to let the user be able to select the approximate spelling of a given last name. We'll add a `LastName` column to a new People table. To facilitate this, all you'd need to do is use the following:

```
CREATE PROCEDURE usp_GetCustomersByLastName
        @LastName VARCHAR (50) INPUT
AS
    SELECT LastName FROM People WHERE LastName LIKE @LastName%
```

This is enhanced somewhat, but if you wanted to have an "Exact search" and a "Like Search," you'd need two procedures to do it this way. Fortunately, you can create an additional parameter, and taking advantage of two T-SQL features — variable declarations and flow-control statements — you can build a really flexible search:

```
CREATE PROCEDURE usp_GetCustomersByLastName
        @LastName VARCHAR (50) INPUT, --Input is the default but we added it for
clarity
        @UseWildcard VARCHAR(5) INPUT
AS
IF UPPER(@UseWildCard) = 'TRUE' BEGIN
        SELECT LastName
        FROM People
        WHERE LastName
        LIKE @LastName%
END
ELSE BEGIN
        SELECT LastName FROM People WHERE LastName = @LastName
END
```

As you can see, by simply adding some variables and using the flow control, we just made our stored procedure a lot more possible. Now let's take it up another level. Assume that our table had some additional columns, such as `FirstName`, `SocialSecurityNumber`, and `DateOfBirth`. Using essentially the same logic used before, we could add a few other parameters and greatly expand what the user can search for:

```
CREATE PROCEDURE usp_CustomerSearch
  @FirstName AS VARCHAR = NULL,
  @LastName AS VARCHAR = NULL,
  @DOB AS DATETIME = NULL,
  @SSN AS DATETIME = NULL,
  @CustomerID AS INT = NULL
AS
SELECT *
FROM People
WHERE
  ((FirstName = @FirstName) OR (@FirstName = NULL)) AND
  ((LastName = @LastName) OR (@LastName = NULL)) AND
  ((DOB = @DOB) OR (@DOB = NULL)) AND
  ((SSN = @SSN) OR (@SSN = NULL)) AND
  ((CustomerID = @CustomerID) OR (CustomerID = NULL))
```

If you're thinking that this is awfully complex just to pull in a few fields, we don't blame you — it is. However, there's a definite method to our madness: We're going to be referring to what we just did shortly.

So what just happened? Essentially, what we did was enable the user to specify a value for any of the given fields of the table. If the user passes in a value, the stored procedure will match only the field(s) that match that value(s). Absent any field being present, no restriction will be used. We set a default value for each parameter so that if the user calls the procedure without passing in a parameter, the query will still succeed.

Structured Exception Handling

In the past, we had very limited capabilities with respect to error handling. The notion of exception handling per se was non-existent, and at best was awkward:

```
ALTER PROCEDURE usp_CustomerSearch
  @FirstName AS VARCHAR      = NULL,
  @LastName AS VARCHAR       = NULL,
  @DOB AS DATETIME           = NULL,
  @SSN AS DATETIME           = NULL,
  @CustomerID AS INT         = NULL
AS
BEGIN TRY
IF(@DOB = 'Bill') Begin
  PRINT 'This should cause and Error'
END
END TRY
BEGIN CATCH
   PRINT 'Error - DateTime can not == Bill'
END CATCH

SELECT *
FROM People
WHERE
    ((FirstName = @FirstName) OR (@FirstName = NULL)) AND
    ((LastName = @LastName) OR (@LastName = NULL)) AND
```

240

```
((DateOfBirth = @DOB) OR (@DOB = NULL)) AND
((SSN = @SSN) OR (@SSN = NULL)) AND
((CustomerID = @CustomerID) OR (CustomerID = NULL))
```

While this is a nonsensical example from a real-world perspective, it does illustrate how you use the TRY/CATCH blocks in T-SQL. Essentially, they work pretty much as you'd expect them to if you mixed .NET exception handling with T-SQL language constructs. The real power, of course, comes not from silly little examples with PRINT commands, but from more advanced uses such as transaction processing:

```
ALTER PROCEDURE usp_CustomerSearch
   @FirstName AS VARCHAR = NULL,
   @LastName AS VARCHAR  = NULL,
   @DOB AS DATETIME      = NULL,
   @SSN AS DATETIME      = NULL,
   @CustomerID AS INT    = NULL
AS
BEGIN TRY
    BEGIN TRAN
        IF(@DOB = 'Bill') Begin

          PRINT 'This should cause and Error'
        END
        ELSE BEGIN
            UPDATE PEOPLE
            SET FirstName = @FirstName,
                LastName = @LastName,
                DateOfBirth = @DOB,
                    SSN = @SSN,
                CustomerID = @CustomerID
        END
    COMMIT
END TRY
BEGIN CATCH
    ROLLBACK
    PRINT 'Error - DateTime cant == Bill'
END CATCH
```

Although we discuss transaction processing in its own context in Chapter 6, structured exception handlers and transactions are a match made in heaven. The following example shows how to handle transaction processing in its simplest form completely from client-side code:

VB.NET

```
Dim tn As SqlTransaction
Const sql As String = "INSERT INTO Employees1(EmpID) VALUES (@UserID)"
Dim cn As New SqlConnection("data source=AUG-SQLSRV;initial
catalog=HumanResources;integrated security=SSPI")
Try
   If (cn.State <> ConnectionState.Open) Then
      cn.Open()
   End If
Catch ex As SqlException
    Debug.Assert(False, ex.ToString)
```

```
End Try
tn = cn.BeginTransaction
Dim cmd As New SqlCommand(sql, cn, tn)
cmd.Parameters.Add("@UserId", SqlDbType.Int).Value = 314

Try
 Dim i As Int32 = cmd.ExecuteNonQuery
 For x As Int32 = 0 To 5
    cmd.Parameters("@UserId").Value = 314 + x
    cmd.ExecuteNonQuery()
 Next
cmd.Parameters("@UserId").Value = 325
cmd.ExecuteNonQuery()
tn.Commit()

Catch ex As SqlException
   tn.Rollback()
Finally
    cn.Close()
End Try
```

C#

```
SqlTransaction tn ;  //declare a transaction
const string sql = "INSERT INTO Employees1(EmpID) VALUES (@UserID)";
SqlConnection cn = new SqlConnection("data source=AUG-SQLSRV;initial
catalog=HumanResources;integrated security=SSPI");

try{if(cn.State != ConnectionState.Open){
cn.Open();}
}
//If we throw an exception on Open, which is a 'risky' operation
//manually make the assertion fail by setting it to false and use
  //ex.ToString() to get the information about the exception.
catch (SqlException ex){
     Debug.Assert(false, ex.ToString());
}
  //Instantiate command with CommandText and Connection and Transaction
  tn = cn.BeginTransaction();
   SqlCommand cmd = new SqlCommand(sql, cn,tn);
   cmd.Parameters.Clear();
   cmd.Parameters.Add("@UserID", SqlDbType.Int).Value = 314;

  try
  {
   //You can test for records affected, in this case we know it
  //would be at most one record.
     int i = cmd.ExecuteNonQuery();
   //If successful, commit the transaction
  //Loop 5 times and just add the id's incremented each time
     for(int x=0; x<5; x++)<BR>       {
          cmd.Parameters["@UserID"].Value = (315 + x);
          cmd.ExecuteNonQuery();
```

```
        }
        cmd.Parameters["@UserID"].Value = (325);
        cmd.ExecuteNonQuery();

        tn.Commit();
    }
    catch(SqlException ex){
        Debug.Assert(false, ex.ToString());
//If it failed for whatever reason, rollback the //transaction
        tn.Rollback();
//No need to throw because we are at a top level call and //nothing is handling
exceptions
    }
    finally{
        //Check for close and respond accordingly
        if(cn.State != ConnectionState.Closed){cn.Close();}
    }
```

If you look at the behavior of both code snippets, it is readily apparent that the logic is identical in both cases (for one, the `Commit` and `Rollback` are handled exclusively on the server, whereas for the other, those behaviors are handled exclusively on the client). As such, you'd want to try a piece of code and then, assuming that it completed successfully, you'd fire a `Commit`. However, if an exception is raised, then it is skipped over and control proceeds to the `catch` block, where at a minimum you would roll back your transaction. It's important to understand the flow of control under structured exception handling. In the following example, we're forcing an exception to occur by trying to compare a `DateTime` value to the literal `'Bill'`:

```
CREATE PROCEDURE usp_CustomerSearch
  @FirstName AS VARCHAR     = NULL,
  @LastName AS VARCHAR      = NULL,
  @DOB AS DATETIME          = NULL,
  @SSN AS DATETIME          = NULL,
  @CustomerID AS INT        = NULL
AS
BEGIN TRY
IF(@DOB = 'Bill') Begin
  PRINT 'This should cause and Error'
  PRINT 'Neither of these lines ever gets to execute'
  PRINT 'AND AS SUCH, both are potentially unreachable'
END
END TRY
BEGIN CATCH

  PRINT 'Error - DateTime can not == Bill'
END CATCH
```

As such, because of the way it's coded, you will never hit any of the following lines:

```
PRINT 'This should cause and Error'
PRINT 'Neither of these lines ever gets to execute'
PRINT 'AND AS SUCH, both are potentially unreachable'
```

Instead, you will only get the following output:

```
Error - DateTime can not == Bill
```

Why is this important? Well, depending on the way your procedure is written, you cannot count on certain lines of code executing. For instance, in the C# language specification, Section 8.1 (End Points and Reachability) indicates that code is deemed reachable in the following manner:

> **"If a statement can possibly be reached by execution, the statement is said to be reachable. Conversely, if there is no possibility that a statement will be executed, the statement is said to be unreachable."**

The section continues and specifies a little more with respect to reachability:

> **"A warning is reported if the compiler determines that a statement is unreachable. It is specifically not an error for a statement to be unreachable. To determine whether a particular statement or end point is reachable, the compiler performs flow analysis according to the reachability rules defined for each statement. The flow analysis takes into account the values of constant expressions (Section 7.15) that control the behavior of statements, but the possible values of non-constant expressions are not considered. In other words, for purposes of control flow analysis, a non-constant expression of a given type is considered to have any possible value of that type."**

While this may appear somewhat irrelevant, we bring it up for a specific reason. In Visual Basic .NET, for instance, the rules of reachability are not the same as they are in C#. As such, you can have unreachable code and the compiler will still head over to the bar and have a few beers with you afterward. Many consider this to be a "problem" with Visual Basic .NET (and the last thing we want to do is start that debate again) and a superiority of C# — you need to remember that T-SQL behaves like Visual Basic in this regard. We have potentially unreachable code throughout the code block specified in the previous example and if you weren't aware of reachability as an issue, you couldn't count on the compiler to help you out. In situations where you are using T-SQL Return Values or output parameters, or you are returning data in one form or another, it's important to account for the new flow of control that occurs within structured exception handler blocks.

At this point, we weren't sure where we should include a discussion of the InfoMessage event and how to handle it, but within the context of structured exception handlers seems as good a place as any.

According to the MSDN documentation on the SqlConnection object's InfoMessage event, the following behavior will be observed:

> **"Clients that want to process warnings or informational messages sent by the server should create an** SqlInfoMessageEventHandler **delegate to listen to this event.**
>
> **The** InfoMessage **event fires when a message with a severity of 10 or less is returned by SQL Server. Messages with a severity between 11 and 20 raise an error, and messages with a severity over 20 will cause the connection to close."**

Consider now the following code. We're creating a procedure that does pretty much nothing but run a `Print` statement. `Print` statements, by the way, are treated as very low severity errors, so if you need to start a dialogue between the client code and your stored procedure, trapping the `InfoMessage` event in conjunction with `Print` statements is often an effective way to accomplish your goal:

```
ALTER PROCEDURE dbo.usp_TestProc
AS BEGIN TRY
   DECLARE @Value DATETIME
   SET @Value = 'cuckoo'
   PRINT 'Cuckoo, Cuckoo'

END TRY
   BEGIN CATCH
         Print 'Catch Cuckoo Exception'
   END CATCH
RETURN
```

As you can see, we're intentionally causing an exception condition by converting the literal `'cuckoo'` to a `DateTime`. Now for the code:

```
SqlConnection cn = null;
private void Form1_Load(object sender, EventArgs e)
{
cn = new SqlConnection(@"Data Source=mycomputer\cuckoobird;Initial
Catalog=Cuckooz;Integrated Security=SSPI;" );
   cn.InfoMessage += new SqlInfoMessageEventHandler(MessageHandler);
   cn.Open();
   SqlCommand cmd = new SqlCommand("usp_TestProc", cn);
   cmd.CommandType = CommandType.StoredProcedure;
   cmd.ExecuteNonQuery();
   cn.Close();
}
private void MessageHandler(object sender, SqlInfoMessageEventArgs args)
{
    MessageBox.Show(args.Message)
};
```

If you run this code, a `MessageBox` object should appear with "Catch Cuckoo Exception" as its text. This is exactly what we'd expect because, as the comments indicate, we're forcing an exception condition.

By using the `TRY`/`CATCH` syntax, we can effectively get code to work that would otherwise cause the application to bomb if the client code wasn't handling the exceptions properly. We could probably write a small book on exception management strategies in .NET alone — so much of it is beyond the scope of what we're discussing here. The point we want to make is that often, in your `TRY`/`CATCH` blocks, you'll try a piece of code that you *know* may have something predictably wrong with it and you respond to it. In most .NET code, you typically try to respond to the exception, and you often use some sort of logging mechanism.

The Microsoft Exception Management Application Block is an excellent example of a fully featured logging mechanism that is used in conjunction with structured exception handling. For one thing, it allows exception/error information to be transmitted to users via e-mail, published to event logs, stored to a database, or written to file or even a message queue. Similarly, depending on the exception being raised, different people can be notified. If you think about it, this is an excellent way to handle such problems. As developers, we have little control over the database going down, for instance (unless our code is really bad), so a connection timeout is probably not something we need to know about—but the network administrator or DBA would need to be notified. Conversely, the DBA wouldn't need to know about a NullReferenceException *caused because we failed to instantiate an object. You can find more information at* www.microsoft.com/downloads/details.aspx?displaylang= en&FamilyID=8CA8EB6E-6F4A-43DF-ADEB-8F22CA173E02

Perhaps one of the most straightforward ways to simulate this sort of functionality is by using InfoMessage and Print statements. Now for the obligatory caveats. As author Bill Ryan's senior lead technical architect—a man named Phil—wrote a while back in an e-mail message: *"Never, never, never, never, never, under any circumstances, catch an exception and do nothing with it unless you have an absolutely compelling reason for doing so."* He went on to say that there are no compelling reasons to do so. Why? For one thing, there's overhead associated with catching exceptions, and many poorly designed applications reflect the use of exception handling when they should have been coded correctly in the first place. A bigger problem, however, is that if you catch/eat an exception and do nothing with it, you are very likely introducing subtle bugs in your application that will be next to impossible to track down. If you catch an exception and do nothing with it, you are effectively eliminating the symptom while leaving the root problem broken. If you make a habit of eating exceptions and not doing anything with them, we can pretty much guarantee that you'll one day find yourself feeling really dumb because you didn't heed the advice in that e-mail message.

We should touch upon something else that was more or less glossed over earlier, and that's addressing a more real-world application of using structured exceptions. To accomplish this, we need to again discuss exception handling "in general." Exception handling should be limited to situations in which the code block in question cannot perform its specific behavior. What it should *not* do is try to "handle" things out of its intended duties or handle things by merely covering them up. To elaborate, consider the following code snippet. It looks like a very simple and very common way of handling things. For the time being, let's equate this sort of code with previous versions of T-SQL code:

```
Private Function ExceptionTest(ByVal divisor As System.Int32) As System.Int32
    Dim Numerator As System.Int32 = 100
    Dim CalculatedValue As System.Int32 = Numerator / divisor
    Return CalculatedValue
End Function
```

Note first that the preceding code is very fragile because someone could pass in a 0 and the code would break. A common way to fix such potential issues is by using a TRY/CATCH block but trapping an inappropriate exception:

```
Dim CalculatedValue As System.Int32
Try
   Dim Numerator As System.Int32 = 100
   CalculatedValue = Numerator / divisor
Catch ex As Exception
   Return 0 'This is a random number chosen to represent an
      'error condition
End Try
Return CalculatedValue
```

This code fixed the divide-by-zero problem, but there's still a lot wrong with it. We blame part of the problem on the Visual Basic implementation in Visual Studio .NET. (This is *not* a shortcoming of the Visual Basic language by any means, just a poor choice of implementation of the IDE.) What specific problem are we talking about? We're now trapping `System.Exception`, the most broad and all-encompassing of the exceptions. If the return of 0 is supposed to signify that a 0 was passed in, how would one differentiate between a 0 being passed in as a parameter and an `OutofMemory` exception? Unfortunately, when this point is raised, many people do a little research and then modify the code to trap `System.ApplicationException` instead of `System.Exception` but change nothing else.

Remember Phil's rule. A better way to handle this scenario is to check for 0 before attempting to divide and either raising an exception or doing whatever it is that you do when business rules are violated. A common example might entail having some Debug assertions in your code, which will signal a problem during smoke test builds but won't compile into the production application. Alternately, you could include some logging information, using something such as Log4Net or the Microsoft Exception Management Block.

> *Log4Net is a superb open-source logging framework hosted by the Apache project. It is available at* `http://logging.apache.org/log4net/`.

We've belabored this point a little, but it's a very big issue when coding outside of T-SQL, and it's an equally big issue when using the new T-SQL constructs. The point is that exception handling should do two things: handle the exception, not just eat it, and do something useful with it. Whether this entails logging it, providing user feedback in the form of a visual cue, supplying alternative values, or whatever else the requirements may demand, the common denominator is that something of value should be done with it. In order to do something of value, you need to be precise. Many of us can recall instances when people complained of a problem and when asked what was wrong, simply replied, "It doesn't work."

Trapping `System.Exception` is essentially like answering "It didn't work." Okay, could we be more precise? "Uh, I was running the SEC Margin Requirement batch and it stopped working." This is like trapping an `ApplicationException` object. At least we know that it has something directly to do with our application, but not much else. Trapping `DivideByZero` is like saying "When I was running the SEC Margin Requirement process, we got an error that said it had already been run and it couldn't run again unless the previous values were cleared out, and I don't know how to clear them out." Now we finally have something useful that we can work with. If you are ever tempted to trap `System.Exception` or trap an exception less specific than necessary, think back to someone telling you, "It doesn't work," and picture yourself being on the other side of the equation — it'll make you want to do the right thing quickly.

Similarly, too often you'll hear people say, "Well, I trap `System.Exception` because I know that under no circumstances do I want the program to crash." Fair enough. Neither do we. But if the program doesn't work correctly, and your strategy to keep it from crashing entails making it virtually impossible to track down the bug in a timely manner, you aren't helping the customer at all. Not too long ago, when Bill Ryan was new to .NET, he trapped `System.Exception` in the deep inner recesses of a class library and just ate the exception. Unfortunately, a problem he never anticipated was causing the routine to blow up, but because he wasn't doing anything meaningful and he was returning a 0, it looked just like it would have if it were behaving normally. By the time he found the problem, after many wild goose chases, he had wasted a lot of time and inconvenienced a lot of people. . . all in the name of never letting the program crash as a convenience to the user.

So what does this have to do with T-SQL exception handling? Well, T-SQL's ability to trap and handle exceptions isn't quite as powerful as .NET's. On the other hand, it's a lot more powerful than `Goto` statements or looking for `@@Error`. In order to do "something useful," you need to know what potential errors can arise and look for them in particular. For instance, take the following simple SELECT statement:

247

```
SELECT *
FROM Customers
```

Is there any chance of raising a Constraint violation? Is there any chance that you'll have a null value violation? Of course not. Therefore, you need to look at the specific task at hand and trap accordingly. This entails thinking about your code in a little more depth, as well as doing a little homework to find the error numbers. Here is an example of what we mean:

```
ALTER PROCEDURE usp_CustomerSearch
        @FirstName AS VARCHAR,
        @LastName AS VARCHAR,
        @DOB AS DATETIME,
        @SSN AS DATETIME,
        @CustomerID AS INT
AS
BEGIN TRY
  BEGIN TRAN
        UPDATE PEOPLE
        SET FirstName = @FirstName,
            LastName = @LastName,
            DateOfBirth = @DOB,
            SSN = @SSN,
            CustomerID = @CustomerID
  COMMIT
END TRY
BEGIN CATCH
  DECLARE @ErrorInfo INT
  SET @ErrorInfo = @@error
  ROLLBACK
  IF @ErrorInfo = 515 BEGIN
   PRINT 'Cannot insert the value NULL into column '%.*ls', table '%.*ls'; column
does not allow nulls. %ls fails.'
  END
  ELSE IF @ErrorInfo = 542 BEGIN
    PRINT 'An invalid datetime value was encountered. Value exceeds the year 9999.'
  END
END CATCH
```

In SQL Server 97, 2000, and Yukon, you can define custom error numbers and messages. To get a full list of the error numbers and corresponding messages that have been defined, you can query the sysmessages table of the Master database (SELECT * FROM sysmessages). This will provide a complete list that includes every system error as well as any that you have defined.

For this modified version of the original procedure, we aren't specifying default values for our parameters, so any of them could be null. It is hoped that our business rules on the client will prevent this condition from ever happening, but you can't control how someone uses your code, so you would want to check this as well. Because we are also passing in a date and no longer checking to ensure the date is valid, we could get a value like January 1, 2 B.C., which would cause an overflow. We could probably come up with a few others, but two are enough to give you an idea of how to proceed. Anyway, by looking up the error codes in the sysmessages table, we find that error 515 is raised when you try to insert a value into a column that doesn't allow nulls. Similarly, if you try to insert a date that is greater than or less than what can be held in a DateTime or SmallDateTime, then error 542 is raised. As far as handling the exception, that again depends on your business rules. Author Bill Ryan is currently working on a project that includes building a system used by the state's technical college system and ensuring that student data is in a valid format. The data comes from several different vendors that have different implementations, but when it's transmitted to the government, it has to be in a very precise format. As such, there are certain generic rules in place, like "If someone's birth date would make them less than 10 years old or older than 100, we'll use the default data of January 1, 1970." The following example shows how you might implement such a requirement (and truth be told, in this system and many others, dummy values are often used when the real data can't be accurately determined):

```
AS
BEGIN TRY
    BEGIN TRAN
        UPDATE PEOPLE
        SET FirstName = @FirstName,
            LastName = @LastName,
            DateOfBirth = @DOB,
            SSN = @SSN,
            CustomerID = @CustomerID
    COMMIT
END TRY
BEGIN CATCH
  DECLARE @ErrorInfo INT
  SET @ErrorInfo = @@error
  ROLLBACK
 IF @ErrorInfo = 515 BEGIN
   PRINT 'Cannot insert the value NULL into column '%.*ls', table '%.*ls'; column
does not allow nulls. %ls fails.'
 END
  ELSE IF @ErrorInfo = 542 BEGIN
  UPDATE PEOPLE
        SET FirstName = @FirstName,
            LastName = @LastName,
            DateOfBirth = '01/01/1970',
            SSN = @SSN,
            CustomerID = @CustomerID

  END
END CATCH
```

We'd like to point out one more thing. When using @@error, every time you reference it, it resets itself. Therefore, if you use PRINT @@Error PRINT @@Error when an error occurs, the first Print statement will print out a value, whereas the second one won't. This is why we created a temporary variable and set it equal to @@Error at a given point in time. If you don't do this, then you'll never trap the exception as expected because the value will reset itself.

OUTPUT

Without a doubt, one of our favorite new features is the output clause. If you look on the microsoft .public.dotnet.framework.adonet newsgroup, you'll see daily questions about retrieving newly created @@Identity values.

> Bill Vaughn has an excellent article on this topic, called "Managing an @@Identity Crisis." You can find it at http://msdn.microsoft.com/library/default.asp?url=/library/en-us/ dnadonet/html/manidcrisis.asp

To get around all the fancy footwork necessary to retrieve newly inserted values, the OUTPUT method is used. In many ways, it resembles a trigger in that it has the inserted record that you can reference:

```
ALTER PROCEDURE usp_ShowHowOutPutWorks
    @FirstName VARCHAR(50),
    @LastName VARCHAR(50)
AS

DECLARE @TempVariable
    TABLE(    ConsultantID   INT,
        FirstName        VARCHAR(50),
        LastName         VARCHAR(50),
          SSN                VARCHAR(50),
          DateOfBirth      DATETIME,
          ProjectHours    INT,
          Award            BIT)


INSERT INTO dbo.PEOPLE (FirstName ,
                        LastName,
                        DateOfBirth,
                        SSN,
                        ConsultantId,
                        ProjectHours,
                        Award)

OUTPUT inserted.* INTO @TempVariable

VALUES(@FirstName,
       @LastName,
       '07/12/1975',
       '072150088',
       20,
       100,
        1)

SELECT *
FROM @TempVariable
```

To call this, you'd simply use the following:

```
usp_ShowHowOutPutWorks 'Jenna', 'Jameson'
```

Top X

The current version of T-SQL includes a TOP operator. To use it, you simply use a syntax such as this:

```
SELECT TOP 10(CustomerID)
FROM People
```

This would return the top 10 values of the CustomerID column if there were at least 10 records; and if there were fewer, it would return whatever values there were. This provides some pretty useful functionality for many scenarios because you often use an `Identity` column, for instance, as a key, and don't know which 10 records you need. Consultants, for example, typically make their money by hourly billing, so time tracking is critical. Each project typically includes a bonus pool. Cost overruns cause that pool to dwindle. However, consultants are rewarded in part for how much they bill. Consequently, their bonuses are based in part on who bills the most for a given project. Slightly modifying the first table we used, imagine that the following table is used as part of our human resources program:

```
CREATE TABLE [dbo].[People](
    [FirstName] [varchar](50) COLLATE SQL_Latin1_General_CP1_CI_AS NULL,
    [LastName] [varchar](50) COLLATE SQL_Latin1_General_CP1_CI_AS NULL,
[DateOfBirth] [datetime] NULL,
    [SSN] [varchar](50) COLLATE SQL_Latin1_General_CP1_CI_AS NULL,
    [ConsultantID] [int] IDENTITY(1,1) NOT NULL,
    [ProjectHours] [money] NULL,
  [Award] [bit],
  CONSTRAINT [PK_People]
PRIMARY KEY CLUSTERED
```

Now suppose that the powers that be decided we would give award money to the five consultants who billed the most. In the current version of T-SQL, the query would be logically identical to the first query, but how would they get that data in there? Previously, it would have taken some slightly fancy footwork, but in the current version of T-SQL, the following would work:

```
UPDATE TOP (5) PEOPLE
SET Award = 1
```

In addition to being able to specify the TOP command with UPDATEs, you can also use it with DELETE statements and it works exactly as the UPDATE does except that you are using the word DELETE:

```
DELETE TOP (5) PEOPLE
```

As convenient as this is, though, an equally cool feature is the capability to specify a parameterized value in the Top function. What that means is that you could use some formula specified in a variable and use it in place of the hard-coded number:

```
DECLARE @NumberOfEmployees  INT
DECLARE @Divisor            INT
DECLARE @TopFactor          INT
SELECT @NumberOfEmployees = COUNT(*) FROM People
SET @Divisor = 2
SELECT  @TopFactor = @NumberOfEmployees/@Divisor
SELECT TOP (@TopFactor) *
FROM PEOPLE
```

Assuming the values we started with at the beginning of this section, the following results will be output:

```
FirstName   LastName   DateOfBirth   SSN  ConsultantID ProjectHours        Award
William     Ryan       1971-08-06    166888888 2          200.00               1
John        Smith      1972-09-05    11111111  4          250.00               1

(2 row(s) affected)
```

Similarly, you can do away with a little of the complexity and nest a complex (or, in this case, a relatively straightforward) function call directly in the TOP command:

```
DECLARE @NumberOfEmployees  INT
DECLARE @Divisor            INT
DECLARE @TopFactor          INT
SELECT @NumberOfEmployees = COUNT(*) FROM People
SET @Divisor = 2

SELECT TOP ((SELECT COUNT(*) FROM PEOPLE)/@Divisor) *
FROM PEOPLE
```

Note that this query does effectively the same thing that the preceding one does. The main difference is that it uses an abbreviated syntax by specifying a new SELECT clause and corresponding restriction statement just as it would a declared variable. Again, the output from the above query outputs to the following:

```
FirstName                                       LastName
DateOfBirth                 SSN
ConsultantID ProjectHours           Award
------------------------------------------------- ---------------------------------
------
William                                         Ryan
1971-08-06   166888888                              1             200.00
1
John                                            Smith
1972-09-05   111111111                              4             250.00
1

(2 row(s) affected)
```

Note one caveat to using any of the new versions of TOP: The value that you are using as the TOP parameter must be decorated with parentheses, like this:

```
UPDATE TOP (5) PEOPLE
SET Award = 1
```

The preceding code will parse and work as expected, whereas this

```
UPDATE TOP 5 PEOPLE
SET Award = 1
```

will not. It's a seemingly trivial distinction, but when getting used to the new language construct, it's an easy thing to get wrong (which in our case led to us wasting about 20 mintues trying to figure out why it wouldn't parse).

Common Table Expressions

Common Table Expressions (CTEs) are another enhancement that get a full 100% cool factor rating. Conceptually, they are similar to Temporary tables in current versions of T-SQL, but in our opinion they are infinitely more elegant and intuitive. In addition to elegance, they afford one the luxury of using recursion, a feature that we'll discuss shortly.

To use a CTE, you give it a name and then specify a command to populate it. Using the People table we provided in the TOP section, here's an example of how this would work:

```
WITH CTE_TABLE(FirstName, LastName)
AS
(SELECT FirstName, LastName
FROM PEOPLE)
SELECT FirstName, LastName
FROM CTE_Table
```

This query will result in the following output:

```
FirstName                                              LastName
-------------------------------------------------     --------------------------------
------
William                                                Ryan
John                                                   Smith
Beamer                                                 Gregory
Wallace                                                McClure
Bill                                                   Gates

(5 row(s) affected)
```

Because there is no restriction clause specified in the SELECT statement defining the CTE, the output will be identical to running the statement SELECT * FROM People.

Now, in order to understand how recursive queries work, you need to understand the notion of a *self join*. Here's a fairly simple example. Assume a very simple schema that contains a Family Member Number, a Family Member name, and a Parental ID, as shown in the following table:

Family Member Number	Family Member	Parental ID
1	Mom	NULL
2	Dad	1
3	Bill	1
4	Sparky	3
5	Rover	3

Given the information in this table, let's say we want to print out who answers to whom. In order to facilitate this, a self join would come in really handy:

```
SELECT  Fam.FamilyMember, Parent.ParentId
FROM FamilyMembers Fam, FamilyMembers Parent
WHERE Fam.FamilityMemberId = Parent.ParentId
```

To use a recursive query, you need two components, an *anchor* and a *joinback*. The anchor is the base query that you'll use; it essentially specifies the values that you're looking for. The joinback has two SELECT statements, the second of which references itself:

```
WITH FAMILYCTE (FamilyMemberNumber, MemberName, ParentID)
AS
   (SELECT Fam.FamilyMemberNumber, Fam.MemberName, Fam.ParentId
    FROM FamilyMembers Fam
    WHERE Fam.ParentID IS NULL
    UNION ALL
    SELECT Fam.FamilyMemberNumber, Fam.MemberName, Fam.ParentId
    FROM FamilyMembers Fam
            INNER JOIN FAMILYCTE ON FAMILYCTE.FamilyMemberNumber = FAM.ParentID
SELECT FamilyMemberNumber, MemberName, ParentID)
FROM FamilyCTE
```

In the preceding code, we began by specifying an anchor (represented by the first SELECT statement). We then took this output as the basis for recursion. The final selection condition is the exit condition, similar to that which is necessary to all recursive statements if you want them to end at any point.

PIVOT

Without a doubt, another features that gets a full 100% cool factor rating is the PIVOT function. To get a feel for it, let's use a typical scenario that most of us are probably familiar with: project management. Assume for a second that we had the following table definition:

```
CREATE TABLE [dbo].[BillingSummary](
  [Hours] [int] NULL,
  [ProjectID] [varchar](50) COLLATE SQL_Latin1_General_CP1_CI_AS NULL,
  [BillingType] [varchar](50) COLLATE SQL_Latin1_General_CP1_CI_AS NULL,
  [BillingPeriod] [int] NULL
) ON [PRIMARY]
```

Now, for the sake of simplicity, assume that the following values are included in the table:

Hours	ProjectID	BillingType	BillingPeriod
250	SCPPP	ProjManagement	1
280	SCPPP	ProjManagement	2
350	SCPPP	ProjManagement	3
125	SCPPP	ProjManagement	4
512	SCPPP	Development	1
645	SCPPP	Development	2
501	SCPPP	Development	4
655	GAPPP	ProjManagement	2
699	GAPPP	Development	2
988	GAPPP	ProjManagement	3
945	GAPPP	Development	3
699	SCPPP	Development	3
198	GAPPP	ProjManagement	1
256	GAPPP	Development	1
233	GAPPP	ProjManagement	4
298	GAPPP	Development	4

```
(16 row(s) affected)
```

Now suppose that the boss wants to know how much we billed per service type, per billing period, per project. In traditional T-SQL, it would be a pain in the you-know-what. But using the T-SQL PIVOT function, it's a breeze. Examine the following query:

```
SELECT * FROM BillingSummary
PIVOT
(SUM(Hours)
FOR [ProjectId]
IN (SCPPP, GAPPP)
)
AS Results
GO
```

It will yield the following results:

BillingType	BillingPeriod	SCPPP	GAPPP
Development	1	512	256
ProjManagement	1	250	198
Development	2	645	699
ProjManagement	2	280	655
Development	3	699	945
ProjManagement	3	350	988
Development	4	501	298
ProjManagement	4	125	233
(8 row(s) affected)			

If we wanted to shift the entire focus to break it down by billing type, we could simply shift the operators around, as so:

```
SELECT * FROM BillingSummary
PIVOT
(SUM(Hours)
FOR [BillingType]
IN (Development, ProjManagement)
)
AS Results
GO
```

That modified query will result in the following output:

ProjectID ProjManagement	BillingPeriod	Development	
GAPPP	1	256	198
SCPPP	1	512	250
GAPPP	2	699	655
SCPPP	2	645	280
GAPPP	3	945	988
SCPPP	3	699	350

| GAPPP | 4 | 298 | 233 |
| SCPPP | 4 | 501 | 125 |

`(8 row(s) affected)`

UNPIVOT

UNPIVOT works the same way PIVOT does, just reversed. In a nutshell, UNPIVOT takes "PIVOTED" data and turns the columns into rows. The only caveat that needs mentioning with UNPIVOT is how nulls are treated. They aren't. They are ignored. Therefore, you need to be well aware of this. Of course, if you need the rows to come back, you can specify default values in cases of null.

```
SELECT * FROM BillingSummary
UNPIVOT
(Hours
FOR [BillingType]
IN (Development, ProjManagement)
)
AS Results
```

Ranking

Traditionally, if you wanted to check the row number of a result set, you'd need to use an Identity in SQL Server. A similar way to get to the same result in ADO.NET was an Expression column in your DataTable. This was accomplished by choosing a column and setting its Autoincrement property to true. You could then specify a Seed value (the value at which the sequence begins) as well as the AutoIncrement value (so you could have everything increase by two or three or whatever). In Oracle, this is roughly analogous to a sequence. In Yukon, there are two new ways to achieve a sequence in your results (in addition, of course, to the previous methods just mentioned). Note that nothing has been taken away; now you just have some more options, the first of which is the ROW_NUMBER function.

ROW_NUMBER()

ROW_NUMBER() is the first of the two new methods and it couldn't be more straightforward to use. Assuming the People table specified at the beginning of the chapter, you could use ROW_NUMBER like so:

```
SELECT  FirstName,
        LastName,
        ROW_NUMBER()
        OVER (ORDER BY ConsultantID) AS IDValue FROM People
```

This would yield the following results:

FirstName	LastName	IDValue
William	Ryan	1
Wallace	McClure	2
Beamer	Gregory	3
John	Smith	4

```
Bill                    Gates                                          5

(5 row(s) affected)
```

The only caveat to using ROW_NUMBER is that you need to specify an ORDER BY clause. This is critical because unlike using an Identify value or some other hard-coded value, this is virtual (which means it's calculated on the fly) and completely contingent upon the ORDER BY clause. To that end, the result is the same as it would be if you were to use the Autoincrement column in a DataTable because using that method, the values of each row/column combination would be virtual and only determined after the query was in effect. You essentially get the same result using ROW_NUMBER. Therefore, by changing the ORDER BY clause, the ROW_NUMBER value will change accordingly:

```
SELECT  FirstName,
        LastName,
        ROW_NUMBER()
OVER (ORDER BY ConsultantID DESC)
AS IDValue
FROM People

FirstName    LastName              IDValue
-----------  ------------------    ---------------------
Bill         Gates                                     1
John         Smith                                     2
Beamer       Gregory                                   3
Wallace      McClure                                   4
William      Ryan                                      5

(5 row(s) affected)
```

The obvious question that comes to mind is what happens when you use an ORDER BY clause that has non-distinct values—namely, values that appear more than once. The answer is that you'll get an undefined (null) value. With this in mind, our previous statement that ROW_NUMBER results in the same result sequence as an expression column in ADO.NET is not entirely true.

RANK()

The corollary to the ROW_NUMBER function is the RANK() function. Virtually identical to ROW_NUMBER, the primary distinction between the two is that RANK() will yield the same value for similar items specified in the ORDER BY clause:

```
SELECT  FirstName,
        LastName,
        RANK() OVER (ORDER BY ConsultantID DESC) AS IDValue
FROM People

FirstName    LastName              IDValue
-----------  ------------------    ---------------------
Bill         Gates                 1
John         Smith                 2
John         Smith                 2
John         Smith                 2
William      Ryan                  5
```

Dense_Rank()

If you examine the Rank() example results, you'll see that the record with FirstName equal to John, LastName equal to Smith, and IDValue equal to 2 appears three times. However, you'll see that we go from 1 to 2 to 5. There is not an uninterrupted sequence, which is what you may need. If you need an uninterrupted sequence, then use Dense_Rank().

Assuming the same data that was used in the Rank() section, Dense_Rank() would look like this:

```
SELECT  FirstName,
        LastName,
        DENSE_RANK() OVER (ORDER BY ConsultantID DESC) AS IDValue
FROM People
```

This in turn would give you the following results:

FirstName	LastName	IDValue
Bill	Gates	1
John	Smith	2
John	Smith	2
John	Smith	2
William	Ryan	3

We've seen this explained in a very confusing manner in most sources, so we want to make sure you understand what happened. The last record (William Ryan 3) has 3 for an IDValue in this example, whereas it was 5 when we used the Rank() function alone. Each time the grouping switches, it will be sequential using Dense_Rank, whereas it will increase with Rank() but there may be gaps depending on the data.

NTile()

The NTile() function is similar to both Rank() and Dense_Rank(), but it has a slightly different purpose. NTile() is essentially a mechanism by which you can assign effective percentiles to different values. You'll often want to put people into percentiles. To accomplish this, you can use the NTile() function, passing in whatever number you want to be used to "percentalize" things with (ideally, an even number). In the preceding example, we'd use NTile() like this (we're going to use 5 because there are five different records).

```
SELECT  FirstName,
        LastName,
        NTILE(5) OVER (ORDER BY ConsultantID DESC) AS IDValue
FROM People
```

This would in turn yield the following:

FirstName	LastName	IDValue
Bill	Gates	1
John	Smith	2

John	**Smith**	**3**
John	**Smith**	**4**
William	Ryan	5

If we used 100, it would break them up into similar percentiles, just as would 1,000 or 1,000,000 (currently, you can pass in anything up to the maximum of Yukon's BIGINT value). What would happen if you used one of these bigger numbers, a number that exceeded the count of records? Well, we can't tell you for sure, other than it will be weird and unpredictable. We've tried running the preceding query using 1,000 and we got really strange values, but basically the highest number that resulted was 10. Suffice it to say that if you use a number greater than the number of records, then the results will be unpredictable.

TABLESAMPLE

In the spirit of the ranking functions just described, TABLESAMPLE is another really slick enhancement. What this enables you to do is essentially select a subset of data in your query's restriction. In many business scenarios, decision-makers employ the use of statistical sampling to get a feel for how things are running in their business. TABLESAMPLE makes doing this a lot easier.

```
SELECT FirstName,
       LastName
FROM People
TABLESAMPLE (4 Rows)


FirstName                      LastName
-------------------------      ------------------------------------
William                        Ryan
John                           Smith
Beamer                         Gregory
Wallace                        McClure
Bill                     Gates
```

Does something look funny up there? If not, look again. You should notice that in the TABLESAMPLE call, we specified four rows, yet five are returned in the query. (For the record, there are five rows in the table.) More interestingly, if we specify the argument to be 3 instead of 4, we get 0 rows back:

```
SELECT FirstName,
       LastName
FROM People
TABLESAMPLE (3 Rows)

FirstName                      LastName
-------------------------      ------------------------------------
0 Rows Returned
```

Why is that? Well, we have yet to figure out the algorithm, but the number that is used is definitely an approximation—so you aren't sure exactly how many will be returned. You'd think that with five rows in a table, any such restriction with a smaller number (in this case three, two, or one) would yield at least a row or two, but it doesn't. Well, at least it doesn't some of the time. We ran the query multiple times and, as the table shows, sometimes values were returned and sometimes they weren't:

Attempt	Rows in Table	Rows Specified	Records Returned
1	5	5	5
1	5	4	5
1	5	3	5
1	5	2	0
1	5	1	0
2	5	5	5
2	5	4	5
2	5	3	0
2	5	2	0
2	5	1	0
3	5	5	5
3	5	4	0
3	5	3	0
3	5	2	0
3	5	1	0

This is particularly noteworthy because if you must have a minimum or specific sample size, you'll have to check the counts of the records returned manually.

Just as you can specify the number of rows to be used using the rows, you can specify percentage using, you guessed it, PERCENT:

```
SELECT  FirstName,
        LastName
FROM People
TABLESAMPLE( 100 PERCENT )
```

We used percentages down to 60% to get a feel for how things behaved under percent versus rows. With five rows, 80% would roughly correlate to four rows, 60% to three rows, and 70% being in the middle. However, the behavior was just as random, as shown in the following table:

Attempt	Rows in Table	Percentage Specified	Records Returned
1	5	100	5
1	5	90	5
1	5	80	5
1	5	70	0

Attempt	Rows in Table	Percentage Specified	Records Returned
1	5	60	0
2	5	5	5
2	5	90	5
2	5	80	0
2	5	70	5
2	5	60	0
3	5	5	5
3	5	90	5
3	5	80	5
3	5	70	0
3	5	60	5

As we mentioned previously, not knowing how many rows will be returned may be a deal-breaker, because in statistics, one of the critical components of the confidence interval is the sample size, and many disciplines demand a given confidence interval in order for results to be considered valid. To address this issue, there's another tool at your disposal, the REPEATABLE modifier.

Using REPEATABLE is very simple in practice but it doesn't work like you might guess. Take a look at the following modification:

```
SELECT  FirstName,
        LastName
FROM People
TABLESAMPLE ( 10 PERCENT)
REPEATABLE (50000)
```

What is the 50,000 number? Well, the REPEATABLE function takes a BIGINT value and if you use the same Seed value, your sample size will remain constant with one caveat: If the underlying table data changes, then all bets are off. This makes sense, after all, because you can't guarantee that the row count will stay the same across queries if you can't guarantee that the rows will even be there.

From what we can tell, if rows are modified but not added or deleted, then you can count on the sample sizes to remain constant. We tried to determine whether we could identify any patterns for how things would work if, for example, half the rows were deleted, but we didn't detect any (that's not to say there aren't any — just that we've been unable to identify any of them).

There's one more word issue worth noting. In just about every context that we've come across in T-SQL in SQL Server 2005, you can drive the functionality with parameters. If you can stick a parameter in somewhere, you can usually get it to work. TABLESAMPLE and REPEATABLE seem to be exceptions to the rule, though. If you were to use either of the following constructs, the query would not parse:

```
DECLARE @SeedValue BIGINT
SET @SeedValue = 50000
SELECT  FirstName,
        LastName
FROM People
TABLESAMPLE( @SeedValue)
REPEATABLE (@SeedValue)

Msg 497, Level 15, State 1, Line 3
Variables are not allowed in the TABLESAMPLE or REPEATABLE clauses.
```

READPAST

In previous versions of SQL Server, the READPAST locking hint was available, but only for SELECT statements. Although a full discussion about locking hints is beyond the scope of this chapter, we mention READPAST in particular because of its applicability in scenarios such as using WAITFOR (discussed next). SQL Server 2000's Books Online defines READPAST as follows:

> **Skip locked rows. This option causes a transaction to skip rows locked by other transactions that would ordinarily appear in the result set, rather than block the transaction waiting for the other transactions to release their locks on these rows. The READPAST lock hint applies only to transactions operating at READ COMMITTED isolation and will read only past row-level locks. Applies only to the SELECT statement.**

Currently, Yukon has added support for both UPDATE and DELETE statements using the READPAST hint. Essentially, this enables multiple processes to handle unlocked rows while ignoring locked ones that other processes are using. With UPDATE and DELETE statements, you can enable multiple parallel processes to handle nonlocked rows and skip locked ones that other sessions are processing.

WAITFOR

Although WAITFOR was available in pre-Yukon versions of SQL Server, it now boasts a few really cool enhancements. WAITFOR in previous versions was defined as WAITFOR { DELAY 'time' | TIME 'time' }. Now you can wait for some procedure to complete.

You could use it to wait for *x* number of minutes/seconds, or you could have it wait until a fixed time in the future. Traditionally, you'd use the WAITFOR command in either of these ways:

```
PRINT GETDATE()
WAITFOR DELAY '00:01:00'
PRINT GETDATE()
```

or

```
PRINT GETDATE()
WAITFOR TIME '00:13:00'
PRINT GETDATE()
```

In the first usage, the second PRINT would print a time that was one minute after the first one. In the second, the process would wait until 13:00. This is analogous to calling Thread.Sleep(Interval) in .NET.

Using the People table referenced in the preceding section, you can see some of the cool new features available:

```
WHILE TRUE
  PRINT GETDATE()
  WAITFOR (DELETE FROM People
  WHERE LastName = 'Ryan')
  PRINT GETDATE()
```

In this instance, we won't know when the second PRINT statement will execute because it will depend on the DELETE statement. With this particular example, it will wait until exactly one row has been deleted. If there are no rows with the LastName of Ryan, then we'll be waiting for a while. Obviously, this is something that needs to be used judiciously with some forethought.

How else can it be used? Well, you can do the same for INSERT, SELECT, UPDATE, and RECEIVE. INSERT, SELECT, and UPDATE are all probably intuitive in light of the preceding example, but RECEIVE may not be. RECEIVE is used to accept a message from a queue. Again, this one should be used judiciously because it has the potential to block for a long time if nothing is in the queue.

Combined with the new READPAST hint, this can be used safely in a very high-volume environment while still maintaining performance. To accomplish this, only slight modifications are needed:

```
WHILE TRUE
  PRINT GETDATE()
  WAITFOR (DELETE FROM People WITH (READPAST)
  WHERE LastName = 'Ryan')
  PRINT GETDATE()
```

DDL Triggers

Without a doubt, one of the biggest features we've been given is DDL triggers. *Every* company we know has had a need for these, and every developer we've spoken with has said they can't wait for these to come out. And the best part is, they're easy to use.

For the complete newbie, a trigger is a mechanism that "fires" whenever an event occurs. Typically, you could use triggers for items such as database inserts, updates, and deletes. These are critical features and lifesavers for many tasks. For instance, if you need to create an audit trail for a given table, triggers enable you to insert a new record into an audit trail table each time something happens to the table. This happens in such a way that it is invisible to end users (unless, of course, you want to notify them), so end users never know the trigger is firing.

DDL triggers are great because they can be used to send a notification to the team each time someone changes a table, or creates a table, or does anything else that typically would constitute a breaking change. Now let's look at a few. If you wanted to stop people from inserting tables (yes, this can be done with permissions but it serves well for illustrative purposes), here's how you'd do it:

```
CREATE TRIGGER DISALLOW_CREATES ON DATABASE FOR CREATE_TABLE
AS
RAISERROR('DATABASE TABLES CAN'T BE CREATED AT THIS TIME.', 10, 1)
ROLLBACK
```

To do the same but disallow drops, you'd just do the reverse:

```
CREATE TRIGGER DISALLOW_DROPS ON DATABASE FOR DROP_TABLE
AS
RAISERROR('DATABASE TABLES CAN'T BE DELETED AT THIS TIME.', 10, 1)
ROLLBACK
```

There are so many uses for these that they are only limited by one's imagination. For instance, you could use these to log user login additions, which might indicate something fishy is going on. You could do it when logons are dropped. You can use them when tables are changed. You can use them everywhere for just about every conceivable DDL function and the syntax shown in the preceding example will work for all of them (when in doubt, take your best guess about the event, such as DROP_TABLE, and chances are good you'll be right).

Summary

This chapter has provided you with a brief overview of the new features that are coming out with Yukon. We've been given a huge new set of features to solve problems that were previously a real pain. We can't begin to tell you the number of times that we've needed a feature like PIVOT or DDL triggers. Actually, we doubt there's a company out there that hasn't wished for DDL triggers.

To date, we have quite a few new features to look forward to. There may well be more coming down the pike, but for now, we can definitely count on these — they're very cool.

For More Information

For more information about the SQL Standard in general, or the T-SQL enhancements available in SQL Server 2005, please refer to the links provided below:

❑ **Chapter 3, "Understanding SQL"; Practical PostgreSQL** — www.faqs.org/docs/ppbook/c1164.htm

❑ **MSDN SQL Server Developer Center article, "SQL Server 2005 Beta 2 Transact-SQL Enhancements** — http://msdn.microsoft.com/SQL/sqlreldata/TSQL/default.aspx?pull=/library/en-us/dnsql90/html/sql_05tsqlenhance.asp

ADO.NET Programming with SQL Server from a Client Application

Within the ADO.NET Framework, Microsoft has provided a high-performance data provider for accessing a Microsoft SQL Server database. With the release of the .NET 2.0 Framework, Microsoft has provided several new items:

❑   Asynchronous operations so that commands may be executed in a nonblocking fashion

❑   Increased data type–specific support in SQL Server

❑   Added support for .NET commands that were previously only available when using an API-based interface, such as dealing with passwords

This chapter explores these and other new features in the SqlClient included in the .NET 2.0 System.Data.SqlClient.

SQL Server and ADO.NET

With the introduction of .NET Framework 1.0, Microsoft introduced a new mechanism to program against SQL Server. This mechanism is called a *.NET Data Provider*. The SQL Server Data Provider is the best tool to use to communicate with SQL Server when writing applications based on the .NET Framework. It's contained within the System.Data.SqlClient, which is in turn stored within the System.Data.dll file. With the release of Microsoft .NET Framework Version 2.0, Microsoft has included a new set of features specifically geared toward the Microsoft SQL Server Database.

The namespace System.Data.SqlClient is designed to communicate with SQL Server 7.0 or later. The System.Data.SqlClient provides a complete set of classes and methods to communicate with SQL Server.

Throughout this chapter, you will see notes regarding which version of SQL Server supports which feature in the ADO.NET namespace.

Asynchronous Commands in ADO.NET

Two of the most important goals of every application are to run as fast as it possibly can and to respond to user requests and input. Single-threaded applications may tie up the user interface while background operations are performed. Depending on the operations that are being run and how fast the back-end database schema is set up to receive them, the users of an application may or may not like the performance they are getting from an application. One way to increase application performance is to have the application perform operations in the background, to avoid tying up the user interface.

With classical COM-based ADO using Visual Basic, there was a mechanism for client-server applications that enabled asynchronous operations to perform the asynchronous operations work in the background. The user could continue inputting data and typing away on screens while the application performed database operations in the background, outside of the user interface's thread in a secondary thread that was created by the classic COM-based ADO components. The same is possible with Visual C++ — a thread can be either created explicitly or not. Unfortunately, asynchronous operations were not true within classical ASP.

When ADO.NET shipped with the .NET 1.0 release, one of the things that did not ship was a mechanism to directly perform database operations outside of the user interface's thread. It was entirely possible to simulate this activity with the use of the System.Threading namespace and a managed thread or a thread-pool thread. The use of threads provided the same level of functionality that had existed with classical COM-based ADO's asynchronous operations when commands and recordsets were defined with the WithEvents mechanism. Unfortunately, while providing the same type of functionality, the threading approach was not very simple or elegant. The situation was exacerbated by the fact that threading is a fairly complicated subject, and seemingly simple operations can become fairly complicated due to the environment.

Another issue regarding the threading approach is that while this technically does not block the user interface thread, the blocking is merely moved from the user interface thread to the thread created to process the request. While this may work fine in a client-server application with a user interface, this was not the best scenario for middle-tier-type applications.

To overcome this problem, Microsoft designed asynchronous command support into the .NET 2.0 Framework. Asynchronous commands enable multiple operations to occur at the same time. For example, assume you have an ASP.NET application that must process several database commands at the same time. With Classic ASP, each command would need to be processed one after the other in a serial fashion. With Classic ADO, support for asynchronous operations was actually implemented by creating a second thread and blocking on that second thread. With ASP.NET 1.x, it was possible to execute the various database commands independently of each other by using the threading support in the .NET Framework; however, this might be complicated, given the skills of the developers, and it might be the fact that this required another namespace to be used. With the asynchronous support in ADO.NET 2, the support for asynchronous operations is built into the System.Data.SqlClient namespace, without the need to use the `System.Threading` namespace. ADO.NET 2 also provides true asynchronous operations. Unlike creating a background thread and blocking the background thread, ADO.NET 2 implements asynchronous operations by using IO Completion ports, which are built into the .NET Framework but are truly asynchronous, with no secondary thread being created and blocked while the UI continues on.

The ADO.NET 2 solution follows the general look-and-feel for the other asynchronous commands within the .NET Framework, as the method names use the standard calling syntax of `BeginABC`/`EndABC`. The `SqlCommand` class provides support for asynchronous commands through the following methods:

- ❑ `BeginExecuteNonQuery`/`EndExecuteNonQuery`

- ❑ `BeginExecuteReader`/`EndExecuteReader`

- ❑ `BeginExecuteXmlReader`/`EndExecuteXmlReader`

These new methods in the `SqlCommand` class provide for a nonblocking implementation of asynchronous commands. Let's look at how to use these commands effectively.

To use asynchronous commands, you will need to add the `async=true;` *parameter to the connection string. Check the* `SqlConnectionStringBuilder` *class covered later in this chapter to properly set the connection string.*

Asynchronous commands are available using SQL 7 and SQL 2000 when not using the shared memory provider. They are also available when using all of the protocols with SQL Server 2005. If the application and the database are running on the same system and that system is not SQL Server 2005–based, you will want to force a protocol, such as TCP/IP, by appending `tcp:` *to the front of the server name.*

BeginExecuteNonQuery

In many situations, it is necessary to merely perform a database operation that does not return any data back to the calling method. With ADO.NET, `ExecuteNonQuery()` is the preferred method to call to execute a command that does not return any results. This method is used for INSERT, UPDATE, and DELETE commands that do not return any values. With the `BeginExecuteNonQuery()` method, these commands can now be performed asynchronously to the main user interface thread. Let's take a look at some source code for performing asynchronous commands.

There are two ways to call the `BeginExecuteNonQuery()`. The basic calling convention would be either of the following:

- ❑ `BeginExecuteNonQuery(AsyncCallBackObject, StateObject)`. These are the full parameters for calling the `BeginExecuteNonQuery` method. The `AsyncCallBackObject` is an object that is created by calling the function defined in `AsyncCallBack(AddressOf CallbackFunctionName)`. The `StateObject` is typically going to be the SQL command object that is passed to the `AsyncCallBackObject`. This version of the method call is the full version and will be useful if you want to perform some type of operation after the SQL command object has finished executing the method on the database server.

- ❑ `BeginExecuteNonQuery()`. Using the `BeginExecuteNonQuery()` method with no parameters will result in the method being called with no callback method. This calling convention will typically be used when multiple asynchronous commands are called and the program needs to wait on all of them to finish.

Along with the `BeginExecuteNonQuery()` method is an `EndExecuteNonQuery()` method. This method is specifically called from within the `AsyncCallBackObject` method. Consider the following code:

```
'private variables within the class
Private gsqlCm As SqlCommand
Private gsqlCn As SqlConnection
 'code within a method
Dim i As Integer = 0
Dim strSql As String
Dim strCn As String = "Initial Catalog=dbBookSampleChapter10;Data
Source=tcp:entrepid\sqlyukonbeta2;User Id=......;Password=.........;async=true;"
Dim iResult As IAsyncResult
gsqlCm = New SqlCommand()
gsqlCn = New SqlConnection(strCn)
gsqlCn.Open()
gsqlCm.Connection = gsqlCn
gsqlCm.CommandType = CommandType.Text
strSql = "insert into tblAsyncExecuteNonQuery ( ClientDateEntered) values ('" &
DateTime.Now.ToString() & "')"
gsqlCm.CommandText = strSql
iResult = gsqlCm.BeginExecuteNonQuery(New System.AsyncCallback(AddressOf
ExecuteNonQueryCallback), gsqlCm)
MsgBox("Command done.")'The callback method.
Private Sub ExecuteNonQueryCallback(ByVal iRes As IAsyncResult)
    gsqlCm.EndExecuteNonQuery(iRes)
gSqlCm.Dispose();
gSqlCm = Nothing
if gSqlCn.State <> ConnectionState.Closed then
     gSqlCn.Close()
end if
gSqlCn.Dispose()
gSqlCn = Nothing
End Sub
```

The first thing you will note in the preceding code that is different is the connection string used by the connection object to communicate with the database. The connection string has a new parameter at the end of the string: `async=true;`. This parameter turns on the asynchronous support when performing commands against the database. Performing an asynchronous command requires some additional operations to set up communications within the database. These asynchronous operations incur an overhead versus standard synchronous operations. If the `async=true;` parameter is not used and an asynchronous command is attempted, an `InvalidOperationException` exception will be raised. With the addition of the `SqlConnectionStringBuilder`, discussed later in this chapter, it is fairly easy to add asynchronous capabilities. The specific property that should be set is `.AsyncProcessing = True`.

> *Due to increased overhead, the only time the* `async=true;` *option should be set in the connection string is when asynchronous operations are actually needed. If asynchronous operations are not necessary, it is best to not set them up in the connection string.*

When the SQL command operation is completed and the callback function is executed, the method `EndExecuteNonQuery` should be called on the SQL command object. This method is necessary to make the results available to the caller and to clean up some system resources. In the case of `EndExecuteNonQuery`, the results that are returned represent the number of rows affected by the operation. Failure to call the `EndExecuteNonQuery()` method may result in a leakage of system resources.

It is possible to call the `EndExecuteNonQuery` *method immediately after calling the* `BeginExecuteNonQuery` *method. This will effectively turn the operation into a synchronous operation at the application level. However, the operation will continue to be treated like an asynchronous operation underneath the application.*

BeginExecuteReader

The `BeginExecuteNonQuery`/`EndExecuteNonQuery` methods are great ways to asynchronously perform operations that do not actually query information from the database. When you do want to actually perform a query and get some data back from the database, the .NET 2.0 Framework's `SqlClient` provides the capability to perform a query asynchronously. The `BeginExecuteReader()`/ `EndExecuteReader()` set of methods are for performing asynchronous operations that return data.

The `BeginExecuteReader` method can be called with four different sets of parameters:

❑   `BeginExecuteReader(AsyncCallBackObject, StateObject, CommandBehavior)` — This is the full set of objects for the `BeginExecuteReader` method. The `AsyncCallBackObject` is the method that will be called when the command is completed on the server and the front end is signaled that the command has been completed. The `StateObject` is the state that is handed to the `AsyncCallBackObject`. The `CommandBehavior` is the behavior that the `DataReader` object will perform after reading the final record. This is the same `CommandBehavior` used with a regular `DataReader`.

❑   `BeginExecuteReader(AsyncCallBackObject, StateObject)` — This method is the same as the preceding method with the difference that the `DataReader` is opened with the default behavior.

❑   `BeginExecuteReader(CommandBehavior)` — This method opens the `DataReader` with the option of having `CommandBehavior` specified. When this method is called, no asynchronous object is called when the `DataReader` is returned to the calling application.

❑   `BeginExecuteReader()` — This method, like the one before it, merely opens the `DataReader` with the default `CommandBehavior`.

Let's take a look at some sample code for calling the `BeginExecuteReader` both with an asynchronous callback object and without one.

Asynchronous Callback Object Version

The `BeginExecuteReader()` set of methods is useful for retrieving a `DataReader` from a database. The following example calls `BeginExecuteReader()` and passes a callback object to the method:

```
Dim strSql As String
Dim strCn As String = gstrAsyncString
Dim iResult As IAsyncResult

sqlCm = New SqlCommand()
sqlCn = New SqlConnection(strCn)
sqlCn.Open()
sqlCm.Connection = sqlCn
sqlCm.CommandType = CommandType.Text
strSql = "select count(*) from tblAsyncExecuteNonQuery"
```

269

```
sqlCm.CommandText = strSql
Me.gdtStart = GetTickCount()
iResult = sqlCm.BeginExecuteReader(New System.AsyncCallback(AddressOf
ExecuteDataReaderCallback), sqlCm, CommandBehavior.Default)

Private Sub ExecuteDataReaderCallback(ByVal iRes As IAsyncResult)
Dim sqlDr As SqlDataReader
Try
    sqlDr = sqlCm.EndExecuteReader(iRes)
    Me.gdtEnd = GetTickCount()
    sqlDr.Read()
    Me.giNum = Convert.ToInt32(sqlDr(0))
    Dim cntDsplay As New DisplayCountDelegate(AddressOf DisplayCount)
    Me.Invoke(cntDsplay)
    sqlDr.Close()
    sqlDr.Dispose()
    sqlDr = Nothing
Catch sqlExc As SqlException
'Perform some type of operation to notify someone that an error has occurred.
'If an exception occurs, show it to the user.
    Dim excDsplay As New DisplayErrorDelegate(AddressOf DisplayError)
    Dim parameterArray(1) As Object
    parameterArray(0) = CType(sqlExc, System.Object)
    Me.Invoke(excDsplay, parameterArray)
Finally
    If sqlCn.State <> ConnectionState.Closed Then
        sqlCn.Close()
    End If
    sqlCn.Dispose()
    sqlCn = Nothing
    sqlCm.Dispose()
    sqlCm = Nothing
End Try
End Sub
```

Asynchronous Operations with No Callback Object

The BeginExecuteReader() method allows for asynchronous operations to be called with no callback object. While not necessarily the optimal way to call asynchronous commands, this may be necessary in some situations. In the following example, the BeginExecuteReader() method is called with no callback object. The calling thread continues to run, and every 50 milliseconds the calling thread will check to determine whether the asynchronous command has completed. The asynchronous operation is tested by looking at the value of the IsCompleted property:

```
Dim iResult As IAsyncResult
Try
    sqlCn.Open()
    sqlCm.Connection = sqlCn
    sqlCm.CommandType = CommandType.Text
    strSql = "select count(*) from tblAsyncExecuteNonQuery"
    sqlCm.CommandText = strSql
    Me.gdtStart = GetTickCount()
    iResult = sqlCm.BeginExecuteReader(CommandBehavior.Default)
    While Not iResult.IsCompleted
```

```
        Thread.Sleep(50)
    End While
    sqlDr = sqlCm.EndExecuteReader(iResult)
    sqlDr.Read()
    MsgBox("Number of Records: " & Convert.ToString(sqlDr(0)))
    sqlDr.Close()
    sqlDr.Dispose()
Finally
    If sqlCn.State <> ConnectionState.Closed Then
        sqlCn.Close()
    End If
    sqlCn.Dispose()
    sqlCn = Nothing
    sqlCm.Dispose()
    sqlCm = Nothing
End Try
```

BeginExecuteXMLReader

Much like `BeginExecuteNonQuery` and `BeginExecuteReader`, another set of commands enables the return of XML-based results in SQL Server asynchronously. These commands will take a query result from SQL Server in an XML format and return an `XmlReader` object to the program. Given a query to send to the database, an `XmlReader` is returned.

There are a couple of different calling options for the `BeginExecuteXMLReader` method. These options are very similar to the `BeginExecuteNonQuery` method's calling syntax.

❑ `BeginExecuteXMLReader(AsyncCallback, Object)` — The `AsyncCallback` object is the method that should be called when the Framework signals that the query has been completed. The `Object` parameter is a user-defined state object that will be passed to the callback procedure. As in the other asynchronous operations, this object may be accessed with the callback procedure using the `AsyncState` property.

❑ `BeginExecuteXMLReader()` — This Initiates the asynchronous execution of the passed SQL `Command` object.

Let's take a look at some code:

```
Dim strSql As String
Dim strCn As String = gstrAsyncString
Dim iResult As IAsyncResult
sqlCm = New SqlCommand()
sqlCn = New SqlConnection(strCn)
sqlCn.Open()
sqlCm.Connection = sqlCn
sqlCm.CommandType = CommandType.Text
strSql = "select * from tblAsyncExecuteNonQuery FOR XML AUTO, XMLDATA"
sqlCm.CommandText = strSql
Me.gdtStart = GetTickCount()
iResult = sqlCm.BeginExecuteXmlReader(New System.AsyncCallback(AddressOf
ExecuteXMLReaderCallback), sqlCm)

Private Sub ExecuteXMLReaderCallback(ByVal iRes As IAsyncResult)
```

```
        Dim xmlR As XmlReader
        Dim lsqlCm As SqlCommand
        Try
            lsqlCm = CType(iRes.AsyncState, SqlCommand)
            xmlR = lsqlCm.EndExecuteXmlReader(iRes)
            Me.gdtEnd = GetTickCount()
            Dim cntDsplay As New DisplayCountDelegate(AddressOf DisplayCount)
            Me.Invoke(cntDsplay)
        Catch sqlExc As SqlException
            'Perform some type of operation to notify someone that an error has
    occurred.
            'If an exception occurs, show it to the user.
            Dim excDsplay As New DisplayErrorDelegate(AddressOf DisplayError)
            Dim parameterArray(1) As Object
            parameterArray(0) = CType(sqlExc, System.Object)
            Me.Invoke(excDsplay, parameterArray)
        Finally
            If sqlCn.State <> ConnectionState.Closed Then
                sqlCn.Close()
            End If
            sqlCn.Dispose()
            sqlCn = Nothing
            sqlCm.Dispose()
            sqlCm = Nothing
        End Try
    End Sub
```

The preceding code is an example of how to get an XMLReader. You issue a command to get the XML through the SQL Server command and begin the operation to get the XML result; and when the XML result is returned, the callback method is called and the EndExecuteXmlReader() method is called to end the asynchronous command.

Asynchronous Operations in ASP.NET

Now that you have had the opportunity to look at the basics of asynchronous operations in ADO.NET, let's look at a more serious example using ASP.NET. This example is derived from a real-world instance related to a search engine system. In that scenario, the management team wanted the following actions to occur after a user submitted a search:

❑ The domain from which the user entered the query would be stored in a database table for future analysis.

❑ The referrer from which the user entered the query would be stored. While this is very similar to the domain, it is not necessarily 100% the same. For example, if multiple domain names pointed at the same search page and there were search pages on other Web sites that pointed to the result pages, these results would not be guaranteed to be the same.

❑ The search term entered by the user for the query would be stored in a database table for future analysis.

❑ Search results would be displayed to the user.

Attempting to code this in classical ASP/COM was not easily done. Coding this type of operation in ASP.NET 1.x was not that difficult. Several other threads could be created to handle operations to log data and return search results. The only problem was that this required some relatively complex coding in setting up threads, getting results, waiting on the results, setting up delegates to communicate the results back, and so on. With ADO.NET 2, using the asynchronous commands, an ASP.NET application can bypass the need to explicitly use a managed thread or the thread pool. This feature is advantageous because if threads from the thread pool are not used extensively, the thread pool provided by ASP.NET for applications is not easily exhausted. The steps for performing the preceding operations are as follows:

1. Begin the ASP.NET request.

2. Create the ADO.NET objects and populate them appropriately.

3. Perform the operations asynchronously. In the following example, a database insertion and query occur using `BeginExecuteNonQuery()` and `BeginExecuteReader()`.

4. Wait for the results from an operation.

5. If the operation is the query result, display that in a grid.

Now that the logical steps have been laid out, let's look at the source code necessary to perform the operation in this manner:

```
Dim i As Integer
Dim strSql As String = String.Empty
Dim strCn As String = "..........."
Dim sqlCnString As New SqlConnectionStringBuilder(strCn)
sqlCnString.AsynchronousProcessing = True
Dim sqlCnInsert As New SqlConnection(sqlCnString.ConnectionString)
Dim sqlCnQuery As New SqlConnection(sqlCnString.ConnectionString)
Dim sqlCmInsert As New SqlCommand()
Dim sqlCmQuery As New SqlCommand()
Dim sqlpmServer As New SqlParameter()
Dim sqlpmReferer As New SqlParameter()
Dim sqlpmSearchTerms As New SqlParameter()
Dim sqlpmDateEntered As New SqlParameter()
Dim sqlpmSearchTermsQuery As New SqlParameter()
Try
    sqlCmInsert.Connection = sqlCnInsert
    sqlCmQuery.Connection = sqlCnQuery
    strSql = "insert into tblSearch (ServerName, Referer, SearchTerms, DateEntered)
values (@ServerName, @Referer, @SearchTerms, @DateEntered)"
    sqlCmInsert.CommandText = strSql
    sqlpmServer.SqlDbType = SqlDbType.VarChar
    sqlpmServer.Size = 100
    sqlpmServer.SqlValue = Request.ServerVariables("Server_Name").ToString()
    sqlpmServer.Direction = ParameterDirection.Input
    sqlpmServer.ParameterName = "@ServerName"
    sqlCmInsert.Parameters.Add(sqlpmServer)
    sqlpmReferer.SqlDbType = SqlDbType.VarChar
    sqlpmReferer.SqlValue = Request.ServerVariables.Item("Http_Referer").ToString()
    sqlpmReferer.Direction = ParameterDirection.Input
    sqlpmReferer.ParameterName = "@Referer"
    sqlCmInsert.Parameters.Add(sqlpmReferer)
    sqlpmSearchTerms.SqlDbType = SqlDbType.VarChar
```

```vbnet
        sqlpmSearchTerms.Size = Me.txtSearchTerm.MaxLength
        sqlpmSearchTerms.SqlValue = Me.txtSearchTerm.Text
        sqlpmSearchTerms.Direction = ParameterDirection.Input
        sqlpmSearchTerms.ParameterName = "@SearchTerms"
        sqlCmInsert.Parameters.Add(sqlpmSearchTerms)
        sqlpmDateEntered.SqlDbType = SqlDbType.DateTime
        sqlpmDateEntered.SqlValue = DateTime.Now
        sqlpmDateEntered.Direction = ParameterDirection.Input
        sqlpmDateEntered.ParameterName = "@DateEntered"
        sqlCmInsert.Parameters.Add(sqlpmDateEntered)
        strSql = "select top 50 Searchurl from tblSearchResults where
    contains(SearchText, '""" & SqlEscape(Me.txtSearchTerm.Text) & """')"
        sqlCmQuery.CommandText = strSql
        sqlCnInsert.Open()
        sqlCnQuery.Open()
        Dim arInputs As IAsyncResult = sqlCmInsert.BeginExecuteNonQuery()
        Dim arSearch As IAsyncResult = sqlCmQuery.BeginExecuteReader()
        Dim whandles(1) As WaitHandle
        whandles(0) = arInputs.AsyncWaitHandle
        whandles(1) = arSearch.AsyncWaitHandle
        For i = 0 To 1
            Dim index As Integer = WaitHandle.WaitAny(whandles, 1000, False) '  secs
            If i = 0 Then
                sqlCmInsert.EndExecuteNonQuery(arInputs)
            ElseIf i = 1 Then
                Dim sqlDr As SqlDataReader = sqlCmQuery.EndExecuteReader(arSearch)
                Me.gvResults.DataSource = sqlDr
                Me.gvResults.DataBind()
                sqlDr.Close()
                sqlDr.Dispose()
                sqlDr = Nothing
            End If
        Next
        Me.pnlResults.Visible = True
    Finally
        If sqlCnInsert.State <> ConnectionState.Open Then
            sqlCnInsert.Close()
        End If
        sqlCnInsert.Dispose()
        If sqlCnQuery.State <> ConnectionState.Open Then
            sqlCnQuery.Close()
        End If
        sqlCnQuery.Dispose()
        sqlCnInsert = Nothing
        sqlCnQuery = Nothing
        sqlCmInsert.Dispose()
        sqlCmQuery.Dispose()
    End Try
    Private Function SqlEscape(ByVal pstrTerm As String) As String
        Dim strTemp As String = String.Empty
        If Not (pstrTerm Is Nothing) Then
            strTemp = pstrTerm.Replace("'", "''")
        End If
        Return (strTemp)
    End Function
```

You've just seen a complete working example of asynchronous operations in ADO.NET 2 being called through ASP.NET. Figure 10-1 shows the output for a sample search criteria.

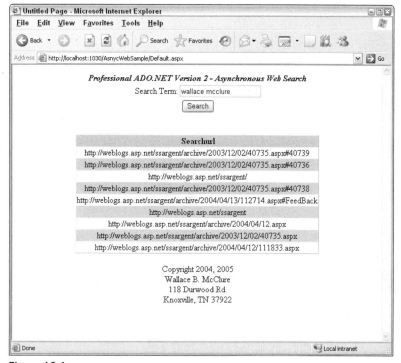

Figure 10-1

IAsyncResult

While not specifically a member of the System.Data.SqlClient namespace, the IAsyncResult interface is important when dealing with asynchronous operations. With ADO.NET, the IAsyncResult interface may be used to poll or wait for results, in addition to being called by the method that ends the asynchronous operation. Overall, the IAsyncResult interface is used to represent the state of an asynchronous operation. The following table shows the properties available to an IAsyncResult object.

IAsyncResult Members

Property	Description
AsyncState	Returns a user-defined object that contains information about an asynchronous operation.
AsyncWaitHandle	Returns a WaitHandle that is used to wait for an asynchronous operation to finish. A WaitHandleis used to wait for exclusive access to shared resources.

Table continued on following page

IAsyncResult Members (continued)

Property	Description
CompletedSynchronously	Returns an indication of whether the asynchronous operation completed synchronously.
IsCompleted	Returns an indication of whether the asynchronous operation is finished.

Final Words of Warning with Asynchronous Operations

Now that you are familiar with asynchronous operations in ADO.NET Version 2, note the following items that must be monitored in a program because they can jump out and bite you if you're not careful:

❑ Multiple commands on a connection — SQL Server 2005 will support multiple commands on one connection. Previous versions of SQL Server do not support multiple commands on a single connection.

❑ The connection and command objects are not thread safe — Great care must be taken when making multiple calls, especially in a winforms application.

❑ Cleanup — Merely because an operation is asynchronous does not mean that commands and connections should not be properly cleaned up.

Multiple Active Result Sets

With Classic ADO and ADO.NET 1.x, there has been a one-to-one relationship between commands and connection objects. With the release of SQL Server 2005 and ADO.NET 2.0, Microsoft has added the capability for multiple command objects to open on a single connection object when executing against a SQL Server 2005 database. This capability is referred to as *Multiple Active Result Sets (MARS)*. Let's look at some code:

```
Dim strSql1 As String = "select top 10 * from tblAsyncExecuteNonQuery"
Dim strSql2 As String = "select top 20 * from tblAsyncExecuteNonQuery"
Dim sqlCn As New SqlConnection(Me.gstrSyncString)
Dim sqlCm1 As New SqlCommand(strSql1, sqlCn)
Dim sqlCm2 As New SqlCommand(strSql2, sqlCn)
Dim sqlDr1 As SqlDataReader
Dim sqlDr2 As SqlDataReader
Dim dsData As New DataSet()
Try
    If Not Page.IsPostBack Then
        sqlCn.Open()
        sqlDr1 = sqlCm1.ExecuteReader()
        sqlDr2 = sqlCm2.ExecuteReader()
        Me.ddl1.Items.Add(String.Empty)
        Me.ddl2.Items.Add(String.Empty)
        Me.ddl1.DataSource = sqlDr1
        Me.ddl2.DataSource = sqlDr2
        Me.ddl1.DataTextField = "ClientDateEntered"
```

```
            Me.ddl1.DataValueField = "tblAsyncExecuteNonQueryId"
            Me.ddl2.DataTextField = "ClientDateEntered"
            Me.ddl2.DataValueField = "tblAsyncExecuteNonQueryId"
            Me.ddl1.DataBind()
            Me.ddl2.DataBind()
            If Not sqlDr1.IsClosed Then
                sqlDr1.Close()
            End If
            If Not sqlDr2.IsClosed Then
                sqlDr2.Close()
            End If
            sqlDr1.Dispose()
            sqlDr2.Dispose()
        End If
        Me.lblError.Visible = False
    Catch sqlEx As SqlException
    'Do something with this error. We are just going to show the message
    ' in a label control
        Me.lblError.Text = "Error: " & sqlEx.Message.ToString()
        Me.lblError.Visible = True
    Finally
        If sqlCn.State <> ConnectionState.Closed Then
            sqlCn.Close()
        End If
        sqlCn.Dispose()
        sqlCn = Nothing
    End Try
```

The interesting thing to note about the preceding code is that there is only one connection object, but two open data readers on that object.

What Is MARS Useful For?

Now that you have seen the basics of MARS, let's take a look at a common scenario in which MARS can be used. ASP.NET includes a Page_Load event, which, along with the Page.IsPostback property, can preload values for an ASP.NET page. For example, you might want to get the values for several drop-down lists. To do so, several commands and connections will be made against a database. These connections may come from the connection pool, but they are still resources and processing that are used up. With MARS, a single connection is opened to a database, and multiple commands are sent over that connection and kept open for processing as necessary.

Technical Issues with MARS

MARS is a great feature, but developers should be careful of several things when using it:

❑   MARS operations are only supported with a .NET 2.0 (or later) front-end application when the application is running with a SQL Server 2005 (or later) database.

❑   MARS operations are synchronous.

❑   MARS statements may contain data manipulation language and data definition language statements. However, these statements must execute atomically, with the result that other MARS statements will be blocked.

❑   No other statements may execute while a `WAITFOR` statement is waiting.

❑   Connections with MARS enabled create a logical session that adds some amount of overhead.

❑   The logical sessions are cached by the `SqlClient`. The cache supports up to 10 MARS sessions.

❑   The cache is on a per-connection basis, and the sessions are not shared across connections.

❑   The sessions are only cleaned up when the associated connection is disposed.

❑   The session cache is not pre-loaded.

❑   MARS operations are not thread safe.

❑   MARS-enabled connections may be connection pooled. If some connections are MARS-enabled and some have MARS disabled, the connections are pulled from different pools.

You need to be aware of these technical issues when working with MARS. As a programmer, you should also be aware of an architectural issue: MARS is very similar to parallel operations, such as asynchronous commands discussed earlier in this chapter. If you need the capability to perform operations in parallel, then a better choice is to perform the necessary commands through the asynchronous commands discussed earlier in this chapter.

MARS is turned off by default. It may be turned on by using the connection string keyword or the property of the SQL connection string builder object.

Enumerating SQL Servers

Have you ever wanted to create an application that knows about all of the database systems on your company's network? Perhaps you need to create an application for a set of database administrators for your SQL Server databases so that they can see a list of all of the SQL Server databases in your company. ADO.NET 2.0 provides this feature through the `DbEnumerator` base class in `System.Data.Common`. When using the `SqlDataSourceEnumerator` and the `DbDataSourceEnumerator`, a `DataTable` is returned.

The following code enumerates SQL Server servers on a network:

```
Dim sdsObj As DataTable = SqlDataSourceEnumerator.Instance.GetDataSources()
Dim src As DataRow
Me.lbServer.Items.Clear()
For Each src In sdsObj.Rows
Me.lbServer.Items.Add(src.Item("ServerName").ToString() & "-" & _
    src.Item("InstanceName").ToString() & "-" & src.Item("Version").ToString())
Next src
```

The preceding code uses the `SqlDataSourceEnumerator` to obtain information about SQL Server running within the local network. The `SqlDataSourceEnumerator` class exposes the information programmatically.

In order to obtain the information correctly from SQL Server 2005, the SQL Server Browser service must be running on the client system.

To enumerate through all of the data providers on the network and the servers associated with them, the DbProvider factory is used:

```
Dim t As DataTable = DbProviderFactories.GetFactoryClasses()
Dim r As DataRow
Dim servers As DataTable
Dim dbe As DbDataSourceEnumerator
Dim factory As DbProviderFactory
For Each r In DbProviderFactories.GetFactoryClasses().Rows
    factory = DbProviderFactories.GetFactory(r)
    dbe = factory.CreateDataSourceEnumerator()
    If Not (dbe Is Nothing) Then
    servers = dbe.GetDataSources()
        For Each src In servers.Rows
            Me.lbServer.Items.Add(src.Item("ServerName").ToString() & "-" &
src.Item(1).ToString() & "-" & src.Item(3).ToString())
        Next
    End If
Next r
```

This code works by enumerating the installed providers on the system. With each provider, all data sources are enumerated. Each data provider and data source will have its own logic for performing enumeration. Additional configuration may be required for additional database data providers.

Value Name	Example/Typical Value
ServerName	Machine name
InstanceName	Name of the Instance. The default instance will return a System.DBNull for value.
IsClustered	Yes/No
Version	9.0.852

Enumerating servers will only find SQL Server 2000 and later versions of the database.

Connection Pooling

Connection pooling has been around for several iterations of data access technologies. ODBC has supported connection pooling for several versions. OleDb has supported a similar pooling mechanism, called *session pooling* or *resource pooling*. With the release of COM+, Microsoft added more technology to assist with connection and session pooling, along with the capability to create a pool of objects for its own usage. With the release of the .NET 1.0 Framework, Microsoft included pooling with the SqlClient, which provided users with some control over the minimum and maximum number of pooled database connections. These values can be set through the MinClient (the default is zero) and MaxClient (the default is 100) values that are passed through the connection string.

With ADO.NET 2.0, Microsoft has added new capabilities to manage the client-side connection pool with the SqlClient. Some new mechanisms clear the connection pool included with the SqlClient. Let's take a look at two of these methods:

❑ ClearPool(ConnectionObject) — The ClearPool method is a shared (static with C#) method that takes a SqlConnection object. When called, the connection pool within the current app domain that would provide the connection object for the provided SqlConnection has all connection objects marked as doomed:

```
Dim sqlCn As New SqlConnection()
sqlCn.ConnectionString = Me.gstrSyncString
sqlCn.ClearPool(sqlCn)
```

❑ ClearAllPools() — The ClearAllPools() method is a shared (static with C#) method that takes no SqlConnection object as a parameter. Calling this method results in all connections on every connection pool within the current app domain being marked as doomed:

```
Dim sqlCn As New SqlConnection()
sqlCn.ConnectionString = Me.gstrSyncString
SqlConnection.ClearAllPools()
```

When a connection is marked as doomed, the connection is not immediately removed from the connection pool. A background process that runs every four to eight minutes will clean up any connections marked as doomed.

There are some additional changes within ADO.NET Version 2.0 regarding how an application uses the connection pool. Although these items are not changeable through a method or property in a class, they still are valuable to know.

In ADO.NET 1.x, assume that you have a connection pool that is filled with good connections. For some reason, the application loses connection with the SQL Server database and the sessions on the database are reset. The application must go through each connection in the pool and attempt to connect, thus draining the pool, until a new connection attempt can be made and a valid connection is made to the database. Each time a "bad attempt" to connect is made, the connection pool is drained of an individual connection. This may be confusing to the user because the application appears to fail until the connection pool is drained and the application mysteriously starts working.

Let's look at the same scenario in ADO.NET 2. Once again, your application loses connection with the SQL Server database and the sessions on the database are reset. The application will attempt to execute a command on one of the invalid connection objects. An exception will be generated once again. However, when this exception is generated, all connection objects within the pool are marked as doomed.

The result of these new features in the System.Data.SqlClient namespace is a more efficient usage of the connection pool — and the capability for a programmer to twist a few knobs in regard to use of the connection pool.

Password Management

Frequently during the course of an application's lifetime, an administrator would like to change the password for the application. With SQL Server 2000 and earlier, this required opening the SQL Server Enterprise Manager to change the password of a user id.

With SQL Server 2005 and ADO.NET 2.0, Microsoft has provided a *shared* (static in C#) method on the SqlConnection object to change the password of a SQL Server user without the need to involve an administrator. This method is named ChangePassword(). The ChangePassword method takes the following parameters: ChangePassword(ConnectionString, NewPassword). The ConnectionString is literally a valid SQL connection string. The NewPassword is a string containing the new password for the user specified within the ConnectionString. The ChangePassword method, when called, will connect to the specified database, change the password, and then close the underlying connection, as shown in the following code:

```
Dim sqlCn As New SqlConnection()
' Create a sqlconnectionstringbuilder object with the current
'    connection string.
Dim scsbObj As New SqlClient.SqlConnectionStringBuilder(Me.gstrSyncString)
Try
scsbObj.Password = Me.txtPassword.Text
'Calling the ChangePassword() method.
SqlConnection.ChangePassword(scsbObj.ConnectionString, Me.txtNewPassword.Text)
'Change the values in the sqlconnectionstringbuilder object.
scsbObj.Password = Me.txtNewPassword.Text
'Get the updated connection string from the sqlconnectionstringbuilder object.
sqlCn.ConnectionString = scsbObj.ConnectionString
sqlCn.Open()
'Save the string into a private string variable.
'    This activity is particular to this example.
Me.gstrSyncString = scsbObj.ConnectionString
MsgBox("Succesful logon with a new password.")
Catch sqlEx As SqlException
'Do something with this error.
MsgBox("Error: " & sqlEx.Message.ToString())
Finally
        'Perform cleanup.
If sqlCn.State <> ConnectionState.Closed Then
   sqlCn.Close()
End If
sqlCn.Dispose()
sqlCn = Nothing
End Try
```

This code changes a user's password. Changing a password is a new feature that requires the .NET 2.0 Framework and SQL Server 2005. This code sample also uses a new feature in the .NET Framework called the SqlConnectionStringBuilder.

The ChangePassword feature works only with SQL Server 2005 and later.

Building a SQL Connection with the SqlConnectionStringBuilder Class

One interesting new feature in the System.Data.Common namespace is the DBConnectionStringBuilder. From that, the SqlClient has implemented the class SqlConnectionStringBuilder. This class will parse your connection string, enabling you to easily make changes without having to go through all the drudgery of writing the parsing routines on your own. The class has a number of very useful properties, described in the following table.

Chapter 10

Properties of the SqlConnectionStringBuilder

Property	Description
ApplicationName	Textual name of the application as presented to the database.
AsynchronousProcessing	Boolean value that specifies whether the connection should be set up to process commands asynchronously.
AttachDBFileName	Textual path to the database file so that the database file may be used as a database without having to explicitly attach to the database engine.
BrowsableConnectionString	Boolean value that specifies whether the connection string is browsable by a visual designer.
ConnectionReset	Boolean value that specifies whether the connection is reset.
ConnectionString	Textual value representing the SQL Server connection string.
ConnectTimeout	Integer value representing the number of seconds before an error is raised.
Count	Integer value representing the number of keys within the connection string maintained by instance.
CurrentLanguage	Textual value representing the current language.
DataSource	Textual value containing the data source value of the connection string.
Encrypt	Boolean value that specifies whether encryption is used when communicating between the client application and the database.
Enlist	Boolean value that specifies whether commands associated with the connection will enlist within a transaction.
FailoverPartner	The failover partner.
InitialCatalog	Textual value representing the InitialCatalog property of the connection string.
IntegratedSecurity	Boolean value that specifies whether integrated Security is used.
IsFixedSize	Determines whether the SqlConnectionStringBuilder has a Fixed size.
IsReadOnly	Boolean read-only value that specifies whether the ConnectionStringBuilder object is read-only.
Item	Gets or sets the value associated with the specified key.
Keys	As ICollection that contains the keys in the SqlConnectionStringBuilder.
LoadBalanceTimeout	The minimum timeout value in seconds.
MaxPoolSize	Integer value representing the maximum size of the connection pool of database connections.

Property	Description
MinPoolSize	Integer value representing the minimum size of the connection pool of database connections.
MultipleActiveResultSets	Boolean value that specifies whether multiple active result sets (MARS) is available.
NetworkLibrary	Textual representation of the network library that will be used to communicate between the client application making the database connection and the database itself.
PacketSize	Integer value representing the packet size for network communications.
Password	Textual value representing the Password value of the connection string.
PersistSecurityInfo	Boolean value that specifies the Persist security value of a connection string.
Pooling	Boolean value that specifies whether connection pooling is enabled.
Replication	Boolean value that indicates whether replication is supported using the connection.
UserId	Textual value representing the UserId value of a connection string.
Values	An ICollection that contains the value in the SqlConnectionStringBuilder.
WorkStationID	Textual value representing the workstation id value of a connection string

As you can see, the properties of the SqlConnectionStringBuilder map to the values that can be specified in the SQL connection string.

The SqlConnectionStringBuilder is a simple class that is included with the SqlClient namespace to provide an easy way to add and change values within a connection string that is passed to a SqlConnection object. Let's look at a simple example of a change from synchronous operations to asynchronous operations:

```
Dim strCn As String = "..............."
Dim sqlCnString As New SqlConnectionStringBuilder(strCn)
sqlCnString.AsynchronousProcessing = True
Dim sqlCnInsert As New SqlConnection(sqlCnString.ConnectionString)
```

SQL Server Types (SqlTypes)

With the introduction of ADO.NET 1.x, Microsoft provided a set of classes for working with the native data types within SQL Server. These classes are stored within the System.Data.SqlTypes namespace. Using these classes will help in several areas:

❏ Fewer errors because code will automatically know the data type it is using

❏ Fewer errors involving a loss of precision

❏ Faster code because the SqlTypes are already used behind the scenes and type conversions are minimized

Structures

Included in the System.Data.SqlTypes namespace are the basic structures for dealing with SQL Server data types. These structures are described in the following table.

Overview of the System.Data.SqlTypes Namespace

SQL Server Data Type	Structure Name	Description of the SqlType Structure	Equivalent SqlDbType
Binary	SqlBinary	The SqlBinary structure represents an unknown length binary data that is to be inserted or retrieved from a database. This binary data is stored in the form of a stream of binary data.	Binary
Bigint	SqlInt64	The SqlInt64 structure maps to the Bigint data type of SQL Server. It is a signed, 64-bit integer that has a valid range of -2^{63} to $2^{63} - 1$.	BigInt
boolean	SqlBoolean	The SqlBoolean structure represents an integer with a value of either 1 or 0 that is to be inserted or retrieved from the database.	Bit
char	SqlString	The SqlString structure represents textual data.	Char
datetime	SqlDateTime	The SqlDateTime represents a standard DateTime data type.	DateTime
decimal	SqlDecimal	The SqlDecimal structure maps to the Decimal/Numeric of SQL Server. It has a fixed precision and scales between $-10^{38} - 1$ and $10^{38} - 1$ when inserted and selected from the SQL Server database.	Decimal
float	SqlDouble	The SqlDouble structure maps to the Double data type of SQL Server. It is a floating-point data type with a range of -1.79×10^{308} to 1.79×10^{308}.	Float

SQL Server Data Type	Structure Name	Description of the SqlType Structure	Equivalent SqlDbType
image	SqlBinary	The SqlBinary structure represents an unknown length binary data that is to be inserted or retrieved from a database. This binary data is stored in the form of a stream of binary data.	Image
int	SqlInt32	The SqlInt32 structure maps to the int data type of SQL Server. It is a signed, 32-bit integer that has a valid range of –2147483647 to 2147483647.	Int
money	SqlMoney	The SqlMoney structure maps to the money data type of SQL Server. It has a valid range of –922,337,203,685,477.5808 to 922,337,203,685,477.5807.	Money
ntext	SqlString	The SqlString structure represents several different string data types within SQL Server.	NText
nvarchar	SqlString	The SqlString structure represents several different string data types within SQL Server.	NVarChar
numeric	SqlDecimal	The SqlDecimal structure maps to the Decimal/Numeric of SQL Server. It has a fixed precision and scales between –10^38 -1 and 10^38 – 1 when inserted and selected from the SQL Server database.	Numeric
real	SqlSingle	The SqlSingle is a single-precision data type.	Real
smalldatetime	SqlDateTime	The SqlDateTime maps to a valid date between January 1, 1753 to December 31, 9999, with an accuracy of 3.33 milliseconds. Note that this is slightly different from the SQL Server smalldatetime, which maps to a valid date between January 1, 1900, to June 6, 2079, with an accuracy of a minute.	SmallDateTime
smallint	SqlInt16	The SqlInt16 structure maps to the smallint data type of SQL Server. It is a signed, 16-bit integer that has a valid range of –32768 to 32767.	SmallInt

Table continued on following page

Overview of the System.Data.SqlTypes Namespace (continued)

SQL Server Data Type	Structure Name	Description of the SqlType Structure	Equivalent SqlDbType
smallmoney	SqlMoney	The SqlMoney structure maps to a valid monetary value between –922,337,203,685,477.5808 and 922,337,203,685,477.5807, with an accuracy to ten thousandths of a monetary value. This is larger than the necessary storage space for a small money structure, which is accurate between –214,748.3648 and 214,748.3647 to ten thousandths of a monetary unit.	SmallMoney
sql_variant	Object	The sql_variant maps to the generic Variant object.	Variant
sysname	SqlString	The SqlString structure represents several different string data types within SQL Server.	VarChar
Text	SqlString	The SqlString structure represents several different string data types within SQL Server.	Text
timestamp	SqlBinary	The SqlBinary structure represents a binary stream of data.	TimeStamp
Tinyint	SqlByte	The SqlByte structure represents an unsigned 8-bit integer.	TinyInt
varbinary	SqlBinary	The SqlBinary structure represents a binary stream of data.	VarBinary
Varchar	SqlString	The SqlString structure represents several different string data types within SQL Server.	VarChar
uniqueidentifier	SqlGuid	The SqlGuid structure maps to the uniqueidentifier data type of SQL Server. It is a 128-bit globally unique identifier.	UniqueId

With the release of .NET 2.0, it is possible to retrieve the SQL server data types of the column as defined by System.Data.SqlTypes. The following code does just that:

```
Dim i As Integer
Dim strSql As String = "select * from tblTest where 1=2"
Dim scsbObj As New SqlConnectionStringBuilder(Me.gstrSyncString)
Dim sqlCn As New SqlConnection(scsbObj.ConnectionString)
Dim sqlCm As New SqlCommand(strSql, sqlCn)
Dim sqlDr As SqlDataReader
Try
```

```
      sqlCn.Open()
      sqlDr = sqlCm.ExecuteReader()
      sqlDr.Read()
      For i = 0 To (sqlDr.FieldCount - 1)
          MsgBox(sqlDr.GetName(i) + vbCrLf + "SqlType: " + _
          Convert.ToString(sqlDr.GetProviderSpecificFieldType(i)) + vbCrLf + _
          "Database Type: " + Convert.ToString(sqlDr.GetDataTypeName(i)) + vbCrLf + _
          ".NET Type: " + Convert.ToString(sqlDr.GetFieldType(i)))
      Next
      If Not (sqlDr.IsClosed = True) Then
          sqlDr.Close()
      End If
      sqlDr.Dispose()
      sqlDr = Nothing
  Catch sqlExc As SqlException
      MsgBox("Error: " & sqlExc.Message.ToString())
  Finally
      sqlCm.Dispose()
      sqlCm = Nothing
      If sqlCn.State <> ConnectionState.Closed Then
          sqlCn.Close()
      End If
      sqlCn.Dispose()
      sqlCn = Nothing
  End Try
```

The methods to pay attention to are `SqlDataReader.GetProviderSpecificFieldType()` and the `SqlDataReader.GetDataTypeName()`.

The `SqlDataReader.GetProviderSpecificFieldType()` method will return the `System.Data.SqlType` that the column is defined as. Valid return values are `System.Data.SqlTypes.SqlInt32`, `System.Data.SqlTypes.SqlString`, and other `SqlTypes` as defined within the `System.Data.SqlTypes` namespace. The `SqlDataReader.GetDataTypeName()` method will return the data type as defined within the database. Valid return values are `int`, `varchar`, and other data types as defined within the SQL Server database.

> *While not necessary in this example, two important command behaviors may need to be passed within the* `.BeingExecuteReader()` *method:* `CommandBehavior.KeyInfo` *and* `CommandBehavior.SchemaOnly`. *For more information about these two* `CommandBehaviors`, *refer to the Appendix, which describes* the `CommandBehavior` *enumeration.*

Using SqlTypes

Let's look at an example that uses the `SqlTypes`:

```
iVarCharOrdinal = sqlDr.GetOrdinal("TestVarchar")
While sqlDr.Read()
   sqltString = sqlDr.GetSqlString(iVarCharOrdinal)
   strSqlAsString = sqltString.ToString()
End While
```

The following table describes the methods that retrieve the `SqlTypes` from your data.

Get Values as SqlTypes

Method	Description
GetSqlBoolean(integer)	Gets the value of the specified column as a SqlBoolean type. The column that is specified must be the ordinal value of the column desired.
GetSqlByte(integer)	Gets the value of the specified column as a SqlByte type. The column that is specified must be the ordinal value of the column desired.
GetSqlBytes(integer)	Gets the value of the specified column as SqlBytes. The column that is specified must be the ordinal value of the column desired.
GetSqlChars(integer)	Gets the value of the column as SqlChars. The column that is specified must be the ordinal value of the column desired.
GetSqlDateTime(integer)	Gets the value of the specified column as a SqlDateTime type. The column that is specified must be the ordinal value of the column desired.
GetSqlDecimal(integer)	Gets the value of the specified column as a SqlDecimal type. The column that is specified must be the ordinal value of the column desired.
GetSqlDouble(integer)	Gets the value of the specified column as a SqlDouble type. The column that is specified must be the ordinal value of the column desired.
GetSqlGuid(integer)	Gets the value of the specified column as a SqlGuid type. The column that is specified must be the ordinal value of the column desired.
GetSqlInt16(integer)	Gets the value of the specified column as a SqlInt16 type. The column that is specified must be the ordinal value of the column desired.
GetSqlInt32(integer)	Gets the value of the specified column as a SqlInt32 type. The column that is specified must be the ordinal value of the column desired.
GetSqlInt64(integer)	Gets the value of the specified column as a SqlInt64 type. The column that is specified must be the ordinal value of the column desired.
GetSqlMoney(integer)	Gets the value of the specified column as a SqlMoney type. The column that is specified must be the ordinal value of the column desired.
GetSqlSingle(integer)	Gets the value of the specified column as a SqlSingle type. The column that is specified must be the ordinal value of the column desired.

Method	Description
GetSqlString(integer)	Gets the value of the specified column as a SqlString type. The column that is specified must be the ordinal value of the column desired.
GetSqlValue(integer)	Gets the value of the specified column as an Object type. The column that is specified must be the ordinal value of the column desired.
GetSqlValues(values())	Gets the value of the specified column as a SqlBoolean type. The parameter passed is an area of type object. If fewer values in the array are passed than items in the row of data, the elements returned are truncated to fit in the array.
GetSqlXml(integer)	Gets the value of the specified column as a SqlXml type. The specified column must be the ordinal value of the column desired.

Except for the GetSqlValues() method, the preceding methods all take an integer as a parameter. This integer represents the zero-based ordinal value of that column. The ordinal value may be obtained by calling SqlDataReader.GetOrginal(ColumnName). This method call will return the ordinal position of the column specified by the parameter ColumnName.

Let's look at some example code:

```
Dim i As Integer
Dim iStart As Integer
Dim iEnd As Integer
Dim iVarCharOrdinal As Integer
Dim strSql As String = "select * from tblTest"
Dim scsbObj As New SqlConnectionStringBuilder(Me.gstrSyncString)
Dim sqlCn As New SqlConnection(scsbObj.ConnectionString)
Dim sqlCm As New SqlCommand(strSql, sqlCn)
Dim sqlDr As SqlDataReader
Dim sqltString As System.Data.SqlTypes.SqlString
Try
    sqlCn.Open()
    iStart = GetTickCount()
    For i = 0 To Me.iLength - 1
        sqlDr = sqlCm.ExecuteReader()
        iVarCharOrdinal = sqlDr.GetOrdinal("TestVarchar")
        While sqlDr.Read()
            sqltString = sqlDr.GetSqlString(iVarCharOrdinal)
        End While
        If Not (sqlDr.IsClosed = True) Then
            sqlDr.Close()
        End If
        sqlDr.Dispose()
    Next
    iEnd = GetTickCount()
    MsgBox(sqltString.ToString())
    MsgBox("Time: " & (iEnd - iStart).ToString())
    sqlDr = Nothing
```

```
Catch sqlExc As SqlException
    MsgBox("Error: " & sqlExc.Message.ToString())
Finally
    sqlCm.Dispose()
    sqlCm = Nothing
    If sqlCn.State <> ConnectionState.Closed Then
        sqlCn.Close()
    End If
    sqlCn.Dispose()
    sqlCn = Nothing
End Try
```

The preceding code shows a call using GetSqlString() to return a string within a routine to calculate the amount of time to make that call in a loop. By calculating the amount of time, the user can perform some performance analysis and determine any performance advantages of using GetSqlString().

Using SqlDbType

Now that you have looked at what the SqlTypes namespace is used for, let's look at how to use SqlTypes. Typically, the SqlType structures are used for calling stored procedures or prepared SQL statements for which the data type is already known. The SqlTypes are used in conjunction with the SqlParameter objects. Using the SqlParameters along with the SqlTypes, code will bypass some extra conversions that are performed as a command is executed if a SqlType is not specified. An additional benefit of using the SqlParameter objects is that it will assist in protecting code from a SQL injection attack. Take a look at the following code samples:

```
Dim iReturn As Integer
Dim strSql As String = "spSimple"
Dim sqlCn As New SqlConnection(Me.gstrSyncString)
Dim sqlCm As New SqlCommand(strSql, sqlCn)
Dim sqlPmDate As New SqlParameter("@pdtClientDate", SqlDbType.DateTime)
Try
    sqlPmDate.Direction = ParameterDirection.Input
    sqlPmDate.IsNullable = False
    sqlPmDate.Value = DateTime.Now
    sqlCm.Parameters.Add(sqlPmDate)
    sqlCm.CommandType = CommandType.StoredProcedure
    sqlCn.Open()
    iReturn = Convert.ToInt32(sqlCm.ExecuteScalar())
    MsgBox("Value returned: " & iReturn.ToString())
Catch sqlExc As SqlException
    MsgBox("Error: " & sqlExc.Message.ToString())
Finally
    If sqlCn.State <> ConnectionState.Closed Then
        sqlCn.Close()
    End If
    sqlCn.Dispose()
    sqlCn = Nothing
    sqlPmDate = Nothing
    sqlCm.Dispose()
    sqlCm = Nothing
End Try
```

Why use the `SqlDbType`? The `SqlDbType` is very useful when used in conjunction with the `SqlParameter` class. Together, the two objects provide for an optimized mechanism to communicate with stored procedures and to properly remove illegal characters from a database operation. For example, taken together, these classes will properly escape an input sequence containing the single apostrophe character, which is often used in a SQL injection attack.

Bulk Copy with SQL Server

Bulk copying of data to and from SQL Server databases is a relatively common practice. For example, you may need to download or upload a large number of records from multiple hardware devices or pull a large number of financial transactions out of a database.

Traditionally, the utility `bcp.exe` has been used to perform bulk-style operations. Underlying the `bcp.exe` utility is the Bulk Copy API. This API exists at the NETLIB and ODBC levels. With the arrival of ADO.NET 2.0, there is now a managed interface into this API. The managed interface is built into the `SqlClient` namespace. Three classes are of interest. The primary class is `SqlBulkCopy`. Two additional supporting classes are `SqlBulkCopyColumnMapping` and `SqlBulkCopyColumnMappingCollection`.

The following simple example takes data from one table and puts it into another:

```
Dim strSql As String
Dim sqlCn As New SqlConnection(Me.gstrSyncString)
Dim sqlBcp As New SqlBulkCopy(sqlCn)
Dim sqlDa As New SqlDataAdapter()
Dim sqlCm As New SqlCommand()
Dim dtData As New DataTable
Try
    sqlCn.Open()
    strSql = "truncate table tblAsyncExecuteNonQuery2"
    sqlCm.Connection = sqlCn
    sqlCm.CommandText = strSql
    sqlCm.CommandType = CommandType.Text
    sqlCm.ExecuteNonQuery()
    strSql = "select tblAsyncExecuteNonQueryId, ClientDateEntered, ServerDateEntered
from tblAsyncExecuteNonQuery"
    sqlDa.SelectCommand.CommandText = strSql
    sqlDa.SelectCommand.CommandType = CommandType.Text
    sqlDa.SelectCommand.Connection = sqlCn
    sqlDa.Fill(dtData)
    sqlBcp.DestinationTableName = "tblAsyncExecuteNonQuery2"
    sqlBcp.WriteToServer(dtData)
Catch sqlExc As SqlException
    MsgBox("Error: " & sqlExc.Message.ToString())
    Catch sqlnvExc As SqlNullValueException
    MsgBox("Error: " & sqlnvExc.Message.ToString())
Finally
    sqlDa.Dispose()
    sqlDa = Nothing
    If sqlCn.State <> ConnectionState.Closed Then
        sqlCn.Close()
    End If
    sqlCn.Dispose()
    sqlCn = Nothing
End Try
```

In this example, the destination table is emptied out and a data table from the source is created, which is then inserted into the destination table.

What about copying data out of a table into a file? The `SqlBulkCopy` object has no support for outputting data to a file. Several objects in the .NET Framework can be used for copying data out of a database table and into a file.

Provider Statistics

Sometimes within an application, the amount of information exposed by the Performance Monitor is not sufficient. With ADO.NET 2, it is now possible for an application to expose statistical information on a SQL connection:

```
Dim strSql As String = "select tblAsyncExecuteNonQueryId, ClientDateEntered,
ServerDateEntered from tblAsyncExecuteNonQuery"
Dim strOut As String = String.Empty
Dim sqlCn As New SqlConnection(Me.gstrSyncString)
Dim sqlDa As New SqlDataAdapter(strSql, sqlCn)
Dim dtData As New DataTable
Dim hashSqlStats As Hashtable
Dim de As IDictionaryEnumerator
Try
    sqlCn.Open()
    sqlCn.StatisticsEnabled = True
    sqlDa.Fill(dtData)
    hashSqlStats = CType(sqlCn.RetrieveStatistics(), Hashtable)
    de = hashSqlStats.GetEnumerator()
    While de.MoveNext()
        strOut += Convert.ToString(de.Key) & ": " & Convert.ToString(de.Value) &
vbCrLf
    End While
    MsgBox(strOut)
Catch sqlExc As SqlException
    MsgBox("Error: " & sqlExc.Message.ToString())
Catch sqlnvExc As SqlNullValueException
    MsgBox("Error: " & sqlnvExc.Message.ToString())
Finally
    sqlDa.Dispose()
    sqlDa = Nothing
    If sqlCn.State <> ConnectionState.Closed Then
        sqlCn.Close()
    End If
    sqlCn.Dispose()
    sqlCn = Nothing
    de = Nothing
    hashSqlStats = Nothing
End Try
```

This code provides some insight into how the connections and commands are performing within an application.

One of the biggest advantages this approach has over merely using the Performance Monitor when attempting to retrieve information is that this approach enables a program to provide specific information about its current state. Relying on the Performance Monitor results in an approximation of what is happening inside of a program when something bad happens. Figure 10-2 displays sample output for the provider statistics.

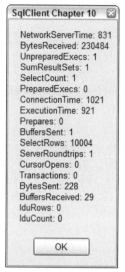

```
SqlClient Chapter 10

NetworkServerTime: 831
BytesReceived: 230484
UnpreparedExecs: 1
SumResultSets: 1
SelectCount: 1
PreparedExecs: 0
ConnectionTime: 1021
ExecutionTime: 921
Prepares: 0
BuffersSent: 1
SelectRows: 10004
ServerRoundtrips: 1
CursorOpens: 0
Transactions: 0
BytesSent: 228
BuffersReceived: 29
IduRows: 0
IduCount: 0

        OK
```

Figure 10-2

SqlCacheDependency

One of the really nice features of ASP.NET 1.x is its capability to cache data from queries on the Web server in the form of the Cache object. In addition to the Cache object is the CacheDependency object, which is designed to work with the Cache object so that when changes are made in the local system on a dependent object, the data stored in the Cache object will be updated based on the CacheDependency object. With the CacheDependency object, it was possible to cache data on the local system based on a timer or a change on the local file system. Unfortunately, the CacheDependency object in .NET 1.x was sealed and could not be extended by being inherited from. The idea is that when a set of values changes within a SQL server database, a cache item would be rebuilt with the updated and necessary data from a predefined SQL server query. With .NET 1.x, it was necessary to go through some mechanism, such as a timer-elapsed, file-system change initiated by a trigger, or other local event to the CacheDependency object, in order for it to realize that it needed to be updated. This resulted in several mechanisms that were somewhat complicated to implement. With .NET 2.0, Microsoft has unsealed the CacheDependency object and created the SqlCacheDependency object. The SqlCacheDependency works with SQL Server 7, 2000, and 2005 to provide a mechanism for updating a client-side cache of data in an easy package.

How to Use the SqlCacheDependency in an ASP.NET Application

Getting database records is a relatively expensive operation. Anything that can be done to minimize the number of round-trips to a database is a good thing. In many applications, several drop-down list boxes are filled from some type of lookup table in a database. The data that would be stored in these list boxes is a great candidate for caching. In Figure 10-3, you can see the time saved when data is stored close to the client system.

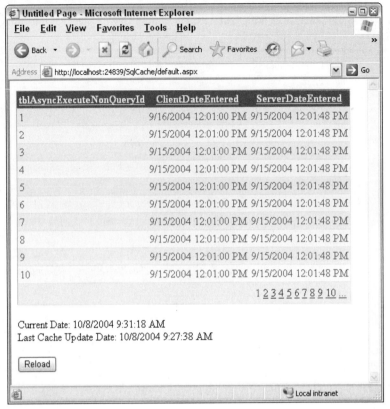

Figure 10-3

SQL Server 2005

SQL Server 2005 databases and tables have the built-in notification support necessary for the database to communicate back to the calling application—in this case, an ASP.NET application—and mark the cached values as invalid. The following code performs this operation:

```
Dim strKey As String = "SqlCacheDependency"
Dim strCn As String = "..........."
Dim strSql As String = "select tblAsyncExecuteNonQueryId, ClientDateEntered,
ServerDateEntered from dbo.tblAsyncExecuteNonQuery"
Dim dsData As New DataSet()
Dim sqlCn As New SqlConnection(strCn)
Dim sqlCm As New SqlCommand(strSql, sqlCn)
Dim sqlDa As New SqlDataAdapter(sqlCm)
Dim sqlDep As SqlCacheDependency
If Cache(strKey) Is Nothing Then
    sqlDep = New SqlCacheDependency(sqlCm)
    sqlDa.Fill(dsData)
    Cache.Insert(strKey, dsData, sqlDep)
    Application("CacheUpdateDate") = Now.ToString()
End If
```

```
Me.lblCurrentDate.Text = Now.ToString()
Me.lblCacheUpdateDate.Text = Application("CacheUpdateDate").ToString()
Me.gvData.DataSource = CType(Cache(strKey), DataSet).Tables(0)
Me.gvData.DataBind()
```

This code provides an example of how you can use the `SqlCacheDepenncy` within an ASP.NET application.

The `Cache.Insert()` method inserts a cacheable item into the `System.Web.Caching.Cache` class. This method includes several overloaded versions that are of interest:

- ❑ `Cache.Insert(key as String, item as Object)` — This version takes a key to identify the cached item.

- ❑ `Cache.Insert(key as String, item as Object, dep as CacheDependency)` — This version builds on the previous version and takes a `CacheDependency` object. The `CacheDependency` object contains the dependencies, such as the `SqlCacheDependency` object.

- ❑ `Cache.Insert(key as String, item as Object, dep as CacheDependency, dt as DateTime, ts as TimeSpan)` — This version builds on the previous version and takes a `datetime` object for setting an absolute expiration time, and a `timespace` for a relative expiration.

- ❑ `Cache.Insert(key as String, item as Object, dep as CacheDependency, dt as DateTime, ts as TimeSpan, cpriority as CacheItemPriority, cir as CacheItemRemovedCallback)` — This version builds on the previous version. The `CacheItemPriority` is an enumeration that instructs the system on the priority of a cached item. The `CacheItemRemovedCallback` is a delegate that may be used to notify the running application when the inserted item is removed from the cache.

SQL Server 7 and 2000

Working with SQL Server 7 and 2000 is slightly different than working with SQL Server 2005. SQL Server 7 and 2000 do not have a built-in way to communicate back to the client when changes have been made. With ASP.NET and ADO.NET Version 2, a built-in mechanism polls for changes to tables. Let's look at some code.

Web.config:

```
<caching>
    <sqlCacheDependency enabled="true">
        <databases>
            <add name="SqlServer2kCacheExample"
connectionStringName="SqlCacheDBConnectionString" pollTime="600000" />
        </databases>
    </sqlCacheDependency>
</caching>
```

Code:

```
Dim strKey As String = "SqlCacheDependencySql2k"
Dim strCn As String = "............"
Dim strSql As String = "select tblAsyncExecuteNonQueryId, ClientDateEntered,
ServerDateEntered from dbo.tblAsyncExecuteNonQuery"
```

```
Dim dsData As New DataSet()
Dim sqlCn As New SqlConnection(strCn)
Dim sqlCm As New SqlCommand(strSql, sqlCn)
Dim sqlDa As New SqlDataAdapter(sqlCm)
Dim sqlDep As SqlCacheDependency

Try
    If Cache(strKey) Is Nothing Then
        sqlDep = New SqlCacheDependency("SqlServer2kCacheExample",
"tblAsyncExecuteNonQuery")
        sqlDa.Fill(dsData)
        Cache.Insert(strKey, dsData, sqlDep)
        Application("CacheUpdateDate") = Now.ToString()
    End If
    Me.lblCurrentDate.Text = Now.ToString()
    Me.lblCacheUpdateDate.Text = Application("CacheUpdateDate").ToString()
    Me.gvData.DataSource = CType(Cache(strKey), DataSet).Tables(0)
    Me.gvData.DataBind()
Finally
    If sqlCn.State <> ConnectionState.Closed Then
        sqlCn.Close()
    End If
    sqlCn.Dispose()
    sqlDa.Dispose()
    sqlCm.Dispose()
    sqlCn = Nothing
    sqlDa = Nothing
    sqlCm = Nothing
End Try
```

Three items must be set up differently when dealing with SQL 7 or SQL 2000 and using the `SqlCacheDependency` object:

❑ The database must be set up for caching. This is handled through a command-line call to `aspnet_regsql.exe` and a call to the shared method `SqlCacheDependencyAdmin`. `EnableTableForNotifications`(db connection string). The `EnableTableForNotifications` method will create a trigger to run on an insert, update, or delete of records within that table.

❑ The `SqlCacheDependency` object must be set up differently when running with SQL 7 or SQL 2000. The connection and table must be specified.

❑ The `web.config` must be set up. A back-end ASP.NET process will connect to the database and look for changes in the specified table.

❑ Caching can only be done at the table level with SQL 7 and SQL 2000.

Uses for SqlCacheDependency

If you are thinking that this is a really good tool that might have useful applications elsewhere, you are right. Let's look at some scenarios:

❑ **Data that changes slowly** — This is the optimal situation in which to use the `SqlCacheDependency` object. If the data being monitored changes slowly, the data can be cached closer to the methods that need the data.

- ❑ **Data that changes rapidly** — The SqlCacheDependency object should probably not be used in a scenario in which the data changes fairly rapidly. If it is used, the back-end processes would be notified by the SqlCacheDependency object and would spend too much time notifying the cache that the cached object should be rebuilt and triggering queries against the database.

- ❑ **Data that is hard to reach** — If for any reason there is a delay in reaching the data, caching it might be very useful.

Ultimately, deciding where and how to cache data is an important architectural issue. What data to cache and when to cache it is an important decision in the scope of architecting an application, and it can only reliably be made by those who are tightly involved with the application.

SqlCacheDependencyAdmin

The SqlCacheDependencyAdmin class is used to perform administrative tasks required on a SQL Server database to add, update, and remove support for the SqlCacheDependency class. This class is a member of the System.Web.Caching namespace. The following table describes the members of this class.

SqlCacheDependencyAdmin Members

Public Methods	Description
DisableNotifications	Connects to a SQL Server database and performs the necessary operations to remove support for change notification for a database.
DisableTableForNotifications	Connects to a SQL Server database and performs the necessary operations to remove support for change notification for a table.
EnableNotifications	Connects to a SQL Server database and performs the necessary operations to add support for change notification for a database.
EnableTableForNotifications	Connects to a SQL Server database and performs the necessary operations to support change notification for a table.
GetTablesEnabledForNotifications	An array of strings is returned with the name of each table that is enabled for change notification in a SQL Server database.

To successfully call these methods, a program needs appropriate security on the SQL Server database. These security rights include the ability to create and remove stored procedures, triggers, and tables.

SqlDependency

Very similar to the SqlCacheDependency class is the SqlDependency class. The SqlDependency object can be used to notify a winforms client-server style application that a change has occurred. The SqlDependency object is bound to a SqlCommand object. Let's look at some source code (and see the tables following the code for SqlDependency properties, methods, and events):

```
Dim strSql As String = "select tblTestId, TestBigInt from dbo.tblTest"
Dim sqlDr As SqlDataReader

sqlCn = New SqlConnection(Me.gstrSyncString)
sqlCm = New SqlCommand(strSql, sqlCn)
sqlCn.Open()
'this does work.
sqlDep = New SqlDependency(sqlCm)
sqlDr = sqlCm.ExecuteReader()
While sqlDr.Read()
    'Do something with the code.
    'I am just using a loop with nothing in it.
End While
sqlDr.Close()
'sqlDep.AddCommandDependency(sqlCm)
AddHandler sqlDep.OnChanged, AddressOf onChangeSqlDep

Private Shared Sub onChangeSqlDep(ByVal caller As Object, ByVal sqlEvent As
SqlNotificationEventArgs)
    MessageBox.Show(sqlEvent.Info.ToString())
    'You will need to rebuild the SqlDependency object here.
End Sub
```

The following is a table containing the properties and methods of the SqlDependency object.

SqlDependency Properties

Properties	Description
HasChanges	Returns a value that indicates whether one of the result sets associated with the SqlDependency object has changed.
Id	A value that uniquely identifies the instance of the SqlDependency class.

SqlDependency Methods

Method	Description
AddCommandDependency	Adds a SqlCommand object to the SqlDependency object. This is similar to setting the SqlCommand object within the constructor.

SqlDependency Events

Event	Description
OnChanged	This event is called when the results of a query change. Note that this event may fire based on a time-out expiration or a failure to set a notification request.

You should be aware of several rules when using the `SqlCacheDependency` and `SqlDependency` objects:

- ❏ The select list cannot use the `*` or `table_name.*` syntax to specify columns. Column names must be explicitly stated.

- ❏ Table names must be qualified with two-part names. Subscription is invalid if three- or four-part names are used.

- ❏ The SQL query must not contain a table column name used as a simple expression, and the column cannot be specified more than once.

- ❏ The SQL query must not contain derived tables.

- ❏ The SQL query must not contain rowset functions.

- ❏ The SQL query must not contain the `UNION` operator.

- ❏ The SQL query must not contain subqueries.

- ❏ The SQL query must not contain outer or self joins.

- ❏ The SQL query must not contain the `TOP` clause.

- ❏ The SQL query must not contain the `DISTINCT` keyword.

- ❏ The SQL query must not contain the `COUNT(*)` aggregate.

- ❏ The SQL query must not contain `AVG`, `MAX`, `MIN`, `STDEV`, `STDEVP`, `VAR`, or `VARP` aggregates.

- ❏ The SQL query must not contain user-defined aggregates.

- ❏ The SQL query must not contain a `SUM` function that references a nullable expression.

- ❏ The SQL query must not contain the full-text predicates `CONTAINS` or `FREETEXT`.

- ❏ The SQL query must not contain the `COMPUTE` or `COMPUTE BY` clause.

- ❏ In the SQL query, if `GROUP BY` is not specified, the select list cannot contain aggregate expressions.

- ❏ In the SQL query, if `GROUP BY` is specified, the select list must contain a `COUNT_BIG(*)` expression, and cannot specify `HAVING`, `CUBE`, or `ROLLUP`.

- ❏ The SQL query must not reference temporal tables or table variables.

- ❏ The SQL query must not reference tables/views from other databases/servers.

- ❏ The SQL query must not reference any other views or inline table-valued functions.

- ❏ The SQL query must not reference any system tables or views.

- ❏ The SQL query must not reference any nondeterministic function — including ranking/windowing functions.

- ❏ The SQL query must not reference any server global variables. These are typically defined as `@@xxx`.

- ❏ The SQL query must reference some base table or view.

- ❏ The SQL query must not contain an `INTO` clause.

❑ The SQL query must not specify FOR BROWSE (or be running with SET NO_BROWSETABLE ON).

❑ The SQL query must not contain conditions that will preclude results from changing (e.g., WHERE 1=0).

❑ The SQL query cannot specify the READPAST locking hint.

❑ The SQL query must not reference any Service Broker QUEUE.

Summary

The SqlClient in ADO.NET Version 2 has seen a significant increase in the number of methods and features that it supports. In this chapter, you learned about the following:

❑ Asynchronous support in ASP.NET and a winforms application

❑ Caching and notifications of updates in ASP.NET and winforms applications

❑ How to manage passwords

❑ How to use the SqlConnectionStringBuilder

For More Information

❑ **.NET Whidbey Books Online documentation**

❑ **SQL Server 2005 Books Online**

❑ **Microsoft SQL Server 2005 Community Technology (CTP) Newsgroups** — http:// communities.microsoft.com/newsgroups/default.asp?icp=sqlserver2005&slcid=us

❑ **"Asynchronous Command Execution in ADO.NET Version 2," by Pablo Castro, PM at Microsoft** — http://msdn.microsoft.com/library/default.asp?url=/library/ en-us/dnvs05/html/async2.asp

❑ **Bob Beauchemin's Weblog on the new features of ADO.NET. Bob is known for his work at Developmenor and now works at SQLSkills.** — http://www.sqlskills.com/blogs/bobb

SQL Server 2005 Server-Side Programming

With the release of Microsoft SQL Server 2005 (aka Yukon), Microsoft has added a significant number of features to their flagship database products. These updates represent many years of study into how developers are using relational databases and what types of needs developers will have in the next few years.

In Chapter 10, you looked at the latest features available for programming against SQL Server on the client side using the System.Data.SqlClient namespace. In this chapter, you will be looking at the new features for programming with SQL Server 2005. Specifically, you will be examining the following:

- ❏ **Common Language Runtime (CLR) Objects** — You will learn how to create stored procedures, functions, triggers, aggregates, and user-defined types (UDTs) that run and reside in the database, along with the Transact-SQL (T-SQL) objects that have been available in previous versions of the SQL Server database.

- ❏ **SQL Management Objects (SMO)** — SMO provides the capability to programmatically create, drop, and manage database objects within SQL Server.

- ❏ **Web Services/XML Endpoint** — Web Services/XML Endpoints provide a mechanism for SQL Server to expose data without the need for Internet Information Server.

Extended Stored Procedures

Before Microsoft SQL Server 2005, when an application needed to implement complicated business logic within the database that was not possible within the Transact-SQL (T-SQL) language, a developer had to use a feature of SQL Server called *extended stored procedures (XPs)*. XPs are pieces of native code that are loaded by SQL Server but are written in a traditional programming language, such as Visual C++. Unfortunately, XPs had several problems, including the following:

❏ **Control** — Once an XP is executing, there is little control over what the XP can and cannot do.

❏ **Reliability** — Problems with an XP can wreak havoc on the SQL Server database. These extended stored procedures run within the address space of SQL Server; however, they have complete access to the memory space of the server. A failure in the extended stored procedures may result in the failure of SQL Server Service, with the result that the database is unavailable. This would be a major problem for applications requiring significant update.

❏ **Data access** — Within an XP, application code has no access back to the database. A loop-back connection must be made. In addition, the loop-back connection must be bound to the existing session's transaction to ensure that the XP is involved with the same transaction.

❏ **Performance** — Open Data Services (ODS) APIs are used by XPs. The ODS API does not include support for the new data types in SQL Server, such as XML, varchar(max), varbinary(max), and so on. Compared to CLR objects, the ODS API is less optimized for sending result sets back to a client application.

❏ **Scalability** — SQL Server has no control over the resources used by an XP. If an XP uses too much CPU or memory, the system SQL Server has no way to stop the misuse of resources.

While XPs tend to perform very well, the problems of scalability and reliability tend to overshadow their performance advantages.

CLR Objects

SQL Server 2005 includes the capability to safely program in the database using the languages of the .NET 2.0 and later Frameworks. Previously, the only language that was supported when running inside the database was T-SQL. Along with T-SQL, it was possible to call COM objects through the use of extended stored procedures. Unfortunately, this was relatively complex and — due to the problems mentioned previously — Microsoft introduced the capability to programmatically use CLR objects within the database. Although XPs have a performance advantage compared to CLR objects because of the native code of XPs and the switching between managed and unmanaged code within a database, the safety of CLR objects will tend to provide a better alternative when all of the issues are taken into account.

With the release of SQL Server 2005, SQL Server can host and run assemblies written in any .NET programming language. These assemblies can simulate the activity of T-SQL database objects such as triggers, stored procedures, aggregates, and functions, along with the capability to define new data types. The objects appear and act just like T-SQL-based database objects, even while they are written in a .NET language, such as Visual Basic .NET or C#.

Set-Based Programming

Before getting into the programming of CLR objects, we need to discuss some basic programming methodologies. In mathematics, we have the concept of *set theory*. A *set* is a collection of objects. These objects can be operated on in nearly any fashion, such as by using AND, OR, XOR, and other set/logical operations. Relational databases are based on this mathematical concept of set theory.

Let's take a look at a SQL statement that will return some data:

```
Select PartNumber, PartDescription, PartCost from PartTable where PartFamily=123
```

This statement is asking for the `PartNumber`, `PartDescription`, and `PartCost` columns from a `PartTable`, where the `PartFamily` value is 123. This is an example of the SQL implementation of set theory. The database is being asked to return all records that match specified criteria. Not only can data be selected in `Insert`, `Update`, and `Delete`, operations may also be done in bulk, or as part of a set of data. This is different from mainstream programming languages, which tend to operate on pieces of data one at a time. Thousands of human-years have been put into optimizing databases for set-based programming using the T-SQL language. As a result, set-based programming is the default mechanism used to access data stored within a database, and it is very tightly embedded into many database products. As a result, the SQL-based implementation provides a high-performance interface into data.

Procedural Programming

Typical procedural programming is a concept with which most programmers are familiar. With *procedural programming*, operations against data tend to happen one at a time in a line-by-line process. This is the metaphor that mainstream programming languages, such as Visual Basic .NET and C#, tend to follow. From the standpoint of a human being performing programming operations, this approach makes a lot of sense. To operate on a set of data within a database in a line-by-line fashion, an object called a *cursor* is typically used. One might think of a cursor as a pointer into a set of data. Unfortunately, cursors within a database and this style of programming are at odds with producing highly optimized database operations. There is significant overhead in operating on rows of data in a database in a line-by-line fashion. As a result, these types of operations should be minimized.

Using CLR Objects

With the release of Microsoft SQL Server 2005, Microsoft has added the capability to execute objects stored and run within the database that are based on the Microsoft .NET Framework, as opposed to relying on T-SQL or the extended stored procedure architecture. There are several advantages to using CLR objects within a SQL Server database versus programming in T-SQL or extended stored procedures, including the following:

❑ An improved programming model over set-based programming. Objects written in a .NET language offer capabilities that are not possible, or are extremely difficult to implement, under the T-SQL programming language.

❑ Enhanced safety and security over using extended stored procedures

❑ .NET languages offer capabilities not available in T-SQL. For example, a CLR object can easily perform complicated string processing and mathematical calculations. The string processing and mathematical calculations would be very difficult within a T-SQL-based object. Furthermore, the addition of the CLR provides the capability to develop aggregates and types not possible with just using TSQL.

❑ .NET languages enable the creation of new capabilities. User-defined types and aggregates are two new features that evolved from the inclusion of the .NET Framework in the database.

❑ Visual Studio .NET as a development tool provides for an improved development experience.

Please check the Wrox Web site (at `www.wrox.com`) for updates or additional information.

Creating CLR Objects

Let's take a quick look at the steps for creating a CLR object for SQL Server 2005. To quickly and easily create a SQL Server 2005 CLR object, a developer needs Visual Studio 2005 and an instance of SQL Server 2005.

1. Create a SQL Server project using Visual Studio .NET 2005. This project type has all of the associated assemblies referenced. It does not allow you to easily add any possible assembly to the list. Only approved assemblies within the .NET 2.0 Framework and other SQL Server projects are currently allowed.

2. Create a class definition. Typically, there will be a separate class for each object type. For example, stored procedures, functions, and triggers would be separated into a stored procedure, function, and trigger class. Each aggregate and user-defined type would be separated into its own individual class. By compiling the code, Visual Studio .NET 2005 will create the assembly.

3. Deploy the assembly. This operation is a separate operation for compiling the code. In this case, the code is uploaded and deployed to the database server. The assembly is stored within a system catalog. This operation in Visual Studio .NET 2005 is analogous to the CREATE ASSEMBLY TSQL statement. You'll look at the CREATE ASSEMBLY statement in the section on manual deployment.

4. T-SQL objects need to be wired to CLR objects so that when specific calls are made to the T-SQL objects, the calls are routed to the appropriate CLR objects. This can be done through the various attributes for triggers, functions, and stored procedures. In T-SQL, this is performed through the T-SQL CREATE procedure, function, trigger, aggregate, and type statements used to wire the objects for operation.

Now that the CLR objects have been created and deployed, these objects may be called and used just like any other database object in T-SQL. Therefore, using a stored procedure written in VB.NET is no different from using a stored procedure written in T-SQL. Figure 11-1 shows you how a stored procedure looks in Visual Studio .NET 2005.

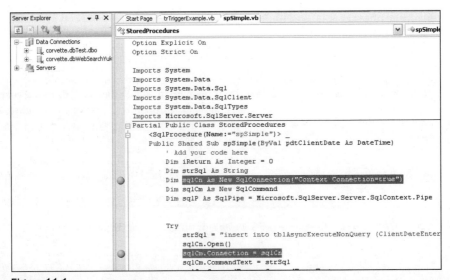

Figure 11-1

In Figure 11-2, you can see how user-defined types are displayed within Visual Studio 2005 and the SQL Management Studio.

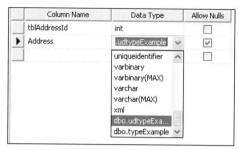

Figure 11-2

Once within the Visual Studio 2005 environment, additional features are available to optimize the development experience. Several of the biggest features include the following:

❑ The capability to open the source code for a CLR object by right-clicking Open from a submenu. Figure 11-3 shows the Open option for editing a CLR object.

❑ A listing of all files associated with that assembly.

❑ Debugging of a CLR object.

❑ The capability to open files associated with an assembly.

Figure 11-3

Just to note, by default the ability to use CLR objects is turned off in SQL Server 2005. This feature needs to be turned on. This is done through the following series of commands:

```
sp_configure 'show advanced options', 1
go
reconfigure
go
sp_configure 'clr enabled', 1
go
reconfigure
go
```

New Namespaces

With the release of SQL Server 2005 and .NET 2.0, two new namespaces are included for programming with the SQL Server 2005 database: `Microsoft.SqlServer.Server` and `System.Data.Sql`. Along with these two namespaces, the `System.Data.SqlClient` namespace has had features added so that it will run within the SQL Server database.

Microsoft.SqlServer.Server

The `Microsoft.SqlServer.Server` namespace provides support for running code within the database. This namespace provides support for the attributes along with the support for the `SqlContext`, `SqlPipe`, and other objects.

System.Data.Sql

The `System.Data.Sql` namespace is a new namespace with the release of .NET 2.0 and SQL Server 2005. This namespace is needed to support the user-defined types within .NET 2.0 and SQL Server 2005. Why is this namespace defined outside of the `Microsoft.SqlServer.Server` namespace? User-defined types are needed by both the client and the server. The server needs to support the new objects and the client needs to be able to process the new objects on the client — hence, the separation of the support into different namespaces.

System.Data.SqlClient

The `System.Data.SqlClient` has been modified so that its objects may run within the SQL Server database engine. With this support, an application has access to the standard ADO.NET objects, such as `SqlConnection`, `SqlDataReader`, and other objects.

SQL Server Projects

Visual Studio 2005 has defined support for SQL Server into a specific project type. This project type makes Visual Studio a top-notch environment in which to develop CLR objects. With this project, numerous features are set up for the developer, including the following:

❑ **Database connection string** — This can be used to define the project to which the object will be deployed.

❑ **Test scripts** — A set of test .sql scripts can be defined so that repetitive tasks may be automated easily.

❑ **Programmability tracking** — Much like the Class viewer in Visual Studio, there is an "Assembly view" within a SQL Server 2005 database through Visual Studio 2005.

Deployment

When a set of CLR objects are created for SQL Server 2005, the objects must be loaded into the database. This is accomplished through one of two methods: manual deployment and the Visual Studio .NET Deploy features.

The manual process to install an assembly is a two-step process:

1. The CREATE ASSEMBLY statement is a T-SQL statement used to load the assembly within the database. In the following code example, the assembly named SqlCLRObjects is created from the listed file:

```
CREATE ASSEMBLY SqlCLRObjects FROM 'C:\Development Projects\
SqlCLRObjects\bin\Debug\SqlCLRObjects.dll' WITH PERMISSION_SET = SAFE
```

2. Now that the assembly exists within the database, a CLR object must be mapped to the CLR method. This is accomplished through one of the following T-SQL commands:

    ❏   CREATE FUNCTION. CREATE FUNCTION functionName RETURNS datatype AS EXTERNAL namespace.class.methodname is the basic calling convention to setup a CLR Function.

    ❏   CREATE PROCEDURE. CREATE PRODCUEDRE sprocname (<@PARAM, DATATYPE> LIST) AS EXTERNAL NAME namespace.class.methodname is the basic calling convention to set up a stored procedure.

    ❏   CREATE TRIGGER. CREATE TRIGGER triggername ON tablename FOR action AS EXTERNAL NAME fullyqualifiedname is the basic calling convention to set up a trigger.

    ❏   CREATE TYPE. CREATE TYPE typename EXTERNAL NAME fullyqualifiedname is the basic calling convention to set up a type.

    ❏   CREATE AGGREGATE. CREATE AGGREGATE methodname (@param datatype) RETURNS datatype EXTERNAL NAME namespace.class.methodname is the basic calling convention to set up an aggregate.

As you can see, the manual process contains a number of options to make the CLR objects operational. The second, more automated, way to create these objects within the database can be performed within the Visual Studio .NET 2005 IDE. This automated deployment is performed in three steps:

1. Use the appropriate CLR attributes in a function, trigger, and such. These are discussed in more detail within the appropriate CLR object section.

2. Set the appropriate deployment settings within Visual Studio .NET 2005 by selecting My Projects and then selecting the Database tab to change deployment options, as shown in Figure 11-4.

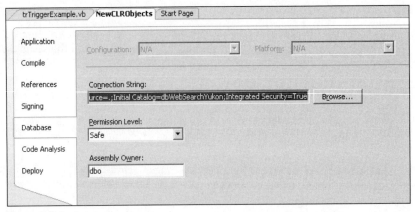

Figure 11-4

3. Deploy the assembly by right-clicking on the project and selecting the Deploy option. This deployment is based on the rules selected in Figure 11-4. Figure 11-5 shows the deployment through Visual Studio 2005.

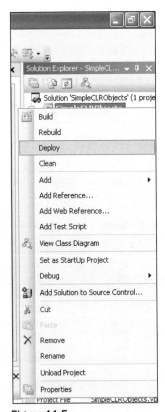

Figure 11-5

Security

An assembly may run within three allowed permissions:

❑ SAFE — This is the most restrictive execution environment that an assembly may run within. With the SAFE permission, code is not allowed to access any external system resources, such as files, networks, the registry, or any environment variables.

❑ EXTERNAL_ACCESS — This permission allows assemblies to access system resources, such as files, networks, environment variables, and the registry.

❑ UNSAFE — This permission set allows assemblies to access resources within SQL Server and outside of the database in an unrestricted manner. Only sysadmin members can create UNSAFE assemblies.

Debugging

Visual Studio 2005 provides for the capability to create CLR objects. It also provides for the capability to debug CLR objects after they have been deployed within SQL Server 2005 and SQL Express. Here are the steps you must take to debug a CLR object:

1. Build and deploy a CLR object.

2. Within Visual Studio, select Debug ➪ Attach to Process.

3. Select the process that needs to be debugged and then select Attach (see Figure 11-6).

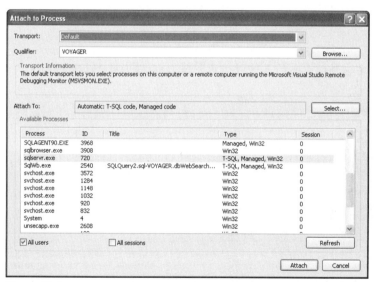

Figure 11-6

4. Select the appropriate line to set breakpoints and begin the debugging session. Figure 11-7 shows the window to debug a CLR trigger.

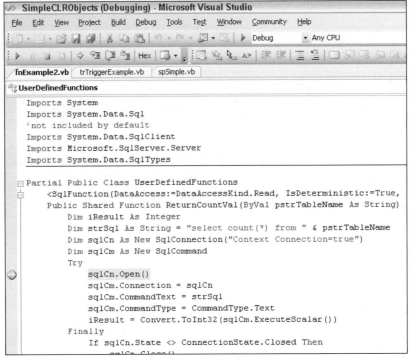

Figure 11-7

Assemblies and CLR Object Tables/Functions

Within each SQL Server 2005 database are a set of tables and functions that contain information regarding CLR objects and assemblies within the database:

❑ sys.assemblies — The sys.assemblies catalog view contains a row for each assembly within a database. This table contains information, including the security permission set, for the assembly.

❑ sys.assembly_files — The sys.assembly_files catalog view contains a row of information for each file that makes up an assembly.

❑ sys.assembly_references — The sys.assembly_references catalog view contains a row for each pair of assemblies that directly reference each other.

❑ sys.assembly_types — The sys.assembly_types catalog view contains a row for each user-defined type specified within a CLR assembly.

❑ sys.types — The sys.types catalog view contains a row for each system and user-defined type within an assembly.

❑ sys.assembly_modules — The sys.assembly_modules catalog view contains a row per function, stored procedure, or trigger within a CLR assembly.

❑ sys.sql_modules — The sys.sql_modules catalog view contains a row per object for items defined within T-SQL.

❏ ASSEMBLYPROPERTY — The ASSEMBLYPROPERTY provides information about the specified property of an assembly.

Its proper usage is as follows:

```
SELECT ASSEMBLYPROPERTY('clr assembly name', 'property name');
```

The allowed properties are as follows:

- ❏ CultureInfo — The locale information for the assembly.
- ❏ PublicKey — The public key of the assembly.
- ❏ VersionMajor — The major component of the version number of the assembly. This is the first part of the four-part version information.
- ❏ VersionMinor — The minor component of the version number of the assembly. This is the second part of the four-part version information.
- ❏ VersionBuild — The build component of the version number of the assembly. This is the third part of the four-part version information.
- ❏ VersionRevision — The revision component of the version number of the assembly. This is the last part of the four-part version information.
- ❏ SimpleName — The simple name of the assembly.
- ❏ Architecture — The processor architecture for which the assembly is compiled.

Triggers

Triggers are one of the basic objects within a database. A special type of stored procedure, triggers are called when an operation occurs that changes data within a table. When an insert, update, or delete operation occurs on a table or view, a database object, a trigger, can be set to fire.

By using a .NET language, a CLR trigger can do the following:

- ❏ Reference the special tables INSERTED and DELETED, which are visible to T-SQL triggers.
- ❏ Calculate the columns that have been changed through the UPDATE operation.
- ❏ Retrieve information about database changes.

Within the .NET Framework, the SqlTriggerContext provided by the method SqlContext.TriggerContext property provides the trigger context so that a program may obtain information about running within the database engine.

SqlTriggerContext

The SqlTriggerContext class is provided by calling the SqlContextTriggerContext property within a SQL Server 2005 CLR trigger. The SqlTriggerContext class provides the contextual information within a CLR trigger. This provides information regarding the action that is to be fired, the columns modified in an UPDATE command, and any EventData contained within a DDL style trigger.

Once the `SqlTriggerContext` is obtained, it is possible to determine the type of operation that has been performed that caused the trigger to fire. This information is provided by the `SqlTriggerContext`'s `TriggerAction` property. Let's look at the possible `TriggerAction` values for DML operations:

- ❑ `TriggerAction.Update`
- ❑ `TriggerAction.Insert`
- ❑ `TriggerAction.Delete`

For DDL operations, the possible number of `TriggerAction` values is much larger. Following are the areas of possible values into which these operations fall:

- ❑ Alter
- ❑ Create
- ❑ Drop
- ❑ Deny
- ❑ Grant
- ❑ Invalid
- ❑ Revoke

These operations can usually run across against the following types of objects:

- ❑ AppRole
- ❑ Assembly
- ❑ Binding
- ❑ Contract
- ❑ EventNotification
- ❑ Function
- ❑ Index
- ❑ MsgType
- ❑ PartitionFunction
- ❑ PartitionScheme
- ❑ Object
- ❑ Procedure
- ❑ Role
- ❑ Route
- ❑ Scheme
- ❑ Secexpr
- ❑ SecurityExpression

- ❏   Synonym

- ❏   Queue

- ❏   Schema

- ❏   Service

- ❏   Statement

- ❏   Table

- ❏   Trigger

- ❏   User

- ❏   View

Note that there is not an action for each object type.

Updating Columns

One of the important operations in a trigger is determining the columns that have been updated due to an insert/update/delete operation. The columns can be found by performing the following sequence of commands of operations within a CLR trigger. This will return the updated columns by their ordinal value. To return the column names, several more operations must be performed:

```
Dim i As Integer = 0
Dim strSql As String = "select * from inserted"
Dim sqlCn As New SqlConnection("Context Connection=true")
Dim sqlCm As New SqlCommand
Dim sqlTrCtx As SqlTriggerContext = SqlContext.TriggerContext
Dim spPipe As SqlPipe = SqlContext.Pipe
Dim sXml As SqlXml = sqlTrCtx.EventData()
Dim strTriggerAction As String
Dim sqlDr As SqlDataReader
spPipe.Send("Total Columns: " & sqlTrCtx.ColumnCount.ToString())
sqlCm.CommandText = strSql
sqlCm.Connection = sqlCn
sqlCn.Open()
sqlDr = sqlCm.ExecuteReader
For i = 0 To (sqlTrCtx.ColumnCount - 1)
    spPipe.Send(sqlDr.GetName(i) & " " & sqlTrCtx.IsUpdatedColumn(i))
Next
```

There are some problems with handling BLOB types with the text, ntext, *and* column *definitions. The preceding code will only work if the tables contain columns that are non-BLOB only. A future version of SQL Server will drop support for these BLOB columns and replace them with* varchar(max) *and* varbinary(max).

EventData for DDL Triggers

When a Data Definition Language (DDL) change event occurs due to the creation, deletion, or other operation performed against the structure of a database object, a DDL trigger can be set to fire. This operation performed against the structure of a database object is most likely going to be performed through a CREATE, ALTER, or DROP command:

```
Dim sqlTrCtx As SqlTriggerContext = SqlContextTriggerContext
Dim spPipe As SqlPipe = SqlContext.Pipe
Dim sXml As SqlXml = sqlTrCtx.EventData()
If Not (sXml Is Nothing) Then
    If (sXml.IsNull <> True) Then
        SqlContext.GetPipe().Send("xml data: " & sXml.Value)
    Else
        SqlContext.GetPipe().Send("No xml data.")
    End If
Else
    spPipe.Send("EventData is nothing.")
End If
```

Notice that the XML that has been returned to the `SqlXml` object is well-formed XML that contains `EventData` information about the DDL operation. This information includes things such as the time of the operation, the user connected, the machine name, and so on.

It is possible for a CLR trigger to execute on a DDL command. The `TriggerAction` enum exposes values for dropping a table, altering a view, and other operations.

Sample Code

The following example code contains many of the options available to a developer building a CLR-based trigger:

```
Option Explicit On
Option Strict On
Imports System
Imports System.Data.Sql
Imports System.Data.SqlClient
Imports System.Data.SqlTypes
Imports System.Diagnostics
Imports Microsoft.SqlServer.Server
Partial Public Class Triggers
    ' EventData should be null in a DML.
    ' ColumnsUpdated should be null in a DDL.
    ' Enter existing table or view for the target and uncomment the attribute line
    <SqlTrigger(Name:="trtblSearchResults", Target:="tblSearchResults", Event:="FOR
INSERT, UPDATE")> _
    Public Shared Sub trtblSearchResults()
        Dim i As Integer = 0
        'dim strSql as String = "select SearchUrl, DateEntered, dateupdated,
ServerName, SearchCode, tblSearchResultsId, DateTimeStamped, DateSearched from
inserted"
        Dim strSql As String = "select * from inserted"
        Dim sqlCn As New SqlConnection("Context Connection=true")
        Dim sqlCm As New SqlCommand
        Dim sqlTrCtx As SqlTriggerContext = SqlContext.TriggerContext
        Dim spPipe As SqlPipe = SqlContext.Pipe
        Dim sXml As SqlXml = sqlTrCtx.EventData()
        Dim strTriggerAction As String
        Dim sqlDr As SqlDataReader
```

```
        Try

                spPipe.Send("Total Columns: " & sqlTrCtx.ColumnCount.ToString())
                sqlCm.CommandText = strSql
                sqlCm.Connection = sqlCn
                sqlCn.Open()
                sqlDr = sqlCm.ExecuteReader
                For i = 0 To (sqlTrCtx.ColumnCount - 1)
                    spPipe.Send(sqlDr.GetName(i) & " " & sqlTrCtx.IsUpdatedColumn(i))
                Next
                If sqlDr.IsClosed = False Then
                    sqlDr.Close()
                End If
                sqlDr.Dispose()
                strTriggerAction = sqlTrCtx.TriggerAction.ToString()
                spPipe.Send("Trigger Action: " & strTriggerAction)
                If Not (sXml Is Nothing) Then
                    If (sXml.IsNull <> True) Then
                        SqlContext.Pipe.Send("xml data: " & sXml.Value)
                    Else
                        SqlContext.Pipe.Send("No xml data.")
                    End If
                Else
                    SqlContext.Pipe.Send("EventData is nothing.")
                End If

        Catch sqlEx As SqlException
                'managed the SqlException.
                'we are just going to log it an then throw it.
                EventLog.WriteEntry("test trigger", sqlEx.Message.ToString(),
    EventLogEntryType.Error)
                Throw
        Finally
                If sqlCn.State <> ConnectionState.Closed Then
                    sqlCn.Close()
                End If
                sqlCn.Dispose()
                sqlCm.Dispose()
        End Try
    End Sub
End Class
```

Working through the code from the top down, let's take a look at some items to which we should pay particular attention (this is only a quick overview; you will learn much more about these items in other sections of the chapter):

❑   Option Explicit and Option Strict are turned on.

❑   A number of standard namespaces are imported.

❑   There is a partial class defining the triggers.

❑   There is a SqlTrigger attribute. This example sets the name of the trigger (Name), the target database object to monitor (Target), and the events to process (Event). This attribute is used to mark the method as a trigger within the database.

❏ The `SqlTriggerContext` is calculated and returned based on the `SqlContext`'s property `TriggerContext`.

❏ The `SqlPipe` object is created. The `SqlPipe` object is used to send data back to the calling method. It is important that the `SqlPipe` not be overused. Calling back to the calling method will result in a method that is slow compared to an object that minimizes its calls back to the calling method.

❏ A DDL trigger, which is new with SQL Server 2005, will provide some type of `EventData`. With this specific trigger, there is no `EventData` that will be returned and the `SqlXml` object is NULL. The code in the code segment takes the EventData into account.

❏ Much like in a T-SQL trigger, it is possible to determine the columns that have been updated. One of the properties of the trigger context is the `ColumnsUpdated` property. This property will return an array of the columns that have been updated by the associated T-SQL statement that caused the trigger to fire.

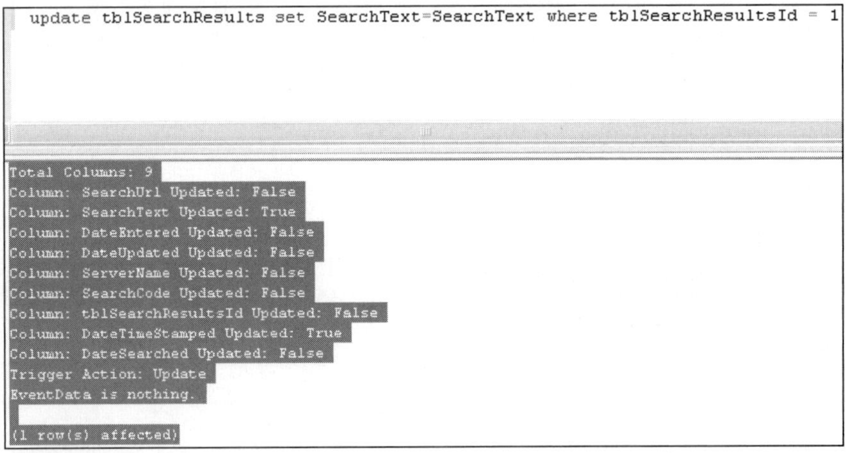

```
update tblSearchResults set SearchText=SearchText where tblSearchResultsId = 1




Total Columns: 9
Column: SearchUrl Updated: False
Column: SearchText Updated: True
Column: DateEntered Updated: False
Column: DateUpdated Updated: False
Column: ServerName Updated: False
Column: SearchCode Updated: False
Column: tblSearchResultsId Updated: False
Column: DateTimeStamped Updated: True
Column: DateSearched Updated: False
Trigger Action: Update
EventData is nothing.

(1 row(s) affected)
```

Figure 11-8

Now let's look at another example of a CLR trigger. This CLR trigger covers the general design goals for a CLR trigger:

```
<SqlTrigger(Name:="tr_tblSearchResults_InsertUpdate", Event:="FOR INSERT,
UPDATE", Target:="tblSearchResults")> _
    Public Shared Sub InsertUpdateSearchResultsTrigger()
    Dim i As Integer
    Dim iSearchCode As Long
    Dim strServerName As String
    Dim strSql As String = String.Empty
    Dim glResults As New Generic.List(Of String)
    Dim sqlCn As New SqlConnection("Context Connection=true")
    Dim sqlCmd As New SqlCommand
    Dim sqlTrCtx As SqlTriggerContext = SqlContext.TriggerContext
    Dim dsData As New DataSet()
    Dim dtData As New DataTable
```

```
        Dim sqlDr As SqlDataReader

    Try
        strSql = "select SearchUrl, tblSearchResultsId from inserted"
        sqlCmd.Connection = sqlCn
        sqlCn.Open()
        sqlCmd.CommandText = strSql
        sqlCmd.CommandType = CommandType.Text

        sqlDr = sqlCmd.ExecuteReader()
        While sqlDr.Read()
            iSearchCode =
CalculateSearchCode(Convert.ToString(sqlDr("SearchUrl")))
            strServerName =
CalculateServerName(Convert.ToString(sqlDr("SearchUrl")))
            strSql = "update tblSearchResults set SearchCode=" &
iSearchCode.ToString() & ", ServerName='" & _
                strServerName.Replace("'", "''") & "', DateUpdated=getdate()
where tblSearchResultsId=" & _
                Convert.ToString(sqlDr("tblSearchResultsId"))
            If sqlTrCtx.TriggerAction = TriggerAction.Insert Then
                strSql = strSql & ";update tblSearchResults set
DateEntered=getdate() where tblSearchresultsId=" & _
                Convert.ToString(sqlDr("tblSearchResultsId"))
            End If
            glResults.Add(strSql)
        End While
        If Not (sqlDr.IsClosed) Then
            sqlDr.Close()
        End If
        For i = 0 To (glResults.Count - 1)
            sqlCmd.CommandText = glResults.Item(i)
            sqlCmd.ExecuteNonQuery()
        Next
        sqlDr.Dispose()
    Catch sqlExc As SqlException
        Dim sqlPipe As SqlPipe = SqlContext.Pipe
        sqlPipe.Send("Error: " & sqlExc.Message.ToString())
        sqlPipe = Nothing
        Throw
    Finally
        If sqlCn.State <> ConnectionState.Closed Then
            sqlCn.Close()
        End If
        sqlCmd.Dispose()
    End Try
End Sub
```

This trigger is based on a personal application that performs a Web search. The trigger is used to parse the information that is inserted and update several of the fields within the search results table.

Stored Procedures

Stored procedures are basic database objects in many databases. With Microsoft SQL Server 2005, SQL Server now has the ability to run objects written in any .NET language within the database. Stored procedures are objects that can return tablelike results and messages, invoke DDL and DML changing statements, and return parameter values to the calling code. CLR stored procedures are public, shared (static in C#) methods within a .NET class.

Outputting Results

With a CLR stored procedure, there are several ways to return data, including output parameters, tablelike results, and messaging.

Using output parameters in a CLR stored procedure is very similar to using output parameters in the client. By passing values into a function by reference and marking the parameters as output parameters, an argument may be passed from the CLR stored procedure back to the calling method.

The `SqlPipe` object, which is new in the .NET 2.0 Framework, can be used to send results to the client. The `SqlPipe` object is provided by the `SqlContextPipe` property. On the `SqlPipe` is the `Send()` method. The `Send` method includes several overloads that may be used to send table-style information (such as a `SqlDataReader`) or textual information back to the calling method. The `SqlPipe` object includes the method `ExecuteAndSendResults()`, which is an optimized mechanism to send data back to the calling method.

SqlProcedure Attribute

The `System.Data.Sql` namespace provides the `SqlProcedure` attribute. This attribute is used to set up a stored procedure. The only property that may be set on the `SqlProcedure` attribute is the name that will be used for this stored procedure.

Sample Code

In the following sample code, the `SqlProcedure` attribute is used to set the name of the procedure as it will appear within SQL Server:

```
<SqlProcedure(Name:="spFunctionCount")> _
Public Shared Sub spFunctionCount()
        ' Add your code here
        Dim iReturn As Integer = 0
        Dim strSql As String
        Dim sqlCn as New SqlConnection("Context Connection=true")
        Dim sqlCm As New SqlCommand
        Dim sqlP As SqlPipe = SqlContext.Pipe
        Try
            strSql = "select count(*) as RecordCount from tblSearchResults"
            sqlCn.Open()
            sqlCm.Connection = sqlCn
            sqlCm.CommandText = strSql
            sqlCm.CommandType = CommandType.Text
            sqlP.ExecuteAndSend(sqlCm)
        Finally
            If sqlCn.State <> ConnectionState.Closed Then
                sqlCn.Close()
```

```
                    End If
                    sqlCn.Dispose()
                    sqlCm.Dispose()
                    sqlCm = Nothing
                    sqlP = Nothing
            End Try
    End Sub
```

By sending the results through the Execute *method, the results are sent directly to the client by transferring data directly to the network buffers without being copied into the managed memory space.*

Functions

User-defined CLR functions are functions that take some type of parameter and return some type of value. Like triggers and stored procedures, functions can be developed in any .NET language. Two types of functions can be developed. *Scalar-valued functions* return a single value. *Table-valued functions,* or *TVFs,* return values in the form of a table.

If you know that your function will not add read data from a table, you can optimize your function by adding DataAccess = DataAccessKind.None *and* SystemDataAccess = SystemDataAccessKind.None *to the definition within the attribute.*

Scalar-Valued Functions

A scalar-valued function is a function that returns a single value. This function is implemented as a method of a class. It can return any Unicode data type except rowversion, text, ntext, or image. Let's look at some sample code:

```
    <SqlFunction(DataAccess:=DataAccessKind.Read, IsDeterministic:=True,
isprecise:=True, Name:="fnTest", SystemDataAccess:=SystemDataAccessKind.Read,
TableDefinition:="")> _
    Public Shared Function ReturnCountVal(ByVal pstrTableName As String) As
SqlInt32
        Dim iResult As Integer
        Dim strSql As String = "select count(*) from " & pstrTableName
        Dim sqlCn As New SqlConnection("Context Connection=true")
        Dim sqlCm As New SqlCommand
        Try
            sqlCn.Open()
            sqlCm.Connection = sqlCn
            sqlCm.CommandText = strSql
            sqlCm.CommandType = CommandType.Text
            iResult = Convert.ToInt32(sqlCm.ExecuteScalar())
        Finally
            If sqlCn.State <> ConnectionState.Closed Then
                sqlCn.Close()
            End If
            sqlCm.Dispose()
            sqlCm = Nothing
        End Try
        Return (New SqlInt32(iResult))
    End Function
```

The preceding scalar function looks very similar to the previous objects that have been created. The `SqlFunction` attribute now is much more complicated, with more options than a CLR trigger and the CLR stored procedure:

❑   The `DataAccess` property is set to `DataAccessKind.Read`. This tells the CLR that the object will be reading from user tables.

❑   The `IsDeterministic` property is set to `True`. A deterministic function is a function that will return the same data to the calling method no matter when it is called.

❑   The `Name` property sets the name that the function will be listed as within SQL Server.

❑   The `IsPrecise` member tells the CLR whether or not the returned value is precise. Strings and integers are considered to be precise; however, singles and doubles are not considered precise. If a UDF is returning a single, double, or some other imprecise value (real number), the method should be marked with `IsPrecise`, and the `IsPrecise` value should be set to `false`. Otherwise, `IsPrecise` should be set to `true`.

❑   The `SystemDataAccess` property tells the system whether the function will be reading from the system tables. The allowed values are `SystemDataAccessKind.Read` and `SystemDataAccessKind.None`.

❑   The `TableDefinition` member defines the table that will be returned. In this case, an empty string is passed.

Table-Valued Functions

A table-valued function (TVF) is a user-defined function that returns results in the form of a table. A TVF may be defined in any .NET-managed language. The data is returned through an `ISqlReader` object.

A T-SQL-defined TVF obtains results of a function from an intermediate table. By using an intermediate table, a T-SQL TVF may support constraints and indexes of a set of results. A CLR-based TVF represents an alternative. The results do not have to be materialized in a single table. Instead, they are streamed to the calling method and may be used immediately after the first row is available. This can improve performance when large numbers of rows are returned.

TVFs are implemented as methods on a class in .NET assembly. TVF code must implement the `ISqlReader`. The `ISqlReader` is an interface provided by the in-proc `System.Data.Sql` provider that supports forward-only, read-only results.

Let's look at some code:

```
Imports System
Imports System.Collections
Imports System.Data
Imports System.Data.Sql
Imports System.Data.SqlTypes
Imports System.IO
Imports Microsoft.SqlServer.Server
Partial Public Class UserDefinedFunctions
    <Microsoft.SqlServer.Server.SqlFunction(FillRowMethodName:="MyFillFunction",
TableDefinition:="RowData nvarchar(4000)")> _
    Public Shared Function fnTVF2(ByVal strFileName As String) As IEnumerable
        ' Add your code here
```

```
        Dim strArray() As String
        Dim strReader As StreamReader = New StreamReader(strFileName)
        Dim line As String
        Dim i As Integer = 0
        Do
            ReDim Preserve strArray(i + 1)
            line = strReader.ReadLine()
            strArray(i) = line
            i += 1
        Loop Until line Is Nothing
        Return strArray
    End Function
    Public Shared Sub MyFillFunction(ByVal obj As Object, ByRef strLine As String)
        strLine = CType(obj, String)
    End Sub
End Class
```

In this code example, a text file is passed to the function. The text file is then parsed on a line-by-line basis.

Figure 11-9 shows the results of a query and uses a LIKE operator to operate on the result.

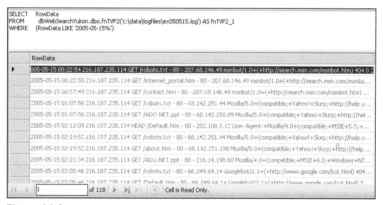

Figure 11-9

Aggregates

An aggregate function is a function that performs a calculation on a set of values and returns a single value. Before SQL Server 2005, developers were limited to the built-in aggregate functions provided by SQL Server and could not define their own aggregate functions. These functions included an arithmetic average (AVG), maximum values (MAX), minimum values (MIN), and other built-in methods.

With SQL Server 2005, developers have the capability to define their own aggregates. For example, it is possible for developers to determine the value second to the maximum.

Before SQL Server 2005, when developers wanted to define their own aggregate, they had to pull the results to the client and then perform the operation on the results, including iterating through the results. This is relatively inefficient, in that all the records necessary are returned to the client for processing, and yet the complete set of records is not needed — merely the aggregate. In addition, processing time is needed on the client to perform the operation. With a CLR attribute running on the server, there is no sending of records across the network and no processing on the client. Processing occurs on the server, which will typically have more resources than a client system.

A CLR aggregate in SQL Server 2005 has several requirements:

- ❑ The `SqlUserDefinedAggregate` attribute shows the attribute members that need to be specified:
  - ❑ `Format` — This specifies the serialization form of the aggregate type.
  - ❑ `MaxByteSize` — This is the maximum size, in bytes, necessary to store the state of the aggregate type. The maximum value is 8000.
  - ❑ `IsInvariantToDuplicates` — True if the aggregate is invariant to duplicates.
  - ❑ `IsInvariantToNulls` — True if the aggregate is invariant to NULLs.
  - ❑ `IsInvariantToorder` — True if the aggregate is invariant to order. If the aggregate is invariant to order, the query optimizer has more flexibility in choosing the execution plan when the aggregate is used.
  - ❑ `IsNullifEmpty` — True if the aggregate returns NULL when no values have been accumulated.
- ❑ The `Init()` method is used to initialize the internal storage of values.
- ❑ The `Accumulate()` method processes data.
- ❑ The `Merge()` method handles data from multiple instances of the aggregate value. Depending on the amount of data and the processing power of a server, multiple instances of the aggregate may be created. The `Merge()` method will be called by SQL Server to integrate the data from multiple instances of the aggregate function.
- ❑ The `Terminate()` method returns the result of the aggregate function:

```
<Serializable()> _
<StructLayout(LayoutKind.Sequential)> _
<SqlUserDefinedAggregate(Format.Native, IsInvariantToDuplicates:=True,
IsInvariantToNulls:=True, isinvariantToOrder:=True, IsNullIfEmpty:=True,
Name:="SecondMax")> _
Public Structure aggExample
    Private gDblHigh As Double
    Private gDblNextHigh As Double

    Public Sub Init()
        ' Put your code here
        gDblHigh = Nothing
        gDblNextHigh = Nothing
    End Sub

    Public Sub Accumulate(ByVal value As Double)
        ' Put your code here
        If gDblHigh = Nothing Then
            gDblHigh = value
        ElseIf gDblNextHigh = Nothing Then
            If value > gDblHigh Then
                gDblNextHigh = gDblHigh
                gDblHigh = value
```

```
                    Else
                        gDblNextHigh = value
                    End If
                ElseIf (Not (IsNothing(gDblHigh)) And Not (IsNothing(gDblNextHigh)))
        Then
                    If value > gDblHigh Then
                        gDblNextHigh = gDblHigh
                        gDblHigh = value
                    ElseIf (value > gDblNextHigh) And (gDblHigh <= value) Then
                        gDblNextHigh = value
                    End If
                End If
            End Sub

            Public Sub Merge(ByVal value As aggExample)
                ' Put your code here
                If Not (IsNothing(value.GetHighValue)) Then
                    Me.Accumulate(Convert.ToDouble(value.GetHighValue))
                End If
                If Not (IsNothing(value.GetNextValue)) Then
                    Me.Accumulate(Convert.ToDouble(value.GetNextValue))
                End If
            End Sub

            Public Function Terminate() As SqlDouble
                ' Put your code here
                Return New SqlDouble(gDblNextHigh)
            End Function

            Public Function GetHighValue() As SqlDouble
                Return (New SqlDouble(gDblHigh))
            End Function

            Public Function GetNextValue() As SqlDouble
                Return (New SqlDouble(gDblNextHigh))
            End Function
            ' This is a place-holder field member
            Public var1 As Integer
        End Structure
```

Calling a CLR User-Defined Aggregate Function

Calling a T-SQL aggregate function is relatively simple. The statement select AVG(col1) from table will easily return the arithmetic average of the column col1 of the specified table. A CLR user-defined aggregate function must obey all of the rules of a built-in aggregate function. In addition to those rules, a CLR user-defined aggregate function must obey the following rules:

❑   The user id for the connection must have permission to EXECUTE on the called user-defined aggregate.

❑   The aggregate must be called using the schema_name.aggregate_name form. For the example code used previously, the calling convention would be to select dbo.SecondMax(TestValue) from tblTestNumeric.

❑ The argument passed to the user-defined aggregate must be the specified type or be able to be implicitly converted to the input type as specified by the CREATE AGGREGATE statement.

❑ The return type of the user-defined aggregate must match the return type of the output in the CREATE AGGREGATE statement.

User-Defined Types

Traditional databases have typically supported simple data types. Microsoft SQL Server 2005 has added support for user-defined types. By integrating the CLR with SQL Server 2005, the capability to extend the simple data types has been added to the database. Whereas CLR triggers, stored procedures, functions, and aggregates were defined as subroutines and methods within a .NET class, a user-defined type (UDT) is equivalent to a class within the .NET Framework. These UDTs enable developers to create complex structured data types within the database.

UDTs provide several benefits for an application architecture. They provide the capability to encapsulate the internal state and the external behaviors of a data type. Once defined, UDTs enable deep integration between the client and the database server.

User-Defined Sample Code

The following code contains the address, city, state, and zip code:

```
Option Explicit On
Option Strict On

Imports System
Imports System.Data.Sql
Imports System.Data.SqlTypes
Imports System.IO
Imports System.Runtime.Serialization

<Serializable()> _
<SqlUserDefinedType(Format.UserDefined, IsByteOrdered:=True, IsFixedLength:=True,
MaxByteSize:=512)> _
Public Structure udtypeExample
    Implements INullable, IBinarySerialize

    Private gblIsNull As Boolean
    Private gstrAddress1 As String
    Private gstrCity As String
    Private gstrState As String
    Private gstrZip As String

    Public Sub Read(ByVal r As BinaryReader) Implements IBinarySerialize.Read
        Address1 = r.ReadString()
        City = r.ReadString()
        State = r.ReadString()
        ZipCode = r.ReadString()
    End Sub

    Public Sub Write(ByVal w As BinaryWriter) Implements IBinarySerialize.Write
        w.Write(Address1)
```

```vbnet
            w.Write(City)
            w.Write(State)
            w.Write(ZipCode)
        End Sub

        Public ReadOnly Property IsNull() As Boolean Implements INullable.IsNull
            Get
                ' Put your code here
                Return (gblIsNull)
            End Get
        End Property

        Public Overrides Function ToString() As String
            Dim strVal As String
            If IsNull Then
                strVal = "NULL"
            Else
                strVal = Convert.ToString(gstrAddress1) & vbCrLf & _
                    Convert.ToString(gstrCity) & ", " & Convert.ToString(gstrState) & Space(1) & _
                    Convert.ToString(gstrZip)
            End If
            Return strVal
        End Function

        Public Shared ReadOnly Property Null() As udtypeExample
            Get
                Dim h As udtypeExample = New udtypeExample
                Return h
            End Get
        End Property

        Public Shared Function Parse(ByVal s As SqlString) As udtypeExample
            If s.IsNull Or s.Value.ToLower().Equals("null") Then
                Return Null
            End If

            Dim u As udtypeExample = New udtypeExample
            Dim strTemp As String = Convert.ToString(s)
            Dim strArray() As String
            strArray = strTemp.Split(Convert.ToChar(";"))
            u.Address1 = strArray(0)
            u.City = strArray(1)
            u.State = strArray(2)
            u.ZipCode = strArray(3)

            Return u
        End Function

        Public Property Address1() As String
            Get
                Return (gstrAddress1)
            End Get
            Set(ByVal value As String)
                gstrAddress1 = value
```

```
                End Set
        End Property

        Public Property City() As String
            Get
                Return (gstrCity)
            End Get
            Set(ByVal value As String)
                gstrCity = value
            End Set
        End Property

        Public Property State() As String
            Get
                Return (gstrState)
            End Get
            Set(ByVal value As String)
                gstrState = value
            End Set
        End Property

        Public Property ZipCode() As String
            Get
                Return (gstrZip)
            End Get
            Set(ByVal value As String)
                gstrZip = value
            End Set
        End Property
    End Structure
```

To get this code to function correctly, both the server and the client must understand the type. This requirement includes the SQL Server Management Studio and Visual Studio 2005 IDE.

Manually Creating Tabular Results

Sometimes a stored procedure must create its own data and then return that data to the client in the form of a result set. This may be done by using the `SqlDataRecord` object and the `SqlMetaData` object. The `SqlDataRecord` is the definition of the result set's columns. The `SqlMetaData` is the definition of each individual column. Consider the following code example:

```
<SqlProcedure(Name:="spReturnData")> _
Public Shared Sub spReturnData()
    Dim i As Integer = 0
    Dim sqlRec As New SqlDataRecord( _
        New SqlMetaData("ID", SqlDbType.Int), _
        New SqlMetaData("DateCalc", SqlDbType.DateTime))
    Try
        SqlContext.Pipe.SendResultsStart(sqlRec)
        For i = 1 To 10
            sqlRec.SetInt32(0, i)
            sqlRec.SetDateTime(1, DateTime.Now)
            SqlContext.Pipe.SendResultsRow(sqlRec)
```

```
            Next
        Finally
            SqlContext.Pipe.SendResultsEnd()
        End Try
    End Sub
```

This code will return an integer, which identifies the results within the result set and the DateTime of the row being created. The data types are defined within the SqlDataRecord, using a type from within the SqlDbType enumeration.

SqlContext

Whenever managed code is called within SQL Server 2005, whether it is a trigger, stored procedure, function, user-defined aggregate, or user-defined type, execution of that code involves the .NET Framework and requires access to the calling context. The calling context is contained within the abstract SqlContext object (defined and provided by the SQL Server namespace Microsoft.SqlServer.Server). The calling context provides access to the following set of objects:

❑ IsAvailable— The IsAvailable property indicates whether or not the program is running within the SQL Server.

❑ Pipe— The Pipe property is the conduit, or pipe, that is used to flow results between the client and the server. Typically, it is used for sending results from the CLR object to the calling method. The Pipe is obtained by calling the SqlContext.Pipe property.

❑ TriggerContext— The TriggerContext object only exists within a CLR trigger. It is used to obtain information about the trigger that is running and the columns that were updated. Some of that information about the trigger specifies whether the trigger is an INSERT, UPDATE, DELETE, or DDL statement.

❑ WindowsIdentity— The WindowsIdentity property returns a WindowsIdentity object detailing information about the connected Windows user.

The Context Connection

When running within a SQL Server CLR object and communicating with the local database, the object will run within a context connection. A context connection is a connection between the CLR object and the local database, bypassing the network protocol stacks. A context connection is specified by the connection string parameter Context Connection=true. Note several restrictions to having a context connection:

❑ Only one context connection may be opened at a given time for a specific connection.

❑ MARS is not supported.

❑ The SqlBulkCopy class will not operate on a context connection.

❑ Update batching is not supported.

❑ SqlNotificationRequest cannot be used.

❑ Canceling commands is not supported.

❑ Asynchronous operations are not supported.

327

❏   `SqlDependency` and related methods are not supported.

❏   When a context connection is used, no other keywords may be used when within the connection string.

Now that you have the capability to communicate within the database, what about connecting to an external database? The capability to communicate with an external database is available within a context connection by opening a second connection object with the appropriate connection strings. When a CLR object opens a second connection, a transaction based on the `System.Transactions` namespace is created. The database transaction is promoted to a full distributed transaction. For more information on the `System.Transactions` namespace, see Chapter 6, "Transactions."

One of the side benefits of using the `Context Connection` keyword and the existing `SqlConnection` object is that code that runs within the database looks very similar to client-side/middle-tier data access.

SQL CLR Architecture

The Common Language Runtime is integrated with the Microsoft SQL Server 2005 database. By integrating the database and the CLR, database programmers can use any .NET language, such as C#, Visual Basic, and Visual C++, to create functions, stored procedures, triggers, aggregates, and user-defined data types.

Placing Business Logic

With the release of Microsoft SQL Server 2005, a new issue has cropped up for application architects and developers. Where should the business logic of an application be placed? Before Microsoft SQL Server 2005, business logic was primarily placed within the "middle tier" of an application. SQL Server 2005 still allows business logic to be placed within the middle tier of an application, but with the capability to program using a .NET language, SQL Server 2005 enables developers to rather easily place business logic within the database. Let's look at some of the advantages of doing this:

❏   By moving logic to the database tier, network traffic can be minimized. There is no reason for the data to be moved from the database to the middle tier for processing and then back to the database.

❏   The data within the database tier can be better validated.

❏   Data integrity can be better enforced. While databases have been able to provide for foreign key relationships for years, it is sometimes hard to enforce integrity and relationships between columns within a row. By having the CLR objects within the database, complex calculations that had to be performed within a middle tier can now be done closer to the data.

The capability to place business logic within the database does not mean that all application logic should be placed within the database. There are several reasons *not* to place all business logic within your SQL Server 2005 database:

❏   Databases are designed and optimized for holding data, not for performing long-running operations that consume a large number of locks and other resources on the server. Successful CLR objects will perform the minimum number of necessary operations and then exit the execution.

❑ CLR objects are written specifically for SQL Server 2005. They are not directly transportable to other databases. If an application needs to run on multiple databases, CLR objects may not be the best choice.

❑ Typically, updates to the user interface and business logic of a Web application can be easily rolled out to users. If an update needs to be rolled back to the previous version, that is also fairly easy. Updates to CLR objects, while not being overly hard, require more sophistication regarding updates and possible rollbacks.

When to Use T-SQL and CLR Objects

One of the questions that came up during the beta cycle for the integration of CLR and Microsoft SQL Server 2005 concerned when it is appropriate to use a CLR object as opposed to a T-SQL object.

If a T-SQL object can be written that is equivalent to a CLR object, the T-SQL object will typically perform better than the CLR object. CLR objects are continuing to use T-SQL to perform operations. If the necessary operations can be performed within a T-SQL object, it is usually best to use the T-SQL object. Because T-SQL objects perform set-based operations, set-based operations will typically perform better than equivalent CLR objects that merely perform set-based operations without additional processing. However, there are several situations in which T-SQL cannot perform the same type of operations that a CLR object can perform:

❑ **Security calculations** — Complex security calculations such as the encoding or decoding of data can typically best be performed within the CLR.

❑ **Scientific calculations** — Complicated scientific calculations can typically best be performed within the CLR.

❑ **Complex CLR operations** — Complex CLR operations that require some type of procedural objects should typically reside in a CLR object.

SQL Server Management Objects

With the release of .NET 1.x and the `SqlClient`, Microsoft released a set of objects that were able to perform typical database operations in a highly optimized manner. One item that was not included in .NET 1.x was a managed interface into SQL Distributed Management Objects (SQL-DMO).

With the release of .NET 2.0 and ADO.NET 2.0, Microsoft has introduced a set of managed objects called *SQL Server Management Objects (SMOs)*. These objects are designed for interacting with the internal aspects of Microsoft SQL Server. SMO can be used to build a customized SQL Server management application. For example, an SMO management application could be used when it isn't practical to use the full Microsoft SQL Server Management Studio. An SMO application for managing SQL Server can be used to manage an embedded application for which the interface must be fairly simple.

The SMO object model replaces the SQL DMO objects. SMO has been tweaked beyond the DMO objects. All of the functionality within DMO has been included in the new SMO objects. SMO will work on Microsoft SQL Server 7.0 and later.

The SMO namespace is `Microsoft.SqlServer.Smo`. SMO is a .NET assembly, which means that the .NET Framework must be installed before SMO may be used.

General Design

SMO has been designed from the ground up to be faster and more efficient (in terms of memory) than DMO. For example, full instantiation of objects is delayed until an object is explicitly referenced. An object is fully instantiated when a requested property is not in the list of initially referenced properties. In addition, some expensive properties are not retrieved unless they are specifically requested (the Size property of the Database object, for example). As a result, the amount of memory used and the amount of time needed to fill the SMO objects has been minimized.

SMO classes call into two classes: instance classes and utility classes.

Instance Classes

SMO instance classes are classes that represent SQL Server objects, such as databases, tables, triggers, and such. The SMO instance objects create a hierarchy that represents the hierarchy of a database server. The top levels are the instances of SQL Server. The databases are underneath the SQL Server instances, tables are underneath the databases, triggers and columns are underneath the tables, and so on. With this type of design, one parent object may have many child objects.

Instance classes can exist in one of three instantiation levels: un-instantiated, partially instantiated, and fully instantiated. The partially instantiated state is somewhat new to programmers. The partially instantiated state is the default state for an object that has not been directly referenced. By partially instantiating an object, memory usage and the time needed to create objects are minimized.

Utility Classes

SMO utility classes support specific tasks that occur in the server. These classes are roughly divided into the Transfer class, Backup and Restore class, and Scripter class.

Execution

With SMO, execution may occur in one of two ways. The usual mechanism is *direct execution*. With direct execution, statements are sent to the SQL Server instance as the statements occur. The second execution method is *capture execution*. With capture execution, statements are collected and then executed as a T-SQL batch. This provides the application with the maximum amount of flexibility. The method of execution is controlled using the ServerConnection object.

WMI Provider

The SMO wraps the WMI Provider objects. By wrapping the WMI Provider, a developer using XMO has a relatively simple object model that resembles the SMO classes without needing to understand the intricacies of the SQL Server WMI Provider.

Scripting

With SMO, the scripting of objects has been moved into the Scripter class. The Scripter class is the main scripting object within SMO. The Scripter class can manage the hierarchy of objects and determine the relationships between those objects. The Scripter object and its supporting set of classes can handle the dependencies and the progression events during execution.

Referencing Objects through URN

One of the key conventions in referencing an object in SMO is the *Unique Resource Name (URN)*. The URN uses XPATH syntax. With SMO, a URN has the two elements *path* and *attribute*. The path is used to specify the object location and the attribute specifies a degree of filtering. A database URN looks something like this:

```
/Server[@Name='Entrepid']/Database[@Name='dbWebSearchYukon']
```

The URN of an object can be retrieved from its URN property. URNs are used as parameters for passing object references to methods contained in the `Scripter` object. URNs may also be used to instantiate an SMO object.

Creating Objects

Using SMO, a program has the capability to add, update, delete, and query the internal objects of SQL Server, along with performing maintenance tasks. This section describes the management of these internal objects as well as the maintenance tasks.

You should understand two *base* objects in SMO before tackling the others: `Microsoft.SqlServer` `.Management.Common.ServerConnection()` and `Microsoft.SqlServer.Management` `.Smo.Server()`.

The `ServerConnection()` object is fairly similar to the `System.Data.SqlClient.SqlConnection()` object. However, it has a few extra commands from the `SqlCommand()` object that allow for the execution of commands to the database.

The `ServerConnection()` has two members that are different and somewhat interesting:

- ❑ `CapturedSql` — The `CapturedSql` property returns SQL commands that would be sent to the database if the `ServerConnection()` object is set to capture the SQL commands.

- ❑ `SqlExecutionModes` — This takes a `SqlExecutionModes` enum and sets the execution mode of the connection. There are several execution modes:

    - ❑ `CaptureSql` — This value instructs the `ServerConnection()` object to merely capture the commands that it would send to the database, as opposed to sending them to the database.

    - ❑ `ExecuteAndCaptureSql` — This value instructs the `ServerConnection()` object to capture and execute commands that are sent to the database.

    - ❑ `ExecuteSql` — This value instructs the `ServerConnection()` object to execute the commands against the database and not save them.

The `Server()` object is an object that represents a particular instance of a SQL Server database server that is currently being pointed at by the `SqlServerConnection()` object. This object has numerous properties that describe the behavior of the installed instance. These properties include server defaults, databases, startup options, memory, language, authentication, version, connection, and other properties of interest. These properties are contained within the `Database`, `Information`, `Settings`, `UserOptions`, and `Configuration` members of the `Server()` object.

The `Database()` object contains information about the databases currently installed on the server. It is through this object and its children that modifications will be made through DDL statements against the database objects.

The `Information()` object contains general information about the instance of the SQL Server database. This information includes processor, platform, the current state of the instance, edition (MSDE, SQLExpress, Standard, Enterprise, or other information), and additional information about this particular instance to which the `Server()` object points.

The `Settings()` object contains settings information about the instance of the SQL Server database. This includes information about the instance of SQL Server. From this object, code can obtain information about default databases, files and directories, current connections, the server account, and other valuable pieces of server setting information.

The `Configuration()` object is a child of the `Server` object. It contains a set of properties that map to the allowed changes within the `sp_configure` stored procedure. These members contain the information that controls the server configuration. Most of the properties themselves are read-only.

The `UserOptions` object is a child of the `Server` object. The `UserOptions()` object has a series of read-only members, along with members that enable the user's options to be changed. Some of the properties that can be changed through the `UserOptions()` object include the Ansi settings, Abort settings, NoCount settings, and others.

Creating a Database

Creating a database is the first step in the life of a database. This is when the database is "born." SMO makes adding a database a rather simple step, although there are some management issues to overcome.

Let's begin with an example. The following code creates a new database on a system:

```
Dim sqlCn as New SqlConnection(strSqlcn)
Dim sqlServerConnection as New ServerConnection(sqlcn)
Dim Server as new Server(sqlServerConnection)
Dim db as new Database(Server, Me.txtDbName.Text)
Dim fgObj as New FileGroup(db, "PRIMARY")
Dim df as New DataFile(fgObj, "SMODataFile")
if server.Databases.Contains(Me.txtDbName.Text) = True then
    db.Drop()
End If
df.Size = 10240
df.Growth = 10
df.GrowthType = FileGrowthType.Percent
df.FileName = Server.Settings.MasterDBPath & "\" & "Test.mdf"
dim lf as New LogFile(db, "SMOLogFile")
lf.Size = df.Size / 5
lf.Growth = df.Growth
lf.GrowthType = df.GrowthType
lf.FileName = Server.Settings.MasterDBLogPath & "\" & "Test.ldf"
fgObj.Files.Add(df)
db.FileGroups.Add(fgObj)
db.LogFiles.Add(lf)
db.Create()
```

Following are the steps involved in creating a database, which you can see in the preceding code:

1. Create a `ServerConnection()` object. This object manages the connection between the `Server()` object and the SQL Server instance. It is fairly similar to the `SqlConnection()` object underneath ADO.NET.

2. Create a `Server()` object that is based on the previous `ServerConnection()` object.

3. Create a new `Database()` object. With this object, the following members of the object should be set:

    ❑   The parent of the database is the `Server()` object.

    ❑   The `Name` property should be set to the name of the database that is desired.

4. Create the file group by adding a new `FileGroup()` object to the `Database()` object.

5. Create the data file by creating a new `DataFile()` object and associating that object with the `FileGroup()` object that was created in Step 4. Several properties of this `DataFile()` object should be set:

    ❑   `GrowthType` — This property sets the type of growth for the data file through an enum. The `GrowthType` enum has three values: `KB`, `None`, and `Percent`.

    ❑   `Growth` — This property sets the amount of growth as necessary.

    ❑   `Size` — This property sets the initial size of the data file.

    ❑   `MaxSize` — This property sets the maximum size of the data file.

6. Create the log file by creating a new `LogFile()` object and associating that object with the `LogFiles` property of the `Database()` object. This can be performed by calling `DataBase().LogFiles.Add(LogFile())`. The same properties of the `DataFile()` object listed before may be set.

7. Create the database by calling the `DataBase().Create()` method.

Along with the creation of a database, you will want to pay attention to the following properties and methods:

❑   `Server().Databases.Contains(database name)` — This method will return a true or a false depending on whether the specified database already exists.

❑   `Server().Settings.MasterDBPath` — This property returns the path to the directory for the Master database files. This is typically the default directory for new database files.

❑   `Database().Drop()` — The Drop method will drop an existing database as pointed to by the `Database()` object. This should only be done by first checking to see whether the database exists.

Figure 11-10 shows the files that were created for the database.

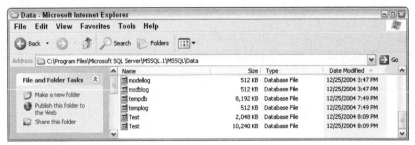

Figure 11-10

Creating a Table, Its Columns, and an Index

Creating and managing tables can be done through the `Database()` and `Table()` objects. Within the SMO hierarchy, the `Table` objects are directly below the `Database()` object.

The following sample code creates a table, its columns, a primary key, and an index:

```
Dim strTableName as String = "tblTest"
Dim sqlCn as New SqlConnection(strSqlcn)
Dim sqlServerConnection as New ServerConnection(sqlCn)
Dim Server as new Microsoft.SqlServer.Management.Smo.Server(sqlServerConnection)
Dim db as Database = Server.Databases(txtDb.Text)
Dim tbl as New Table(db, strTableName)
if db.Tables.Contains(strTableName) then
    db.Tables(strTableName).Drop()
End If
Dim colpk as New Column(tbl, strTableName & "ID")
colpk.DataType = DataType.Int
colpk.Nullable = False
colpk.Identity = True
colpk.IdentityIncrement = 1
colpk.IdentitySeed = 1
tbl.Columns.Add(colpk)
Dim idxpk as New Index(tbl, "idx" & strTableName)
Dim idxcol as New IndexedColumn(idxpk, colpk.Name)
idxpk.IndexKeyType = IndexKeyType.DriPrimaryKey
idxpk.IndexedColumns.Add(idxcol)
tbl.Indexes.Add(idxpk)
Dim colTest as New Column(tbl, "VarcharField")
colTest.DataType.MaximumLength = 50
colTest.DataType.SqlDataType = SqlDataType.VarChar
tbl.Columns.Add(colTest)
tbl.Create()
```

Here are the steps for creating a table in the database:

1. Create a `Database()` and associate it with the appropriate `Server()` instance object.

2. Create a `Table()` object. Set the following properties:

   ❑ `Parent` — The `Parent` property of the `Table()` object is the `Database()`.

   ❑ `Name` — The name of the `Table()` object is the name of the table.

   ❑ `Schema` — The `schema` of the table will most likely be the default schema of the database. This may be set by using the `Database().DefaultSchema` property. If a different schema is needed, then a separate string may be passed into the `Schema` property.

3. Create the columns next. The first column that should be created is the primary key column. This column is contained within a `Column()` object and `Index()` object. The properties of the `Column()` are as follows:

   ❑ `Parent` — The `Parent` property of the `Column()` object is the `Table()` object.

   ❑ `Name` — The `Name` property of the `Column()` object is a string name of the `Index()` object.

   ❑ `DataType` — The `DataType` property takes a `DataType` enum. Typically, this will be a `DataType.Int`, but it might also be a `DataType.BigInt`, `DataType.SmallInt`, `DataType.TinyInt`, or a `DataType.UniqueIdentifier`.

   ❑ `Nullable` — The `Nullable` property of a column that will be a primary key must be set to `false`. The default value is `true`.

   ❑ `Identity` — The `Identity` property of a primary column is typically set to `true`. This allows the database to automatically increment (for integers) the column for inserts.

   ❑ `IdentitySeed` — The `IdentitySeed` property is the starting value for the `Identity` field.

   ❑ `IdentityIncrement` — The `IdentityIncrement` property is the value that the column will be incremented by on each insert.

   ❑ The `Column` must be added to the table through the `Table().Columns.Add()` method.

4. Create an `Index()` object and associate that with the primary key column. The following properties and methods should be set:

   ❑ `Parent` — The `Parent` property of the `Index()` object is the `Table()` object.

   ❑ `Name` — The `Name` property of the `Index()` object is the name of the index within the database.

   ❑ The `Index()` needs to be added to the `Table()` object through `Table().Indexes.Add()`.

   ❑ The `Index` must have the columns added by using the `Index().IndexedColumns.Add()` method. This will also be used for creating a primary key through the `IndexKeyType` property.

   ❑ `IsClustered` — The `IsClustered` property is set to `True` or `False`.

❏ IsUnique—The IsUnique property is set to True for a primary key.

❏ IndexKeyType—The IndexKeyType property is set to an enum value. The enum values are IndexKeyType.DriPrimaryKey, IndexKeyType.DriUniqueKey, IndexKeyType.DriNone. For a primary key, the property should be set to IndexKeyType.DriPrimaryKey.

5. Call the Index() object's .Create() method.

Within the Table() object is the IndexCollection member. This is a collection of the indexes associated with the table. Each Index() object contains a collection of IndexedColumn objects. This enables multiple columns to be associated within an index.

If necessary, the index can be dropped by calling the index() object's Drop() method. If the index needs to be disabled, the Index() object contains a Disable() method. To re-enable an Index() object, there is an Enable() method. The Enable() method takes an enum of type IndexEnableAction. The values of the enum are IndexEnableAction.Rebuild and IndexEnableAction.Recreate.

Creating a User

To create a user, the User() object will be used. The User() object is an SMO object that contains information about a specific user in a SQL Server instance. This object will be used with the Server() and Database() objects.

Let's look at some sample code to create a user:

```
Dim sqlCn as New SqlConnection(strSqlcn)
Dim sqlServerConnection as New ServerConnection(sqlcn)
Dim Server as New Server(sqlServerConnection)
Dim db as Database = Server.Databases(txtDb.Text)
Dim strUser as String = Me.txtUserId.Text
Dim usr as New User(db, strUser)
if db.Users.Contains(strUser) then
    db.Users(strUser).Drop()
End If
usr.Login = strUser
usr.Create()
```

This code will work with SQL Server Authentication.

Here are the steps for creating a user with the User() object:

1. Create SqlServerConnection(), Server(), and Database() objects, as done previously. Note that the Database() object is not created by creating a new instance of a database object, but by referencing the existing database instance through the Server() object.

2. Create a User() object. The User() object should have the following properties set:

❏ Parent—The Parent property is the database to which this user will be assigned.

❏ Name—The Name property is the name that will be assigned to this user.

3. Assign the `Login` property to the `User()` object. The `Login` property is a string with the user's name.

4. Call the `User()` object's `Create()` method to create the defined user.

Within the `User()` class are several properties and methods that may be interesting for the SMO programmer:

❑ `Drop()` — This method will drop a user.

❑ `Deny()` — This method takes a `Permission()` object and allows permissions to be set on objects through SMO.

❑ `DefaultSchema` — The `DefaultSchema` property will return the `Schema` associated with the defined user.

❑ `Grant()` — This method takes a `Permission()` object and gives the `User()` object access to the specified objects defined by the `Permission()` object.

❑ `HasDBAccess` — This property will return a Boolean indicating whether a `User()` object has access to a specified database.

Creating a Foreign Key

Foreign keys are a mechanism within a database to relate data in two different tables. SMO provides a mechanism to create those objects in SQL Server through the `ForeignKey()` object.

Let's look at the code necessary to create the foreign key:

```
Dim strTableNameBase as String = "tblItem"
Dim strTableNameForeign as String = "tblBill"
Dim strColBase as String = "tblBillId"
Dim sqlCn as New SqlConnection(strSqlcn)
Dim sqlServerConnection as New ServerConnection(sqlCn)
Dim Server as new Microsoft.SqlServer.Management.Smo.Server(sqlServerConnection)
Dim db as Database = Server.Databases(txtDb.Text)
Dim tblBase as Table = db.Tables(strTableNameBase)
Dim tblForeign as Table = db.Tables(strTableNameForeign)
Dim colBase as column = tblBase.Columns(strColBase)
Dim colForeign as column = tblForeign.Columns(strColBase)
Dim forkey as New ForeignKey(tblBase, "fk" & strTableNameBase)
Dim forkeyCol as new ForeignKeyColumn(forkey, colForeign.Name, colForeign.Name)
forkey.ReferencedTable = tblForeign.Name
forkey.Columns.Add(forkeyCol)
forkey.Create()
```

Here are the steps for building a database foreign key in SQL Server:

1. Create `SqlServerConnect()`, `Server`, `Database()`, and appropriate `Column()` objects for the two tables that will be used.

2. Create a `ForeignKey()` object. The `ForeignKey()` object should have the following properties set:

❑ Parent — The Parent property is the Table() object of the base table that will be used for the foreign key.

❑ Name — The Name property is the name of the foreign key.

❑ ReferencedTable specifes the table to reference.

3. Create a ForeignKeyColumn() object. The properties of the ForeignKeyColumn that need to be set are as follows:

❑ Parent — The parent of the ForeignKeyColumn() object is the ForeignKey() object.

❑ Name — The name of the ForeignKeyColumn() object.

❑ ReferencedColumn — The ReferencedColumn specifies the reference column.

4. Specify the ReferencedTable property on the ForeignKey() object.

5. Add the ForeignKeyColumn object to the ForeignKey object.

6. Call the Create() method. Figure 11-11 has the foreign key relationship within Visual Studio.

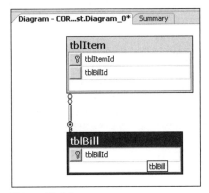

Figure 11-11

Creating a Backup

You already know how to create objects when using SMO. SMO is also capable of performing other operations. The two most common operations within SQL Server are backup and restore.

Backup

Backing up a database is the most common management operation performed against a database. The backup operation is contained within an SMO object called Backup().

Let's look at the code necessary to perform a backup:

```
dim strFileName as String
dim bkdb as New Backup()
Dim sqlCn as New SqlConnection(strSqlcn)
Dim sqlServerConnection as New ServerConnection(sqlCn)
```

```
Dim Server as new Microsoft.SqlServer.Management.Smo.Server(sqlServerConnection)
Dim db as Database = Server.Databases(me.txtDbBackup.Text)
me.sfdBackupDatabase.AddExtension = True
me.sfdBackupDatabase.DefaultExt = ".bak"
me.sfdBackupDatabase.ShowDialog()
strFileName = me.sfdBackupDatabase.FileName
bkdb.Database = db.Name
bkdb.Action = BackupActionType.Database
bkdb.BackupSetName = "BackupSet " & db.Name & DateTime.Now
bkdb.Devices.Add(New
Microsoft.SqlServer.Management.Smo.BackupDeviceItem(strFileName, DeviceType.File))
bkdb.Initialize = True
bkdb.SkipTapeHeader = True
bkdb.UnloadTapeAfter = True
bkdb.SqlBackup(Server)
```

Now let's take a look at the steps necessary to perform a backup:

1. Create the necessary SqlServerConnection, Server, and Database objects.

2. Create a Backup() object.

3. Set the Action property. The Action property of the Backup() object should be set as appropriate from the BackupActionType enum. The allowed values are as follows:

   ❑ BackupActionType.Database — This will set the action type to back up a database.

   ❑ BackupActionType.Files — This will set the action type to back up a set database file.

   ❑ BackupActionType.Logfiles — This will set the action type to back up a set of database log files.

4. BackupSetName. The BackupSetName sets the name of the backup.

5. Database. The Database property will set the name of the database to back up. This property can be set by the using the Name property of the database object.

6. Devices. Typically, a program will need to merely add a new device in the type BackupDeviceItem. This type is based on a string that points to a filename and the DeviceType.

7. DeviceType. The DeviceType accepts an enum with the following allowed values:

   ❑ DeviceType.File

   ❑ DeviceType.LogicalDevice

   ❑ DeviceType.None

   ❑ DeviceType.Pipe

   ❑ DeviceType.Tape

   ❑ DeviceType.VirtualDevice

8.   `Initialize`—The `Initialize` property determines whether this is the backup in the set.

9.   `RetainDays`—The `RetainDays` sets the number of days to retain the backup.

10.   `SkipTapeHeader`—If the backup is done to a file, this property should be set to `true`.

11.   `UnloadTapeAfter`—If the tape is to be unloaded after the backup is completed, the property is set to `true`.

12.   `SqlBackup()`—Calling the `SqlBackup()` routine and passing the `Server()` object starts the backup process.

This will start a backup process running on the server. A backup process can take a significant amount of time, so it may be performed asynchronously with intermittent updates. To set the backup operation to run asynchronously, the following commands must be added before the backup is started:

1.   `PercentCompleteNotification`—This property sets the value of the backup completion that will result in an event being raised on the client.

2.   `PercentComplete`—A handle for the `PercentComplete` event should be specified. The two parameters that the `PercentComplete` event should accept are as follows:

    ❑   `Sender`—This is a standard parameter passed to methods that process events.

    ❑   `PercentCompletedEventArgs`—This parameter contains information about the current percentage status of the backup.

In addition, the `.SqlBackupAsync()` method must be called to start the processing asynchronously.

Restore

Restoring a database is a very similar process to backing up a database. The restore operation is contained within the SMO `Restore()` object.

Let's look at some code to perform a restore:

```
Dim strFileName as String
Dim rstdb as New Restore()
Dim sqlCn as New SqlConnection(strSqlcn)
Dim sqlServerConnection as New ServerConnection(sqlCn)
Dim Server as new Microsoft.SqlServer.Management.Smo.Server(sqlServerConnection)
Dim db as Database = Server.Databases(me.txtDbRestore.Text)
me.ofdRestoreDatabase.AddExtension = True
me.ofdRestoreDatabase.DefaultExt = ".bak"
me.ofdRestoreDatabase.ShowDialog()
strFileName = me.ofdRestoreDatabase.FileName
rstdb.Database = db.Name
rstdb.Action = RestoreActionType.Database
rstdb.Devices.Add(New
Microsoft.SqlServer.Management.Smo.BackupDeviceItem(strFileName, DeviceType.File)
rstdb.UnloadTapeAfter = True
rstdb.ReplaceDatabase = true
rstdb.SqlRestore(Server)
```

Here are the steps necessary to restore a database from backup:

1. Create the necessary `SqlServerConnection()`, `Server()`, and `Database()` objects.

2. Create a `Restore()` object.

3. The `Database` property of the `Restore()` object needs to be set to the database that is being restored to. The name of the database can be obtained by the `Database().Name` property.

4. A `Device` needs to be added to the `Restore()` object. This is done by using `Restore().Devices.Add(new BackupDeviceItem(FileName, DeviceType))`, where the string is the filename of the backup file.

5. The `DeviceType` must be set. The allowed `DeviceType` enum values are mentioned in the previous backup section.

6. Set the Boolean `ReplaceDatabase` property. `True` will result in the database being overwritten.

7. The Boolean `UnloadTapeAfter` property specifies whether or not the tape should be unloaded after the restore is completed.

8. The `SqlRestore(SqlServerConnection)` will begin the restore.

To perform the updated commands asynchronously and have the updates communicated back to the calling application, the `SqlRestoreAsync` will need to be called to start the restore process asynchronously. The `PercentCompleteNotification` property and a handle must be specified for the `PercentComplete` method for the restore to be properly performed asynchronously.

Scripting with SMO

The `Scripter()` object is the object designed to create scripts from SMO objects. Let's take a look at some code that uses the `Scripter()` object. The following example is taken from the create database example described previously:

```
Dim strScript as String = String.Empty
Dim strcolScript as StringCollection
Dim strTableName as String = "tblTest"
Dim sqlCn as New SqlConnection(strSqlcn)
Dim sqlServerConnection as New ServerConnection(sqlCn)
Dim Server as new Microsoft.SqlServer.Management.Smo.Server(sqlServerConnection)
Dim db as Database = Server.Databases(txtDb.Text)
Dim tbl as New Table(db, strTableName)
Dim smoObj(1) as SqlSmoObject
Dim scrptObj as New Scripter(Server)
if db.Tables.Contains(strTableName) then
    db.Tables(strTableName).Drop()
End If
Dim colpk as New Column(tbl, strTableName & "ID")
colpk.DataType = DataType.Int
colpk.Nullable = False
colpk.Identity = True
colpk.IdentityIncrement = 1
colpk.IdentitySeed = 1
tbl.Columns.Add(colpk)
Dim idxpk as New Index(tbl, "idx" & strTableName)
```

```
Dim idxcol as New IndexedColumn(idxpk, colpk.Name)
idxpk.IndexKeyType = IndexKeyType.DriPrimaryKey
idxpk.IndexedColumns.Add(idxcol)
tbl.Indexes.Add(idxpk)
Dim colTest as New Column(tbl, "VarcharField")
colTest.DataType.MaximumLength = 50
colTest.DataType.SqlDataType = SqlDataType.VarChar
tbl.Columns.Add(colTest)
smoObj(0) = tbl
smoObj(1) = idxpk
strcolScript = ScrptObj.Script(smoObj)
for each item as String in strColScript
    strScript &= item & ";"
Next
Me.txtResults.Text = strScript
tbl.Create()
```

Let's examine what this code does:

1. The necessary objects have been created, such as `ServerConnection()`, `Server()`, `Database()`, `Table()`, `Column()`, `Index()`, and so on.

2. A `StringCollection` object is created to hold the output of the `Scripter()` object. The `Scripter()` object is created, with the `Server` property set.

3. An array of generic `SqlSmoObject` types has been created. A list of URN types could also be used.

4. The array of `SqlSmoObject` type is filled.

5. The `Script()` method of the `Scripter()` object is called. This will return a `StringCollection` object.

6. Iterate through the `StringCollection` to display the values.

Figure 11-12 shows the output of the database table creation in a script.

Simple Scripting

Sometimes the `Scripter()` object is too complex for some reason. Many of the SMO objects contain a `Script()` method that can be used to create the script necessary for that single object. The biggest difference between the `Script()` method of an individual SMO object and the `Scripter()` object is that the `Script()` method can take a `ScriptOptions` object to specify the options in creating the SQL script.

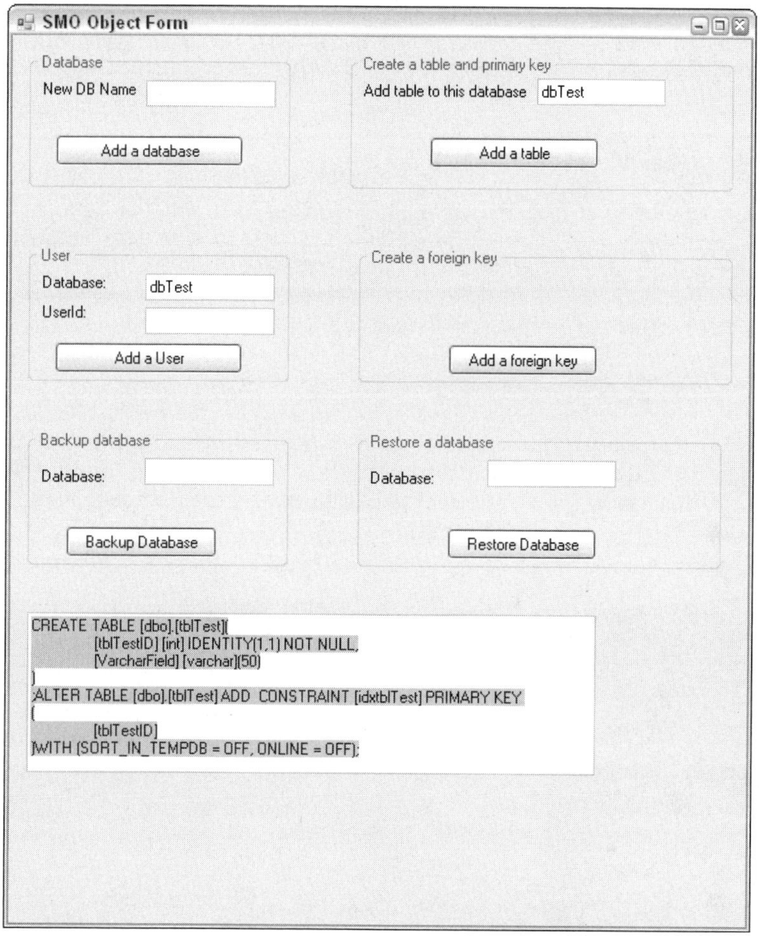

Figure 11-12

XML Web Services Processing in the Database

With SQL Server 2005, Microsoft has added the capability to process XML Web Services directly in the database tier. This enables SQL Server 2005 to act as an HTTP listener. This in turn enables SQL Server 2005 to directly process XML Web Services without the need for an intermediate listener, such as the Microsoft Internet Information Server (IIS). SQL Server 2005 will be able to expose an XML Web Service so that SQL statements, functions, and procedures may be directly executed. Query results may be returned in an XML format.

The capability to be an HTTP listener is similar in concept to the original SOAP toolkit for COM, released several years ago. With the HTTP listener, the XML Web Services request is mapped to a command within the database.

The capability of SQL Server 2005 to listen to XML Web Services requests is limited to systems with http.sys, *which, at the time of this writing, is Windows 2003 Server and WindowsXP Service Pak 2.*

Creating an Endpoint

With the release of SQL Server 2005, the capability to process XML and Web Services is included in the database. This capability is implemented through the DDL CREATE ENDPOINT command. The commands necessary to run an example CREATE ENDPOINT are as follows:

```
EXEC sp_reserve_http_namespace N'http://voyager:80/sql2k5';
```

In the preceding code, the system name is voyager.

The sp_reserve_http_namespace explicitly reserves the namespace necessary to allow subsequent DDL commands to be executed against that namespace without requiring administrator privileges on the SQL Server 2005 database server. The next step is the DROP ENDPOINT statement.

```
DROP ENDPOINT sql_endpoint;
```

The DROP ENPOINT command merely drops a defined endpoint:

```
CREATE ENDPOINT sql_endpoint
STATE = STARTED
AS HTTP(
    PATH = '/sql2k5',
    AUTHENTICATION = (INTEGRATED ),
    PORTS = ( CLEAR ),
    SITE = '*'
    )
FOR SOAP (
    WEBMETHOD 'http://tempUri.org/'.'spFunctionCount'
            (name='dbWebSearchYukon.dbo.spFunctionCount',
             SCHEMA=STANDARD ),
    WEBMETHOD 'spFunctionCount'
            (name='dbWebSearchYukon.dbo.spFunctionCount'),
    WSDL = DEFAULT,
    DATABASE = 'dbWebSearchYukon',
    NAMESPACE = DEFAULT
)
```

The CREATE ENPOINT command defines the endpoint that a Web Service can call and the method to which the ENDPOINT is mapped. The URL http://servername/sql2k5?wsdl shows that the system displays the wsdl associated with the preceding defined endpoint. Figure 11-13 shows a view of the wsdl exposed by the Web Service.

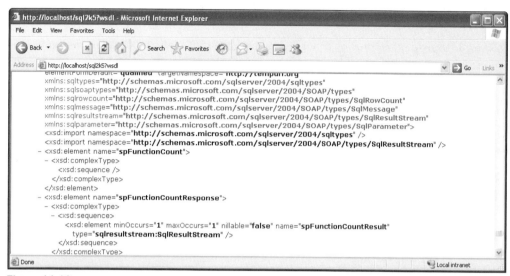

Figure 11-13

Once the Web Service is created, it needs to be consumed by an application. Visual Studio .NET has the capability to set up and consume an XML Web Service. Figure 11-14 shows a SQL Server 2005 XML Web Service being consumed by Visual Studio .NET 2005.

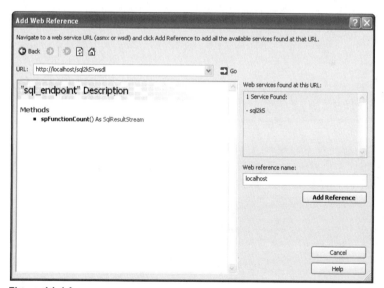

Figure 11-14

The table sys.endpoints displays all of the endpoints contained within a database.

Summary

This chapter provided information about programming the SQL Server 2005 database engine. You looked at the development of CLR objects that run within the database. These CLR objects can be triggers, stored procedures, functions, aggregates, and user-defined types. You also learned how to create database objects, such as a database, tables, and users, and perform backups and restores using SQL Management Objects (SMOs). Last, but not least, you created a Web Service to communicate with a SQL Server 2005 function directly, without the need for an intermediary such as IIS.

For More Information

To complement the information in this chapter, take a look at the following resources:

❑ **MSDN article titled "Using CLR Integration in SQL Server 2005"** — `http://msdn.microsoft.com/data/default.aspx?pull=/library/en-us/dnsql90/html/sqlclrguidance.asp`

❑ **MSDN article titled "An Overview of SQL Server 2005 for the Database Developer"** — `http://msdn.microsoft.com/library/default.asp?url=/library/en-us/dnsql90/html/sql_ovyukondev.asp`

❑ **The Weblog by Niels Berglund of Developmentor** — `http://staff.develop.com/nielsb/`

❑ **Data Samples and Tools page, by Bob Beauchemin of SQLSkills and formerly of Developmentor** — `www.sqlskills.com/blogs/bobb`.

12

Notification Services

Notification Services was originally released as a downloadable add-on for Microsoft SQL Server 2000, much like Analysis Services and Reporting Services. Because it wasn't released as part of SQL, many people haven't used it yet simply because they don't know it exists. This chapter covers the basics of creating a Notification Services application and highlights the new features available for Notification Services in SQL 2005.

If you have been developing for a while, chances are good that you have had the need to create an application that sends notifications when an event occurs, or on a periodic basis. Some examples of these types of applications include the following:

- ❏ Flight schedule changes
- ❏ Task reminders
- ❏ Minimum account balance warnings
- ❏ Stock updates
- ❏ Weather updates
- ❏ Server monitoring
- ❏ News updates
- ❏ Task approval notifications
- ❏ Many other line-of-business applications

Notification Services is designed to make creating these types of applications easier. It does this by providing a framework containing the core functionality, which means you just need to specify the configuration and provide the method for subscribing to notifications.

Major Components

When you are building your first Notification Services application, you face a steep learning curve. There isn't a simple "Hello World" example to start with that enables you to build your knowledge in small steps and see results along the way. With Notification Services, you need to define many functions before creating your first application. Don't worry; you'll examine each of these functions in detail throughout the chapter, but first you should look at the major components and how they interact. Figure 12-1 shows just that, providing the "big picture" level.

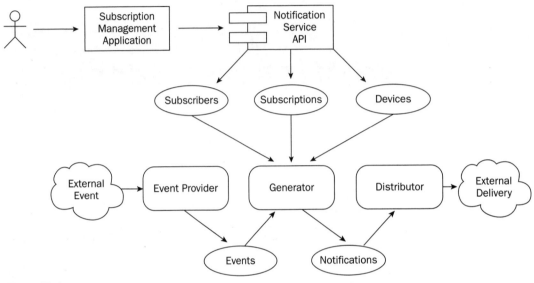

Figure 12-1

Subscription Management Application

The subscription management application is responsible for collecting information from the user and adding it to SQL Notification Services (SQL NS). This includes a list of who the subscribers are, what types of devices the subscribers have, and the services to which they wish to subscribe.

Microsoft exposes a NS API for doing this. Your responsibility is building the interface to collect the data and send it to the API. This is usually done in the form of a Web application that enables the user to define his or her own subscriptions. This could be in the form of a desktop app, a service that monitors an e-mail account, or a bulk import from another system.

This is typically the only part of a NS application that requires writing code. The rest of the application is defined by XML files. The key components of the subscription management application are as follows:

❑ **Subscriber**—Who or what will be receiving the notification. There's usually only one entry per person, even when the user wishes to subscribe to several services offered or receive notification on several different devices.

❑ **Subscriber Device** — What to send the notification to. A user of your application may wish to receive an e-mail message at work when one type of event has occurred, another at home for a second event, a page for some other events, and so on. The subscriber devices are the delivery endpoints that may be used by a subscriber's subscriptions.

❑ **Subscription** — A subscription merges the information of when and where to send a notification. It describes the conditions for being notified, such as a flight being delayed or a work item awaiting approval. It also indicates the device to which the subscription should be sent.

Event Provider

An event provider is designed to watch for an event to occur outside of Notification Services and then create an NS event, such as when a file shows up on a server, when the results of a query change, or when the contents of a Web site change.

An event provider is not required for an NS application. The NS events can be added manually through the NS API or stored procedures, but creating an NS event is much quicker and easier in most circumstances. There are two built-in event providers for monitoring a SQL database or file system, but you also have the option of creating your own custom event providers. Here are some key terms you'll need to fully understand event providers:

❑ **External Event** — Something that occurs outside of the NS application that may or may not be used to trigger events within the NS application.

❑ **Event** — This is an XML representation of the action that occurred, which is stored within the NS application. It contains any relevant data needed for determining which notifications should be sent and any data that needs to be included in them.

❑ **Event Batches** — When multiple events occur at the same time, they are grouped together into event batches for processing as a single group.

❑ **Hosted Event Providers** — These are event providers that run within the NS application.

❑ **Non-Hosted Event Providers** — These are also sometimes referred to as *independent event providers*. They are not hosted by the NS application, but rather run independently of it, possibly even on a different server.

Generator

The generator performs the majority of the work in a NS application. Its role is to evaluate the events that have occurred and check them against the subscriptions on file. It then determines whether any notifications need to be generated, and if so, generates them. The major components of the generator are as follows:

❑ **Rules** — These are used by the generator to determine which notifications need to be generated for a given event. All the data you need to determine this has been stored in SQL Server tables by the event providers and the subscription management application. Writing the rule is as simple as creating a join between these two sets of data and inserting the results into another table using SQL syntax.

❑ **Quantum** — A quantum is the interval during which the generator checks for notifications that need to be generated. This interval is adjustable through the instance configuration file, described later in this chapter.

❑ **Chronicles** — These store information about an event over the series of multiple event firings. They are useful if you wish to be notified of certain information that isn't typically tabulated, such as how many sales took place in a given hour if your events only report single sales as they occur.

Distributor

The role of the distributor is to deliver the notifications to the users, which can be done via e-mail, a pager, a net send command, the delivery of a file, an FTP transfer, and so on. In many cases, a single event can generate thousands of notifications. Delivery of these notifications can be rather intensive. The distributor consists of the following three major parts:

❑ **Formatters** — These translate the raw XML data about the notification into the presentation format. Formatters usually take the form of an XSL stylesheet, the only built-in formatter, but you can also create your own formatters.

❑ **Delivery Protocols** — These are the basic formats available for delivering a message, such as SMTP, FTP, or HTTP.

❑ **Delivery Channel** — This is an instance of a delivery protocol that specifies which server, port, and additional information to use.

Instances and Applications

As mentioned earlier, the majority of the configuration of a NS application is defined by two XML files: the *instance configuration file* and the *application definition file*.

A notification server instance is a named copy of Notification Services. You can have multiple NS instances running on a single machine. For each instance, a separate copy of all the NS components is created. Each instance can contain multiple NS applications, which are usually contained within one logical group. This is the level at which the subscribers and their devices are defined. It also contains information such as the machine on which the event providers, generator, and distributor will run.

Configuring the Instance

Let's get started building your first NS application. To create a new instance, start by creating a new XML file. First you'll need to create the root node of NotificationServicesInstance and reference the appropriate namespace. Inside this tag, you need to define the instance and SQL Server names. The instance name is what you want this copy of SQL NS to be called. It will be used to name the Windows services and SQL database. You also have the option to specify the SQL Server that stores the data for this NS application as a different machine than the one that runs it. In most cases, you'll specify the local machine name.

```
<?xml version="1.0" encoding="utf-8"?>
<NotificationServicesInstance xmlns="http://www.microsoft.com/↩
MicrosoftNotificationServices/ConfigurationFileSchema">
   <InstanceName>WeatherInstance</InstanceName>
   <SqlServerSystem>YourMachineName</SqlServerSystem>
</NotificationServicesInstance>
```

The next step is to define the `ParameterDefaults` section. Parameters are used for values that may change when deploying the app to different environments. This provides a single point to change these values. The Notification Services GUI provides screens for specifying these values when creating the instance. The `ParameterDefaults` section isn't necessary to use parameters; it simply sets the default values for each parameter.

For this application, configure four parameters for the following: the local computer name, the base directory in which your configuration files will be stored, the address of the SMTP server you wish to use, and the e-mail address from which notifications should come. This and the rest of the configuration settings outlined in this section are contained within the `NotificationServicesInstance` tag:

```
<ParameterDefaults>
  <Parameter>
    <Name>ComputerName</Name>
    <Value>YourMachineName</Value>
  </Parameter>
  <Parameter>
    <Name>BaseDirectoryPath</Name>
    <Value>C:\NS</Value>
  </Parameter>
  <Parameter>
    <Name>SmtpServer</Name>
    <Value>localhost</Value>
  </Parameter>
  <Parameter>
    <Name>EmailAddress</Name>
    <Value>name@domain.com</Value>
  </Parameter>
</ParameterDefaults>
```

It's time to tell the instance about the applications it will be running. For this example, we'll only have one, but an instance can run multiple applications. The first thing it needs to know about the application is its name. This name will also be used to create the corresponding SQL tables, views, and stored procedures. You also need to specify the base directory path. The parameters you defined earlier will come in handy here. You can pass in the value of the parameter by referencing the name surrounded by percent symbols.

The application definition file (ADF) path specifies the name of the ADF file. Each application can also have its own set of parameters. Here we are passing in the local computer name for the distributor and generator. We are also specifying the base directory path for the XSLT file that will format the notification, and passing in the e-mail address from which the notifications will come. These values will be consumed later in the ADF file:

```
<Applications>
  <Application>
    <ApplicationName>WeatherAlert</ApplicationName>
    <BaseDirectoryPath>%BaseDirectoryPath%</BaseDirectoryPath>
    <ApplicationDefinitionFilePath>WeatherAlert.xml</ApplicationDefinitionFilePath>
    <Parameters>
      <Parameter>
        <Name>Distributor</Name>
        <Value>%ComputerName%</Value>
      </Parameter>
```

```
      <Parameter>
        <Name>Generator</Name>
        <Value>%ComputerName%</Value>
      </Parameter>
      <Parameter>
        <Name>XsltDirectory</Name>
        <Value>%BaseDirectoryPath%</Value>
      </Parameter>
      <Parameter>
        <Name>FromEmail</Name>
        <Value>%EmailAddress%</Value>
      </Parameter>
    </Parameters>
  </Application>
</Applications>
```

The last part to define in the instance configuration file is the delivery channels that will be used in this application. The sample app will only deliver notifications via e-mail, so you'll need to specify one delivery channel. The delivery channel name can be anything you want. The protocol must be SMTP because we're sending e-mails. In the arguments section, pass in the `SmtpServer` parameter for the SMTP server argument. If you leave it as `localhost` in the parameters section, be sure to verify that the mail service is running on your machine.

```
<DeliveryChannels>
  <DeliveryChannel>
    <DeliveryChannelName>EmailChannel</DeliveryChannelName>
    <ProtocolName>SMTP</ProtocolName>
    <Arguments>
      <Argument>
        <Name>SmtpServer</Name>
        <Value>%SmtpServer%</Value>
      </Argument>
    <Arguments>
  </DeliveryChannel>
</DeliveryChannels>
```

That's it. You're done defining the instance configuration file. Save it as WeatherInstance.xml and proceed to create the application definition file. You'll use the configuration file again later in the chapter.

The Application Definition File

It is now time to define your application. In this section, you'll specify what data you need to gather in the events, what data is needed from the subscribers, and what will be included in the notification, as well as what triggers the notification. It is a bit more involved than the configuration file. Once again, begin by making the shell. You'll need a root, `Application` node that points to the namespace specified in the following code sample. You'll also need to specify the machine on which the distributor and generator will run. If you want them to run on the same machine, you can use the `%Distributor%` and `%Generator%` parameters that were passed in from the instance configuration file you just created.

```xml
<?xml version="1.0" encoding="utf-8" ?>
<Application xmlns="http://www.microsoft.com/↵
MicrosoftNotificationServices/ApplicationDefinitionFileSchema">
  <Distributors>
    <Distributor>
      <SystemName>%Distributor%</SystemName>
    </Distributor>
  </Distributors>

  <Generator>
    <SystemName>%Generator%</SystemName>
  </Generator>
</Application>
```

Next, you need to define what data will be expected on the events in the `EventClasses` section. This consists of providing a name and the schema for the data that will be collected. In this case, you'll need to know the zip code for the temperature update and the current temperature in that zip code. This will later be used to create corresponding SQL tables and views. The field types you specify need to be valid SQL Server field types.

```xml
<EventClasses>
  <EventClass>
    <EventClassName>WeatherAlertEvent</EventClassName>
    <Schema>
      <Field>
        <FieldName>ZipCode</FieldName>
        <FieldType>varchar(5)</FieldType>
      </Field>
      <Field>
        <FieldName>CurrentTemperature</FieldName>
        <FieldType>float</FieldType>
      </Field>
    </Schema>
  </EventClass>
</EventClasses>
```

You'll also need to specify the provider for the events. The provider specifies how the events will be populated. There are two types of providers: *hosted* and *nonhosted*. Hosted providers run within the NS application scope and usually consist of monitoring a SQL table for changes or waiting for a file to show up. Nonhosted providers indicate that the data will be populated into events by something outside of NS; you still need to add an entry for them, though. For now, specify a nonhosted provider:

```xml
<Providers>
  <NonHostedProvider>
    <ProviderName>WeatherAlertProvider</ProviderName>
  </NonHostedProvider>
</Providers>
```

Now you need to specify what the output format will be. To send a message of "The current temperature is X degrees," the only piece of data you need is the current temperature. In the schema section, specify this field with a type of float.

To format the message as previously stated, specify the content formatter. To do this, add the `ContentFormatter` node and specify the built-in `XsltFormatter` for the class name. You'll need to specify the path to your XSLT file by using the `XsltDirectory` parameter, and specify the name of the XSLT file you wish to use.

Now you need to specify which protocols specified in the instance configuration file will be used by this notification class, and provide the parameters to be used. For the subject, priority, and body format, you can hard-code the values. To do this, be sure to pass the values surrounded by single quotes and encode these quotes for XML. The only parameter that changes is the To address. You just need to specify `DeliveryAddress` for this value, which will be passed in from the subscriber's device:

```xml
<NotificationClasses>
  <NotificationClass>
    <NotificationClassName>WeatherAlertNotification</NotificationClassName>
    <Schema>
      <Fields>
        <Field>
          <FieldName>CurrentTemperature</FieldName>
          <FieldType>float</FieldType>
        </Field>
      </Fields>
    </Schema>
    <ContentFormatter>
      <ClassName>XsltFormatter</ClassName>
      <Arguments>
        <Argument>
          <Name>XsltBaseDirectoryPath</Name>
          <Value>%XsltDirectory%</Value>
        </Argument>
        <Argument>
          <Name>XsltFileName</Name>
          <Value>WeatherAlert.xslt</Value>
        </Argument>
      </Arguments>
    </ContentFormatter>
    <Protocols>
      <Protocol>
        <ProtocolName>SMTP</ProtocolName>
        <Fields>
          <Field>
            <FieldName>Subject</FieldName>
            <SqlExpression>
              &apos;Weather Alert.&apos;
            </SqlExpression>
          </Field>
          <Field>
            <FieldName>From</FieldName>
            <SqlExpression>
              &apos;%FromEmail%&apos;
            </SqlExpression>
          </Field>
          <Field>
            <FieldName>To</FieldName>
            <SqlExpression>
```

```
                    DeviceAddress
                  </SqlExpression>
                </Field>
                <Field>
                  <FieldName>Priority</FieldName>
                  <SqlExpression>
                    &apos;Normal&apos;
                  </SqlExpression>
                </Field>
                <Field>
                  <FieldName>BodyFormat</FieldName>
                  <SqlExpression>
                    &apos;html&apos;
                  </SqlExpression>
                </Field>
              </Fields>
            </Protocol>
          </Protocols>
        </NotificationClass>
      </NotificationClasses>
```

The last piece you need in order to have a complete NS application defined is the subscription information. This section contains three parts: the class name and schema, which are defined in this section, and the event rules, defined in the next section. The first two are very similar to what you've already done. Specify the class name you want. On the schema, we need several pieces of information: the zip code for which the subscriber wishes to receive notifications, the name of the device on which they wish to receive them, and the maximum and minimum temperature thresholds so they can determine when they should receive notifications:

```
<SubscriptionClasses>
  <SubscriptionClass>
    <SubscriptionClassName>WeatherAlertSubscriptions</SubscriptionClassName>
    <Schema>
      <Field>
        <FieldName>ZipCode</FieldName>
        <FieldType>varchar(5)</FieldType>
      </Field>
      <Field>
        <FieldName>DeviceName</FieldName>
        <FieldType>varchar(255)</FieldType>
      </Field>
      <Field>
        <FieldName>MaxTemperature</FieldName>
        <FieldType>float</FieldType>
      </Field>
      <Field>
        <FieldName>MinTemperature</FieldName>
        <FieldType>float</FieldType>
      </Field>
    </Schema>
  </SubscriptionClass>
</SubscriptionClasses>
```

The event rules section is a bit different from the others. It defines a SQL query that merges the event data with the subscriber data to populate the notification data. You should already be familiar with how to write such a query, so we won't walk you through it, but you can see an example in the following code. It references several views that do not yet exist. These views will be created at the time the NS instance is created. You have already defined the names and schema for them, however, so it's pretty easy to go ahead and write the query. Be sure to encode any characters, such as the greater than and less than symbols, for XML.

```
<EventRules>
  <EventRule>
    <RuleName>WeatherAlertRule</RuleName>
    <Action>
      INSERT INTO WeatherAlert(
        SubscriberId, DeviceName, SubscriberLocale, CurrentTemperature)
      SELECT s.SubscriberId, s.DeviceName,'en-US',
        e.CurrentTemperature
      FROM WeatherAlertEvent e
      INNER JOIN WeatherAlertSubscriptions s
      ON e.ZipCode=s.ZipCode AND (
        e.CurrentTemperature&gt;s.MaxTemperature OR
        e.CurrentTemperature&lt;s.MinTemperature)
    </Action>
    <EventClassName>WeatherAlertEvent</EventClassName>
  </EventRule>
</EventRules>
```

The application definition file is now complete, and you're almost ready to create your NS application. The last thing you need to do is define the contents of the XSLT file previously referenced in the content formatters section. This can be as simple or elaborate as you like, but we'll go with simple for our example:

```
<?xml version="1.0" encoding="utf-8"?>
<xsl:stylesheet xmlns:xsl="http://www.w3.org/1999/XSL/Transform" version="1.0">
  <xsl:template match="*/notification">
      The current temperature is <xsl:value-of select="CurrentTemperature"/>.
  </xsl:template>
</xsl:stylesheet>
```

Adding the SQL NS Instance

You have completely configured your first NS application, and we haven't even looked at the interface yet. It's time to take a look now. Begin by opening the SQL Server Management Studio. Right-click the Notification Services node and choose the option to add a new instance. You'll see a dialog box with a Browse button. Use it to browse to and select the instance configuration file you created earlier and then click OK. SQL NS is now aware of this instance and the application contained within it.

Next, you need to register the NS instance. This will create the associated Windows service and performance counters. It is also where you specify which account that service will run as, along with which account to connect to the database as. After that, you'll need to enable the services. This will turn on all of the subcomponents — the event providers, the generators, the distributors, and the subscriptions. Finally, you need to start the service.

Your application is now running and ready to send notifications. All you need to do now is set up some subscriptions and then fire events. If you need to make changes to your configuration later, just stop and disable the service. Then choose the update option to point to the updated configuration file and re-enable and restart the service again.

Building the Subscription Management Application

You need to provide the users of this application with a way to subscribe. Microsoft has provided an API for Notification Services, but it is up to you to create the interface for collecting the subscription information. In most cases, this is provided via a Web application. For this example, we create a single admin interface for setting up subscribers; you may also wish to enable subscribers to edit their own information in your application.

In this section, you'll learn the steps necessary for adding subscribers, defining what devices each subscriber has, and adding subscriptions for those subscribers. You will need to create a new Web project and add a reference to `Microsoft.SqlServer.NotificationServices`. You'll also need to add an `Imports` statement referencing `Microsoft.SqlServer.NotificationServices` to each of the pages outlined in this section.

Retrieving a List of Subscribers

The first step for our admin application is to create a screen that will retrieve a list of subscribers already set up, and then allow the admin to choose one to edit or create a new one. To do this, create a new page, called subscriberlist.aspx. In the HTML section, add a datagrid with a single hyperlink column. The text for this column will be the value of the `SubscriberId` property, and the link will point to subscriberedit.aspx, passing in the hyperlink parameter. Also add a link that points to subscriberedit.aspx, with no parameters, in order to add a new subscriber.

Use the following code to populate the datagrid. You first need to get a copy of the Notification Services instance. This is something that will be reused throughout the application, so it's best to define it in a shared method. This method, `GetNsInstance`, is defined in the `Utils` class in the following section. Next, create a new instance of the `SubscriberEnumeration` object, passing in the NS instance. This will return a populated list of all subscribers, which you can then bind to your datagrid.

```
Sub Page_Load(ByVal sender As Object, ByVal e As System.EventArgs) Handles Me.Load
    Dim ns As NSInstance
    Dim subscribers As SubscriberEnumeration

    ns = Utils.GetNsInstance()
    subscribers = New SubscriberEnumeration(ns)

    SubscriberGrid.DataSource = subscribers
    SubscriberGrid.DataBind()
End Sub
```

This page references the GetNsInstance method in the Utils class. You'll need to create this class and method in the Code directory. It is fairly simple and just consists of retrieving the instance name from the web.config file, creating a new NSInstance object with that name, and returning the object:

```
Public Shared Function GetNsInstance() As NSInstance
  Dim instanceName As String
  Dim ns As NSInstance
  instanceName =
System.Configuration.ConfigurationSettings.AppSettings("InstanceName")
  ns = New NSInstance(instanceName)
  Return ns
End Function
```

Adding/Removing a Subscriber

You now need to define subscriberedit.aspx, referenced by the previous page. There's really only one field you must be able to define for the subscriber: the subscriber id. Create a Web form with a field for the subscriber id, a Save button, and a Delete button.

Also add two hyperlinks to the page: one to edit the devices for this subscriber and one to edit the subscriptions. These hyperlinks should have the visible property set to false by default.

In the Page_Load event, request the subscriber id from the query string. If it isn't blank, store it in ViewState for future use, update the SubscriberIdText textbox with the value, and call the EnableSubscriber method to make the appropriate links and buttons visible:

```
Sub Page_Load(ByVal sender As Object, ByVal e As System.EventArgs) Handles Me.Load
  If Not IsPostBack Then
    Dim subscriberId As String
    subscriberId = Request("SubscriberId")
    If subscriberId <> "" Then
      ViewState("SubscriberId") = subscriberId
      SubscriberIdText.Text = subscriberId
      EnableSubscriber()
    End If
  End If
End Sub
```

If this is an existing subscriber, you need to enable the links to edit the devices, subscriptions, and Delete button, as well as disable the Save button. You'll also need to specify the link URLs, passing in the subscriber id, the subscription class name, and the application name:

```
Sub EnableSubscriber()
  Dim subscriberId As String
  subscriberId = Convert.ToString(ViewState("SubscriberId"))

  SubscriberIdText.Enabled = False
  SaveButton.Visible = False
  DeleteButton.Visible = True
  DevicesLink.Visible = True
  DevicesLink.NavigateUrl = "DeviceList.aspx?subscriberId=" & subscriberId

  AlertSubscriptionsLink.Visible = True
```

```
   AlertSubscriptionsLink.NavigateUrl =
  "SubscriptionList.aspx?applicationName=WeatherAlert&subscriptionClassName⊃
  =WeatherAlertSubscriptions&subscriberId=" & subscriberId
  End Sub
```

Saving the subscriber is pretty straightforward. You just need to call the same shared method used earlier to retrieve the Notification Services instance. Then create a new subscriber object, passing in the NS instance. Set the subscriber name property and call the `Add` method. Then call the `EnableSubscriber` method to populate the links:

```
Sub SaveButton_Click(ByVal sender As Object, ByVal e As System.EventArgs)
   Dim instanceName As String
   Dim ns As Microsoft.SqlServer.NotificationServices.NSInstance
   Dim subscriber As Microsoft.SqlServer.NotificationServices.Subscriber

   ns = Utils.GetNsInstance()
   subscriber = New Microsoft.SqlServer.NotificationServices.Subscriber(ns)
   subscriber.SubscriberId = SubscriberIdText.Text
   subscriber.Add()
   ViewState("SubscriberId") = subscriberId
   EnableSubscriber()
End Sub
```

To delete a subscriber, load the NS instance. Call a new shared method to retrieve the subscriber by its subscriber id. Call the `Delete` method on the subscriber object and transfer the user back to the subscriber list:

```
Sub DeleteButton_Click(ByVal sender As Object, ByVal e As System.EventArgs)
   Dim instanceName As String
   Dim ns As NSInstance
   Dim subscriber As Subscriber
   Dim subscribers As SubscriberEnumeration

   ns = Utils.GetNsInstance()
   subscriber = Utils.GetSubscriber(subscriberId)
   subscriber.Delete()
   Server.Transfer("SubscriberList.aspx")
End Sub
```

You now need to create the `GetSubscriber` method in the `Utils` class referenced by the last code block. It will also be used in several other places in the application. Create the new NS instance by calling the shared `GetNsInstance` method. Then, create a new `SubscriberEnumeration` object, passing in the NS instance. Next, request the subscriber object from the collection by the subscriber id and return that subscriber object:

```
Public Shared Function GetSubscriber(ByVal subscriberId As String) As Subscriber
   Dim ns As NSInstance
   Dim subscriber As Subscriber
   Dim subscribers As SubscriberEnumeration

   ns = GetNsInstance()
   subscribers = New SubscriberEnumeration(ns)
   subscriber = subscribers.Item(subscriberId)
   Return subscriber
End Function
```

Device List

The next step we're going to cover is building the device list, devicelist.aspx. This page will show which devices each subscriber has and enable the user to add new devices. Figure 12-2 shows a simple example of how this page may look.

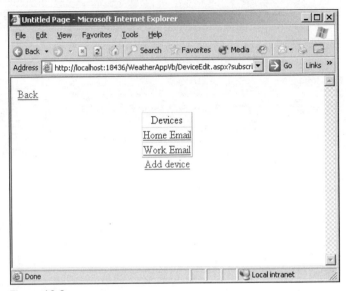

Figure 12-2

As with the subscriber list, create a new datagrid in your .aspx page and two hyperlinks for adding a device and returning to the previous page. In the code-behind, the first thing that you're going to need is the subscriber id. Request it from the query string and place it in a local variable. Use it to populate the Back link and Add Device link, and then call the GetSubscriber method to return the current subscriber object. You can then call the GetDevices method of the subscriber object and simply databind it to the grid:

```
Sub Page_Load(ByVal sender As Object, ByVal e As System.EventArgs) Handles Me.Load
    Dim subscriberId As String
    Dim subscriber As Subscriber
    Dim devices As SubscriberDeviceEnumeration

    subscriberId = Request("SubscriberId")
    BackLink.NavigateUrl = "SubscriberEdit.aspx?subscriberId=" +
subscriberId.ToString()

    subscriber = Utils.GetSubscriber(subscriberId)
    devices = subscriber.GetDevices()

    DeviceGrid.DataSource = devices
    DeviceGrid.DataBind()
    Me.AddDeviceLink.NavigateUrl = "DeviceEdit.aspx?subscriberId=" + subscriberId
End Sub
```

Device Edit

Next you'll need to add a page similar to the one shown in Figure 12-3 to enable users to edit or add devices.

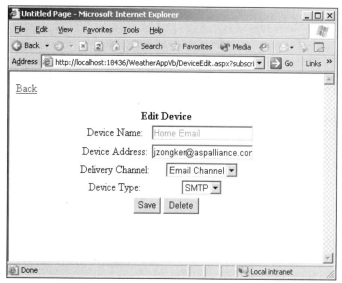

Figure 12-3

For the Edit Device screen, you'll need textbox fields for setting the device name and address, and drop-down menus for selecting the delivery channel and device type. You'll also need a Save and Delete button and a link to go back. In the code-behind, we'll use the values of the subscriber id and device name several times. This will be easier if you create properties for them. In these properties, just store the value in `ViewState` and pull it back out in the `Set` and `Get` methods, respectively:

```
Private Property SubscriberId() As String
  Get
    Return Convert.ToString(ViewState("SubscriberId"))
  End Get
  Set(ByVal value As String)
    ViewState("SubscriberId") = value
  End Set
End Property

Private Property DeviceName() As String
  Get
    Return Convert.ToString(ViewState("DeviceName"))
  End Get
  Set(ByVal value As String)
    ViewState("DeviceName") = value
  End Set
End Property
```

In the `Page_Load` method, you just need to request the subscriber id and device name. Then populate the Back link; and if the device name isn't empty, call the `PopulateDevice` method:

```
Sub Page_Load(ByVal sender As Object, ByVal e As System.EventArgs) Handles Me.Load
   If Not IsPostBack Then
      SubscriberId = Request("SubscriberId")
      DeviceName = Request("Devicename")

      BackLink.NavigateUrl = "DeviceList.aspx?subscriberId=" +
SubscriberId.ToString()

      If DeviceName <> "" Then
         PopulateDevice()
      End If
   End If
End Sub
```

The `PopulateDevice` method loads the device using the new `GetDevice` shared method and populates the fields on the page with the values stored within Notification Services when you're editing an existing device. It also disables the name so that it cannot be changed and enables the Delete button:

```
Sub PopulateDevice()
   Dim device As SubscriberDevice
   device = Utils.GetDevice(SubscriberId, DeviceName)

   DeviceNameText.Text = device.DeviceName
   DeviceAddress.Text = device.DeviceAddress
   DeliveryChannelList.Items.FindByValue(device.DeliveryChannelName).Selected = True
   DeviceTypeList.Items.FindByValue(device.DeviceTypeName).Selected = True

   DeviceNameText.Enabled = False
   DeleteButton.Enabled = True
End Sub
```

In the `Utils` class, you must add a new method of `GetDevice`. It calls the `GetSubscriber` shared method to get the subscriber object. The `GetDevices()` method of the subscriber object retrieves all of the devices and then returns the device matching the specified device name:

```
Public Shared Function GetDevice(ByVal subscriberId As String, ByVal deviceName As
String) As SubscriberDevice
   Dim subscriber As Subscriber
   Dim devices As SubscriberDeviceEnumeration
   Dim device As SubscriberDevice

   subscriber = GetSubscriber(subscriberId)
   devices = subscriber.GetDevices()
   device = devices.Item(deviceName)
   Return device
End Function
```

To save the device, either create a new `SubscriberDevice` object if it is a new subscriber or use the `GetDevice` method to load an existing device. Update each of the properties with the values inputted on the screen, and then call either the `Add` or `Update` method, accordingly. Then transfer the user back to the DeviceList page:

```
Sub SaveButton_Click(ByVal sender As Object, ByVal e As System.EventArgs)
   Dim device As SubscriberDevice


   If (DeviceName = "") Then
     'Add device
     device = New SubscriberDevice(Utils.GetNsInstance)
     device.SubscriberId = SubscriberId
     device.DeviceName = DeviceNameText.Text
     device.DeviceAddress = DeviceAddress.Text
     device.DeliveryChannelName = DeliveryChannelList.SelectedItem.Value
     device.DeviceTypeName = DeviceTypeList.SelectedItem.Value
     device.Add()
   Else
     'Update device
     device = Utils.GetDevice(SubscriberId, DeviceName)
     device.SubscriberId = SubscriberId
     device.DeviceAddress = DeviceAddress.Text
     device.DeliveryChannelName = DeliveryChannelList.SelectedItem.Value
     device.DeviceTypeName = DeviceTypeList.SelectedItem.Value
     device.Update()
   End If
   Server.Transfer("DeviceList.aspx")
End Sub
```

For the `Delete` method, get the device using the shared method, call the `Delete` method on it, and transfer the user back to the DeviceList page:

```
Sub DeleteButton_Click(ByVal sender As Object, ByVal e As System.EventArgs)
   Dim device As SubscriberDevice
   device = Utils.GetDevice(SubscriberId, DeviceName)
   device.Delete()
   Server.Transfer("DeviceList.aspx")
End Sub
```

Subscription List

The last set of pages you'll need to make are the subscription management pages. First you need a page to list the subscriptions. The subscription class name is being passed into the page, so this will be a filtered list. Begin by adding a datagrid, Back link, and Add Device link as you did for the other list pages. In the code-behind, request the `SubscriberId`, `ApplicationName`, and `SubscriptionClassName` from the query string. Then call a new method in the `Utils` class of `GetSubscriptions` to return a `SubscriptionEnumeration` object. Bind the subscriptions and populate the two links:

```
Protected subscriberId As String
Protected applicationName As String
Protected subscriptionClassName As String


Sub Page_Load(ByVal sender As Object, ByVal e As System.EventArgs) Handles Me.Load
   Dim subscriptions As SubscriptionEnumeration

  subscriberId = Request("SubscriberId")
```

```
    applicationName = Request("ApplicationName")
    subscriptionClassName = Request("SubscriptionClassName")
    subscriptions = Utils.GetSubscriptions(applicationName, ⤸
subscriptionClassName, subscriberId)

    SubscriptionGrid.DataSource = subscriptions
    SubscriptionGrid.DataBind()

    BackLink.NavigateUrl = "SubscriberEdit.aspx?subscriberId="⤸
  + subscriberId.ToString()
    AddSubscriptionLink.NavigateUrl = "SubscriptionEdit.aspx?subscriberId="⤸
  + subscriberId + "&applicationName=" + applicationName + ⤸
"&subscriptionClassName=" + subscriptionClassName


End Sub
```

Of course, you now need to add the GetSubscriptions method you just called to the Utils class. Call the GetNsApplication method, which is another new method you will add to this class in a moment. Then create a new SubscriptionEnumeration class, passing in the application object, subscription class name, and subscriber id. Now return the SubscriptionEnumeration object:

```
Public Shared Function GetSubscriptions(ByVal applicationName As String,⤸
  ByVal subscriptionClassName As String, ByVal subscriberId As String) As⤸
SubscriptionEnumeration
    Dim app As NSApplication
    Dim subscriptions As SubscriptionEnumeration

    app = GetNsApplication(applicationName)
    subscriptions = New SubscriptionEnumeration(app, subscriptionClassName,⤸
  subscriberId)
    Return subscriptions
End Function
```

The GetNsApplication method needs to call GetNsInstance to create a new NS instance and then create a new NSApplication object, passing in the NS instance and application name and returning that object:

```
Public Shared Function GetNsApplication(ByVal applicationName As String)⤸
  As NSApplication
    Dim instanceName As String
    Dim ns As NSInstance
    Dim app As NSApplication

    ns = Utils.GetNsInstance()
    app = New NSApplication(ns, applicationName)
    Return app
End Function
```

Subscription Edit

We're at the last and most complex page in the subscription management application. Begin by creating the HTML layout, including textboxes for zip code, max temperature, and min temperature. Also add a drop-down menu for the device name. Add the usual Save and Delete buttons and a link to go back.

In the code-behind, add properties for the application name, subscriber id, subscription class name, and subscription id that store their values in `ViewState`:

```
Private Property ApplicationName() As String
  Get
    Return Convert.ToString(ViewState("ApplicationName"))
  End Get
  Set(ByVal value As String)
    ViewState("ApplicationName") = value
  End Set
End Property

Private Property SubscriberId() As String
  Get
    Return Convert.ToString(ViewState("SubscriberId"))
  End Get
  Set(ByVal value As String)
    ViewState("SubscriberId") = value
  End Set
End Property

Private Property SubscriptionClassName() As String
  Get
    Return Convert.ToString(ViewState("SubscriptionClassName"))
  End Get
  Set(ByVal value As String)
    ViewState("SubscriptionClassName") = value
  End Set
End Property

Private Property SubscriptionId() As String
  Get
    Return Convert.ToString(ViewState("SubscriptionId"))
  End Get
  Set(ByVal value As String)
    ViewState("SubscriptionId") = value
  End Set
End Property
```

In the `Page_Load` event, populate all of the properties from their appropriate query string values. Set the URL on the Back link and populate the Device List drop-down menu using the same shared method you used to populate the devices on the devicelist.aspx page. Call the `PopulateSubscription` method if the subscription id is not empty, and make the alert info section visible if this is an alert subscription:

```
Sub Page_Load(ByVal sender As Object, ByVal e As System.EventArgs) Handles Me.Load
  If Not IsPostBack Then
    SubscriberId = Request("SubscriberId")
    SubscriptionClassName = Request("SubscriptionClassName")
    SubscriptionId = Request("SubscriptionId")
    ApplicationName = Request("ApplicationName")

    BackLink.NavigateUrl = "SubscriptionList.aspx?applicationName=" +
  ApplicationName + "&subscriptionClassName=" + SubscriptionClassName +
```

```
    "&subscriberId=" + SubscriberId

      DeviceList.DataSource = Utils.GetSubscriber(SubscriberId).GetDevices()
      DeviceList.DataBind()

      If SubscriptionId <> "" Then
          PopulateSubscription()
      End If

    End If
End Sub
```

The `PopulateSubscription` method calls a new shared method of `GetSubscription` to load the subscription object. Use the `GetFieldValue` method of the subscription object to retrieve the value of any property that is defined in the ADF file. Next, populate the appropriate textboxes and select the appropriate items in the list boxes using this data. Lastly, enable the Delete button:

```
Sub PopulateSubscription()
   Dim subscription As Microsoft.SqlServer.NotificationServices.Subscription
   subscription = Utils.GetSubscription(Applicationname, SubscriptionClassName,
   SubscriberId, subscriptionId)

   SubscriptionIdLabel.Text = subscription.SubscriptionId
   ZipCodeText.Text = Convert.ToString(subscription.GetFieldValue("ZipCode"))
   DeviceList.Items.FindByValue(
   Convert.ToString(subscription.GetFieldValue("DeviceName"))).Selected = True

   MaxTemperatureText.Text =
   Convert.ToString(subscription.GetFieldValue("MaxTemperature"))

   MinTemperatureText.Text =
   Convert.ToString(subscription.GetFieldValue("MinTemperature"))

   DeleteButton.Enabled = True
End Sub
```

Now add the `GetSubscription` method to the `Utils` class. This method calls the shared `GetSubscriptions` method to retrieve a list of subscriptions for the specified application and returns the subscription matching the specified subscription name:

```
Public Shared Function GetSubscription(ByVal applicationName As String, ByVal⤸
 subscriptionClassName As String, ByVal subscriberId As String, ByVal⤸
 subscriptionId As String) As Subscription
  Dim subscriptions As SubscriptionEnumeration
  subscriptions = GetSubscriptions(applicationName, subscriptionClassName,
subscriberId)
  Return subscriptions.Item(subscriptionId)
End Function
```

To save the subscription, either create a new subscription object if adding a new subscription, or call the shared method to load a subscription if editing an existing one. Use the `SetFieldValue` method, passing in the parameter names you defined in the ADF file and the values for the parameters that apply to this subscription type. Call `Add` or `Update` depending on the subscription, and redirect the user back to the subscription list:

```
Sub SaveButton_Click(ByVal sender As Object, ByVal e As System.EventArgs)
    Dim subscription As Subscription

    If (SubscriptionId = "") Then
      'Add device
      subscription = New Subscription(Utils.GetNsApplication(ApplicationName),
    SubscriptionClassName)
      subscription.SubscriberId = SubscriberId
      subscription.SetFieldValue("ZipCode", ZipCodeText.Text)
      subscription.SetFieldValue("DeviceName", DeviceList.SelectedItem.Value)
      subscription.SetFieldValue("MaxTemperature",
    Convert.ToDouble(MaxTemperatureText.Text))
      subscription.SetFieldValue("MinTemperature",
    Convert.ToDouble(Me.MinTemperatureText.Text))
      subscription.Add()
    Else
      'Update device
      subscription = Utils.GetSubscription(ApplicationName,
    SubscriptionClassName, SubscriberId, SubscriptionId)
      subscription.SubscriberId = SubscriberId
      subscription.SetFieldValue("ZipCode", ZipCodeText.Text)
      subscription.SetFieldValue("DeviceName", DeviceList.SelectedItem.Value)
      subscription.SetFieldValue("MaxTemperature",
    Convert.ToDouble(MaxTemperatureText.Text))
      subscription.SetFieldValue("MinTemperature",
    Convert.ToDouble(Me.MinTemperatureText.Text))
      subscription.Update()
    End If
    Server.Transfer("SubscriptionList.aspx")
End Sub
```

Add code to the Delete button that calls the shared `GetSubscription` method to get the subscription object. Then call the `Delete` method on that object and transfer the user back to the subscription list:

```
Sub DeleteButton_Click(ByVal sender As Object, ByVal e As System.EventArgs)
    Dim subscription As Subscription
    subscription = Utils.GetSubscription(Applicationname, SubscriptionClassName,
    SubscriberId, SubscriptionId)
    subscription.Delete()
    Server.Transfer("SubscriptionList.aspx")
End Sub
```

You finally have a complete subscription management application. Run it and set up at least one subscriber, device, and subscription.

Firing an Event

You may recall that you configured the application to use a nonhosted provider. This means you are responsible for firing the events. This can be done by calling three stored procedures specific to this NS instance: NSEventBeginBatchWeatherAlertEvent, NSEventWriteWeatherAlertEvent, and NSEventFlushBatchWeatherAlertEvent.

As mentioned before, events are submitted in batches. Even if you are only submitting a single event, you must still create a batch for it. Use the NSEventBeginBatchWeatherAlertEvent stored procedure to do this. You must pass in the name of the provider you wish to use and the batch id as an output parameter.

Once you have the batch id, you can submit events to it using NSEventWriteWeatherAlertEvent. For this stored procedure, you must pass in the batch id and the parameters defined for the event in the ADF. Be sure to pass in the zip code you have subscribed to and a temperature that falls outside of the range you specified in order to trigger the notification. If you wish to submit more than one event, call this stored procedure as many times as necessary.

You must now close the event batch by calling NSEventFlushBatchWeatherAlertEvent and passing in the batch id. Within a few minutes of submitting the batch, you should receive an e-mail notification:

```
DECLARE @BatchId bigint
exec NSEventBeginBatchWeatherAlertEvent 'WeatherAlertProvider', @BatchId OUTPUT

exec NSEventWriteWeatherAlertEvent
 @EventBatchId=@BatchId,
 @ZipCode='74011',
 @CurrentTemperature=31

exec NSEventFlushBatchWeatherAlertEvent @BatchId
```

Summary

This chapter has only scratched the surface of what Notification Services can do. Many topics, such as scheduled subscriptions, nonhosted providers, chronicles, and performance tuning, simply can't be covered in a single chapter. It is hoped that you can see what is possible with Notification Services and are now well on your way to understanding how to use it.

For More Information

For additional information on SQL 2005 Notification Services, we suggest the following resources:

- ❑ **Microsoft SQL Server Home Page** — www.microsoft.com/sql/

- ❑ **Microsoft SQL Server 2005 Developer Center** — http://msdn.microsoft.com/sql/2005/

- ❑ **MSDN Webcast: Introducing Notification Services in SQL Server 2005** — http://msevents .microsoft.com/cui/WebCastEventDetails.aspx?EventID=1032263436

13

Service Broker

To better understand the queue mechanism known as *Service Broker,* we'll begin this chapter with an analogy. A crying baby is a common form of asynchronous communication (the parent's normal response time may make it seem synchronous, but it's actually asynchronous). Here's a breakdown of the communication pattern that results when a parent hears his or her baby crying (yes, this will make sense soon enough):

> Sending Service: Baby
>
> Receiving Service: Parent
>
> Message: Baby cries out
>
> Message Type: Baby cries with a specific tone
>
> Contract: Baby expects parent to help
>
> Queue: Parent in the middle of something that cannot be dropped immediately, so message is not acted on immediately
>
> Service Program: Parent changes diaper
>
> Dialog: Parent reassures baby and no more messages are queued

Okay, this may not be the best analogy, but it does represent the basic outline of each part of Service Broker. As we proceed through the chapter, you will learn about the following concepts: Service, Service Program, Message, Message Type, Queue, and Dialog.

An Introduction to Service Broker

When you hear the term *Service Broker,* one of the first products that may come to mind is Microsoft Message Queue (MSMQ). To many, Service Broker is a SQL Server–based replacement for MSMQ. However, while it can certainly fulfill the role of replacement, Service Broker is more than just a new queue mechanism. Here are some of its features:

❑ **Message Ordering:** Service Broker has the capability to order messages to ensure they are processed in the correct order. Each message in a unit is marked with a unique identifier to easily determine the task to which each message is tied.

❑ **Message Locking:** Service Broker locks all messages relating to the same task, ensuring that the messages are processed as a unit. This facility reduces the likelihood of incomplete transactions leaving the data in an inconsistent state.

❑ **Coordination:** Service Broker has a built-in mechanism to ensure that each message is only delivered once, eliminating the risk of messages being processed twice.

❑ **Database integration:** The Service Broker service is tightly integrated with SQL Server 2005. The queues are stored as tables in a database. This makes it very easy to use built-in SQL Server tools to back up and restore queues, as well as create highly available solutions.

❑ **Automatic Activation:** Service Broker is a service and not directly implemented inside the database. What this means is that numerous instances of the Service Broker service can automatically be activated when message load is heavy. These instances can also be shut down as the workload decreases.

❑ **Asynchronous Communication:** Service Broker is an asynchronous service. When a server goes down, messages can be queued until the service is back up and running. As asynchronous communication is loosely coupled, Service Broker can be configured to distribute the workload across multiple servers with very little work on the part of either a developer or a DBA.

The components of Service Broker include the following (in normal order of creation):

❑ **Message Types:** Every communication in Service Broker must adhere to a specific message type. Message types can be set up to allow complete flexibility (useful for binary communication) or they can be set up to rigidly adhere to a specific schema.

❑ **Contracts:** Dialogs have to be set up as a group of conversational pieces, each adhering to a specified message type. The layout of the conversation is set up in a contract, which cannot be changed without destroying and recreating the contract.

❑ **Queue:** A queue is a storage place for messages. As Service Broker is asynchronous, queues persist messages until they either are picked up or expire.

❑ **Service:** We are concerned with two types of service — those that initiate conversations (the INITIATOR) and those that receive messages in conversations (the TARGET). These can also be called *sending services* and *receiving services*.

❑ **Dialog:** When discussing Service Broker, there is a bit of confusion over the use of the words "dialog" and "conversation." Think of a conversation as communication from one queue to another. The fact that Microsoft chose to use the syntax CREATE DIALOG CONVERSATION further exacerbates the problem. If a conversation is communication between queues, then a dialog is a conversation between two queues with messages sent in both directions, with mechanisms to ensure that messages are received and processed in order. By setting up contracts with two-way messaging (with proper message types for each type of message sent), you initiate a dialog. Service Broker allows for very complex "dialog conversations."

❑ **Route:** A route is a pathway of communication from service to service (queue to queue). Routes indicate where one service should send messages to communicate with another service. They are extremely important when communicating from server to server, which is the norm when using Service Broker.

The basic layout of Service Broker is shown in Figure 13-1. On each end, you have a queue with a service on top. Between the two queues is a route over which a dialog (or conversation) takes place. These conversations use messages that adhere to a specific message type (in best practice, XML validated by a schema). The message types are listed in a contract that is placed at both ends as an agreement to what is going to be said.

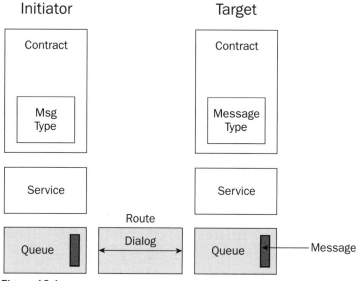

Figure 13-1

Working with Service Broker: A Simple Example

Before we dive into Service Broker, we'd like to give credit for the inspiration for the sample in this section, which has been adapted from guidance in the Microsoft course 2733 (*Updating Your Database Administration Skills to Microsoft® SQL Server 2005*). This particular example was chosen for adaptation for several reasons. First, it is simple enough to give you the basic concepts of Service Broker without getting you bogged down in too many details. Second, it is easy to expand on with other types of code. Finally, the example makes sense operating in a single database, even in a real-world scenario (that is, you do not have to install two instances to make it fit a scenario you might encounter in your career).

Scenario

In this example, you will play the part of a SQL Server developer for Adventure Works, an online retailer of bicycle parts. You are given the task of setting up a mechanism to send an e-mail message to new users when they sign up on your e-commerce site. As the site occasionally experiences heavy loads, you have been asked to ensure that the sign-up service does not interfere with transactions. The natural choice of tools is Service Broker.

> *In order to work through this example, you will need the Adventure Works sample database installed on your SQL Server 2005 instance. If you have not installed SQL Server 2005 yet, you can choose a custom install and install the sample database(s) as part of setup. If you have already installed SQL Server, there is a script for the Adventure Works database in the samples folder, located at %Program Files%\Microsoft SQL Server\90\Tools\Samples\AdventureWorks OLTP. Run the file instawdb.sql to install.*

In the following example, you will set up both the sending and receiving service in the same instance of SQL Server, acting on the same database. This is fine considering the requirements of the example, but you would normally be setting up sending and receiving queues on different server instances (or at least different databases). We will point out where you have to duplicate efforts when working on two databases. The scenario in mind is illustrated in Figure 13-2.

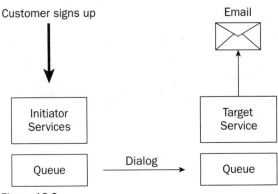

Figure 13-2

When a user signs up on the Web form, his or her information is sent to the contacts table. In addition, the information is sent to a customer service queue (outgoing queue), which is hooked up to an e-mail queue (incoming queue).

Setup

Before getting started, we have to do a couple of setup tasks. The first task is to set up the database to support Service Broker. By default, databases do not allow queues. In the following code, there are two queries. The first query enables the Service Broker, while the second disables it. Please note that you only have to enable Service Broker once for the database, regardless of how many queues you might wish to set up:

```
-- SCRIPT = EnableServiceBroker.sql
-- 1. Enable Service Broker in Adventure Works OLTP database
USE Master
ALTER DATABASE AdventureWorks SET ENABLE_BROKER
GO


/*
-- 2.Disable Service Broker
USE Master
ALTER DATABASE AdventureWorks SET DISABLE_BROKER
GO


*/
```

Now that the Service Broker service is enabled, we should also ensure we have a user under whom the service can run. If you wish to skip this step, you can set up the message type with the authorization of 'dbo', as you are most likely running as the database owner while you play with the scripts in this chapter. Understand, however, that this is not a best practice.

To follow best practices, we are going to perform the following steps:

1. Create a login.
2. Create two schemas.
3. Create a user in the AdventureWorks database for the login created in step 1.
4. Grant rights for this user.

The script to set up this user is shown here:

```
-- SCRIPT = Logins.sql
USE Master
GO


-- 1. Create a Login
CREATE LOGIN [Chapter13Login] WITH PASSWORD=N'pass@word1',
DEFAULT_DATABASE=[AdventureWorks], DEFAULT_LANGUAGE=[us_english],
CHECK_EXPIRATION=ON, CHECK_POLICY=ON
GO


USE [AdventureWorks]
GO


-- 2. Create the User
CREATE USER [Chapter13AWUser] FOR LOGIN [Chapter13Login]
GO


-- 3a.Create Signup Schema
CREATE SCHEMA CustomerSignUpService
  AUTHORIZATION [Chapter13AWUser]
GO


-- 3b.Create Email Schema
CREATE SCHEMA EmailServiceSchema
  AUTHORIZATION [Chapter13AWUser]
GO


-- 4. GRANT rights
-- User needs DDL rights to create Service Broker objects
EXEC sp_addrolemember N'db_ddladmin', N'Chapter15AWUser'

-- Table rights to make it easier to put all objects under one user
/* MISSING */

GO
```

You are now ready to begin working with Service Broker. Before heading into the next section, you should log in as the Chapter13Login account. If you don't, there is no major issue, as long as you are logged in under an account that has dbo rights for the AdventureWorks database, but understand that you might alter the ownership of objects without an AUTHORIZATION clause, which will change the examples listed slightly.

Please check the Wrox Web site (at www.wrox.com) for updates to this section or for additional information.

Message Types

You have to have an agreed-on means of communicating to have meaningful communication. In Service Broker, message types are the method of establishing an agreed-on format for communication. At its simplest, you can set up a message type using the text shown in the code listing that follows. One thing to note: When you set up a message type, you only have 128 characters for the message name. While this is not a major issue in most cases, you can run out of space when you heavily nest a type for organization, like `AdventureWorks.com/SalesApplications/ECommerce/Portals/AdventureWorks-CustomerWebApplication/NewCustomerSignup/CustomerInformation`, which weighs in at 129 characters.

```
-- SCRIPT = CreateMessageType.sql
USE AdventureWorks
GO

-- Create a message type for both services
CREATE MESSAGE TYPE [CustomerInformationMessageType]
    AUTHORIZATION [Chapter13AWUser]
GO
```

When you set up a message as shown in this code, you are using the defaults for both authorization and validation. The default for authorization is the account that you are currently running this script under, while the default for validation is None. What this means is you now have a message type called `CustomerInformation`, which is authorized to your account (most likely `sa` or `dbo` for most of you) that accepts any message sent. We are not overly concerned with authorization, as that sets the owner of the queue; we are, however, concerned about validation.

Let's take a moment to discuss VALIDATION = None, which is the default. While using this form of validation is extremely flexible, it is not a wise form of validation to use when not needed, as it allows an authorized sender to send you anything they desire. If you do not have a thorough check on the messages, you may end up attempting to process a message that causes errors. When you set up a garbage pail, there is a potential someone will throw in some garbage. Make sure you cannot express your message type as XML before heading for None.

We can, however, think of a very good reason to use VALIDATION = None: performance. We say this with a bit of trepidation, however, as many people err on the side of performance whenever they are given a chance. This is a mistake, especially when your application accepts messages from partners outside of your organization. If you require additional performance, particularly with internal services, you can remove validation and gain a few more cycles, realizing that this move will force you to add additional checking on the back end. With complex dialogs, there is the potential you will lose any performance gains you have initiated by turning off validation.

Another option we have seen written up numerous times is VALIDATION = WELL_FORMED_XML. We see this form of validation as only a notch above None. With WELL_FORMED_XML, you can still send garbage messages to the queue, as long as you take the time to create XML messages. Internally, the danger here is someone not formatting their XML message correctly. Externally, it only forces the hacker to format as XML to attempt to cause errors.

WELL_FORMED_XML is not a bad option in all cases, as you might want to use the queue to store to an XML data type column. We cannot envision such a scenario at the moment, but we will agree it is possible. In this case, WELL_FORMED_XML is a much better option than None.

Another potential reason to use XML without a schema is in a case where you have one queue that handles multiple types of XML snippets. While you certainly could accept all sorts of XML messages with a single message type with no validation, we disagree with this reasoning on many levels:

❑ There is a greater likelihood of confusing a colleague about what you are accomplishing. When you set up a message type that accepts many different types of XML snippets, you have effectively obfuscated what your service is set up to handle. It is very flexible, of course.

❑ It is far more maintainable to have a single message type for each specific message format. When you allow multiple message formats in a single message type, you end up writing a lot of logic to determine how to handle the different formats. In most cases, there is more overhead associated with determining where to send a message and adding some form of back-end type checking than there is with setting up multiple queues.

❑ The system is already extremely flexible without creating message types that accept garbage. As you will see, you have the capability to create any number of message types in a contract. The capability to create multiple message types in a single contract allows you to create extremely complex and long running conversations. You can also write to any number of queues, as long as you have a service for each queue.

The following table lists all of the options available for validation, with an explanation of what each type of validation allows. Of these message types, we would stick to `Empty` or `VALID_XML WITH SCHEMA COLLECTION`. Which of the two you choose depends on whether you require "parameters" to get work done. In a queue that fires off work without needing any additional information, you should use `Empty`. Any queue with a message type should use `VALIDATION = VALID_XML WITH SCHEMA COLLECTION`.

Validation Type	Description
None	Any type of message body is acceptable to the service. This is, by far, the most flexible option, but also the most prone to error, as a sender can send anything.
Empty	The message contains no data in the body. This option enables you to use a queue to fire off services that require no parameters to work.
WELL_FORMED_XML	The message body must be well-formed XML. This is only a slight step above None, as a user can send messages you cannot consume, although they will be in an XML format.
VALID_XML WITH SCHEMA COLLECTION	The message body must contain well-formed XML, with a valid schema attached. Note that you must include a schema collection name when using this option.

As our message queue will require information, we will now alter the message type from the earlier code listing to use XML and a schema. To do this, however, we must create a schema for the message type. Because our service is going to be used for customer information, we will get the first and last name, along with the e-mail address, a sign-on name, and a password.

The easiest way to create a schema is with Visual Studio 2005 (or Visual Studio .NET, as the .xsd schema format is present in older versions of Visual Studio, as well):

```
-- SCRIPT = CustomerInfoSchema.sql
CREATE XML SCHEMA COLLECTION CustomerInfoSchema AS
N'<?xml version="1.0" encoding="utf-16"?>
<xsd:schema xmlns:xsd="http://www.w3.org/2001/XMLSchema"
targetNamespace="http://Adventure-Works.com/schemas/expenseReport"
xmlns:expense="http://Adventure-Works.com/schemas/expenseReport"
elementFormDefault="qualified">
    <xsd:complexType name="Customer">
        <xsd:sequence>
            <xsd:element name="FirstName" type="xsd:string" />
            <xsd:element name="LastName" type="xsd:string" />
            <xsd:element name="Password" type="xsd:string" />
            <xsd:element name="EmailAddress" type="xsd:string" />
        </xsd:sequence>
    </xsd:complexType>
</xsd:schema>'
GO
```

You have now created a schema called `CustomerInfoSchema`. You need to alter the message type to use this schema for validation. The name of the schema used to validate is shown in bold in the following code listing. Please note that if you did not already create the message type, change from `ALTER` to `CREATE` in the following script:

```
-- SCRIPT = AlterMessageType.sql
USE AdventureWorks
GO

-- Create a message type for both services
ALTER MESSAGE TYPE [CustomerInformationMessageType]
    VALIDATION = VALID_XML WITH SCHEMA COLLECTION CustomerInfoSchema
GO
```

You now have a message type set up that validates to a particular schema. Only messages that validate to that schema will be accepted once you set up the contract for this service.

In order to create a message type, the user must have permissions. The fixed database roles `db_owner` and `ddl_admin` supply these rights, as does the `sysadmin` fixed server role. This was the reason behind the statement `EXEC sp_addrolemember N'db_ddladmin', N'Chapter13AWUser'` in our setup area, which gave our Chapter 13 user rights to create objects. The `owner`, `db_owner`, and `sysadmin` will have `REFERENCE` permission to the message type. This is important when creating a contract that uses this particular message type.

In the example in this section, both the sending and receiving service are in the same database. You only have to run the message type script once in this case. If you were setting up the sending and receiving services on separate servers, you would need the message type on both servers. This does not necessarily mean the message type must be identical on both instances, however. The rules are as follows:

❏ The name of the message type must be the same on both server instances.

❏ The validation type must be compatible, meaning you cannot have an empty message sent to a service that requires XML, with or without schemas. In most cases, you will want to match types to avoid problems.

Every database has a message type called DEFAULT *that is created with the database. If you want to test a service prior to figuring out your XML schema, you can use this message type to test with. We suggest you only use this message type for demo purposes, however, as it has no validation (*VALIDATION=None*). The script for the* DEFAULT *Message type is shown below:*

```
USE [AdventureWorks]

GO

CREATE MESSAGE TYPE [DEFAULT] AUTHORIZATION [dbo] VALIDATION = NONE
```

Contracts

To facilitate communication between two services with an agreed-on message type name, the next step is setting up a contract. A contract is an agreement between services over how communication is going to take place. The important parts of the contract are the message type being used and the sender of the communication. Before elaborating on the details, let's take a quick look at a simple contract:

```
-- SCRIPT = CreateContract.sql
USE AdventureWorks
GO

-- Illustration only, so no reason to create schema
CREATE MESSAGE TYPE [CreateCustomer] VALIDATION = WELL_FORMED_XML
CREATE MESSAGE TYPE [CustomerCreated] VALIDATION = WELL_FORMED_XML
GO

CREATE CONTRACT [SendCustomerContract]
(
  [CreateCustomer]
  SENT BY INITIATOR,
  [CustomerCreated]
  SENT BY TARGET
)
GO
```

If you get nothing else from this section, make sure you understand that a contract is an agreement between an INITIATOR (a service sending the message) to a TARGET (a service receiving the message) with agreed-on message types specified.

In order to create contracts, the account you are logged in under must be part of the fixed database roles ddl_admin or db_owner or the fixed server role sysadmin. The account must also have REFERENCE permission to the Message Type(s) specified in the contract. All of these roles will have REFERENCE permission on the contract created.

If this example were set up on two servers, you would need to have the contract placed on both servers to fulfill communication.

As with Message types, there is a default contract in each database for SQL Server. The default contract uses the default *message and allows it to be sent by either* INTEROGATOR *or* TARGET. *As with Message Types, this contract should only be used for demo purposes. The script for the default contract is shown here:*

```
USE [AdventureWorks]

GO

CREATE CONTRACT [DEFAULT] AUTHORIZATION [dbo] ([DEFAULT] SENT BY ANY)
```

Queues

Queues are temporary storage places for messages. When you set up a queue in SQL Server 2005, you are creating a specialized type of table. The benefit of this setup is that you can use disaster recovery techniques on queues in the same manner you can for other database objects. One example is backing up queues as part of your nightly backup. We see this as having limited benefit, except in cases where the queue is servicing a person who logs onto the network from a remote location. Most other types of queues will either be cleared out too quickly to have the backup be of any benefit or have messages that expire before restore is completed.

> *You do not have to set up a message type or contract prior to setting up a queue. As the queue is just a special type of table, you have the option of setting it up as the first step. We prefer to wait until the message type and contract are complete, as we believe contract-first development is the best style when working with Service Broker.*

To set up a simple queue, you simply need a name for the queue. The name must be unique, which means you cannot name it with the same fully qualified name as another table (that is, you cannot use the same database schema and table name). While you can give the queue the same name as a table if you use a different schema, we would not advise this, as it is likely to lead to confusion.

The next code listing shows two queues created in the AdventureWorks database. The first queue is used for the E-mail a Customer service, while the second is used for the Customer Sign-up service. Please notice that we have the queue turned off when we set it up. This is not the default behavior, but it is a good practice. You should have queues disabled to ensure they are not used until you are finished setting up the service. You can then alter the queue with an ALTER QUEUE statement and set STATUS = ON.

```
-- SCRIPT = QueueSetup.sql
USE AdventureWorks
GO


-- queue for emailing the new customer
CREATE QUEUE EmailServiceSchema.SignUpEmailQueue
  WITH
    STATUS = OFF
GO

-- queue used by Customer service to receive responses
CREATE QUEUE CustomerSignUpService.NewCustomerSignUpQueue
  WITH
    STATUS = OFF
GO
```

You will notice that the example in this listing is far simpler than creating a table. There are two reasons for this. First, a queue is an extremely simple type of table; after all, it only requires an identifier and a "bucket" to store the messages. Second, you can set other options. Why don't we show you? We're so glad you asked. The options available are shown in the following table.

Options	Information
STATUS	A queue can either be ON or OFF. By default, queues are ON, if you do not explicitly set a status. If you set STATUS to OFF, the queue is completely unavailable, which means you cannot add any messages to the queue. It also means you cannot get any messages out of the queue.
RETENTION	RETENTION can be set to ON or OFF. RETENTION indicates whether messages are cleared from the queue as soon as it is processed or if it is retained for the entire duration of the dialog. By default, retention is set to OFF. As performance degrades when RETENTION is set to ON, you should only retain messages when you need a mechanism to roll back through messages in case of a failure.
ACTIVATION *	With ACTIVATION, you name a stored procedure used to process messages thrown into a queue. ACTIVATION has four sub-options: STATUS, PROCEDURE_NAME, MAX_QUEUE_READERS, and EXECUTE AS.
* STATUS	ACTIVATION STATUS is either ON or OFF. When set to ON, the default, Service Broker will automatically invoke the stored procedure when additional processes have to be started to handle message load.
* PROCEDURE_NAME	Any valid, fully qualified stored procedure name.
* MAX_QUEUE_READERS	This value specifies the maximum number of queue readers that can be running at any one time. The value of MAX_QUEUE_READERS must be between 0 and 32767.
* EXECUTE AS	As mentioned in Chapter 9, this is the account under which the procedure runs. The account that owns the queue must have access to this stored procedure, but setting it to a highly privileged account makes it possible to use objects to which the queue account does not have access.
ON {filegroup}	As a queue is a table, you can place it on any file group available in the database. If you do not specify one, the default is DEFAULT. The main purpose for this option is for organization and performance. In general, this option should be set by a member of your DBA team.

Unlike a contract, you can restructure your queue as needed. This enables you to add a stored procedure that is automatically invoked after you have the queue set up. The following code listing shows the ALTER statement necessary to enable our queue:

```
-- SCRIPT = TurnOnCustomerQueue.sql
USE AdventureWorks
GO

-- queue used by Customer service to receive responses
ALTER QUEUE CustomerSignUpService.NewCustomerSignUpQueue
  WITH
    STATUS = ON
GO
```

If you were setting this up on two servers, the e-mail queue would go on the server that handles sending the e-mail, while the customer sign-up queue would go on the server that stores customer information. Please note that we have only activated one queue at this point. When we get to implementation, you will see the reason for this.

As with other objects mentioned thus far, to create a queue, the account you are logged in under must be in the fixed database roles ddl_admin or db_owner or in the fixed server role sysadmin. Each of these roles, along with the owner, will have permission to reference the queue, while all but ddl_admin will have the right to receive from the queue.

> *Unlike Message Types and contracts, there is no DEFAULT queue available for your use. Three queues are used by the Service Broker itself (EventNotificationErrorsQueue, QueryNotificationErrorsQueue, and ServiceBrokerQueue). Do not attempt to use these queues for your own work.*

Services

Each queue must have a service. Like most of the objects we have created thus far, declaring a service is a simple process. For an outgoing queue you must, at minimum, declare a name for the service and the queue name. This is shown for the customer service queue. For an incoming queue, you also specify the contract name. This is shown for the e-mail service queue. Both are shown in the following code:

```
-- SCRIPT = CreateServices.sql
USE AdventureWorks
GO
-- The Email service
CREATE SERVICE [EmailConfirmationService]
    AUTHORIZATION [Chapter13AWUser]
ON QUEUE EmailServiceSchema.SignUpEmailQueue
([SendCustomerInformationContract])

-- The Customer service
CREATE SERVICE [CustomerSignUpService]
    AUTHORIZATION [Chapter13AWUser]
ON QUEUE CustomerSignUpService.NewCustomerSignUpQueue
GO
```

The rules of the service are simple. If a queue is a TARGET, or accepts incoming messages, a contract must be specified. If no contract is specified, a queue is set up as an INITIATOR, or a sender of messages.

When you set up a service, you must have permissions. By default, the `ddl_admin` and `dbo_owner` fixed database roles have permission to set up a service, as does the `sysadmin` fixed server role. Each of these roles, as well as the owner, has permission to REFERENCE the service, but the `ddl_admin` is excluded from SEND rights.

Note that we have explicitly set the owner of the services. As with other Service Broker objects, if you do not specify an owner, with AUTHORIZATION, the account you are logged in under will be the owner.

Processing Messages

We now have all of the objects in place to communicate. In addition to this infrastructure, we need some plumbing to get things working. When a customer visits the Adventure Works Web site, there is a sign-up form for an account. Sign-up is synchronous, but the e-mail sent back to the customer is not.

The Web Application

The entry point for the entire system is the form with which the user signs up. This is a simple form that asks for the new customer's first and last name, the e-mail address, and a password. Please note that this is not a book on ASP.NET, so there is no input checking on the form, nor any validation. If we were to move this to a working app, we would add these best practices. The ASPX, or tagged, portion of this page is shown in the following code:

```
<%@ Page Language="VB" AutoEventWireup="false" CodeFile="CustomerSignUp.aspx.vb"
Inherits="CustomerSignUp" %>

<!DOCTYPE html PUBLIC "-//W3C//DTD XHTML 1.1//EN"
"http://www.w3.org/TR/xhtml11/DTD/xhtml11.dtd">

<html xmlns="http://www.w3.org/1999/xhtml" >
<head id="Head1" runat="server">
  <title>Customer Sign Up Form</title>
</head>
<body>
  <form id="form1" runat="server">
  <div>
    <h1>Customer Sign Up</h1>
    <table>
      <tr>
        <td style="width: 127px">First Name:</td>
        <td style="width: 191px">
          <asp:TextBox ID="txtFirstName" runat="server"></asp:TextBox></td>
      </tr>
      <tr>
        <td style="width: 127px">Last Name:</td>
        <td style="width: 191px">
          <asp:TextBox ID="txtLastName" runat="server"></asp:TextBox>
        </td>
      </tr>
      <tr>
        <td style="width: 127px">Email Address:</td>
        <td style="width: 191px">
          <asp:TextBox ID="txtEmailAddress" runat="server"></asp:TextBox>
        </td>
```

```
        </tr>
        <tr>
          <td style="width: 127px">Password:</td>
          <td style="width: 191px">
            <asp:TextBox ID="txtPassword" runat="server"></asp:TextBox>
          </td>
        </tr>
        <tr>
          <td style="width: 127px"></td>
          <td style="width: 191px">
            <asp:Button ID="btnSubmit" runat="server" Text="Submit" /></td>
        </tr>
      </table>
    </div>
  </form>
</body>
</html>
```

To handle the Submit button click, we will create a routine that sends the customer information to a stored procedure called AddNewCustomer, which is detailed a bit later in this section. The Submit button click handler is shown in the following code listing. Note that the code here is very similar to code in earlier sections, so we will not cover it in great detail. If you skipped the ADO.NET sections of this book (yes, we're dreaming), here is a brief list of the steps:

1. Create a connection string. Normally, this would be pulled from somewhere other than the page, per best practices.

2. Create a string for the stored procedure name.

3. Create a SqlConnection object.

4. Create a SqlCommand object. The CommandType must be set to StoredProcedure, or this will be a short ride.

5. Create a parameter object for every one of the parameters in the stored procedure and attach the parameters to the command object parameter collection.

6. Open the connection and execute the command.

7. Clean up the connection object with Dispose(). We have this coded in a Finally statement to ensure that cleanup occurs even if there is a problem executing the command.

```
Imports System.Data.SqlClient

Partial Class CustomerSignUp
    Inherits System.Web.UI.Page

    Protected Sub btnSubmit_Click(ByVal sender As Object, _
                 ByVal e As System.EventArgs) Handles btnSubmit.Click

        Dim connString As String = _
             "Server=(local);Database=AdventureWorks;UID=sa;PWD=pass@word1"
        Dim sproc As String = "AddNewCustomer"

        Dim conn As New SqlConnection(connString)
```

```
            Dim cmd As New SqlCommand(sproc, conn)

            cmd.CommandType = Data.CommandType.StoredProcedure

            Dim param As New SqlParameter("@FirstName", Data.SqlDbType.NVarChar)
            param.Value = txtFirstName.Text
            cmd.Parameters.Add(param)

            param = New SqlParameter("@LastName", Data.SqlDbType.NVarChar)
            param.Value = txtLastName.Text
            cmd.Parameters.Add(param)

            param = New SqlParameter("@EmailAddress", Data.SqlDbType.NVarChar)
            param.Value = txtEmailAddress.Text
            cmd.Parameters.Add(param)

            param = New SqlParameter("@Password", Data.SqlDbType.NVarChar)
            param.Value = txtPassword.Text
            cmd.Parameters.Add(param)

            Try
                conn.Open()
                cmd.ExecuteNonQuery()
            Finally
                conn.Dispose()
            End Try

        End Sub
End Class
```

You now have a Web form to submit data. If you were to run it right now, it would throw an error, as the stored procedure to handle the customer sign-up is not complete.

Customer Sign-Up Service

The stored procedure that starts the chain of events for sign-up is shown in the following code. We will run through each of the sections after we take a brief look at the sample. Please note that we are not inserting anything into the database, as this is a Service Broker example. We have added a TODO comment where you would place code to insert into the Contact table if this were a live sign-up form.

```
-- SCRIPT = AddNewCustomer.sql
USE AdventureWorks
GO

SET QUOTED_IDENTIFIER ON
GO

-- stored procedure to send customer details to Email service
CREATE PROCEDURE CustomerSignUpService.AddNewCustomer
(
    @FirstName      nvarchar(50),
    @LastName       nvarchar(50),
    @EmailAddress   nvarchar(50),
    @Password       nvarchar(8)
```

```
)
AS
BEGIN
  DECLARE @message NVARCHAR(MAX)
  SET @message = NCHAR(0xFEFF)
    + '<Customer>'
        + '<FirstName>' + @FirstName + '</FirstName>'
        + '<LastName>' + @LastName + '</LastName>'
        + '<EmailAddress>' + @EmailAddress + '</EmailAddress>'
        + '<Password>' + @Password + '</Password>'
    + '</Customer>'

  --TODO: INSERT INTO Contact table here

  DECLARE @conversationHandle UNIQUEIDENTIFIER

  BEGIN DIALOG @conversationHandle
   FROM SERVICE [CustomerSignUpService]
   TO SERVICE 'EmailConfirmationService'
   ON CONTRACT [SendCustomerInformationContract];

  SEND ON CONVERSATION @conversationHandle
      MESSAGE TYPE [CustomerInformationMessageType]
     (@message)

END
GO
```

The basic setup for a stored procedure has been highlighted in Chapter 9, so we're not concerned about the top portion. The first section of interest is the one that creates our XML string. This is a very low-tech solution to our problem, as we're simply creating a string and storing it in an nvarchar(MAX) variable. Next, we have the code that creates the XML, along with the schema created earlier:

```
/* Stored Procedure Code */
  DECLARE @message NVARCHAR(MAX)
  SET @message = NCHAR(0xFEFF)
    + '<Customer>'
        + '<FirstName>' + @FirstName + '</FirstName>'
        + '<LastName>' + @LirstName + '</LastName>'
        + '<EmailAddress>' + @EmailAddress + '</EmailAddress>'
        + '<Password>' + @Password + '</Password>'
    + '</Customer>'

/* Schema the Stored Procedure adheres to */
CREATE XML SCHEMA COLLECTION CustomerInfoSchema AS
N'<?xml version="1.0" encoding="utf-16"?>
<xsd:schema xmlns:xsd="http://www.w3.org/2001/XMLSchema"
targetNamespace="http://Adventure-Works.com/schemas/expenseReport"
xmlns:expense="http://Adventure-Works.com/schemas/expenseReport"
elementFormDefault="qualified">
    <xsd:complexType name="Customer">
        <xsd:sequence>
            <xsd:element name="FirstName" type="xsd:string" />
            <xsd:element name="LastName" type="xsd:string" />
```

```
            <xsd:element name="Password" type="xsd:string" />
            <xsd:element name="EmailAddress" type="xsd:string" />
        </xsd:sequence>
    </xsd:complexType>
</xsd:schema>'
GO
```

It's important that an element be created for every required element in the schema. If not, the Message Type will be invalidated, creating an error from the queue. The next step is the creation of a conversation. This is shown in the following code listing. A dialog requires a conversation handler, which is created by the Service Broker service. If you are sending multiple messages to a queue, you will have to retain this handle for subsequent messages.

```
DECLARE @conversationHandle UNIQUEIDENTIFIER

BEGIN DIALOG @conversationHandle
    FROM SERVICE [CustomerSignUpService]
    TO SERVICE 'EmailConfirmationService'
    ON CONTRACT [SendCustomerInformationContract];
```

In this example, we simply have to specify a FROM SERVICE and a TO SERVICE, as both are in the same database. If we were dealing with two databases, our example would get a bit more complex, as we would have to specify the Service Broker GUID for the target database. Provided the database is on the same server, it is simply a matter of pulling the information from the sys.databases catalog view.

The following code shows how to alter a stored procedure when you are dealing with two different databases for the initiating and target services. In this example, we are assuming that the database with the e-mail send is some form of CRM database. Note that this code is for illustrative purposes only, as the CRM database does not exist in any of the samples:

```
DECLARE @TargetDatabaseID uniqueidentifier

SELECT @TargetDatabaseID = service_broker_guid
FROM sys.databases
WHERE [name] = 'AdventureWorksCRMDatabase'

DECLARE @conversationHandle UNIQUEIDENTIFIER

BEGIN DIALOG @conversationHandle
    FROM SERVICE [CustomerSignUpService]
    TO SERVICE 'EmailConfirmationService'
            , @TargetDatabaseID
    ON CONTRACT [SendCustomerInformationContract];
```

The final step for the customer sign-up side is to actually send the message to the queue, as shown in the following code. Initially, the message will be sent to the customer sign-up queue. Provided the e-mail service queue is not disabled, it will be sent over to that queue, where it will be handled by the e-mail service:

```
SEND ON CONVERSATION @conversationHandle
    MESSAGE TYPE [CustomerInformationMessageType]
  (@message)
```

Before continuing, you should fill out the form from the Web app and submit a couple of new customers. As an alternative option, you can run the following script, which will create our new customers:

```
-- Add customers
USE AdventureWorks
GO
EXEC CustomerSignUpService.AddNewCustomer
   'Jane',
   'Roe',
   'jane@somewhere.com',
   'pass@word1'

EXEC CustomerService.AddNewCustomer
   'John',
   'Doe',
   'john@nowhere.com',
   'pass@word1'
```

At this point in time, the customer service queue is up and running, but the e-mail queue is not. This means we now have messages in the customer service queue, but none in the e-mail queue. To test this, run the following script:

```
USE AdventureWorks
GO

SELECT * FROM CustomerSignUpService.NewCustomerSignUpQueue
GO
```

You should see the messages you created, either from the preceding script or the Web application. To get the messages to forward, you need to enable the e-mail queue. At this point, we have no stored procedure to handle the e-mail queue, so we are simply going to turn it on. Later in the chapter, we will show you how to alter this again to automatically use a stored procedure as a service handler. Run the following ALTER script, followed by the SELECT from the e-mail queue and you should see your messages appear in the e-mail queue in short order:

```
USE AdventureWorks
GO

ALTER QUEUE EmailServiceSchema.SignUpEmailQueue
   WITH
     STATUS = ON
GO

SELECT * FROM EmailServiceSchema.SignUpEmailQueue
GO
```

E-mail Sending Service

Now that we have sent a message to the queue and it has been forwarded to the e-mail service queue, the next step is to process this message. The stored procedure that handles this queue is shown in the following code (we will go through this step by step in this section):

```
-- stored procedure to read and process messages from queue
CREATE PROCEDURE EmailServiceSchema.ProcessMessages
AS
  WHILE (1 = 1)
  BEGIN
    DECLARE @conversationHandle UNIQUEIDENTIFIER,
      @messageTypeName NVARCHAR(256),
      @messageBody NVARCHAR(MAX);

    RECEIVE TOP(1)
      @conversationHandle = conversation_handle,
      @messageTypeName = message_type_name,
      @messageBody = message_body
    FROM NewCustomerEmailQueue

    IF  @messageTypeName = 'http://schemas.microsoft.com/SQL/ServiceBroker/Error'
OR
      @messageTypeName = 'http://schemas.microsoft.com/SQL/ServiceBroker/EndDialog'
    BEGIN
      END CONVERSATION @conversationHandle
      CONTINUE
    END

    IF @messageTypeName <> 'CustomerDetails'
    BEGIN
      END CONVERSATION @conversationHandle
        WITH ERROR = 500
          DESCRIPTION = 'Invalid message type.'
      CONTINUE
    END

    DECLARE @customerName nvarchar(50)
            , @emailAddress nvarchar(50)
            , @password nvarchar(8)

  -- Get our information to email
  EXEC sp_xml_preparedocument @idoc OUTPUT, @XMLstring

  SELECT  @customerName = CustomerName,
     @emailAddress = EmailAddress
  FROM OPENXML (@idoc, '/Customer',2)
  WITH (CustomerName  Name, EmailAddress Name)

  EXEC sp_xml_removedocument @idoc

    -- send an email using SQLiMail
    EXEC sendimail_sp @profile_name = 'Email Service Mail Profile',
            @recipients= @emailAddress,
            @subject='Thank your for signing up at Adventure Works',
            @body='Your account has been created with the email address '
                  + @emailAddress + ' and the password '
                  + @password

    END CONVERSATION @conversationHandle
  END
GO
```

The first step in this procedure is to pull the message information from the queue. The important bits of information, as this is a one-way queueing mechanism, are the message type name, the message body, and the conversation handler:

```
DECLARE @conversationHandle UNIQUEIDENTIFIER,
    @messageTypeName NVARCHAR(256),
    @messageBody NVARCHAR(MAX);

RECEIVE TOP(1)
    @conversationHandle = conversation_handle,
    @messageTypeName = message_type_name,
    @messageBody = message_body
FROM NewCustomerEmailQueue
```

After we pull the information from the queue, the next step is to ensure that we have not pulled a message with an error or one that states we should end the conversation. We also have to ensure that the MessageType is not something other than what we were expecting. If any of these conditions are true, we should abort the conversation immediately.

```
-- Service Broker messages.
IF  @messageTypeName = 'http://schemas.microsoft.com/SQL/ServiceBroker/Error' OR
        @messageTypeName = 'http://schemas.microsoft.com/SQL/ServiceBroker/EndDialog'
    BEGIN
        END CONVERSATION @conversationHandle
        CONTINUE
    END

-- Wrong message type
IF @messageTypeName <> 'CustomerDetails'
    BEGIN
        END CONVERSATION @conversationHandle
            WITH ERROR = 500
                DESCRIPTION = 'Invalid message type.'
        CONTINUE
    END
```

The syntax for END CONVERSATION is rather simple. At a minimum, you simply pass in the conversation handler and end the dialog. If you would like to specify an error, you use the WITH ERROR statement, followed by an error number that you designate (this number should be documented, as Service Broker examples can get far more complex over time). In addition, you can add a DESCRIPTION to send back to the initiator.

In END CONVERSATION, there is one additional option that you can specify: WITH CLEANUP. WITH CLEANUP runs through the queue and deletes all of the messages in this particular conversation, cleaning up the queue. Make sure you cannot salvage the conversation before invoking this option, however, because WITH CLEANUP simply clears out its own queue. There is no notification to the other side of the conversation that this has happened.

The next step is to create an e-mail message and send it to the customer. Currently, we have only XML sent to us, so we have to, at minimum, pull the information we need from the message body. The code to do this is shown here:

```
DECLARE @docPointer int
EXEC sp_xml_preparedocument @docPointer OUTPUT, @XMLstring

SELECT @customerName = CustomerName,
       @emailAddress = EmailAddress,
       @password     = Password
FROM OPENXML (@docPointer, '/Customer', 2)
WITH (CustomerName  nvarchar(50), EmailAddress nvarchar(50),
      Password nvarchar(50))

EXEC sp_xml_removedocument @idoc
```

In this code, we make a call to the system stored procedure sp_xml_preparedoc. This has two parameters: an integer for the document pointer and the XML string we are feeding to this procedure. After this, we use OPEN XML to open the document, using the document pointer, the node we wish to start at, and a flag to indicate whether the mapping is attribute-centric (1), element-centric (2), or both (3). In our case, we have used elements, so this is set to 2.

The next step is to send the e-mail message and end the conversation. To send the message, we are using the SQL Server 2005's new SQL iMail feature. The stored procedure takes a profile name, a recipient(s) list, a subject, and a body:

```
-- send an email using SQLiMail
EXEC sendimail_sp @profile_name = 'Email Service Mail Profile',
        @recipients= @emailAddress,
        @subject='Thank your for signing up at Adventure Works',
        @body='Your account has been created with the email address '
              + @emailAddress + ' and the password '
              + @password

END CONVERSATION @conversationHandle
```

As the e-mail queue was disabled when we started this process, you will have to run the following script to process the e-mail messages. In the code samples for this book, we have the actual e-mail send commented out. If you have SQL iMail configured on your server, you can uncomment the section and send test e-mails. The command to fire off the stored procedure is shown in the following code. There is also a test statement to ensure messages were processed.

```
USE AdventureWorks
GO

EXEC EmailServiceSchema.ProcessMessages
GO

SELECT * FROM EmailServiceSchema.SignUpEmailQueue
GO
```

Automating the Entire Service

We need to add a couple of alterations to automate the entire process. First, we have to alter our e-mail queue again to make sure it automatically invokes the stored procedure. The alteration is shown here:

```
ALTER QUEUE EmailServiceSchema.SignUpEmailQueue
   WITH
     STATUS = ON
   WITH ACTIVATION
     (PROCEDURE_NAME = EmailServiceSchema.ProcessMessages,
       EXECUTE AS [Chapter13AWUser])
GO
```

In addition, we have to make sure that only one message is processed. To do this, comment out the line WHILE (1 = 1) in the ProcessEmail stored procedure. You can now sign up on the Web site and run the e-mail service.

We have included a couple of tweaks to the samples in this chapter, which you can download with the book samples. Once you have fully automated the services, you will not see any output if you do not have SQL iMail enabled. To ensure that the services are, in fact, working, we have a script that creates a log table and logs the information from both queues in this table. If you run this script, you can query the log table to see what has transpired as the services fire.

Routes

A *route* is a pathway for communication, from service to service. Dialogs take place over routes. In the example shown in this section, there was no need for a route, as all of the communication took place in one database. This is fine, because the portion we were worried about bogging down our server was the sending of an e-mail message, which can be done at any time. A route can be created as simply as the statement in this code:

```
USE AdventureWorks
GO

CREATE ROUTE MyRoute
    AUTHORIZATION [Chapter13AWUser]
WITH
    ADDRESS = 'TCP://MyNewServer:1433'
GO
```

The route in this code is largely useless, however, as it establishes nothing other than a route from one server to another. If you were to create a route like this, you would have a pathway without any information on the service being contacted. For our purposes, this is not a useful route.

To make this more applicable, let's suppose that Adventure Works has built a new SQL Server machine to handle e-mailing customers. This server will handle e-mailing new customers who are signing up, as well as order fulfillment and sending out e-mails when orders are fulfilled. To run this sample, you will need two computers, two Virtual PC images, or two separate instances running on a single machine.

In order to do this, we have to create the queue, contract, message type(s), and e-mail service on the new database. This is done by running the following script on the new database. The downloadable sample also includes a script to create the new AWFulfillment database and turn on Service Broker in this database:

```
USE Master
GO
-- 1. Create a Login
CREATE LOGIN [Chapter13Login] WITH PASSWORD=N'pass@word1',
DEFAULT_DATABASE=[AdventureWorks], DEFAULT_LANGUAGE=[us_english],
CHECK_EXPIRATION=ON, CHECK_POLICY=ON
GO


USE [AWFulfillment]
GO


-- 2. Create the User
CREATE USER [Chapter13AWUser] FOR LOGIN [Chapter13Login]
GO


-- 3.Create Email Schema
CREATE SCHEMA EmailServiceSchema
  AUTHORIZATION [Chapter13AWUser]
GO


-- 4. Create the Schema Collection for the Message Type
CREATE XML SCHEMA COLLECTION CustomerInfoSchema AS
N'<?xml version="1.0" encoding="utf-16"?>
<xsd:schema xmlns:xsd="http://www.w3.org/2001/XMLSchema"
targetNamespace="http://Adventure-Works.com/schemas/expenseReport"
xmlns:expense="http://Adventure-Works.com/schemas/expenseReport"
elementFormDefault="qualified">
    <xsd:complexType name="Customer">
        <xsd:sequence>
            <xsd:element name="FirstName" type="xsd:string" />
            <xsd:element name="LastName" type="xsd:string" />
            <xsd:element name="Password" type="xsd:string" />
            <xsd:element name="EmailAddress" type="xsd:string" />
        </xsd:sequence>
    </xsd:complexType>
</xsd:schema>'
GO


-- 5. Create the Message Type
CREATE MESSAGE TYPE [CustomerInformationMessageType]
    AUTHORIZATION [Chapter13AWUser]
    VALIDATION = VALID_XML WITH SCHEMA COLLECTION CustomerInfoSchema
GO


-- 6. Create the Contract
CREATE CONTRACT [SendCustomerInformationContract]
(
    AUTHORIZATION [Chapter13AWUser]
  [CustomerInformationMessageType]
  SENT BY INITIATOR
)
GO


-- Create stored procedure
CREATE PROCEDURE EmailServiceSchema.ProcessMessages
```

```
AS
  WHILE (1 = 1)
  BEGIN
    DECLARE @conversationHandle UNIQUEIDENTIFIER,
      @messageTypeName NVARCHAR(256),
      @messageBody NVARCHAR(MAX);

    RECEIVE TOP(1)
      @conversationHandle = conversation_handle,
      @messageTypeName = message_type_name,
      @messageBody = message_body
    FROM NewCustomerEmailQueue

    IF  @messageTypeName = 'http://schemas.microsoft.com/SQL/ServiceBroker/Error'
OR
      @messageTypeName = 'http://schemas.microsoft.com/SQL/ServiceBroker/EndDialog'
    BEGIN
      END CONVERSATION @conversationHandle
      CONTINUE
    END

    IF @messageTypeName <> 'CustomerDetails'
    BEGIN
      END CONVERSATION @conversationHandle
        WITH ERROR = 500
          DESCRIPTION = 'Invalid message type.'
      CONTINUE
    END

    DECLARE @customerName nvarchar(50)
          , @emailAddress nvarchar(50)
          , @password nvarchar(8)

  -- Get our information to email
  EXEC sp_xml_preparedocument @idoc OUTPUT, @XMLstring

  SELECT  @customerName = CustomerName,
    @emailAddress = EmailAddress
  FROM OPENXML (@idoc, '/Customer',2)
  WITH (CustomerName  Name, EmailAddress Name)

  EXEC sp_xml_removedocument @idoc

    -- send an email using SQLiMail
    EXEC sendimail_sp @profile_name = 'Email Service Mail Profile',
            @recipients= @emailAddress,
            @subject='Thank your for signing up at Adventure Works',
            @body='Your account has been created with the email address '
                + @emailAddress + ' and the password '
                + @password

    END CONVERSATION @conversationHandle
  END
```

```
GO

-- Create the QUEUE
CREATE QUEUE EmailServiceSchema.SignUpEmailQueue
  WITH
    STATUS = ON
  WITH ACTIVATION
    (PROCEDURE_NAME = EmailServiceSchema.ProcessMessages,
      EXECUTE AS [Chapter13AWUser])
GO

-- Create the Service
CREATE SERVICE [EmailServiceSchema.EmailConfirmationService]
    AUTHORIZATION [Chapter13AWUser]
ON QUEUE EmailServiceSchema.SignUpEmailQueue
([SendCustomerInformationContract])
GO
```

In order to facilitate the route, one more step has to be performed on the new database. Run the script in the following code to get the `id` of the Service Broker instance for the new database:

```
USE Master
GO

SELECT service_broker_guid
FROM sys.databases
WHERE [name] = 'AWFulfillment'
GO
```

Next, we have to create a route from one server to another. In this instance, we are dealing with what is essentially a one-way route, as we are only sending messages from our customer service queue to our e-mail queue. The route script in the preceding code listing is, therefore, only run on the original database. Paste the `service_broker_guid` from this code into the first bolded section of the script. You will also need either the machine name or the IP address of the new server. We assume the service is on a machine called `FulfillmentServer` for the purposes of this exercise; this is also bolded in the script, as you will have to use the IP address or name of your server:

```
USE AdventureWorks
GO

DECLARE @service_broker_guid uniqueidentifier
SET @service_broker_guid = '{Paste GUID here}'

CREATE ROUTE EmailServiceRoute
  AUTHORIZATION [Chapter13AWUser]
WITH
  SERVICE_NAME = EmailServiceSchema.EmailConfirmationService,
  BROKER_INSTANCE = @service_broker_guid,
  LIFETIME = NULL,
  ADDRESS = 'TCP://FulfillmentServer:1433'
GO
```

Finally, we have to delete the service on the old server in order to have it use the service on the new server (via the route we are creating). Here is the script that accomplishes this:

```
USE AdventureWorks
GO

DROP SERVICE EmailServiceSchema.EmailConfirmationService
GO
```

You now can test the route by running through the test scripts presented earlier in this section. If you turn off the e-mail queue, you will now see messages retained on the original server.

Technical Bits

This section deals with what goes on under the hood in Service Broker. The first part of this section deals with the queue table(s) and gives you brief information about how to query a queue. As you have already queried a queue in the previous section, the main focus is on the columns in a queue, what data they contain, and which items are linked to other tables or views.

The second part of this section covers catalog views included in all SQL Server 2005 databases that you can query to find out more about the internal workings of Service Broker.

Queues

As mentioned earlier in the chapter, when you create a queue in SQL Server 2005, it is created as a specialized type of table. There are few options, as the structure of the table is already set. Without hacking deep into SQL Server, you do not have access to alter this table structure, which is a good thing. Understanding the structure, however, gives you an understanding of how a queue works. The table structure is in the following table.

Column Name	Data Type	Description
status	tinyint	The current status of a message in the queue. Valid values are as follows: 0 = Ready 1=Received message 2=Not yet complete 3=Retained sent message Note that you must have RETENTION=ON to retain the message.
queueing_order	bigint	This is the message order number in the queue.

Column Name	Data Type	Description
conversation_group_id	uniqueidentifier	Identifier for the conversation group to which the message belongs. This is the same as `conversation_group_id` in the catalog view `sys.conversation_groups`.
conversation_handle	uniqueidentifier	The handle of the conversation. When you begin to receive a conversation, you can query the handle and use it to later end a conversation.
message_sequence_number	bigint	Sequence number of a message in a conversation. This is the order in which the message is placed under a particular `conversation_group_id` or `conversation_handle`.
service_name	nvarchar(512)	Name of the service handling the conversation.
service_id	int	SQL Server object id for the service handling the conversation. This is the same value as `ID` in the `sys.sysobjects` catalog view.
service_contract_name	nvarchar(256)	Name of the contract under which this conversation is held.
service_contract_id	int	The id for the contract under which the conversation is held. This is the same as `service_contract_id` in the `sys.service_contracts` catalog view.
message_type_name	nvarchar(256)	Name of the message type that describes this message.
message_type_id	Int	The id for the message type that describes this message. This is the same as `message_type_id` in the `sys.service_message_types` catalog view.
validation	nchar(2)	Type of validation used for the message type. This is the same as the field validation in the `sys.service_message_types` catalog view.
message_body	varbinary(MAX)	The body of the message. Depending on the validation type, this can be converted to an XML message or left as binary information.

The following code listing has a script you can use to get information from the e-mail queue table you have worked with in this chapter. We could have linked to service views as well, but much of the queue is denormalized (information pulled over from other views and tables for performance), so it is an unnecessary step.

```
USE AdventureWorks
GO

SELECT e.message_body
        , CASE e.status WHEN 0 THEN 'Ready'
                WHEN 1 THEN 'Received Message'
                WHEN 2 THEN 'Not yet complete'
                ELSE 'Retained' END AS Status
        , e.message_type_name
        , e.service_contract_name
        , e.service_name
FROM EmailServiceSchema.SignUpEmailQueue e
GO
```

Service Broker Catalog Views

Realizing the danger one could get into poking around at Service Broker tables, Microsoft has hidden these tables. Because there are situations in which you need information about Service Broker, the SQL Server team has made information available through catalog views. The catalog views for Service Broker are shown in the following table. We have included the columns in each of these views, as well as their primary keys (PKs) and foreign keys (FKs).

Catalog View	Description
sys.service_contract_message_usages	Each side of a Service Broker dialog has an endpoint. This view contains a row for each endpoint. This view is a junction between `sys.service_contracts` and `sys.service_message_types`. COLUMNS: `service_contract_id` (FK to `sys.service_contracts.contract_id`), `message_type_id` (FK to `sys.service_message_types.message_type_id`), `is_sent_by_initiator`, and `is_sent_by_target`
sys.service_contract_usages	This view contains a row showing the linkage between Message Types and Contracts. Each row contains the `message_type_id` and `service_contract_id` as well as 2 bits to indicate whether it is initiated by the INITIATOR or TARGET. This view is a junction between `sys.service_contracts` and `sys.services`. COLUMNS: `service_id` (FK to `sys.services.service_id`), and `service_contract_id` (FK to `sys.service_contracts.service_contract_id`)

Catalog View	Description
sys.conversation_groups	This view contains a row for each service in a conversation group. COLUMNS: `conversation_group_id` (PK), `service_id` (FK to `sys.services.service_id`), `is_system`
sys.remote_service_bindings	This view contains a row for each binding to a remote service. COLUMNS: `[name]`, `remote_service_binding_id` (PK), `principal_id` (FK to `sys.sysuers.uid`), `remote_service_name`, `service_contract_id` (FK to `sys.service_contracts.service_contract_id`), `remote_principal_id` (FK to `sys.remote_logins.local_principal_id`), and `is_anonymous_on`
sys.routes	Service broker uses routes to locate a network address for a service. Each row contains a single route. COLUMNS: `[name]`, `route_id` (PK), `principal_id` (FK to `sys.sysusers.uid`), `remote_service_name`, `broker_instance`, `lifetime`, `address`, `mirror_address`
sys.service_contracts	This view contains a row for each contract used by Service Broker. COLUMNS: `[name]`, `service_contract_id` (PK), `principal_id` (FK to `sys.sysusers.uid`)
sys.service_message_types	This view contains a row for each message type, including the schema used (if you have validated XML as your type). COLUMNS: `[name]`, `message_type_id` (PK), `principal_id` (FK to `sys.sysusers.uid`), `validation`, `validation_desc`, `xml_collection_id` (FK to `sys.xml_schema_collections.xml_collection_id`)

Table continued on following page

Catalog View	Description
sys.services	This view contains a row for each service for use in Service Broker. COLUMNS: [name], service_id (PK), principal_id (FK to sys.sysusers.uid), service_queue_id (FK to sys.service_queues.object_id or sys.sysobjects.[id])
sys.service_queues	This view contains a row for every queue used by Service Broker. COLUMNS: [name], object_id (PK & FK to sys.sysobjects.[id]), principal_id (FK to sys.sysusers.uid), schema_id (FK to sys.schemas.schema_id), parent_object_id (FK to sys.sysobjects.[id]), type, type_desc, create_dat, modify_date, is_ms_shipped, is_published, is_schema_published, max_readers, activation_procedure, execute_as_principal_id, is_activation_enable, is_receive_enabled, is_enqueue_enabled, is_retention_enabled

To get an idea of how to use these views, it is best to look at an example. Let's say you want to find out all contracts and their associated message types as well as the owners of both the contracts and the message types. In addition, you would like to know whether a message can be sent by the INITIATOR or TARGET, as well as the validation type and the schema name, if XML with schema. The SQL query necessary to get this information is shown below:

```
SELECT c.service_contract_id As ContractID
     , c.[name] As ContractName
     , su2.[name] As ContractOwner
     , mt.[name] As MessageTypeName
     , su.[name] As MessageTypeOwner
     , mt.validation_desc
     , CASE WHEN (mu.is_sent_by_initiator=1)
             AND (mu.is_sent_by_target = 1) THEN 'ANY'
         WHEN (mu.is_sent_by_initiator=1) THEN 'INITIATOR'
         ELSE 'TARGET' END AS SentBy
     , CASE WHEN mt.xml_collection_id IS NULL THEN 'None'
         ELSE x.[name] END AS ValidationSchema
FROM sys.service_message_types mt
JOIN sys.service_contract_message_usages mu
        ON mt.message_type_id = mu.message_type_id
JOIN sys.service_contracts c
        ON mu.service_contract_id = c.service_contract_id
JOIN sys.sysusers su
        ON mt.principal_id = su.uid
```

```
JOIN sys.sysusers su2
        ON c.principal_id = su2.uid
LEFT JOIN sys.xml_schema_collections x
        ON mt.xml_collection_id = x.xml_collection_id
ORDER BY c.service_contract_id, mt.message_type_id
```

Making It Easier

Niels Berglund has created a tool for administering Service Broker called *SSB Admin*. You can download a copy from his site by searching the blog at `http://staff.develop.com/nielsb/`. (We have the most current link for the source project in the "For More Information" section of this chapter. We aren't going to go into great detail about the product, but we did want to give you a quick overview, as this tool can save you a lot of typing.)

When you open SSB, you are greeted with a screen similar to the one shown in Figure 13-3. We say "similar," as we have already opened the database tree to show the Service Broker information found in the AdventureWorks database. The tool will prompt you to log on when you choose a server.

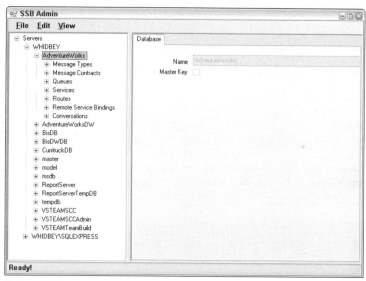

Figure 13-3

To create the message type we have worked with in this chapter, you would simply right-click Message Types and click New. You will be greeted by the screen shown in Figure 13-4.

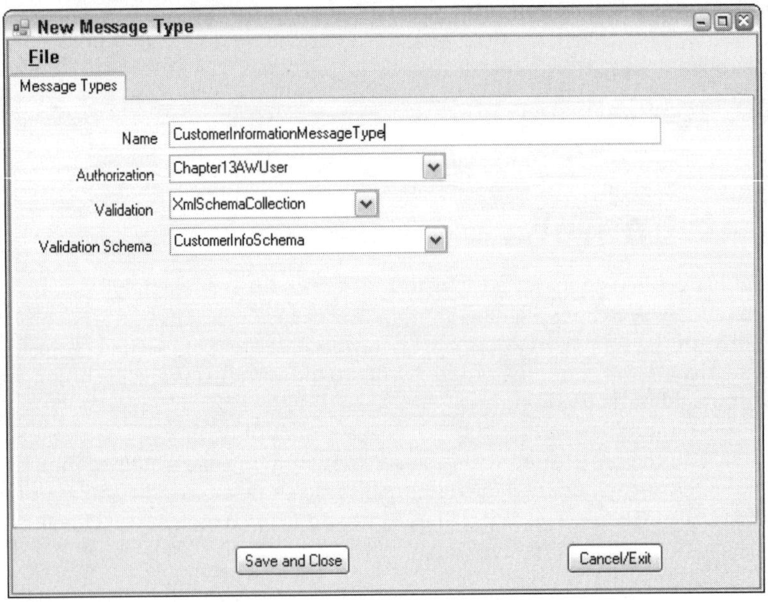

Figure 13-4

The resulting message type is shown here:

```
CREATE MESSAGE TYPE CustomerInformationMessageType
    AUTHORIZATION Chapter13AWUser
    VALIDATION = VALID_XML WITH SCHEMA COLLECTION CustomerInfoSchema
GO
```

Dan Sullivan has created a tool called SQL Service Broker Explorer, which can be downloaded from the SQL Service Broker community site, located at www.sqlservicebroker.com; the direct link is www.sqlservicebroker.com/forums/ShowPost.aspx?PostID=80. Currently, we have been unable to get a good build of the tool.

Summary

In this chapter, you learned how to set up asynchronous applications using Service Broker. The key concepts you learned focus mostly on the objects you use with Service Broker:

❑ **Message Type:** Message types are used to set up the format of the communication. You have the option to validate against a schema, allow XML only, allow empty messages only, or allow any type of message (NONE).

❑ **Contracts:** In Service Broker, the contract specifies which of the parties is going to communicate: the sender (INITIATOR), the receiver (TARGET), or both (ANY). It also specifies which message types (formats) are going to be used in the communication.

❑ **Queue:** A queue is a specialized type of table in SQL Server 2005. Because it is a table, you can use any of the High Availability and Disaster Recovery mechanisms on a queue. As a best practice, you should initially set up a queue in a disabled (STATUS = OFF) state.

❑ **Service:** An endpoint of communication. Services watch queues for messages or send messages through queues.

❑ **Dialog:** Two-way communication between two services connected via queues.

❑ **Route:** A pathway for communication between services located on different instances or servers.

For More Information

To complement the information in this chapter, take a look at the following resources:

❑ **MSDN SQL Server site** — http://msdn.microsoft.com/SQL/. This is the first place to search for information about Service Broker. Currently, you have to make an additional click to get to SQL Server 2005–specific information, but this will likely change in the future.

The MSDN site also has a great article that introduces you to the basic concepts of SQL Server. According to developer/evangelist Kirk Evans (Microsoft's Atlanta field office), it is the best article for those starting to delve into this technology (of course, he hasn't read this chapter yet). The article is a bit dated now, but it still contains a very useful overview: http://msdn.microsoft.com/library/en-us/dnsql90/html/sqlsvcbroker.asp.

❑ **The Microsoft Events site** — www.microsoft.com/events. Here you can find Webcasts, chats, and local events. To find Service Broker–specific events and others, use the advanced search engine, located at www.microsoft.com/events/AdvSearch.mspx. Check out these Webcasts in particular (note that the links require additional clicks, as the direct links are rather long):

  ❑ In April 2005, there was a Webcast on using Service Broker in SQL Server Express. Look for the event on April 21 at www.microsoft.com/events/webcasts/library/200504.mspx.

  ❑ In December 2004, there was a Webcast introducing Service Broker.

Microsoft has all of its sessions labeled as either 100, 200, 300, or 400. Level 100 sessions are very high level with very little technical content, if any. Level 200 is a bit deeper of an overview, with demos that include code samples. The level 300 sessions are quite a bit deeper and delve into the particulars of the subject, generally with a much narrower scope. Finally, level 400 sessions are very advanced, dealing with topics that require a good knowledge of the subject before attending.

You can also download a couple of GUI tools to make Service Broker easier to implement. Both take the basic Service Broker idea and break it down into a Windows Explorer-like view:

❑ **Neils Berglund's SSB Admin** — http://staff.develop.com/nielsb/PermaLink.aspx?guid=0f036cd1-2692-4362-837a-81cb2587acc2 (as of this writing, this link was set up to host the latest version).

❑ **Dan Sullivan's Service Broker Explorer** — You can find the zip for download at `www.sqlservicebroker.com/forums/ShowPost.aspx?PostID=80`.

Here are a couple of blogs we find interesting when dealing with Service Broker:

❑ Rushi Desai, a developer on the SQL Server database engine team, blogs about a variety of functionality. Of particular interest is his entry on **integrating Service Broker with InfoPath** — `http://blogs.msdn.com/rushidesai/archive/2005/02/18/375873.aspx`. This is a wonderful real-world sample.

❑ You can also find Service Broker entries and links at **Kent Tegel's SQL Junkies site** — `www.sqljunkies.com`.

14

Full-Text Searching

Historically, all databases have supported the ability to perform lookups based on exact values (=), ranges (>,<, and such), and patterns (LIKE). Full-Text Search is a relatively new feature for SQL Server, enabling users to perform lookups based on large amounts of textual data in a very fast and efficient way. In this chapter, we will look at Full-Text Search primarily in SQL Server, focusing on the following topics:

❑   The terminology involved with full-text searching

❑   The Full-Text Search Architecture

❑   Setting up Full-Text Search Indexing

❑   Querying a Full-Text Index

What Is Full-Text Searching?

One of the basic features of most databases is the ability to perform searches that match a certain pattern using the LIKE SQL operator, as shown in the following example:

```
Select col1, col2 from table where col3 like '%ADO.NET%'
```

This is an example query for performing a lookup. The problem with using the LIKE SQL operator is that this query does not generally use a set of indexes. The result is that the preceding query would typically result in an expensive table scan. Attempting to perform this search within a table that contains several million records could result in a query that takes several minutes to run.

While using the LIKE keyword is relatively simple, it has a performance problem. The LIKE keyword will not use an index and may force a table scan. For performance reasons, it is a good idea to eliminate table scans. Full-text searching was developed to overcome some of the problems that result when using the LIKE operator. With full-text searching, it is possible to perform searches based on more complicated situations and with higher performance than if you merely base them on pattern matching . Here are some of the search options and advantages that full-text search provides:

- ❑ Higher performance than what you can obtain with the LIKE operator.
- ❑ Searching for words based on their proximity.
- ❑ Searching for words that are derived from a common word foundation. For example, the terms "walk" and "walking" would likely return a similar result.
- ❑ Words and phrases close to the search terms.

Terminology

Let's take a look at the terminology associated with full-text searching in SQL Server 2005:

- ❑ **Full-Text Index** — A full-text index is the storehouse for the significant words within a column and their respective locations within a given column. This information allows a full-text engine to quickly find necessary words and combinations of words within the desired column.

- ❑ **Full-Text Catalog** — A full-text catalog contains the full-text indexes. It resides on a local hard drive associated with a SQL Server Instance. Each catalog contains the full-text indexes of every table within a database. Full-text catalogs cannot be stored on nonlocal hard drives. As a result, a catalog cannot exist on a removable drive, network drive, or floppy drive, unless this is a read-only database.

- ❑ **Word Breaker** — A word breaker is the mechanism to tokenize text, based on the rules of a given language.

- ❑ **Token** — A token is a word within a language that has been identified by the breakup performed by a word breaker.

- ❑ **Stemmer** — Within a specific language, a stemmer is a mechanism to generate specific forms of a given word based on the rules of the given language. As a result, stemmers are specific for a given language. Stemmers and word breakers are included for several versions of Chinese, Brazilian, British English, Danish, Dutch, English, French, German, Italian, Japanese, Korean, Polish, Portuguese, Russian, Spanish, Swedish, Thai, and Turkish languages.

- ❑ **Filter** — A filter is the mechanism that extracts text from a file stored in a BLOB column (such as varbinary(max) or image). Filters are specific for a given file type. To obtain a list of the filters installed, the sp_help_fulltext_extensions stored procedure can be called. Because a document stored in a table has no file extension, the file extension must be stored within a column. Typically, it is stored within a FileExtension column.

- ❑ **Population/Crawl** — A population is a process for creating and updating a full-text index. A population is an operation that typically requires a significant amount of CPU time and hard drive access.

- ❑ **Noise Words** — Noise words are words that are ignored to prevent a full-text index from becoming too large while not providing any value. For example, in English, words such as "a," "and," "the," and other small words are considered to be noise words. These words typically provide no value to a full-text index.

How Does Full-Text Indexing Work?

A full-text index is a special type of index within SQL server. It is built and maintained by the SQL Server full-text service. Building a full-text index is different from building a typical index. Typically, indexes are made from a B-tree structure based on a specific value within a particular row. Once an index is created, inserts, updates, and deletes result in changes to a standard index. Creating a full-text index is a different mechanism.

Microsoft Full-Text Engine for SQL Server Service

The Microsoft Full-Text Engine for SQL Server (MSFTESQL) is a service that provides full-text indexing and the ability to search. MSFTSQL is built on Microsoft Search and is fully integrated into the SQL Server 2005 Database. The MSFTESQL provides several features:

❑ **Index Support** — The MSFTESQL service manages the full-text catalogs and indexes for a database.

❑ **Query Support** — The MSFTESQL service implements the full-text queries. It processes the full-text query and returns the results of the query.

❑ **Management** — The MSFTESQL service is responsible for managing the full-text indexes and catalogs. These catalogs are not stored in the database, but in the file system.

SQL Server and the MSFTESQL Service must run under the same account to work properly together.

What Does a Full-Text Index Look Like?

To understand how SQL Server Full-Text Search works, it helps to understand the full-text index structure. Let's look at a couple of example rows in a table. For this example, we'll look at a table from our full-text search table, and in particular, at a small portion of the search results table.

tblSearchResultsId	SearchText
1	Welcome to Weblogs. This is a list of the latest posts.
2	Welcome to NOAA. United States weather reports online.

Here's a somewhat simplified look at the resulting full-text index:

Word	ColId	DocId	Occ
Welcome	1	1	1
weblogs	1	1	3
This	1	1	4
List	1	1	
Latest	1	1	7

Table continued on following page

Word	ColId	DocId	Occ
Posts	1	1	10
Welcome	1	2	1
NOAA	1	2	3
United	1	2	4
States	1	2	5
Weather	1	2	6
reports	1	2	7
Online	1	2	8

The Word column contains the single word (token) created at the time of indexing. Word breakers are used to determine the contents of a word or token. The ColId column contains a value that represents the specific table and column that is being full-text indexed. The DocId column contains values for a Word/ColId set that maps to a particular full-text key value in a full-text indexed table. Typically, this will be the primary key of the row from which the particular word (token) came. The Occ column contains an integer value that contains the location within a column marked for full-text searching. This is used for the proximity and phrase matches. The DocId and Occ column values are represented internally to the database as a compressible 4-byte integer value. This is done primarily to save space and minimize processing.

This section represents only a simple overview of the SQL Server 2005 Full-Text Index. Note that additional pieces of information are stored within the full-text index tables.

How Is a Full-Text Index Populated?

You know what a full-text index looks like, but how is it populated? The full-text index is populated not by SQL Server, but by the Full-Text Engine for SQL Server (MSFTESQL).

MSFTESQL supports four types of full-text index population: full population, change tracking-based population (automatic and manual), and incremental timestamp-based population.

Full Population

A full population will typically occur when a full-text catalog or index is first created and populated. During a full population, the index entries for all of the tables within the catalog and all of the rows in those tables are built. As a result, this may be a time-consuming process for the SQL Server Instance.

Automatic Change Tracking Population

An automatic change tracking population is a population that occurs based on changes to the table being tracked. By tracking changes soon after they are made, the full-text index very closely mirrors the data stored within the table being tracked. The full-text data is up-to-date in almost real time.

Manual Change Tracking Population

With a manual change tracking population, the index is updated only when the full-text population is specified. The change tracking can be specified with the following command:

```
ALTER FULLTEXT INDEX ON tableName START UPDATE POPULATION
```

In this code example, the `tableName` is replaced with the name of the table whose index is to be updated. When a manual population occurs, only the changes that have not previously been made to the index are sent to the full-text index.

Incremental Timestamp-Based Population

An incremental population is a population of a full-text index based on the set of rows that have been added, updated, or deleted since the last population was started. As a result, records added since the last update was started are added in the next update. To perform an incremental population, the database table(s) being indexed must have a column with the type of timestamp. If a timestamp column does not exist within each table, an incremental population cannot be performed and a full population is performed instead.

When an incremental population request is started, the SQL Gatherer receives the request. The Gatherer scans the tables for rows that have had their contents changed since the last population was started. The Gatherer then groups these rows in a set of batch jobs. Each batch job is sent to the Microsoft Full-Text Engine for SQL Service (MSFTESQL). Within the MSFTESQL, the batch jobs are sent to the filter daemon. Once a row is finished within the filter daemon, the SQL Protocol Handler indexes each row within a batch. Once the population is completed, the SQL Gatherer sets the new timestamp value, which is used when the next incremental population is started.

If any data, such as columns, indexes, or full-text index definitions, change between incremental populations, a full population of the full-text index is performed.

Setting up Full-Text Indexing

Setting up full-text indexing in SQL Server 2005 has changed from previous versions. Previous versions of SQL Server used system stored procedures to create, drop, and change catalogs and full-text indexes. The existing stored procedures for managing these objects should continue to work. However, there will most likely be no additional changes to them. As a result, we will look at using the DDL commands and the new options in SQL Server Management Studio for managing full-text indexes.

DDL Setup

With the release of SQL Server 2005, Microsoft has included DDL statements for managing full-text operations. To create a full-text index, follow these steps:

1. **Create the full-text catalog.** The full-text catalog can be created through the following DDL statement:

```
CREATE FULLTEXT CATALOG catName WITH ACCENT_SENSITIVITY = ON|OFF
```

where catName is the name of the catalog that is to be created. Additional options are possible with the CREATE FULLTEXT CATALOG statement, including the following:

❑ ON FILEGROUP filegroup name — This is the name of the filegroup with which the created catalog will be associated. By default, this is the primary filegroup of the database. The catalog is treated like a file. The physical location of the catalog is contained within the path of sys.master_files. The filename of the full-text catalog is a combination of "sysft_" and the name of the catalog.

❑ IN PATH root path — This is the root directory for a catalog. If a 'root path' is not included, the catalog will be created in the directory specified during the setup of SQL Server.

2. **Create the full-text index.** The full-text index can be created through the DDL statement

```
CREATE FULLTEXT INDEX ON tableName
(
    columnName TYPE COLUMN FileExtensionColumnName Language 0X0
)
KEY INDEX uniqueIndexName ON CatalogName
WITH CHANGE_TRACKING AUTO
```

where tableName is the name of the table that will have the full-text index. The columnName is the name of the column containing the column of the file extension for the filter (discussed later in this chapter). The Language keyword is the language that will be used to filter the specified column. In this example, the 0X0 value is the neutral language. The uniqueIndexName is the name of the unique index that covers the specified table. The catalogName is the catalog that will be used to store the full-text index. The last option listed is the setting for the population.

Setup with the SQL Server Management Studio

With the SQL Server Management Studio, use the following steps to graphically create a full-text index:

1. Open the SQL Server Management Studio and right-click the table that needs to be full-text indexed.

2. Select the Full-Text option and then select Define Full-Text Index.

3. Once the wizard opens, select the primary key of the table.

4. Select the column that will be used and the language associated with that column.

Figure 14-1 shows the columns that may have a full-text index.

Figure 14-1

5. Select the schedule for updating the full-text index, as shown in Figure 14-2.

Figure 14-2

6. Select the catalog that will be used to store the full-text index. Figure 14-3 shows the catalog selection.

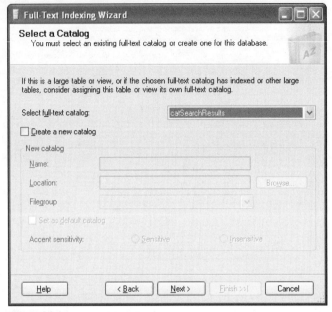

Figure 14-3

7. Select the appropriate table and catalog populations, as shown in Figure 14-4.

Figure 14-4

8. Set the table and catalog population schedules. Figure 14-5 shows the table population schedule options.

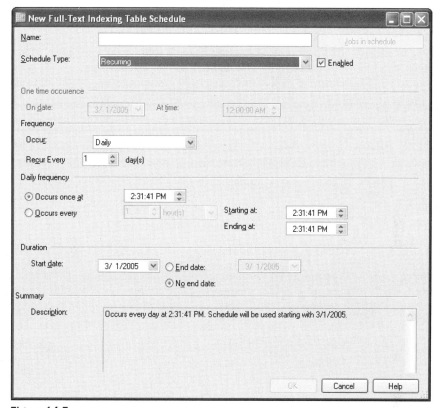

Figure 14-5

Full-Text Properties

The Full-Text Search Engine provides a mechanism for viewing the properties of a full-text index. The function is named FULLTEXTCATALOGPROPERTY('CATNAME', 'PROPERTYNAME'). The CATNAME is the name of the full-text catalog. The PROPERTYNAME is the name of the property that is being viewed. The allowed entries are as follows:

❑ **AccentSensitivity** — A value of 0 is accent-insensitive. A value of 1 specifies that the catalog is accent-sensitive.

❑ **IndexSize** — The IndexSize shows the size of the full-text catalog in megabytes.

❑ **ItemCount** — The ItemCount shows the number of full-text indexed items in a catalog.

❑ **LogSize** — The LogSize is a value that enables backward compatibility.

❑ **MergeStatus** — A value of 0 means that a master merge is not currently occurring. A value of 1 means that a master merge is currently in progress.

❑ **PopulateCompletionAge** — This property is the difference between the completion of the last full-text index population and January 1, 1900. If no population has previously occurred, the value 0 is returned. This value is updated only on full and incremental crawls.

❑ **PopulateStatus** — This property shows the current status of the population. The values are defined as follows: 0 = idle, 1 = full population is in progress, 2 = paused, 3 = throttled, 4 = recovering, 5 = shutdown, 6 = incremental population in progress, 7 = building index, 8 = disk is full and the index population is paused, and 9 = change tracking.

❑ **UniqueKeyCount** — This property shows the number of unique keys in the specified full-text catalog.

These properties can be determined through the following command sent to the database:

```
SELECT fulltextcatalogproperty(' catSearchResults', 'ItemCount')
```

Predicates, Programming, and the Results

Full-text searching is somewhat different from typical SQL-based programming. With typical SQL-based programming, the results returned are based on specific criteria. Results from a full-text query are based on approximate results.

Queries

Writing full-text queries in SQL Server requires that the programmer be very familiar with the CONTAINS, FREETEXT, CONTAINTABLE, and FREETEXTTABLE functions/predicates and that he or she also understand what full-text can and cannot do and how results rank works. Let's take a look at all of these query options.

CONTAINS

CONTAINS is one of the full-text search predicates that can be used to search textual columns for matches to words, phrases, word proximity, words that are related to each other, synonyms (through a thesaurus), and weighted matches. These searches can also be used to check for the proximity of words to determine whether words are within a certain distance of each other.

The syntax for the CONTAINS predicate looks like the following:

```
CONTAINS ( { column_name or (columnlist) | * }, 'search criteria'  [, LANGUAGE
value] )
```

❑ column_name represents the name of a column.

❑ (columnlist) represents a list of columns to search. This list of columns can be either a specific column_name or a list of columns, but not both.

❑ The 'search criteria' from the preceding query may represent a relatively complex set of criteria. It looks similar to the following:

❑ A *simple term* may be a word or phrase that matches exactly, such as "Web Logs." If a noise word is used in a search by itself, an error is returned stating that only noise words were contained within the search.

❑ A *prefix term* may be a word or phrase that matches a set of words or phrases beginning with the specified text. To create a prefix term, enclose the term in double quote marks (") and add the asterisk (*) before the ending quotation mark. If the double quotes are not used, the full-text engine will treat the "*" as any other character. The word breakers will typically ignore the "*".

❑ A *generational term* may be a simple set of terms that include variants of the original word being searched.

❑ An *inflectional* term specifies the language-dependent stemmer to be used on the specified simple term.

❑ *Proximity terms* are words or phrases that are near each other. This closeness operates very similarly to the AND term. NEAR is a term that looks for terms in the same proximity:

```
term1 NEAR term2 NEAR term3
```

❑ *Weighted terms* specify that the matching rows are weighted based on specified values.

❑ LANGUAGE refers to the language that will be used for the query.

These searches may be concatenated through T-SQL-based AND and OR operators to produce the appropriate search results. Let's look at a couple of examples:

```
SELECT * FROM TBLSEARCHRESULTS WHERE CONTAINS(SEARCHTEXT, 'PRESIDENT')
```

The preceding example returns the columns for all rows where the term 'PRESIDENT' is contained within the column SEARCHTEXT of the table TBLSEARCHRESULTS. Here's another:

```
SELECT * FROM TBLSEARCHRESULTS WHERE CONTAINS(SEARCHTEXT, 'PRESIDENT AND BUSH')
```

This example returns the columns for all rows where the term 'PRESIDENT' and 'BUSH' are contained within the column name. Figure 14-6 shows the results of a query using the CONTAINS predicate. Note that only three rows are returned.

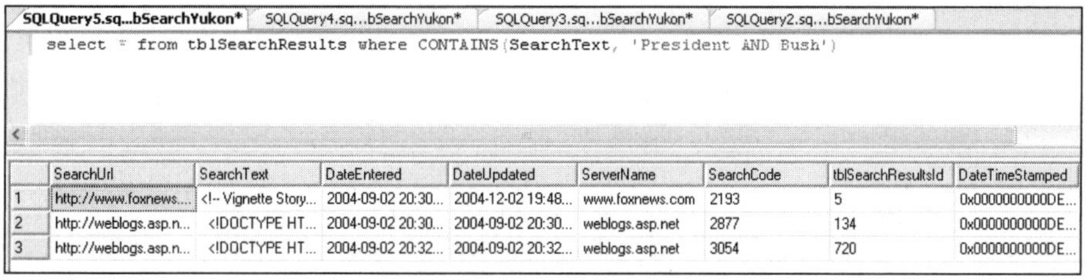

Figure 14-6

The following example returns the columns for all rows containing a term that starts with the prefix 'PRESIDENT':

```
SELECT * FROM TBLSEARCHRESULTS WHERE CONTAINS(SEARCHTEXT, 'PRESIDENT*')
```

FREETEXT

FREETEXT is a predicate used to search columns of textual data for values that have a similar meaning—however, not necessarily the exact wording of the words in the search term. When the FREETEXT command is used, the FTS engine performs the following actions:

- The string is divided into individual words based on word boundaries.
- Inflectional forms of the words are generated through stemming.
- The list of expansions and replacements for the terms are generated based on matches in the thesaurus.

The general syntax for the FREETEXT command is as follows:

```
FREETEXT( { column_name or (column_list)  or * } , 'text string' [, LANGUAGE
language_term ] )
```

The column_name, a list of columns, or all columns listed as being full-text searchable may be used for the search. The 'text string' is the text that will be searched for within the specified columns. The language_term is the language that will be used for word breaking, stemming, thesaurus, and noise word removal during the FREETEXT query. The language_term is optional. The language term may be specified as a string, integer, or hexadecimal value corresponding to the locale identifier (LCID) or a language. If the language_term is not used, the full-text language of the column is used.

Let's review one example where the FREETEXT predicate is used:

```
SELECT * FROM TBLSEARCHRESULTS WHERE FREETEXT(SEARCHTEXT, 'PRESIDENT AND BUSH')
```

This query will return rows that have the terms PRESIDENT and BUSH in the column SEARCHTEXT within the table TBLSEARCHRESULTS. Figure 14-7 shows the results of the preceding query.

Full-text queries with the FREETEXT are less precise than same, or similar, queries using CONTAINS.

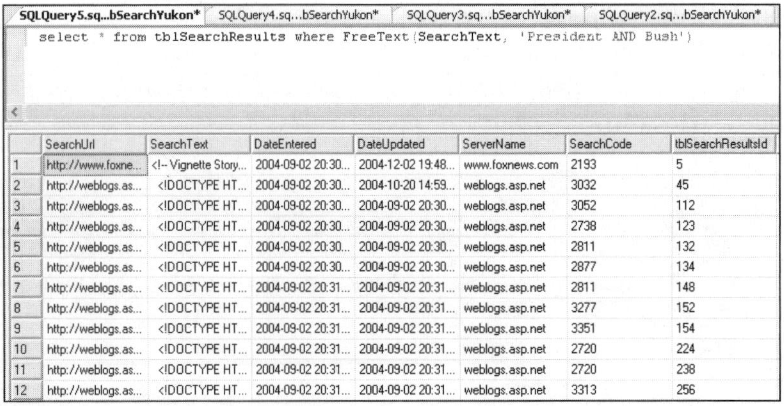

	SearchUrl	SearchText	DateEntered	DateUpdated	ServerName	SearchCode	tblSearchResultsId
1	http://www.foxne...	<!-- Vignette Story...	2004-09-02 20:30...	2004-12-02 19:48...	www.foxnews.com	2193	5
2	http://weblogs.as...	<!DOCTYPE HT...	2004-09-02 20:30...	2004-10-20 14:59...	weblogs.asp.net	3032	45
3	http://weblogs.as...	<!DOCTYPE HT...	2004-09-02 20:30...	2004-09-02 20:30...	weblogs.asp.net	3052	112
4	http://weblogs.as...	<!DOCTYPE HT...	2004-09-02 20:30...	2004-09-02 20:30...	weblogs.asp.net	2738	123
5	http://weblogs.as...	<!DOCTYPE HT...	2004-09-02 20:30...	2004-09-02 20:30...	weblogs.asp.net	2811	132
6	http://weblogs.as...	<!DOCTYPE HT...	2004-09-02 20:30...	2004-09-02 20:30...	weblogs.asp.net	2877	134
7	http://weblogs.as...	<!DOCTYPE HT...	2004-09-02 20:31...	2004-09-02 20:31...	weblogs.asp.net	2811	148
8	http://weblogs.as...	<!DOCTYPE HT...	2004-09-02 20:31...	2004-09-02 20:31...	weblogs.asp.net	3277	152
9	http://weblogs.as...	<!DOCTYPE HT...	2004-09-02 20:31...	2004-09-02 20:31...	weblogs.asp.net	3351	154
10	http://weblogs.as...	<!DOCTYPE HT...	2004-09-02 20:31...	2004-09-02 20:31...	weblogs.asp.net	2720	224
11	http://weblogs.as...	<!DOCTYPE HT...	2004-09-02 20:31...	2004-09-02 20:31...	weblogs.asp.net	2720	238
12	http://weblogs.as...	<!DOCTYPE HT...	2004-09-02 20:31...	2004-09-02 20:31...	weblogs.asp.net	3313	256

Figure 14-7

The FREETEXT *query returned 49 records from our database table, whereas the same query using* CONTAINS *returned only three records.*

CONTAINSTABLE

The CONTAINSTABLE T-SQL command returns a table consisting of zero or more rows for the columns containing textual data types. The queries that use the CONTAINSTABLE function take the same set of search parameters as the CONTAINS predicate. Note several differences between the CONTAINS and the CONTAINSTABLE TSQL objects:

❑   CONTAINSTABLE returns a relevance ranking value called RANK and a full-text key called KEY for each row returned.

❑   The table name of the table to be searched by FTS must be specified within the CONTAINSTABLE function.

❑   CONTAINSTABLE can be referenced in the FROM clause of a SELECT statement. The CONTAINS predicate is referenced within the WHERE clause of a SELECT statement.

An example of the values returned through the CONTAINSTABLE function is shown in Figure 14-8.

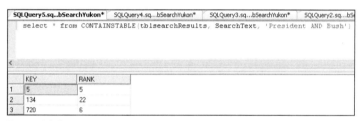

Figure 14-8

Here's an example of using the CONTAINSTABLE function:

```
SELECT * FROM TBLSEARCHRESULTS A JOIN CONTAINSTABLE(TBLSEARCHRESULTS, SEARCHTEXT,
'PRESIDENT AND BUSH') B ON A.TBLSEARCHRESULTSID = B.KEY
```

The preceding query will return the columns of the rows in the TBLSEARCHRESULTS table that match the criteria specified in the CONTAINSTABLE function.

FREETEXTTABLE

The FREETEXTTABLE T-SQL command returns a table consisting of zero or more rows for the columns containing textual data types. The queries that use the FREETEXTTABLE function take the same set of search parameters as the CONTAINS predicate. Note several differences between the FREETEXT and the FREETEXTTABLE T-SQL objects:

❑   FREETEXTTABLE returns a relevance ranking value called RANK and a full-text key called KEY for each row returned.

❑   The table name of the table to be searched by FTS must be specified within the FREETEXTTABLE function.

❑   The top set of ranked results can be returned by specifying the top_n_by_rank option, as shown in the following example:

```
FREETEXT( { column_name or (column_list)  or * } , 'text string' [, LANGUAGE
language_term ] [, top_n_by_rank])
```

- FREETEXTTABLE can be referenced in the FROM clause of a SELECT statement. The FREETEXT predicate is referenced within the WHERE clause of a SELECT statement.

Figure 14-9 shows the results of a query merely using the FREETEXTTABLE function.

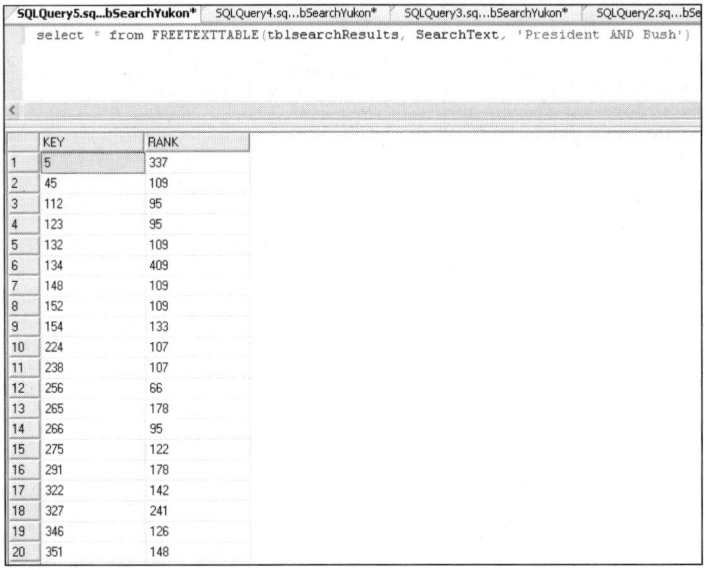

	KEY	RANK
1	5	337
2	45	109
3	112	95
4	123	95
5	132	109
6	134	409
7	148	109
8	152	109
9	154	133
10	224	107
11	238	107
12	256	66
13	265	178
14	266	95
15	275	122
16	291	178
17	322	142
18	327	241
19	346	126
20	351	148

Figure 14-9

Here's an example of using the FREETEXTTABLE function:

```
SELECT * FROM TBLSEARCHRESULTS A JOIN FREETEXTTABLE(TBLSEARCHRESULTS, SEARCHTEXT,
'"MOTLEY CRUE"') B ON A.TBLSEARCHRESULTSID = B.KEY
```

The preceding query will return the ROWS of the products in the TBLSEARCHRESULTS table that match the criteria specified in the FREETEXTTABLE function.

Precomputed Rank with the FREETEXTTABLE Query

The top_n_by_rank option in the FREETEXTTABLE function also offers the capability to precompute the rank. This option may be set through the sp_configure stored procedures sp_configure and sp_fulltext_service. The precompute rank option is used to improve the performance of queries based on FREETEXTTABLE that use top_n_by_rank.

FORMSOF

There are times within a full-text search when it is necessary to use associated terms in the search. To enable the associated terms, the FORMSOF object is used. With the FORMSOF object, an inflectional (single or plural) form of a word or related form (through a thesaurus) is used.

INFLECTIONAL

It is possible to search for all of the different tenses of a verb as well as the plural and singular forms of a noun. Such a search can be performed by passing the INFLECTIONAL parameter in a T-SQL query:

```
SELECT * FROM TBLSEARCHRESULTS WHERE CONTAINS(SEARCHTEXT, 'FORMSOF(INFLECTIONAL,
record)')
```

In the preceding example, searches are performed for "record," "records," and so on in the SEARCHTEXT field of the TBLSEARCHRESULTS table.

THESAURUS

It is also possible to search for related word in a search. The related word is found through a search using a thesaurus. The THESAURUS parameter is passed in a T-SQL query, like this:

```
SELECT * FROM TBLSEARCHRESULTS WHERE CONTAINS(SEARCHTEXT, 'FORMSOF(THESAURUS,
record)')
```

In the preceding example, searches are performed for "record," "disks," and so on in the SEARCHTEXT field of the TBLSEARCHRESULTS table.

ISABOUT

The ISABOUT object works with the WEIGHT object. ISABOUT is used to specify the weighted term keyword.

WEIGHT

In a simple full-text search query, it is possible to put a search weight on the different words that are being searched. This weighting is based on a decimal number between 0.0 and 1.0, with the 0.0 value being the lowest and the 1.0 value being the highest. Consider the following query:

```
SELECT URL FROM TBLSEARCHRESULTS WHERE CONTAINS (SEARCHTEXT, 'ISABOUT("MOTLEY*",
CRUE WEIGHT(0.8), CREW WEIGHT(0.2))')
```

In the preceding example, the rows that contain the term MOTLEY CRUE will be ranked higher than those that contain the term MOTLEY CREW.

NEAR

The NEAR operator is used to indicate that the word or phrase on the left-hand side of a NEAR operator is close to the word or phrase on the right-hand side of the NEAR operator. The NEAR operator may be used to chain operations together. SQL Server ranks the distance between words operated on by the NEAR operator. A low-ranking value (0) indicates that the words are fairly far apart from each other.

The following example will return rows in which the words MOTLEY and CRUE are near each other:

```
SELECT URL FROM TBLSEARCHRESULTS WHERE CONTAINS(SearchText, 'MOTLEY NEAR CRUE')
```

Query Linked Servers

To perform a full-text query against a linked server, a full-text index must be created on the remote tables and columns on the linked server. After the full-text indexes are created, the remote server may be created as a linked server. Once this is done, the linked server may be queried using the four-part name of `RemoteServer.database.Owner.Table`.

Multi-Column Queries

With Microsoft SQL Server 2000 and prior releases, a T-SQL statement was limited to using only one column per predicate/function. SQL Server 2005 offers the capability to query multiple columns with the `CONTAINS` and `FREETEXT` predicates, along with the `CONTAINSTABLE` and `FREETEXTTABLE` functions. These may be specified by either a list of columns or as a '*', where the '*' functions as a list of all columns with a full-text index on them.

Language Settings

The `LANGUAGE` setting is an optional value that represents the language of the textual data stored in a column. This textual data may be stored in a char, nchar, varchar, nvarchar, text, or ntext datatype. The `LANGUAGE` setting is a string, integer, or hexadecimal value that corresponds to the locale identifier (LCID) of a language. If the language of a column is unknown or multiple languages are to be stored in a column, the neutral language setting (0x0) is used.

When choosing a language, several items must be considered. One is the tokenizing of words. Word boundaries are used to divide words for indexing. In some languages, these boundaries are merely white space or a punctuation mark, such as a comma or period. Other languages may combine words with no visible separator beyond the reader's ability to understand that the words have been combined. As a result, the choice of a column-level language should best represent the language expected to be stored as textual data in the rows of the column. When in doubt, a neutral word breaker should be used. Another consideration is stemming. *Stemming* is the process of searching for all inflectional forms, such as the tenses of a verb and the single/plural forms of a noun.

The full-text data engine supports the following languages:

- German
- French
- Japanese
- Danish
- Spanish
- Italian
- Dutch
- Norwegian
- Portuguese
- Finnish
- Swedish
- Czech
- Hungarian
- Polish
- Romanian
- Croatian
- Slovak
- Slovenian
- Greek
- Bulgarian

❑   Russian   ❑   Brazilian

❑   Turkish   ❑   Traditional Chinese

❑   British- English   ❑   Korean

❑   Estonian   ❑   Simplified Chinese

❑   Latvian   ❑   Arabic

❑   Lithuanian   ❑   Thai

Ranking

A full-text query in SQL Server can produce a ranking value indicating how relevant the returned data is believed to be. This rank value is returned on a per-row basis. The higher the rank value for a row, the more relevant the row when compared to other rows.

The algorithms for creating a rank depend on several items. For example, different work breakers tokenize textual data differently. The matching and ranking of the same words when in different languages may be broken up differently, assuming different languages are specified. If the words are broken differently, the length of the resulting token results in a different value.

> *The ranking values of different searches do not have a relationship between searches. For example, the ranking of query 1 has no relationship to the ranking returned from a separate query.*

Some commonly used properties when calculating a ranking include the following:

❑   **Property** — A property is an attribute of a document. This corresponds to a column in SQL Server.

❑   **Document** — The document is the entity returned in a query. This corresponds to a row in SQL Server. A document may have multiple properties, just as a row may have multiple full-text indexed columns.

❑   **Index** — Many query statistics are determined relative to an individual index in which the match occurred.

❑   **Catalog** — A catalog is a collection of indexes treated as a single entity for queries. Catalogs are a mechanism of organization visible to the database administrator.

❑   **Word** — A word is the unit that is to be matched in the full-text search engine. Text is broken into words by a language-specific word breaker.

❑   **Occurrence** — An occurrence is the work offset in a document property as made by the word breaker. The first word is at occurrence 1, the second at occurrence 2, and so on. The first word of a sentence has an occurrence value eight times greater than the last word of the previous sentence. The first word of a paragraph has an occurrence value that's 128 higher than the last word of the previous sentence. The Occurrence value is taken into account when creating the weighting of a result.

❑   **Key** — A key is a combination of a property and a word.

❑   **HitCount** — The HitCount is the number of times a key occurs in a query result.

❑   **Log2** — The Log2 is the logarithm in base 2. The Log2 offers higher performance when compared to a logarithm in base 2 or base e.

❑ **IndexDocumentCount** — The `IndexDocumentCount` is the total number of documents within an index.

❑ **KeyDocumentCount** — The `KeyDocumentCount` is the number of documents in the index containing the key.

❑ **MaxOccurrence** — The `MaxOccurrence` is the largest occurrence within an index for a given property in a document.

❑ **MaxQueryRank** — This is the maximum rank, 1,000, which is returned by the Microsoft Full-Text Search Engine for SQL.

How Results Are Ranked

The computing of rank is difficult. Ranking depends on a number of factors. Different word breakers break streams of text into words differently. Ranking and matching vary depending on the language used. Different languages break words differently, which will result in different document lengths. Much like the word breakers, statistics, such as `IndexDocumentCount` and `MaxOccurrence`, can vary depending on a number of factors. Documents are normalized based on the following list:

```
{ 16, 32, 128, 256, 512, 725, 1024, 1450, 2048, 2896, 4096, 5792, 8192, 11585,
  16384, 23170, 28000, 32768, 39554, 46340, 55938, 65536, 92681, 131072, 185363,
  262144, 370727, 524288, 741455, 1048576, 2097152, 4194304 };
```

The normalization means that a document of length 300 and length 400 will be treated as having the same length because they fall within the same range. In this case, the documents of length 300 and length 400 are both between 256 and 512. As a result, they are treated as having a length of 512.

`CONTAINSTABLE`, `ISABOUT`, and `FREETEXT` have ranking capabilities inherent within them. The ranking for `CONTAINSTABLE` is as follows:

```
StatisticalWeight = Log2( ( 2 + IndexDocumentCount ) / KeyDocumentCount )
Rank = Min( MaxQueryRank, HitCount * 16 * StatisticalWeight / MaxOccurrence )
```

Phrase matches are ranked similarly to individual keys except that the property `KeyDocumentCount` is estimated and may be inaccurate. As a result, phrases may receive higher weights than individual keys.

`ISABOUT` uses a vector-space query based on traditional information retrieval terminology. The default ranking algorithm that is used is Jaccard. The ranking is based on the following statistics:

```
ContainsRank = same formula used for CONTAINSTABLE ranking of a single term.
Weight = the weight specified in the query for each term.  MaxQueryRank is the
default weight.
WeightedSum = _[key=1 to n] ContainsRankKey * WeightKey
Rank = ( MaxQueryRank * WeightedSum ) / ( ( _[key=1 to n] ContainsRankKey2 )
+ ( _[key=1 to n] WeightKey2 ) - ( WeightedSum ) )
```

The sum data is computed using unsigned 4-byte integers. All other math is performed with 8-byte integers.

FREETEXT ranking is based on an OKAPI BM25 formula. Each term in the query is ranked, and these values are summed. Words are added to the query through inflection. The added words are treated as different terms. These different terms have no special weighting or relationship to the words from which they are generated. The synonyms used from the thesaurus are treated as separate terms that are weighted equally:

```
Rank = _[Terms in Query] w ( ( ( k1 + 1 ) tf ) / ( K + tf ) ) * ( ( k3 + 1 ) qtf /
( k3 + qtf ) ) )
Where:
w is the Robertson-Sparck Jones weight.
Originally, w is defined as:
w = log10 ( ( ( r + 0.5 ) * ( N - n - R + r + 0.5 ) ) / ( ( R - r + 0.5 ) * ( n - r
+ 0.5 ) ) )
This was simplified to:
w = log10 ( ( ( r + 0.5 ) * ( N - R + r + 0.5 ) ) / ( ( R - r + 0.5 ) * ( n - r +
0.5 ) ) )
R is the number of documents marked relevant by a user. This is not implemented in
SQL Server 2005 full-text search, and thus is ignored.
r is the number of documents marked relevant by a user containing the term. This is
not implemented. N is the number of documents with values for the property in the
query.
n is the number of documents containing the term.
K is ( k1 * ( ( 1 - b ) + ( b * dl / avdl ) ) ).
dl is the document length, in word occurrences.
avdl is the average document length of the property over which the query spans, in
word occurrences. k1, b, and k3 are the constants 1.2, 0.75, and 8.0, respectively.
tf is the frequency of the term in a specific document.
qtf is the frequency of the term in the query.
```

Accent Sensitivity

With accent sensitivity, words that differ only according to whether or not they are accented are determined to be the same. For example, if accent sensitivity is set to on, the string "cafe" is not the same as "café." If accent sensitivity is set to off, then the string "cafe" is the same as "café."

Accent sensitivity can be set in the CREATE FULLTEXT CATALOG statement along with the ALTER FULLTEXT CATALOG statement.

Transforming Noise Words

Languages tend to include a lot of words that don't necessarily provide value to the meaning of a phrase. For example, the phrase "The full-text search engine is running" contains the noise words "the" and "is." Other English noise words are "a" and "and." A noise word is left out of an index and its occurrence value is not used.

> *The noise word file is stored in $SQL_SERVER_INSTALL_PATH\Microsoft SQL Server\MSSQL.1\ MSSQL\Binn\FTERef\ directory. Editing a noise-word file means that a full-text catalog must be repopulated.*

SQL Server includes an option to "transform noise words." This option is used to remove error messages if noise words cause a Boolean operation on a full-text query to fail. The default setting for "transform noise words" is set so that noise words are not transformed and the value is 0. The default setting means that when noise words in a full-text query would cause a failure, SQL Server returns an error instead.

When the Transform Noise Words option is set to 1, SQL Server will replace noise words with an asterisk "*" in phrase queries:

```
sp_configure 'transform noise words', 1;
go
reconfigure;
go
```

The preceding T-SQL code sample set the Transform Noise Words option to 1.

Searching XML and BLOBs

So far, we have discussed the ability of SQL Server to search textual information, such as information in char, varchar, and varchar(max) datatype columns.

XML

With the introduction of Microsoft SQL Server 2005, the XML data type has been added. This data type allows for the storage of XML fragments and documents. Full-Text Search in SQL Server supports the creation of full-text indexes and searches on the XML data type. Full-text queries against an XML data type column will return rows in which the search parameters exist anywhere within the column.

BLOBs

Data, such as a Microsoft Word Document and Adobe Acrobat files, can be stored within a varbinary(max) or images column. Data may be stored within one of these data type columns and then queried against using a filter, which implements the IFilter interface. The filter will extract text based on a specific file format.

There are several steps to perform the search on a BLOB:

1. Create a table to hold the BLOB. In this example, the table has the following definition:

```
CREATE TABLE [dbo].[tblFile](
        [tblFileId] [int] IDENTITY(1,1) NOT NULL,
        [ContentData] [varbinary](max) NULL,
        [FileType] [varchar](10) COLLATE SQL_Latin1_General_CP1_CI_AS NULL,
        [MimeType] [varchar](50) COLLATE SQL_Latin1_General_CP1_CI_AS NULL,
  CONSTRAINT [PK_tblFile] PRIMARY KEY CLUSTERED
(
        [tblFileId] ASC
) ON [PRIMARY]
) ON [PRIMARY]
```

The column tblFileId is a primary key and is an identity field. The column ContentData is the column that holds the BLOB data. The FileType column contains the file extension of the uploaded file. The MimeType column contains the mime type for the BLOB data as determined by the ASP.NET file upload control.

2. Create code that will upload a table. For this example, our code looks like this:

```
Dim iLength As Integer
Dim strFile As String
Dim strSql As String
Dim byteBuffer() As Byte
Dim httpFile As HttpPostedFile
Dim sqlCn As New SqlConnection()
Dim sqlCm As New SqlCommand()
Dim sqlDa As New SqlDataAdapter()
Dim drData As DataRow
Dim dsData As New DataSet()
Dim cmdBld As New System.Data.SqlClient.SqlCommandBuilder(sqlDa)
Try
    iLength = Me.fuplControl.PostedFile.ContentLength
    If (iLength > 0) Then
        strFile = Right(Me.fuplControl.PostedFile.FileName, 3)
        httpFile = fuplControl.PostedFile
        ReDim byteBuffer(iLength)
        httpFile.InputStream.Read(byteBuffer, 0, iLength)
        sqlCn.ConnectionString = strCn
        sqlCm.Connection = sqlCn
        strSql = "select tblFileId, FileType, MimeType, ContentData from
tblFile where 1=2"
        sqlDa.MissingSchemaAction = MissingSchemaAction.AddWithKey
        sqlCm.CommandText = strSql
        sqlDa.SelectCommand = sqlCm
        sqlDa.Fill(dsData, "tblFile")
        drData = dsData.Tables("tblFile").NewRow()
        drData("MimeType") = httpFile.ContentType
        drData("FileType") = strFile
        drData("ContentData") = byteBuffer
        dsData.Tables("tblFile").Rows.Add(drData)
        sqlDa.Update(dsData, "tblFile")
        Call DisplayFilesInDb()
    End If
Finally
    If sqlCn.State <> ConnectionState.Closed Then
        sqlCn.Close()
    End If
    sqlCn.Dispose()
    sqlCm.Dispose()
End Try
```

3. The final step in the process is to run a full-text search. An example full-text search query will result in data like that shown in Figure 14-10.

Figure 14-11 shows the selection of a language along with the file type to use for filtering when performing a full-text search on a BLOB. The choice of the file type column will directly change the filter that is used in the gathering process. In Figure 14-11, we are setting the column that contains the file type to the column named [FileType].

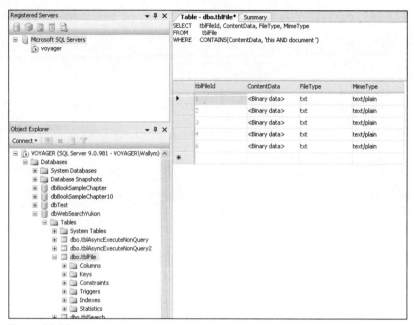

Figure 14-10

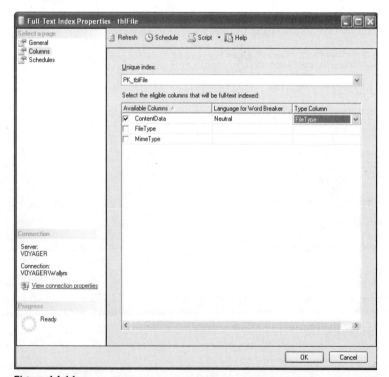

Figure 14-11

Extending Full-Text Search with Filters

When creating a full-text search, it is possible to search on columns that hold BLOB-style data. This data can be stored in a `varbinary(max)` column while another column holds the file type. This data is extracted using what is called a *filter*. SQL Server 2005 ships with a number of filters for common file types, including Microsoft Office documents. Full text searching on these documents will work out of the box.

What happens when you would like to filter on different file types? Let's look at filtering on an Adobe Acrobat PDF file type. Here are the steps to filter a PDF file:

1. Remember that your table must have a BLOB field, such as a `varbinary(max)`, and a column to specify the file type to the full-text index Create Index commands or the full-text index wizard in SQL Server Management Studio.

2. Download and install the Adobe Acrobat PDF Filter.

3. Execute the following commands against your SQL Server 2005 instance:

```
sp_fulltext_service 'load_os_resources',1
```

The preceding command tells the Microsoft Search Service to load OS-specific word breakers, stemmers, and so on.

Do not verify that the binaries are signed:

```
sp_fulltext_service 'verify_signature', 0
```

4. Bounce the SQL Server Service and MSFTESQL. Figure 14-12 shows the execution of the stored procedure `sp_help_fulltext_extensions`. The result is the full-text extensions that are installed, which the Microsoft Search Service can use.

5. Create your full-text index.

6. Issue the necessary command(s) to (re)index. This can be done through the SQL Server Management Studio or by issuing T-SQL commands.

	file extension	clsid	fullpath	version
22	.htw	E0CA5340-4534-...	C:\Program Files\Microsoft SQL Server\MSSQL.2\MSSQL\Binn\nlhtml.dll	12.0.4524.1
23	.htx	E0CA5340-4534-...	C:\Program Files\Microsoft SQL Server\MSSQL.2\MSSQL\Binn\nlhtml.dll	12.0.4524.1
24	.hxx	C7310720-AC80-...	C:\Program Files\Microsoft SQL Server\MSSQL.2\MSSQL\Binn\msfte.dll	12.0.4524.1
25	.ibq	C7310720-AC80-...	C:\Program Files\Microsoft SQL Server\MSSQL.2\MSSQL\Binn\msfte.dll	12.0.4524.1
26	.idl	C7310720-AC80-...	C:\Program Files\Microsoft SQL Server\MSSQL.2\MSSQL\Binn\msfte.dll	12.0.4524.1
27	.idq	C1243CA0-BF96-...	C:\WINDOWS\system32\query.dll	5.1.2600.2180
28	.inc	C7310720-AC80-...	C:\Program Files\Microsoft SQL Server\MSSQL.2\MSSQL\Binn\msfte.dll	12.0.4524.1
29	.inf	C7310720-AC80-...	C:\Program Files\Microsoft SQL Server\MSSQL.2\MSSQL\Binn\msfte.dll	12.0.4524.1
30	.ini	C7310720-AC80-...	C:\Program Files\Microsoft SQL Server\MSSQL.2\MSSQL\Binn\msfte.dll	12.0.4524.1
31	.inx	C7310720-AC80-...	C:\Program Files\Microsoft SQL Server\MSSQL.2\MSSQL\Binn\msfte.dll	12.0.4524.1
32	.js	C7310720-AC80-...	C:\Program Files\Microsoft SQL Server\MSSQL.2\MSSQL\Binn\msfte.dll	12.0.4524.1
33	.log	C7310720-AC80-...	C:\Program Files\Microsoft SQL Server\MSSQL.2\MSSQL\Binn\msfte.dll	12.0.4524.1
34	.m3u	C7310720-AC80-...	C:\Program Files\Microsoft SQL Server\MSSQL.2\MSSQL\Binn\msfte.dll	12.0.4524.1
35	.mht	C7310720-AC80-...	C:\Program Files\Microsoft SQL Server\MSSQL.2\MSSQL\Binn\msfte.dll	12.0.4524.1
36	.obd	F07F3920-7B8C-1...	C:\Program Files\Microsoft SQL Server\MSSQL.2\MSSQL\Binn\offfilt.dll	12.0.4524.1
37	.obt	F07F3920-7B8C-1...	C:\Program Files\Microsoft SQL Server\MSSQL.2\MSSQL\Binn\offfilt.dll	12.0.4524.1
38	.odc	E0CA5340-4534-...	C:\Program Files\Microsoft SQL Server\MSSQL.2\MSSQL\Binn\nlhtml.dll	12.0.4524.1
39	.pdf	4C904448-74A9-1...	C:\Program Files\Adobe\PDF IFilter 6.0\PDFFILT.dll	6.0.0.0

Figure 14-12

Once the necessary commands have been run, the table may be queried using the existing full-text search commands. Figure 14-13 shows the results of a full-text search query for which a PDF file is returned.

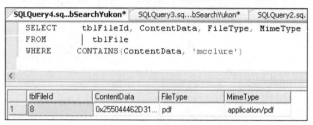

Figure 14-13

Summary

This completes our look at the full-text capabilities of SQL Server and, in particular, SQL Server 2005. In this chapter, you learned the basics of full-text searching and examined the full-text indexing of files in the database. In addition, you examined different searching options.

For More Information

To complement the information in this chapter, take a look at the following resources:

❑   **SQL Server 2005 Books Online**

❑   **SQL Server 2005 newsgroups**

❑   **MSDN article titled "SQL Server 2005 Full-Text Search: Internals and Enhancements," by Andrew Cencini** — http://msdn.microsoft.com/library/default.asp?url= /library/en-us/dnsql90/html/sql2005ftsearch.asp

❑   **John Kane's Weblog** — http://spaces.msn.com/members/jtkane

15

Reporting

Originally, this chapter was titled "Business Intelligence (BI)." The direction changed when we considered that BI, in the Microsoft vernacular, deals more with Online Analytic Processing (OLAP) than anything else. While certain aspects of BI are very difficult, if not impossible without OLAP, other aspects are quite easy to create against a transactional data store. Consider the following:

❑   The key purpose of technology is to support business.

❑   Technology is concerned with the storing of data.

❑   Business is run on information.

❑   Data is not information.

❑   Therefore, one of the most important aspects of technology is turning data into information.

For the purposes of this chapter, BI is the process of turning pieces of data into meaningful information in order to make business decisions. In most cases, this information is conveyed in the form of a report. While reporting is not the sole focus of this chapter, a great deal of data analysis and business intelligence work ends with building some form of report or another. This means a great deal of the material will focus on Reporting Services. Some of the material will apply to SQL Server 2000 as well, so we will let you know the portions that require SQL Server 2005.

The database we will be using is the AdventureWorks database. To install this database, do a custom install of SQL Server 2005 and install the sample applications. This database is also available on the Microsoft downloads site for SQL Server 2000 (surf to www.microsoft.com/downloads and look for "Adventure Works"). As of the writing of this chapter, the latest copy is from 2003 and requires the .NET 1.0 Framework to install. Please note that some of the scripts will require alteration if you go the SQL Server 2000 route.

There is a lot of ground to cover when it comes to reporting in SQL Server 2005. Much of the material in this chapter is introductory in nature and designed to whet your appetite for more information. As the model has been greatly simplified, this is not a code-intensive chapter. Rather, the focus is on increasing your toolset to expand your horizons. By the end of this chapter, you will see that it is possible to move more work to the business analyst and spend time developing the more difficult parts of your application.

An Introduction to Reporting

While reports are one of the least favorite parts of application development for most developers, ultimately they are one of the most important aspects from a business standpoint. In addition, whether you realize it or not, you are constantly building reports of one type or another. In some instances, you will work with a formal reporting tool, such as Crystal Reports or Reporting Services, but many times building reports is just another aspect of your UI development. Anytime you aggregate data, you are, by definition, building a report.

This section focuses on a reporting scenario that is similar to the daily operations for many developers, albeit quite a bit simpler. The reason for choosing a simple report is that much of the work in this chapter is done without code. While showing a few different ways to render a complex report might be more exciting and create a bigger book, complex reports are not necessary to cover the breadth of the toolset available in Visual Studio 2005 and SQL Server 2005. To get the most out of this chapter, you will have to play around with the tools.

Scenario

You were just hired as a senior developer at Adventure Works, a global company that sells bicycle parts. Your boss, Jean Trenary, just got a call from Brian Welckler, the vice president of sales. He wants a report of total sales for all sales representatives for the first quarter of 2003, including bonuses and quotas. You have been tasked to implement this report in a Web application.

Implementation

After the conversation with Ms. Trenary, you quickly get back to your chair, thankful that the assignment was a very easy one. To finish this assignment, you will write a stored procedure, create a logon in SQL Server (optional), and add a few items to a Web page.

SQL Server Setup

To get data from SQL Server, you will create a stored procedure. There are a couple of reasons for this. The most obvious reason is because it is far easier to secure database access through a stored procedure, as you can restrict who has access to the procedure. With SQL Server 2005, you can also set a user under whom the stored procedure can run, allowing a user with very limited rights to still gain access to the database (this feature is not available if you are using SQL Server 2000).

The stored procedure that will deliver our simple sales report is shown in the following code. Please note that this particular stored procedure covers many schema names. The account the procedure runs as must have access to all of the schema names.

```
-- SCRIPT = SimpleReportExercise.sql

USE AdventureWorks
GO

CREATE PROCEDURE [Sales].[sspGetSalesTotals]
WITH EXECUTE AS 'dbo'
AS
BEGIN
 SELECT c.FirstName, c.MiddleName, c.LastName, s.SalesQuota, s.Bonus
       , s.SalesYTD, s.SalesLastYear
 FROM Sales.SalesPerson s
        JOIN HumanResources.Employee e
              ON s.SalesPersonID = e.EmployeeID
        JOIN Person.Contact c
              ON e.ContactID = c.ContactID
END;
```

As mentioned in Chapter 9, we are using the new EXECUTE AS function. In this case, we have EXECUTE
AS 'dbo' to have this stored procedure run under the credentials of the dbo account. This is unnecessary if you have an account that has proper rights to the database (i.e., has access to each of the schemas
represented). If so, you can change this to EXECUTE AS CALLER to have it run under the account that is
calling the stored procedure. Remember that dbo execution does not mean that anyone has rights to run
this stored procedure. You will still have to GRANT that right. Running as dbo, we guarantee that any
person with rights to run the stored procedure has rights to access the tables it calls — in this case,
Sales.SalesPerson, HumanResources.Employees, and Person.Contact.

The next thing you will do is create a logon to run the stored procedure. When using Windows
Authentication, this is completely unnecessary. We add this step primarily for those who have a problem
running under Windows Authentication. We would rather offer this solution than have the developer
give database dbo rights to the Internet Guest account (yes, people really do this, and often). The SQL
script necessary to create your login is as follows:

```
-- SCRIPT = Chapter15User.sql
USE master
GO

CREATE LOGIN [Chapter15User] WITH PASSWORD=N'pass@word1',
DEFAULT_DATABASE=[AdventureWorks], DEFAULT_LANGUAGE=[us_english],
CHECK_EXPIRATION=ON, CHECK_POLICY=ON
GO
```

The final step is giving the account rights to the database and granting execute rights for the
sspGetSalesTotal stored procedure. As mentioned before, the stored procedure itself runs as dbo, so
we do not have to grant rights to all of the objects used in the stored procedure. Creating a user and
granting execute rights is shown in the following code:

```
--SCRIPT = Chapter15AWUser.sql
USE AdventureWorks
GO

CREATE USER [Chapter15AWUser] FOR LOGIN [Chapter15User]
```

```
WITH DEFAULT_SCHEMA = Sales
GO

GRANT EXECUTE ON Sales.sspGetSalesTotals
TO [Chapter15AWUser]
GO
```

Now that you are finished with the database, it is time to move to the Web application.

Web Application, or "Look Ma, No Code ..." (Part One)

Although this is not a book on Web applications, reporting and the Web seem to go together. With ASP.NET 2 and Visual Studio 2005, you can create this very simple report without writing one line of code. Here is a quick step by step:

1. Drag a DataGridView control on the page.

2. Configure the data source of the DataGridView to a SqlDataSource that points to the AdventureWorks database.

3. On the GridView tasks menu, select Auto Format ⇨ Professional.

4. On the GridView tasks menu, select Edit Columns and add BoundField objects for FirstName, MiddleName, LastName, SalesQuota, Bonus, SalesYTD, and SalesLastYear.

5. In the same window, uncheck the Auto-Generate Fields checkbox.

6. Add the format {0:c} for each of the monetary columns.

The formatting is optional, but it creates a report page that looks better. In addition, you can auto-generate the fields, but understand that you will have to alter the stored procedure to return a properly formatted currency string if you choose this route. The resulting code from the steps taken is shown in the next code snippet:

```
<h1>
    Sales Report
</h1>
<asp:GridView ID="GridView1" runat="server" DataSourceID="ReportSource1"
AutoGenerateColumns="False" CellPadding="4" ForeColor="#333333" GridLines="None">
    <Columns>
        <asp:BoundField DataField="FirstName" HeaderText="First Name" />
        <asp:BoundField DataField="MiddleName" HeaderText="Middle Initial" />
        <asp:BoundField DataField="LastName" HeaderText="Last Name" />
        <asp:BoundField DataField="SalesQuota" DataFormatString="{0:c}"
            HeaderText="Sales Quota" />
        <asp:BoundField DataField="Bonus" DataFormatString="{0:c}"
            HeaderText="Bonus" />
        <asp:BoundField DataField="SalesYTD" DataFormatString="{0:c}"
            HeaderText="Sales YTD" />
        <asp:BoundField DataField="SalesLastYear" DataFormatString="{0:c}"
            HeaderText="Sales Last Year" />
    </Columns>
    <FooterStyle BackColor="#5D7B9D" Font-Bold="True" ForeColor="White" />
```

```
            <RowStyle BackColor="#F7F6F3" ForeColor="#333333" />
            <PagerStyle BackColor="#284775" ForeColor="White"
              HorizontalAlign="Center" />
            <SelectedRowStyle BackColor="#E2DED6" Font-Bold="True"
              ForeColor="#333333" />
            <HeaderStyle BackColor="#5D7B9D" Font-Bold="True" ForeColor="White" />
            <EditRowStyle BackColor="#999999" />
            <AlternatingRowStyle BackColor="White" ForeColor="#284775" />
        </asp:GridView>
<asp:SqlDataSource ID="ReportSource1" runat="server" ConnectionString="Data
    Source=(local);Initial Catalog=AdventureWorks;Integrated Security=True"
    ProviderName="System.Data.SqlClient" SelectCommand="Sales.sspGetSalesTotals"
    SelectCommandType="StoredProcedure"></asp:SqlDataSource>
```

When you run this page in a browser, you will see the report shown in Figure 15-1.

Figure 15-1

Don't you wish all reports were that easy?

Now we will look at how to change the application to use the account we created in SQL Server. The only change required to the page is a change in the connection string for the SqlDataSource, as shown here:

```
<asp:SqlDataSource ID="ReportSource1" runat="server" ConnectionString="Data
    Source=(local);Initial Catalog=AdventureWorks;Persist Security Info=False;
    User ID=Chapter15User;Password=pass@word1;"
ProviderName="System.Data.SqlClient" SelectCommand="Sales.sspGetSalesTotals"
    SelectCommandType="StoredProcedure"></asp:SqlDataSource>
```

If you hear a funny sound right now, it is us beating the guy who thought that embedding a tag in an ASPX page was a nifty idea. While Microsoft has ensured us that a hacker can never get at the tags of the page, we're a bit paranoid about this one. Although a full explanation is beyond the scope of this book, one potential option is moving the connection string to the web.config file, where you can later add encryption using either the `DataProtectionConfigurationProvider` or the `RSAProtectedConfigurationProvider`. The code change necessary for the initial move is shown here:

```
<!-- web configuration file addition -->
<connectionStrings>
    <add name="Chapter15ConnString" connectionString="Data Source=(local);Initial
Catalog=AdventureWorks;Persist Security Info=False;User
ID=Chapter15User;Password=pass@word1;" providerName="System.Data.SqlClient"/>
</connectionStrings>

<!-- Change ASPX page -->
<asp:SqlDataSource ID="ReportSource1" runat="server"
  ConnectionString="<%$ ConnectionStrings:Chapter15ConnString %>"
  ProviderName="<%$ ConnectionStrings:Chapter15ConnString.ProviderName %>"
ProviderName="System.Data.SqlClient" SelectCommand="Sales.sspGetSalesTotals"
  SelectCommandType="StoredProcedure"></asp:SqlDataSource>
```

Normally, we would spend a little more time on this report to utilize more ADO.NET, but we won't do that, however, as this report is nothing more than a simple segue into the main topic of this chapter, which is Reporting Services.

Reporting Services

For many of us, Reporting Services was revealed at the Yukon Summit in 2003. The idea of having a server that takes the complexity of creating reports off the developer's plate is just too cool for words. While you can move the work to business people, there will be resistance to using the Business Intelligence *Developer* Studio, largely due to that word in italics. As many of the functions available in the BI Developer Studio are way out of the league of the sales manager, keeping Pandora out of the box might be a wise decision. Later in the chapter, we will touch on a better way to have businesspeople create reports, and leave development to the developers.

When you install Reporting Services, you have the option of setting up the URL with SSL or without. If you set up Reporting Services without SSL, you will have to use http:// *instead of* https:// *at the beginning of all of your URLs.*

Our Simple Report in Reporting Services, or "Look Ma, no Code ..." (Part 2)

Once again, you are called into Jean Trenary's office. She says, "I am a bit disappointed that you decided to build that report in ASP.NET. We spent quite a bit of money on SQL Server 2005 and feel that using the Reporting Services feature will better justify the cost of moving to the new platform. I need you to go back and redo that report using Reporting Services."

While this illustrates why business decisions are often made for the wrong reasons, we agree that Reporting Services is a better way to go than building a report in ASP.NET. As the chapter progresses, the reasons for using Reporting Services will become very clear. For the moment, however, the task is building the same report using a different tool.

The first step to producing the Sales By Sales Person report is opening the Business Intelligence Development Studio, aka Visual Studio 2005, with a different name. In other words, if you already have Visual Studio 2005 open, you do not have to close it to open another tool; the business intelligence projects are included in the new project window, so simply create a new project.

The type of project you need to create is a Report Server project. While you can create a report without thinking in the Reports Server Project Wizard project, we won't go quite that brain-dead at this time. Once you have the project open, right-click the Reports folder and choose Add ⇨ New Item ⇨ New Report. If you are tempted, you can choose Add ⇨ New Report, but you will go directly to wizard land, and not pass Go. For the rest of this section, you will be creating a report for the Sales By Sale Person functionality called `SalesBySalesPerson`.

Configure a data source by right-clicking the Shared Data Sources folder. A dialog box will pop up. In the Name textbox, call the data source `Chapter15DataSource`. In the Connection String textbox, add a connection to your SQL Server database. If you are using Windows Authentication on your local box, you can use the string `Data Source=(local);Initial Catalog=AdventureWorks`. If you cannot use Windows Authentication, the connection string for a local box should read `Data Source=(local);Initial Catalog=AdventureWorks;Persist Security Info=False;User ID=Chapter15User;Password=pass@word1`. Click OK and exit the dialog box.

Right-click the Reports folder, click Add ⇨ New Item and choose Report. When you right-click, the Add New Report items will use the report wizard, as will Add ⇨ New Item and choosing Report Wizard. Feel free to experiment with the wizard later.

The next step is to click the DataSet drop-down, in your new report, and choose <New DataSet ...>. In the dialog box that appears, name the DataSet `SalesBySalesPersonDataSet` and choose `Chapter15DataSource (shared)` in the Data Source drop-down. Change the Command Type drop-down to `Stored Procedure` and type `Sales.sspGetSalesTotals` in the Query String box and click OK.

To complete the report, flip to the toolbox and drag a Table onto the report design. Type the title "Sales By Sales Person" in the header. Then, drag a Matrix object under the header. Finally, click from the toolbox to the DataSet tab and drag items from the DataSet onto the second row of the Matrix. To complete the full report, add cells and pull them in to fit underneath the header.

As with the ASP.NET report, you will have to configure the currency fields. The formula for the sales quota field is `=FormatCurrency(Fields!SalesQuota.Value,2,true,true,true)`. You can do this by right-clicking on the cell and choosing Properties, but we find it more informative to open the Report Definition Language (RDL) file in code view. To do this, click the code button in the Solution Explorer and view the code. When you open the code, you will see a document that looks strangely like XML. This is because it is, in fact, XML, although some rules are a bit more restrictive, such as the fact that you cannot add comments to the file.

In this example, shown in the following code, we are focusing on the section of the file that takes the data elements and places them in the file. You are searching for `=Fields!SalesQuota.Value`. When you find it, change it to =FormatCurrency(Fields!SalesQuota.Value, 2, true, true, true). The bolded sections are the pieces you are adding to this report:

```xml
<TableCell>
 <ReportItems>
  <Textbox Name="SalesQuota">
   <rd:DefaultName>SalesQuota</rd:DefaultName>
   <ZIndex>3</ZIndex>
   <Style>
    <PaddingLeft>2pt</PaddingLeft>
    <PaddingTop>2pt</PaddingTop>
    <TextAlign>Right</TextAlign>
    <PaddingBottom>2pt</PaddingBottom>
    <PaddingRight>2pt</PaddingRight>
   </Style>
   <CanGrow>true</CanGrow>
   <Value>=FormatCurrency(Fields!SalesQuota.Value,2,true,true,true)</Value>
  </Textbox>
 </ReportItems>
</TableCell>
<TableCell>
 <ReportItems>
  <Textbox Name="Bonus">
   <rd:DefaultName>Bonus</rd:DefaultName>
   <ZIndex>2</ZIndex>
   <Style>
    <PaddingLeft>2pt</PaddingLeft>
    <PaddingTop>2pt</PaddingTop>
    <TextAlign>Right</TextAlign>
    <PaddingBottom>2pt</PaddingBottom>
    <PaddingRight>2pt</PaddingRight>
   </Style>
   <CanGrow>true</CanGrow>
   <Value>=FormatCurrency(Fields!Bonus.Value,2,true,true,true)</Value>
  </Textbox>
 </ReportItems>
</TableCell>
<TableCell>
 <ReportItems>
  <Textbox Name="SalesYTD">
   <rd:DefaultName>SalesYTD</rd:DefaultName>
   <ZIndex>1</ZIndex>
   <Style>
    <PaddingLeft>2pt</PaddingLeft>
    <PaddingTop>2pt</PaddingTop>
    <TextAlign>Right</TextAlign>
    <PaddingBottom>2pt</PaddingBottom>
    <PaddingRight>2pt</PaddingRight>
   </Style>
   <CanGrow>true</CanGrow>
   <Value>=FormatCurrency(Fields!SalesYTD.Value, 2, true, true, true)</Value>
  </Textbox>
 </ReportItems>
</TableCell>
```

```
<TableCell>
 <ReportItems>
  <Textbox Name="SalesLastYear">
   <rd:DefaultName>SalesLastYear</rd:DefaultName>
   <Style>
    <PaddingLeft>2pt</PaddingLeft>
    <PaddingTop>2pt</PaddingTop>
    <TextAlign>Right</TextAlign>
    <PaddingBottom>2pt</PaddingBottom>
    <PaddingRight>2pt</PaddingRight>
   </Style>
   <CanGrow>true</CanGrow>
   <Value>=FormatCurrency(Fields!SalesLastYear.Value,2 ,true, true, true)</Value>
  </Textbox>
 </ReportItems>
</TableCell>
```

You have just edited your first RDL document. Later in the chapter, we will cover a bit more on RDL, including how to programmatically render RDL from your own code. When you are finished editing, click Preview to see the results of your work. You should see a report that looks like the screenshot shown in Figure 15-2.

\multicolumn{7}{c}{Sales By Sales Person}						
First Name	**Middle Name**	**Last Name**	**Sales Quota**	**Bonus**	**Sales YTD**	**Sales Last Year**
Stephen	Y	Jiang		$0.00	$677,558.47	$0.00
Michael	G	Blythe	$300,000.00	$4,100.00	$4,557,045.05	$1,750,406.48
Linda	C	Mitchell	$250,000.00	$2,000.00	$5,200,475.23	$1,439,156.03
Jillian		Carson	$250,000.00	$2,500.00	$3,857,163.63	$1,997,186.20
Garrett	R	Vargas	$250,000.00	$500.00	$1,764,938.99	$1,620,276.90
Tsvi	Michael	Reiter	$300,000.00	$6,700.00	$2,811,012.72	$1,849,640.94
Pamela	O	Ansman-Wolfe	$250,000.00	$5,000.00	$0.00	$1,927,059.18
Shu	K	Ito	$250,000.00	$3,550.00	$3,018,725.49	$2,073,506.00
José	Edvaldo	Saraiva	$250,000.00	$5,000.00	$3,189,356.25	$2,038,234.65
David	R	Campbell	$250,000.00	$3,500.00	$3,587,378.43	$1,371,635.32
Amy	E	Alberts		$0.00	$636,440.25	$0.00
Jae	B	Pak	$250,000.00	$5,150.00	$5,015,682.38	$1,635,823.40
Ranjit	R	Varkey Chudukatil	$250,000.00	$985.00	$3,827,950.24	$2,396,539.76
Tete	A	Mensa-Annan	$300,000.00	$3,900.00	$1,931,620.18	$0.00
Syed	E	Abbas		$0.00	$219,088.88	$0.00
Rachel	B	Valdez	$250,000.00	$75.00	$2,241,204.04	$1,307,949.79
Lynn	N	Tsoflias	$250,000.00	$5,650.00	$1,758,385.93	$2,278,548.98

Figure 15-2

Be careful using Preview. While Visual Studio 2005 against a SQL Server 2005 Reporting Services instance will allow you to get back to design view, this is not the case with Reporting Services against SQL Server 2000. If you select Preview in SQL Server 2000, you are pretty much hosed. As a result, you will have to restart your project to get back to design view.

A Brief Primer on Report Definition Language

As you will find, we see very little value in expanding on the formats of most of the XML derivatives in this chapter, as most of the derivatives are way too complex to be covered adequately in such as short space. RDL is an exception, however, as it is useful to see how Reporting Services is working underneath the hood. In addition, there will be times when you need to edit RDL directly, as we did in the last section. We won't go into great detail on every element in the RDL file; we'll save that for another book, *RDL for Dummies* (yes, that's a joke).

Rather than show the entire RDL for the simple report, which encompasses more than 25 pages, let's take a quick trip through a much simpler report. In this case, we made a report called `rdlReport` and dragged the `firstName` onto the report. Because the data is the same source, much of the material here can be used to edit the Sales by Sales Person report.

The first section to look at is `<DataSources>`. We can have two types of data sources: shared and single report. With a shared data source, we get a name, an id (in the form of a globally unique identifier, or GUID), and a reference. The reference refers back to an rds file, with the name of Chapter15DataSource.rds. The link to the RDS file is shown in the following code:

```
<DataSources>
  <DataSource Name="Chapter15DataSource">
    <rd:DataSourceID>559a2b48-7b75-42f3-94d0-18276f3b3cd1</rd:DataSourceID>
    <DataSourceReference>Chapter15DataSource</DataSourceReference>
  </DataSource>
</DataSources>
```

The RDS data source (shared data source) contains the information that would be embedded in the page if this were a non-shared data source. It is pulled out into a separate XML file so it can easily be shared by multiple reports. Highlighted in bold are the pieces that pertain to the connection string:

```
<?xml version="1.0" encoding="utf-8"?>
<RptDataSource xmlns:xsi="http://www.w3.org/2001/XMLSchema-instance"
xmlns:xsd="http://www.w3.org/2001/XMLSchema">
  <Name>Chapter15DataSource</Name>
  <DataSourceID>81c6df8b-5368-4723-915b-989164ecafd2</DataSourceID>
  <ConnectionProperties>
    <Extension>SQL</Extension>
    <ConnectString>Data Source=(local);Initial
Catalog=AdventureWorks</ConnectString>
    <IntegratedSecurity>true</IntegratedSecurity>
  </ConnectionProperties>
</RptDataSource>
```

If you had created a non-shared data source, the connection string would have been embedded in the RDL, as shown in the following code:

```
<DataSources>
  <DataSource Name="Chapter15DataSource2">
    <ConnectionProperties>
      <DataProvider>SQL</DataProvider>
      <ConnectString>Data Source=(local);Initial
Catalog=AdventureWorks</ConnectString>
```

```
        <IntegratedSecurity>true</IntegratedSecurity>
      </ConnectionProperties>
      <rd:DataSourceID>cf744c43-70b4-473d-a9a3-33d337f34186</rd:DataSourceID>
   </DataSource>
</DataSources>
```

The main difference here is where the information to connect is located. Both of these methods will work identically, although the data source embedded in the RDL will only apply to a single report. Note one other thing about the two XML snippets. When embedded in the RDL, the tag is `<DataProvider>`, whereas it is `<Extension>` in an RDS file. Why? That is a great question for which we have no reasonable answer.

The next section of the RDL page deals with how the page is rendered. The height and width of the report are included, as well as the margins. Finishing up, there is a bit of information about the grid on the page, which is used in the designer, as well as the language of the report and the Report ID (another GUID). This section is shown here:

```
<InteractiveHeight>11in</InteractiveHeight>
<InteractiveWidth>8.5in</InteractiveWidth>
<TopMargin>1in</TopMargin>
<BottomMargin>1in</BottomMargin>
<LeftMargin>1in</LeftMargin>
<RightMargin>1in</RightMargin>
<Width>6.5in</Width>
<rd:DrawGrid>true</rd:DrawGrid>
<rd:SnapToGrid>true</rd:SnapToGrid>
<Language>en-US</Language>
<rd:ReportID>6d3dc829-bb8d-46d1-84a7-fa1073457bd4</rd:ReportID>
```

As we move down a bit farther, we get to the meat of the report. The `<Body>` tag wraps around the rendered section of the report, much like a `<Body>` tag in HTML wraps around the rendered HTML content of the page. The use of a `<TableRows>` collection enables an item to repeat once for every record in the page. The following code shows the report if only the `FirstName` field is added:

```
<Body>
    <TableRows>
      <TableRow>
          <Height>0.25in</Height>
            <TableCells>
              <TableCell>
                 <ReportItems>
                   <Textbox Name="FirstName">
                    <Width>2in</Width>
                    <rd:DefaultName>FirstName</rd:DefaultName>
                    <Top>0.125in</Top>
                    <Style>
                       <PaddingLeft>2pt</PaddingLeft>
                       <PaddingTop>2pt</PaddingTop>
                       <PaddingBottom>2pt</PaddingBottom>
                       <PaddingRight>2pt</PaddingRight>
                    </Style>
                    <Left>0.125in</Left>
```

```
                    <CanGrow>true</CanGrow>
                    <Height>0.25in</Height>
                    <Value>=Fields!FirstName.Value</Value>
                </Textbox>
              </ReportItems>
            </TableCell>
          </TableCells>
        </TableRow>
      </TableRows>
   <Height>2in</Height>
   <Style />
 </Body>
```

The final section of the file that we will look at is shown in the following code. This is the `DataSets` section, which contains the fields from the `DataSet` we created earlier in this section. The `Value` tag (above) contains the link to the `FirstName` field (below) in the `DataSet` for the page, which is bolded:

```
<DataSets>
  <DataSet Name="DataSet1">
    <Fields>
      <Field Name="FirstName">
        <DataField>FirstName</DataField>
        <rd:TypeName>System.String</rd:TypeName>
      </Field>
... Snipped out code for rest of fields
      <Query>
        <DataSourceName>Chapter15DataSource2</DataSourceName>
        <CommandType>StoredProcedure</CommandType>
        <CommandText>Sales.sspGetSalesTotals</CommandText>
      </Query>
    </DataSet>
  </DataSets>
```

While this short primer is certainly not enough to build full-scale RDL reports by hand, it should give you a good heads-up for editing reports without the designer.

Using the Reporting Service Server

To go to the next level, you will have to deploy the report by right-clicking the solution and choosing Deploy. Once you deploy the solution, you can surf to the report by using the URL http:// hostname/Reports. When you do this, you will see a screen that contains all of the projects you have deployed to Reporting Services. From here, select SimpleReport ➪ SalesBySalesPerson. You now see your report in all its shining glory, as shown in Figure 15-3.

Okay, maybe doesn't look so special on the surface. What's going on underneath the hood, however, is a bit more impressive. When you render a report, two applications are serving up the report. The application you see the report in is called Reports, while the application doing all of the work is called ReportServer. The Reports application is of little use to us at the moment; we will concentrate on the ReportServer.

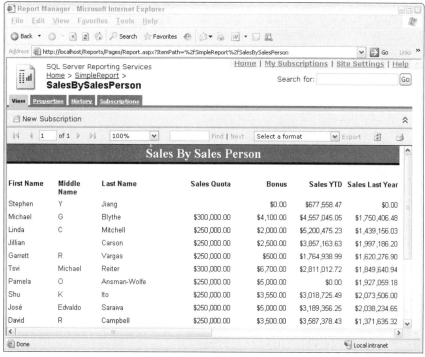

Figure 15-3

Please be aware that Visual Studio does not always fill in the production values for you to deploy your reports. If you get an error on deployment, right-click the Solution and choose Properties. Next, you change the drop-down on the Properties dialog box to read `Active (Production)` *and type values next to* `TargetServerURL` (`http://localhost/ReportServer` *for a development machine) and a value for the* `TargetDataSourceFolder`. *The* `TargetDataSourceFolder` *is controlled by Reporting Services, and you can name it whatever you like. (We use* `DataSources`, *but any name you like will work.) As it is controlled by Reporting Services, you must specify a name; you cannot use an absolute path such as* `C:\MyDataSources`.

Contacting Reporting Services via an URL

One of the easiest ways to contact Reporting Services from another application is through a URL. Microsoft has built in a rather extensive array of parameters that can be sent to the ReportServer application to render reports in a variety of formats. Control of the rendered report is achieved by sending commands through either the query string or the form collection. If you are not familiar with Web applications, don't worry; we'll give you enough rope to hang yourself, but we'll also show you how to cut the branch before you jump.

If you experiment, you will find that you can run many of the commands in this section against the Reports application. Because of this, you might be tempted to use Reports instead of ReportServer. Avoid this temptation; it will only add weight to your application. Remember that the ReportServer is called from Reports. If you use Reports, you will be using two applications instead of one.

To control the server, you will have to learn a little bit about a couple of namespaces: namely, rs and rc. Rather than create a long-winded intro, we believe it's better to give an example. If you type the following URL into a browser (substituting the server name for hostname, of course), you will see the Sales By Sales Person report created in the last section, assuming you deployed it, that is:

```
http://hostname/ReportServer/Pages/ReportViewer.aspx?/SimpleReport/
SalesBySalesPerson&rs:Command=Render&rc:Toolbar=false
```

Below is a breakdown of what is happening with this URL:

❑   http://localhost/ReportServer/Pages/ReportViewer.aspx is the page in the ReportServer application that renders reports.

❑   /SimpleReport/SalesBySalesPerson is our first query string element, which indicates we are rendering the sales by sales person report in the SimpleReport project.

❑   rs:Command=Render indicates that we would like to view the rendered report.

❑   rc:Toolbar=false indicates we do not want the toolbar to show up when we render the report.

Looking at the URL, you see two namespaces: rs and rc (these are bolded in the preceding list). The first is rs, which stands for report server. You will use this namespace to send parameters that tell the Report Server what to do. The second namespace is rc, which stands for rendering controller. You use this to determine how the UI is rendered.

As you proceed through this section, we recommend working through the commands in a browser, where applicable, and viewing the results; this will give you a much better grasp of what is going on behind the scenes.

The rs Namespace

The first set of parameters we are going to look at are those that control the Report Server itself. In the rs namespace are the parameters Command (what we would like the server to do), Format (how we would like to examine the report), Snapshot (saving a rendered report), SessionID, and ClearSession:

❑   rs:Command — This parameter specifies which command should be applied to the path you are working with.

❑   Render — This parameter renders the specified resource. In the following code sample, the sales by sales person, from the Simple Report project created earlier, is rendered:

```
http://hostname/ReportServer/Pages/ReportViewer.aspx?/SimpleReport/SalesBySalesPers
on&rs:Command=Render
```

❑   ListChildren — ListChildren is most commonly used to list the reports under a specific project deployed to the Report Server. As an example, the following URL is used to view links to all of the reports in the SimpleReport application created earlier in this chapter. The list will only contain one report at this time.

```
http://hostname/ReportServer/SimpleReport?/SimpleReport&rs:Command=ListChildren
```

❑   GetResourceContents — This renders a specified resource and displays it in an HTML page:

```
http://hostname/ReportServer/SimpleReport?/SimpleReport&rs:Command=GetResource
Contents
```

❑ GetDataSourceContents — This parameter displays the properties of a given shared data source. If you have created individual, non-shared data sources for your reports, this value is useless for the Command parameter:

```
http://hostname/ReportServer/SimpleReport?/SimpleReport&rs:Command=GetDataSource
Contents
```

❑ rs:Format — This is by far the easiest rs parameter to understand. It indicates the format of the rendered report. Valid values for this parameter are HTML3.2, HTML4.0, HTMLLOWC (HTML with Office Web Components), MHML (Web Archive Format), IMAGE, EXCEL, CSV (a comma-delimited text file), PD, and XML. You can also create custom rendering extensions for Reporting Services and add them to the list.

```
http://hostname/ReportServer/SimpleReport?/SimpleReport&rs:Format=HTML4.0&rs:Comman
d=Render
```

❑ rs:Snapshot — This parameter renders a snapshot to the Report Server. This is a good option for particularly complex reports that a lot of users access. The value for this parameter is a timestamp in the format YYYY-MM-DDThh:mm:ss (Y=Year, M=Month, D=Day, T=time from this point on, H=Hour, m=Minute and S=Second). Example January 1, 2006 at 2:05:03 AM = 2006-01-01T02:05:03.

```
http://hostname/ReportServer/SimpleReport?/SimpleReport&rs:Snapshot=2005-06-07T13:
40:02
```

❑ rs:SessionID — This identifies the session access the Report Server. This option is useful when you are not using session cookies. If a Report Server has been configured to not use session cookies, the first hit on a report will cause a redirect using the Session ID, whether you specify this or not. Subsequent hits on this report from the same session will need the Session ID attached.

```
http://hostname/ReportServer/SimpleReport?/SimpleReport&rs:SessionID=DA215DE6-0206-
401C-8C9D-823337722CBE&rs:Command=Render
```

❑ rs:ClearSession — This parameter tells the browser to clear the currently cached copy of a report. The only valid value for this parameter is true. Note that this will clear all copies of this report currently associated with a particular user.

```
http://hostname/ReportServer/SimpleReport?/SimpleReport&rs:ClearSession=true
```

❑ rs:ParameterLanguage — This indicates the language in which the report should be rendered. Note that this parameter is not useful for a report that uses a data source containing only one language.

```
http://hostname/ReportServer/SimpleReport?/SimpleReport&rs:ParameterLanguage=en-
US&rs:Command=Render
```

The rc Namespace

The second namespace is for the rendering controller. The parameters available are `Toolbar`, `Parameters`, `Zoom`, `Section`, and `LinkTarget`:

❏ `rc:Toolbar` — This indicates whether the toolbar should be shown or not. Valid values are `true` and `false`, with the default being `true`. For most reports in a separate application, the value will be `false`.

❏ `rc:Parameters` — This parameter indicates whether the parameters area of the toolbar should be shown or not. Valid values are `true`, `false` and `Collapsed`, with the default being `true`.

❏ `rc:Zoom` — This is the zoom factor, as a percentage, to zoom in or out on a report. Valid values are positive numbers (although you should not get stupid on this one and create a zoom that is completely unreadable), `Page Width` and, `Whole Page`, with the default being `100` (or 100 percent).

❏ `rc:Section` — This indicates which page you wish to render. `Section` must be an integral number (i.e., no decimals) of a valid page in the report, with a default value of 1. Note that you must have a multi-page report to take advantage of this parameter.

❏ `rc:LinkTarget` — Useful for reports with a hyperlink column, this parameter sets the target for browser-driven reports:

  ❏ `_blank` — Creates a new, unnamed window. If you click multiple hyperlinks, you will end up with multiple windows.

  ❏ `_self` — The new report will render in the same window as the old report.

  ❏ `_parent` — Parent window of the window to which you are sending the command. Please note that this value is fairly useless if you have not spawned off a new window for Report Server queries.

  ❏ `_top` — Uses the full window. This is useful when you are using frames and want the hyperlink to open the link in the full window instead of inside the same frame as the report.

  ❏ `{window_name}` — If you specify a window name as a target, any links clicked with this value will render in the same window.

❏ `rc:FindString` — This is used to find a string in a particular report. This parameter is useful to find a particular item in a multi-page report. You can further refine your search with the parameters `StartFind` and `EndFind`. In addition, you can set a page to show whether the search results end up with no hits.

  ❏ `rc:StartFind` — Page to start a search for the string parameter for `FindString`.

  ❏ `rc:EndString` — Page to stop a search for the string parameter for `FindString`.

  ❏ `rc:FallbackPage` — Page to show when a search fails.

❏ `rc:StyleSheet` — Indicates which cascading stylesheet (CSS) to use when rendering a report. Do not include the .css extension when specifying a stylesheet. The stylesheet used must be deployed to the server to be valid.

URL Parameters in Action

Setting the stage, let's suppose the VP of Sales told Ms. Trenary that he would like you to provide a way to view the report on the company intranet. With the simple report, you would most likely use a hyperlink to send all parameters through the query string. The following example links to the Sales by Sales Person report created earlier in this chapter. If you are typing this in, remember to change the `hostname` to the actual name for the machine hosting Reporting Services, as shown here:

```
<%@ Page Language="VB" AutoEventWireup="false" CodeFile="Default.aspx.vb"
Inherits="_Default" %>
<!DOCTYPE html PUBLIC "-//W3C//DTD XHTML 1.1//EN"
"http://www.w3.org/TR/xhtml11/DTD/xhtml11.dtd">
<html xmlns="http://www.w3.org/1999/xhtml" >
<head id="Head1" runat="server">
    <title>Chapter 15 web - Launch page</title>
</head>
<body>
    <form id="form1" runat="server">
    <div>
       <ul>
          <li>
<a href="
http://hostname/ReportServer/Pages/ReportViewer.aspx?/SimpleReport/SalesBySales
Person&rs:Command=Render&rc:Toolbar=false">Sales By Salesperson</a>
          </li>
       </ul>
    </div>
    </form>
</body>
</html>
```

Suppose you would like to render a report and specify values for parameters. Fortunately, this is quite easy, as you can send the parameters as part of a form send. To show a form sending to the Report Server, we will use the Quarterly Sales for a Sales Rep report.

In the first run at the page, the page is going to submit directly to the Report Server for the rendered report. To accomplish this easily, we will short-circuit the normal ASP.NET feature and have the form run as a normal HTML form. This can be done by removing the `runat="server"` attribute in the form tag and using HTML elements on the page. You can see this in the following code:

```
<%@ Page Language="VB" AutoEventWireup="false" CodeFile="FormSubmit.aspx.vb"
Inherits="FormSubmit" %>
<!DOCTYPE html PUBLIC "-//W3C//DTD XHTML 1.1//EN"
"http://www.w3.org/TR/xhtml11/DTD/xhtml11.dtd">
<html xmlns="http://www.w3.org/1999/xhtml" >
<head runat="server">
    <title>Untitled Page</title>
</head>
<body>
  <form id="form1"
action="http://hostname/ReportServer/Pages/ReportViewer.aspx?/SimpleReport/SalesBy
SalesPerson"
  method="post" target="_blank">
```

```
<div>
  <h1>Form for report</h1>
    <table style="width: 257px">
      <tr>
        <td style="width: 106px">
          Employee ID:</td>
        <td>
          <INPUT type="text" ID="EmployeeID" />
        </td>
      </tr>
      <tr>
        <td style="width: 106px">
        </td>
        <td>
          <INPUT type="submit"  value="View" />
        </td>
      </tr>
      <tr>
        <td style="width: 106px">
        </td>
        <td>
        </td>
      </tr>
    </table>
    <input type="hidden" name="rs:Command" value="Render" />
    <input type="hidden" name="rs:Format" value="HTML4.0" />
    <input type="hidden" name="rc:Toolbar" value="false" />
  </div>
  </form>
</body>
</html>
```

The downside of contacting the Report Server directly is that there is no validation on the controls in the form. In this example, a person could easily type in an alphanumeric string and return no results. To correct this, we have two basic options. The first is to add a JavaScript form handler and the second is to move to ASP.NET and handle the form submit, building the URL to open on the fly. Of the two, JavaScript will work within the page we have already created without altering anything else except the form tag. The JavaScript routine is shown here:

```
<head runat="server">
    <title>Untitled Page</title>
    <script language="Javascript">
    function CheckForm()
    {
        var field = form1.EmployeeID;
        var regex = /^\d*$/

        if(regex.test(field.Value))
        {
          return (true);
        }
        else
        {
```

```
                alert('Employee ID must be a number');
                return (false);
        }     }
      </script>
  </head>
  <body>
      <form id="form1" onsubmit="return CheckForm()" ...
```

The second method of checking is to return to query string arguments and build the page using ASP.NET server controls. The simple ASP.NET form is shown here:

```
<%@ Page Language="VB" AutoEventWireup="false" CodeFile="FormSubmit2.aspx.vb"
Inherits="FormSubmit2" %>
<!DOCTYPE html PUBLIC "-//W3C//DTD XHTML 1.1//EN"
"http://www.w3.org/TR/xhtml11/DTD/xhtml11.dtd">
<html xmlns="http://www.w3.org/1999/xhtml" >
<head runat="server">
    <title>Form Submit 2</title>
</head>
<body>
  <form id="form1" runat="server">
  <div>
    <h1>Form for report</h1>
      <table style="width: 257px">
        <tr>
          <td style="width: 106px">
            Employee ID:</td>
          <td>
            <asp:TextBox ID="EmpID" runat="server"></asp:TextBox>
          </td>
        </tr>
        <tr>
          <td style="width: 106px">
          </td>
          <td>
            <asp:Button ID="SubmitButton" runat="server" Text="Button" />
          </td>
        </tr>
        <tr>
          <td style="width: 106px">
          </td>
          <td>
          </td>
        </tr>
      </table>
  </div>
    <asp:TextBox ID="CommandTextBox" runat="server"
        Visible="False">Render</asp:TextBox>
    <asp:TextBox ID="FormatTextBox" runat="server"
        Visible="False">HTML4.0</asp:TextBox>
    <asp:TextBox ID="ToolbarTextBox" runat="server"
        Visible="False">false</asp:TextBox>
  </form>
</body>
</html>
```

To finish this off, we will set up a CodeBeside page that handles the Submit button click event. As it is best practice to always check form submission on the server side as well, we are checking `Page.IsValid` prior to sending the user to the Report page. The CodeBeside file is shown here:

```
Partial Class FormSubmit2
    Inherits System.Web.UI.Page

    Protected Sub SubmitButton_Click(ByVal sender As Object, _
        ByVal e As System.EventArgs) Handles SubmitButton.Click
        If (Page.IsValid) Then
            SubmitFormAndRedirect()
        Else
            'TODO: Add error message here
        End If
    End Sub

    Private Sub SubmitFormAndRedirect()
        Dim command As String = CommandTextBox.Text
        Dim format As String = FormatTextBox.Text
        Dim toolbar As String = ToolbarTextBox.Text
        Dim fullURL As String

        Dim urlBuilder As New StringBuilder()
        urlBuilder.Append("http://localhost/ReportServer/Pages/ReportViewer.aspx?")
        urlBuilder.Append("/SimpleReport/SalesBySalesPerson")

        If (command.Length <> 0) Then
            urlBuilder.Append("&rs:Command=")
            urlBuilder.Append(command)
        End If

        If (format.Length <> 0) Then
            urlBuilder.Append("&rs:Format=")
            urlBuilder.Append(format)
        End If

        If (toolbar.Length <> 0) Then
            urlBuilder.Append("&rc:Toolbar=")
            urlBuilder.Append(toolbar)
        End If

        fullURL = urlBuilder.ToString()

        'Redirect on client side
        Response.Redirect(fullURL, True)
    End Sub
End Class
```

If you do not want the user to see the parameters on the query string, you have the option of hiding it by using `Server.Transfer` instead of `Response.Redirect`.

Using SOAP to Contact the Report Server

At this point, we assume that everyone knows what Service Oriented Architecture Protocol (SOAP) and Web Service Description Language (WSDL) are. Just in case a few of you who have been napping, both SOAP and WSDL are XML derivatives used for Web services. Yes, we realize SOAP has other uses, but they are not germane to this chapter. For the purposes of this chapter, WSDL is the means by which the Report Server exposes its Web services, while SOAP is the format with which it communicates.

Creating WSDL (pronounced "Whiz-dull" or "Whiz-dill") is far beyond the scope of this chapter, or this book for that matter. In fact, it is way off the map for most books, as WSDL is a rather complex contract language. To get an idea of the complexity, here is part of the WSDL for the simple Hello World sample that's created when you add a new ASMX page in Visual Studio:

```
<?xml version="1.0" encoding="utf 8" ?>
<wsdl:definitions xmlns:soap="http://schemas.xmlsoap.org/wsdl/soap/"
xmlns:s="http://www.w3.org/2001/XMLSchema" targetNamespace="http://tempuri.org/"
xmlns:wsdl="http://schemas.xmlsoap.org/wsdl/">
  <wsdl:types>
  <s:schema elementFormDefault="qualified" targetNamespace="http://tempuri.org/">
  <s:element name="HelloWorld" />
  <s:element name="HelloWorldResponse">
  <s:complexType>
  <s:sequence>
  <s:element minOccurs="0" maxOccurs="1" name="HelloWorldResult" type="s:string" />
  </s:sequence>
  </s:complexType>
  </s:element>
  </s:schema>
  </wsdl:types>
  <wsdl:message name="HelloWorldSoapIn">
  <wsdl:part name="parameters" element="tns:HelloWorld" />
  </wsdl:message>
  <wsdl:message name="HelloWorldSoapOut">
  <wsdl:part name="parameters" element="tns:HelloWorldResponse" />
  </wsdl:message>
  <wsdl:portType name="HelloWorldSoap">
  <wsdl:operation name="HelloWorld">
  <wsdl:input message="tns:HelloWorldSoapIn" />
  <wsdl:output message="tns:HelloWorldSoapOut" />
  </wsdl:operation>
  </wsdl:portType>
  <!-- Lots more stuff removed here -->
</wsdl:definitions>
```

Note that this is only around 30% of the WSDL needed to set up a single method with no parameters. The size increases dramatically with just a few parameterized Web methods. In fact, the WSDL for Reporting Services would weigh in at about 120 pages if placed in this book (great "thunk" factor, low educational value = tastes great, less filling). If you would like to study the WSDL, you can surf over to `http://hostname/ReportServer/ReportService.asmx?WSDL` and take a gander.

Because all major vendors we know of have a tool to create WSDL, there is no need to learn the intricacies of building it by hand. In Visual Studio 2005 (or Visual Studio .NET for that matter), you set up a proxy for a WSDL contract by adding a Web reference. By the same token, you do not have to actually know SOAP to use SOAP in Reporting Services, as Visual Studio will handle fulfilling the contract for you when you create a Web reference.

Setting up the Web Application

In this section, you'll learn how to set up a Web application that renders a report. To show you the power of the Report Server, we are going to render the report as an image and then click on that image to create the desired report.

The first step is creating a Web reference. Most of you have probably done this before, but we don't want to assume anything. To set up a Web reference, right-click on the project and choose Add Web Reference. This will bring up a screen like the one shown in Figure 15-4.

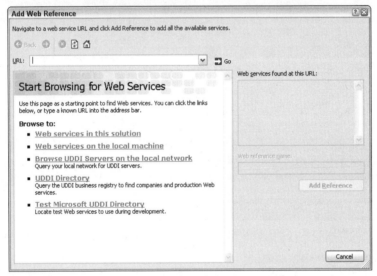

Figure 15-4

If you want, you can click on Web Services on the local machine and find the Report Server Web Service. Another method to get to the service is to click in the URL textbox and type in `http://localhost/ReportServer/ReportService.asmx?WSDL`. Give the Web service the name `AdventureWorksReports` and click the Add Reference button.

What you have done is create a proxy object that will contact the Web service you have referenced. This proxy object will handle the SOAP for you, which is why we stated earlier that knowing SOAP is not a mandatory skill to set up a report.

One other setup step is necessary to render a report using the user's credentials. You will have to make sure impersonation is set to `true` in the web.config file:

```
<identity impersonate="true"/>
```

The second step is to add a page in which to render the report. We called this page RenderReport.aspx. At the top, type in a header and then drag an image button onto the form. Call the image button `imgSalesBySalesPerson`. This is the image button that will hold a pictorial version of the report. Below that, add a panel and call it `pnlReport`. Set the visible property of this panel to `false`. This is the panel that will handle the rendered report. The resulting ASP.NET page is shown here:

```
<%@ Page Language="VB" AutoEventWireup="false" CodeFile="ReportImage.aspx.vb"
Inherits="ReportImage" %>

<!DOCTYPE html PUBLIC "-//W3C//DTD XHTML 1.1//EN"
"http://www.w3.org/TR/xhtml11/DTD/xhtml11.dtd">

<html xmlns="http://www.w3.org/1999/xhtml" >
<head runat="server">
    <title>Report Rendering Page</title>
</head>
<body>
    <form id="form1" runat="server">
    <div>
        <h1>Choose a report</h1>
        <asp:ImageButton ID="imgSalesBySalesPerson" runat="server" /><br />
        <asp:Panel ID="pnlReport" runat="server" Height="384px" Visible="False"
                Width="705px">
        </asp:Panel>
    </div>
    </form>
</body>
</html>
```

To set up the initial state of the page, move to the code view (click on the ReportSelector page and then click the View Code button at the top of the Solution Explorer). At the top of the editor window, click the left-most drop-down list and choose Form1 events; in the right drop-down list, choose Load. In the `Page_Load` event created, add the following code:

```
Protected Sub Page_Load(ByVal sender As Object, _
        ByVal e As System.EventArgs) Handles Me.Load

    If (Page.IsPostBack = False) Then
        BindImage()
    End If

End Sub
```

The next step is to build the `BindImage()` subroutine, which will hold the code to render our image in the image button. Following are step-by-step instructions for setting up the Bind Image routine.

First, create an object for the Web service proxy class (the class created when you added your Web reference). Setting up the Web reference is shown here:

```
Dim rs As New AdventureWorksReports.ReportingService()
rs.Credentials = System.Net.CredentialCache.DefaultCredentials
rs.Url = "http://localhost/ReportServer/ReportService.asmx"
```

On this Web proxy object, we are setting the default credentials, which are covered a bit more in the next paragraph. In addition, we are setting the URL for the Report Server. You may wonder why we are doing this, as the Web proxy object already contains this URL. For the answer, think for a moment about the most common change you make in a Web application, which is moving an application from development to test, or even production. If you prefer to hack your proxy object and recompile every time you move to a new Report Server, then this step is completely unnecessary.

Back to the credentials! Imagine a scenario in which you are rendering a report, or part of a report, to a user who has no access to the Report Server. In these cases, you could create a Credentials object that contained a user who did have access to the Report Server, and deliver the report in your Web application. To do this, you must set up a NetworkCredential object, like this:

```
rs.Credentials = System.Net.NetworkCredential("UserName", "Password", "DomainName")
```

Note that you would not embed a username and password into the code. Sure, .NET is compiled, but it is only compiled to IL code. Anyone who finds a way to hack your app has access to your Report Server, so put the secrets in a better spot.

The next step is setting up the parameters for the Render method of our proxy object. The signature for the Render method is shown here:

```
Public Function Render(ByVal Report As String, ByVal Format As String, _
ByVal HistoryID As String, ByVal DeviceInfo As String, _
ByVal Parameters() As AdventureWorksReports.ParameterValue,_
ByVal Credentials() As AdventureWorksReports.DataSourceCredentials, _
ByVal ShowHideToggle As String, ByRef Encoding As String, _
ByRef MimeType As String, _
ByRef ParametersUsed() As AdventureWorksReports.ParameterValue, _
ByRef Warnings() As AdventureWorksReports.Warning, _
ByRef StreamIds() As String) As Byte()
```

Rather than gloss over this, it is better to step through each of the parameters:

❑   Report: The name of the report we are rendering.

```
Dim reportName As String = "/SimpleReport/SalesBySalesPerson"
```

❑   Format: The Format parameter is the format in which the report will be rendered. The types of valid rendering formats were covered previously in the section on rs Parameters. Currently, we are setting this to IMAGE, but we will focus on an HTML4.0 rendered report later.

```
Dim format As String = "IMAGE"
```

❑   HistoryID: The HistoryID deals with snapshots, which we are not going to cover in this chapter. For our purposes, this is set to Nothing.

❑   DeviceInfo: DeviceInfo tells us a bit about the rendering of the Report. We explain this after we finish the rest of the parameters.

```
Dim devInfo As String =
"<DeviceInfo><OutputFormat>GIF</OutputFormat></DeviceInfo>"
```

❑   Parameters: These are the input parameters for a report. As the report we are rendering does not have parameters, this is set to Nothing.

❑   Credentials: The credentials necessary to render the report. As we are using impersonation, this is set to Nothing in our Web application.

❑   ShowHideToggle: The show/hide toggle is useful for times when you are rendering the header bar. For our purposes, this is set to Nothing.

❑   Encoding: This is the encoding type of the text in the report returned to you. Our advice? Go ahead and get this string, even if you are not using it now.

❑   MimeType: This is the mime type of the report returned to you. Once again, go ahead and get this string, even if you are not using it now.

❑   ParametersUsed: This is a list of parameters used in rendering this report. This may or may not match the Parameters collection seen earlier in the list. For example, let's assume you are rendering more than one report in your page. If so, you can set up all of the parameters in a collection. Those that are returned are the parameters that were actually used. There is no reason to gather this information if you are not using parameters, so we have set it to Nothing.

❑   Warnings: This is a list of warnings returned from the report. You should always grab this information, as it is the first indicator of a problem — unless you have an exception thrown, of course.

❑   StreamIds: These are the ID values returned to you for each page in the rendered report. You should always get these ID values.

To render the report, each of these parameters is sent to the server and a report is returned for the page selected. If you did not specify a particular page, you will get page 1. To render the rest of the reports, you call the service again with the StreamId of the page you would like to render. Setting up the report capture is shown here:

```
Dim report As Byte() = rs.Render(reportName, format, historyID, _
        devInfo, parameters, credentials, showHideToggle, encode, mimeType, _
        parametersUsed, warnings, streamIDs)
```

Finally, we are going to render the image and place it in the rendered report as an image button. In order to do this, you must pull the image from the stream of bytes. The only way to do this under the current Framework is to place the byte array into a System.Drawing.Image object. You then save the image and read it from a relative URL path:

```
Dim filePath As String = Server.MapPath(".") + "\Report.gif"
Dim img As System.Drawing.Image = _
    System.Drawing.Image.FromStream(New System.IO.MemoryStream(report))

Dim thumbnail As System.Drawing.Image = _
    img.GetThumbnailImage(100, 200, Nothing, Nothing)
thumbnail.Save(filePath)

'Bind to the image button
imgSalesBySalesPerson.ImageUrl = "report.gif"
```

When you are finished, you should have a page that has a cute little version of your report rendered as an image button, as shown in Figure 15-5.

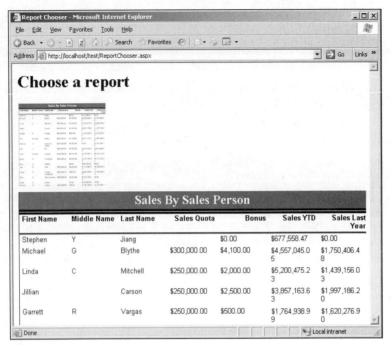

Figure 15-5

When you click the image button, you will render the report for the image button you clicked. In this instance there is only one, which is our famous Sales By Sales Person report. The code necessary to render an HTML report is pretty close to the code necessary to render an image. The changes necessary to do this are shown in bold:

```
Protected Sub imgSalesBySalesPerson_Click(ByVal sender As Object, _
        ByVal e As System.Web.UI.ImageClickEventArgs) _
        Handles imgSalesBySalesPerson.Click
    'Set up the service
    Dim rs As New AdventureWorksReports.ReportingService()
    rs.Credentials = System.Net.CredentialCache.DefaultCredentials
    rs.Url = "http://localhost/ReportServer/ReportService.asmx"

    'Set up parameters to return an image
    Dim reportName As String = "/SimpleReport/SalesBySalesPerson"
    Dim format As String = "HTML4.0"
    Dim historyID As String = Nothing
    Dim devInfo As String = _
        "<DeviceInfo><StreamRoot>/SimpleReport/resources/</StreamRoot>" & _
        "<StyleStream>True</StyleStream><HtmlFragment>True</HtmlFragment>" & _
        "</DeviceInfo>"
    Dim parameters() As AdventureWorksReports.ParameterValue = Nothing
    Dim credentials() As AdventureWorksReports.DataSourceCredentials = Nothing
    Dim showHideToggle As String = Nothing
    Dim encode As String = Nothing
    Dim mimeType As String = Nothing
```

```
    Dim parametersUsed() As AdventureWorksReports.ParameterValue = Nothing
    Dim warnings() As AdventureWorksReports.Warning = Nothing
    Dim streamIDs() As String = Nothing

    'Get the report as an Image
    Dim report As Byte() = rs.Render(reportName, format, historyID, _
        devInfo, parameters, credentials, showHideToggle, encode, mimeType, _
        parametersUsed, warnings, streamIDs)

    'Return the page count (not used in this example)
    Dim pageCount As Integer = streamIDs.Length

    'Turn into a string
    Dim encodingVal As New System.Text.ASCIIEncoding
    Dim page As String = encodingVal.GetString(report)

    Dim ctl As New LiteralControl(page)
    pnlReport.Controls.Add(ctl)
    pnlReport.Visible = True
End Sub
```

At the end of the report, you will notice that we are rendering the report by turning it into a string. If you are rendering the report to a particular place in the HTTP stream, this is an unnecessary step, as you can simply bind the following routine to the form and output the report as a stream of bytes:

```
Response.BinaryWrite(report)
```

There is a practical reason to sacrifice a bit of performance and render as a string. When you create a string, you have the option of replacing strings in the output. One reason for doing this is to replace hyperlinks that point directly to the Report Server. If you simply hand the report over to the user, every hyperlink will point to the Report Server and not your applications. This is true of drill-down reports as well. A simple code fix looks something like this:

```
page.Replace("ReportServer/", "reportHandler.aspx?/ReportServer")
```

You will then have to create the report handler page that renders the report from the hyperlink.

DeviceInfo

We have shown you DeviceInfo a couple of times in the preceding section and we are not happy with the amount of XML you have to write to use the SOAP interfaces. After the initial shock wears off, you find that this is not really all that complex, although there is a lot to learn. In an ideal world, the IDE would help you with some of this work — perhaps in the 3.0 Framework. For now, however, you will have to roll up your sleeves and write a bit of XML. To cover this subject correctly, we have to break this down by the type of format you are going to use.

In the following sections, we cover each of the XML tags, what they are used for, and acceptable values. The default value, where applicable, is **bolded**.

Please check the Wrox Website (at www.wrox.com) for updates to this section or for additional information.

CSV

Comma Separated Values (CSV) produces a flat file with cells in a row, separated by a comma, by default. In reality, you can use any separator if you specify a CSV file format.

Tag	Purpose	Acceptable Values
Encoding	Determines the text encoding of the comma separated file.	ASCII, UTF-7, UTF-8, or **Unicode**
Extension	File extension for the resulting file.	Default is **.CSV**
FieldDelimiter	Delimiter to separate columns in tabular data. Note: Value should be URL encoded (UNIX encoded), so a tab would be %09.	Default is comma (,)
NoHeader	Specifies whether to include column names in a header row. If true, it means there is no header row in the file.	true or **false**
Qualifier	If you want each field (column) to be delimited on each side, you will specify the character here.	Default is quotation mark (")
RecordDelimiter	Character or character combination to terminate a row.	Default is **<cr><lf>**
SuppressLineBreaks	Indicates whether line breaks are absent from the output. If you set this value to true, you cannot use a space for field delimiter, record delimiter, or qualifier.	true or **false**

Here's an example:

```
Dim devInfo As String = "<DeviceInfo><Encoding>ASCII</Encoding>" & _
        "<Extension>.TXT</Extension><NoHeader>true</NoHeader>" & _
        "<Qualifier>'</Qualifier><RecordDelimiter><cr></RecordDelimiter>" & _
        "<SuppressLineBreaks>false</SuppressLineBreaks></DeviceInfo>"
```

EXCEL

Excel means that the report is rendered in Microsoft® Excel format.

Tag	Purpose	Acceptable Values
OmitDocumentMap	Indicates whether or not you should omit the document map for reports t hat can use it.	true or **false**
OmitFormulas	Indicates whether or not formulas are omitted from the rendered report.	true or **false**
RemoveSpace	Determines the minimum space of an empty column smaller than a specific size.	Integer or decimal value followed by "in"; the default is **0.125in**
SimplePageHeader	Determines whether the page header is separate from the rest of the report. If you state false, the header is the first row.	true or **false**

Here's an example:

```
Dim devInfo As String = "<DeviceInfo><OmitDocumentMap>true</OmitDocumentMap>" & _
    "<OmitFormulas>true</OmitFormulas><RemoveSpace>0.5</RemoveSpace>
    "<RemoveSpace>false</RemoveSpace></DeviceInfo>"
```

HTML

HTML rendering can be done in HTML 3.2, HTML 4.0, or HTML for the Office Web components (HTMLOWC).

Tag	Purpose	Acceptable Values
BookmarkID	Tag for the bookmark you would like to go to in the report.	Only applicable when there are bookmarks
DocMap	Determines whether the report document map is visible or not.	**true** or false
DocMapID	The document map ID to scroll to when the report is rendered.	The document map ID to scroll to in the report
EndFind	SEARCH functionality: The last page to examine if there is a search for a particular item. Used with StartFind.	Integral value
FallbackPage	SEARCH functionality: The page to show when no results are found.	Integral value
FindString	SEARCH functionality: Text to search for.	The default is an empty string.
GetImage	Gets an icon for the HTML viewer.	Gets a particular icon for the HTML Viewer user interface.

Table continued on following page

Tag	Purpose	Acceptable Values
HTMLFragment	Indicates whether the report is rendered as a full HTML page or a snippet. If you are embedding this page in an ASP.NET application, you should set this to true.	true or **false**
Icon	Icon for a particular rendering extension.	The icon of a particular rendering extension.
JavaScript	Indicates whether JavaScript is supported in the rendered report.	true or **false**
LinkTarget	Target URL for any hyperlinks in the report.	Default is **_self**
Parameters	Specifies whether the parameter toolbar shows or is hidden.	**true** or false
ReplacementRoot	Root path for any hyperlink	The default is ReportServer.
Section	Page number of the report to render.	Integral value. The default is **1**.
StartFind	SEARCH functionality: The first page to examine if there is a search for a particular item. Used with StartFind.	Integral value
StreamRoot	If there are images in the report, this is the root location for these images.	The default is **/ReportServer/resources**.
StyleStream	Specifies whether cascading stylesheets and JavaScript files are streamed separately from the report.	true or **false**
Toolbar	Specifies whether the main toolbar shows or is hidden. If you set this to false, the parameters toolbar is also hidden.	**true** or false
Type	Browser abbreviation as defined in the browscap.ini file.	
Zoom	Amount to zoom into on the report.	Can be an integral value between 1 and **100** or the words Page Width or Whole Page.

Here's an example:

```
Dim devInfo As String = "<DeviceInfo><HTMLFragment>true</HTMLFragment>" & _
    "<JavaScript>true</JavaScript><StyleStream>0.5</StyleStream>" & _
    "<StreamRoot>/ReportServer/Resources/</StreamRoot></DeviceInfo>"
```

IMAGE

IMAGE is used to render a report as an image. Valid types are Bitmapped Pictures (BMP), Extended Metafile (EMG), Graphics Interfile Format (GIF), Joint Photographers Extension Group (JPEG), Portable Net Graphics (PNG), or Tagged Image File Format (TIFF). You are now ready to try your luck in the Image category on Jeopardy as well.

Tag	Purpose	Acceptable Values
ColorDepth	Number of bit to use for colors.	1,4,8,**24**, or 36.
Columns	Number of columns for the report. This will override the report's original settings.	Any positive integer or decimal value.
ColumnSpacing	Spacing between columns. This will override the report's original settings.	Any positive integer or decimal value (larger values create larger graphics).
DpiX	Horizontal resolution.	The default value is **96**.
DpiY	Vertical resolution.	The default value is **96**.
EndPage	The last page of the report to render. A value of 0 means all pages.	The default value is the same as StartPage.
MarginBottom	Bottom margin value, expressed as an integer or decimal. Must be followed by "in". This will override the report's original settings.	A positive integer or decimal value. A value of 1in means a 1-inch margin.
MarginLeft	Left margin value, expressed as an integer or decimal. Must be followed by "in". This will override the report's original settings.	A positive integer or decimal value. A value of 1in means a 1-inch margin.
MarginRight	Right margin value, expressed as an integer or decimal. Must be followed by "in". This will override the report's original settings.	A positive integer or decimal value. A value of 1in means a 1-inch margin.
MarginTop	Top margin value, expressed as an integer or decimal. Must be followed by "in". This will override the report's original settings.	A positive integer or decimal value. A value of 1in means a 1-inch margin.
OutputFormat	Any valid GDI format for a graphic.	BMP, EMF, GIF, JPEG, PNG, or TIFF. No default; must be specified.
PageHeight	Page height, in inches. Must be followed by "in". This will override the report's original settings.	A positive integer or decimal value. A value of 11in means a page height of 11 inches.

Table continued on following page

457

Tag	Purpose	Acceptable Values
PageWidth	Page width, in inches. Must be followed by "in". This will override the report's original settings.	A positive integer or decimal values. A value of 8.5in means a page width of 8.5 inches.
StartPage	The first page of the report to render. A value of 0 means all pages.	The default value is **1**.

Here's an example:

```
Dim devInfo As String = "<DeviceInfo><DpiX>200</DpiX>" & _
        "<DpiY>300</DpiY><StartPage>1</StartPage><EndPage>10</EndPage>" & _
        "<OutputFormat>JPEG</OutputFormat></DeviceInfo>"
```

MTHML

MHTML is used for the Web archive format. It is, by far, the simplest to set the DeviceInfo for, as there are only two options.

Tag	Purpose	Acceptable Values
JavaScript	Specifies whether JavaScript is supported in the rendered report.	true or **false**
MHTMLFragment	Indicates whether the report is rendered as a full HTML page or a snippet. If you are embedding this page in an ASP.NET application, you should set this to true.	true or **false**

Here's an example:

```
Dim devInfo As String = "<DeviceInfo><JavaScript>false</JavaScript>" & _
        "<MHTMLFragment>true</MHTMLFragment></DeviceInfo>"
```

PDF

PDF is used to render Portable Document Files, aka Adobe Acrobat documents. PDF is a rebranded version of PostScript underneath the hood.

Tag	Purpose	Acceptable Values
Columns	Number of columns for the report. This will override the report's original settings.	Any positive integer or decimal value.
ColumnSpacing	Spacing between columns. This will override the report's original settings.	Any positive integer or decimal value (larger values create larger PDF files).

Tag	Purpose	Acceptable Values
DpiX	Horizontal resolution.	The default value is **300**.
DpiY	Vertical resolution.	The default value is **300**.
EndPage	The last page of the report to render. A value of 0 means all pages.	The default value is the same as StartPage.
MarginBottom	Bottom margin value, expressed as an integer or decimal. Must be followed by "in". This will override the report's original settings.	A positive integer or decimal value. A value of 1in means a 1-inch margin.
MarginLeft	Left margin value, expressed as an integer or decimal. Must be followed by "in". This will override the report's original settings.	A positive integer or decimal value. A value of 1in means a 1-inch margin.
MarginRight	Right margin value, expressed as an integer or decimal. Must be followed by "in". This will override the report's original settings.	A positive integer or decimal value. A value of 1in means a 1-inch margin.
MarginTop	Top margin value, expressed as an integer or decimal. Must be followed by "in". This will override the report's original settings.	A positive integer or decimal value. A value of 1in means a 1-inch margin.
PageHeight	Page height, in inches. Must be followed by "in". This will override the report's original settings.	A positive integer or decimal value. A value of 11in means a page height of 11 inches.
PageWidth	Page width, in inches. Must be followed by "in". This will override the report's original settings.	A positive integer or decimal values. A value of 8.5in means a page width of 8.5 inches.
StartPage	The first page of the report to render. A value of 0 means all pages.	The default value is **1**.

Here's an example:

```
Dim devInfo As String = "<DeviceInfo>StartPage>1</StartPage>" & _
    "<EndPage>10</EndPage></DeviceInfo>"
```

XML

XML renders the report in the eXtended Markup Language format.

459

Tag	Purpose	Acceptable Values
XSLT	Path for an XSLT file to render the report. Note that setting this value overrides the OmitSchema tag.	Any valid relative path (also known as an item path) on the report server. The XSLT must be published on Report Server to be used.
MIMEType	MIME type of the XML file	Any valid MIME type.
UseFormattedValues	Indicates whether the formatted value of a textbox is used, or the underlying, unformatted value is used.	Indicates whether to render the formatted value of a textbox when generating the XML data. A value of false indicates that the underlying value of the textbox is used.
Indented	Indicates whether the XML should be indented.	True or **false**
OmitSchema	Indicates whether the Schema name should be omitted, as well as the XSD.	True or **false**
Encoding	A valid character encoding.	ASCII, **UTF-8**, or Unicode
FileExtension	File extension for the file created.	The default is **.xml**.
Schema	Indicates whether the schema is rendered or the XML. True means schema, false means XML.	True or **false**

Here's an example:

```
Dim devInfo As String = "<DeviceInfo><XSLT><ReportServer/XSLT</ReportServer>" & _
    "<UseFormattedValues>true</UseFormattedValues>" & _
    "<Idented>true</Idented></DeviceInfo>"
```

Building Report Models, or How to Slough Some of the Work off on the Biz Guys!

For many of you, this is the only information you really wanted in this chapter. After all, developers develop and business guys tell developers what to develop. Face it, coders like to code, not build Excel spreadsheets. That is what biz guys do best. Fortunately, Microsoft understands this and gives us the means to push the boring analysis garbage onto those who find it interesting. Unfortunately, very little of this tool is about coding.

Report models are essentially an abstraction layer between the database and the Report Server. In a model, you are exposing bits of information you would like the business analyst to have access to in a particular context. From there, the business analyst can take the bits you have exposed and move them around the page to his or her heart's content, even building multiple reports without one phone call to your boss.

The majority of the work you will perform to build a model is wizard-driven. The hardest part of the task is figuring out which items will be necessary for reporting.

Creating the Model

Open the Business Intelligence Development Studio. You will want to create a new project using the Report Model Project template. When the project opens, complete the following steps:

1. Create a new data source for you model.

   a. Right-click the `Data Sources` folder in Solution Explorer and choose `Add New Data Source`.

   b. Create a connection to the AdventureWorks database on your SQL Server box by clicking New and then filling in the Server and Database textboxes.

   c. When you click to the next box in the wizard, check the connection string (it should be `Data Source=(local);Initial Catalog=AdventureWorks;Integrated Security=True`, unless you are using a specific user account, in which case it should be `Data Source=(local);Initial Catalog=Northwind;Persist Security Info=False;User ID=Chapter15User;Password=pass@word1;`). Name the data source `Chapter15AdvWorks` and click Finish.

2. Create a new `Data Source View` for your model.

   a. Right-click on the `Data Source View` folder in the Solution Explorer and choose `Add New Data Source View`.

   b. In the first wizard step, make sure your Chapter15AdvWorks data source is selected and click Next.

   c. In the next wizard step, scroll down the list of available objects and add `HumanResources.Employee, Person.Contact, Sales. Customer, Sales. Individual, Sales.SalesOrderDetail, Sales.SalesOrderHeader, Sales. SalesPerson` and click Next.

   d. Name the Data Source View `dsvSalesOrders` and click Next.

3. Create a `Report Model`

   a. Right-click on `Report Models` and choose `Add New Report Model`.

   b. In the first wizard step, ensure that the `dsvSalesOrders` Data Source View is chosen and click Next.

   c. In the next wizard step, click Select All and then Next.

   d. Leave the default of Update Statistics Before Generating and click Next.

   e. In the final wizard step, name the Report model SalesOrders and click Run.

The resulting Report model should look like the screenshot shown in Figure 15-6.

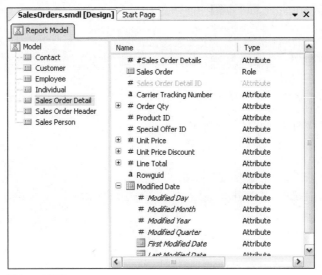

Figure 15-6

These bits of information have been aggregated and saved as an XML file. To finish the exercise, right-click on the project folder in Solution Explorer and click Deploy.

Creating a Report

This is the step where our business analyst comes in. When a person goes to the Reports application `http://hostname/Reports`, there is a button on the toolbar labeled Report Builder. Have the user click the Models hyperlink and then press the Report Builder button.

> *Make sure that you inform your report builder user to click Models before clicking the Report Builder button, as the Report Builder crashes when clicked outside of the Models section of the Reports application.*

The Report Builder is a new feature of SQL Server 2005 Reporting Services. When clicked, users will have to choose a data source from the models you have deployed. They can then begin fashioning a report by dragging elements on the page. The Report Builder application looks like the screenshot shown in Figure 15-7.

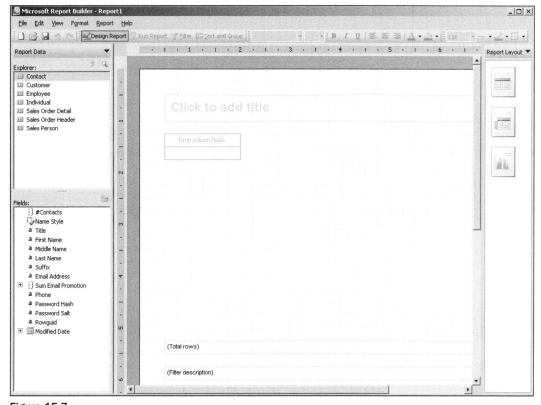

Figure 15-7

To create a meaningful report, you have to start with one of the tables. For example, follow these steps to create an employee report of salespeople, showing hire date and birth date:

1. Select `Contact` in Explorer.

2. Drag `Last Name` and `First Name` onto the report.

3. Once the name is on the form, you have the option to drill down from Employee and add the `Hire Date` and `Birth Date` fields.

The resulting report, when previewed, looks like the screenshot shown in Figure 15-8.

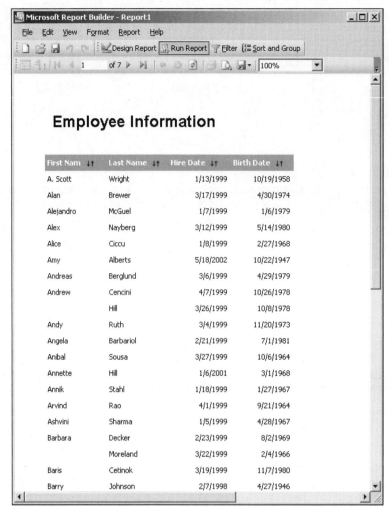

Figure 15-8

Summary

Reporting is an integral part of business, as aggregation of data is necessary to make proper business decisions. Prior to the advent of tools, much of reporting was hand-coded. As tools mature, however, more and more of the work is moved off of the developer's plate to the business analyst's.

In this chapter, we first looked at building a report in ASP.NET. With the new data source controls, we were able to do this without writing any code. You can easily tailor this, using the examples in Chapter 3, to use more ADO.NET.

The core of the chapter focused on Reporting Services. The first example was a report built using the Business Intelligence Developer Studio, whereby a report can easily be fashioned without writing a line of code. We pushed a bit deeper, however, into the Report Definition Language to give you a basic grounding in what is going on behind the scenes.

We then delved into the ReportServer application and contacting, both via a URL string and the SOAP interface. This was the most code-intensive part of the chapter, although much of the coding was fairly simple due to the objects Microsoft has made available through Reporting Services. The most difficult task for the developer, as demonstrated, is working with the `DeviceInfo` parameter for rendering reports. It is hoped that this will be simplified in future versions of the product, as this is the area in which errors are most likely to crop up.

Finally, we built a Report Model and explored the Report Builder using that model. While the examples are fairly simple, it should be evident that this is where the real power lies, as you, the developer, have the ability to give your users the power to create their own information.

For More Information

Unfortunately, this whirlwind tour is over. While we covered a great deal of ground, much more information has been left uncovered. Here are a few resources you can use to further hone your SQL Server reporting skills:

- **Community Content** — In late 2003, Microsoft made a huge push to increase its online content. In 2004, this culminated in community sites for each of the Microsoft technologies. The community sites with content for SQL Server are the SQL site, the TechNet site, and the MSDN site:

    - **SQL** — www.microsoft.com/sql/community/default.mspx.

    - **TechNet** — www.microsoft.com/technet/community/default.mspx.

    - **MSDN** — http://msdn.microsoft.com/community/. Note, however, that Microsoft Webcasts have a completely different URL: http://msdn.microsoft.com/webcasts. Another good page to start your search for developer content is the MSDN shows and Webcasts launch page: http://msdn.microsoft.com/showsandwebcasts/.

- **Webcasts** — We advise searching the community sites for Webcasts, as a very large body of information is available. Specific to this chapter, we suggest a couple of Webcasts at different levels: Level 100 (a very high-level overview), level 200 (an overview with lightly technical demos), level 300 (intermediate-level content), and level 400 (advanced sessions).

    - **Introduction to Reporting Services (level 200)** — A good overview of SQL Server 2005 Reporting Services, at http://msevents.microsoft.com/CUI/EventDetail.aspx?EventID=1032263305

    - **Advanced Reporting with SQL Server 2005 Reporting Services (level 200)** — http://go.microsoft.com/fwlink/?LinkId=43725.

    - **Ad Hoc Reporting with SQL Server 2005 Reporting Services (level 200)** — https://msevents.microsoft.com/cui/WebCastEventDetails.aspx?EventID=1032259394.

Chapter 15

❑ **Hands on Labs** — You can find lab manuals for offline work, or you can sign up and use one of Microsoft's virtual servers to complete various labs (great for those who have not yet installed SQL Server 2005).

    ❑ **Lab Manuals** — `http://msdn.microsoft.com/SQL/2005/2005Labs/default.aspx`.

    ❑ **Hosted Labs** — To launch the hosted experience, surf over to `http://msdn.demoservers.com/login.aspx?group=sql2005`.

16

ADO.NET 2 and
Open-Source Databases

While SQL Server and Oracle are well-established commercial databases that Bill Gates and Larry Ellison each believe provide the only genuine solution for data applications, there are other options. Not only do other databases exist, but many are freely available for download. This chapter provides a survey of several popular open-source databases, what features they provide, and, most importantly for this book, how they work with .NET 2.0. MySQL leads the crowd as the perennial open-source favorite, holding the "M" position in LAMP (Linux, Apache, MySQL, Perl). Firebird, Ingres, and MaxDB — from Borland, Computer Associates, and SAP, respectively — are also covered, representing a group of databases that were once commercial but are now open. PostgreSQL, BerkeleyDB, and SQLite are also covered — these quality databases have always been open and are well established among open-source advocates, although they may not be as well known outside of that community. Along with each of these databases, we provide some sample code demonstrating fundamental capabilities of the available drivers, and references to relevant Web sites for that community. It is hoped that this chapter will entice you to try some of the alternatives for your next project.

Open Source and Licensing

What is open-source software? Well, metaphorically, for some it's a floor wax, while for others it's a dessert topping. For many, if not most, *open source* implies software developed by a community of developers that can be freely obtained and distributed. Some organizations, however, have hijacked the term for marketing purposes, and may provide access to the source code but only under very limited conditions, and they do not support any sort of community process. While that may be a misuse of the term, the reality is that calling something "open source" does not guarantee much. What truly matters is the process that surrounds the product development and the license that accompanies the source code.

The *Open Source Initiative (OSI)* at opensource.org provides the most widely recognized definition of open-source software based upon the contents of a software product's license. This definition can be found at `www.opensource.org/docs/definition.php`. This approach makes sense given that copyright law governs all software, and the license that governs the product will be the final statement of permitted use of the software. There are many OSI-approved licenses, and while they all adhere to the principles put forth in the OSI definition, they vary in ways that are important to understand. In addition, some open-source software is dual-licensed, meaning the software may be governed by one license under one condition and a different license for another — that is, a product may be free for noncommercial use, but royalties are charged for any commercial distribution. Furthermore, if you plan on using an open-source database in a commercial application, you should have the license reviewed by an attorney who understands copyright law.

Besides the license, there is the community that surrounds a software project, so while the software is governed by a given license, the process for modifying and producing the product may be more or less open. A small group of people may produce a product under the BSD license, which would allow you to acquire, modify, and distribute the software, but they may or may not include your or anybody else's changes into their version of the software. Therefore, when choosing to work with an open-source product, carefully consider the community with whom you will be working, as you will often be dependant upon them for support, especially at the outset.

Databases

This part of the chapter covers seven databases from the open-source world. The discussion of each database takes the same form and the material for each database can be covered independently. Each section opens with the background of the database and the license under which it is currently released. Then it provides you with the information needed to download and install the software and links to the primary discussion forums. This is followed by a review of the level of support each database provides for SQL and .NET, as well as any specific features of the database. Finally, of course, we provide examples showing how to use the database in conjunction with .NET 2.

MySQL

MySQL is probably the best known of the open-source databases. It likely achieved most of this celebrity by being included in the LAMP acronym, the vanguard combination of open-source technologies that dominated dynamic Web content in the early part of the Internet boom. Ironically, early on, MySQL did not support much of the SQL standard. It was a purely utilitarian implementation of an ISAM database with data access provided via a daemon running on port 3306. However, good open-source software evolves rapidly, and MySQL has been no exception.

The current recommended release is 4.1, and version 5.0 is currently in beta testing. With the 4.1 version of MySQL, a large portion of standard SQL syntax and features are supported, including ACID-compliant transactions when using the InnoDB table type; and with version 5.0, many more features will be supported. However, as 4.1 is the currently recommended version, this section is based upon the features and usage of 4.1. Where appropriate, any significant new features coming in version 5 will be noted.

MySQL is a dual-licensed product. You can find information about MySQL licensing at `www.mysql.com/company/legal/licensing/`. In short, MySQL is licensed under the GPL, and if you do not intend to comply with the requirements of the GPL, then you will need to purchase a license for MySQL.

To understand the details of the licensing implications, you should consult an attorney with experience in copyright law.

SQL Compliance

For an in-depth treatment of ANSI SQL compliance and details of MySQL syntax, you should refer to the MySQL online documentation found at `http://dev.mysql.com/doc/mysql/en/compatibility .html`. Here we will examine some of the more central aspects of the MySQL database implementation and how they may affect cross-platform compatibility. When considering these implementation issues, it is worth remembering the origins of the database as a server daemon providing access to ISAM data. Therefore, because there is nothing particularly special about an ISAM database, the more important feature of MySQL is as data provider to a back-end data engine. MySQL has largely evolved along these lines by providing support for other back-end data engines, and this, as you will see, greatly affects the notion of SQL compliance.

Since its humble beginnings with ISAM, MySQL has grown to support eight additional storage engines as of version 4.1 and will add a ninth with version 5.0. The following table itemizes and describes the supported storage engines. The original ISAM engine has been deprecated in favor of the now standard MyISAM format. At the other end of the time line, the Federated storage engine arriving in version 5.0 will support SQL operations against remote data. In between are several other interesting storage engines.

The Merge storage engine allows a table space to be divided among multiple files, enabling a single table to manage data that would exceed the file capacity limits on some operating systems. The Merge data engine could also be used to distribute database activity to multiple files. The Memory engine stores all data in heap memory. This, of course, is volatile; however, the SELECT performance is excellent against data in the Memory table type. The other operations are fast as well, but the Memory data engine is particularly useful for directory information for which inserts and updates are rare in comparison to reads. If you need data stored in a compressed format, there is the Archive storage engine; be forewarned, however, that this storage type only supports INSERT and SELECT. If you need data in plain, old CSV, there is a storage engine for that, too. Berkeley databases are also supported, but the BDB engine is still considered experimental. If your database requires ACID (Atomic, Consistent, Isolated, and Durable) transactions, InnoDB is the default table type for that purpose. Finally, there is the Example engine, which provides a template should you desire to implement a data engine of your own.

Table Type	Description
ISAM	Original MySQL table type (deprecated)
MyISAM	Current default table type
Merge	Allows one logical table to be split into multiple physical tables
Memory	Table stored in heap memory
InnoDB	The default table type for supporting ACID-compliant transactions
BDB	Provides storage in a Berkeley database format (MySQL to BDB interface considered gamma quality)
Archive	Stores non-indexed table data in a compressed format
Example	Demonstrates how to implement a new storage engine

Table continued on following page

Table Type	Description
CSV	Provides storage tables in comma-separated values format
Federated	Coming in version 5, allowing queries against remote data tables (beta)

The MyISAM and InnoDB storage engines will receive most of the focus here. MyISAM is the default table type for MySQL; and, if transactions are required, InnoDB is the default storage engine contained in all of the MySQL-Max binary distributions. The idea that transactions may not be required may seem odd. After all, aren't transactions central to any relational database management system?

Well, maybe, but for the creators of MySQL, the issue at the time was the practical storage of data as opposed to creating an RDBMS in compliance with the concepts of E. F. Codd and others (which, in fact, was one purpose behind PostgreSQL, discussed later in this chapter). In short, while ACID transactions are good, the philosophy of the MySQL creators was oriented to storing data and using techniques within the application to achieve data consistency. To them, transactions were a trade-off between DBMS complexity and application complexity.

> If the name E. F. Codd doesn't ring a bell, he was the IBM researcher who first developed the relational model in 1970, which is the basis for the relational database.

For most developers with complex data systems, transactions seemed to be a better way to go, which resulted in pressure for MySQL to support transactions; and in 2002, the InnoDB storage engine for MySQL was completed, enabling MySQL to fully support transactions. The InnoDB storage engine also supports row-level locking and foreign keys, features that most developers expect from their database system.

While it may seem that we have drifted far afield from this section's topic of SQL compliance, the reality is that all of this information is central, both to understanding MySQL and addressing the issue of compliance. For instance, it has already been noted that the Archive storage engine supports only inserts and selects, and does not maintain any indexes on Archive table type data. Therefore, with the Archive storage engine, there really is no sense in asking about SQL compliance, as it is a specialized table type for a supposedly equally specialized application. The question of SQL compliance can be reasonably limited to the MyISAM and InnoDB storage engines. Nonetheless, MySQL provides multiple modes that also affect SQL compliance issues.

Modes were introduced into MySQL to enable an administrator to select specific syntactic features or database behaviors to allow for backward compatibility or the controlled implementation of newer database features. The twelve modes listed in the following table apply to version 4.1 databases, and several additional modes will be available with version 5 that are related to behavioral features introduced in version 5.

Most of the mode descriptions are straightforward, but some deserve special mention. For instance, with ANSI_QUOTES, the behavior of MySQL to allow both single and double quotes to identify strings is altered to only allow single quotes. This is important if you are porting a statement like the following to MySQL:

```
SELECT SYSTEM_USERS.ID FROM SYSTEM_USERS WHERE SYSTEM_USERS."LastName" = 'CROFT';
```

The default behavior for MySQL would be to treat `"LastName"` as a string literal, which it isn't. Another syntactical item of note is `PIPES_AS_CONCAT`. The default behavior is to treat double pipes (||) as a logical `or`, which while common in programming languages, is not the typical SQL behavior of string concatenation. `NO_AUTO_VALUE_ON_ZERO` alters the behavior of auto-increment fields. If an `INSERT` statement is executed against a table with an auto-increment field and the field is set to null or zero in the statement, then an auto-incremented value is generated and placed into the field. Therefore, if you have auto-incremented data starting from zero that needs to be imported, then the row with an auto-increment value of zero would normally, and unexpectedly, generate a new value and replace the zero. The final mode worth special mention is `IGNORE_SPACE`. MySQL typically requires the opening parenthesis for a function's parameter values to immediately follow the function name, as demonstrated with the `BIN` function, which returns the binary representation of a number:

```
SELECT BIN(32);
```

This way, functions cannot be confused with database fields. `IGNORE_SPACE` would allow the following:

```
SELECT BIN  (32);
```

Now, however, function names — in this case, `BIN` — are treated as reserved words. However, if you have a table — say, `INVENTORY_ITEM` — with a field called `BIN`, then that field would have to be referenced with double quotes to distinguish it from the `BIN` function:

```
SELECT INVENTORY_ITEM."BIN" FROM INVENTORY_ITEM;
```

The rest of the modes are explained in the following table.

Mode	Description
ANSI_QUOTES	Restricts text string identifiers to single quotes (') and reserves double quotes (") for database entity identifiers.
IGNORE_SPACE	Allows space between a function name and its opening parenthesis. This results in all function names becoming reserved words and requires the use of double quotes to access database fields that have the same names as functions.
NO_AUTO_VALUE_ON_ZERO	Causes an auto-increment value not to be generated when a zero (0) is inserted into an auto-increment column.
NO_DIR_IN_CREATE	Ignores INDEX DIRECTORY and DATA DIRECTORY directives when a table is created.
NO_FIELD_OPTIONS	Omits all MySQL-specific field options when a SHOW CREATE TABLE command is executed.
NO_KEY_OPTIONS	Omits all MySQL-specific index field options when a SHOW CREATE TABLE command is executed.
NO_TABLE_OPTIONS	Omits all MySQL-specific table options when a SHOW CREATE TABLE command is executed.

Table continued on following page

Mode	Description
NO_UNSIGNED_SUBTRACTION	Does not cast the result of a subtraction to unsigned if one of the operands is unsigned.
ONLY_FULL_GROUP_BY	Prevents a nonselected column from being referenced in the GROUP BY clause of the SELECT statement.
PIPES_AS_CONCAT	Causes double pipes (||) to be treated as a concatenation instead of a logical OR.
REAL_AS_FLOAT	Treats REAL as an alternate for FLOAT, instead of DOUBLE.

While a MySQL administrator could implement any combination of the preceding modes, for most purposes there are shorthand modes. The *shorthand modes,* or *combined modes,* are listed in the following table. Combined modes are largely for providing compatibility with different RDBMSs, but note that these modes do not provide complete compatibility with the identified system. To quote the MySQL documentation on the ANSI mode, the ANSI mode will ". . . change syntax and behavior to be more conformant to standard SQL." The definition of "more conformant" isn't precisely stated.

Combined Modes	Description
ANSI	REAL_AS_FLOAT, PIPES_AS_CONCAT, ANSI_QUOTES, IGNORE_SPACE
DB2	PIPES_AS_CONCAT, ANSI_QUOTES, IGNORE_SPACE, NO_KEY_OPTIONS, NO_TABLE_OPTIONS, NO_FIELD_OPTIONS
MAXDB	PIPES_AS_CONCAT, ANSI_QUOTES, IGNORE_SPACE, NO_KEY_OPTIONS, NO_TABLE_OPTIONS, NO_FIELD_OPTIONS, NO_AUTO_CREATE_USER
MSSQL	PIPES_AS_CONCAT, ANSI_QUOTES, IGNORE_SPACE, NO_KEY_OPTIONS, NO_TABLE_OPTIONS, NO_FIELD_OPTIONS
MYSQL323	NO_FIELD_OPTIONS, HIGH_NOT_PRECEDENCE
MYSQL40	NO_FIELD_OPTIONS, HIGH_NOT_PRECEDENCE
ORACLE	PIPES_AS_CONCAT, ANSI_QUOTES, IGNORE_SPACE, NO_KEY_OPTIONS, NO_TABLE_OPTIONS, NO_FIELD_OPTIONS, NO_AUTO_CREATE_USER
POSTGRESQL	PIPES_AS_CONCAT, ANSI_QUOTES, IGNORE_SPACE, NO_KEY_OPTIONS, NO_TABLE_OPTIONS, NO_FIELD_OPTIONS

The InnoDB and BDB storage engines only support transactions that meet the ACID test, and the BDB storage engine is not ready for production environments. From a practical standpoint, InnoDB is the only storage engine to support transactions. Therefore, when considering SQL compliance, if you don't use the InnoDB table type for your application, you will not have transactional capabilities. If you do not have a complex database schema with numerous integrity constraints, then the default table type (MyISAM) should be fine.

Stored procedures are not supported by any of the versions prior to the upcoming 5.0, so if you have to port a database with stored procedures to MySQL, you will need to either wait for 5.0 to become suitably stable or implement the functionality in the application. Stored procedures provide a nice place to compartmentalize some database activities and to control access to those activities, but MySQL 5.0 will not support GRANT EXECUTE so that may still be a limiting concern. On a positive note, MySQL stored procedures will be conformant to the SQL2003 syntax standard.

Triggers are another feature that do not exist prior to version 5.0. This is annoying because triggers are a great place for putting code that generates audit logs and such, relieving the application from a lot of pedantic code.

Views are also being added with version 5.0, currently in beta. Views will support two different algorithms: MERGE or TEMPTABLE. MERGE is the internally preferred algorithm if none is specified, as it is expected to be more efficient, but the TEMPTABLE algorithm may lead to shorter lock times. Therefore, depending on your application, the TEMPTABLE algorithm may be a preferred strategy. Additionally, MySQL 5.0 will support updateable views. For a view to be updateable, it must use the MERGE algorithm whereby there must be a one-to-one relationship between the rows in the view and the rows in the underlying table. There are additional requirements too. For example, an updateable view may not contain an aggregate function, may not be based upon a derived table, and may not be based upon a non-updateable view. For all of the details, check with the documentation. The rules for updateable views are in line with other databases.

The InnoDB table type supports foreign keys in MySQL since version 3.23.44, and MySQL says that foreign keys will be implemented for MyISAM tables at some point in the future. Those tables that have foreign keys will also support cascading DELETE statements. Foreign keys may be temporarily disabled while loading data from backup.

Primary keys and unique constraints are also supported by both MyISAM and InnoDB table types, but because one table type supports transactional rollback and the other doesn't, it is important to note the different behaviors that will occur when an error condition occurs. In general, if a constraint is violated during a transactional operation, the transaction will be rolled back; and if the operation is not transactional, the process will terminate and whatever records have been written are essentially "committed." With nontransactional operations, the IGNORE option will let the process continue while simply skipping records that fail a constraint.

How MySQL handles invalid data is also worth noting. Prior to version 5, MySQL will try a best fit on certain illegal data, particularly with NULL values. For instance, if you try to insert a NULL value into a numeric column that is defined as NOT NULL, MySQL will automatically convert the NULL to a zero; and for CHAR and VARCHAR columns, it will convert the NULL to a zero-length string (''). In addition, MySQL will not validate dates, so you can store 2/31/05 in the database. These are the most notable items that may cause a "gotcha" experience if you are coming from another RDBMS, but there are others, and reviewing the documentation on this matter is worthwhile.

To summarize, the current production version of MySQL, 4.1 does not support stored procedures, triggers, or views. In addition, when not using the InnoDB table type, MySQL does not support transactions. All of these features will be arriving soon, but the current stable release doesn't compare particularly well with many other major database management systems.

Database Features

The real features of MySQL are simplicity and ubiquity. Notwithstanding the previous discussion about all of the possible configurations of MySQL, the "out-of-the-box" binary installation provides a quick setup that will allow for easy data storage in a largely SQL-like manner. The overall point of the previous discussion reflects more on the RDBMS feature set of MySQL. On a practical basis, INSERT, UPDATE, DELETE, and SELECT statements work the way you would expect, and MySQL has a slick graphical administration tool, shown in Figure 16-1. With all of that, why not go with a database that has more features?

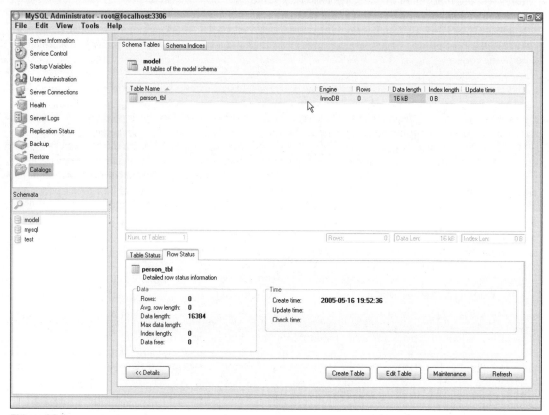

Figure 16-1

Database constraints are shown in the following table:

Condition	Limit
Maximum size for a database	64 TB with InnoDB engine
Maximum size for a table	64 TB with InnoDB engine
Maximum size for a row	Not including VARCHAR, BLOB, and TEXT columns, the maximum row size is about 8K; and total row size must be less than 4G with InnoDB
Maximum size for a field	2 GB
Maximum number of columns in a table	1000 with InnoDB
Maximum number of indexes on a table	1024 bytes

Well, to quote an unknown source: quantity is not quality, but quantity has a quality all its own. MySQL is all over the place. Moreover, it is installed by default in a great number of Linux distributions and it has probably reached the critical point where people are using it simply because other people are using it. If you find yourself needing a cross-platform or Linux-based solution, MySQL may already be set up, or you may need to provide access to existing data in a MySQL database. Either way, it is likely that at some point you will have reason to bridge the divide between your application and a MySQL database.

For our purposes, the database will be set up using InnoDB and run in ANSI mode. This will provide data storage behavior that is most in line with other major database management systems. Setup and configuration are explained in the following section.

Installation

Installing MySQL on Windows is as simple as installing most Windows software. Go to `mysql.com` and select Products ➪ Downloads. Follow the MySQL 4.1 link to the Downloads page. Find the Windows downloads, and get the Windows (x86) download. This will provide a Windows setup executable with all of the bells and whistles. You can run the setup program and accept all of the default settings if you have enough disk space on your C: drive. At the end of the setup procedure, the program will prompt you to configure the MySQL server. Go ahead and do that now, again accepting all of the defaults, assuming you are intending to use this installation as a development server.

Level of .NET Support

MySQL has a .NET Connector package that contains a 1.1-compatible data adapter that is at version 1.04 at the time of writing. This is the package that is used for the sample code, so download and install the package now if you haven't already done so. In addition to the 1.1 data adapter, MySQL also supports ODBC, so as an alternative, you could use the ODBC driver and Microsoft's `OdbcConnection` object to establish a connection to the database.

Working with .NET

The following code shows a basic console application for VB establishing a connection to the database and performing a `SELECT` operation against a table called `PERSON_TBL`. Before running this example, you will need to open MySQL Administrator and create a new database called `MODEL`. In the new database, create a table called `PERSON_TBL`. The following `CREATE TABLE` statement can be used to create the table:

```
CREATE TABLE PERSON_TBL (
    PER_ID          VARCHAR(38) NOT NULL,
    PER_CODE        VARCHAR(16),
    PER_PUBID       VARCHAR(16),
    PER_LASTNAME    VARCHAR(32),
    PER_FIRSTNAME   VARCHAR(32),
    PER_MIDDLENAME  VARCHAR(32),
    PER_ORDINAL     VARCHAR(8),
    PER_CALLEDNAME  VARCHAR(32) NOT NULL,
    PER_HONORIFIC   VARCHAR(8),
    PER_DOB         DATE,
    PER_GENDER      VARCHAR(1),
    PER_CREATED     TIMESTAMP NOT NULL,
    PER_CREATED_BY  VARCHAR(8),
    PER_UPDATED     TIMESTAMP NOT NULL,
    PER_UPDATED_BY  VARCHAR(8)
);
```

Once the database and table have been created, simply open a new console application for VB, change the name of `Module1` to `MySQLTest`, and then add the remaining code shown here:

```
Imports MySql.Data.MySqlClient

Module MySQLTest

    Sub Main()

        Dim connectionString As String
        Dim dbcon As IDbConnection
        Dim dbcmd As IDbCommand
        Dim sql As String
        Dim reader As IDataReader
        Dim dataValue As Object
        Dim strValue As String

        Console.WriteLine("MySQLTest - start.")
        connectionString = "server=localhost;user id=root;" & _
                          "password=mypassword;database=model;pooling=false"

        dbcon = New MySqlConnection(connectionString)
        dbcon.Open()
        dbcmd = dbcon.CreateCommand()
        sql = "SELECT * FROM PERSON_TBL"
        dbcmd.CommandText = sql
        dbcmd.Transaction = dbcon.BeginTransaction()
        reader = dbcmd.ExecuteReader()

        Do While reader.Read() = True

            dataValue = reader.GetValue(0)
            strValue = dataValue.ToString()
            Console.WriteLine("Value: " + strValue)

        Loop

        'Clean up
        reader.Close()
        dbcmd.Dispose()
        dbcon.Close()

        reader = Nothing
        dbcmd = Nothing
        dbcon = Nothing

        Console.WriteLine("MySQLTest - end.")

    End Sub

End Module
```

This program establishes connectivity, selects all of the data from the PERSON_TBL, and then prints the PER_ID field. Check the Web site for an enhanced version of the program that also demonstrates inserting, updating, and deleting data.

Resource Information

This section lists important online sites for information about MySQL. First are the sites from which the software for this section was downloaded, followed by a list of drivers, including third-party drivers not used in this section, and finally a section covering support and product comparisons.

Downloads

For this section all of the software can be downloaded from MySQL or one of the MySQL mirrors. The software downloaded for this section was MySQL 4.1 Windows Binary package.

- ❑ `http://dev.mysql.com/downloads/` — Main page for MySQL downloads
- ❑ `http://dev.mysql.com/downloads/mirrors.html` — List of MySQL mirrors

Drivers

The two .NET connectors used for this section were the MySQL Connector/ODBC 3.51 and the MySQL Connector/Net 1.0, and both were downloaded from MySQL.

- ❑ `http://dev.mysql.com/downloads/` — Main page for MySQL downloads
- ❑ `http://sourceforge.net/projects/mysqlnet/` — SourceForge project for open-source, fully managed drivers for an ADO.NET/MySQL connector
- ❑ `http://crlab.com/mysqlnet/` — A third-party provider of MySQL/.NET connectivity

Support

In addition to coordinating the development of MySQL, MySQL AB provides professional service and support contracts, but for getting started or comparing other products to MySQL, here are two useful pages, one that links to all the documentation and another that generates feature comparison lists:

- ❑ `http://dev.mysql.com/doc/` — The primary page for the MySQL documentation.
- ❑ `http://dev.mysql.com/tech-resources/features.html` — This page has a comparison tool that provides a detailed comparison chart between multiple, selectable databases.

MaxDB (formerly SAPdb)

MaxDB was formerly SAPdb, the default database server that SAP provided with its ERP (Enterprise Resource Planning) system. Given that SAP was frequently implemented on other database systems, such as Oracle, DB2, and others, SAPdb was not business critical. Therefore, SAP released SAPdb under the GPL in 2001. SAP continued to provide support and development guidance after the GPL release (providing a more friendly transition to open source than what happened with InterBase and Borland, which are covered later). Interestingly, in 2004, MySQL AB took over SAPdb and renamed it MaxDB, where it is now dual-licensed in the same manner as MySQL. This also explains why this section follows the MySQL section.

It is somewhat ironic that on the MySQL Web site, the Web site for the database system that many argued could do anything that needed to be done, there is now an offering for MaxDB, which, to quote, is "for the most demanding enterprise applications." However, on a more serious note, MaxDB is

SAP/R3-certified and boasts 6,000 major installations of the core technology. Clearly, MaxDB is a serious database and provides a good fit for MySQL AB's business strategy.

Given that MySQL AB also controls MaxDB, it shouldn't be surprising that MaxDB is also a dual-licensed product governed by the same licenses as MySQL. Information about MaxDB licensing can be found at www.mysql.com/company/legal/licensing/. In short, MaxDB is licensed under the GPL, and if you do not intend to comply with the requirements of the GPL, then you will need to purchase a license for MaxDB.

SQL Compliance

MaxDB, along with the rest of the databases in this chapter, was initially designed to be a transactional, relational database system with support for SQL. As a consequence, MaxDB broadly supports most SQL and RDBMS features. Additionally, MaxDB supports the SQL modes described in the following table:

Mode	Description
INTERNAL	MaxDB SQL definition
ANSI	ANSI SQL-92 entry level definition
DB2	DB2 version 4 definition
ORACLE	Oracle version 7 definition

MaxDB provides support for foreign keys and referential integrity. Foreign keys may consist of one or more primary key columns and may be defined in either the CREATE TABLE statement or the ALTER TABLE statement. MaxDB supports four options with regard to the ON DELETE behavior of related rows. These options are described in the following table:

Mode	Description
ON DELETE RESTRICT	System prevents the deletion of rows referenced by a foreign key
ON DELETE CASCADE	System cascades the delete of a row in a master table to the rows in the foreign key table
ON DELETE SET NULL	On the deletion of a record referenced by a foreign key, the foreign key values are set to null
ON DELETE SET DEFAULT	On the deletion of a record referenced by a foreign key, the foreign key values are set to a default value

MaxDB queries contain both sub-selects and outer joins. Outer joins may be defined as LEFT, RIGHT, or FULL. Any FROM clause may contain a query statement that will be executed to fill the place of a table at that position in the query. If a subquery contains an OUTER JOIN clause, it will have additional restrictions that are explained within the documentation.

MaxDB has both stored procedures and triggers, which really are merely stored procedures that are tied to data events on a given table. The CREATE DBPROC statement is used to create a stored procedure. The stored procedure defines parameters as either IN, OUT, or INOUT, causing a parameter to be exclusively for input, output, or for both input and output, respectively. MaxDB supports TRY..CATCH blocks, which work as expected: If an error is generated in the TRY block, the execution drops to the CATCH statement where the return code, held in the $rc environment variable may be evaluated. MaxDB procedures may also return a cursor if the procedure is defined with the RETURNS CURSOR modifier.

Triggers are defined in MaxDB using the CREATE TRIGGER statement, and triggers may be defined to be before and after INSERT, UPDATE, or DELETE. The body of a trigger is like a stored procedure, but an UPDATE trigger provides an IGNORE TRIGGER statement to prevent infinite recursion of changes on a table. A minor annoyance is that MaxDB offers no way to disable a trigger on an active database other than dropping the trigger.

MaxDB supports updateable views. Views are updateable if the CREATE statement for the view does not contain DISTINCT, GROUP BY, HAVING, EXCEPT, INTERSECT, or UNION clauses. In addition, updateable views may not contain subqueries or outer joins. Furthermore, for a view to be updateable, if it contains more than one base table, then the base tables in the view must have referential constraints based on a foreign or primary key that are reflected in the JOIN predicate for each table in the view. Finally, an updateable view table may have no fields that are complex expressions. From a permissions standpoint, the user performing an update, insert, or delete against the view must have update, insert, or delete privileges on all of the tables contained in the create view table. These conditions are generally applicable to most databases that allow updateable views.

MaxDB also supports both subtransactions and nested subtransactions. These are implemented with the SUBTRANS BEGIN, SUBTRANS END, and SUBTRANS ROLLBACK statements, which behave much as expected. The SUBTRANS BEGIN marks the starting point for a subtransaction, and these statements may be nested. A SUBTRANS END causes the last SUBTRANS BEGIN to be popped off the SUBTRANS stack, which, within the context of the transaction, essentially causes any work done since the SUBTRANS BEGIN to be retained by the current transaction. A SUBTRANS ROLLBACK would discard the work back to the previous SUBTRANS BEGIN. For all of the work to be retained, the current transaction must be committed or rolled back. In addition, a subtransaction will not affect any locks held by the parent transaction.

Database Features

MaxDB provides the graphical Installation Manager tool for installing MaxDB, and for setting up and migrating specific database instances. The graphical interface is available on Windows and Linux, and it is built with wxWidgets.

The Database Manager utility is provided for, you guessed it, database management. The manager has both a command-line interface (CLI) and a graphical-user interface. The CLI is available for every platform on which MaxDB runs, whereas the GUI is available for Windows and Linux.

Since version 7.4, the Database Analyzer has been provided as a monitoring tool to determine the performance characteristics of a running database. A default configuration is provided, but the configuration may be changed as needed.

MaxDB provides three tools for querying a database: SQL Studio, WebSQL, and SQLCLI. SQL Studio is a graphical client that provides an interface much like that of SQL Server Enterprise manager. WebSQL is a Web-based interface for executing SQL statements and scripts. Finally, there is always the typical command-line interface.

Backups for MaxDB can be run in either online or administration (offline) mode. Online backups can be run from either the Database Manager or the Computing Center Management System, but offline backup may only be run from the Database Manager. Data backups may be full or incremental, but note that backing up the data is independent of backing up the log files. Log file backups are only incremental and will always run from the point of the last backup.

High availability features of MaxDB are primarily available through the clustering technologies of the underlying operating system. MaxDB can be clustered on Windows 2003 Sever when you use Microsoft cluster server. However, the details of setting up Microsoft cluster server and installing MaxDB into the cluster are beyond the scope of our discussion. On Linux or other systems that have clustering capabilities, MaxDB may be clustered as well, but custom configuration scripts must be written that are specific to the clustering solution.

In addition to database clustering, MaxDB supports a *hot standby* configuration. When a database is setup with a hot standby, a duplicate database is maintained in administrative state. Log files from the active database are sent to the standby server where they are applied to the standby database. If the primary database fails, the standby database can be brought online. The standby database will only be as current as the last log file applied, so whenever possible, the last database log needs to be brought over and applied to the system to retain all of the data.

MaxDB also has a Synchronization Manager to support the synchronization of one or more distributed MaxDB databases. The upcoming MinDB, a small footprint, Java-based database for mobile clients, will also have synchronization support.

Web Distributed Authoring and Versioning (WebDAV) is an extension to HTTP 1.1, detailed in RFC 2518, intended to facilitate collaborative work on the Internet. MaxDB directly supports WebDAV, which enables MaxDB to serve as a Web-based document and XML repository.

MaxDB supports both implicit and explicit schemas. When a user is created, any database objects created by that user will automatically be assigned to the schema that was implicitly created with the same name as their username. However, MaxDB also supports the explicit creation of database schemas with the CREATE SCHEMA command.

MaxDB provides support for server-side cursors using the DELCARE CURSOR, OPEN CURSOR, and FETCH commands. Cursors can be used independently or returned from stored procedures. In addition, MaxDB cursors may be updateable (there are some constraints, but most simple cursors will be updateable). MaxDB cursors are also scrollable.

MaxDB supports temporary tables in a rather elegant way. If you create a table within the TEMP schema, it is a temporary table. While you use the same CREATE TABLE command to create a temporary table, temp tables do not support referential integrity. Therefore, specifying a referential constraint during the creation of a temp table will generate an error.

As with most ACID-compliant databases, MaxDB makes extensive use of locking, and both implicit and explicit locking of rows and tables is supported. Objects in the database catalog may also be locked, but only explicitly. The isolation level in place determines the implicit locking behavior of MaxDB, and MaxDB supports five isolation levels: 0, 10, 15, 20, and 30. Isolation level 0 corresponds to uncommitted read, so a transaction operating at level 0 may see different results from a single query executed at two different times within the transaction. For rows to be inserted, updated, or deleted, exclusive locks are implicitly requested. For isolation level 10, committed reads, a shared lock is requested for each row read; this guarantees that no other transaction has an exclusive lock on the row being read. In addition, for rows read during an SQL query, there is a guarantee that at the time a row is read, there are no exclusive locks on the row by any other transactions. Again, exclusive locks are requested for inserts, updates, and deletes at isolation level 10.

As you might guess, level 15 provides an isolation level between committed read, 10, and repeatable read, 20. Therefore, level 15 provides all of the isolation of level 10, but also requests shared locks on any table referenced by an SQL SELECT statement. Repeatable reads are achieved by isolation level 20, so within the transaction, shared locks will be placed on all rows read by the transaction as well as all tables referenced by an SQL query, and these locks are not released until the transaction ends or the result table is closed. The shared locks requested on rows read by the transaction may be explicitly released before the end of the transaction with an unlock statement. At isolation level 30, serialized, shared locks are acquired in the same manner as level 20; but in this case, the locks can be released only by the termination of the transaction. Moreover, while it is always true that long-running transactions should be avoided, it should be especially clear that long-running transactions with an isolation level of 20 or 30 would destroy the concurrency of your MaxDB database. For an in-depth discussion of the explicit locking options, consult the documentation.

Condition	Limit
Maximum size for a database	32 TB (using an 8k page size)
Maximum size for a table	Limited by database size
Maximum size for a row	8088 bytes (This represents the internal row definition; an actual row could have a BLOB or LONG VARCHAR field, which could contain 4 GB or 2 GB each, respectively.)
Maximum size for a field	1 GB
Maximum number of rows in a table	Limited by database size
Maximum number of columns in a table	1024 with primary key
Maximum number of indexes on a table	255

Installation

The installation process for the base MaxDB package for version 7.5 is guided by a simple command-line program. A graphical installation should be available in version 7.6, but 7.6 is not yet the generally available release. MaxDB is also available at the MySQL Web site. Go to mysql.com and select Products ⇨ MaxDB. Go to the Download Version 7.5 page and under Server Downloads, select Microsoft Windows (x86). Once the download completes, unzip the package and execute the SDBINST.exe file. This will start a brief interview at the command line. The first question requires an affirmative answer regarding which components to install. Enter 10 to get everything and from then on you can press Enter to select the defaults. When the installation completes, you will see a screen like the one shown in Figure 16-2. You can reboot from there.

After rebooting, return to the MySQL Web site and to the Download Version 7.5 page. This time, follow the link under Client Downloads. On the Client Downloads page, download the DBMGUI for Windows, shown in Figure 16-3, as well as SQL Studio and the ODBC driver. Install all of these with the Windows setup package in which they are bundled. You should now have all the requisite MaxDB software installed.

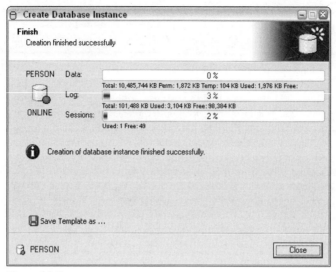

Figure 16-2

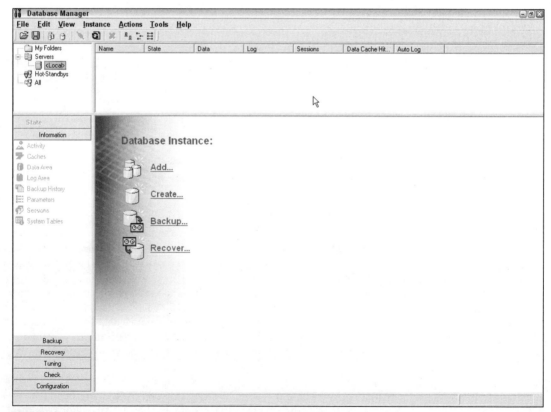

Figure 16-3

Level of .NET Support

MaxDB has full support for ODBC 3.51, but it does not yet have a .NET DataAdapter. The ODBC driver is installed with the database installation routine, and the example that follows demonstrates a DSN-less connection to the database.

Working with .NET

The following code is a simple variation on the MySQL example. It demonstrates basic database connectivity and data selection. It is the same in content as the prior example, so before running it, go into the Database Manager for MaxDB, shown earlier in Figure 16-3, and create a new database called MODEL. Within the database, create a table called PERSON_TBL (you can use the same CREATE TABLE statement as before):

```
Imports System.Data.Odbc

Module MaxDBTest

    Sub Main()

        Dim connectionString As String
        Dim dbcon As IDbConnection
        Dim dbcmd As IDbCommand
        Dim sql As String
        Dim reader As IDataReader
        Dim dataValue As Object
        Dim strValue As String

        Console.WriteLine("MaxDBTest - start.")

        'Note that password has to be upper case
        'DSN connection string
        'connectionString = "DSN=MODEL;UID=DBA;PWD=DBA"
        'DSN-less connection string
        connectionString = "driver={MaxDB};server=127.0.0.1;" & _
                           "uid=DBA;pwd=DBA;database=MODEL;OPTION=3"

        dbcon = New OdbcConnection(connectionString)
        dbcon.Open()
        dbcmd = dbcon.CreateCommand()
        sql = "SELECT * FROM PERSON_TBL"
        dbcmd.CommandText = sql
        dbcmd.Transaction = dbcon.BeginTransaction()
        reader = dbcmd.ExecuteReader()

        Do While reader.Read() = True

            dataValue = reader.GetValue(0)
            strValue = dataValue.ToString()
            Console.WriteLine("Value: " + strValue)

        Loop

        'Clean up
```

```
            reader.Close()
            dbcmd.Dispose()
            dbcon.Close()

            reader = Nothing
            dbcmd = Nothing
            dbcon = Nothing

            Console.WriteLine("MaxDBTest - end.")

        End Sub

    End Module
```

Again, check the Web site for an enhanced example.

Resource Information

This section lists important online sites for information about MaxDB. First we list the sites from which the software for this section was downloaded, followed by drivers (including third-party drivers not used in this section), and finally resources that provide support and product comparisons.

Downloads

For this section, all the software can be downloaded from MySQL or one of the MySQL mirrors. The software downloaded for this section was the MaxDB 7.5.0.24 Windows Binary package.

- ❑ http://dev.mysql.com/downloads/ — Main page for MySQL downloads
- ❑ http://dev.mysql.com/downloads/mirrors.html — List of MySQL mirrors

Drivers

The .NET connector used for this section was the MaxDB ODBC client interface.

- ❑ http://dev.mysql.com/downloads/maxdb/clients_75.html#Documentation — Main page for MaxDB client downloads

Support

In addition to coordinating the development of MaxDB, MySQL AB provides professional service and support contracts, but for getting started or comparing other products to MySQL, here are two useful pages, one that links to all the documentation and another that generates feature comparison lists:

- ❑ http://dev.mysql.com/doc/maxdb/index.html — The primary page for the MaxDB documentation.
- ❑ http://dev.mysql.com/tech-resources/features.html — This page has a comparison tool that provides a detailed comparison chart between multiple, selectable databases.

Firebird

Firebird is an open-source RDBMS that stems from a product with a long and stable track record. Firebird supports, and has always supported, all the key features of an RDBMS, including ACID transactions, stored procedures, triggers, foreign keys, and views. Firebird also has an architecture based on record versioning that provides solid performance without many of the issues associated with lock escalation on other systems. The installation is easy and compact, making it easy to distribute with applications. Firebird also has an interesting corporate history.

Firebird originated back in the mid-eighties as a conventional development effort by a fairly typical software startup. The company was based in Groton, Massachusetts, which resulted in the database files having a .GDB extension (for Groton database). The original business plan to private label the database didn't work out quite as expected, and the company became InterBase. Ashton-Tate, of DBase fame, bought InterBase in 1991; and Borland bought Ashton-Tate not long thereafter. This author, along with most others, was exposed to InterBase, as it was the client-server database that Borland pushed with their Delphi (Visual Pascal) product. The world was client-server, Borland had a great combo-package, and all was good.

However, the better mousetrap doesn't always win. Delphi never approached the popularity of Visual Basic, and more people in the VB world opted for Access or SQL Server over anything else. This, coupled with the schizophrenic renaming of Borland to Inprise and then back to Borland later, didn't help market share either. Ultimately, Borland reached the conclusion that InterBase was essentially a dead product, but with the encouragement of some staff who believed in the product, Borland open-sourced InterBase 6 in August of 2000. Open-sourcing InterBase generated plenty of activity and interest by many who believed in the database; and after seeing all of the interest, Borland decided to continue the product and has since released a number of updates to the closed-source product. However, the ink was in the water, and while Borland had decided to abandon an open-source strategy, a number of committed people in the community began to enhance the product from the 6.01 base and then officially forked the project under the name Firebird.

The current stable release of Firebird is version 1.52, and Firebird 2.0 is now in alpha testing. The InterBase Public License under which the InterBase 6.01 source code was originally released covers Firebird. The copy of the InterBase Public License can be found on the following page: `http://info.borland.com/devsupport/interbase/opensource/IPL.html`.

SQL Compliance

Given that Firebird started out with the goal of providing a robust and transactional database system, the question of SQL compliance is much easier than with MySQL. Firebird 1.5 implements full SQL-92 Entry-Level Support and most of the SQL-99 standard.

Therefore, along with the SQL compliance, Firebird supports views and sub-selects. It also supports full fine-grained user permission handling with roles and grants. It also provides support for domains, field check constraints, and referential integrity. In short, Firebird has solid support for all of the fundamentals.

Database Features

One of the broad features of the Firebird database is that it is based on a multigenerational architecture, which prevents reads from blocking writes and vice-versa. That is, in the relational database world, there are two ways to skin the concurrency cat: *record locking* and *record versioning*. With record locking, whenever a consistent view of a set of records is required, a lock is placed on the records while the consistent view needs to be maintained. This directly impacts concurrency, which is why transactions should always be short lived.

With record versioning, instead of locking the records and preventing data activity against the records in question, multiple versions of the record are maintained and associated with the transaction that created them. Each transaction has a unique, sequential identifier, so a transaction always has the ability to find the state of any record at the time that the transaction began by examining the record and determining whether its transaction number is less than or equal to the current transaction number. By the way, this functionality is available in MaxDB, but only as a proprietary extension from SAP. While this mode of operation improves concurrency generally, it is particularly important for OLAP situations in which read transactions cannot be guaranteed to be short lived.

Before discussing some of the other features of the Firebird database, let's address a feature that is surprisingly missing. Firebird does not come bundled with a visual database management tool. While a visual database management tool is not essential and really has nothing to do with the performance or functionality of the database itself, a good visual management tool is just handy and convenient. So, what are your options? Several commercial and freeware products are available, as well as some open-source offerings. They are listed at the IBPhoenix Web site mentioned later in this chapter. Two are highly recommended: Marathon, an open-source offering at SourceForge, and IBExpert, which has a free personal edition at www.ibexpert.com. These applications are shown somewhat later in this section, in Figures 16-4 and 16-5, respectively.

The Firebird database can be run with one of two architectures: Classic Server or Super Server. The Classic Server architecture provides one process per connection, while the Super Server architecture provides a single server process with each connection handled by a thread. The following table provides a comparison of the two architectures:

Classic Server	Super Server
Mature on Linux. This was the original mode of operation for Linux running from inetd. This architecture was ported more recently to Windows.	Mature on Windows and Linux
The database cache exists in each client process, resulting in lower with resource usage if the number of connections is low.	Database cache is in the shared process space; scales better more connections.
Allows fast, direct connections to database files for local connections on Linux via the local protocol. On Windows, only remote connections are allowed through the localhost interface.	On Linux, only remote connections are allowed via localhost. On Windows, the local protocol is available for direct local connections, but these are not as fast as the "Classic" processes on Linux and are not thread safe.

Classic Server	Super Server
On Linux, the Services Manager interface is fully implemented, allowing remote administration capability. On Windows, the Services Manager interface is only partially implemented. Backup/restore and database shutdown can be performed remotely but other administrative tasks require the use of local client utilities.	The Services Manager interface is fully supported on both Windows and Linux.
SMP (symmetrical multi-processor) support, allowing better performance with a limited number of connections.	No SMP support, and on multi-processor Windows machines, the `CpuAffinityMask` parameter in the configuration file firebird.conf must be set to prevent processor hopping and a severe degradation in performance.

With that said, the examples in this chapter will be run on the Windows Super Server implementation. In addition to those two implementations, there is also an embedded database version, though for coverage of that you will have to refer to the Firebird site and documentation.

Firebird has support for selectable stored procedures. This is better than a stored procedure that simply returns data; it allows a stored procedure, along with its parameters, to be used in a SELECT statement anywhere a table would be used. This feature, along with the fact that Firebird is a versioned database engine, can actually be used to eliminate the need for temp tables. The creators did not implement temp tables in InterBase, and so Firebird does not have them either. Some may consider this a feature, but for many people used to solutions that require temp tables, this seems more like a missing feature. However, temp tables are planned for Firebird 2.0.

Firebird provides full support for referential integrity and foreign keys as well as field check constraints and domains. Along with this is the capability to cascade deletes and updates, and, of course, the capability to stop you from doing bad things with your data.

Firebird supports the creation of user-defined functions (UDFs). If an additional function is required beyond those provided with Firebird's procedural SQL, you might define a function that is available in an external library module and use that function with your procedural SQL statements. On Windows, this means accessing a function in a DLL, while on Linux the function would be found in a shared object (.so) file.

Windows, Linux, Mac OS X, BSD, HP-UX, and AIX can all run Firebird. Firebird also has support for multiple collations and character sets. Character sets can be implemented at the database level as a default, and on individual columns if an override to the default is necessary. Note, however, that if you use a default character set other than CHARACTER SET NONE, then you have to specify the same character set for any client connection or transliteration errors will occur.

Client applications may also register with the database events interface to receive notification about defined data events within the system. The important point here is that the client will be notified of the event asynchronously without the client polling. When the event occurs, all clients that have registered for the event will be notified that it occurred.

Firebird defines a number of error and exception codes that may be generated while working on the database. These exceptions can be caught and handled within a stored procedure or passed back to the client. In addition to the system-defined exceptions, you can also define custom exceptions that may likewise be handled either within a stored procedure or trigger or be sent back to the client.

Firebird does not support auto-number columns; instead it provides a more general feature in the form of generators. Generators are selectable items that produce a transaction-safe series of unique numbers. The following code creates a generator:

```
CREATE GENERATOR ID_GEN;
```

You can then set the value of ID_GEN to 1000 (the default would be 0 if you didn't bother) with this line:

```
SET GENERATOR ID_GEN TO 1000;
```

Then you can get an id value with a SELECT statement:

```
SELECT GEN_ID (ID_GEN, 1) FROM RDB$DATABASE;
```

This statement generates a new id by adding 1 to the current value of the generator, so the returned value would be 1001. You can pre-select the id value that is needed or you can add similar code to an ON INSERT trigger to accomplish an auto-number type behavior.

Condition	Limit
Maximum size for a database	32TB
Maximum size for a table	32TB
Maximum size for a row	64 Kb, not including BLOBs
Maximum size for a field	32Kb or 2 GB for a BLOB
Maximum number of rows in a table	2^32 Rows
Maximum number of columns in a table	Limited by column types and row size
Maximum number of indexes on a table	255

Installation

The installation of Firebird for this chapter is straightforward. First, visit the Firebird site at SourceForge and download the Windows setup package for Firebird version 1.5. Run the setup program and accept all of the defaults. That is all that is required to set up the server.

Second, return to the SourceForge site and download the latest Firebird Data Adapter for .NET. As of this writing, the latest version is 1.7-RC3. This is a .NET 1.1 data adapter, so you will need .NET 1.1 installed on the target system. In addition, the installation will run gacutil.exe to register the assembly, and gacutil.exe will require msvcr71.dll, so ensure that it is present on your system. The adapter is packaged in a Windows installation program; and given the aforementioned prerequisites, you can run the installation with all of the defaults.

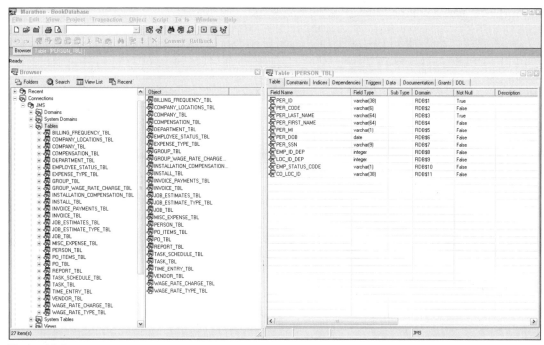

Figure 16-4

Finally, go to ibexpert.com, and download the free personal edition; again, follow the Windows installation and accept any defaults. We recommend Marathon for the examples, but at the time of this writing, version 3 is still in beta. However, by the time you read this, a stable version may be completed, so check it out.

Level of .NET Support

Firebird currently supports ODBC and .NET 1.1. In the example that follows, we are relying on the 1.7 version of the .NET data adapter that can be found at the Firebird site at SourceForge. Make sure that this is installed prior to building the test program.

Working with .NET

Here again we see our friendly neighborhood sample program, this time updated to run against the Firebird database. Go into IBExpert and create the new database. Immediately after creating the database, you will be given a database registration form. Change the Server Version to Firebird 1.5, and then click the Register button. Once the database is registered, double-click it in the database explorer window to connect to it and create our ubiquitous PERSON_TBL. Following this, you will need to edit the aliases.conf file found in the Firebird_1_5 directory. This file matches simple names with the location of the database file on disk. Add the following line to this file:

```
model = C:\dbfiles\firebird\MODEL.FDB
```

Everything should now be set to go for the sample code that follows:

```
Imports FirebirdSql.Data.Firebird

Module FirebirdTest

    Sub Main()

        Dim connectionString As String
        Dim dbcon As IDbConnection
        Dim dbcmd As IDbCommand
        Dim sql As String
        Dim reader As IDataReader
        Dim dataValue As Object
        Dim strValue As String

        Console.WriteLine("FirebirdTest - start.")
        connectionString = "Database=model;" & _
                            "User=SYSDBA;" & _
                            "Password=masterkey;" & _
                            "Dialect=3;" & _
                            "Server=localhost"

        dbcon = New FbConnection(connectionString)
        dbcon.Open()
        dbcmd = dbcon.CreateCommand()
        sql = "SELECT * FROM PERSON_TBL"
        dbcmd.CommandText = sql
        dbcmd.Transaction = dbcon.BeginTransaction()
        reader = dbcmd.ExecuteReader()

        Do While reader.Read() = True

            dataValue = reader.GetValue(0)
            strValue = dataValue.ToString()
            Console.WriteLine("Value: " + strValue)

        Loop

        'Clean up
        reader.Close()
        dbcmd.Dispose()
        dbcon.Close()

        reader = Nothing
        dbcmd = Nothing
        dbcon = Nothing



        Console.WriteLine("FirebirdTest - end.")

    End Sub

End Module
```

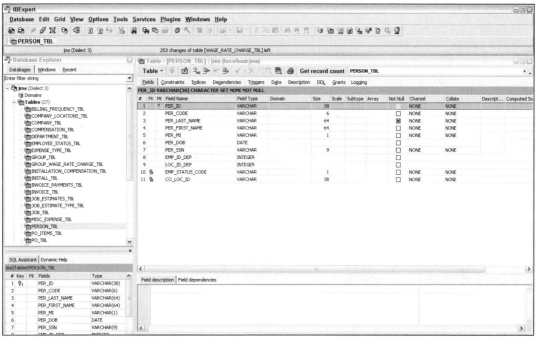

Figure 16-5

Resource Information

This section lists important online sites for information about Firebird. First are the sites from which the software for this section was downloaded, followed by a list of drivers (including third-party drivers not used in this section), and finally resources that provide support and product comparisons.

Downloads

The Firebird project is hosted at SourceForge and all of the downloads for this section can be found at the following Web site as well as from download links at the main support sites found later in this chapter:

❑   http://sourceforge.net/projects/firebird — Main SourceForge page for Firebird
    downloads

Drivers

The .NET provider for Firebird can be found at SourceForge at the location in the following list. Also shown is the link for the project ODBC driver. A number of other freeware and closed-sourced drivers are available, and links to those may be found at the IBPhoenix Web site.

❑   http://firebird.sourceforge.net/index.php?op=files&id=netprovider — The
    Firebird data provider for .NET and Mono

❑   http://firebird.sourceforge.net/index.php?op=files&id=odbc — The Firebird
    ODBC driver

Support

Following are the two main Web sites for Firebird information, as well as the location for the ever-useful Firebird discussion forums:

- ❑ `http://firebird.sourceforge.net/index.php` — The home page for Firebird at SourceForge.

- ❑ `www.ibphoenix.com/` — A very useful site for all things InterBase and Firebird. This is also an organization that sells professional support services.

- ❑ `http://firebird.sourceforge.net/index.php?op=guide` — The location of the novice's guide, with links to other documentation.

- ❑ `http://groups.yahoo.com/group/Firebird-support/` — The Firebird and InterBase discussion forum hosted at Yahoo and monitored by plenty of very helpful people.

Ingres

Ingres was the first commercially available RDBMS, initially released over 20 years ago. It was developed at Berkeley and became commercially available in 1980. In 1994, it was acquired by Computer Associates (CA). Ingres is embedded in most of CA's applications, with some of the most notable being Unicenter and ETrust.

In 2004, Computer Associates became yet another company to release a lagging database product to the open-source community. On top of that, when they open-sourced the product, they offered a $1 million purse with prizes of up to $400,000 for tools to automate the conversion of Oracle, Microsoft, Sybase, DB/2, Informix, and MySQL databases to Ingres. Ingres is an enterprise-level system that offers high availability clustering, scalable Linux database clusters, table partitioning, parallel query processing, and online table and index reorganization. There are also 64-bit versions of the database.

Why should a company give away a quality product like Ingres? Because the reality is that the big three databases — Oracle, Microsoft SQL Server, and DB/2 — occupy a huge share of the market. Therefore, a company that is going to spend money on a database will likely spend money where others are spending it, which makes their investment more secure. After all, none of the big three will be discontinued anytime soon, and the prospective company will be able to find professionals with necessary skill sets to maintain their database. For the database vendor, this can cause a death spiral: Smaller market share leads to fewer sales leads to even smaller market share.

Open-sourcing the product can theoretically provide a way out. The company forgoes initial licensing fees but has the opportunity to sell service, support, and consulting. Companies that use the software no longer have to worry that the product won't be available and they don't have any up-front costs, so it is easier to get them to at least try the product. Finally, it is easier to cultivate a developer base when developers can freely and easily access the product. Will it work? With a product as robust and sophisticated as Ingres, it might.

The Ingres database is licensed under the CA Trusted Open Source License (CATOSL). This license is OSI-approved, and information about the license, along with the license itself, can be found at `www3.ca.com/Files/Licensing/`.

SQL Compliance

Ingres R3 is SQL-92 entry-level-compliant, and it includes a large number of more advanced SQL features. R3 provides support for all the expected features of a relational database system, including foreign keys, check constraints, and cascading updates and deletes. In addition, it offers common support for both triggers and stored procedures. In short, there are no real surprises in the area of SQL behavior and compliance.

Database Features

With a long history as a commercial product, a lot of time was invested in end-user tools for database management and performance analysis. These tools include the Visual DBA for database administration, Import Manager and Export Manager for importing and exporting data, and the Journal Analyzer for examining recovery journals.

Ingres R3 provides some fairly straightforward performance features, including read-ahead caching, deferred writes, and group commits. In addition, Ingres provides some very sophisticated performance options, including parallel query execution. This enables the system to fully utilize a multi-processor environment to divide a query into pieces for execution.

R3 provides a number of options for partitioning the data in the database. Ingres has long had the capability to partition different tables and indices to meet storage configuration requirements. The latest of these partitioning capabilities is *key range table partitioning*. This divides the physical table into segments determined by different key ranges. This feature coupled with parallel query execution can provide a great boost to database retrieval times.

Ingres also provides a number of distributed data features. The first is the Distributed Query Option, which enables queries to be executed against a remote system. R3 also provides a replication option that enables remote sites to synchronize their data in a two-way exchange. There is also a Web Deployment option, which is used to hook an HTTP server to the database server for the deployment of a data-driven Web application.

Another feature that is uncommon, especially among open-source databases, is support for clustering (and it is included with the R3 basic download). Clustering is supported on both Linux and Windows along with cluster fail-over capabilities.

CA uses Ingres as the default database for a wide range of its applications, but many applications were originally designed to run against Oracle. This led CA to add features in Ingres that provide support for it in these products and allow for straightforward conversion of systems that support Oracle to Ingres. This should make porting from Oracle to Ingres easier than most large database conversions.

Ingres is not an object-relational database, but it does provide for some user-defined extensions. These features include the capability to create user-defined functions, data types, and operators. The Ingres Object Manager handles these user extensions. Ingres also has a component known as the Knowledge Manager. The Knowledge Manager enables business rules to be tied to data events much like the more general check constraint. When the event occurs, the initial rule is fired — that is, there can be a number of rules that run in either a forward chained or recursive fashion. There is no limit to the number of rules that may be assigned to a table.

Database alerts are also available in Ingres. These alerts are asynchronous messages that are sent out to listening client programs, and once the client program receives the message, it may forward the message via e-mail or instant messaging.

Ingres databases allow the specification of the page size, but row-level locking is only available in databases for which the page size is larger than 2K. By default, at page sizes larger than 2K, Ingres R3 will use shared read locks for row-level locking, which produces a read-committed isolation level. However, Ingres has a LOCKMODE command that can be used to alter the transaction level for the current connection, enabling a user to alter the locking behavior.

Ingres has very broad platform support that goes beyond the typical x86/Windows/Unix combinations. Due to Ingres's history and enterprise credentials, R3 scales all the way to the mainframe, but it also extends support down to lower-end systems. The R3-supported platforms include Windows 98, WindowsNT/2000/XP, OpenVMS, Solaris, HP-UX, AIX, Linux on Intel, and zSeries mainframes. Ingres also has 64-bit support for both Itanium and Opteron systems that enables you to fully leverage the latest server technology. With that said, it is worth noting that Advantage Enterprise Access and Advantage EDBC features, which provide some interconnectivity features in mainframe environments, are not available under open source.

Installation

While Ingres R3 does have a Windows installer, some additional work is required to set up Ingres. It involves setting up a special user on the system. The Ingres Getting Started guide provides a good step-by-step description of the process, but the quick-and-dirty procedure is briefly described here. First, create a user named ingres on the machine, assign a password to the new user, and add the user to the Administrators group. Then go to the Local Security Settings in Administrative Tools. Add the ingres user to the policies for "Act as part of the operating system" and "Logon as a service."

Once that is done, log in as the ingres user. Start up the installation program and accept all of the defaults. Be forewarned: If you change any of the default paths (we changed the path for the data files because we put all the database data files under a single directory tree for ease of offline backups), the install program may not create them. It didn't create an alternate data directory, and at the end of the installation it couldn't start the database and we had to read the error log to find out that it had produced a "directory not found" error. After creating the required directory and rerunning the install with the repair option, everything went fine.

The Ingres installation installs the database along with all of the required graphical tools, documentation, and client connectivity drivers, including a data adapter for .NET. The Visual DBA tool for Ingres is shown in Figure 16-6.

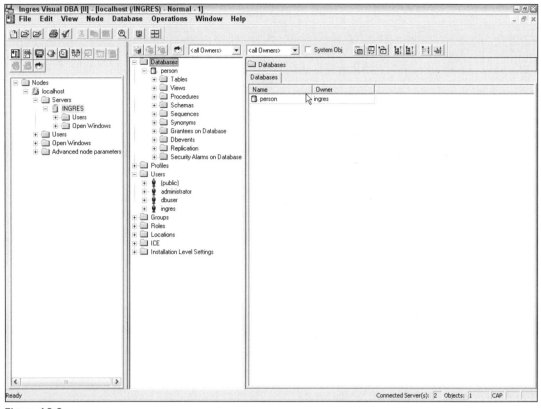

Figure 16-6

Level of .NET Support

CA provides both an ODBC driver and a .NET data adapter with the base installation. The .NET adapter, like the others, is a 1.1 adapter at this point. However, just as with the others, if the 1.1 Framework is installed, you should be good to go.

Working with .NET

Let's look at our sample program modified to work with Ingres R3. Again, ensure that you have created a database called MODEL and a table called PERSON_TBL. The CREATE TABLE statement from before will need to be altered slightly to execute on Ingres. Change the TIMESTAMP fields to DATE, which supports the same time-date accuracy as TIMESTAMP:

```
Imports Ca.Ingres.Client

Module IngresTest

    Sub Main()

        Dim connectionString As String
        Dim dbcon As IDbConnection
```

```
        Dim dbcmd As IDbCommand
        Dim sql As String
        Dim reader As IDataReader
        Dim dataValue As Object
        Dim strValue As String

        Console.WriteLine("IngresTest - start.")
        connectionString = "Host=localhost;" & _
                           "Database=model;" & _
                           "User ID=ingres;" & _
                           "PWD=ingres;"

        dbcon = New IngresConnection(connectionString)
        dbcon.Open()
        dbcmd = dbcon.CreateCommand()
        sql = "SELECT * FROM PERSON_TBL"
        dbcmd.CommandText = sql
        dbcmd.Transaction = dbcon.BeginTransaction()
        reader = dbcmd.ExecuteReader()

        Do While reader.Read() = True

            dataValue = reader.GetValue(0)
            strValue = dataValue.ToString()
            Console.WriteLine("Value: " + strValue)

        Loop

        'Clean up
        reader.Close()
        dbcmd.Dispose()
        dbcon.Close()

        reader = Nothing
        dbcmd = Nothing
        dbcon = Nothing

        Console.WriteLine("IngresTest - end.")

    End Sub

End Module
```

Again, look at the code online for a more in-depth sample.

Resource Information

This section lists important online sites for information about Ingres. First are the sites from which the software for this section was downloaded, followed by a list of drivers (including third-party drivers not used in this section), and finally a section covering support and product comparisons.

Downloads

For this section, all the software can be downloaded from CA's Ingres site. The software downloaded for this section was the Ingres R3 Windows Binary package:

- ❏ http://opensource.ca.com/projects/ingres — Main page for Ingres downloads

Drivers

The .NET connector used for this section was the Ingres ADO.NET Connector installed with the main package:

- ❏ C:\Program Files\CA\Ingres [II]\ingres\dotnet\assembly\v1.1 — Default location of the installed assembly

Support

Ingres support information can be found online at the following pages:

- ❏ http://opensource.ca.com/projects/ingres/documents — The primary page for the Ingres documentation.
- ❏ http://opensource.ca.com/projects/ingres/forum — Discussion forums.
- ❏ http://opensource.ca.com/projects/ingres/lists — This is the mailing list site for Ingres.
- ❏ http://opensource.ca.com/projects/ingres/support/support — For professional support.

PostgreSQL

PostgreSQL is an Object Relational Database Management System (ORDBMS) that was forked from POSTGRES 4.2, which was developed at UC-Berkeley. The university POSTGRES development effort came to an end in 1994; coincidentally, in 1995, Marc Fournier was looking for a database back-end for an accounting application and MySQL wasn't working for the expected loads. He tried Postgres95, a patch to the 4.2 code base, found he liked it, and pulled together the PostgreSQL open-source project.

Given that PostgreSQL started in an academic environment, it implemented many core ideas of solid database design and included many more experimental ideas as well, including object-oriented inheritance and a high level of extensibility. Although it didn't support SQL initially (it had its own query language, known as PostQUEL), that was addressed early on in the PostgreSQL project.

PostgreSQL is licensed under the BSD License, which provides very liberal terms for modification, distribution, and usage. A copy of the BSD License and the PostgreSQL licensing philosophy can be found at www.postgresql.org/about/licence.

SQL Compliance

PostgreSQL supports fully ACID-compliant transactions to ensure data integrity. Postgres, which was the forbearer of PostgreSQL, quite deliberately did not support SQL, but instead implemented a procedural language. PostgreSQL was formed in part to provide ANSI SQL support, and now supports all of the SQL-92 entry-level requirements. It also supports many features from the SQL-99 standard. PostgreSQL provides full inner and outer join support as well as the less commonly implemented INTERSECT construct.

PostgreSQL provides full support for views and updateable views. In addition, it has a feature known as *materialized views*, which are views that hold pre-generated results. This, of course, greatly speeds up the response time when selecting data from the materialized view.

The database provides full support for foreign keys and referential integrity, including CASCADE, UPDATE, and DELETE. PostgreSQL also supports other forms of constraints, including CHECK constraints. In addition, you can define custom data types with embedded constraint behavior.

Triggers and stored procedures are part and parcel of PostgreSQL. Both BEFORE and AFTER triggers are available. Stored procedures can be written in SQL or several other compatible procedural languages, including Perl and C.

Database Features

The broadest and most interesting feature of PostgreSQL is that it is an object relational database. In addition to all of the relational aspects of the database, it also provides many object-oriented features as well. First and foremost among these is inheritance. You can define a base table and then define a table as an extension of that table. The extension table automatically possesses all of the fields of the base table plus any additional fields it defines, and it is logically handled as a single table.

In addition to inheritance, you can gain functionality in PostgreSQL by defining and implementing your own functions, aggregate functions, and indexing methods. Any of these may be implemented using one of the supported procedural languages discussed in a moment.

Part of the object-oriented nature of the system is an inherent capacity for extensibility, so aside from any of the default data types found in the system, you may define new ones. Furthermore, you can define the behavior of the functions and operators that work on them. A good example of an extended data type is actually provided by default: an IP address data type. The database has an understanding of the nature of IP addresses, so a query can be run against a table of IP addresses using an IP address and, subnetwork mask combination. The database understands that the "=" operator applied to an address means that both the IP address and the subnetwork mask must match.

In addition to the IP address, PostgreSQL also possesses complex geometric types such as points, lines, and circles. Jumping from the subject of geometry to the related field of geography, PostGIS is available as a downloadable add-on to allow for the implementation of a geographic information system.

Other open add-ons include OpenFTS, for full text search capabilities. These capabilities include indexing, relevance ranking, and metadata filtering. OpenFTS also supports multiple languages and uses a natural language format for query search values.

Replication is supported through yet another download, this time of the Slony-I project. This replication mechanism provides a master to multiple slaves. The goal of this sort of replication is to provide fail-over support to a data center and is geared toward operation with all slaves normally available. It is not for two-way synchronization or mobile usage.

PostgreSQL implements what they call *multi-version concurrency control,* which is similar to the multi-generational architecture referred to in the Firebird discussion, and it serves the same purpose. In PostgreSQL, writers don't block readers, and readers don't block writers. This is accomplished through the use of a record-versioning mechanism for concurrency instead of a locking mechanism.

A number of procedural languages are supported for writing functions within PostgreSQL. Within the main download, four procedural languages are supported: PL/pgSQL, PL/Tcl, PL/Perl, and PL/Python. In addition, downloads are available for procedural languages based on PHP, Java, and R. If you are really ambitious, there is a standard interface for developing procedural languages to be used with PostgreSQL, so you could write an interface to allow for PL/C# on Windows systems.

You can also find several good additional add-on tools for this database system. In particular are some nice graphical database management clients, including pgAdmin III for a client-based solution and phpPgAdmin for a Web-based management system. Links to all of these tools may be found at the PostgreSQL Web site at www.postgresql.org/download/.

Condition	Limit
Maximum size for a database	Unlimited (32 TB databases exist)
Maximum size for a table	32 TB
Maximum size for a row	1.6 TB
Maximum size for a field	1 GB
Maximum number of rows in a table	Unlimited
Maximum number of columns in a table	250–1600 depending on column types
Maximum number of indexes on a table	Unlimited

Installation

PostgreSQL 8.0, now in general release, is the first version of PostgreSQL to natively support Windows. Prior versions could be run on Windows within Cygwin, but that was not a great solution. Now there is a Windows version and it comes with an installer. Even better, the installer also includes all of the other necessary tidbits, such as the graphical database manager, pgAdminIII, and the ODBC driver and the .NET adapter. The installer recommends reading a FAQ concerning the Windows installation, and we recommend it too. It's short, but it explains some potential gotchas regarding the need for NTFS and permissions for the account that runs the PostgreSQL database process. These are mostly common sense things, and you don't have to do anything but run the installer and accept the defaults, as per usual. Nevertheless, read the FAQ, just in case.

Once installed, you will be able to manage the database with the pgAdminIII tool (shown in Figure 16-7) and proceed to the sample program.

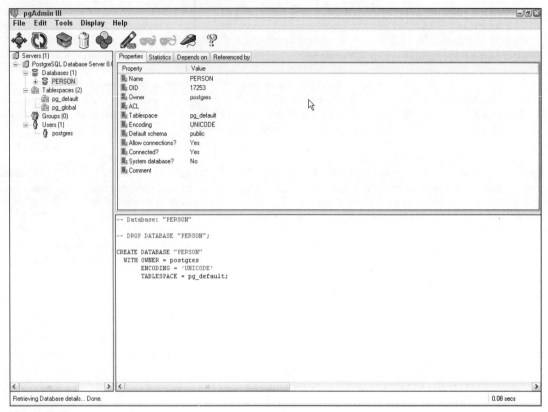

Figure 16-7

Level of .NET Support

PostgreSQL provides support for ODBC, OleDB, and .NET 1.1. All of these connectors are installed by the Windows installer process. For this example, we will use the .NET data connector in the NpgSQL package.

Working with .NET

This is our basic example reworked with PostgreSQL. Again, you will need to go into the database management tool, pgAdminIII, and create a database called model; within that database, create the PERSON_TBL. The original CREATE TABLE statement may be used without alteration. Once these steps are out of the way, you can proceed to the sample program:

```
Imports Npgsql

Module PostgreSQLTest

    Sub Main()

        Dim connectionString As String
        Dim dbcon As IDbConnection
        Dim dbcmd As IDbCommand
```

```
            Dim sql As String
            Dim reader As IDataReader
            Dim dataValue As Object
            Dim strValue As String

            Console.WriteLine("PostgreSQLTest - start.")
            connectionString = "Database=MODEL;" & _
                               "User=postgres;" & _
                               "Password=postgres;" & _
                               "Server=localhost;" & _
                               "Port=5432;"

            dbcon = New NpgsqlConnection(connectionString)
            dbcon.Open()
            dbcmd = dbcon.CreateCommand()
            sql = "SELECT * FROM PERSON_TBL"
            dbcmd.CommandText = sql
            dbcmd.Transaction = dbcon.BeginTransaction()
            reader = dbcmd.ExecuteReader()

            Do While reader.Read() = True

                dataValue = reader.GetValue(0)
                strValue = dataValue.ToString()
                Console.WriteLine("Value: " + strValue)

            Loop

            'Clean up
            reader.Close()
            dbcmd.Dispose()
            dbcon.Close()

            reader = Nothing
            dbcmd = Nothing
            dbcon = Nothing

            Console.WriteLine("PostgreSQLTest - end.")

        End Sub

End Module
```

Resource Information

This section lists important online sites for information about PostgreSQL. First are the sites from which the software for this section was downloaded, followed by a list of drivers (including third-party drivers not used in this section), and finally sources that provide support information support.

Downloads

For this section, all the software can be downloaded from PostgreSQL. The software downloaded for this section was the PostgreSQL 8 Windows Binary package.

❑ www.postgresql.org/ftp/win32/ — Location for the Win32 installer

Drivers

The .NET connector used for this section was shipped with PostgreSQL, but you can also visit
`http://gborg.postgresql.org/project/npgsql/projdisplay.php`.

Support

PostgreSQL support information can be found online at the following pages:

❑ `www.postgresql.org/docs/` — The primary page for the PostgreSQL documentation.

❑ `www.postgresql.org/community/` — Provides links to the mailing lists and newsgroups.

❑ `www.postgresql.org/support/professional_support` — If you are interested in professional support or custom modifications, this page provides links to companies that provide support and hosting services.

BerkeleyDB

BerkeleyDB is a transactional database that is more widely used than any other open-source database. The BerkeleyDB is an embedded database that runs behind many open source applications, not the least of which is SendMail. Sleepycat Software makes and distributes BerkeleyDB, which is a fork of yet another database developed at UC-Berkeley. That database was licensed under BSD, and Netscape intended to use the database for a directory server. However, in 1996, BerkeleyDB had shortcomings in the areas of concurrency and robustness, so Sleepycat was formed to build up the BerkeleyDB at that time, and they just kept on going. Sleepycat and BerkeleyDB now assist a wide range of corporations, including Google and Amazon, with specialized, high-performance data requirements.

Sleepycat now provides three products, two of which are described in this section. The first is the plain BerkeleyDB, version 4.3. The other is BerkeleyDB XML, which provides a native XML database over BerkeleyDB. This product understands XML Schema as well as XPath and XQuery. This enables these expressions to be evaluated by the database against XML documents stored in the database instead of having to process the documents in your application.

BerkeleyDB is another product that is dual-licensed. The software has the Sleepycat Public License for open-source projects, and Sleepycat can provide proprietary licenses for those who need them. The licensing information regarding BerkeleyDB can be found at `http://sleepycat.com/download/licensinginfo.shtml`.

SQL Compliance

BerkeleyDB has no support for SQL, and thus no ANSI SQL compliance. BerkeleyDB provides a database interface for a very fundamental table structure. While this may seem odd compared to the other databases, and in the context of ADO.NET, it is actually a feature for the problem space that BerkeleyDB attacks.

Database Features

Sleepycat Software calls BerkeleyDB 4.3 a developer's database, which might sound more than a bit like marketing-speak. Most people would call BerkeleyDB a database API, but this probably connotes a tool that is much simpler than BerkeleyDB. BerkeleyDB is in fact an API; and while the API is compact, it is quite sophisticated. The API manages a database that is not like a generic x-base, ISAM type file.

As an API, BerkeleyDB provides two related features: it is not client-server and it has a small footprint. The libraries that support a BerkeleyDB require less that 500 K, and the fact that it is not a database server makes it easy to embed into an application and to install on a target system. In addition, the data structure for a table is very simple, a key-value pair. The key or value can be up to 2 G, but the keys and values are not defined by the database. The application must understand what is being stored in each row. This is good if the application is using a predefined and immutable data structure, because it will be fast. If you need data flexibility, return to a SQL-oriented database.

BerkeleyDB provides a data store that supports a very high level of concurrency. This concurrency extends not only to multiple threads within a process but also to multiple independent processes on a given system. BerkeleyDB uses a fine-grained locking system to ensure that in spite of potential multi-process access, the data will be accessible and consistent. Therefore, the data store will be accessible given virtually any access strategy that your system might use.

BerkeleyDB implements a truly transactional data store. BerkeleyDB couples write-ahead logging with logically atomic transactions to ensure that any database operation commits or rolls back appropriately. The write-ahead logging also provides the capability to recover from a crash condition by playing back the log.

High-availability solutions are available by implementing single-master replication. With single-master replication, all updates are handled via a single, master database. This database then replicates changes to any number of replicas. All replicas are always available for data retrieval so that any given replica can fail without impacting data retrieval capabilities. If the update master fails, then any one of the replicas may take over that role.

For the highest level of data access performance, BerkeleyDB supports in-memory transaction logs and databases. Configured in this manner, an application can eliminate most disk I/O and have very fast access times.

The API enables you to configure different data store types. The basic data store is available for a single writer with multiple readers. The concurrent data store allows multiple readers and writers. The transactional data store provides the capabilities of the concurrent data store and adds support for ACID-compliant transactions, hot backups, group commits, and system recovery. Finally, a replicated data store adds high availability.

As mentioned earlier, in addition to the basic BerkeleyDB, Sleepycat also puts out BerkeleyDB XML, now at version 2.0. With this, your application can store any given data in the key and value of a data row. BerkeleyDB XML adds an XML layer to the BerkeleyDB that enables an application to easily store and search XML data.

BerkeleyDB XML enables container-based document management whereby the storage container possesses an understanding of XML and XML structure. For instance, it allows for the indexing of XML nodes, attributes, elements, and metadata. The XML layer also understands XPath statements and XML namespaces. This means that you can use XQuery to directly query documents without having to load and parse documents in separate operations. You will examine this in the examples in this section.

Condition	Limit
Maximum size for a database	256 TB
Maximum size for a table	256 TB
Maximum size for a row	4 GB
Maximum size for a field	4 GB
Maximum number of rows in a table	Direct function of row size
Maximum number of columns in a table	2 — one key and one value column
Maximum number of indexes on a table	Application-dependant

Installation

Installing the BerkeleyDB library is straightforward. Download the Windows installation packages from sleepycat.com. Run the installations and accept the defaults. This will give you the base packages. To run the database from managed code requires a managed wrapper. The wrapper will be built from the source provided under the build_win32 directory under the previously created installation directory.

Also download and install the BerkeleyDB XML package, accepting all of the defaults in the Windows installer. Building the library will be covered shortly.

Level of .NET Support

As noted in the installation section, support for the BerkeleyDB products is in the form of an API, and building the API is covered in the next section.

Working with .NET

Building the BerkeleyDB API for C++ .NET is the most ambitious project in this chapter. We will run through it here, but for more coverage you may want to look at some of the following Web sites:

- ❑ www.cs.sunysb.edu/documentation/BerkeleyDB/ref/build_win/intro.html
- ❑ www.cs.sunysb.edu/documentation/BerkeleyDB/ref/build_win/faq.html
- ❑ www.huihoo.com/berkeley/dbxml-1.2.1/docs/ref_xml/xml_win/intro.html
- ❑ www.huihoo.com/berkeley/dbxml-1.2.1/docs/ref_xml/xml_win/examples.html

Building the API from Visual Studio 2005 is a bit tedious but not fundamentally difficult. Keep in mind that ours was done with the 2.1.7 build of the BerkeleyDB XML product; by the time you read this, the issues mentioned here may have already been fully addressed. Open Visual Studio and select Open ➪ Project/Solution and then navigate to the build_win32 directory under your BerkeleyDB XML installation directory. Open the DBDXML_all project, and Visual Studio should convert the project for you.

Before building the solution, there are three additional dependencies to deal with. The DBDXML_all project also builds interfaces for Java, Tcl, and Python, so install the Java SDK from the Sun Web site; you can download and install Tcl and Python from ActiveState.com. All of these can be installed using the default installation settings. Now select Tools ⇨ Options in Visual Studio. Then, in the options tree under Projects and Solutions in VC++ Directories, you need to make changes to both the Include Files list and the Library Files list. To the Include Files list, add the include directories from the Python, Tcl, and Java installations. Add another path to the win32 directory under the Java include directory. After that, add the lib directory for Java and Tcl to the Library Files list, and add the libs directory under the Python installation. Now build the project.

The project will generate a bunch of errors, all related to implicit casting. These can all be corrected by explicitly casting the variable involved. Rebuild the project. Now the errors should be reduced to those caused by missing libraries. In one case, the project was looking for tcl84g.lib and Tcl had tcl84.lib. Simply change the additional library settings for the related projects to use the right library. There should only be a few of these. Now rebuild again.

You are now ready to create and run the BerkeleyDB XML example for this chapter. Unlike the other examples, this example is C++ code used to create an interface wrapper to utilize the Berkeley XML database system. The first block shows a sample main program that uses the `SimpleXMLWrapper` object to store some simple XML documents and then run a query to retrieve them:

```cpp
#using <mscorlib.dll>

#include "dbxml/DbXml.hpp"
#include "db_cxx.h"
#include "SimpleXMLWrapper.hpp"

using namespace std;
using namespace DbXml;
using namespace XMLWrapper;
//some exception handling omitted for clarity

int main(void)
{
  _CrtSetReportMode( _CRT_ASSERT, 0 ) ;
  SimpleXMLWrapper* wrapper = new SimpleXMLWrapper();
  wrapper->createEnvironment(".");
  wrapper->createContainer("myNewContainer.dbxml");
  wrapper->openContainer("myNewContainer.dbxml");
  wrapper->insertDocument(
          "<book><title>book1</title><chap>chapter 1</chap></book>");
  wrapper->insertDocument(
          "<book><title>book2</title><chap>chapter 1</chap></book>");
  wrapper->insertDocument(
          "<book><title>book3</title><chap>chapter 1</chap></book>");

  wrapper->queryDocuments("/book");

  cout << wrapper->nextResult() << std::endl;

  return 0;
}
```

This next block of code shows the header file for the `SimpleXMLWrapper`:

```
#ifndef __SIMPLEXMLWRAPPER_HPP
#define __SIMPLEXMLWRAPPER_HPP

#using <mscorlib.dll>

#include "dbxml/DbXml.hpp"
#include "db_cxx.h"

using namespace std;
using namespace DbXml;

namespace XMLWrapper
{
  class SimpleXMLWrapper
  {
  private:
    const char* envPath;
    const char* containerName;
    DbEnv* env;
    XmlManager* db;
    XmlContainer* xmlContainer;
    XmlResults* xmlResults;

  public:
    SimpleXMLWrapper ();
    void createEnvironment(const char*);
    void createContainer(const char*);
    void openContainer(const char*);
    void insertDocument(const char*);
    void queryDocuments(const char*);
    std::string nextResult();
  };
}

#endif
```

Finally, this is the implementation of the wrapper object:

```
#using <mscorlib.dll>

#include "dbxml/DbXml.hpp"
#include "db_cxx.h"
#include "SimpleXMLWrapper.hpp"

using namespace std;
using namespace DbXml;

namespace XMLWrapper {

  SimpleXMLWrapper::SimpleXMLWrapper ()
  {
    envPath = ".";
```

```
    }

    void SimpleXMLWrapper::createEnvironment ( const char* environmentLocation )
    {
      envPath = environmentLocation;
      env = new DbEnv(0);
      env->set_cachesize(0, 64 * 1024 * 1024, 1);
      env->open(envPath,
              DB_INIT_MPOOL|DB_CREATE|DB_INIT_LOCK|DB_INIT_LOG|DB_INIT_TXN, 0);
    }

    void SimpleXMLWrapper::createContainer ( const char* containerName )
    {
      this->containerName = containerName;
      db = new XmlManager(env);
      db->createContainer(containerName);
    }

    void SimpleXMLWrapper::openContainer ( const char* containerName )
    {
      xmlContainer = new XmlContainer(db->openContainer(containerName));
    }

    void SimpleXMLWrapper::insertDocument ( const char* strDoc )
    {
      XmlUpdateContext myContext = db->createUpdateContext();
      XmlDocument xmlDoc = db->createDocument();
      xmlDoc.setContent( strDoc );
      xmlContainer->putDocument(xmlDoc, myContext, DBXML_GEN_NAME);
    }

    void SimpleXMLWrapper::queryDocuments ( const char* strQuery )
    {
      std::string fullQuery = "collection('" + xmlContainer->getName() + "')" +
                          strQuery;

      XmlQueryContext context = db->createQueryContext();
      xmlResults = new XmlResults( db->query(fullQuery, context) );
    }

    std::string SimpleXMLWrapper::nextResult ( )
    {
      XmlValue value;
      xmlResults->next(value);
      return value.asString();
    }
}
```

With the previous files, you can create a managed DLL. This is then used as a reference with any other managed application. Using this basic interface along with the Berkeley DB XML libraries, you are free to store and query XML documents at will.

Resource Information

This section lists important online sites for information about BerkeleyDB. First are the sites from which the software for this section was downloaded, followed by a list of drivers (including third-party drivers not used in this section), and finally sources that provide support information.

Downloads

For this section, all of the software can be downloaded from Sleepycat. The software downloaded for this section was Berkeley DB 4.3 and Berkeley DB XML 2.1.

❑   `http://sleepycat.com`—Main page for BerkeleyDB downloads

Drivers

In this section, no drivers were used.

Support

Berkeley DB support information can be found online at the following pages:

❑   `http://sleepycat.com/supports/documentation.shtml`—The primary page for the Berkeley DB documentation

❑   `http://pybsddb.sourceforge.net/ref/intro/dbisnot.html`—BerkeleyDB reference guide

❑   `http://sleepycat.com/supports/index.shtml`—For professional support options

SQLite

SQLite is a great little product, oriented toward being simple and embedded. How simple? SQLite has one executable file with no external dependencies. It reads and writes directly to a single database file, yet it has ACID-compliant transactions. It is a serverless database that is very compact and requires no configuration, yet it supports most of the SQL-92 standard.

SQLite was first released in 2000, and it is now at version 3.2.1, which was released in March of 2005. It started out as a C API for an embedded database, but has grown to support many other interfaces, including ADO.NET 2. The ADO.NET 2 provider is officially beta until Visual Studio 2005 is released, but because this is a book on ADO.NET 2, it seemed appropriate to put the provider through some beta testing.

SQLite is not actually licensed. The software has been donated to the public domain, so you can do anything you want with it. There is no license page, but for a discussion of SQLite and its public domain status, look to the following page: `www.sqlite.org/copyright.html`.

SQL Compliance

Despite its simplicity, SQLite implements most of the SQL-92 standards, with some of the key exceptions contained in the following table. For a full discussion, check the documentation or the online Wiki.

SQL Feature	Behavior
CHECK constraints	Parsed, but only NOT NULL and UNIQUE constraints are enforced.
FOREIGN KEY constraints	Parsed, but not enforced.
Triggers	Incomplete. Recursive triggers are not supported. Triggers must operate on a FOR EACH ROW as opposed to FOR EACH STATEMENT.
ALTER TABLE	Incomplete. Only RENAME TABLE and ADD COLUMN are allowed.
Nested Transactions	Only one transaction may be active at a time.
COUNT (DISTINCT value)	Not supported. An equivalent workaround is provided by the following: SELECT COUNT(value) FROM (SELECT DISTINCT value FROM table);
OUTER JOIN	Incomplete. Only LEFT OUTER JOIN is supported. RIGHT and FULL outer joins are not supported.
Views	Incomplete. Views are read-only; there are no views that support updates.
GRANT, REVOKE	Not supported.

Another item that is not in the table, because it requires some additional explanation, is static typing. SQLite provides no static type checking except for some specific instances. Static typing is generally taken for granted — after all, you wouldn't expect to put a string value into a double field, but with SQLite you can. This isn't catastrophic given that SQLite is targeted at single-user, embedded implementations, but it is important to note.

A second key point regarding SQLite is concurrency. SQLite is serverless, and it is not thread safe. Again, this is a reflection of the product's use as the back-end for an embedded system. The idea is that one application will be using the database. However, this doesn't mean that you can't use SQLite in a server environment. It can be, and is, used for the back-end of Web sites. These are not very high-volume Web sites, but given the quickness of the SQLite engine, it can handle a fair load. Therefore, if you do implement SQLite in a server environment, you will have to ensure synchronized access to the database yourself.

Database Features

The fact that SQLite is serverless is really a key feature. For instance, suppose you want to create a .NET and Winform application that will be distributed to the desktop. Further, this application, like most, will have data storage and manipulation requirements. In many cases, a full-blown database server is too much, and a database server adds complexity to the installation and many possible support headaches. Therefore, if you have client programs that need data functionality but not a full server, and whose data access code needs to be SQL for future use, SQLite may well be your tool of choice.

Other key features of the database also revolve around its minimalist approach. The first of these is that there are zero configuration requirements. Now, when many vendors say they have zero configuration and administrative requirements, they really mean is that they have only a few requirements that any reasonably technical but nondatabase-oriented person can manage. After all, most of them are servers that require network ports to be available, and so on. With SQLite, it really is zero: no network ports, no infrequently used configuration file, nothing.

SQLite is also small, with a tiny footprint. It is a single library, and it is usable from the command line as a single executable less that 350 K in size. That really is tiny, which makes it an easily distributed embedded database component.

Yet for all this smallness and simplicity, it is still pretty snappy. It can insert 25,000 rows into an indexed table in about a second, assuming that all the inserts happen within a single transaction. This is a side benefit of not having to communicate through a server port. However, it is important to use a transaction around a large block of activity; otherwise, the additional file access for each update will become detrimental.

Installation

The base installation of SQLite is the simplest of all the databases described here. SQLite has one single executable that can be downloaded from sqlite.org, and you can copy it wherever you need it. The latest version at the time of writing is version 3.2.1. While you are there, also download the SQLite Analyzer, and the SQLite DLL without the TCL bindings.

Level of .NET Support

Given that SQLite provides an API, you will need a .NET wrapper to use it in a .NET application. There are a couple floating about, but we will use the ADO.NET SQLite wrapper found at ADO.NET SQLite at SourceForge and listed in the "Driver Information" section below.

Working with .NET

Here we examine a basic program that opens and interrogates a simple SQLite database. SQLite doesn't have any graphical tools. Go to a command prompt and start SQLite 3 with the following command:

```
Sqlite3 model.db
```

This will start SQLite and put you at the SQLite prompt. You can paste the CREATE TABLE statement used previously into the command prompt and press Enter to create the PERSON_TBL. Then type .exit at the SQLite prompt to exit the program. This procedure will create a new database with the PERSON_TBL in it. Now, download the x86 DLL package from the SourceForge site. The package contains one managed DLL and two supporting DLLs. All of these need to be available to the test program for it to run.

```
Imports Finisar.SQLite

Module SQLiteTest

    Sub Main()

        Dim connectionString As String
        Dim dbcon As IDbConnection
```

```
            Dim dbcmd As IDbCommand
            Dim sql As String
            Dim reader As IDataReader
            Dim dataValue As Object
            Dim strValue As String

            Console.WriteLine("SQLiteTest - start.")
            connectionString = "Data Source=C:\dbfiles\sqlite\model.db;" & _
                               "Compress=True;" & _
                               "Synchronous=Off;" & _
                               "Version=3"

            dbcon = New SQLiteConnection(connectionString)
            dbcon.Open()
            dbcmd = dbcon.CreateCommand()
            sql = "SELECT * FROM PERSON_TBL"
            dbcmd.CommandText = sql
            dbcmd.Transaction = dbcon.BeginTransaction()
            reader = dbcmd.ExecuteReader()

            Do While reader.Read() = True

                dataValue = reader.GetValue(0)
                strValue = dataValue.ToString()
                Console.WriteLine("Value: " + strValue)

            Loop

            'Clean up
            reader.Close()
            dbcmd.Dispose()
            dbcon.Close()

            reader = Nothing
            dbcmd = Nothing
            dbcon = Nothing

            Console.WriteLine("SQLiteTest - end.")

        End Sub

    End Module
```

Violà! Connectivity for an embedded database; check online for a more in-depth sample.

Resource Information

This section lists important online sites for information about SQLite. First are the sites from which the software for this section was downloaded, followed by a list of drivers (including third-party drivers not used in this section), and finally sources that provide support information.

Downloads

For this section, all of the software can be downloaded from SQLite. The software downloaded for this section was the SQLite 3.2.1 Windows Binary package:

❑ `www.sqlite.org/download.html` — Main page for SQLite downloads

Drivers

The two .NET connectors used for this section were the SQLite ADO.NET 2 connector and a SQLite C# wrapper:

❑ `http://sourceforge.net/projects/adodotnetsqlite` — SourceForge site for SQLite downloads for .NET

❑ `http://sqlite-dotnet2.sourceforge.net` — SourceForge site for SQLite downloads for .NET 2

❑ `www.ag-software.com/DownLoad.aspx?DownLoadID=6` — AG-Software wrapper for SQLite access in C#

❑ `www.phpguru.org/downloads/csharp/SQLite.NET/` — A C# wrapper for accessing SQLite

Support

SQLite support information can be found online at the following pages.

❑ `www.sqlite.org/docs.html` — The primary page for the SQLite documentation.

❑ `sqlite-users-subscribe@sqlite.org` — This is the mailing list for SQLite support.

❑ `www.hwaci.com/sw/sqlite/prosupport.html` — If you are interested in professional support or custom modifications, this is the business site for the primary author of SQLite.

Summary

So there you have it: seven open-source databases to check out. If you're wondering which one is the best open-source database to use with .NET, the answer depends on your environment and what you want to do. If you need an embedded database for a standalone application, SQLite is a clear winner. If someone already has a MySQL database running and you need to talk to it, then the choice has been made for you. If you need a native XML solution, Berkeley DB has one for you. If your environment is an open field and you need to implement a medium- to heavy-weight database server, you have choices to make.

PostgreSQL, Firebird, Ingres, MySQL, and MaxDB could all potentially fit the bill, so it is worth analyzing performance details for your application. MySQL might be weaker in the concurrency department, but if your application has mostly reads, MySQL is solid and it will likely be deployed wherever you need to be. If you can leverage the object-relational features of PostgreSQL in your application, you could save development time. Firebird is just easy to use and has a very active community. Ingres is a serious heavy-weight with may sophisticated capabilities, but its user community is not as well-established. Still, if you have a large amount of data and can leverage such features as key-range partitioning, it is probably your best bet. Now, go give some of these databases a try — with open source, it won't cost you anything!

For More Information

To highlight the information in this chapter, the resources presented earlier are summarized here:

MySql

❑   `http://dev.mysql.com/downloads/` — Main page for MySQL downloads.

❑   `http://sourceforge.net/projects/mysqlnet/` — SourceForge project for open source, fully-managed drivers for an ADO.NET/MySQL connector.MaxDB.

❑   `http://dev.mysql.com/downloads/` — Main page for MySQL and MaxDB downloads.

❑   `http://dev.mysql.com/downloads/maxdb/clients_75.html#Documentation` — Main page for MaxDB client downloads.

Firebird

❑   `http://sourceforge.net/projects/firebird` — Main SourceForge page for Firebird downloads.

❑   `www.ibphoenix.com/` — A very useful site for all things InterBase and Firebird. This is also an organization that sells professional support services.

BerkeleyDB

❑   `http://sleepycat.com` — Main page for BerkeleyDB downloads.

❑   `http://pybsddb.sourceforge.net/ref/intro/dbisnot.html` — BerkeleyDB reference guide.

Ingres

❑   `http://opensource.ca.com/projects/ingres` — Main page for Ingres downloads.

❑   `http://opensource.ca.com/projects/ingres/documents` — The primary page for the Ingres documentation.

PostgreSQL

❑   `www.postgresql.org/ftp/win32/` — Location for the Win32 installer.

❑   `www.postgresql.org/community/` — Provides links to the mailing lists and newsgroups.

SQLite

❑   `www.sqlite.org/download.html` — Main page for SQLite downloads.

❑   `www.sqlite.org/docs.html` — The primary page for the SQLite documentation.

17

Oracle and ADO.NET

Oracle is one of the leading database vendors, and this chapter explores how Oracle and ADO.NET work together. ADO.NET, using its managed provider framework, attempts to provide a consistent interface for you to use when developing applications, regardless of which database vendor you are using. We will discuss how to access the Oracle database using ADO.NET and how to choose between the Microsoft Oracle provider and the Oracle Data Provider (ODP) that Oracle makes available.

Until recently, Oracle has been providing support for .NET on a half-hearted basis; however, that is changing with their current 10g R1 release. This release makes it clear that they are beginning to focus on providing adequate support both in terms of making their provider consistent with the Microsoft ADO.NET feature set and by introducing tools to integrate an Oracle Database Explorer as a Visual Studio add-in. At the time of this writing, the add-in works with Visual Studio 2003, but Oracle anticipates that a supported version of this for Visual Studio .NET 2005 will be available shortly after the release of Visual Studio .NET 2005 by Microsoft.

This chapter builds on what you've learned in previous chapters about ADO.NET and provides specific information that is relevant to using ADO.NET with Oracle. We also cover how to use the new tools that Oracle provides that integrate with Visual Studio .NET. The Oracle database is constantly evolving, and we will highlight a few of the features from the current release, 10g R2, and describe how to use them with your applications. All 10g R2 discussions are based on Oracle Beta 3 and may change slightly by the time of final release of the Oracle database.

Choosing an Oracle Data Provider

If you're targeting Microsoft SQL Server, your choice of ADO.NET providers is a pretty short list, for a number of reasons. If you are targeting Oracle, however, that choice is a little more complex. Two popular data providers are readily available for Oracle. Microsoft provides one that ships with the .NET Framework in the `System.Data.OracleClient` namespace. Oracle provides

ODP.NET as a free download from their Web site. Deciding which to use may be simple or complicated depending on your application and the version of the Oracle database software used. This section provides a high-level overview of each provider and their differences, as well as some recommendations for deciding when use of one is more appropriate than use of another.

One of the first things to help decide which provider to use centers around what version of Oracle the application will be using. Oracle's ODP.NET provider will only work with Oracle 8i or later. The Microsoft Oracle provider will work with version 7.3 and later.

For the most basic operations, such as fetching, inserting, and deleting, both of the providers are almost identical and can be interchanged simply by reference to the assembly and changing the `using` statement (C#) or `Import` statement (VB.NET). As you start looking at Oracle database–specific features, you will start noticing a greater difference between the two providers.

Regardless of the provider chosen, taking the approach of trying to isolate vendor-specific code will always serve you well. A good strategy to help this along is using consistent data access layer utilities and leveraging code generation where appropriate. This means that if you place SQL or calls to SQL throughout your application or Web forms and you decide to use a different database or provider, it is more difficult than if you had put them in a common library that the applications used.

The less you use vendor-specific code, the more options you have. For example, by not going out of your way to use Oracle-specific features, you leave the door open for later conversion to another database with reduced complications.

It is important to mention that there are other ADO.NET providers that vendors have integrated with ADO.NET and that provide access to Oracle databases. Some focus on solving specific problems, while others sit on top of the Oracle OCI client interface. We believe that for most purposes, using either Microsoft Oracle provider or the Oracle ODP.NET will satisfy the needs of most applications. Therefore, this chapter focuses on those two providers.

Common Provider Classes

The following table describes the classes that are common to both the Microsoft Oracle provider and the Oracle ODP.NET provider. While certain methods or properties will vary between the implementations, the high-level concept is generally the same.

Class	Description
OracleBFile	Provides reference access and manipulation of Oracle's BFile LOB type.
OracleCommand	SQL statement or name of the stored procedure; inherits from the DbCommand class.
OracleCommandBuilder	Handles the auto-generation of SQL in conjunction with a dataset and a data adapter.
OracleConnection	Represents the connection to the database; inherits from DbConnection.

Class	Description
OracleDataAdapter	Oracle-specific data adapter that is used to fill and update datasets or data tables.
OracleDataReader	Provides for forward-only reading of results.
OracleException	Thrown when errors occur using the Oracle provider methods and exposes SQL-related error information specific to Oracle.
OracleInfoMessageEventArgs	Used to pass info and warning messages back to a user-registered callback.
OracleParameter	Used to define a parameter for adding to an OracleCommand.
OracleParameterCollection	Collection of OracleParameter classes
OracleTransaction	Returned by BeginTransaction and then used to perform additional actions on the current transaction.
OracleRowUpdateEventArgs	Passed to callback handler for RowUpdated event when DataAdapter update is called; called after the update has occurred.
OracleRowUpdatingEventArgs	Passed to the callback handler for RowUpdating event when DataAdapter update is called; called before the update has occurred.

Microsoft Oracle Provider

The Microsoft Oracle provider furnishes all the basic support to enable standard database activities. Microsoft has even gone so far in the version that ships with .NET 2.x to include a little more support for some of the features that are Oracle-specific. For example, REF Cursor support is now available, along with specialized classes for dealing with Oracle's large object types.

In general, the Microsoft Oracle provider will always lag behind and not implement as many Oracle-specific features. On the other hand, it will typically have a more complete set of the features that make it play well with .NET and the Visual Studio .NET IDE. For example, if you are interested in better built-in Visual Studio .NET wizard support or the capability to use the more generic DbProviderFactories programming model, then you will enjoy the support provided by the Microsoft Oracle provider. If you use the designers provided with Visual Studio .NET and specify Oracle as the provider, you will be using the Microsoft Oracle provider.

The following classes are specific to the System.Data.OracleClient namespace.

Class	Description
OracleClientFactory	Inherits from DbProviderFactory and implements the necessary interface to support the new ADO.NET factory concept. This object would typically be returned from a call to DbProviderFactories.GetFactory.
OracleLob	Represents Blob, CLob, and Nlog types. Used when the file data is stored in the database instead of a physical file in the operating system, which would use an OracleBFile.
OracleConnectionStringBuilder	Allows type-safe building of an Oracle-specific connection string and has Oracle unique properties such as LoadBalanceTimeout that are specific to Oracle.
OraclePermission	Used to help the Framework determine whether the caller has code access security to access the provider in a partial trust environment.
OraclePermissionAttribute	Intended for future use to define attributes for code access security.

Oracle Data Provider for .NET (ODP.NET)

ODP.NET is Oracle's provider. It implements all of the standard requirements to be a first-class ADO.NET provider. Oracle has been aggressively releasing upgrades to the provider since it was released and has ensured that it keeps current with the full Oracle database feature set. For example, support for XmlType, array parameters, and statement caching — to name a few — are all provided only in the Oracle ODP.NET provider.

Because Oracle is dependent on Microsoft as they evolve ADO.NET, in general you will always see a little delay as .NET/ADO.NET features are available for Oracle to implement. For example, Oracle will be waiting to add full support for the new base class model in ADO.NET until after ADO.NET/.NET 2.x is released.

One of the features that is only supported using the Oracle ODP.NET provider is *statement caching*. Statement caching eliminates the need to reparse each statement prior to execution. It is performed on a per-connection basis, and provides a benefit only when a statement is executed multiple times. For some applications, this can result in a large saving of processing resources.

If you are using the more current version of Oracle 10gR2, then you also have access to the Change Notification support that is only available using the ODP.NET provider. We cover this in more detail later in the chapter and provide a couple of examples that show how to use it to invalidate cache in your ASP.NET application.

If your application is heavily dependent on Oracle and leverages some of the more advanced features, then using the ODP.NET provider will probably make more sense.

The following classes are specific to the Oracle ODP.NET provider.

Class	Description
OracleError	Represents an error returned by Oracle; you can access it via the Errors collection on the Oracle provider's OracleException class.
OracleErrorCollection	Represents a collection of OracleError classes.
OracleDependency	Represents a dependency between an application and a database; typically used to track and receive notifications when results of a query have been invalidated due to a table modification.
OracleClob	Provides a class to manipulate a CLOB object.
OracleRefCursor	Used to access a REF CURSOR returned as an output parameter on a SQL statement.

Oracle Developer Tools for Visual Studio .NET

This is a new add-in for Visual Studio .NET that enables the developer to access database designer capabilities without having to leave Visual Studio .NET. The release of this tool represents a big step toward making a .NET developer more productive when working with the Oracle database. In the past, developers had to use third-party tools and never had much of an integrated experience in the Visual Studio .NET IDE.

You can download Oracle Developer Tools from the Oracle site at www.oracle.com/technology/tech/dotnet/tools/

Using the new integrated tool set, a developer in Visual Studio .NET can manipulate Oracle database objects from version 8i forward, regardless of the platform on which the database runs within Visual Studio .NET. For example, even if your database resides on a UNIX server, you can still access it via the add-in.

The main interaction for the developer will be with the new Oracle Explorer window. Using this window provides access to all of Oracle's features. This is not just a generic provider on top of any database — through this window, you can access most Oracle-specific features.

Figure 17-1 illustrates the view you have from the Oracle Explorer window. This tree view provides you with navigation for all of the Oracle database schema objects you have access to using the current connection credentials.

Dragging and dropping schema objects from the Oracle Explorer window will invoke automation that generates code for you. The generated code will use ODP.NET calls, unlike code generated from the built-in Visual Studio .NET wizards that use the Microsoft Oracle provider.

Using the add-on capabilities of Visual Studio .NET, Oracle developers will continue to see improvements in the integration and capabilities for using the Oracle database from within Visual Studio .NET.

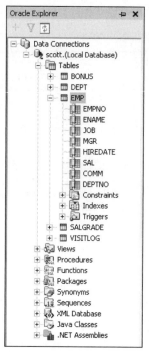

Figure 17-1

The Oracle Explorer window enables you to have multiple connections to servers. These servers can be on platforms other than Windows. You can add connections to the Explorer window, but you must have defined the Oracle database in your local tnsnames.ora file in order for it to be available to add. By dragging an object such as a table from the Oracle Explorer window, you can cause automation to generate code.

If you have access to a large number of schemas, you can use the Apply Filters dialog, shown in Figure 17-2, to reduce the schemas shown in the Oracle Explorer window. The Apply Filters window is accessed by right-clicking a connection in the OE window.

Keep in mind that Oracle Explorer is not specific to a project/solution in Visual Studio .NET. Therefore, if you filter a connection on a schema and later wonder why it is gone when you view it from a different project/solution than you had used it in before, all you have to do is reset the filter on that connection.

As you can see in Figure 17-3, the Table Designer enables you to create/modify the design of a table from within the Visual Studio .NET IDE. Here you can add and remove columns and specify the appropriate data type information for the column. You can also specify or adjust constraints as well as define indexes.

As shown in Figure 17-4, the Data Window enables you to retrieve data from a table as well as edit and insert new data.

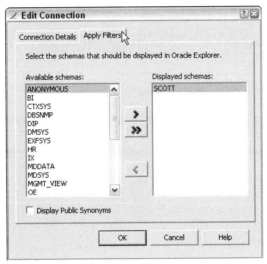

Edit Connection
Connection Details
Apply Filters
Select the schemas that should be displayed in Oracle Explorer.
Available schemas:
ANONYMOUS
BI
CTXSYS
DBSNMP
DIP
DMSYS
EXFSYS
HR
IX
MDDATA
MDSYS
MGMT_VIEW
OE
Displayed schemas:
SCOTT
Display Public Synonyms
OK
Cancel
Help

Figure 17-2

Start Page
ORACLE://scot...TT/EMP[Design]
Schema name:
SCOTT
Table type:
Relational
Table name:
EMP
Columns
Constraints
Indexes
Storage
Columns:
Name
Data type
EMPNO NUMBER
ENAME VARCHAR2
JOB VARCHAR2
MGR NUMBER
HIREDATE DATE
SAL NUMBER
COMM NUMBER
DEPTNO NUMBER
Column Properties
Name: EMPNO
Data type: NUMBER
Default:
Allow null
Precision: 4
Scale: 0
Add
Remove

Figure 17-3

Start Page
ORACLE://sco...OTT/EMP[Data]
EMPNO ENAME JOB MGR HIREDATE SAL COMM DEPTNO
7369 SMITH CLERK 7902 17-DEC-80 1990.66 20
7499 ALLEN SALESMAN 7698 20-FEB-81 3981.31 300 30
7521 WARD SALESMAN 7698 22-FEB-81 3110.4 500 30
7566 JONES MANAGER 7839 02-APR-81 7402.75 20
7654 MARTIN SALESMAN 7698 28-SEP-81 3110.4 1400 30
7698 BLAKE MANAGER 7839 01-MAY-81 7091.71 30
7782 CLARK MANAGER 7839 09-JUN-81 6096.38 10
7788 SCOTT ANALYST 7566 19-APR-87 7464.96 20
7839 KING PRESIDENT 17-NOV-81 12441.6 10
7844 TURNER SALESMAN 7698 08-SEP-81 3732.48 0 30

Figure 17-4

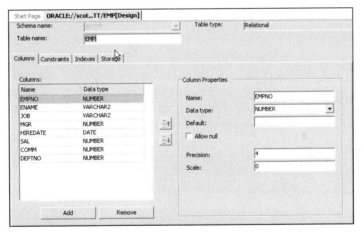

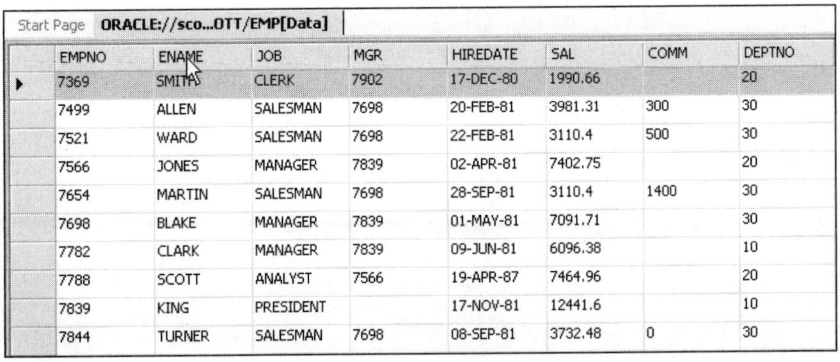

Getting Started with Oracle Explorer

After you install Oracle's Tools for Visual Studio .NET, you will find a new item on your View menu in the IDE labeled Oracle Explorer. When you bring that up the first time after installation, you will not yet have any connections defined.

One of the things you must do before you can add a connection is use the Oracle Net Configuration Wizard or edit your tnsnames.ora file manually to define a data source. The Net Configuration Wizard will walk you through a few screens and update the tnsnames.ora file for you. If you decide to modify this file or just wish to look at what the wizard did, you can find the tnsnames.ora file in your ORACLE_HOME/network/admin directory.

The following example defines an entry that would show up in the Data Source list in the Oracle Explorer Add Connection dialog:

```
PROADODB =
  (DESCRIPTION =
    (ADDRESS_LIST =
      (ADDRESS = (PROTOCOL = TCP)(HOST = 192.168.20.228)(PORT = 1521))
    )
    (CONNECT_DATA =
      (SERVICE_NAME = proadodb)
    )
  )
```

Once you have accomplished the above, or if you already had a valid specification in your tnsnames.ora file from past use, you can click the + on the toolbar in Oracle Explorer or right-click the Data Connection item in the tree and select Add Connection. Upon doing so, you will see the dialog shown in Figure 17-5.

Figure 17-5

Now that you have successfully defined a connection to Oracle Explorer, you can begin exploring your Oracle schema objects.

Support for Large Objects

The following table contains the data types that Oracle supports for dealing with large objects.

Data Type	Comments
BFile	Provides support for external large objects — actual storage of the object is done in the file system. This column is read-only and can reference data that is up to 4 GB.
BLOB	Used to store large amounts of binary data — for example, images or other multimedia files.
CLOB	Large character data support — the first 4,000 are stored like a varchar2 and inline with the row data.
NCLOB	Similar to CLOB but provides support for the National Character Set.

Getting a Connection

The OracleConnection class facilitates the creation of a unique connection to the Oracle database.

The most important property or constructor parameter is the Connection String. Ideally, your connection string would be obtained from your configuration file or some other centralized location to prevent it from being duplicated in multiple places in your application. ASP.NET also has a new section for storing connection strings that enables built-in protection. Having them removed from your code also makes it easier to deal with differences between development, test, and production environments.

If it is necessary to manipulate the connection string or to build it from scratch in the application, the Microsoft Oracle provider OracleConnectionStringBuilder class provides type-safe Oracle-specific properties with which you can manipulate the string.

The following is a simple connection string that uses an alias, proadodb, from tnnames.ora:

```
Data Source=proadodb;Persist Security Info=True;User ID=proadouser;Password=proad
```

It is also possible to create a connection string without using a tnsnames.ora alias. Instead of specifying the alias in the Data Source attribute, the entire connect descriptor is provided. The following example is the same connection string but does not depend on tnsnames.ora:

```
Dim con As OracleConnection

Dim conStr As String

conStr = "User Id=scott; Password=tiger;" + _
        "Data Source=(DESCRIPTION = (" + _
        "ADDRESS_LIST = (ADDRESS = (PROTOCOL = TCP)" + _
        "(HOST = YourHostName)(PORT = 1521)) )" + _
        "(CONNECT_DATA = (SERVER = DEDICATED) " + _
        "(SERVICE_NAME = ProADO2DB)));"

Try
```

```
        con = New OracleConnection(conStr)
        con.Open()
        con.Close()
    Catch ex As Exception
        MessageBox.Show(ex.Message)
    End Try
```

If this method is used, it would be best to move the actual connection string to your application configuration file instead of inline in the code.

The actual options that you can provide on a connection string vary between the two providers. The following tables highlight the options that are similar, and unique, to each of the providers.

Common Properties

Following are connection string properties that both the Oracle ODP.NET and the Microsoft Oracle provider recognize and support, and which share similar behaviors:

Property	Comments
Enlist	Determines whether the connection is automatically enlisted in distributed transactions.
PersistSecurityInfo	Determines whether security-sensitive information is returned with a connection object once it is opened.
Min Pool Size	Minimum number that will be retained for the pool.
Max Pool Size	Maximum number of pooled connections that will be kept.

Microsoft Oracle Provider–Specific Properties

The following table describes connection string properties that are specific to the Microsoft Oracle provider.

Property	Comments
LoadBalanceTimeout	Determines whether the connection is automatically enlisted in distributed transactions.
Pooling	Determines whether connection pooling will be used — the default is true.
IntegratedSecurity	Indicates whether integrated security should be used; if desired, you also should not set user/password — the default value is false.
Unicode	Specifies whether the client is Unicode-capable — the default is false.
ConnectionTimeout	The Microsoft provider does not support using this property.

ODP.NET Provider–Specific Properties

The following table describes connection string properties that are specific to the Oracle ODP.NET provider.

Property	Comments
DBA Privilege	Blank by default; set to SYSDBA or SYSOPER to request administrative privileges.
ValidateConnection	Causes the connection to be validated prior to being returned if it is from the pool. Keep in mind that this causes a server round-trip, so it may cause unnecessary overhead if overused.
Statement Cache Purge	Causes the statement cache to be purged when the connection is returned to the pool — the default is false.
Statement Cache Size	Enables statement caching and sets the cache size — the default is 0.
Proxy User ID	User ID for the proxy ID; provides support for the User ID to pass through a client-specific account or auditing, but have an application server account for actual access authorization.
Proxy Password	Password for the proxy ID.
Incr Pool Size	Number of connections that are established if all of the connections in the pool are in use and pool size is below the max pool size.
Decr Pool Size	Number of connections that are dismantled and closed when excessive connections are not in use.

Once you have opened a connection, be sure to explicitly call the Close method. This ensures that resources are freed, and, if you are using connection pooling, the connection is returned to the pool for use by other callers. A common problem is getting a data reader and not closing the underlying connection when an error occurs.

Both the Oracle and Microsoft provider support the concept of connection pooling and enable it by default. As you have seen, you can gain some amount of control over how the pool is managed. The pool capabilities in the Microsoft Oracle provider use similar techniques to those used in the Microsoft SQL Client provider.

If you want to use Windows authentication, it is supported by both providers using a concept referred to as *integrated security*. Microsoft has a property on the connection string called IntegratedSecurity that you set to true and for which you do not pass a user/password. Oracle's provider expects the connection string to have the User ID=/ to indicate integrated security.

Failover Notification

The Oracle provider has the capability to register a callback for notification in the event that Transparent Application Failover is invoked. While the application should not see any loss of connection as long as at least one instance is left, the application may want to log or notify the caller of the delay that may be incurred.

The following sample shows how to register a failover handler:

```
OracleConnection con = new OracleConnection();
Con.Failover += new OracleFailoverEventHandler(MyFailOverHandler);
```

Only the last failover handler will be invoked if multiple handlers are registered on a connection.

Binding Parameters

Because there are generic .NET types and Oracle-specific DBTypes such as OracleString, there are options for how you handle the binding of parameters.

In most cases for input parameters, the providers can determine the type of the item based on the Parameter Value property type. For output parameters, you have the option of retrieving the data using .NET types or Oracle types. How this happens is different for each of the providers.

Microsoft provides a property on the parameter object named OracleType that can be used to establish the type. This property is linked to the DbType property of the object, and when one changes, the other will be set to an appropriate compatible type.

The Oracle ODP.NET provider will determine how the data is returned based on whether the type specified on the parameter is an OracleDbType or a .NET DbType. For example, if you bind as an OracleDbType.Char, the output is returned as an OracleString type.

Array Binding

One of the features unique to using ODP.NET is the capability to bind to an array of values and pass that via the OracleParameter. This capability would be useful to applications that need to insert multiple rows at once into a table. For example, a logging application that logs every 50 rows would, by using this, reduce round-trips to the database from 50 times to one time. Keep in mind that because this is an Oracle ODP.NET–specific feature, using it would render code incompatible with using the Microsoft provider.

Somewhere, you need to have the data defined in an array that will be passed. For example purposes here, we use a simple static array of numbers:

```
//define array of lucky numbers
int[] luckyNumberArr = {70,25,32,77};
```

To use this feature, you must set the ArrayBindCount on the OracleCommand object. This is an important step, as otherwise, you are likely to get an error such as an invalid cast exception, because the parameter is not expecting to find an array for the value:

```
//inform the command of number in array
cmd.ArrayBindCount = luckyNumberArr.Length;
```

Setting up a parameter itself is pretty straightforward and very similar to a single value operation:

```
OracleParameter luckyNumberParm = new
OracleParameter("luckynum",OracleDbType.Int32);
luckyNumberParm.Direction = ParameterDirection.Input;
luckyNumberParm.Value = luckyNumberArr;
cmd.Parameters.Add(luckyNumberParm);
```

The following code is a more complete example that shows how to use more than a single parameter. In this example, you are adding rows to a visit log table and using the array binding to optimize the round trips to the database engine:

```
string conStr =
        "User Id=scott;Password=tiger;Data Source = ProAdo2DB;";

int[] userIDs = {1,2,3,4};
string[] urls = {"home.aspx","view.aspx","edit.aspx","print.aspx"};
DateTime[] visitDates =
{
    DateTime.Now.AddHours(1),DateTime.Now.AddHours(1),
    DateTime.Now.AddHours(1),DateTime.Now.AddHours(1)
};

string sql = "insert into VisitLog(UserID,URL,VisitDate)" +
             "     values(:userid,:url,:visitdate)";

using (OracleConnection con = new OracleConnection(conStr))
{
    con.Open();

    OracleCommand cmd = new OracleCommand(sql,con);
    cmd.ArrayBindCount = userIDs.Length;

    OracleParameter parmUserID =
            new OracleParameter("userid",OracleDbType.Int32);
    parmUserID.Direction = ParameterDirection.Input;
    parmUserID.Value = userIDs;
    cmd.Parameters.Add(parmUserID);

    OracleParameter parmUrls =
        new OracleParameter("url",OracleDbType.Varchar2);
    parmUrls.Direction = ParameterDirection.Input;
    parmUrls.Value = urls;
    cmd.Parameters.Add(parmUrls);

    OracleParameter parmVisitDate =
        new OracleParameter("visitdate",OracleDbType.Date);
    parmVisitDate.Direction = ParameterDirection.Input;
    parmVisitDate.Value = visitDates;
    cmd.Parameters.Add(parmVisitDate);

    cmd.ExecuteNonQuery();

    con.Close();
```

```
        con.Dispose();

    }
```

Errors encountered during array binding can be more complex to deal with. If an error occurs during the array binding, an `OracleException` will be thrown. The `Errors` property (`OracleErrorCollection`) will contain one or more of the errors that occurred. To make it easier for you to figure out which row caused the problem, each `OracleError` object that is in the collection will have the `ArrayBindIndex` property set. Using that value, you can determine which row is at fault.

The following example shows how you could modify the previous example to include a `try` / `catch` and a message to the user about the row that caused the problem.

Some code has been omitted to preserve space.

```
string conStr =
        "User Id=scott;Password=tiger;Data Source = ProAdo2DB;";

    int[] userIDs = {1,2,3,4};
    string[] urls = {"home.aspx",null,"edit.aspx","print.aspx"};
    DateTime[] visitDates =
    {
        DateTime.Now.AddHours(1),DateTime.Now.AddHours(1),
        DateTime.Now.AddHours(1),DateTime.Now.AddHours(1)
    };

    string sql = "insert into VisitLog(UserID,URL,VisitDate)" +
                "    values(:userid,:url,:visitdate)";

    using (OracleConnection con = new OracleConnection(conStr))
    {
        con.Open();

        OracleCommand cmd = new OracleCommand(sql,con);
        cmd.ArrayBindCount = userIDs.Length;

        //Code to setup parameters omitted to save space

        try
        {
            cmd.ExecuteNonQuery();
        }
        catch(OracleException oracleEx)
        {
            string errorMessage =
            String.Format("OracleException {0} ", oracleEx.Message);
            foreach(OracleError errorDet in oracleEx.Errors)
            {
              if (errorDet.Number != 24381)
                errorMessage += String.Format(" Array Error {0} occurred at parm
{1}",
                    errorDet.Message,errorDet.ArrayBindIndex);
            }

            MessageBox.Show(errorMessage);
```

```
        }

    con.Close();
    con.Dispose();

}
```

In the preceding example, to cause the error, we set the value of the second URL to null. This also assumes that the table definition for this is set so as not to allow nulls. The other thing we did is add the try / catch. Notice that we skipped the OracleError object that had an error number value of 24381; that object is not specific to an array item and just gives you a generic error. Something else to know is that all you get back is the row index and not a specific indication of which parameter caused the problem. It would probably be a good idea to include the value of the item at the error index in your error message or in any logging that is done.

Filling a DataTable

The following code will fill a data table using the OracleDataAdapter. Please note that the following example works with either the Microsoft or ODP.NET provider. The only difference in this particular code would be that the using statement of Oracle.DataAccess.Client would be changed to System.Data.OracleClient to use the Microsoft provider:

```
using System;
using System.Data;
using Oracle.DataAccess.Client;
using System.Collections.Generic;
using System.Text;
using MSOracleProviderLib.Properties;

namespace MSOracleProviderLib
{
    public class DBEventODP
    {
        public static DataTable GetRecentEvents(TimeSpan timeSpan)
        {
            //Determine Start Date
            DateTime startDate = DateTime.Now.Subtract(timeSpan);
            using (OracleConnection con = new OracleConnection())
            {
                //use the property from the config file to get the
                //connection string this uses the new settings class
                //that allows type safe properties to config settings
                con.ConnectionString = Settings.Default.ConnectionString;
                con.Open();
                OracleCommand command = new OracleCommand();
                command.Connection = con;
                command.CommandText = "SELECT EVENTID, TITLE, ABSTRACT," +
                    "EVENTDATE FROM EVENT where EVENTDATE >= ":startdate and" +
                    " eventdate <= :enddate";
                command.CommandType = System.Data.CommandType.Text;
                command.Parameters.Add(
                    new OracleParameter("startdate", startDate));
                command.Parameters.Add(
```

```
            new OracleParameter("enddate", DateTime.Now));

        OracleDataAdapter dataAdapter =
            new OracleDataAdapter(command);

        DataTable dataTable = new DataTable();
        dataAdapter.Fill(dataTable);
        con.Close();
        return dataTable;
        }
    }
  }
}
```

Generically Filling a DataTable

In the prior example, we showed how you could use the Oracle-specific provider classes to fill a data table. In this example, we will use the new DbProviderFactories to accomplish the same thing, but with more generic code. Keep in mind that while this code will work with the Microsoft Oracle provider, the ODP.NET provider does not currently provide support for the provider factory model. Oracle expects to release an updated version of ODP.NET in the future to support this capability.

```
public static DataTable GetRecentEvents(TimeSpan timeSpan)
{
    //Determine Start Date
    DateTime startDate = DateTime.Now.Subtract(timeSpan);
    //get the provider invarient from config file
    DbProviderFactory factory =
    DbProviderFactories.GetFactory(Settings.Default.DBProvider);

    using (DbConnection con = factory.CreateConnection())
    {
        con.ConnectionString =
                Settings.Default.ConnectionString;
        con.Open();
        //get the marker string for parameters from utility function
        string parmMarkerFormat = GetParameterMarkerFormat(con);

        DbCommand command = factory.CreateCommand();
        command.Connection = con;
        command.CommandText = "SELECT EVENTID, TITLE, ABSTRACT," +
            "EVENTDATE FROM EVENT where EVENTDATE >= " +
            FormatParameterName(parmMarkerFormat, "startdate") +
            " and eventdate <= " +
        FormatParameterName(parmMarkerFormat, "enddate");
        command.CommandType = System.Data.CommandType.Text;
        DbParameter startParm =  factory.CreateParameter();
        startParm.ParameterName =
        FormatParameterName(parmMarkerFormat, "startdate");
        startParm.Value = startDate;
        command.Parameters.Add(startParm);
        DbParameter endParm = factory.CreateParameter();
        endParm.ParameterName =
        FormatParameterName(parmMarkerFormat, "enddate");
        endParm.Value = DateTime.Now ;
```

```
        command.Parameters.Add(endParm);

        DbDataAdapter dataAdapter = factory.CreateDataAdapter();
        dataAdapter.SelectCommand = command;

        DataTable dataTable = new DataTable();
        dataAdapter.Fill(dataTable);
        con.Close();
        return dataTable;
    }
}
```

Using the OracleDataReader

The OracleDataReader in both the ODP.NET and Microsoft's Oracle provider enable you to retrieve data in a forward-only stream of data. Using a data reader can be more efficient if you only need forward-only access to your data. Both of the providers give you access to the data in .NET types, as well as Oracle types.

Oracle Type Methods

The following table describes specific methods provided on the DataReader to return data in Oracle database types.

Method	Comments
GetOracleBFile	Obtains an instance of OracleBFile and allows manipulation of the BFile column.
GetOracleBinary	Returns an OracleBinary structure that represents a variable-length stream of binary data.
GetOracleDateTime	Returns an OracleDateTime structure that is capable of representing date and time from Jan 1, 4712 B.C., to Dec 31, 4712 A.D.
GetOracleLob	Returns an OracleLob, which represents a large object that has been stored on the server, unlike the OracleBfile that simply contains a reference to the file.
GetOracleMonthSpan	Returns the value as an OracleMonthSpan object, which will represent the time internval in months.
GetOracleNumber	Returns the value as an OracleMonth, which represents numeric values between -10^{27} and 10^{27}.
GetOracleString	Returns the value as an OracleString, which represents a variable-length stream of characters.
GetOracleTimeSpan	Returns an OracleTimeSpan structure, which contains an interval of time in days, hours, minutes, and seconds.
GetOracleValue	Returns an Oracle type for the column at the ordinal specified on the call.
GetOracleValues	Provides a way to receive all columns at once, rather than having to call methods for each column.

Inserting New Rows

Inserting data into an Oracle table is similar to inserting it with other databases, with one exception: Oracle does not have the same concept of *identity columns* as Microsoft SQL Server. Oracle handles the concept differently using a database object called a *Sequence*.

The `Sequence` database object enables you to generate a unique sequence number. Each user of the sequence can increment it and obtain numbers for their use. Using the sequence is independent of a transaction that is in progress. If you increment the sequence and your transaction rolls back, the sequence number will still have been incremented. Because multiple users can obtain sequence numbers, there is no guarantee that the numbers you get will not have gaps. It is also possible that you will have gaps in the resulting table because of rollbacks that have happened. A sequence does not have to be related to a single table, and therefore could be used to provide unique numbers to multiple tables. As a general rule, having one sequence object per table or at least one for each major table results in easier diagnostics and a better overall experience.

The following code will create a schema database object with the basic options. You can also specify several other more advanced options to control the sequence.

```
CREATE SEQUENCE "PROADOUSER"."SEQ_EVENT"
START WITH 1
CACHE 5
MAXVALUE 100000000000000000000000000000000
```

The following utility method shows an example of how to select the `NEXTVAL` from a sequence. Upon calling this, the sequence value is incremented by 1:

```
public static decimal GetNextSequenceValue(OracleConnection con,
            string sequenceName)
    {
        string sql = "SELECT " + sequenceName + ".NEXTVAL FROM DUAL";

        OracleCommand command = new OracleCommand(sql,con);

        object seqValue = command.ExecuteScalar();

        return (decimal)seqValue;

    }
```

The following code shows an example of an insert method that takes a data class that has properties for the various fields and uses the preceding utility sequence method to get the `EventID` populated prior to invoking the insert:

```
public static decimal CreateEvent(Event eventData)
    {
    using (OracleConnection con = new OracleConnection())
    {

        con.ConnectionString =
            Settings.Default.ConnectionString;
```

```
    con.Open();
    //Go get the next value from the sequence
    eventData.EventID =
        GetNextSequenceValue(con, "SEQ_EVENT");
    OracleCommand command = new OracleCommand();
command.Connection = con;
command.CommandText =
        "INSERT INTO EVENT ( EVENTID, TITLE, ABSTRACT," +
        "EVENTDATE) VALUES(:EVENTID,:TITLE,:ABSTRACT,:EVENTDATE)";
    command.CommandType = System.Data.CommandType.Text;
    command.Parameters.Add(new
    OracleParameter("EVENTID", eventData.EventID));
    command.Parameters.Add(new
    OracleParameter("TITLE", eventData.Title));
    command.Parameters.Add(new
    OracleParameter("ABSTRACT", eventData.Abstract));
    command.Parameters.Add(new
    OracleParameter("EVENTDATE", eventData.EventDate));
    command.ExecuteNonQuery();
    con.Close();
    return eventData.EventID;

    }
}
```

Common Oracle Errors

When developing an application that uses a database, it is almost impossible to avoid having to try to figure out some weird exception message that was thrown as a result of one of your database calls. One of the things you will ultimately encounter if you are developing an application targeting the Oracle database is one of the cryptic messages you get when exceptions occur that are output from the providers and the database engine.

Unfortunately, not every error message you get will provide you with meaningful information to help you solve the problem that was encountered. Many, if not most, offer only a vague indication of what went wrong, and leave it up to you to find the specific issue in your code.

Knowing this up front, it would be wise to implement good error handling and tracing capabilities in your application. For example, a practice of tracing out your parameters and associated values in the event that an exception occurs on a command using parameters would speed up debugging efforts.

This section highlights a few of the common errors that can occur and provides some insight into how you can handle these specific errors.

OracleException Class

When an error is generated during an Oracle call, the type of exception that is thrown is typically an OracleException. This class varies slightly in implementation between the two providers.

The ODP.NET exception class has a property, Errors, that is a collection of OracleError class instances. These will contain the individual errors generated by the database.

The Microsoft provider uses the Data list dictionary property that is inherited by its implementation of `OracleException` from `ExternalException`.

ORA-01008: Not all variables bound

This error typically occurs when you have specified one or more bind variables in your query, but you have not added the same number of parameters to your command object. This can also occur if you have provided the parameter but the names don't match. Another scenario, one of our favorites, is to create the parameter but fail to add it to the parameters collection. Like many other Oracle messages, we only wish it would tell you the name that it thinks is not bound. You would think if they could detect the fact that one is missing, they could enumerate the list to make it less of a search for the needle in the haystack!

ORA-01858: A nonnumeric character was found where a numeric was expected

Another one of our favorite exceptions typically occurs on an `INSERT` or `UPDATE` statement to which you are binding parameters and you mess up the order. By default, binding is done by order and not by name; you can change that by setting the `BindByName` property on the `Command` object. The other option is to be sure that your parameters are, in fact, in the same order in which they are used in the query.

System.DllNotFoundException: Unable to load DLL (oci.dll)

This error typically occurs when trying to connect to Oracle and the user the process is running does not have access to the Oracle/bin directory where the .dll resides. Check your access permissions.

Using Tracing to Find Problems

One of the tools you can use if you are using ODP.NET is the tracing capability. ODP.NET Tracing is controlled via settings in your registry for the Oracle Home that you are working with. Here is the registry key for this:

```
HKEY_LOCAL_MACHINE\SOFTWARE\ORACLE\<HOME NAME>\ODP.NET
```

You should replace `<HOME NAME>` with your own specific home as installed on your system.

Figure 17-6 shows the registry settings that you have to enable, described in the following table.

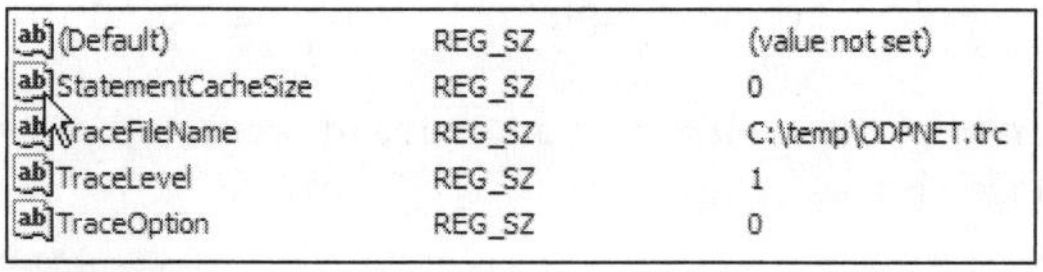

ab) (Default)	REG_SZ	(value not set)
ab) StatementCacheSize	REG_SZ	0
ab) TraceFileName	REG_SZ	C:\temp\ODPNET.trc
ab) TraceLevel	REG_SZ	1
ab) TraceOption	REG_SZ	0

Figure 17-6

Item	Comments
TraceFileName	Name in which to store the trace log entries.
TraceLevel	0 – no logging 1 – Entry/Exit 2 – Connection Pooling statistics 4 – Distributed transaction information Values are accumulative, so if you set the value to 4, you will also see the logging information for 1 and 2.
TraceOption	0 – Single trace file 1 – Multiple trace files; the thread ID will be appended to the file name specified in TraceFileName.

Figure 17-7 shows what you will get in the trace file.

```
TIME:2005/ 5/ 1- 0:26: 6:844 TID:13f8  (ENTRY) GetRegTraceInfo()
TIME:2005/ 5/ 1- 0:26: 6:844 TID:13f8  (EXIT)  GetRegTraceInfo(): RetCode=0 Line=524
TIME:2005/ 5/ 1- 0:26: 6:844 TID:13f8  (ENTRY) OracleConnection::OracleConnection(1)
TIME:2005/ 5/ 1- 0:26: 6:844 TID:13f8  (EXIT)  OracleConnection::OracleConnection(1)
TIME:2005/ 5/ 1- 0:26: 6:874 TID:13f8  (ENTRY) OracleConnection::open()
TIME:2005/ 5/ 1- 0:26: 6:874 TID:13f8  (ENTRY) opsConAllocvalctx()
TIME:2005/ 5/ 1- 0:26: 6:874 TID:13f8  (EXIT)  opsConAllocvalctx(): RetCode=0 Line=134
TIME:2005/ 5/ 1- 0:26: 6:874 TID:13f8  (ENTRY) OpsConOpen()
```

Figure 17-7

Understanding Packages

Packages are a feature that is unique to the Oracle database. They provide for container-like encapsulation or the grouping of schema items such as stored procedures, functions, cursor definitions, and variables.

Packages are not required, and if you create a stored procedure without one, it is said to be a standalone object. The goal of packages is to make life easier by providing a convenient grouping of items for handling grants, and, if nothing else, for improved organization.

Simple Package Definition

Figure 17-8 shows an example of a simple package definition that defines a ref cursor and a procedure using that cursor.

```
PACKAGE "PROADOPACKAGE" AUTHID DEFINER
IS
    type event_cursor is ref cursor;

    procedure geteventsbyidrange(minID number,maxID number,
                    eventdataCursor out event_cursor);

END;
```

Figure 17-8

535

Simple Package Body

Figure 17-9 shows the body, or the actual implementation, of the procedure defined in the package definition shown in Figure 17-8.

```
PACKAGE BODY "PROADOPACKAGE"
IS
    procedure geteventsbyidrange(minID number, maxID number,
                    eventdataCursor out event_cursor) is

    begin
       open eventDatacursor for
       select eventid,eventtitle from event;
    end;
END;
```

Figure 17-9

Overloading Packaged Functions

One of the more obscure uses of packages is to overload functions. These are functions that have the same name, but different parameters:

```
CREATE OR REPLACE PACKAGE PROADOPACKAGE IS
  FUNCTION calceventdurationhours(minutes NUMBER) return Number;
  FUNCTION calceventdurationhours(start DATE,end DATE) return Number;
END;
```

Understanding the State of Your Package

One of the things to keep in mind about your package is whether it is reusable. This is important because you can define variables inside of your package. By default, these, along with their associated values, stay in existence for the life of the session stored in user global area (UGA) memory. This can cause problems if you have a large number of connected users or if you expect the value to be reset for you on each request.

Packages have an option called Serially Reusable that enables you to specify that you do not depend on the values to be retained between requests, which enables Oracle to reuse the memory and not maintain it for the life of the session. The following sample demonstrates how to mark a package as serially reusable:

```
CREATE OR REPLACE PACKAGE PROADOPACKAGE IS
  PRAGMA SERIALLY_REUSABLE;
  MyFavoriteNumber NUMBER := 75;
END;
```

Regular Expression Support

Regular expressions are a popular way to search for patterns within a string of data. Oracle started providing support for regular expressions in the 10g R1 version of their database. Oracle has implemented regular expression in compliance with the POSIX Regular Expression Standard. You might have used regular expressions before, either in ASP.NET validation controls or other places where you wanted to match or extract string data. Oracle regular expression support now provides that same capability, but running inside the database engine. This can result in both significant flexibility and improved performance when compared to performing the function on the data once it is returned.

You can use regular expressions via the provided function either in queries or to enforce constraints on columns in your database tables. The following table describes the functions that Oracle provides to implement regular expressions.

Function	Description
REGEXP_LIKE	Similar to using LIKE. However, instead of using the simple syntax of LIKE, you have the full power of the regular expression syntax
REGEXP_REPLACE	Allows for complex replace operations that use regular expressions — for example, you could use it to format account numbers from one format to another
REGEXP_INSTR	Provides a more powerful version of the INSTR function and enables you to search a string, returning an integer that indicates the beginning or end of the matched string
REGEXP_SUBSTR	Allows for searching a string, returning a substring matching pattern

The following examples show how you can add a constraint to a column to ensure that a properly formatted e-mail is only allowed in the e-mail column:

```
CREATE TABLE Person
(
    PersonName    VARCHAR2(30),
    Email         VARCHAR(75)
    CONSTRAINT Person_Email_Valid
    Check(REGEXP_LIKE(Email,'^.+@[^\.].*\.[a-z]{2,}$'))
)
```

The following example uses a regular expression in a query:

```
public static DataTable GetRecentEvents(string regEx)
  {

    using (OracleConnection con = new OracleConnection())
    {
        con.ConnectionString = Settings.Default.ConnectionString;
        con.Open();
        OracleCommand command = new OracleCommand();
        command.Connection = con;
        command.CommandText = "SELECT EVENTID, TITLE, ABSTRACT," +
            "EVENTDATE FROM EVENT where REGEXP_LIKE(TITLE,:regexp)";
        command.CommandType = System.Data.CommandType.Text;
        command.Parameters.Add(new
        OracleParameter("regexp", regEx));
        OracleDataAdapter dataAdapter =
                new OracleDataAdapter(command);

        DataTable dataTable = new DataTable();
        dataAdapter.Fill(dataTable);
```

```
            con.Close();
            return dataTable;


    }
}
```

Database Change Notification

One of the new features in ODP.NET Release 10g R2 is support for requesting to be notified when there is a change in your query result, a database object, or the state of the database. The goal of the notification is to advise you that your query result set is now invalidated by events that have occurred. This can be an insert, a delete, or a modification of the underlying table.

This capability is similar in concept to support in Microsoft SQL Server; however, the implementation and usage is different. Currently, this is supported only by the ODP.NET provider.

Think about all the places this can be used. Keep in mind that notification requires resources to track and deliver the notifications. Ideally, this is best used on tables that are lookup-oriented and do not have frequent changes. A good example of a table that would make a good candidate is something that stores your product list. A bad table would be a table that stores views of pages on the site. Clearly, the later would constantly be triggering the notification events and could affect performance on both the client and database server.

OracleDependency is a new class provided by ODP.NET that defines the relationship between your application and the database. Creating an instance of this class does not set up the notification channel with the database that occurs when the OracleDependency object is associated with an OracleCommand and that command is executed. Behind the scenes, this class sets up a listener that will receive the notifications from the database engine.

One thing to keep in mind about notification is that the host on which the application is running must have a port open in order for the database engine to send the notification back to the listener. By default, the port is randomly picked by ODP.NET when the first registration occurs. You can set a fixed port using the static property OracleDependency.Port.

The user with which you plan to use change notification must be granted that privilege; otherwise, an exception will occur. The following statement will grant that authority to the user:

```
grant change notification to proadouser
```

Once you have registered to receive notification, it will stay active until one of the following occurs to cause it to end. First, you can call OracleDependency.RemoveRegistration to cause it to be removed from the notification list. If you had set the Timeout property on the OracleNotificationRequest object and the time span specified has elapsed, the notification will automatically stop. Second, that same object also has a notify once property (IsNotifiedOnce), which if set prior to registration will auto-terminate the notification after the first notification is received.

The following shows how to create an instance of OracleDependency and associate it with your command. After this association, when you execute the command, the change notification registration will occur:

```
OracleDependecy dependency = new OracleDependency(command);
```

As indicated previously, you can establish the port on which that notification will occur. Keep in mind that in most production environments containing one or more firewalls or routers, it is generally a good idea to agree on a port to use with your network administrator. It would be a good idea to have that discussion early in the development process to avoid last-minute surprises. The following will establish the port that is used:

```
OracleDependency.Port = 1595;
```

The next thing that you need to do is establish a callback that will be invoked when the notification occurs. If you do not establish a callback, you could also poll the `HasChanges` property on the dependency instance. The following example establishes a callback (this should happen prior to execution/registration of the notification):

```
Dependency.OnChanged += new OnChangedEventHandler(MyNotification_Handler);
```

Using Notification with ASP.NET

As you learned in previous chapters using the `SqlCacheDependecy` object, you can leverage the notification capabilities of Microsoft SQL Server to have it invalidate an ASP.NET cache entry upon change of the item in the database. While Oracle supplies an `OracleDependency`, it does not currently tie that into the ASP.NET cache infrastructure.

It's likely that in the future, ODP.NET might provide this capability, so check with the current version. However, to demonstrate how notification works, let's implement our own simplified version of `SqlCacheDependency` to allow a cache key to invalidate when the Oracle change notification occurs.

We'll first define our own version of `OracleCacheDependency`. It will inherit from `System.Web` `.Caching.CacheDependency` so that we can pass it as required to the Cache API calls. If you're not familiar with the `System.Web.Caching.CacheDependency` class, its purpose is to define a relationship between an ASP.NET cache item and a file, another cache key, or another dependency object. Or, in this case, we are extending it to integrate with Oracle change notification capabilities:

```
public class OracleCacheDependency : System.Web.Caching.CacheDependency
{

    public OracleCacheDependency(OracleCommand command)
    {
        m_Dependency = new OracleDependency(command);

        //work around a beta bug that threw error if you tried to
        //set this after there was already a request
        try
        {
            OracleDependency.Port = 1005;
        }
        catch { }

        m_Dependency.OnChange += new OnChangeEventHandler(HandleChangeNotification);
```

```
    }

    void HandleChangeNotification(object sender,
                        OracleNotificationEventArgs eventArgs)
    {
        this.NotifyDependencyChanged(this, EventArgs.Empty);
    }


    private OracleDependency m_Dependency;

    public OracleDependency Dependency
    {
        get { return m_Dependency; }
        set { m_Dependency = value; }
    }

}
```

In the preceding code sample, your constructor takes an Oracle Command object instance and associates it with the OracleCommand object instance. At the same time, the OnChanged event is handled to detect when the result set of the query has changed. Finally, when the notification occurs, you call the NotifyDependencyChanged method of CacheDependency, which will result in the associated ASP.NET cache entry being deleted.

The next thing we need to do is see how we can use this object when we cache data into the ASP.NET Cache. The goal here is to simply show how change notification works, and to demonstrate how to tie it into the cache dependencies. Much more elaborate things could be done here, but they are beyond the scope of this book.

In the following example, we are going to first determine whether the DataSet is in the ASP.NET Cache. If not, we will proceed to execute the query. For the query, we will tie it to an OracleDependency that is exposed from the OracleCacheDependency object. By doing this, we can then add the item to the ASP.NET cache and associate that cached item to our OracleCacheDependency instance that will get the notification. When that notification occurs, it will cause the CacheDependency to trigger, thereby removing the item from the ASP.NET Cache:

```
public class EmployeeManager
{

    public  DataSet GetEmployees()
    {

        if (HttpContext.Current.Cache["Employees"] != null)
            return HttpContext.Current.Cache["Employees"] as DataSet;


        string conStr = "User Id=scott; Password=tiger;" +
            "Data Source=(DESCRIPTION = (" +
            "ADDRESS_LIST = (ADDRESS = (PROTOCOL = TCP)" +
            "(HOST = 192.168.75.2)(PORT = 1522)) )" +
            "(CONNECT_DATA = (SERVER = DEDICATED) " +
```

```
                 "(SERVICE_NAME = ProADO2DB)));";

        using (OracleConnection con = new OracleConnection())
        {

            con.ConnectionString = conStr;
            con.Open();
            OracleCommand command = new OracleCommand();
            command.Connection = con;
            command.CommandText = "select * from emp where rownum < 5";
            command.CommandType = System.Data.CommandType.Text;
            OracleCacheDependency cacheDep = new OracleCacheDependency(command);

            OracleDataAdapter dataAdapter = new OracleDataAdapter(command);

            DataSet ds = new DataSet();
            dataAdapter.Fill(ds);
            con.Close();

            HttpContext.Current.Cache.Insert("Employees", ds, cacheDep);


        return ds;


    }
  }
}
```

The preceding method simply checks whether the data is in the ASP.NET cache; if not, it will perform the query and register to receive the change notification. After the query is performened, it will place a copy of the DataSet into the ASP.NET cache and return the data to the caller.

In our example, the caller is an ASP.NET Web form that has a `GridView` and gets its data from an `ObjectDataSource`. The following shows how the `EmployeeManager` class along with the `OracleCacheDependency` class can be used with a page:

```
<asp:GridView ID="GridView1" runat="server" DataSourceID="ObjectDataSource1" />
<asp:ObjectDataSource ID="ObjectDataSource1" runat="server"
SelectMethod="GetEmployees" TypeName="EmployeeManager" />
```

No other markup or code is required on the Web form to use the example classes. A complete discussion of the `ObjectDataSource` and other associated data-binding classes can be found in Chapter 7.

When the Web form is accessed, the following list of employee data is provided in the grid (see Figure 17-10).

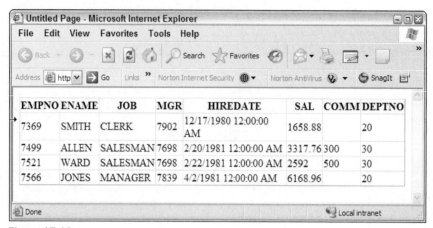

Figure 17-10

Since this was the first time the query was run, it would have registered the change notification request with Oracle. You can check to see whether your notification registration is active by using the following query:

```
select * from user_change_notification_regs;
```

Using this query, you can confirm that the registration did happen. The `CallBack` column returned by this query can be helpful in determining the host that the server will attempt to notify when change occurs. The column will contain the host and the port on which notification will occur.

To trigger the notification, issue the following command to update the salaries on each employee row:

```
update emp set sal = sal * 1.2;
commit;
```

The preceding SQL statement will increase the salary of each employee by 20 percent and then commit the change. Upon commitment of the change, the notification event will occur, and your notification handler will be called. Figure 17-11 shows the output after the page is refreshed and the change notification has been received.

As demonstrated, change notification provides a powerful way to create dependencies on data in the Oracle database. While the example focused on how to integrate the notification with the ASP.NET cache, the same capabilities can be accomplished by a Windows Form application or a Windows Service. The important thing to remember about using change notification is to make sure to use it only on tables that are not subject to a high volume of data changes.

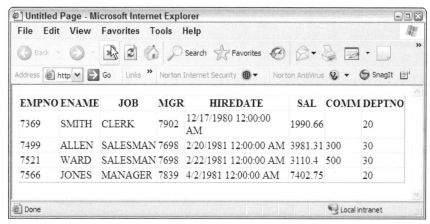

Figure 17-11

Using the BFile Type

As we discussed earlier, the BFile data type provides for storage external to the database in the file system of up to 4 GB of data. This data type is best used where you are consistently storing large amounts of unstructured data and you want to keep that data separate from your database. Because the BFile type provides the capability to retrieve partial amounts of the associated data, it can be advantageous to only retrieve the portion of the referenced item that you need for continued processing, not all of the referenced data.

A nice feature of the BFile data type is that it supports the concept of reference copying. Use this when you want to perform a copy and have only the reference to the data copied and not the file data itself. This can save a tremendous amount of time if you are doing the operation frequently. A unique feature is that the referenced file does not have to exist at the time the reference is created, only when you attempt to use the reference. This could enable you to create a placeholder that is later filled in by your application.

The System.Data.OracleClient data provider that Microsoft ships with ADO.NET 2.x provides support for the BFile using the OracleBFile class.

Oracle Services for Microsoft Transaction Server

Oracle Services for MTS provides for the integration of Oracle databases as resource managers when performing transactions that are coordinated by MTS. Oracle Services interacts with the Microsoft Distributed Transaction Coordinator (MSDTC) to enable all COM components to participate in a global transaction.

Using this capability would enable you to conduct a transaction that spanned multiple database instances, including a mixed environment. For example, you could coordinate work across a Microsoft SQL Server or an Oracle database running on a different operating system, and even include MSMQ activities as part of a single transaction coordinated by MSDTC.

In version 9i of Oracle, improvements were made in the architecture to extend scalability by placing an instance of the Oracle Services within each MTS process. In release 9iR2 that followed, support was also added to enable transactional .NET applications to use Oracle as a resource manager.

Oracle Database Extensions for .NET

Starting with Oracle 10g Release 2, developers will be able to write stored procedures and functions in managed code that will execute within the Oracle database engine. This support is similar to the support that Microsoft SQL Server provides for hosting the CLR Framework. This capability is available on Oracle databases running on the Windows platform, but is not available on other platforms at this time.

From a coding point of view, a stored procedure or function can be written in any CLR-supported language, such as C# or VB.NET. Database access must be accomplished using a server-side version of the Oracle Data Provider (ODP.NET). The main difference is that you already have a database session and you cannot start a local or distributed transaction. The `Oracle.DataAccess.Server` namespace provides access to the ODP.NET provider.

Oracle runs the CLR and associated stored procedures and functions inside a process external to the database main process (`extproc.exe`). You must have the .NET Framework installed on your database server; however, it may be version 1.0 or later. You can debug your stored procedure or function by attaching to this process from within Visual Studio .NET and setting breakpoints in your class.

Deployment support is performed via the Oracle Deployment Wizard, which is integrated with the Oracle Developer Tools for Visual Studio .NET. During the deploy process, the Deployment Wizard will take a copy of your assembly and place it in ORACLE_BASE\ORACLE_HOME\bin\CLR.

Installation of the Database Extensions

You must install the Oracle Database Extensions to use this feature. If you have already created a database and later want to enable this feature, you must first install the Database Extensions and then run the Database Configuration Assistant to enable support.

Your development machine should have the Oracle Developer Tools for Visual Studio .NET installed, so you will be able to deploy the .NET code to the database.

Building a .NET Stored Procedure

In order to be deployed, the stored procedure must be implemented as a static (shared in VB.NET) method and not be a constructor or destructor. The parameter types that you use must be compatible with the Oracle native database types. When deployment happens, they must be mapped by the Deployment Wizard.

The following steps will walk you through the process of creating a .NET stored procedure that will work with the Oracle database.

Step 1 — Set Up a Project to Hold the Class

There is no special type of project for Oracle .NET extensions as there is for Microsoft SQL Server managed-code stored procedures. Class library projects make the best type of project to hold the stored procedure you are going to create. Using other types of projects, such as an executable or Windows application project, is not recommended. Because these are special classes and you may want to have special deployment processes for them, keeping them in their own library, separate from other class libraries that might hold your common business logic, is a good recommendation.

Step 2 — Add a Class and Define Your Method

The following example is a class that we have added to our new class library project. In this example, we will query the emp table, determine the number of rows in it, and return the count:

```
Imports Oracle.DataAccess.Client

Public Class EmployeeProcs

    Public Shared Function GetEmployeeCount() As Int32

        Dim con As OracleConnection

        con = New OracleConnection("context connection=true")

        con.Open()

        Dim cmd As OracleCommand
        cmd = con.CreateCommand()
        cmd.CommandText = "select count(*) from emp"

        Dim empCount As Int32

        empCount = cmd.ExecuteScalar()

        cmd.Dispose()

        con.Close()

        Return empCount

    End Function
```

Step 3 — Deploy the New Stored Procedure

Now that you have built a class that implements a stored procedure, the next step is to deploy the assembly so that it can be seen by the database. To accomplish this, you use the Oracle Data Tools and click the .NET Assembly ⇨ Deploy .NET Assembly menu item. This will start the deployment wizard to help walk you through the process. Figure 17-12 shows the first step in the deploy process.

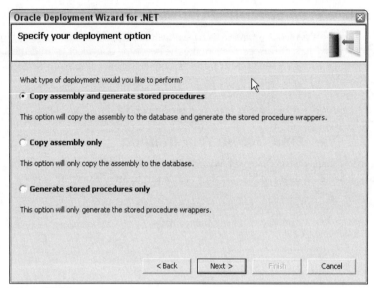

Figure 17-12

You select the Copy Assembly and Generate Stored Procedures option. The wizard will copy your assembly from its current location to ORACLE_HOME\bin\clr. On future pages, you will be able to select whether you want to create a subdirectory inside the clr folder for your specific assembly. This is a good idea if you have multiple applications using the same server and you want to keep some separation between the applications.

Once you have selected to copy the assembly and generate stored procedures, the wizard will move along to collect information on which of the methods in the selected assembly you wish to deploy. This is also where you identify the parameter mapping and the associated security. Figure 17-13 shows how to perform method selection.

Mapping parameter data types on stored procedures is an important part of deploying a managed-code stored procedure. Figure 17-14 shows the wizard screen that helps you through mapping. Consult the ODP.NET reference manual for further details on recommended mappings.

Once you have completed these steps, you will be presented with a summary of your options. You will also have the option to save the script to a file for later use. If you were to take a look at the proposed script, it would look similar to the following:

```
CREATE OR REPLACE LIBRARY SIMPLESPROC_DLL AS
'$ORACLE_HOME\bin\clr\SimpleSProc.dll';
GRANT EXECUTE ON SIMPLESPROC_DLL TO SCOTT;
GRANT EXECUTE ON DBMS_CLR TO SCOTT;
GRANT EXECUTE ON DBMS_CLRTYPE TO SCOTT;
GRANT EXECUTE ON DBMS_CLRPARAMTABLE TO SCOTT;
CREATE OR REPLACE FUNCTION SCOTT.GETEMPLOYEECOUNT RETURN BINARY_INTEGER;
```

This script will run after the assembly is already copied to the bin\clr directory. The first line of the script defines the library to the Oracle database. Next, the grants will provide access to the owner to use the stored procedure. Finally, the actual function that you want to use is defined.

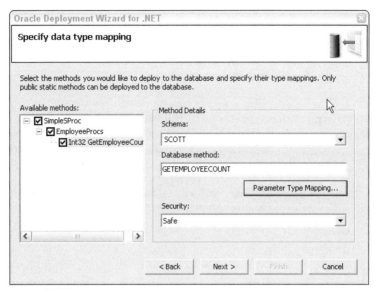

Figure 17-13

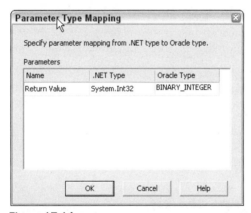

Figure 17-14

Summary

Covering all of the features and capabilities of ADO.NET and the Oracle database would be impossible without dedicating a complete book (or books) to the topic. In this chapter, we tried to provide you with a foundation for using ADO.NET with the Oracle database.

You learned that your choice of providers and the specific feature set in Oracle that you will use is critical. Additionally, your commitment to follow an architectural design that will isolate your database calls to a layer within your application will also provide you with ongoing flexibility to make decisions as your application evolves.

The new Oracle Tools for Visual Studio .NET represent tangible evidence of Oracle's commitment to provide first-class tools for working with their database from within Visual Studio .NET. Using these tools, you will be more productive and have quick access to schema information as you develop your application.

The Oracle database continues to evolve and add new and progressive features, such as Change Notification and Extensions for .NET that represent significant advances for the database engine. Keep in mind that these are not the only new features Oracle has added, and you are encouraged to learn about and explore the other features not highlighted in this chapter.

Using any database is associated with learning the specifics of that vendor's product. If every database provided the same support, there would be no competition between database vendors. ADO.NET, while not perfect, provides significant abstraction on top of vendor specifics, yet provides you with the flexibility to access the low-level vendor-specific capabilities needed by your application. As you read about how ADO.NET works, absorbing the specifics of the different databases we cover in the book, take a few minutes to reflect on the similarities.

In addition to the content covered in this chapter, Oracle provides a wealth of information in their production documentation. Another great place to get questions answered is on the Oracle Web site, `www.oracle.com`, where key members of the Oracle team, in addition to the community, provide responses to questions posted to their forums.

For More Information

To complement the information in this chapter, take a look at the following resources:

- **Oracle .NET Developer Center**—`www.oracle.com/technology/tech/dotnet/`
- **Download Oracle Developer Tools for Visual Studio .NET**—`www.oracle.com/technology/tech/dotnet/tools/`

Constants/Enums in ADO.NET

This appendix provides the set of constants/enums that are included with ADO.NET with Version 2.0 of the .NET Framework and with SQL Server 2005.

Parent Name	Enum	Description
Microsoft.SqlServer.Server.TriggerAction Enum.		
TriggerAction	Invalid	The Invalid TriggerAction event.
TriggerAction	Insert	The Insert TriggerAction occurs when a row is inserted into a table. This is a DML trigger.
TriggerAction	Update	The Update TriggerAction occurs when a row is updated in a table. This is a DML trigger.
TriggerAction	Delete	The Delete TriggerAction occurs when a row is deleted from a table. This is a DML trigger.
TriggerAction	CreateTable	The CreateTable TriggerAction occurs when a table is created. This is a DDL trigger.
TriggerAction	AlterTable	The Alter TriggerAction occurs when a table is altered. This is a DDL trigger.

Table continued on following page

Parent Name	Enum	Description
`TriggerAction`	`DropTable`	The `DropTable` `TriggerAction` occurs when a table is dropped. This is a DDL trigger.
`TriggerAction`	`CreateIndex`	The `CreateIndex` `TriggerAction` occurs when an index has been created. This is a DDL trigger.
`TriggerAction`	`AlterIndex`	The `AlterIndex` `TriggerAction` occurs when an index has been altered. This is a DDL trigger.
`TriggerAction`	`DropIndex`	The `DropIndex` `TriggerAction` occurs when an index has been dropped. This is a DDL trigger.
`TriggerAction`	`CreateSecurity Expression`	This is a DDL trigger.
`TriggerAction`	`DropSecurity Expression`	This is a DDL trigger.
`TriggerAction`	`CreateSynonym`	The `CreateSynonym` `TriggerAction` occurs when a synonym has been created. This is a DDL trigger.
`TriggerAction`	`DropSynonym`	The `DropSynonym` `TriggerAction` occurs when a synonym has been dropped. This is a DDL trigger.
`TriggerAction`	`CreateView`	The `CreateView` `TriggerAction` occurs when a view has been created. This is a DDL trigger.
`TriggerAction`	`AlterView`	The `AlterView` `TriggerAction` occurs when a view has been altered. This is a DDL trigger.
`TriggerAction`	`DropView`	The `DropView` `TriggerAction` occurs when a synonym has been created. This is a DDL trigger.
`TriggerAction`	`CreateProcedure`	The `CreateProcedure` `TriggerAction` occurs when a procedure has been created. This is a DDL trigger.
`TriggerAction`	`AlterProcedure`	The `AlterProcedure` `TriggerAction` occurs when a procedure has been altered. This is a DDL trigger.
`TriggerAction`	`DropProcedure`	The `DropProcedure` `TriggerAction` occurs when a procedure has been dropped. This is a DDL trigger.

Parent Name	Enum	Description
TriggerAction	CreateFunction	The CreateFunction TriggerAction occurs when a function has been created. This is a DDL trigger.
TriggerAction	AlterFunction	The AlterFunction TriggerAction occurs when a function has been altered. This is a DDL trigger.
TriggerAction	DropFunction	The DropProcedure TriggerAction occurs when a function has been dropped. This is a DDL trigger.
TriggerAction	CreateTrigger	The CreateTrigger TriggerAction occurs when a trigger has been created. This is a DDL trigger.
TriggerAction	AlterTrigger	The AlterProcedure TriggerAction occurs when a trigger has been altered. This is a DDL trigger.
TriggerAction	DropTrigger	The DropTrigger TriggerAction occurs when a trigger has been dropped. This is a DDL trigger.
TriggerAction	CreateEvent Notification	The CreateEventNotification TriggerAction occurs when an event has been created. This is a DDL trigger.
TriggerAction	DropEvent Notification	The DropEventNotification TriggerAction occurs when an event has been dropped. This is a DDL trigger.
TriggerAction	CreateType	The CreateType TriggerAction occurs when a type has been created. This is a DDL trigger.
TriggerAction	DropType	The DropType TriggerAction occurs when a type has been dropped. This is a DDL trigger.
TriggerAction	CreateAssembly	The CreateAssembly TriggerAction occurs when an assembly has been created. This is a DDL trigger.
TriggerAction	AlterAssembly	The AlterAssembly TriggerAction occurs when a procedure has been altered. This is a DDL trigger.
TriggerAction	DropAssembly	The DropAssembly TriggerAction occurs when an assembly has been dropped. This is a DDL trigger.

Table continued on following page

Parent Name	Enum	Description
TriggerAction	CreateUser	The CreateUser TriggerAction occurs when a user has been created. This is a DDL trigger.
TriggerAction	AlterUser	The AlterUser TriggerAction occurs when a user has been altered. This is a DDL trigger.
TriggerAction	DropUser	The DropUser TriggerAction occurs when a user has been dropped. This is a DDL trigger.
TriggerAction	CreateRole	The CreateRole TriggerAction occurs when a role has been created. This is a DDL trigger.
TriggerAction	AlterRole	The AlterRole TriggerAction occurs when a role has been altered. This is a DDL trigger.
TriggerAction	DropRole	The DropRole TriggerAction occurs when a role has been dropped. This is a DDL trigger.
TriggerAction	CreateAppRole	The CreateAppRole TriggerAction occurs when an AppRole has been created. This is a DDL trigger.
TriggerAction	AlterAppRole	The AlterAppRole TriggerAction occurs when an AppRole has been altered. This is a DDL trigger.
TriggerAction	DropAppRole	The DropAppRole TriggerAction occurs when an AppRole has been dropped. This is a DDL trigger.
TriggerAction	CreateSchema	The CreateSchema TriggerAction occurs when a schema has been created. This is a DDL trigger.
TriggerAction	AlterSchema	The AlterProcedure TriggerAction occurs when a procedure has been altered. This is a DDL trigger.
TriggerAction	DropSchema	The DropSchema TriggerAction occurs when a schema has been dropped. This is a DDL trigger.
TriggerAction	CreateLogin	The CreateLogin TriggerAction occurs when a login has been created. This is a DDL trigger.

Parent Name	Enum	Description
TriggerAction	AlterLogin	The AlterLogin TriggerAction occurs when a login has been altered. This is a DDL trigger.
TriggerAction	DropLogin	The DropLogin TriggerAction occurs when a login has been dropped. This is a DDL trigger.
TriggerAction	CreateMsgType	The CreateMsgType TriggerAction occurs when a MsgType has been created. This is a DDL trigger.
TriggerAction	DropMsgType	The DropMsgType TriggerAction occurs when a MsgType has been dropped. This is a DDL trigger.
TriggerAction	CreateContract	The CreateContract TriggerAction occurs when a contract has been created. This is a DDL trigger.
TriggerAction	DropContract	The DropContract TriggerAction occurs when a contract has been dropped. This is a DDL trigger.
TriggerAction	CreateQueue	The CreateQueue TriggerAction occurs when a queue has been created. This is a DDL trigger.
TriggerAction	AlterQueue	The AlterQueue TriggerAction occurs when a queue has been altered. This is a DDL trigger.
TriggerAction	DropQueue	The DropQueue TriggerAction occurs when a queue has been dropped. This is a DDL trigger.
TriggerAction	CreateService	The CreateService TriggerAction occurs when a service has been created. This is a DDL trigger.
TriggerAction	AlterService	The AlterService TriggerAction occurs when a service has been altered. This is a DDL trigger.
TriggerAction	DropService	The DropService TriggerAction occurs when a service has been dropped. This is a DDL trigger.
TriggerAction	CreateRoute	The CreateRoute TriggerAction occurs when a route has been created. This is a DDL trigger.

Table continued on following page

Parent Name	Enum	Description
TriggerAction	AlterRoute	The AlterRoute TriggerAction occurs when a route has been altered. This is a DDL trigger.
TriggerAction	DropRoute	The DropRoute TriggerAction occurs when a route has been dropped. This is a DDL trigger.
TriggerAction	GrantStatement	The GrantStatement TriggerAction occurs when access to a statement is granted. This is a DDL trigger.
TriggerAction	DenyStatement	The DenyStatement TriggerAction occurs when access to a statement is denied. This is a DDL trigger.
TriggerAction	RevokeStatement	The RevokeStatement TriggerAction occurs when access to a statement is revoked. This is a DDL trigger.
TriggerAction	GrantObject	The GrantObject TriggerAction occurs when access to an object is granted. This is a DDL trigger.
TriggerAction	DenyObject	The DenyObject TriggerAction occurs when access to a statement is denied. This is a DDL trigger.
TriggerAction	RevokeObject	The RevokeObject TriggerAction occurs when access to an Object is revoked. This is a DDL trigger.
TriggerAction	CreateBinding	The CreateBinding TriggerAction occurs when the Create Binding. This is a DDL trigger.
TriggerAction	AlterBinding	The AlterBinding TriggerAction occurs when the Alter Binding statement was executed. This is a DDL trigger.
TriggerAction	DropBinding	The DropBinding TriggerAction occurs when Drop Binding statement is executed. This is a DDL trigger.
TriggerAction	CreatePartition Function	The CreatePartitionFunction TriggerAction occurs when the Create Partition Function is executed. This is a DDL trigger.
TriggerAction	AlterPartition Function	The AlterPartitionFunction TriggerAction occurs when an Alter Partition Function is executed. This is a DDL trigger.

Parent Name	Enum	Description
TriggerAction	DropPartition Function	The DropPartitionFunction TriggerAction occurs when a Drop Parition Function is executed. This is a DDL trigger.
TriggerAction	CreatePartition Scheme	The CreateParitionScheme TriggerAction occurs when the Create Parition Scheme statement is executed. This is a DDL trigger.
TriggerAction	AlterPartition Scheme	The AlterParitionScheme TriggerAction occurs when the Alter Partition Scheme statement is revoked. This is a DDL trigger.
TriggerAction	DropPartition Scheme	The DropPartitionScheme TriggerAction occurs when the Drop Partition Scheme. This is a DDL trigger.
System.Data.AcceptRejectRule Enum		
AcceptRejectRule	None	No action occurs (default).
AcceptRejectRule	Cascade	Changes are cascaded across the relationship.
System.Data.Common.CatalogLocation Enum		
CatalogLocation	Start	The Start value indicates the positon of the catalogn name occurs before the schema portion of a full qualified table name in a text command
CatalogLocation	End	The End value indicates the positon of the catalog name occurs after the schema portion of a full qualified table name in a text command
System.Data.CommandBehavior Enum		
CommandBehavior	Default	The query may return multiple result sets. Execution of the query may affect the database state. Calling ExecuteReader (CommandBehavior.Default) is functionally equivalent to calling ExecuteReader().
CommandBehavior	SingleResult	The query returns a single result set.
CommandBehavior	SchemaOnly	The query returns column information only and does not affect the database state.
CommandBehavior	KeyInfo	The query returns column and primary key information. The query is executed without any locking on the selected rows.

Table continued on following page

Parent Name	Enum	Description
CommandBehavior	SingleRow	The query is expected to return a single row. Execution of the query may affect the database state. Some .NET Framework data providers may, but are not required to, use this information to optimize the performance of the command. If your SQL statement is expected to return only a single row, specifying SingleRow can also improve application performance. It is possible to specify SingleRow when executing queries that return multiple result sets. In that case, multiple result sets are still returned, but each result set has a single row.
CommandBehavior	SequentialAccess	Provides a way for the DataReader to handle rows that contain columns with large binary values. Rather than load the entire row, SequentialAccess enables the DataReader to load data as a stream. You can then use the GetBytes or GetChars method to specify a byte location to start the read operation, and a limited buffer size for the data being returned.
CommandBehavior	CloseConnection	When the command is executed, the associated Connection object is closed when the associated DataReader object is closed.
System.Data.CommandType Enum		
CommandType	Text	An SQL text command. (Default)
CommandType	StoredProcedure	The name of a stored procedure.
CommandType	TableDirect	The name of a table.
System.Data.ConflictOption Enum		
ConflictOption	CompareAll SearchableValues	Update and delete statements will include all searchable columns from the table in the WHERE clause. This is equivalent to specifying CompareAllValuesUpdate | CompareAllValuesDelete.
ConflictOption	Compare RowVersion	If any Timestamp columns exist in the table, they are used in the WHERE clause for all generated update statements. This is equivalent to specifying CompareRowVersionUpdate | CompareRowVersionDelete.

Parent Name	Enum	Description
ConflictOption	OverwriteChanges	All update and delete statements include only `PrimaryKey` columns in the `WHERE` clause. If no `PrimaryKey` is defined, all searchable columns are included in the `WHERE` clause. This is equivalent to `OverwriteChangesUpdate | OverwriteChangesDelete`.
System.Data.ConnectionState Enum		
ConnectionState	Closed	The connection is closed.
ConnectionState	Open	The connection is open.
ConnectionState	Connecting	The `Connection` object is connecting to the data source. (This value is reserved for future versions of the product.)
ConnectionState	Executing	The `Connection` object is executing a command. (This value is reserved for future versions of the product.)
ConnectionState	Fetching	The `Connection` object is retrieving data. (This value is reserved for future versions of the product.)
ConnectionState	Broken	The connection to the data source is broken. This can occur only after the connection has been opened. A connection in this state may be closed and then reopened. (This value is reserved for future versions of the product.)
System.Data.DataRowAction Enum		
DataRowAction	Nothing	The row has not changed.
DataRowAction	Delete	The row was deleted from the table.
DataRowAction	Change	The row has changed.
DataRowAction	Rollback	The most recent change to the row has been rolled back.
DataRowAction	Commit	The changes to the row have been committed.
DataRowAction	Add	The row has been added to the table.
DataRowAction	ChangeOriginal	The original version of the row has been changed.
DataRowAction	ChangeCurrent AndOriginal	The original and the current versions of the row have been changed.

Table continued on following page

Parent Name	Enum	Description
`System.Data.DataRowState Enum`		
DataRowState	Detached	The row has been created but is not part of any datatable. A datarow is in this state immediately after it has been created and before it is added to a collection, or if it has been removed from a collection.
DataRowState	Unchanged	The row has not changed since `update` was last called.
DataRowState	Added	The row has been added to a datatable, and `update` has not been called.
DataRowState	Deleted	The row was deleted using the `delete` method of the datarow.
DataRowState	Modified	The row has been modified and `update` has not been called.
`System.Data.DataRowVersion Enum`		
DataRowVersion	Original	The row contains its original values.
DataRowVersion	Current	The row contains current values.
DataRowVersion	Proposed	The row contains a proposed value.
DataRowVersion	Default	The default version of datarow. For a `DataRowState` value of `Added`, `Modified`, or `Current`, the default version is `Current`.
`System.Data.SerializationFormat Enum`		
SerializationFormat	Xml	Serialize as XML content. This is the default.
SerializationFormat	Binary	Serialize as binary content. This format was added with .NET 2.0.
`System.Data.DataSetDateTime Enum`		
DataSetDateTime	Local	`DateTime` is always stored in Local. If Utc or Unspecified is assigned to a column in this mode, it is first converted into Local. Serialization in this mode is always performed in Local. There is an offset during serialization.
DataSetDateTime	Unspecified	`DateTime` is always stored in Unspecified. If Local or Utc is assigned to a column in this mode, it is first converted into Unspecified. Serialization in this mode does not cause an offset.

Parent Name	Enum	Description
DataSetDateTime	UnspecifiedLocal	`DateTime` is stored in Unspecified. If Local or Utc is assigned to a column in this mode, it is first converted into Unspecified. Serialization in this mode causes offset. This is the default behavior and is backward compatible. This option should be thought of as being Unspecified in storage but applying an offset that is similar to Local during serialization.
DataSetDateTime	Utc	`DateTime` is stored in Universal Coordinated Time (UTC). If Local or Unspecified is assigned to a column in this mode, it is first converted into Utc format. Serialization in this mode is always performed in Utc. There is no offset during serialization.

System.Data.DataViewRowState Enum

Parent Name	Enum	Description
DataViewRowState	None	None.
DataViewRowState	Unchanged	An unchanged row.
DataViewRowState	Added	A new row.
DataViewRowState	Deleted	A deleted row.
DataViewRowState	ModifiedCurrent	A current version, which is a modified version of original data (see `ModifiedOriginal`).
DataViewRowState	CurrentRows	Current rows including unchanged, new, and modified rows.
DataViewRowState	ModifiedOriginal	The original version (although it has since been modified and is available as `ModifiedCurrent`).
DataViewRowState	OriginalRows	Original rows, including unchanged and deleted rows.

System.Data.DbType Enum

Parent Name	Enum	Description
DbType	AnsiString	A variable-length stream of non-Unicode characters ranging between 1 and 8,000 characters.
DbType	Binary	A variable-length stream of binary data ranging between 1 and 8,000 bytes.
DbType	Byte	An 8-bit, unsigned integer ranging in value from 0 to 255.
DbType	Boolean	A simple type representing Boolean values of true or false.

Table continued on following page

Parent Name	Enum	Description
DbType	Currency	A currency value ranging from -2^{63} (or $-922,337,203,685,477.5808$) to 2^{63-1} (or $+922,337,203,685,477.5807$) with an accuracy to a ten-thousandth of a currency unit.
DbType	Date	Date and time data ranging in value from January 1, 1753, to December 31, 9999, to an accuracy of 3.33 milliseconds.
DbType	DateTime	A type representing a date and time value.
DbType	Decimal	A simple type representing values ranging from 1.0×10^{-28} to approximately 7.9×10^{28} with 28–29 significant digits.
DbType	Double	A floating point type representing values ranging from approximately 5.0×10^{-324} to 1.7×10^{308} with a precision of 15–16 digits.
DbType	Guid	A globally unique identifier (or GUID). A GUID has 2^{128} unique values.
DbType	Int16	An integral type representing signed 16-bit integers with values between -32768 and 32767.
DbType	Int32	An integral type representing signed 32-bit integers with values between -2147483648 and 2147483647.
DbType	Int64	An integral type representing signed 64-bit integers with values between -9223372036854775808 and 9223372036854775807.
DbType	Object	A general type representing any reference or value type not explicitly represented by another DbType value.
DbType	SByte	An integral type representing signed 8-bit integers with values between -128 and 127.
DbType	Single	A floating-point type representing values ranging from approximately 1.5×10^{-45} to 3.4×10^{38} with a precision of 7 digits.
DbType	String	A type representing Unicode character strings.
DbType	Time	Date and time data ranging in value from January 1, 1753, to December 31, 9999, to an accuracy of 3.33 milliseconds.

Parent Name	Enum	Description
DbType	UInt16	An integral type representing unsigned 16-bit integers with values between 0 and 65535.
DbType	UInt32	An integral type representing unsigned 32-bit integers with values between 0 and 4294967295.
DbType	UInt64	An integral type representing unsigned 64-bit integers with values between 0 and 18446744073709551615.
DbType	VarNumeric	A variable-length numeric value.
DbType	AnsiString FixedLength	A fixed-length stream of non-Unicode characters.
DbType	StringFixed Length	A fixed-length string.
DbType	Xml	A parsed representation of an XML document or fragment.

System.Data.IsolationLevel Enum

Parent Name	Enum	Description
IsolationLevel	Chaos	The pending changes from more highly isolated transactions cannot be overwritten.
IsolationLevel	ReadUncommitted	A dirty read is possible, meaning that no shared locks are issued and no exclusive locks are honored.
IsolationLevel	ReadCommitted	Shared locks are held while the data is being read to avoid dirty reads, but the data can be changed before the end of the transaction, resulting in nonrepeatable reads or phantom data.
IsolationLevel	RepeatableRead	Locks are placed on all data used in a query, preventing other users from updating the data. Prevents nonrepeatable reads but phantom rows are still possible.
IsolationLevel	Serializable	A range lock is placed on the rows, preventing other users from updating or inserting rows into the dataset until the transaction is complete.
IsolationLevel	Snapshot	Reduces blocking by storing a version of data that one application can read while another is modifying the same data. Indicates that from one transaction, you cannot see changes made in other transactions, even if you requery.

Table continued on following page

Parent Name	Enum	Description
IsolationLevel	Unspecified	An isolation level other than the one specified is being used, but the level cannot be determined.

System.Data.LoadOption Enum

Parent Name	Enum	Description
LoadOption	OverwriteChanges	The incoming values for this row will be written to both the current value and the original value versions of the data for each column.
LoadOption	PreserveChanges	The incoming values for this row will be written to the original value version of each column. The current version of the data in each column will not be changed.
LoadOption	Upsert	The incoming values for this row will be written to the current version of each column. The original version of each column's data will not be changed.

System.Data.MappingType Enum

Parent Name	Enum	Description
MappingType	Element	The column is mapped to an XML element.
MappingType	Attribute	The column is mapped to an XML attribute.
MappingType	SimpleContent	The column is mapped to a System.Xml.XmlText node.
MappingType	Hidden	The column is mapped to an internal structure.

System.Data.MissingMappingAction

Parent Name	Enum	Description
Missing MappingAction	Passthrough	The source column or source table is created and added to the DataSet using its original name.
Missing MappingAction	Ignore	The column or table not having a mapping is ignored. Returns null.
Missing MappingAction	Error	An error is generated if the specified column mapping is missing.
Missing SchemaAction	Add	Adds the necessary columns to complete the schema.
Missing SchemaAction	Ignore	Ignores the extra columns.
Missing SchemaAction	Error	An error is generated if the specified column mapping is missing.

Parent Name	Enum	Description
Missing SchemaAction	AddWithKey	Adds the necessary columns and primary key information to complete the schema. To function properly with the .NET Framework Data Provider for OLE DB, AddWithKey requires that the native OLE DB provider obtains necessary primary key information by setting the DBPROP_UNIQUEROWS property, and then determines which columns are primary key columns by examining DBCOLUMN_KEYCOLUMN in the IColumnsRowset. As an alternative, the user may explicitly set the primary key constraints on each column. This ensures that incoming records that match existing records are updated instead of appended. When using AddWithKey, the .NET Framework Data Provider for SQL Server appends a FOR BROWSE clause to the statement being executed. Users should be aware of potential side effects, such as interference with the use of SET FMTONLY ON statements. See SQL Server Books Online for more information.
System.Data.ParameterDirection Enum		
ParameterDirection	Input	The parameter is an input parameter.
ParameterDirection	Output	The parameter is an output parameter.
ParameterDirection	InputOutput	The parameter is capable of both input and output.
ParameterDirection	ReturnValue	The parameter represents a return value from an operation such as a stored procedure, built-in function, or user-defined function.
System.Data.Rule Enum		
Rule	None	No action is taken on related rows.
Rule	Cascade	Delete or update related rows. This is the default.
Rule	SetNull	Set values in rows related to DBNull.
Rule	SetDefault	Set values in related rows to the value contained in the DefaultValue property.
System.Data.SchemaType Enum		
SchemaType	Source	Ignore any table mappings on the DataAdapter. Configure the schema using the incoming schema without applying any transformations.

Table continued on following page

Parent Name	Enum	Description
SchemaType	Mapped	Apply any existing table mappings to the incoming schema. Configure the System.Data.DataSet with the transformed schema.
System.Data.SchemaSerializationMode Enum		
SchemaSerializationMode	IncludeSchema	Includes schema serialization for a typed DataSet. The default.
SchemaSerializationMode	ExcludeSchema	Skips schema serialization for a typed DataSet.
System.Data.SqlDbType Enum		
SqlDbType	BigInt	A 64-bit signed integer.
SqlDbType	Binary	A fixed-length stream of binary data ranging between 1 and 8,000 bytes.
SqlDbType	Bit	An unsigned numeric value that can be 0, 1, or null.
SqlDbType	Char	A fixed-length stream of non-Unicode characters ranging between 1 and 8,000 characters.
SqlDbType	DateTime	Date and time data ranging in value from January 1, 1753 to December 31, 9999 to an accuracy of 3.33 milliseconds.
SqlDbType	Decimal	A fixed precision and scale numeric value between -10^{38-1} and 10^{38-1}.
SqlDbType	Float	A floating-point number within the range of $-1.79E+308$ through $1.79E+308$.
SqlDbType	Image	A variable-length stream of binary data ranging from 0 to 2^{31-1} (or 2,147,483,647) bytes.
SqlDbType	Int	A 32-bit signed integer.
SqlDbType	Money	A currency value ranging from -2^{63} (or $-922,337,203,685,477.5808$) to 2^{63-1} (or $+922,337,203,685,477.5807$) with an accuracy to a ten-thousandth of a currency unit.
SqlDbType	NChar	A fixed-length stream of Unicode characters ranging between 1 and 4,000 characters.
SqlDbType	NText	A variable-length stream of Unicode data with a maximum length of 2^{30-1} (or 1,073,741,823) characters.

Parent Name	Enum	Description
SqlDbType	NVarChar	A variable-length stream of Unicode characters ranging between 1 and 4,000 characters. Implicit conversion fails if the string is greater than 4,000 characters. Explicitly set the object when working with strings longer than 4,000 characters.
SqlDbType	Real	A floating-point number within the range of –3.40E +38 through 3.40E +38.
SqlDbType	UniqueIdentifier	A globally unique identifier (or GUID).
SqlDbType	SmallDateTime	Date and time data ranging in value from January 1, 1900, to June 6, 2079, to an accuracy of 1 minute.
SqlDbType	SmallInt	A 16-bit signed integer.
SqlDbType	SmallMoney	A currency value ranging from –214,748.3648 to +214,748.3647 with an accuracy to a ten-thousandth of a currency unit.
SqlDbType	Text	A variable-length stream of non-Unicode data with a maximum length of 2^{31-1} (or 2,147,483,647) characters.
SqlDbType	Timestamp	Automatically generated binary numbers, which are guaranteed to be unique within a database. Timestamp is used typically as a mechanism for version-stamping table rows. The storage size is 8 bytes.
SqlDbType	TinyInt	An 8-bit unsigned integer.
SqlDbType	VarBinary	A variable-length stream of binary data ranging between 1 and 8,000 bytes. Implicit conversion fails if the byte array is greater than 8,000 bytes. Explicitly set the object when working with byte arrays larger than 8,000 bytes.
SqlDbType	VarChar	A variable-length stream of non-Unicode characters ranging between 1 and 8,000 characters.
SqlDbType	Variant	A special data type that can contain numeric, string, binary, or date data as well as the SQL Server values Empty and Null, which is assumed if no other type is declared.
SqlDbType	Xml	An XML value.

Table continued on following page

Parent Name	Enum	Description
SqlDbType	Udt	A SQL Server 2005 user-defined type (UDT).
System.Data.StatementType Enum		
StatementType	Select	An SQL query that is a SELECT statement.
StatementType	Insert	An SQL query that is an INSERT statement.
StatementType	Update	An SQL query that is an UPDATE statement.
StatementType	Delete	An SQL query that is a DELETE statement.
StatementType	Batch	An SQL query that is a batch of statements.
System.Data.UpdateRowSource Enum		
UpdateRowSource	None	Any returned parameters or rows are ignored.
UpdateRowSource	OutputParameters	Output parameters are mapped to the changed row in the datatable.
UpdateRowSource	FirstReturned Record	The data in the first returned row is mapped to the changed row in the datatable.
UpdateRowSource	Both	Both the output parameters and the first returned row are mapped to the changed row in the datatable.
System.Data.UpdateStatus Enum		
UpdateStatus	Continue	The data update is to continue processing rows.
UpdateStatus	ErrorsOccurred	The event handler reports that the update should be treated as an error.
UpdateStatus	SkipCurrentRow	The current row is not to be updated.
UpdateStatus	SkipAll RemainingRows	The current row and all remaining rows are not to be updated.
System.Data.XmlReadMode Enum		
XmlReadMode	Auto	Default.
XmlReadMode	ReadSchema	Reads any inline schema and loads the data.
XmlReadMode	IgnoreSchema	Ignores any inline schema and reads data into the existing schema. If any data does not match the existing schema, it is discarded. If the data is a DiffGram, IgnoreSchema has the same functionality as DiffGram.

Parent Name	Enum	Description
XmlReadMode	InferSchema	Ignores any inline schema, infers schema from the data, and loads the data. If the table already contains a schema, the current schema is extended by adding new tables or adding columns to existing tables. An exception is thrown if the inferred table already exists but with a different namespace, or if any of the inferred columns conflict with existing columns.
XmlReadMode	DiffGram	Reads a `DiffGram`, applying changes from the `DiffGram` to the table.
XmlReadMode	Fragment	Reads XML fragments, such as those generated by executing `FOR XML` queries, against an instance of SQL Server.
XmlReadMode	InferTypedSchema	Ignores any inline schema, infers a strongly typed schema from the data, and loads the data. If the type cannot be inferred from the data, it is interpreted as string data.
System.Data.XmlWriteMode Enum		
XmlWriteMode	WriteSchema	Writes the current contents of the schema as XML data, with the relational structure as inline XSD schema.
XmlWriteMode	IgnoreSchema	Ignore any inline schema. Rely on the Data's existing schema.
XmlWriteMode	DiffGram	Writes the entire contents as a `DiffGram`, including original and current values.
System.Data.KeyRestrictionBehavior Enum		
KeyRestrictionBehavior	AllowOnly	Default. Identifies the only additional connection string parameters that are allowed. Identifies additional connection string parameters that are not allowed.
KeyRestriction Behavior	PreventUsage	Identifies additional connection string parameters that are not allowed.
System.Data.Common.GroupByBehavior Enum		
GroupByBehavior	Unknown	The support for the GROUP BY clause is unknown.
GroupByBehavior	NotSupported	The GROUP BY clause is not supported.
GroupByBehavior	Unrelated	There is no relationship between the columns in the GROUP BY clause and the nonaggregated columns in the SELECT list. You may group by any column.

Table continued on following page

Parent Name	Enum	Description
GroupByBehavior	MustContainAll	The GROUP BY clause must contain all nonaggregated columns in the select list, and can contain other columns not in the select list.
GroupByBehavior	ExactMatch	The GROUP BY clause must contain all nonaggregated columns in the select list, and must not contain other columns not in the select list.
System.Data.Common.IdentifierCase Enum		
IdentifierCase	Unknown	The data source has ambiguous rules regarding identifier case and cannot discern this information.
IdentifierCase	Insensitive	The data source ignores identifier case when searching the system catalog. The identifiers "ab" and "AB" will match.
IdentifierCase	Sensitive	The data source distinguishes identifier case when searching the system catalog. The identifiers "ab" and "AB" will not match.
System.Data.Common.SupportedJoinOperators Enum		
Supported JoinOperators	None	The data source does not support join queries.
Supported JoinOperators	Inner	The data source supports inner joins.
Supported JoinOperators	LeftOuter	The data source supports left outer joins.
Supported JoinOperators	RightOuter	The data source supports right outer joins.
Supported JoinOperators	FullOuter	The data source supports full outer joins.
System.Data.Odbc.OdbcType Enum		
OdbcType	BigInt	Exact numeric value with precision 19 (if signed) or 20 (if unsigned) and scale 0 (signed: $+-2^63 - 1$, unsigned:0 $2^64 - 1$) (SQL_BIGINT).
OdbcType	Binary	A stream of binary data (SQL_BINARY). This maps to Byte.
OdbcType	Bit	Single-bit binary data (SQL_BIT). This maps to Boolean.

Parent Name	Enum	Description
OdbcType	Char	A fixed-length character string (SQL_CHAR). This maps to String.
OdbcType	DateTime	Date data in the format yyyymmddhhmmss (SQL_TYPE_TIMESTAMP). This maps to DateTime.
OdbcType	Decimal	Signed, exact numeric value with a precision of at least p and scale s, where $1 \le p \le 15$ and $s \le p$. The maximum precision is driver-specific (SQL_DECIMAL).
OdbcType	Numeric	Signed, exact, numeric value with a precision p and scale s, where $1 \le p \le 15$, and $s \le p$ (SQL_NUMERIC).
OdbcType	Double	Signed, approximate, numeric value with a binary precision 53 (zero or absolute value 10[–308] to 10[308]) (SQL_DOUBLE).
OdbcType	Image	Variable-length binary data. Maximum length is data source–dependent (SQL_LONG-VARBINARY).
OdbcType	Int	Exact numeric value with precision 10 and scale 0 (signed: $-2[31] \le n \le 2[31] - 1$, unsigned: $0 \le n \le 2[32] - 1$) (SQL_INTEGER).
OdbcType	NChar	Unicode character string of fixed string length (SQL_WCHAR).
OdbcType	NText	Unicode variable-length character data. Maximum length is data source–dependent. (SQL_WLONGVARCHAR).
OdbcType	NVarChar	A variable-length stream of Unicode characters (SQL_WVARCHAR).
OdbcType	Real	Signed, approximate, numeric value with a binary precision 24 (zero or absolute value 10[–38] to 10[38]) (SQL_REAL).
OdbcType	UniqueIdentifier	A fixed-length, globally unique identifier (GUID) (SQL_GUID).
OdbcType	SmallDateTime	Data and time data in the format yyyymmddhhmmss (SQL_TYPE_TIMESTAMP).
OdbcType	SmallInt	Exact numeric value with precision 5 and scale 0 (signed: $-32{,}768 \le n \le 32{,}767$, unsigned: $0 \le n \le 65{,}535$) (SQL_SMALLINT).

Table continued on following page

Parent Name	Enum	Description
OdbcType	Text	Variable-length character data. Maximum length is data source–dependent (SQL_LONG-VARCHAR).
OdbcType	Timestamp	A stream of binary data (SQL_BINARY).
OdbcType	TinyInt	Exact numeric value with precision 3 and scale 0 (signed: $-128 \leq n \leq 127$, unsigned: $0 \leq n \leq 255$) (SQL_TINYINT).
OdbcType	VarBinary	Variable-length binary. The maximum is set by the user (SQL_VARBINARY).
OdbcType	VarChar	A variable-length stream character string (SQL_CHAR).
OdbcType	Date	Date data in the format yyyymmdd (SQL_TYPE_DATE).
OdbcType	Time	Date data in the format hhmmss (SQL_TYPE_TIMES).
System.Data.OleDb.OleDbLiteral Enum		
OleDbLiteral	Invalid	An invalid value. This maps to DBLITERAL_INVALID.
OleDbLiteral	Binary_Literal	A binary literal in a text command. This maps to DBLITERAL_BINARY_LITERAL.
OleDbLiteral	Catalog_Name	A catalog name in a text command. This maps to DBLITERAL_CATALOG_NAME.
OleDbLiteral	Catalog_Separator	The character that separates the catalog name from the rest of the identifier in a text command. This maps to DBLITERAL_CATA-LOG_SEPARATOR.
OleDbLiteral	Char_Literal	A character literal in a text command. This maps to DBLITERAL_CHAR_LITERAL.
OleDbLiteral	Column_Alias	A column alias in a text command. This maps to DBLITERAL_COLUMN_ALIAS.
OleDbLiteral	Column_Name	A column name used in a text command or in a data-definition interface. This maps to DBLITERAL_COLUMN_NAME.
OleDbLiteral	Correlation_Name	A correlation name (table alias) in a text command. This maps to DBLITERAL_CORRE-LATION_NAME.
OleDbLiteral	Cursor_Name	A cursor name in a text command. This maps to DBLITERAL_CURSOR_NAME.

Parent Name	Enum	Description
OleDbLiteral	Escape_ Percent_Prefix	The character used in a LIKE clause to escape the character returned for the DBLITERAL _LIKE_PERCENT literal. For example, if a percent sign (%) is used to match zero or more characters and the backslash (\) is used, the characters "abc\%%" match all character values that start with "abc%". Some SQL dialects support a clause (the ESCAPE clause) that can be used to override this value. This maps to DBLITERAL_ESCAPE_PERCENT_PREFIX.
OleDbLiteral	Escape_ Underscore _Prefix	The character used in a LIKE clause to escape the character returned for the DBLITERAL_LIKE_UNDERSCORE literal. For example, if an underscore (_) is used to match exactly one character and the backslash (\) is used, the characters "abc_ _" match all character values that are five characters long and start with "abc_". Some SQL dialects support a clause (the ESCAPE clause) that can be used to override this value. This maps to DBLIT- ERAL_ESCAPE_UNDERSCORE_PREFIX.
OleDbLiteral	Index_Name	An index name used in a text command or in a data-definition interface. This maps to DBLITERAL_INDEX_NAME.
OleDbLiteral	Like_Percent	The character used in a LIKE clause to match zero or more characters. For example, if this is a percent sign (%), the characters "abc%" match all character values that start with "abc". This maps to DBLITERAL_LIKE_ PERCENT.
OleDbLiteral	Like_Underscore	The character used in a LIKE clause to match exactly one character. For example, if this is an underscore (_), the characters "abc_" match all character values that are four characters long and start with "abc". This maps to DBLITERAL_LIKE_UNDERSCORE.
OleDbLiteral	Procedure_Name	A procedure name in a text command. This maps to DBLITERAL_PROCEDURE_NAME.
OleDbLiteral	Quote_Prefix	The character used in a text command as the opening quote for quoting identifiers that contain special characters. This maps to DBLITERAL_QUOTE_PREFIX.

Table continued on following page

Parent Name	Enum	Description
OleDbLiteral	Schema_Name	A schema name in a text command. This maps to DBLITERAL_SCHEMA_NAME.
OleDbLiteral	Table_Name	A table name used in a text command or in a data-definition interface. This maps to DBLITERAL_TABLE_NAME.
OleDbLiteral	Text_Command	A text command, such as an SQL statement. This maps to DBLITERAL_TEXT_COMMAND.
OleDbLiteral	User_Name	A user name in a text command. This maps to DBLITERAL_USER_NAME.
OleDbLiteral	View_Name	A view name in a text command. This maps to DBLITERAL_VIEW_NAME.
OleDbLiteral	Cube_Name	The name of a cube in a schema (or the catalog if the provider does not support schemas).
OleDbLiteral	Dimension_Name	The name of the dimension. If a dimension is part of more than one cube, then there is one row for each cube/dimension combination.
OleDbLiteral	Hierarchy_Name	The name of the hierarchy. If the dimension does not contain a hierarchy or has only one hierarchy, then the current column contains a null value.
OleDbLiteral	Level_Name	Name of the cube to which the current level belongs.
OleDbLiteral	Member_Name	The name of the member.
OleDbLiteral	Property_Name	The name of the property.
OleDbLiteral	Schema_Separator	The character that separates the schema name from the rest of the identifier in a text command. This maps to DBLITERAL_SCHEMA_SEPARATOR.
OleDbLiteral	Quote_Suffix	The character used in a text command as the closing quote for quoting identifiers that contain special characters. 1.x providers that use the same character as the prefix and suffix may not return this literal value and can set the lt member of the DBLITERAL structure to DBLITERAL_INVALID if requested. This maps to DBLITERAL_QUOTE_SUFFIX.

Parent Name	Enum	Description
OleDbLiteral	Escape_Percent_Suffix	The escape character, if any, used to suffix thecharacter returned for the `DBLITERAL_LIKE_PERCENT` literal. For example, if a percent sign (%) is used to match zero or more characters and percent signs are escaped by enclosing in open and close square brackets, `DBLITERAL_ESCAPE_PERCENT_PREFIX` is "[", `DBLITERAL_ESCAPE_PERCENT_SUFFIX` is "]", and the characters "abc[%]%" match all character values that start with "abc%". Providers that do not use a suffix character to escape the `DBLITERAL_ESCAPE_PERCENT` character do not return this literal value and can set the `lt` member of the `DBLITERAL` structure to `DBLITERAL_INVALID` if requested. This maps to `DBLITERAL_ESCAPE_PERCENT_SUFFIX`.
OleDbLiteral	Escape_Underscore_Suffix	The character used in a `LIKE` clause to escape the character returned for the `DBLITERAL_LIKE_UNDERSCORE` literal. For example, if an underscore (_) is used to match exactly one character and the backslash (\) is used, the characters "abc_ _" match all character values that are five characters long and start with "abc_". Some SQL dialects support a clause (the `ESCAPE` clause) that can be used to override this value. This maps to `DBLITERAL_ESCAPE_UNDERSCORE_SUFFIX`.

System.Data.OleDb.OleDbType Enum

Parent Name	Enum	Description
OleDbType	Empty	No value (`DBTYPE_EMPTY`).
OleDbType	SmallInt	A 16-bit signed integer (`DBTYPE_I2`).
OleDbType	Integer	A 32-bit signed integer (`DBTYPE_I4`).
OleDbType	Single	A floating-point number within the range of –3.40E +38 through 3.40E +38 (`DBTYPE_R4`).
OleDbType	Double	A floating-point number within the range of –1.79E +308 through 1.79E +308 (`DBTYPE_R8`).
OleDbType	Currency	A currency value ranging from -2^{63} (or –922,337,203,685,477.5808) to 2^{63-1} (or +922,337,203,685,477.5807) with an accuracy to a ten-thousandth of a currency unit (`DBTYPE_CY`).

Table continued on following page

Parent Name	Enum	Description
OleDbType	Date	Date data, stored as a double (DBTYPE_DATE). The whole portion is the number of days since December 30, 1899, while the fractional portion is a fraction of a day.
OleDbType	BSTR	A null-terminated character string of Unicode characters (DBTYPE_BSTR).
OleDbType	IDispatch	A pointer to an IDispatch interface (DBTYPE_IDISPATCH).
OleDbType	Error	A 32-bit error code (DBTYPE_ERROR).
OleDbType	Boolean	A Boolean value (DBTYPE_BOOL).
OleDbType	Variant	A special data type that can contain numeric, string, binary, or date data, as well as the special values Empty and Null (DBTYPE_VARIANT). This type is assumed if no other is specified.
OleDbType	IUnknown	A pointer to an IUnknown interface (DBTYPE_UNKNOWN).
OleDbType	Decimal	A fixed precision and scale numeric value between -10^{38-1} and 10^{38-1} (DBTYPE_DECIMAL).
OleDbType	TinyInt	An 8-bit signed integer (DBTYPE_I1).
OleDbType	UnsignedTinyInt	An 8-bit unsigned integer (DBTYPE_UI1).
OleDbType	UnsignedSmallInt	A 16-bit unsigned integer (DBTYPE_UI2).
OleDbType	UnsignedInt	A 32-bit unsigned integer (DBTYPE_UI4).
OleDbType	BigInt	A 64-bit signed integer (DBTYPE_I8).
OleDbType	UnsignedBigInt	A 64-bit unsigned integer (DBTYPE_UI8).
OleDbType	Filetime	A 64-bit unsigned integer representing the number of 100-nanosecond intervals since January 1, 1601 (DBTYPE_FILETIME).
OleDbType	Guid	A globally unique identifier (or GUID) (DBTYPE_GUID).
OleDbType	Binary	A stream of binary data (DBTYPE_BYTES).
OleDbType	Char	A character string (DBTYPE_STR).
OleDbType	WChar	A null-terminated stream of Unicode characters (DBTYPE_WSTR).
OleDbType	Numeric	An exact numeric value with a fixed precision and scale (DBTYPE_NUMERIC).

Parent Name	Enum	Description
OleDbType	Udt	A SQL Server 2005 user-defined type (UDT).
OleDbType	DBDate	Date data in the format yyyymmdd (DBTYPE_DBDATE).
OleDbType	DBTime	Time data in the format hhmmss (DBTYPE_DBTIME).
OleDbType	DBTimeStamp	Data and time data in the format yyyymmdd-hhmmss (DBTYPE_DBTIMESTAMP).
OleDbType	PropVariant	An automation PROPVARIANT (DBTYPE_PROP_VARIANT).
OleDbType	VarNumeric	A variable-length numeric value.
OleDbType	Xml	An xml data type.
OleDbType	VarChar	A variable-length stream of non-Unicode characters.
OleDbType	LongVarChar	A long string value.
OleDbType	VarWChar	A variable-length, null-terminated stream of Unicode characters.
OleDbType	LongVarWChar	A long null-terminated Unicode string value.
OleDbType	VarBinary	A variable-length stream of binary data.
OleDbType	LongVarBinary	A long binary value.
System.Data.PropertyAttributes Enum		
PropertyAttributes	NotSupported	The property is not supported by the provider.
PropertyAttributes	Required	The user must specify a value for this property before the data source is initialized.
PropertyAttributes	Optional	The user does not need to specify a value for this property before the data source is initialized.
PropertyAttributes	Read	The user can read the property.
PropertyAttributes	Write	The user can write to the property.
Microsoft.SqlServer.Server.DataAccessKind Enum		
DataAccessKind	None	The method or function does not access user data.
DataAccessKind	Read	The method or function reads user data.

Table continued on following page

Appendix A

Parent Name	Enum	Description
Microsoft.SqlServer.Server.SystemDataAccessKind Enum		
SystemDataAccessKind	None	The method or function does not access system data.
SystemDataAccessKind	Read	The method or function reads system data.
Microsoft.SqlServer.Server.Format Enum		
Format	Unknown	The serialization format is unknown.
Format	Native	The Native serialization format uses a very simple algorithm that enables SQL Server to store an efficient representation of the UDT on disk. Types marked for Native serialization can only have value types (structs in Microsoft Visual C#, and structures in Microsoft Visual Basic .NET) as members. Members of reference types (such as classes in Visual C# and Visual Basic), either user-defined or those existing in the framework (such as String), are not supported.
Format	UserDefined	The UserDefined serialization format gives the developer full control over the binary format through the IBinarySerialize.Write and IBinarySerialize.Read methods.
System.Data.SqlClient.SqlBulkCopyOptions Enum		
SqlBulkCopyOptions	Default	Use the default values for all options.
SqlBulkCopyOptions	KeepIdentity	Preserve source identity values. When not specified, identity values are assigned by the destination.
SqlBulkCopyOptions	CheckConstraints	Check constraints while data is being inserted. By default, constraints are not checked.
SqlBulkCopyOptions	TableLock	Obtain a bulk update lock for the duration of the bulk copy operation. When not specified, row locks are used.
SqlBulkCopyOptions	KeepNulls	Preserve null values in the destination table regardless of the settings for default values. When not specified, null values are replaced by default values where applicable.
SqlBulkCopyOptions	FireTriggers	When specified, causes the server to fire the insert triggers for the rows being inserted into the database.

Parent Name	Enum	Description
SqlBulkCopyOptions	UseInternal Transaction	When specified, each batch of the bulk-copy operation will happen within a transaction. If you indicate this option and also provide a SqlTransaction object to the constructor, a System.ArgumentException occurs.

System.Data.SqlClient.SqlNotificationAuthType Enum

Parent Name	Enum	Description
SqlNotification	None	Default. The connection to the client does not AuthType use any authentication. Any connection used is considered to be valid.
SqlNotification AuthType	Integrated	Specifies that the server should try to communicate using integrated security on operating systems that support it. This also means that the service account running SQL Server 2005 must be a recognized account on the client computer requesting the notification.

System.Data.SqlClient.SqlNotificationEncryptionType Enum

Parent Name	Enum	Description
SqlNotification EncryptionType	None	Default. Message data is exchanged in plain text.
SqlNotification EncryptionType	Certificate	Use a server certificate to create an encrypted Secure Sockets Layers (SSL) channel between the client and the server.

System.Data.SqlClient.SqlNotificationInfo Enum

Parent Name	Enum	Description
SqlNotificationInfo	Truncate	One or more tables were truncated.
SqlNotificationInfo	Insert	Data was changed by an INSERT statement.
SqlNotificationInfo	Update	Data was changed by an UPDATE statement.
SqlNotificationInfo	Delete	Data was changed by a DELETE statement.
SqlNotificationInfo	Drop	An underlying object related to the query was dropped.
SqlNotificationInfo	Alter	An underlying server object related to the query was modified.
SqlNotificationInfo	Restart	The server was restarted (notifications are sent during restart.).
SqlNotificationInfo	Error	An internal server error occurred.
SqlNotificationInfo	Query	A SELECT statement that can be notified or was provided.
SqlNotificationInfo	Invalid	A statement was provided that cannot be notified (for example, an UPDATE statement).

Table continued on following page

Parent Name	Enum	Description
SqlNotificationInfo	Options	The SET options were not set appropriately at subscription time.
SqlNotificationInfo	Isolation	The statement was executed under an isolation mode that was not valid (for example, Snapshot).
SqlNotificationInfo	AlreadyChanged	The SqlDependency object already fired, and new commands cannot be added to it.

System.Data.SqlClient.SqlNotificationSource Enum

Parent Name	Enum	Description
SqlNotificationSource	Data	Data has changed; for example, an INSERT, UPDATE, DELETE, or TRUNCATE operation occurred.
SqlNotificationSource	Timeout	The subscription time-out expired.
SqlNotificationSource	Object	A database object changed; for example, an underlying object related to the query was dropped or modified.
SqlNotificationSource	Database	The database state changed; for example, the database related to the query was dropped or detached.
SqlNotificationSource	System	A system-related event occurred. For example, there was an internal error, the server was restarted, or resource pressure caused the invalidation.
SqlNotificationSource	Statement	The Transact-SQL statement is not valid for notifications; for example, a SELECT statement that could not be notified or a non-SELECT statement was executed.
SqlNotificationSource	Environment	The runtime environment was not compatible with notifications; for example, the isolation level was set to snapshot, or one or more SET options are not compatible.
SqlNotificationSource	Execution	A runtime error occurred during execution.
SqlNotificationSource	Client	A client-initiated notification occurred, such as a client-side time-out or as a result of attempting to add a command to a dependency that has already fired.

System.Data.SqlClient.SqlNotificationTransports Enum

Parent Name	Enum	Description
SqlNotification Transports	None	This value is not used when defining a notification transport protocol. It is returned when applying CAS policy and two notification objects return different notification transport values.

Parent Name	Enum	Description
SqlNotification Transports	Tcp	Use TCP as the protocol to perform callback notification.
SqlNotification Transports	Http	Use HTTP as the protocol to perform callback notification.
SqlNotification Transports	Any	Use HTTP as the protocol to perform callback notification if available; otherwise, use TCP.
System.Data.SqlClient.SqlNotificationType Enum		
SqlNotificationType	Change	Data on the server being monitored changed. Use the item to determine the details of the change.
SqlNotificationType	Subscribe	There was a failure to create a notification subscription. Use the object's item to determine the cause of the failure.
System.Data.SqlClient.SqlCompareOptions Enum		
SqlCompareOptions	None	Specifies the default option settings for comparisons.
SqlCompareOptions	IgnoreCase	Specifies that comparisons must ignore case.
SqlCompareOptions	IgnoreNonSpace	Specifies that comparisons must ignore non-space combining characters, such as diacritics. The Unicode Standard defines combining characters as characters that are combined with base characters to produce a new character. Non-space combining characters do not take up character space by themselves when rendered. For more information on non-space combining characters, see the Unicode Standard at www.unicode.org.
SqlCompareOptions	IgnoreKanaType	Specifies that comparisons must ignore the Kana type. Kana type refers to Japanese hiragana and katakana characters, which represent phonetic sounds in the Japanese language. Hiragana is used for native Japanese expressions and words, while katakana is used for words borrowed from other languages, such as "computer" or "Internet." A phonetic sound can be expressed in both hiragana and katakana. If this value is selected, the hiragana character for one sound is considered equal to the katakana character for the same sound.

Table continued on following page

Parent Name	Enum	Description
SqlCompareOptions	IgnoreWidth	Specifies that comparisons must ignore character width. For example, Japanese katakana characters can be written as full-width or half-width, and if this value is selected, the katakana characters written as full-width are considered equal to the same characters written in half-width.
SqlCompareOptions	BinarySort2	Performs a binary sort.
SqlCompareOptions	BinarySort	Specifies that sorts should be based on a character's numeric value, rather than its alphabetic value.

System.Data.SqlClient.StorageState Enum

Parent Name	Enum	Description
StorageState	Buffer	Buffer size.
StorageState	Stream	Stream.
StorageState	UnmanagedBuffer	Unmanaged buffer.

System.Data.OracleClient.OracleLobOpenMode Enum

Parent Name	Enum	Description
OracleLobOpenMode	ReadOnly	The LOB is opened in read/only mode.
OracleLobOpenMode	ReadWrite	The LOB is opened in read/write mode.

System.Data.OracleClient.OracleType Enum

Parent Name	Enum	Description
OracleType	BFile	An Oracle BFILE data type that contains a reference to binary data with a maximum size of 4 GB that is stored in an external file.
OracleType	Blob	An Oracle BLOB data type that contains binary data with a maximum size of 4 GB.
OracleType	Char	An Oracle CHAR data type that contains a fixed-length character string with a maximum size of 2,000 bytes.
OracleType	Clob	An Oracle CLOB data type that contains character data, based on the default character set on the server, with a maximum size of 4 GB.
OracleType	Cursor	An Oracle REF CURSOR.
OracleType	DateTime	An Oracle DATE data type that contains a fixed-length representation of a date and time, ranging from January 1, 4712 B.C. to December 31, 4712 A.D., with the default format dd-mmm-yy. To bind B.C. dates, use a String parameter and the Oracle TO_DATE or TO_CHAR conversion functions for input and output parameters, respectively.

Parent Name	Enum	Description
OracleType	IntervalDay ToSecond	An Oracle INTERVAL DAY TO SECOND data type (Oracle 9i or later) that contains an interval of time in days, hours, minutes, and seconds, and has a fixed size of 11 bytes.
OracleType	IntervalYear ToMonth	An Oracle INTERVAL YEAR TO MONTH data type (Oracle 9i or later) that contains an interval of time in years and months, and has a fixed size of 5 bytes.
OracleType	LongRaw	An Oracle LONGRAW data type that contains variable-length binary data with a maximum size of 2 GB.
OracleType	LongVarChar	An Oracle LONG data type that contains a variable-length character string with a maximum size of 2 GB.
OracleType	NChar	An Oracle NCHAR data type that contains a fixed-length character string to be stored in the national character set of the database, with a maximum size of 2,000 bytes (not characters) when stored in the database. Note: The size of the value is dependent on the national character set of the database. See your Oracle documentation for more information.
OracleType	NClob	An Oracle NCLOB data type that contains character data to be stored in the national character set of the database, with a maximum size of 4 GB (not characters) when stored in the database. Note: The size of the value is dependent on the national character set of the database. See your Oracle documentation for more information.
OracleType	Number	An Oracle NUMBER data type that contains variable-length numeric data with a maximum precision and scale of 38.
OracleType	NVarChar	An Oracle NVARCHAR2 data type that contains a variable-length character string stored in the national character set of the database, with a maximum size of 4,000 bytes (not characters) when stored in the database. Note: The size of the value is dependent on the national character set of the database. See your Oracle documentation for more information.

Table continued on following page

Parent Name	Enum	Description
OracleType	Raw	An Oracle RAW data type that contains variable-length binary data with a maximum size of 2,000 bytes.
OracleType	RowId	The base64 string representation of an Oracle ROWID data type.
OracleType	Timestamp	An Oracle TIMESTAMP (Oracle 9i or later) that contains date and time (including seconds), and ranges in size from 7 to 11 bytes.
OracleType	TimestampLocal	An Oracle TIMESTAMP WITH LOCAL TIMEZONE (Oracle 9i or later) that contains the date, the time, and a reference to the original time zone, and ranges in size from 7 to 11 bytes.
OracleType	TimestampWithTZ	An Oracle TIMESTAMP WITH TIMEZONE (Oracle 9i or later) that contains the date, the time, and a specified time zone, and has a fixed size of 13 bytes.
OracleType	VarChar	An Oracle VARCHAR2 data type that contains a variable-length character string with a maximum size of 4,000 bytes.
OracleType	Byte	An integral type representing unsigned 8-bit integers with values between 0 and 255. This is not a native Oracle data type, but is provided to improve performance when binding input parameters.
OracleType	UInt16	An integral type representing unsigned 16-bit integers with values between 0 and 65535. This is not a native Oracle data type, but is provided to improve performance when binding input parameters.
OracleType	UInt32	An integral type representing unsigned 32-bit integers with values between 0 and 4294967295. This is not a native Oracle data type, but is provided to improve performance when binding input parameters.
OracleType	SByte	An integral type representing signed 8-bit integers with values between –128 and 127. This is not a native Oracle data type, but is provided to improve performance when binding input parameters.

Parent Name	Enum	Description
OracleType	Int16	An integral type representing signed 16-bit integers with values between –32768 and 32767. This is not a native Oracle data type, but is provided to improve performance when binding input parameters.
OracleType	Int32	An integral type representing signed 32-bit integers with values between –2147483648 and 2147483647. This is not a native Oracle data type, but is provided for performance when binding input parameters.
OracleType	Float	A single-precision, floating-point value. This is not a native Oracle data type, but is provided to improve performance when binding input parameters.
OracleType	Double	A double-precision, floating-point value. This is not a native Oracle data type, but is provided to improve performance when binding input parameters.

System.Xml.Xsl.Runtime.SetIteratorResult Enum

Parent Name	Enum	Description
SetIteratorResult	NoMoreNodes	This enumeration supports the .NET Framework infrastructure and is not intended to be used directly from your code.
SetIteratorResult	InitRightIterator	This enumeration supports the .NET Framework infrastructure and is not intended to be used directly from your code.
SetIteratorResult	NeedLeftNode	This enumeration supports the .NET Framework infrastructure and is not intended to be used directly from your code.
SetIteratorResult	NeedRightNode	This enumeration supports the .NET Framework infrastructure and is not intended to be used directly from your code.
SetIteratorResult	HaveCurrentNode	This enumeration supports the .NET Framework infrastructure and is not intended to be used directly from your code.

System.Xml.Xsl.Runtime.IteratorResult Enum

Parent Name	Enum	Description
IteratorResult	NoMoreNodes	This enumeration supports the .NET Framework infrastructure and is not intended to be used directly from your code.

Table continued on following page

Parent Name	Enum	Description
IteratorResult	NeedInputNode	This enumeration supports the .NET Framework infrastructure and is not intended to be used directly from your code.
IteratorResult	HaveCurrentNode	This enumeration supports the .NET Framework infrastructure and is not intended to be used directly from your code.

Index

Index

SYMBOLS

A